# THOMAS MANN

TM in Pacific Palisades, February 1946

Etching by Günter Böhmer, 1975

# THOMAS MANN
## *A Life*

## DONALD PRATER

'It is no easy matter to be a German.... This people ... suffers under its own nature to the point of revulsion. ... There is something most deeply irrational about the German soul which, to the mind and judgement of other, more superficial peoples appears disturbing, agitating, alien, indeed repellent and offensive.'

(Thomas Mann, Thoughts in the War, 1914)

OXFORD UNIVERSITY PRESS

1995

Oxford University Press, Walton Street, Oxford OX2 6DP

Oxford New York
Athens Auckland Bangkok Bombay
Calcutta Cape Town Dar es Salaam Delhi
Florence Hong Kong Istanbul Karachi
Kuala Lumpur Madras Madrid Melbourne
Mexico City Nairobi Paris Singapore
Taipei Tokyo Toronto
and associated companies in
Berlin Ibadan

Oxford is a trade mark of Oxford University Press

Published in the United States
by Oxford University Press Inc. New York

British Library Cataloguing in Publication Data
Data available

Library of Congress Cataloging in Publication Data
Prater, Donald A., 1918–
Thomas Mann: a life / Donald Prater.
Includes bibliographical references.
1. Mann, Thomas, 1875–¹955—Biography.   2. Novelists, German—20th
century—Biography.   I. Title.
PT2625.A44Z7658   1995
833'.912—dc20   [B]   94-44522
ISBN 0–19–815861–0

1 3 5 7 9 10 8 6 4 2

Typeset by Best-set Typesetter Ltd., Hong Kong
Printed in Great Britain
on acid-free paper by
Bookcraft Ltd,
Midsomer Norton, Avon

For Carolyn, Nicholas, and Jeremy

# Preface

Goethe excepted, more has been written about Thomas Mann than about
any other German writer, as much probably as about any author in the
world; but attempts at a comprehensive biography have been few. Some
'life and work' accounts appeared during his lifetime (by Arthur Eloesser in
1925, for example, and Ferdinand Lion in 1947) and soon after his death
(such as that by Eberhard Hilscher in 1966); other contemporary aspirants
to the enterprise, however, like Agnes Meyer, recoiled from the challenge.
By the centenary year of 1975, the events of his long life had become
known in such detail, and were so well documented, that the task became
intimidating; the two decades since have brought further material to light,
notably his diaries, to an extent which makes it even more forbidding. It
may well be true, as Julian Barnes said in *Flaubert's Parrot*, that 'if you love
an author, it is impossible to know too much'; the difficulty comes in trying
to press it all between two covers.

Peter de Mendelssohn, as the centenary approached, began the first full-
scale attempt. His model may have been the master's *The Buddenbrooks*, but
his method was more that of the *Joseph*—the same 'epic pedantry', starting
like Mann deep in the 'well of the past' and, it seems, dredging up everything. Before he died, however, he was able to complete only a first volume,
covering the life to the end of the First World War and published in 1975:
an imposing 1200-page torso, standing as a monument to German
*Gründlichkeit* and in style and treatment a devoted tribute to its subject. A
work on this scale (of his draft sequel two chapters alone, for the important
years 1919 and 1933, now published, take up nearly 200 pages) needs an
athletic readership, and must rank more as a mine of reference—which it
has been for me—than a story which can be absorbed by the ordinary
mortal. Richard Winston also began a full-length biography in 1970, in
brisker style, but was cut off before he could progress beyond *Death in
Venice*; posthumously published, that too, regrettably, had to remain a
torso. Nigel Hamilton in 1978 chose to portray together the lives of the
brothers Thomas and Heinrich, and had necessarily to be more restricted
on each. All these attempts sprang from the perceived need, in view of
Mann's importance, to present both life and works, which naturally vastly
enlarged the scope of the undertaking. And of those mentioned, only
Winston's and Hamilton's are available in English.

To the English public, Thomas Mann's has been a name long familiar, and his principal works are still in print, with at last some good new translations,[1] while film, television, and opera bring him repeatedly to the fore. For those, however, who have no German and wish to learn more of his remarkable career through two world wars and the rise and fall of Nazism, little has been to hand. To fill the gap is the purpose of this book. It deals with his works only briefly (since much of the great mass of critical literature is already available in English) but sufficiently to show how they developed, and to give something of the flavour of the best of his fiction, a taste of its peculiar fascination—the early novellas; *Death in Venice*; *Felix Krull*; *Joseph and his Brothers*; *The Holy Sinner*. The main aim, however, is to present in some detail the events of a life unremitting in dedication to renown, and unique in its illustration of that 'German problem' so vitally important for the Europe of today.

The story of Thomas Mann, for me at least, has a fascination more historical than literary. From the pre-eminent position he achieved in German letters, he became a symbol, in emigration, of the Germany which was to survive the dark years of National Socialist rule; and what he had to say (with all its hesitations and contradictions) through the whole period, from the 1920s through to the post-war nuclear age, is as significant as the statements and memoirs of those in the important political and military positions of the time. And the distance we enjoy now, forty years after his death, will, I hope, have proved of advantage in taking a new look at some aspects of this protean character, a man easier to admire than to love.

While making full use of the latest information and research, I have aimed to produce a readable story that is not too unwieldy in length and avoids the cumbersome 'apparatus' which, for a general reader, risks turning any work on Thomas Mann into a grim and uncomfortable scholastic exercise. Thus—lest the mind, in Samuel Johnson's words, be 'refrigerated by interruptions'—I have restricted footnotes to minimum references only, confident that the experts will recognize well enough my other sources and my indebtedness to my forerunners.

Having seen, I think, all the material directly relating to Mann's life— letters (his own and those from others), diaries and autobiographical writings, memoirs of others, notably of the family—I have based every statement in my narrative on such more or less direct evidence. To reach the summit of the mountain of secondary literature was impossible (and in any case, as Mann commented to a would-be collector of 'material' on him, if the work couldn't be done without what others had written, then better

---

[1] e.g. David Luke's excellent new version of *Death in Venice* (with 'Other Stories': Toronto: Bantam Books, 1988, and as 'Selected Stories', Harmondsworth: Penguin, 1993), with his introduction.

leave it alone). What I have used is shown in the Select Bibliography, and the few instances of direct drawings are referenced in the footnotes. Opinions and all translations are my own, except where indicated; emphases in the translations are as in the original.

A definitive biography in the accepted sense remains elusive. It was a touch unnerving, as I read Mann's diary for 1948, to realize that I was almost exactly the same age as he was then—and that for the long road ahead of me I might not have the further seven years granted to him. I had to hope too that there was no omen in the fate which had overtaken de Mendelssohn and Winston. The limits were therefore set: a life-story which could not possibly include every detail and must eschew that 'fanaticism of the *ab ovo*' which had characterized my subject.

I have been greatly indebted to surviving members of the Mann family— until his recent death, Professor Golo Mann; Professor Elisabeth Mann Borgese, in Halifax, Nova Scotia; Mrs Gret Mann in California—as well as to the extensive resources and assistance of the Thomas Mann Archive in Zurich (Hans Wysling, his successor Thomas Sprecher, and an always helpful staff). I was fortunate too to receive invaluable advice from T. J. Reed (Oxford) after he had read some of my draft. For great generosity with documentation my sincere gratitude is due, among many others, to Jeffrey B. Berlin (Philadelphia), Suzanne Biäsch-Schaub (Basle), Klaus Gräbner (Bamberg), Frederic Bürin (Villars sur Ollon), Gert Heine (Allerød), Klaus W. Jonas (Munich), Michael Limberg (Düsseldorf), the late Hans-Ulrich Lindken (Freilassing), Evgenij I. Netscheporuk (Simferopol), Georg P. Salzmann (Munich), Ferenc Szász (Budapest), and Günther Ullmann (Frankfurt/Main). To the editors of Mann's diaries (de Mendelssohn, and for the later volumes Inge Jens) I owe much for their comprehensive commentaries; of especial value as I was concluding my work was an advance copy, kindly supplied by the S. Fischer Verlag, Mann's publishers, of the text for the final years 1953–5, not yet in print, which spared me probable mistakes in deciphering the originals. My thanks, finally, to the Oxford University Press, for their great forbearance over a too-long gestation period.

D.P.

*Gingins, Switzerland*
*July 1994*

# Contents

# Abbreviations

*(for full titles, refer to Bibliography).*

The following abbreviations are used in the Notes.
References to the works (I, II, III, etc.) are to the thirteen-volume *Gesammelte Werke* (Frankfurt a.M.: S. Fischer Taschenbuch-Verlag, 1990).
Year/number references (e.g. 05/13, N 05/3) are to the five-volume *Regesten und Register* of the letters, ed. H. Bürgin and H.-O. Mayer (Frankfurt a.M.: S. Fischer, 1976–87).

| | |
|---|---|
| *A & N* | *Altes und Neues*, 1976. |
| *Amann Br.* | Thomas Mann, *Briefe an Paul Amann*, 1959. |
| *AM Brw.* | Thomas Mann, *Briefwechsel mit Agnes Meyer 1937–1955*, 1992. |
| Berlin | Thomas Mann, 'Unpublished Correspondence . . . H. E. Jacob', ed. J. B. Berlin, 1992. |
| *Bl.* 1, 2, etc. | *Blätter der Thomas-Mann-Gesellschaft*, Zurich. |
| *Br.* i, ii, iii | Thomas Mann, *Briefe*, ed. Erika Mann, 1961–5. |
| *Br. OG-BE* | Thomas Mann, *Briefe an Otto Grautoff . . . und Ida Boy-Ed . . .*, 1975. |
| *Brw. Aut.* | Thomas Mann, *Briefwechsel mit Autoren*, 1988. |
| *Brw. HM* | Thomas Mann, *Briefwechsel mit Heinrich Mann*, 1984. |
| *Chr.* | H. Bürgin and H.-O. Mayer, *Thomas Mann: Eine Chronik . . .*, 1965. |
| *DüD.* i, ii, iii | *Dichter über ihre Dichtungen*, 1975–81. |
| *EB Br.* | Thomas Mann, *Briefe an Ernst Bertram*, 1960. |
| *EM Br. Antw.* i, ii | Erika Mann, *Briefe und Antworten*, 1984–5. |
| Faesi | Thomas Mann, *Briefwechsel mit Robert Faesi*, 1962. |
| Franke | P. R. Franke, *Der Tod des Hans Hansen . . .*, 1991. |
| *Fr./Antw.* | V. Hansen and G. Heine (eds.): *Frage und Antwort*, 1983. |
| *GBF Brw.* | Thomas Mann, *Briefwechsel mit . . . Bermann Fischer*, 1973. |
| *GM Erinn.* | Golo Mann: *Erinnerungen . . .*, 1986. |
| Häntzschel | H. Häntzschel, '"Pazifistische Friedenshyänen"', 1992. |
| *HH Brw.* | Thomas Mann, *Briefwechsel mit Hermann Hesse*, 1975. |
| Janka | W. Janka, *Spuren eines Lebens*, 1991. |
| *Jb.* 1, 2, etc. | E. Heftrich and H. Wysling (eds.), *Thomas Mann Jahrbücher*, 1988–92. |
| JM | Julia Mann, *Ich spreche so gern . . .*, 1991. |
| Kahn | H. Kahn-Reach, 'Thomas Mann, mein Boss', 1973. |
| *KK Brw.* | *Thomas Mann–Karl Kerényi: Gespräch in Briefen*, 1960. |
| *KlM Br. Antw.* | Klaus Mann, *Briefe und Antworten*, 1987. |
| *KlM Tb.* | Klaus Mann, *Tagebücher*, 1989–90. |

| | |
|---|---|
| KM | Katia Mann, *Meine ungeschriebenen Memoiren*, 1975. |
| Krüll | M. Krüll, *Im Netz des Zauberers* . . . , 1990. |
| Lühe | I. von der Lühe, *Erika Mann* . . . , 1993. |
| Matter i, ii, iii | Thomas Mann, *Aufsätze* . . . , ed. H. Matter, 1983–6. |
| MM *Erinn.* | Monika Mann, *Vergangenes* . . . , 1956. |
| Motsch. | G. Motschan, *Thomas Mann—von nahem erlebt*, 1988. |
| *Nb.* 1, 2, etc. | Thomas Mann, *Notizbücher*, 1991–2. |
| PdM | P. de Mendelssohn, *Der Zauberer* . . . , 1975. |
| PdM ii | Id., *Nachgelassene Kapitel* . . . , 1992. |
| *Pfeff.* | H. Keiser-Hayne, *Die 'Pfeffermühle'*, 1990. |
| Piana | Theo Piana, *Thomas Mann*, 1968. |
| Reed | T. J. Reed, *Thomas Mann: The Uses of Tradition*, 1974. |
| SF *Brw.* | S. Fischer/H. Fischer, *Briefwechsel mit Autoren*, 1989. |
| Sprecher | T. Sprecher, *Thomas Mann in Zürich*, 1992. |
| Stahlb. | P. Stahlberger, *Der Zürcher Verleger* . . . , 1970. |
| *Tb.* i, ii, etc. | Thomas Mann, *Tagebücher*, 1977–93. |
| *TM Stud.* | H. Wysling *et al.* (eds.), *Thomas Mann Studien*, iii, iv, viii, x, 1974–92. |
| Tubach | F. C. and S. Tubach (eds.), *Michael Mann* . . . , 1983. |
| *Ungarn* | A. Mádl and J. Györi (eds.), *Thomas Mann und Ungarn*, 1977. |
| *Urteil* | K. Schröter, *Thomas Mann im Urteil* . . . , 1969. |
| Wiedem. | H.-R. Wiedemann (ed.), *Thomas Manns Schwiegermutter* . . . , 1985. |
| *Zeitalter* | Heinrich Mann, *Ein Zeitalter* . . . , 1945. |

# FAMILY TREE OF THE MANNS

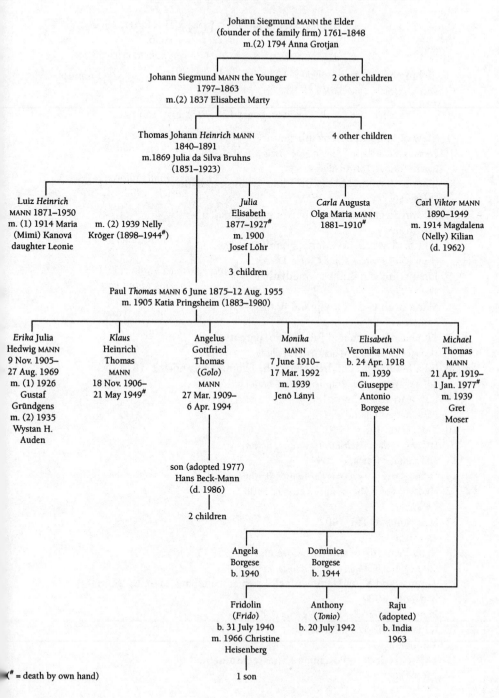

Johann Siegmund MANN the Elder
(founder of the family firm) 1761–1848
m.(2) 1794 Anna Grotjan

Johann Siegmund MANN the Younger
1797–1863
m.(2) 1837 Elisabeth Marty

2 other children

Thomas Johann *Heinrich* MANN
1840–1891
m.1869 Julia da Silva Bruhns
(1851–1923)

4 other children

Luiz *Heinrich*
MANN 1871–1950
m. (1) 1914 Maria
(Mimi) Kanová
daughter Leonie

m. (2) 1939 Nelly
Kröger (1898–1944#)

*Julia*
Elisabeth
1877–1927#
m. 1900
Josef Löhr

3 children

*Carla* Augusta
Olga Maria MANN
1881–1910#

Carl *Viktor* MANN
1890–1949
m. 1914 Magdalena
(Nelly) Kilian
(d. 1962)

Paul *Thomas* MANN 6 June 1875–12 Aug. 1955
m. 1905 Katia Pringsheim (1883–1980)

*Erika* Julia
Hedwig MANN
9 Nov. 1905–
27 Aug. 1969
m. (1) 1926
Gustaf
Gründgens
m. (2) 1935
Wystan H.
Auden

*Klaus*
Heinrich
Thomas
MANN
18 Nov. 1906–
21 May 1949#

Angelus
Gottfried
Thomas
(*Golo*)
MANN
27 Mar. 1909–
6 Apr. 1994

*Monika*
MANN
7 June 1910–
17 Mar. 1992
m. 1939
Jenö Lányi

*Elisabeth*
Veronika MANN
b. 24 Apr. 1918
m. 1939
Giuseppe
Antonio
Borgese

*Michael*
Thomas
MANN
21 Apr. 1919–
1 Jan. 1977#
m. 1939
Gret
Moser

son (adopted 1977)
Hans Beck-Mann
(d. 1986)

2 children

Angela
Borgese
b. 1940

Dominica
Borgese
b. 1944

Fridolin
(*Frido*)
b. 31 July 1940
m. 1966 Christine
Heisenberg

Anthony
(*Tonio*)
b. 20 July 1942

Raju
(adopted)
b. India
1963

1 son

(# = death by own hand)

# List of Plates

# I

## DECLINE OF A FAMILY
## 1875–1900

'I am not unhappy to see myself as a late, a last comer, closing
and completing the record'                          (TM, aged 76)

### 1

*'Education is not won in dull toil and labour; rather it is the fruit of
freedom and apparent idleness. . . . For one must, after all, be of
educable stuff in order to be educated. No one grasps what he has
not possessed from birth'*                          (Felix Krull)

At a quarter past ten in the morning on Sunday, 6 June 1875, a second son,
Paul Thomas, was born to Thomas Johann Heinrich Mann, merchant and
Netherlands Consul in the Hanseatic city of Lübeck, in the patrician house
at 36 Breite Strasse he and his wife Julia had bought three years before. The
planetary aspect was favourable (like Goethe's), wrote Thomas many years
later: his horoscope, experts in that art had assured him, augured a 'long
and happy life and a gentle death'. Long indeed his life was to prove, his
death gentle enough; as to happiness, that he would always find in diligent
labour, the success and comparative wealth it brought him, and the well-
being a hypochondriac can be relied on to ensure for himself.

Certainly all was in place to give him a happy childhood. His father,
master in the third generation of a still-flourishing grain business, was of
high standing in the city, where he would join the Senate in two years' time.
His mother, Julia, had been born in Brazil to the emigrant Lübeck merchant
and plantation-owner Johann Bruhns; after the death of her Portuguese-
Creole mother she had been brought back to Lübeck in 1858 as a girl of 7,
at 18 had captivated his father with her southern beauty and, after their
marriage in 1869 and the birth of their first son, Luiz Heinrich, two years
later, had established with him a household of fitting status. When Thomas

was 6, the Senator's continuing success in business allowed him to buy and develop a bigger house, at 52 Beckergrube, near the River Trave. Here the ivory-complexioned half-Brazilian hostess at their soirées and occasional masked balls made an exotic attraction for the more stolid of their social equals; but the admirers who flocked around her did not disturb what was evidently a happy marriage. Amid the demands of social life she found time to devote to her children—two daughters arrived, Julia in 1877 and Carla in 1881, finally another son, Viktor, in 1890—and Thomas's happiest memories were of her free evenings, when he could curl up and listen to her stories of a childhood on the South American coast 'between sea and primeval forest'; to her readings from Theodor Storm, the brothers Grimm, Fritz Reuter, or Hans Andersen; to the 'small but quite lovely voice' in the songs of Schumann, Schubert, or Brahms, or to her 'well-practised and sensitive' renderings of Chopin, Mozart, or Beethoven at the piano. Unlike his fair-haired brother Heinrich, he was dark like her, and felt himself the nearest of the children to her heart. All indeed were closer to 'Dodo', as she liked them to call her, than to their more remote father, a figure of respect rather than of love. He was always busy with his affairs, not just with his duties at the Senate, where he had charge of the finance portfolio, but also in the big house at 4 Meng Strasse nearby. In the grandfather's day, the latter, 'dominus providebit' inscribed over its portal, had served as counting-house and depot as well as family home, but now, while still the seat of business, housed his mother, up to her death in 1890.

Though he had had to leave school early, Thomas senior had developed wide interests, standing out among his compeers not only with his London-made suits and indulgence in Russian cigarettes but also in the taste for music and the arts he shared with his wife. On business travels, when she sometimes accompanied him, he did not omit visits to art galleries, and enjoyed concert, theatre, and opera performances of a higher standard than was on offer in Lübeck: *Siegfried* in Munich, *Don Juan* and the *Meistersinger* in Frankfurt am Main. One of Zola's novels—in plain wrapper—accompanied him on one summer holiday. His intelligence and knowledge of world affairs were high above those of most of his associates, thought the Lübeck novelist Ida Boy-Ed, whose talent he was one of the few to admire: 'he was a figure of attractive dignity, highly cultivated, and with good humour towards all'.[1]

Lübeck at that time, with its stately gabled houses, still showed something of the power it had once enjoyed as the leading city of the Hanseatic League. Within its moated walls, between the River Trave and its tributary the Wakenitz, still a busy Baltic port, it had scarcely changed in size since

---

[1] Quoted *Br. OG-BE* xviii.

its foundation by Henry the Lion in the twelfth century, near the original Christian-Wendish settlement Liubice ('the charming'), which the later Holsteiners had rechristened Lübeck. Since the time of Emperor Friedrich II in the thirteenth century, and through the Second Reich after 1871, it had retained its status as a Free City (and was to retain it in fact until the assertive head of a Third Reich put an end to such freedom in 1937). Apart from the splendid Town Hall, begun in the year of Luther's Wittenberg theses, the five churches with their seven spires—the cathedral, St Peter's, the Ratskirche St Mary, where Thomas was confirmed, the Ägidienkirche, and the monastery of St John—and the stepped-gable façades of the mercantile quarter, not much remained of the Gothic architecture of the city's medieval past, for the Lübeckers were more redevelopers than preservers. But in the labyrinth of the city's streets one could still sense, so Thomas thought later, the atmosphere of the fifteenth century, some remnant of the hysteria of the late Middle Ages, in which at any moment a 'Children's Crusade, St Vitus's Dance, or some mystical popular excitement over a miracle of the Cross' might break out. Not difficult indeed to picture, in one of the low-ceilinged chambers off the courtyards, a Doctor Faustus crouched by tallow-light over his incantations. The more dubious area near the port, with taverns, cabarets, and whore-houses, was a forbidden zone for the children of the patrician families, but there is no doubt, as is clear from Heinrich's later novel *Professor Unrat*, that he at least ventured its exploration during his last years at school, and the film version *The Blue Angel* made by Joseph von Sternberg in 1929 is a striking record of that seamier side.

At all events, it was a city with a long tradition which, reinforced by that of his family, held fascination for Thomas Mann from an early age. Greatly treasured was a 1661 edition of the Bible, to which his great-great-grandfather from Rostock, brewer and merchant, had begun to attach a continuation of the customary record of the family's births and deaths, but which also contained a chronicle of more exciting events from his youth as cabinboy on North Sea voyages. The great-grandfather, Johann Siegmund Mann the elder, founder of the grain-dealing and forwarding firm in Lübeck, had not continued the traditional entries. But his son Johann Siegmund the younger, Thomas's grandfather, wrote a special essay to accompany the Bible, recording in lively detail his autobiography and the progress of the firm through the profitable Napoleonic era to its prosperity in the wholesale trade it now concentrated on—following always, 'as best I could', the precept of his father of hard work, but 'only on such business as will allow us to sleep peacefully at night'.[2] The chronicle was preserved, though

---

[2] Quoted PdM 35.

not continued in such detail, and stimulated in the young Thomas an interest in his forebears which would continue to absorb him.

It was a prolific and thoroughly German—in the male line almost entirely North German—family from which he sprang. The earliest established records show his seventeenth-century ancestors as merchants, tailors, and drapers, rising to become aldermen and councillors, in Parchim and Grabow, in the Duchy of Mecklenburg. After a move to Rostock during the following century, one branch had continued there, in successful trade; another came to Lübeck, where Thomas's great-grandfather gained citizenship in 1794 and, after a favourable marriage to the daughter of a wealthy Hamburg grain-dealer, became firmly established in the councils of the city. The occupation by Napoleon's troops in 1806 brought disaster to many, but the great-grandfather's business benefited considerably from their need for supplies. His *Plattdeutsch* had a droll admixture of French, as might be expected, and he remained outward-looking, making a month-long visit to London in 1836. His son, Thomas's grandfather, had, however, to make his own way in the business rather than simply step into his father's shoes; and after some unsuccessful attempts to develop export trade, with visits to France, Holland, and Brabant, he correctly realized that development must lie, not with the traditional Hanseatic entrepôt business between Scandinavia, Russia, and the West, but rather with wholesale trade in the products of the Lübeck region itself. His initiative gained his father's trust, and as part-owner at 26 he was able to set a highly prosperous course. Early widowed from his first marriage, from which there were five children, he married again, this time to the much younger Swiss-born Elisabeth Marty, with whom he finally set up in the house at 4 Meng Strasse in 1841.

Mainly North German, then, Thomas Mann's origins, and thoroughly bourgeois: but his family's early seafaring and foreign-trade connections, continued in the consular links with the Netherlands and Brazil, lent them a wider outlook. And a South German influence may not have been lacking, for a laconic entry in the chronicle indicated even earlier ancestors hailing from Nuremberg in Bavaria—'craftsmen', Thomas speculated later, 'of the type that Germany sent throughout the world'. Be that as it may, his quintessentially German make-up did not lack a touch of the cosmopolitan, with an element of the exotic south from his mother. And, like Goethe again, he could say that he too had 'from my father the "serious approach to life", but from my mother my . . . artistic-sensual direction and—in the widest sense of the word—the "urge to story-telling" '.[3]

Imagination played a great part in the games of his childhood. Among his toys, new or inherited from Heinrich, was an elaborate shop, well-

[3] xi 386; 98.

stocked, with counter and scales, a storehouse attached like his father's granary down near the river, and even a working crane to hoist up the sacks. But always more exciting for him was make-believe: re-enacting the myths from Homer and Virgil his mother read from her own school anthology, much of which he later learned by heart—donning the winged sandals of Hermes; flashing the fearful lightnings of Zeus from a table serving as the citadel of the gods; as Achilles dragging a luckless sister three times round the walls of Ilion. A life-size rocking-horse, with 'the most faithful glass eyes in the world', he dubbed Achilles. Best of all were musical-dramatic performances, behind closed doors, with a puppet-theatre Grandmother Elisabeth Marty had presented to Heinrich, the actors carefully dressed and standing in little blocks, Heinrich's talent for drawing used for effective backdrops, and music provided by voice and drum. It was a game Tommy never tired of, long after his brother had given it up; but he also found satisfaction in pure fantasy, with its added advantage that no props were needed. Waking one morning, he would decide to be an eighteen-year-old prince named Karl, and the day could be spent 'proud and happy in the secret of my dignity'—no lessons, walks, or being read to need interrupt the game for a moment, and the character could be changed at will from day to day. Later he wrote real plays to be staged with his sisters for parents and aunts, 'stupid little pieces, one I remember with the title "You Can't Poison Me!"' [4] No one then thought to detect an authorial talent in the making, but in his own recollection there seemed no sharply defined dividing-line between his games as a child and the beginnings of his art. Such an early penchant for role-playing, at all events, was not without significance for his later life and career.

Lessons began for him at 7, in the preparatory school his father and Heinrich had attended before him. Six years here were supposed to qualify the boys for entry into middle secondary school; but Tommy, though not alone in taking seven years to reach that stage, by his own confession 'hated school and right to the end never satisfied its demands'—as was certainly borne out by his subsequent performance at secondary level. A dreamy indolence, lethargy even, and a desire to follow his own direction in reading, made him indifferent to the efforts of the admittedly poor teachers there. All the happier the annual escape to the family's four-week holiday on the nearby Baltic coast, mostly at Travemünde, but once in a rented house in Niendorf. These idyllic stays remained a treasured memory. Here he could luxuriate in idleness, spend long hours on the beach searching for amber, read whatever he liked when he wanted, and, at the five-course table d'hôte meals in the Travemünde hotel, go and lie down after the soup

[4] xi 328; x. 511.

and be wakened when the pudding was on. Later, after he had begun violin lessons, he could even join in the orchestral concerts (if we are to believe his reminiscence at an advanced age) in the pavilion which then stood in front of the *Kurhaus*: 'under a little gypsy-like conductor named Hess I played first violin, with such enthusiasm that he used to tell his musicians, when we went into our folk-song pot-pourri, to follow my lead nicely. It was the first orchestral music I'd heard and played in.'[5] Whether this was real playing, or only the make-believe he later imagined for his hero Felix Krull, is less important than the lasting influence he acknowledged of the sea and the music of Travemünde's 'paradise' on the epic prose that would be his life's work. 'I like to think that the rhythm, the musical transcendency of the sea is somehow omnipresent in all my books . . . the sea of my childhood, the Bay of Lübeck. . . . If my colours have been found subdued rather than luminous, the reason may be certain glimpses through silvery beechwood trunks of pastel-pallid sea and sky, when I was a child and happy.'

## 2

*'An anxious time, school, anything but serene; being young's a fraud . . . I wouldn't like to be 13 or 20 again'*     (TM, aged 71)

The Katharineum secondary school, by the time Thomas started there in 1889, had lost much of its former repute. After the founding of the Reich in 1871, a Prussian regime in education, as in all administrative affairs, had succeeded the liberal methods of more independent times in the 'High School', as it was still known, just as the city's garrison now formed part of the 9th Prussian Army Corps. In the 1880s and 1890s the Katharineum was 'the worst of German schools', recalled Otto Grautoff, a contemporary of Tommy's: incompetently run, its sixth-rate teachers stifling any interest in either classics or languages, the discipline and tone of this 'state within a state' that of the barrack-room.[6] 'General Dr von Staat' was the scornful term Thomas, like Heinrich, would often use for the authoritarian military–academic complex of the time, where education for state service seemed the only path to advancement (and the later mania for fleet construction put children, including his own, into sailor suits). Not that the Mann household was of an anti-Prussian mood: the Senator, though of a sceptical turn of mind, admired the politics of Bismarck, if not the theatricality of the Kaiser, and Thomas would always count the *Reichsgründer* of 1871 with Luther and Goethe as the greatest men of Germany. Against the

[5] *Fr./Antw.* 356.     [6] Piana 8.

school's harsh regime, however, which left his dreamy nature little scope for the independent reading he liked, he offered passive resistance—though he long acknowledged the influence of one exceptional teacher in his introduction to Schiller's works ('this is not just any reading for you: it is the very best you could have!').

Heinrich, destined for university and the distinction of learning the family had so far lacked, was more actively rebellious, but had stayed the humanities course in Latin, Greek, and French with success, and was clearly expected to gain the *Abitur* qualification required. Tommy, however, proved a signal failure in his secondary class, where he took English instead of Greek, which his father hoped would fit him to succeed in the business. He was put back twice before reaching the upper form, and only scraped through the leaving examination, which carried entitlement to one year's voluntary military service instead of three as a conscript (but for that bait, it seems likely he would have dropped out).

School hours were morning only, from eight to midday, with plenty of homework set for the afternoon. Apart from the daily walk to and fro, physical exercise was limited to the shirt-sleeved hour in the gym, where Tommy showed the same passive resistance he displayed in his lessons, grasping the bars 'barely symbolically and with a glazed look of contempt'.[7] The slim figures of the boys in the photographs of those days seem all the more surprising given the powerful eating-habits then customary. Not only did the boys join in the family's four daily meals—breakfast, second breakfast, the big lunch at four (after the Senator's long morning at counting-house, Town Hall, and Exchange), and usually the late cold dinner—but they also had sandwiches to take to school and their own earlier evening meal.

Both boys began early to write, and neither thought much of the Senator's plans for them. In his final school year, just after Thomas had entered the Katharineum, Heinrich had two short novellas published in a local paper, under initials which made an easily penetrated disguise, and another under his own name in a Berlin journal. The success lent him a sudden resolve not to follow the prescribed path to law studies at university, and only a few months before his *Abitur* he discharged himself from school. The Senator, much against his will, had to compromise with a solution which to his mind would at least provide some grounding for a career, and sent him as a bookseller's apprentice to Dresden. Though Heinrich hated the work, it at least got him away from Lübeck, whose materialistic money-grubbing and social injustice had already roused him to write an article (mercifully then unpublished), *Fantasies about my Hometown L.*, bitterly

---

[7] PdM 113.

sarcastic on the city's philistinism—a prelude to the social critique which was to characterize his later novels. For him, the apprenticeship was one in writing, not bookselling: over a hundred poems and ten fictional 'attempts', written between 1886 and 1891, were found in his papers.

Thomas, on the other hand, was proud to sign himself in the first letter we have of his, in October 1889, as 'lyric-dramatic poet', and to quote in it from a drama, *Aischa*, he had just written. Deep in Schiller, he had progressed from his earlier children's performance texts to 'works' in their own right: imitative verse-dramas—one, to the dismay of his pious grandmother, in a tendentious anti-clerical vein. 'Funny, the notions that came to me,' he wrote later. 'But no one, I think, least of all myself, saw any basis for future prospects there. If one then continues, as I did, with poetry and indifferent scribblings . . . it becomes a serious matter and for the family only a worry. At 15 I was nothing but a bad scholar.'[8] The budding poet was decidedly not popular with the teachers, who felt such aspirations were an unwelcome distraction from the homework that was supposed to occupy his afternoons. Heine and Storm were his idols here, the models to be imitated in the verse that expressed his first youthful passions. Attempts in prose too were not lacking, diary entries as well as philosophical essay fragments; but, despite the stimulus of his mother's readings, it was not until his last year at school that he discovered this bent.

Musical interest, and a certain talent, he had inherited from his mother. There were musical evenings in the Beckergrube house, when she would accompany the leader of the city theatre orchestra; one of its members became Thomas's violin teacher, and Thomas was fond of improvising on the piano. The Travemünde pavilion may or may not have been his first experience of orchestral music: among the groundlings at the city theatre, while still a schoolboy, he certainly heard his first Wagner operas, *Tannhäuser* and *Lohengrin*, ' "transported", as the French say' by these often far from first-rank performances, 'never has the theatre had a more receptive or enthusiastic listener than I on those magical evenings'. After his encounter, much later, with the writings of Nietzsche, he could claim that he had never 'really believed in Wagner': but he admitted the strength of the latter's emotional appeal, quite irresistible, and to the end of his life *Tristan* could bring tears to his eyes. He kept up his violin-playing until well into his twenties: but his pleasure in music was as listener rather than performer. 'The sensations of sound have had influences [on me] far surpassing those of vision,' as he wrote much later.[9]

At school, though he made many friends, he was disdainful of the 'average', already conscious of a certain superiority over his fellows, not

---

[8] PdM 107.    [9] 40/650.

simply as the scion of such a patrician family, but in intellect. And he could impress them, in figure and accomplishments—notably once when he read the class some satirical verses on a temporary teacher, who, coming in half-way through, was generous enough to ask him for a copy. The superior attitude remained, inspiring for the later successful author respect but rarely affection, and lending him a stiffness in personal relationships which others found it hard to overcome (only a handful of the friends in his life ever graduated from the formal *Sie* to the more intimate *Du*, and then usually only after many years of familiarity). Looking back on his schooldays, he felt they had been a source 'of arrogance as well as of melancholy and suffering, though I would not then have been able to put a name to it'.[10]

If melancholy there was, it undoubtedly derived from a homosexual tendency which developed early, to last his life through. Though never pronounced, or taking what is known as a 'practising' course, it dared not speak its name—either then (even if he had been able to put a name to it) or later. At school he developed an attachment to a slightly younger boy, Armin Martens, to whom he wrote poems of vague passion, but who, himself more interested in the sister Julia, reacted only with good-humoured contempt (against one refrain, 'What has pale death done to you?', he marked each time, though probably not for the poet's eye, 'Dunno, better ask him').[11] 'It was my first love,' Thomas recalled at the end of his life, 'a more tender, more bitter-sweet was never granted me,' and the thought of this passion remained 'a treasured memory'[12]—though the two did not meet again after leaving school and Martens later came to a sad and obscure end in Africa. He became the model for Hans Hansen in Thomas's later story *Tonio Kröger*:

Tonio loved Hans Hansen, and had already suffered a great deal on his account. Whoever loves the more is at a disadvantage and must suffer—life had already imparted this hard and simple truth to his fourteen-year-old soul; and his nature was such that when he learned something in this way he took careful note of it, inwardly writing it down, so to speak, and even taking a certain pleasure in it . . .

Heinrich, by now in contrast a vigorous skirt-chaser, heard in Dresden, from a friend, of his 'poor brother's suffering', and expressed his view of this nonsense: 'a thorough course of sleeping with a passionate . . . and not too damaged girl will soon cure him'.[13] At this stage, Tommy's affections were as ambivalent as Tonio Kröger's, and he wrote poems to the 'brown-tressed' partner at his regular dancing-lessons, accepting this love too, with all its frustration, 'abandoning himself utterly and nourishing it with all the strength of his spirit, for he knew it would enrich him and make him more

---

[10] xi 452.    [11] PdM 115.    [12] *Br.* iii, 387.    [13] Krüll 442.

fully alive'. In such adolescent confusion, Heinrich's advice—if in fact he received it—was not likely to be followed, even if he had the opportunity.

A close friendship, untroubled by any homosexual overtones, was that with Otto Grautoff. Son of a bookseller, short, unattractive, myopic, the lad seemed an unlikely comrade, but his literary enthusiasms doubtless commended him to the superior Tommy, who already dreamed of the laurels one day to adorn his brow. In 1893, their last year at school, they were to edit together a short-lived journal, *Spring Storm*. How far Grautoff contributed to the two numbers is not clear, but Tommy, under the pseudonym Paul Thomas, seems to have been well to the fore, with a short prose sketch, *Vision*, in true *fin de siècle* style; some poems; an essay on Heine; and a theatre review on an Ibsen production. He also shone, in his own estimation, as 'philosophical-subversive leader-writer'. The worthy city of Lübeck, dusty and lethargic, he wrote in the foreword, needed a spring storm to waken it to life: their journal would drive 'with word and thought into the plethora of dust-laden minds and ignorance, the narrow-minded, self-important philistinism all around us'. Vague protest this, weak compared with Heinrich's *Fantasies*, and hardly comparable with his contemporary Rilke's *Wegwarten* ('Songs as a Gift to the People'), distributed free three years later in Prague: but his prose at least gave some promise of the accomplishments to come. Whatever his technical failure at school, of which, in false modesty, he made much later, he had in fact been better educated than he was prepared to allow.

In May 1890, shortly after the birth of his young brother Viktor, came the centenary of the firm. Overshadowed for the Senator by his forebodings for the future, as social democrat election successes eroded Bismarck's majority in the Reichstag and the Chancellor in whom he trusted was summarily dismissed by the Kaiser, the celebrations were the occasion for beflagging the whole city, and delegations of visitors succeeded each other in the Beckergrube mansion to congratulate the worthy representative of a hundred years of successful enterprise. The children still at home looked on in awe: but Heinrich did not attend, for his father had received unsettling reports from his Dresden employers, knew of the literary ambitions which, to his mind, held no future, and had left him in no doubt of his disappointment at his apathy towards his work. The centenary, as he wrote to Heinrich afterwards, 'when there was so much talk of hopes in my sons', was clouded for him by such conduct. Tommy, for his part, watched with an uneasy conscience.

At 14, 15, you are more advanced and conscious of the future than the grown-ups realize, and if they nourish unsuitable hopes for you, you know, painfully and in your secret heart, that you are going to disappoint them. So I knew then that I wouldn't be the successor. What I would and could do instead, I had no idea.[14]

The political prospects and disappointment in his sons were not the only clouds on the Senator's horizon. A few months before, the family's reputation in the city had suffered unwelcome damage with the prosecution and sentencing for fraud of his niece's husband, a director of an insurance firm. The case made a great sensation for the press, and the disappearance of the offender after his release, leaving his wife with a second child just born and his company bankrupt, gave rise to gossip, it seems, of a family on the downward path. The Senator, still only 50, might have been expected to see hope for the continuation of its business in the arrival of a third son; but the economic upturn which had followed the unification of Germany had left Lübeck somewhat bypassed, with Kiel selected for the North Sea–Baltic canal and the ports of Hamburg and Stettin outstripping it in development, and the Mann affairs, he thought, were far from flourishing. When his mother died, at the end of the year, he decided at once to sell her house in the Meng Strasse, which for over half the hundred years had been the seat of the enterprise, had made for his children a second and more exciting home, and was always the setting for Christmas Eve. It was the only property of the Manns to survive the Second World War.


3

*'Tommy will weep for me. He must never neglect prayer, respect for his mother, and diligent work'*          (*Senator Mann's will, 1891*)

In April 1891 letters came from Dresden to deepen the Senator's concern for his eldest son's future. Heinrich wanted to abandon his post to find something more suited to a literary career, and, still only just 20, sought his father's permission. From his employers, however, came a report that indicated imminent dismissal. Posting at once to Dresden, the Senator found himself faced with a *fait accompli*: to avert the storm, Heinrich had already arranged for himself an unpaid position with the publishing and bookselling firm of S. Fischer in Berlin, and an immediate interview there seems to have impressed his father. The repute of Samuel Fischer, who had started as an independent publisher only five years before and whose list already included Tolstoy, Ibsen, Gerhart Hauptmann, and Knut Hamsun, as well as the journal *Freie Bühne*, may have been not unknown to him. At

[14] PdM 126.

all events, he was persuaded, and within a few days Heinrich had started in Berlin (still, of course, supported by his father).

How far the Senator was aware of Tommy's unwillingness to succeed him is not clear; but there is no doubt of his growing conviction that all he had struggled for was in irreversible decline. The feeling was soon reflected in his health. In July 1891 an operation for stone became necessary, dangerous enough at that time to warrant revising yet again the will long since drawn up. From this (or rather these, for he added a codicil the day before the operation) it was clear that he fully expected to die under the knife, and that his death would mark the end of an era. After precise instructions for the funeral arrangements, including the text of the announcement, he prescribed the total liquidation of the firm and the sale of all the associated properties, within the year. The proceeds were to be invested by his trustee to yield an annual income for his widow (that, as sole heir, she should have no call on the capital, was not actually specified, but this turned out to be the trustee's interpretation). From this income she was to provide for the children, for whom, as was the custom then, two guardians were appointed, responsible to the city court of guardianship. On these guardians he laid the duty of seeing that the children received a '*practical* upbringing':

As far as lies in their power, they should oppose my eldest son's leanings to so-called literary activity [for which] I think he lacks the requirements: adequate study and wide knowledge. . . .

My second son is susceptible to gentler ideas, has a good temperament and will find himself a practical profession. Him I may expect to be a support to his mother.

Julia, my elder daughter, needs strict supervision. Her lively temperament must be held in check.

Carla I think will be easier to handle, and with Thomas will bring an element of tranquillity.

Our little 'Vicco'—may God protect him. Late-born children are often favoured intellectually—the child has such good eyes.

May my wife show herself firm to them all and keep them always dependent upon her. Should she ever waver, I commend her to read *King Lear*.

In a codicil he asked his brother to use his influence on Heinrich, to ensure that he took the 'right road' and kept 'the end in view, not his temporary wishes'.

Tommy will weep for me. He must never neglect prayer, respect for his mother, and diligent work. The children love each other and all love their mother deeply. All my hopes are built on that, and they will be fulfilled if my wife never shows weakness.[15]

[15] PdM 132 f.

The operation, since the city boasted no surgical clinic, had to be performed at home, the ballroom cleared and converted and the surgeons living in. Though he did not then die, the testamentary precautions proved justified: for the intervention revealed an advanced and inoperable cancer of the bladder, and within three months he indeed lay on his deathbed, from 'blood-poisoning', it was stated. The city's concern was profound; straw was laid in the Beckergrube to silence the clatter of traffic, and there were constant enquiries as to his progress. He was far from being exhausted or tired of life, Viktor recounts, from what his mother told him later: 'I would so like to have remained with you,' he said to her. In fever once, thinking himself in a Senate session, he spoke out clearly: 'Gentlemen, on the 13th at half-past five I shall start an inspection tour'—*se non è vero, è ben trovato*, for the premonition was exact, and on 13 October 1891 at that hour his time came.

Both Heinrich, who had hurried from Berlin, and Thomas have left significant accounts of the experience. In wishful thinking perhaps, Heinrich claimed that the dying man expressed at the last his true sentiment towards him: 'I want to help you.' To become a writer, that is: 'both knew it, the one kissed the other's hand, and kisses it still today'. That his filial piety was deeply felt, despite their differences and the negative attitude of the will, is shown in the moving sketches he made, much later, of the scene. Thomas, however, chiefly remembered the pastor's interminable prayers at the deathbed, interrupted by a loud 'Amen!' from his father: the pastor did not let it disturb his flow, 'whereas I, though still a youngster, had realized at once it meant nothing more than "Enough." That Amen rings in my ear whenever I am asked about my attitude to religion, just as my whole life as long as I can remember was strongly oriented towards my father—which may also perhaps be something to do with religion.'[16] He was to live his life without religion, in the sense his father had known; but he was the only one to follow the course his father had foreseen in his will, achieving greater honours than those offered by a city senate.

Certainly the widow, still only just 40, showed no intention of keeping the strict control over her children her husband had prescribed, whether or no she was familiar with *King Lear*. Unlike him, she thoroughly approved, indeed was proud, of her sons' literary ambitions, and although compelled to follow the financial restrictions he had laid down, would do all she could to favour their efforts. The liquidation of the assets yielded a total fortune of around 400,000 marks, a much more favourable result than the Senator's gloomy appreciation of his position, and her income was more than adequate. 'We're not rich, but well-to-do,' she told the children, as Thomas

---

[16] PdM 133.

would tell his own one day. Though the sale of the Beckergrube house had not been specified, she had no wish to follow her mother-in-law's example, sooner or later to be abandoned to a lonely existence in a mansion of ghostly memories; and to keep it up, with the social life she enjoyed and the large team of servants it needed, was out of the question. She decided at once it should be sold, and in 1892 moved with Julia, Carla, and Viktor to the more modest villa they owned just outside the city gates.

Tommy was left to board, like many of his contemporaries, in an establishment run by a teacher of more congenial repute than most, moving shortly after to another, where the regime was stricter. Here he remained, to sit out the rest of his time at school, when his mother, in July 1893, moved to Munich. Her father, Johann Bruhns, who had long since exchanged the plantations of Brazil for business in Germany, had just died in Kassel; and, as Heinrich remarked, it was as though only now she felt really free to start a new life. The Bavarian south had long appealed to her, since her visits there with her husband, and Munich offered her a wider social scene than Lübeck. Her apartment was in the Ramberg Strasse, in Schwabing or nearly, home to many of Munich's artists and writers. Though relatively modest and overstuffed with the best of the Beckergrube furniture, its salon was soon thronged with numerous uncles and aunts for little Vikko—musicians, actors, littérateurs, bankers, and officers—for the widow was still a beautiful woman, and as her daughters grew up could still rival them in attraction.

Heinrich had meanwhile made good progress with what he felt was the right preparation for a literary career: a few spare-time lectures at Berlin University, but, more important, independent studies, cultivation of the right contacts, and observation of life in the streets of Berlin. During the winter of 1891–2 his first attempts at essays appeared in Michael Georg Conrad's *Die Gesellschaft*, the leading journal in Germany of the naturalist movement, for which Fischer's publications of Ibsen and Gerhart Hauptmann, and especially his journal *Freie Bühne*, were giving notable impetus. For Heinrich, however, following Hermann Bahr, naturalism was already superseded by the new romanticism of Paul Bourget, which he celebrated in an essay for the weekly *Die Gegenwart*. His ideas were probably not without influence on Thomas, whose diaries of this time were full of 'slavish' copies of Bahr and who was following with admiration his brother's apparent successes on the path he himself hoped to take. In January 1892 Heinrich suffered a lung haemorrhage, and after a long convalescence did not return to Berlin. He had decided finally to strike out on his own, the monthly allowance from his mother seeming adequate; and during a stay in the Black Forest and the winter in Lausanne, he began his first novel, before returning to Lübeck to help with the family's move.

For Thomas, the final stages of his less than brilliant school career were a relatively contented time. In his pension, the company of young Mecklenburg nobles and sons of the Holstein gentry brought flattery for his ego; for Willri Timpe, the son of the teacher who ran it, he conceived his second great passion, though this time, it seems, with less heartache, the faithful Grautoff his confidant. His 'publications', in the *Spring Storm*, were the beginning of the real work which, he was dimly convinced, would one day bring him success, and even the refusal by a Lübeck paper of one of his prose sketches (*Vision*, perhaps) seemed a step on the right road ('if you often have ideas like this,' wrote the *feuilleton* editor, 'you should do something about it').[17] Ida Boy-Ed took an interest in him, and it may have been she who secured his first truly public appearance in print, in Conrad's *Gesellschaft*, where one of the *Spring Storm* poems appeared later in 1893. The school, meanwhile, now evidently resigned over this mediocre pupil, made few demands: it 'left me to my fate, which to myself remained dark, but whose uncertainty, since I felt myself clever and healthy, failed to cast me down'. His final report, at Easter 1894, was probably more benevolent than he deserved: industry and attentiveness 'on the whole' satisfactory, conduct 'generally good', but his subjects, even German, all no more than satisfactory; and he lost no time in packing and leaving to join the family in Munich.

4

'. . . to learn something, as I intend to do now; neither of us has actually learned anything yet, and for the most intellectual of the arts, that of words, not only feeling and technique are needed, but also knowledge'      (TM to Grautoff, September 1894)

As his father would doubtless also have done, had he lived, the guardian, with his mother's agreement, had arranged for Thomas to join the office of a fire-insurance company in Munich, and he began there on 1 April. As with Heinrich in Dresden, it was an unpaid position, designed to start him on a 'sensible' career and steer him away from hopeless dreams of literary achievement; and, as for Heinrich, the unappealing drudgery was no more than a temporary necessity until he could see his own way clear. He was comfortably housed in the Ramberg Strasse apartment, and the monthly income from his mother of some 160 marks was adequate to cover modest city lunches, a contribution to the household expenses, and his tailor's bills (now, as later, he set store on elegance). His mother admitted afterwards

[17] PdM 143.

that her insistence on pushing him into a city career was probably due to his disappointing school-record, making her lose faith in his talent, and she may have thought to dampen his poetic fire by encouraging this more solid apprenticeship. If so, it was labour lost: for at his desk, between copying out insurance accounts, he began his first serious attempt at a novella, *Fallen*, which he hoped would persuade her otherwise and free him to follow in his brother's footsteps. The title appeared at the head of a list of projects he had made at school, in a notebook he had started—along with his diary, a habit which he would keep up for almost all his life. At the time it had held mostly memos of homework and expenditure; but scattered among them were ideas for novellas and sketches, and increasingly from now on he noted references and quotations, direct or indirect, in great profusion from his wide reading. It marked the beginning of the craftsmanlike approach which would turn the writing-desk of his maturity into a workshop of book-making, rather than the scene of inspiration, his material carefully assembled and items struck through as they were used. 'The devil lies in the detail,' he said towards the end of his life, in the excerpts and notes to be made, a preparation 'taking hours and days . . . the actual writing is more a question of discipline'.[18]

That kind of work came later: no such lengthy preparation was needed for his story of a fallen woman, which an older man at a bachelor dinner-party recounts to cap a discussion on women's emancipation, the romantic tones of his narrative of young love between actress and student dispelled by the cynical conclusion that, if a woman falls today for love, she will fall tomorrow for money. That no sexual experience lay behind the veil of fine words is evident from his decorous treatment of the night of love. In his notebook he had recorded Paul Bourget's warning against two contemporary types: 'l'homme cynique et volontiers jovial, dont la religion tient dans un seul mot, jouir, et celui qui a toutes les aristocraties des nerfs, toutes celles de l'esprit, et qui est un épicurien intellectuel et raffiné'—and the second was no doubt how Thomas Mann, at 19, liked to see himself. (In a friend's album, the following year, he wrote: 'My favourite occupation? to poetize *without* writing; favourite characters in poetry? Hamlet, Tristan, Faust *and* Mephisto, Parsifal; my temperament? contemplative, Hamletish, sicklied o'er with the pale cast of thought.'[19])

Submitted to *Die Gesellschaft*, the story was immediately accepted, an achievement impressive enough to justify asking his mother to let him quit his clerk's stool. Knowing her reluctant, he was clever enough to ask her lawyer to advise her in favour, and before the summer was out had gained

---

[18] Motsch. 29 f.        [19] Franke 8 f.

his point. Admittedly, he was still to 'learn something', and for this he was only too ready, if he was to prepare himself for the 'most intellectual of the arts, that of words'. The solution that suited both himself and his guardians was that he should enrol in November as an outside student at the university and Technische Hochschule, and become a journalist. Whatever this vague term might mean, the lecture courses he attended through the winter (culture and world history, economics, German literature, foundations of aesthetics, and Shakespeare) were not without their usefulness. His most copious notes, surprisingly, were on economics, seen by the professor as a 'modern and moral science' in lectures which for him often held 'deep philosophical moments'. On aesthetics, however, he was provoked in his notes to argue: 'the professors never distinguish between classical aesthetics and that of decadence, and do not realize that the classical they teach must be totally foreign to our age'. What he learned and noted on art history, notably on ancient Egypt, from Professor Hertz's stimulating lectures on courtly poetry and the Nordic sagas, and, after he had exchanged economics for history, on Napoleon and Germany, would leave impressions to be recalled, and material to be used, many years later. His independent reading in Nietzsche too, at this time, left traces in his notebook as well as in his style: *Beyond Good and Evil* and *The Wagner Case* were clearly already familiar.

Free until the late-afternoon lecture sessions, he was happier than ever before. *Fallen* had appeared in October, and brought him an unexpected accolade: a letter from Richard Dehmel, the Berlin poet he had long admired, full of praise for his 'wonderful story' and its 'simple, soulful prose', so rarely met with now. 'If you have further tales of similar maturity, I would like to ask you to send me the manuscripts for the arts journal *Pan*, just now being started, for which I am on the editorial board (rates: 10–15 marks per printed page),' wrote Dehmel—though he criticized the title, suggesting 'The Cynic' as more apt, and added, meanwhile, some technical comments designed to improve the style 'for the later edition in book form'. He could hardly have asked for a more promising start, and he never forgot his pride as a beginner at receiving such praise and advice. He was particularly struck by Dehmel's assumption, with no idea what else he had written, that he must have a volume of collected novellas in view. He had indeed; ideas were not lacking, but the invitation had taken him by surprise. He promised, however, to respond as soon as he had something suitable to offer; and in November sent a further story, *The Little Professor*, 'much shorter than *Fallen* (sorry—*The Cynic*!) but marking, I think, some slight progress from the literary point of view'. Too short for *Pan*, was Dehmel's reply: he had no doubt of his talent, but *Pan* demanded more ambitious stuff, for which 'great art' was required. (The novella, also refused by *Die Gesellschaft*, was probably the first version of *Little Herr Friedemann*, which only later would see the light.)

Single-minded devotion to the art of words proved over that winter to be more difficult than might have been expected. Munich offered so much, he wrote to Grautoff in January: carnival time was approaching, and 'for better or worse you have to amuse yourself'; there were always 'new introductions, to actors, poets, artists—it never stops . . . hardly time to breathe'; the lecture courses continued; and he had joined Ernst von Wolzogen's 'Academic-Dramatic Club'. In this 'coffee-house company with theatrical and literary ambitions' the author of *Fallen* enjoyed an immediate welcome, though he made no real friends there. Mainly but not entirely made up of students, the company went in for serious productions, and he was soon heavily involved in rehearsals for Ibsen's *Wild Duck*, which he had recommended and in which he was to play Werle. The performance in June 1895, its première in Germany, was successful enough, 'against the protests of a conservative audience', to warrant a second, and the notices gave praise too for Thomas Mann. It was his one and only try as an actor, though he was a hilarious success at carnival time in 'village idiot' mask over full evening dress—and it would be by no means his last public appearance.

Pure dissipation, he admitted in his letters to Grautoff. The rehearsals were followed by long sessions in the Café Luitpold; he was often not abed before daybreak, 'three-quarters of the day and three-quarters of the night away from the writing-desk'. A start at learning shorthand—an 'outside support' against his 'decadent nature', and he might after all become a journalist—remained little more than a good intention. But he was not as idle as he claimed, and by May was able to send another, longer novella, *Walter Weiler*, to Dehmel, asking with some hesitation whether it marked any progress. Dehmel was highly encouraging, and on a visit to Munich in June told him it was accepted for *Pan*; but the rest of the editorial board apparently did not share his enthusiasm, for it never appeared, and he did not offer it elsewhere.

The manuscript has not survived, and we know only that the theme was of a 'useless decadent'—'very much like you', as he wrote in his usual mocking tone to Grautoff—so that it was probably the original form of the story *Der Bajazzo* (*The Joker*), which he was to rewrite two years later. In spite of all Mann's new contacts in Munich, Grautoff remained his only real friend and confidant at this time, and they maintained an active correspondence. He was by no means so favourably placed as Thomas, being forced, after the bankruptcy of his father, to settle to real work at a bookseller's in Brandenburg; a touch bitter for him, doubtless, to hear so constantly of the comparative luxury and stimulating company enjoyed by his friend in Munich, and especially of his success with *Fallen*, for he too had literary aspirations. His poems and prose pieces received good-humoured but merciless criticism: 'useless verses', plagiarizing Heine, but 'a certain, if still-undeveloped talent'; a novella no more than 'a charcoal sketch . . . preparatory work for an artist to work into a bigger creation . . . but *good* as a study'; 'as a story-writer you lack *invention* . . . you still have no idea of dialogue'. A year older, Thomas felt it incumbent on him to offer fatherly advice in matters financial, and had succeeded in stopping him from the 'stupid' step of exchanging his office stool in Brandenburg for the uncertainty of journalism in Berlin. But he set store by the other's comments on his own work, waiting to hear what he thought of *Walter Weiler* before submitting it to Dehmel, and the often *de haut en bas* tone of his long letters betrayed his lack of any real affection.

During most of 1894 the family had been together in the Ramberg Strasse. For the youngest, it was a household of uncles and aunts, rather than brothers and sisters, with all that that implied in distance: the moustachioed 'Ommo' seemed serious, but always had a joke for him; 'Heini', in beard, dark suit, and watch-chain, was awesome and remote; 'Lula' and Carla, as older sisters will, tended to exert the heavy hand of discipline on mother's behalf; but he loved them all. Heinrich, though unsuccessful with his first novel, which reached print only at his mother's expense, had produced a flow of short stories and novellas after a first visit to Italy, and Thomas's admiration knew no bounds. After Heinrich had left for another extended stay in Italy, early in 1895, Thomas wrote to Grautoff: 'he is an artist, a poet'—a giant even the knees of whom they could not reach; and he drew for his friend a significant sketch of the three sons of Senator Mann.

Heinrich is already a poet, but also a 'writer', with a powerful intellectual talent, versed in criticism, philosophy, politics. . . . I am only an artist, only a poet, only a creature of moods, intellectually weak, socially useless. Would it be surprising if the third son finally followed the most vague of arts, music? That may be called degeneration. But I find it devilish neat.

Significant too his note about this time of the Turkish proverb: 'When the house is completed, then comes death.' The perception of his family in decline (as it was regarded, so he heard, among the gossips of Lübeck), from the hard-headedness of business to the intellectual pursuit of the arts, would find its expression in his first novel. For the moment, the pose of decadent dilettante, 'creature of moods', was maintained, and he was delighted to accept his brother's suggestion that he join him in Italy. Between July and October, in Rome and during a short stay in Palestrina, he completed no fewer than four manuscripts—a production tempo, under the influence perhaps of Heinrich's, he would never again achieve; but only one, the novella *The Will to Happiness*, survived for publication. He also helped with a monthly journal, *Das zwanzigste Jahrhundert*, a publication of reactionary, anti-Semitic, and polemical line which Heinrich was editing and to a great extent writing, mainly, no doubt, for the money. Thomas contributed a number of reviews and commentaries, and, as will be seen, absorbed political views from this association that would last longer with him than with his brother; neither cared in their later autobiographical writings to enlarge on the episode, which lasted barely a year. His intervention, in one commentary, in a public dispute between a dramatist and the prominent Berlin critic Alfred Kerr, earned him the lasting enmity of the latter.

Unlike Heinrich, he was incapable of letting himself go: reading and psychologizing were no substitute for life, and he lacked the breadth of experience which his brother used to good effect in his stories. His own of this time—*The Will to Happiness*, and *Little Herr Friedemann*, rewritten early in 1896 from the first version—exploited with virtuosity such life as he knew, from his schooldays, or in Munich and Rome, and the sober narrative style contrasted with Heinrich's breathless raciness; but there was inevitably an air of unreality in his treatment of sexual relationships, given the still-uncertain direction of his own. Uneasy at the homosexual revelations of his diaries, he decided to burn the lot after his return from Italy (though the compulsion to a daily record persisted, and another was immediately started). 'Uncomfortable and painful, to have such a mass of secret—*very* secret—writings lying around,' he told Grautoff in February 1896; and he described his practice of cold douches every morning to damp down the urges and 'chain up the dogs lurking underground'. Among other Nietzsche quotations, he had noted from *Beyond Good and Evil*: 'Sensuality often outstrips the growth of love, so that the root remains weak and is easily torn out.' There was a girl in Munich to whom he spoke of sending roses; but this seems to have been but the half-hearted attempt of a 'degenerate weakling', as he said himself, his mood still one of 'indolence and a bad social conscience', though combined with a sure confidence in his latent capabilities.[20]

That this last was not an illusion was confirmed when *The Will to Happiness* was accepted in August 1896 for the journal *Simplicissimus*, just started by Albert Langen in Munich. Its sharply satirical line and often outrageous cartoons he found an attractive contrast to the 'childish mannerism of *Pan*', especially when, unlike the latter, it was ready to publish him; and it was a memorable day when he received cash payment in gold

[20] xi 104.

at the hands of Jakob Wassermann, on Langen's editorial staff and himself one of the promising young authors of Munich. He had spoken earlier of continuing university study in Berlin, but was spurred now to drop everything 'like a true vagabond', and set off in October with Heinrich for another stay in Italy. Meanwhile he entered another story, *Death*, for the prize offered by the journal for the best novella in which sex played no part. Though published the following year, this dreamlike musing, in diary form, on a terminal cardiac condition did not win the 'golden laurels' he had been bold enough to aspire to: these were captured by Wassermann.

The brothers travelled together first to Zurich, from where Heinrich went direct to Rome, while Thomas spent three weeks in Venice, before going on via Ancona and Rome to Naples, where he spent most of November, in the hope of an 'exquisite sensation mingling Rome and the Orient'. He had not, of course, let everything lie: the manuscript of *Little Herr Friedemann* was with him, and already his next novella, *Disillusionment*, set in Venice, was taking shape. The theme of *Friedemann* continued to disturb him: 'the longing for a neutral nirvana' and the 'incursion of sexuality into a sheltered existence', destroying his hero; and he pondered much, as he wrote to Grautoff in November, on his personal problem:

What am I suffering from? . . . knowledge? is that then to destroy me? . . . sexuality? will that destroy me? How I hate this knowledge, this science, which compels even art to follow it! How I hate this sexuality, which claims for itself everything that is beautiful! It's the poison that lurks in all beauty! . . . How can I free myself from science? through religion? from sexuality? by eating rice?

The indefatigable pimps in the Naples streets, offering 'very beautiful girls . . . and not only girls', were hard to fight off. 'They don't seem to know I've almost decided to live on nothing but rice, just to free myself from sexuality.' As the ironic tone showed, the torment was far from unbearable: it was more an unease that refused to be dispelled, at its root the conflict between homosexual and heterosexual compulsions which he would never succeed in resolving and which needed 'discreet forms and masks' in the work he put before the public. With *Friedemann* he felt that he had found the way for this.

Once in Rome, he did not share Heinrich's *pensione* in the Via Argentina, but secured a room in the Via del Pantheon nearby for the first months of their stay. Not that there was coolness between them, his admiration for Heinrich was too great for that; they spent much time together, enjoying the wine and excellent *crochette di pollo* of the local restaurant 'Genzano' and an evening game of dominoes in a café, and sedulously avoiding any contact with other Germans. Separate quarters, however, seemed right for what had become almost a competition in production, for both were more than usually busy. Their far from lavish monthly allowances gave a more favourable yield in Italian currency, adequate for their so far unregulated lives and giving them a social freedom they could not have found in Munich, as they worked on their stories and waited for fame. A light-hearted break in their work was a joint manuscript as a present for Carla's confirmation on Palm Sunday 1897: a 'Picture-Book for Good Children', with ballads both scurrilous and idyllic, parodies, and satirical comments on family, social, and literary life, illustrated with Simplicissimus-type caricatures from both their hands. How their sister, not yet 15, reacted to this most unsuitable but evidently highly amusing production, is not recorded: but the book became a family favourite and source for quotation, particularly later with Thomas's own children, until its loss in 1933, with only a few of the drawings surviving.

Of the brothers, Heinrich was a comparatively well travelled man, having seen much more of Germany, and with stays in Paris and Lausanne behind him, and was better able to appreciate the attraction of the 'colours and lines' he found in Italy's art and countryside. For Thomas, apart from two short visits to Austria, the Italian journeys were his first ventures abroad; yet he found the south as such to hold little appeal. He preferred hearing a mass in St Peter's to visiting the standard tourist sites, for which he felt respectful admiration rather than enthusiasm, and the Vatican's sculptured antiquities said more to him than the paintings of the Renaissance. His stories show how closely he observed the scene; Italy's traditional magnetism for German writers and artists, however, was clearly eminently resistible.

Over the winter, 'in the smoke of innumerable 3-centesimi cigarettes', he devoured Scandinavian and Russian literature, and went on with his writing. There was now an aim to it: for, having ventured to send *Friedemann* from Italy directly and unintroduced to Fischer's *Neue Rundschau*, he had received, to his delight, from the editor Oscar Bie, early in 1897, a letter not only praising and accepting it, but also asking him to send everything else he had written. The implication was that Fischer already intended publishing a whole volume of his stories, as indeed later proved the case; and he had to decide now which of those so far produced he would send in. *Fallen* he felt was too slight; *The Will to Happiness* and *Death* could be included, and *Disillusionment* and *Tobias Mindernickel*, just written, but to round out the volume a revised version of *Walter Weiler* now became urgent. By April this had become *The Joker*, and the five manuscripts were sent in to add to *Friedemann*. At the end of May he heard from the publisher himself that he proposed to include them with an illustrated jacket in the cheap 'Fischer Collection' edition:

I offer you 150 marks for the rights, subject to publishing *The Joker*, which I presume has not yet appeared, in the *Rundschau*. I cannot offer you a good royalty for the 'Collection' edition, which I produce at a very cheap price; but I would be very pleased if you would give me the opportunity of publishing a larger prose work, perhaps a novel if not too long. I can pay far better royalties for this kind of work . . . and will be pleased to do all I can for your production, on condition, of course, that we have exclusive rights.[21]

This was indeed a decisive turn in his writing career, towards achievement more permanent than a series of journal contributions, and in his hitherto 'wholly temporary and experimental way of life'. Introduced now to a publisher of repute who recognized his potential, he was spared the usual disappointments of a beginner, and in this sense was more fortunate than his brother. The offer to promote his work, with exclusive rights, alongside that of established giants like Hauptmann and Bjørnson, could hardly be more encouraging, and marked, as he wrote later, his real 'breakthrough into literature'. It was the birth too of a mutual loyalty between Fischer and himself which would endure for the rest of his life.

He had wondered, after sending off the novellas, whether they would in fact be advantageous for his reputation: 'all the stuff I've written so far,' he had confessed to Grautoff, 'seems grey and tedious in comparison with the singular things I have in my head'. After *Friedemann*, though, he had found the 'discreet forms and masks' under which he could go before the public, 'whereas before, just to speak to myself, I had to make use of a private diary'. *The Joker* was just such discreet autobiography: the self-confessed dilettantism of a young man left like himself, after the death of his father, with adequate means but lacking a purpose in his life. By July, however, once the volume was being printed, he felt his hands free for the artistic expression of 'my love, my hate, my sympathy, my contempt, my pride, my scorn and my complaints'. There were indeed 'singular things' in his head. *Tobias Mindernickel*—caricature of a weirdly named solitary figure, butt of the local children, and his love–hate relationship with a dog bought on impulse to share his life—was followed by the bitter story of *Little Lizzy*. Foreshadowed by a cartoon in the picture-book for Carla ('Attorney Jacoby and his wife, from popular poet Thomas Mann's delightful novella, which is most warmly to be recommended to the German public'), this tragicomic tale of a deceiving wife's contemptuous ridiculing of the husband's doglike devotion by forcing him into an absurd song-and-dance number, dressed like a Shirley Temple *avant la lettre*, at the entertainment she has organized, ending with his collapse and death at the final curtain, made a grotesque

[21] SF *Brw*. 394.

elaboration of the theme of *Friedemann*, the ironic treatment harsher and less benevolent. 'A strange and ugly tale, as befits my present view of people and the world,' he told Grautoff.

At this time, so he claimed much later, he was firmly convinced 'that the short story, as I'd learned it in the school of Maupassant, Chekhov, and Turgenev, was my genre; never, so I believed, would I be able to attempt the wider form of the novel'.[22] But his ambition had been stirred by Fischer's mention of a longer prose work for the production he wished to promote, and not least by the more substantial royalties this might promise. The idea, already mooted by Heinrich, that some aspects of their own family history might offer interesting material for a novel had appealed to him too; but he had hitherto thought only in terms of a novella, a narrative dealing with the problem of the sensitive late-comer to a family in decline, but more directly related to his own childhood experience than had been the case in *The Joker*, and still in his short-story vein. Why not try it in the longer form? His wide reading during the stay in Italy had provided plenty of current examples of such family chronicles. Zola he had not yet encountered, but the Goncourt brothers' *Renée Mauperin* had aroused his admiration for its felicitous composition in short chapters: 'I thought something like that could well be attempted'; among the Scandinavians the novels of Jonas Lie and Alexander Kielland made even closer models as he considered the links between his Hanseatic home and Denmark and Norway. Within two months of receiving Fischer's letter he had decided on a shortish novel of 250 pages, in fifteen chapters. His notebook began to fill with snatches of dialect conversation, brief characterizations, names, even the opening and closing scenes of the work; and when he and Heinrich left the heat of Rome for Palestrina, early in August 1897, the outline was clear to him.

## 5

*'You won't always be writing four-volume novels, so a publisher can probably . . . take a chance with you'*
(Fischer to TM, March 1901)

The title, Thomas thought, might be 'Downhill': the story in essence that of the Manns of Lübeck, from his great-grandfather's time to his own, and ending with the death of little Johann (Hanno), the last of the line, too sensitive to survive or succeed. The names must, of course, be changed, and it was not long before he hit on that of Buddenbrook for the family

---

[22] xiii 137.

(whether this was suggested by his brother, as much later he thought he recalled, or by someone else, or was taken from Fontane, does not much matter). But he found that though the general story was familiar, he did not 'know enough'; more factual material was needed to fill out the details if he was to give a realistic portrayal of the 'Decline of a Family', which was to be his subtitle; and he drew up long lists of questions to be resolved.

Many were sent to Wilhelm Marty, Lübeck merchant and Portuguese consul, his father's cousin, asking for all kinds of information on the city's life before and after the establishment of the Reich: the French occupation, trade and business policy and practice and the reasons for failures, grain prices, the old and the new currencies in use, the Prussian influence, the customs union, the opening of the railways, post and telegraph communications, army details, even the kind of street lighting. Marty's painstaking replies, still extant, can be found almost all woven into the final text, often in the actual words—an early example of the technique he termed 'montage' and which became a characteristic of his work. His mother contributed what she knew of recipes used for the substantial meals served in the old days. She may well also have entrusted to the mail the family papers, accompanying the old Bible, which were in her charge: for the genealogical table of the Buddenbrooks he drew up now was based very exactly on that of the Manns, though simplified and setting back his timing a quarter-century or so for the novel's events, for which he established a chronological framework. Another valuable source was his sister Julia, who in September sent him a lengthy account, in facts and anecdotes, of their aunt Elisabeth, her two marriages, and her daughter Alice (wife of the fraudulent insurance-man whose case had been of such concern to the Senator in 1890). She impressed on him the need for great discretion in using her information: 'remember, several of the persons mentioned are still alive . . . and be specially careful in your treatment of Alice's story'. But she was sure he would handle it all tactfully.[23]

All these contributions proved of capital importance as *The Buddenbrooks*[24] took shape, providing not only historical and lively anecdotal details, but also elements vital to his tale. Thomas Buddenbrook's speculation in the purchase of standing grain, for example, a significant stage in his ethical and financial decline, was directly based on Marty's information on the practice, while the reincarnation of Aunt Elisabeth in Antonie ('Tony') Buddenbrook, suitably adapted, would become the central figure of the novel (and he did not hesitate later to consult his aunt directly). In Palestrina lengthy jottings accumulated to accompany the basic genealogy and chronology. He made lists of names, some real, some

[23] *Sinn und Form*, 25/2–3 (1963), 480
[24] I prefer David Luke's correct English version, to *Buddenbrooks tout court*.

invented, for the minor characters; worked out details of the Buddenbrook finances in each generation, adapted from those of the Manns so as to bring out more strongly the theme of decline; collected Lübeck and family sayings, in *Plattdeutsch* and French; recorded the changes in dress and fashions; and made extensive notes on the main Buddenbrook characters Thomas, Christian, Tony, and Hanno, especially on the latter's schooldays. When he returned in October to Rome, to spend the winter with Heinrich in the *pensione* in the Via Argentina, he was ready to begin. He had a clear idea of the structure of the work, and as it developed was to hold closely to this, even though (as would so often be his case) it soon manifested a will of its own, to extend far beyond his original concept of the length. By December, as he told Grautoff, he was already on the fifteenth chapter, and his head was full of story themes as well.

Meanwhile he was impatient to see the first Thomas Mann book, his novella volume, in print. Fischer had delayed it, to allow for the prior *Rundschau* publication of *Tobias Mindernickel*, following similar separate appearances of *Friedemann* and *The Joker* in May and September (good business for the publisher, since he paid no additional royalties for these). The volume was not finally out until the following May; but he had his first copies in his hands before the end of the year, and one made a Christmas present for his brother, with a pencilled portrait of the author suitably caricaturing the poetic dilettante with moustache, high collar, and sloping shoulders. His list of presentation copies was long: the family first, not forgetting Aunt Elisabeth and Wilhelm Marty, then Ida Boy-Ed and twenty or so of the Munich friends and contacts, including *Simplicissimus* and *Die Gesellschaft*, who might be expected to prove useful for his future, and finally his Lübeck schoolmasters and trustee and the local papers, as a demonstration of the progress since his departure. Though in sales terms a comparative failure and disappearing in a few years with the rest of the 'Fischer Collection', his first-born, with the pre-prints in the *Rundschau*, made him something of a name—'note this author', ran one of the few reviews, 'a pure artist, assured, experienced'—and achieved, as Fischer wrote later, 'a literary success greater than its sales would suggest'. And, though still 'an unknown beginner in the art of the word',[25] he had the comforting assurance of the publisher's continuing interest.

His mother had meanwhile reminded him that his one-year military service could be falling due in April 1898, so he should save up for an early return to Munich if, as she already planned, a claim for deferment on medical grounds was to be arranged: 'it would be nice if you could be freed from it, and I'll have an extra present for you then'. (A complaisant doctor

---

[25] PdM 329, 323.

of her acquaintance would indeed secure two successive deferments, by attesting his patient's narrow-chestedness and 'nervous heart'.) After eighteen months in Italy, and with his money running short, he was ready anyway to return. Towards the end of April he set off by train, carrying the already bulky manuscript of *The Buddenbrooks*, and making a brief stopover to see Florence for the first time. He found the family now installed in a slightly smaller apartment in the Herzog Strasse, in Schwabing—the first of a series of moves his mother, ever restless, was to make over the coming years. After a few days he escaped from these over-cramped conditions to take a lodging of his own, in the Theresien Strasse, where he soon felt comfortably at home with his books, pictures, piano, and violin, 'as far as a poor neurasthenic can feel at home', he told Grautoff. The cost proved too high, however, as did another in the Barer Strasse, and by October he had abandoned this last 'expensive, bourgeois, banker's apartment' to settle in two rooms in the Markt Strasse in Schwabing, quite near his mother. It would be his home for about a year. The vagabond life of Italy gave way now to the elegance that was truly his style; his first act on returning had been to visit his tailor. 'I returned pretty ragged from the trip,' he had written to Korfiz Holm, an older school-fellow from Lübeck who was now an editor with *Simplicissimus*: 'as soon as I am half-way presentable I'll take the liberty of calling on you'.[26] Presentability, the need to appear as a solid citizen, was and would remain a prime consideration for him. But like most of his contemporaries he had been bitten by the cycling-bug, and became passionately devoted to his 'velocipede', on which he went out in all weathers and which he carried up the three flights to its home in the kitchen, where it would be scrupulously cleaned.

Once presentable, he felt at ease to continue with the novel, which indeed made great strides during the summer and autumn but for which Oscar Bie at the Fischer Verlag had to contain his impatience: for though by the end of the year Thomas reckoned he had it two-thirds done, the narrative was carrying him far beyond his early estimate of its length. The general opinion of the family, to whom, in ceremonious session, he would occasionally read extracts from the manuscript, was that it was more a hobby, or a protracted exercise, than a serious attempt at literary fame. At times he himself felt tempted to think no more highly of it—though the poem in *terza rima* 'Monologue', written in January 1899 and published in *Die Gesellschaft*, showed, for all its coquettish false modesty, that the dream of 'a slender laurel-wreath one day' to adorn his brow was in earnest. The verses of 'Thos the poet' appeared frequently at this time in notebook, letters, and dedications; but he was aware of his shortcomings, and his

---

[26] PdM 327.

efforts were more often humorous than serious. His head was still full of ideas for novellas too. Of a dozen figuring in his notebook, only one, stimulated by his studies of Savonarola after the Florence visit, would actually be written, and that some years later (*Gladius Dei*). But in a few days at the end of November he produced *The Wardrobe*, a fantasy quite outside the world of the Buddenbrooks, mingling dream and reality, its scene, though the city described seems to be Lübeck, clearly his lodging in the Markt Strasse in Munich. Dedicated to Carla, it was accepted for the *Neue Rundschau*, where it appeared in June 1899; a month later came a pirated and unrecompensed reprint in a New York German-language paper ('the American nation deserves sincere congratulations', was his comment on this news); in November, as one of four read by an actor to the Munich Literary Society, it proved a disaster and was hissed off by an unappreciative audience.

Though there can be no doubt that he was continuing his diary, none is extant for this time: we have therefore no idea what may have prompted this extraordinary, almost surrealistic tale, 'full of riddles', as he subtitled it—apart, that is, from the backless wardrobe which was part of the sparse furniture provided by his own landlady. In a 1906 article, he noted one novella, perhaps this one, as an exception to his rule of working mornings only and of never using alcohol—'and it shows'. The hero's strange, erotic vision of a lovely nude girl appearing through the back of the wardrobe, and her story, with its violent end hinting at sex murder, seem to indicate a continuing preoccupation with the problem of sexuality which had disturbed the author in Italy; and this is even more explicit in the short sketch *Avenged*, written a few months later, in which the narrator, confessing to 'unbridled desires', is attracted to a liberated Russo-German woman, a *jolie laide* with 'totally mannish brain', but finds his advances rebuffed. But we gain no pointer to his actual feelings from the rather prissy mode of life we otherwise know was his at the time and from the respectable and solid façade he was careful to present. A reserved nature, recalled a contemporary, of polite formality, his cool superiority discouraging any intimacy.[27]

It remained a habit in his work to have several irons at once in the fire, and often this 'jumbled' method, as he called it, far from hampering production, acted as a stimulant. But at this point a new distraction had arisen which was to slow his progress on the novel. The running of the journal *Simplicissimus* and of Albert Langen's publishing house had been seriously affected, after a lampoon on the Kaiser's visit to Jerusalem, by charges of *lèse-majesté* against Langen, who was obliged to take refuge in Paris, and by

---

[27] *Nb.* 3, 186.

the departure for Vienna of Jakob Wassermann. This left Korfiz Holm, at 26, virtually solely responsible for the journal, while Reinhold Geheeb, brother of the educationist and later founder of the Odenwaldschule Paul Geheeb, handled the literary side. Meeting Thomas Mann by chance in the street, Holm offered him on the spot a post with Langen at 100 marks a month. Despite the time which would be lost to his writing, it was an offer he was glad to accept (and which his family welcomed as a sign of more regular employment): for after all it was in *Simplicissimus* that he had made his real début, with *The Will to Happiness*, and its satirical approach had always appealed to him. Beginning before the end of the year, he found himself responsible not only for the preliminary selection of publishable stories but also for work as general reader for the Langen Verlag. The tendency to caricature in his characters, foreshadowed in the 'Picture-Book' sketches for Carla and already manifest in *Tobias Mindernickel* and *Little Lizzy*, owed a great deal in his later fiction to the two years he was now to spend in the *Simplicissimus* ambience and to his observation of the Munich scene from this vantage-point.

To it he also owed one of the few friendships that developed there. Kurt Martens (no relation to the Lübeck schoolboy Armin), five years older than Thomas Mann, like him a beginner in the literary sphere but with more published work to his credit, had recently arrived in Munich from Leipzig, and in May 1899 received an acceptance letter for a short story from the *Simplicissimus* junior editor. They were soon on visiting terms, and he was one of the few outside the family who was privileged to hear not only excerpts from the manuscript of *The Buddenbrooks*, but also impromptu performances by the amateur violinist in his latest lodging in the Feilitzsch Strasse. Martens, well brought up and carefully dressed, was a more congenial spirit than the bohemians of the artistic world of Munich, and his outspoken admiration for the novel made a welcome counterweight to Thomas Mann's still-lingering doubts of his own capacity. 'I already believed in his great and special worth and in his future,' wrote Martens later, 'when he himself was still hesitantly feeling his way forward. . . . I regarded myself as his precursor, the successes he achieved as the fulfilment of my own artistic ideals.'[28]

Neither Martens nor Grautoff, however, had much to offer him: when Grautoff now came to Munich, his doglike, sometimes querulous, devotion, which had been easy to fend off with ironic letters, became more a burden than a pleasure. Neither could fulfil his longing for real friendship, which his reserved and aloof manner did not encourage. It was different with the Ehrenberg brothers, of Dresden, both talented musically, about

[28] PdM 352.

his own age, and known to him from Lübeck days. Carl, the younger, had studied at the Dresden conservatoire, and taken a post with a theatre orchestra when he arrived in Munich in 1898; while Paul, gifted equally as a painter, had come earlier to study at the Munich Academy of Art, and was now much in demand for portrait commissions, as well as exhibiting often in Munich. Paul he met first, it seems, among the circle his mother had established, Carl not until a year or two later; and to Paul he was attracted as he had been to Armin Martens so long before. They were almost at once on familiar *Du* terms, sharing the same interests, including cycling and making music together; and the friendship with the two brothers he recalled thirty years later as one never paralleled in his life. For Paul, however, it was love he felt. 'To long for love to the point of dying,' he wrote in his notebook later, 'and yet to despise anyone who loves you. Happiness is *not*: to be loved, that is a satisfaction, mixed with disgust, for one's vanity. Happiness is: to love and seek to find subtle approaches to the object of one's love.'[29] His search for happiness that way would in the end prove vain, for Paul, like Armin, had pronounced heterosexual leanings, and their relationship frequently suffered from Mann's over-sensitive reactions. But for the next few years his friendship with the brothers lent his life the sunshine it had lacked, notably in fostering his love for music; with Paul 'experiences which cannot be told', 'highly unliterary, unpretentious and lively', though he admitted it was mere schoolboy love, could lift him out of occasional depressions, showing him that there was 'something honest, warm and good, and not just "irony"' in his nature.

He was conscientious in his editorial work, which he could conveniently divide between home and office; but its impact on the timetable for his novel made itself felt. 'You wouldn't believe how time-consuming the nonsense is!' he wrote to Martens, excusing his delay over a promised visit: even the pleasantest distractions had to be renounced if he was to 'spare two miserable hours a day to roll my novel on a bit'. With it taking so long to complete, he felt that he must give the public an interim reminder of his existence, and there was no difficulty in placing *Avenged* in the August 1899 issue of *Simplicissimus*. 'Very poor quality', he admitted to Martens; and writing to Dehmel to ask for a contribution, he cited it as evidence of the dearth of good material reaching the journal. Martens invited him for a summer holiday at his house in Gmund, on the Tegernsee, where he had enjoyed a previous stay; but he preferred, he said, to spend the summer clearing his editorial desk and then get away in September, northwards this time to Scandinavia, to the sea rather than the mountains.

[29] *Nb.* 4, 210.

His destination was Aalsgard, the Danish resort on the Sund, near Hamlet's Elsinore; as reading, he took with him Goncharov's *Oblomov*. But it was the chance to stop on the way in Lübeck that really drew him—an urge to return, after five years, to his origins. Revisiting that scene was, of course, timely, for in his narrative he was about to describe the death of Senator Buddenbrook's mother and the sale of the family house. But a more likely motive, if unadmitted, was a desire to see how far the moderate fame he had achieved had become known in his native province. If that was indeed in his mind, he was to be disappointed, for as he registered at the Hotel zur Stadt Hamburg there was no recognition of the former Senator's son, let alone of an author of some repute. And as he walked the familiar streets ('how small it all seemed!') he remained anonymous, even when calling in at the old family homes in Beckergrube and Meng Strasse, the latter now in part a public library (and one day to be known as the 'Buddenbrook House'). He seems to have decided to keep it that way, for he made no move to make contact with any old friends, not even Wilhelm Marty, who had been so helpful with data, or Ida Boy-Ed. As he was about to take ship for Copenhagen, he found himself held by the police in mistake for a confidence man they sought, and in some difficulty (in those days of no passports or identity cards) before he could establish his bona fides; but even then he did not make himself known to the hotel owner, whose son had been a schoolmate and who could at once have vouched for him. It was an experience he would not have missed, however, for the theme of confidence man as artist (or artist as confidence man) would emerge in the later memoirs of *Felix Krull*; while the whole journey— Lübeck, Copenhagen, where he spent a few days, Helsingør, and a short stay in Aalsgard before returning to Munich—was already taking shape in his mind as the story of *Tonio Kröger*, directly autobiographical and one of his finest.

But first the novel, wearying though he was of it, must be brought to an end. He could not hasten his pace: as he wrote later, 'presto is a tempo foreign to my nature. A work may be difficult—to the point of being unbearable—but it has to go slowly.'[30] Fischer's report in January 1900 that the sales of *Friedemann* had not yet reached a quarter of the total print-run of 2,000 was scarcely encouraging; but the publisher added how pleased he was to hear the novel would soon be on his desk, and, not yet aware of its inordinate length, wrote: 'I am greatly looking forward to seeing a bigger work from your pen.' Even then, in what was becoming his habit, yet another novella had interposed itself, *The Way to the Churchyard*: a tale in

[30] Ibid. 242.

the same ironically humorous vein as *Tobias Mindernickel* and with a similarly caricatured figure, Praisegod Piepsam, at odds with the world of normal life; and notwithstanding the spur of Fischer's encouragement, it was not until 18 July that the last line of *The Buddenbrooks* was written.

He anticipated a further three months' work to get the manuscript in order, the earlier chapters, as he thought now, 'repellent in their stupidity' and needing revision. But there was another, different pressure now: called again by the army in June, he had this time been found medically fit, and was to 'take up my rifle, to the horror of all enemies of the Fatherland, on 1 October'.[31] The corrections were done within a month; on 13 August he parcelled up the 'impossible' pile of pages, closely written on both sides, and, since it was the only copy, sealed and registered it for a value of a 1,000 marks. The postal clerk's smile, and the burn he gave himself from his clumsy handling of the hot wax, lent an ironic touch to his oft-told tale in later years of this significant moment.

[31] *Br.* iii, 423.

# II

## BEYOND DECADENCE TO PRESTIGE
## 1901–1914

'I dare not deny that he set more of his affections, during a great part of his life, upon worldly things, wealth among others, than might have become such an intellect'
(Lockhart on Walter Scott)

1

' "Isn't it a great grind, sir?" "A very great grind, as you call it. And there may be the grind without the success. But . . . it is the grind that makes the happiness." '
(Anthony Trollope, The Duke's Children, 1880)

Though his friend Kurt Martens thought the prospect of military service frightful for a writer of his nature, Thomas Mann himself was, after all, by no means averse. 'In my arrogant decadence, I find it encouragingly refreshing', he wrote to Paul Ehrenberg, 'to spend a year exposed to ruthless and energetic abuse, for which I shall no doubt offer every excuse. . . . Maybe they'll turn me loose again after a few weeks: but I'm hoping for the best.' He had felt vaguely guilty at having been turned down before; now, with the novel launched, and nothing further yet on the stocks, the timing was right, and he was ready to accept the loss of a year almost with pleasure. His preference would have been the cavalry, as less physically demanding than the infantry, but it was to the Leib-Infanterie-Regiment he was finally assigned, to report on 1 October in the uniform which, like all one-year 'volunteers', he had to provide himself. In the interval, he cleared his editorial desk (for his job with *Simplicissimus* must, of course, now come to an end), went to the opera and to art exhibitions, played his violin, and tried to possess his soul in patience as he waited for the publisher's news on the novel. 'Money and mass applause can hardly be expected . . . but even if it's only a small literary success, I shall be proud and thankful.'

It was to be a longer wait than he had expected. Fischer, on holiday, would not be able to read the manuscript before his return to Berlin; a brief meeting in Munich towards the end of August, at which, of necessity, he could bring no news of acceptance or publication, left his author depressed ('might have been better if we had never met', Mann commented to Grautoff, fearful that he had made a poor personal impression; 'what is to become of my novel is a dark problem'). But his mood lightened when he put on the elegant blue Leib-Infanterie uniform with red collar and silver braid and began his training: Vikko, watching the recruits through the grille of the Türken Strasse barracks, thought he looked every inch a 'proper soldier'. His appearance in full dress lent colour to the occasion of his sister Julia's society wedding on 9 October to the banker Josef Löhr, who, fully fifteen years older, had finally decided to offer for her rather than her mother, and who at the time seemed to Thomas (ever susceptible to the attractions of money) a highly suitable match. To Heinrich, who stayed away in Italy, the union was less appealing; he reserved his affection for Carla, now almost 20, and in the years to come developed a strong aversion for the 'Löhr gentry'. The departures of the couple for their honeymoon in Switzerland and of Carla for her first stage-assignment in Zwickau marked the family's virtual breakup.

Back in barracks, the new recruit found the regime of 'shouting, time-wasting and spit-and-polish' far from the stimulus he had expected. He felt hopelessly cut off from the civilized world, under a 'fearful pressure of authority', yet with 'an extraordinarily heightened enjoyment of inner freedom', as he whistled something from *Tristan* during clumsy attempts to clean his rifle.[1] He blessed the moment, after only three weeks of duty, when the marching made him lame in the right foot, and laid him up in the barracks hospital. 'Tendo-vaginitis', he recorded almost proudly in his later account: caused quite simply by flat feet which neither he nor his medical examiners had remarked. The younger doctors, not strangers to his work, encouraged him to look forward to early release if he could continue to emphasize the pain: for one who never made light of his ailments, this was no problem. Meanwhile, hospital tedium was relieved by the books and correspondence Grautoff brought him, and he could even go on with his notes for a drama on the Florence of Savonarola and Lorenzo de' Medici he had started to plan. Set now on release, and with the military slow to decide on his future, he did not hesitate to bring influence to bear through his

---

[1] *Brw. HM* 121.

mother's doctor, who was a friend of the senior medical officer: by the end of the year, he was finally certified unfit and, although later placed on the reserve, was to all practical purposes once more free. Pure malingering, wrote the Lübeck trustee to his mother, which so incensed him that he sent him 'the most malicious letter of my life', almost provoking a lawsuit. *Qui s'excuse, s'accuse*, we may think: his showing over the episode was an indication of the egoism which was his least attractive trait, and which over the years, apparently to his surprise, often made him enemies. For him, the evidence of the army medical system's manipulability was duly noted for later use, as a telling example later of the artistry of confidence man Felix Krull, and as amusing material for Heinrich, himself never accepted as fit for service, in his later novel on Wilhelmine Germany, *Man of Straw*.

Free: but still without definite news about his novel. At the end of October he had heard for the first time from Fischer, who had not yet read it all, but enclosed part of his reader's report. He judged it far too long to be a commercial proposition—who in that day and age could find the time and concentration for a book of such length?—and he criticized the wealth of detail, which too often over-emphasized the trivial at the expense of the essential. But he was prepared in principle to publish if it could be shortened by about half. This the author downright refused to do; he would accept any terms but this demand to sacrifice three years' work. 'He must bring out the book as it is,' he wrote to Heinrich, 'and I've told him it's not by any means the last I'll give him.' It all depended on whether Fischer was prepared to believe in his talent. In the end, after a gentle threat to offer it to Langen instead, his efforts succeeded. Fischer assured him he had no intention of dropping him: the novel would be published, and if he was keen meanwhile to make himself heard again, a second volume of novellas could be considered. Finally, in April 1901, the novel went to the printer, as a two-volume work rather than the three or even four which at first had seemed necessary. As a publisher, wrote Fischer, he was still 'not exactly delighted' over the unusual length. 'But you won't always be writing four-volume novels, and so a publisher, even though he has to take a commercial view, can well . . . take a chance with you.'[2] The contract he offered allowed for royalties of 20 per cent on the selling-price (which he assured Mann was the level for even his most successful authors), for six years, renewable, and with options on all his production except dramas. After the months of waiting, bringing renewed doubts, Mann found this handsome indeed: 'The time seems at hand, when this work of three years' torment is beginning to bring me a little satisfaction, contentment, and joy.' He was

[2] SF *Brw.* 398 f.

especially proud of the reader's remark, in his final assessment (Fischer had, of course, not sent him all the earlier, more adverse, comments): 'I am astonished how the book's satirical and grotesque elements not only do not disturb the great epic form, but actually enhance it.' Greatness after all, then! he exulted to Heinrich: it was good that it started so modestly, yet by the end developed, not into a run-of-the-mill novel, but into something quite different and perhaps more rare. Though it would be autumn before the book appeared, and he would have to wait a long time to see any money from it, the contract was signed, its duration finally fixed at five years. It was a decision neither he nor the publisher would regret: for that original contract was to be regularly renewed for fully half a century, and to prove lucrative for both.

Unacknowledged, but certainly an element in his exultation, was the fact that he was now by way of overtaking his brother. Though Heinrich's latest novel, *In the Land of Cockaigne*, had just appeared with Langen and after good reviews was already into a second printing, he had never so far achieved such favourable terms as Fischer's; nor had he ever taken the stage for a public reading from his work, which was his brother's privilege in January 1901, sharing the evening with Kurt Martens and offering to some acclaim *The Way to the Churchyard*—by no means the last time he would enjoy displaying his histrionic talent. Underlying Thomas's dream of success there had probably always been an urge to rival and surpass his brother, and their close association in Italy while he was writing *The Buddenbrooks* had given him ample opportunity to profit from Heinrich's experience and ideas, to exploit the relationship as he exploited that with others. While still in barracks, he had thought of nothing but joining him again, this time in Florence, to get on, in his company, with studies for the Renaissance drama, as well as with further novellas, for Fischer thought those available inadequate to make a volume.

But once released, his mood over the winter, determined by his relationship with Paul Ehrenberg, had fluctuated between 'indescribable, pure, unhoped-for happiness of the heart' and 'truly acute depressions with seriously meant ideas of doing away with myself'. Or so he had confessed to Heinrich—hastening soon after to allay his fears that suicide had ever been a serious thought:

it's all metaphysics, music, the eroticism of puberty . . . things that must not be exaggerated. It's not a love-affair, at least not in the usual sense, but a friendship which is understood, returned, rewarded; which at certain times, as I admit without affectation, especially at times of depression and loneliness, takes on a rather too tormented character. . . . My nervous constitution and philosophical turn of mind has made the thing unbelievably complicated, it has a hundred sides, from the simplest to the spiritually most adventurous. But my main feeling is a deeply joyous astonishment over a responsiveness never again expected in this life.[3]

Heinrich was all for another Italian stay together, and by March had discovered a *cinque-lire pensione* in Florence. But the plain fact was that even this was for the moment financially impossible, apart from the fact that a new novella, *Tristan*, was already taking shape, and that with spring he was 'fairly wallowing' in his desire 'for enthusiasm, devotion, trust, the pressure of a hand, loyalty, after so long a fast', for Paul had started his portrait. 'I shall dedicate the novella volume to him, or a chapter of *The Buddenbrooks*, which he knows and loves, whichever comes out first. My gratitude knows no bounds.'

But at the end of April he tore himself away, to spend three weeks with Heinrich in 'the most charming city in the world', returning 'more stimulated and satisfied than ever before from a journey'. 'Writing a Savonarola became a much more definite possibility,' he wrote to Paul later, 'even if I've other things to do for the moment.' Following in the steps of Fra Girolamo, drinking in the seductive splendours of Signoria, Uffizi, cathedral, Pitti Palace, he spent much time in the monastery of San Marco, making detailed notes on the ambience and the monks' comportment; collected or ordered photographs; noted book titles on Renaissance art, architecture, bookbinding. To Grautoff, making the journey after him in November, he expressed envy at his taking this 'beautiful road to the lofty stage of my heroes, scene of my symbols', and pressed him to make notes for him on the interior of the Villa Medici in Careggi, where Lorenzo had died and which he himself had missed: 'with that you might be very useful to me'.

Less lofty during his own brief stay, however, was a sentimental experience, not normally unexpected for a twenty-five-year-old but certainly new for one whose inclinations so far had been towards his own sex. Sharing the brothers' table at the pension were two English girls, Edith Smith and her younger sister Mary, and when Heinrich returned from a trip to Naples, a lively foursome developed over hands of cards and other diversions, despite his brother's complete lack of English and his own very moderate command. Mary, 'looking like a Botticelli, only much jollier', he found highly attractive, and what had begun as a carefree flirtation later took on 'a quite remarkably serious character'—on both sides, surprisingly, with talk even of marriage. Their leave-taking, he told Paul after his return, was 'worthy of a play—though it's actually mean to speak of it in such a tone; but I'm speculating on your inborn coldness of heart'. At 55, in an autobiographical sketch for public consumption, he claimed he had been

[3] *Brw. HM* 21 f.

restrained by the feeling that such a step was premature for him, as well as by misgivings, which Mary herself seemed to share, over marrying a foreigner. Possibly so: and a further deterrent, for one so eager for financial success and the elegant life-style this could bring, was that he was virtually penniless, while a Miss Mary Smith in a *cinque-lire pensione* is hardly likely to have been well endowed. But at the time he seems to have been nervous at what he might be getting into, rather than just sensible about the future, and was anxious for Heinrich's support, urging him to cut short a stay in Naples and return:

My recent Munich experiences and the change of air are beginning to lose their effect, and I'm going through moments hard to bear. . . . Miss Mary, whose birthday was the day before yesterday—I gave her a basket of candied fruit—has been a great joy to me. But now I think I'm getting too melancholy. She is so very clever [this in English] and I'm silly enough always to love those who are clever, even though in the end I can't keep up.[4]

Keeping up with a quick wit, especially in English, may well have been hard for the more phlegmatic North German, better on paper than in repartee. But a more likely reason for his hesitation was alarm at an entanglement so different from that with Paul: to this, for all its emotional problems, he still clung and, with his flippant references to Mary in his letters, no doubt sought to inject into it an element of jealousy. The stage-worthy parting would not be the last word on the affair, he told him: 'but if you don't hold your tongue about it, stupid . . . I'll have your blood'.[5] They may in fact have kept in touch for a while, and the novella he wrote later that summer, *Gladius Dei*, he dedicated in English 'To M. S. in remembrance of our days in Florence'. It 'ended in nothing', however, and he never himself referred again privately to this first fleeting thought of a 'normal' union. Before long, the right time was to come, and then the short experience in *galanterie* may not have been without its value.

Meanwhile, when he returned with Heinrich to Munich at the end of May, there was work to do. *Tristan* was only half-completed; the first proofs of the novel awaited him, to be quickly followed by the page-proofs; and he spent an intensive month of June clearing away both tasks. (In individual dedications of a few parts of *The Buddenbrooks*, his mother and Aunt Elisabeth got no acknowledgement for their help.) The novella, planned to fill up the volume of stories with which he could 'make himself heard' until *The Buddenbrooks* could appear, had a disappointing impact when finally ready. Bie declared it unsuitable for separate publication in the *Neue Rundschau*, and the newly founded literary magazine *Die Insel*, though accepting it, later proposed that its successor, Insel-Verlag, should publish the whole volume. This, of course, was ruled out by his

---

[4] Ibid. 27.     [5] PdM 437 ff.

contract with Fischer—but Fischer was in no hurry to bring out the volume himself, and *Tristan* did not appear, as the title-piece for six stories, until 1903.

The 'burlesque', as he had at first called it to Heinrich, was in a similar vein of caricature to *The Way to the Churchyard*, a humorous presentation of the antithesis of life and death, but in less cruel fashion. The detailed, sardonic description of the central figure, the neurasthenic literary man Detlev Spinell, was immediately recognizable as that of the writer Arthur Holitscher, an acquaintance from *Simplicissimus* days who owed much to Thomas's support for the publication of his first novel, had been an enthusiastic supporter of *The Buddenbrooks*, and so was far from pleased when he finally saw *Tristan*. But as the author justifiably pointed out later, there was in fact more of Thomas Mann than of Holitscher in the character of Spinell, for the story was intended to castigate the weaknesses of the artistic temperament he recognized in himself: slow polisher of phrases ('to see him at work, one would conclude that a writer is a man to whom writing comes harder than to others . . . but it must be admitted that what eventually emerged did give the impression of smooth spontaneity and vigour, despite its odd and dubious, often even unintelligible content'); his preciosity and aesthetic attitudinizing; the antagonism towards robust bourgeois life, which he is ready to express on paper but is too weak to justify face to face; above all the attraction of the music of *Tristan*—with fatal consequences in the story for the gentle wife of the insupportable Klöterjahn.

Patience had still to be his watchword, for although the setting of *The Buddenbrooks* went ahead with some speed (one can only marvel at the printer's capacity to deal with his difficult script), the two volumes were not in his hands until October. The intensive work and long waiting-time for results increased a preoccupation with his health, and especially the digestive tract, which was rarely trouble-free: all his problems seemed to settle in his stomach, as he commented later to Grautoff. He made notes of the doctor's detailed recommendations for diet and physical jerks, and incidentally also of Savonarola's complaint, in an earlier century, of the effect on 'stomach and other organs' of the 'continual . . . intellectual labour' to which he was exposed.[6] A summer break was indicated, and he spent a few weeks with his brother at the spa of Mitterbad, near Merano in the then Austrian South Tyrol, where Heinrich, already with long experience of 'cures', knew the doctor. With mountain air and long walks, even climbs, the hypochondriac soon stopped complaining, though he decided to take up the doctor's suggestion of a treatment under a stricter regime at his winter sanatorium at Riva, on Lake Garda, later in the year;

[6] *Nb.* 5, 271.

and before his return to Munich at the end of August had finished his *Gladius Dei* novella.

Here for the first time he made his setting explicit: instead of the anonymous, Lübeck-like surroundings of his previous stories, a resplendent Munich, 'where art rules the day', its inhabitants engaged in more agreeable pursuits than 'feverish commercial competition'. An imitation Florence, it is the scene of the conflict between the sensuousness of the visual arts and the ascetic puritanism of a young religious fanatic, a modern Savonarola protesting against latter-day Medicis: the expression in another form of Mann's own inner conflict between life and art. The monk-like Hieronymus (or Girolamo, like Savonarola) is bundled ignominiously out of an art-shop, after demanding in vain the destruction of a sensuously depicted Madonna and perorating to deaf ears on true art, whose mission should be, not a 'seductive stimulus to confirm and strengthen the lusts of the flesh', but 'the divine fire to set the world aflame, until the world with all its infamy and anguish burns and melts away in redeeming compassion'; and he conjures up a vision of a bonfire of the worldly vanities like Savonarola's on the Piazza della Signoria, calling down 'the sword of the Lord, swiftly and soon!' The narrative's tone is detached and ironic, like that of *Tristan*, but the antithesis of robust 'normal' life and the aspirations of the aesthete is less simple here. Both Spinell and Hieronymus are gently ridiculed; but in using Hieronymus to stress the sexual aspect of art Mann was expressing the doubts about sexuality which had continued to trouble him since the days in Italy—that 'poison which lurks in all beauty', yet was the mainspring of the life he sought to find outside his own art.

As with *Tristan*, a try for publication with the Insel-Verlag failed, and *Gladius Dei* too would have to await the later Fischer volume, after appearing first in a Vienna journal in June 1902. His hopes for the moment had to rest with *The Buddenbrooks*. It was disappointing that Paul had been absent from Munich for most of the summer; his longing to resume their relationship had to be satisfied with the company of the brother. But temporary work again as reader with Langen was enough to distract him from any emotional thoughts, as well as easing his purse and curbing his impatience to see the first notices of the novel, with which he hoped at last to see the recognition he had longed for.

An invitation to another public reading from his work on 18 November gave a welcome chance to do something himself to boost its reception. This time the evening was all his, and he gave them *Gladius Dei* as well as a sample from *The Buddenbrooks*—the school chapter into which he had woven so much of his own experience in Lübeck. The sensitive schoolboy Hanno, last of the Buddenbrook line, his school-fellows and the teachers, remarked the next day's *Münchner Neueste Nachrichten*, were all vividly portrayed with a humour 'spiced here and there with striking psychological observations' which was far livelier than the often forced irony of the novella and the 'disproportionately pretentious breadth of detail' in its descriptions of Munich. An incomprehensible and cold review, leaving a bitter after-taste, wrote Mann to Grautoff, when he himself had thought his performance very good, 'not to say brilliant'. He had promised himself from it an increased interest in the novel. By then, indeed, the advance notices had spoken of a novel in the grand style, 'a truly German work of art', and 'that is practically all I want to hear . . . Fame seems not entirely to want to fail me, *in spite* of my craving for it.'[7]

It had been a worthwhile delay in his departure for Riva. But even more satisfying was the chance beforehand to see Paul again, who had just returned to Munich. He was unchanged, he confided to Grautoff,

and I too: I'm still so weak, so easily seduced, so unreliable and so little to be taken seriously in my philosophy, that I seize the hand of life as soon as it is extended laughingly to me. Strange! Every year, when nature declines, life breaks into the summer's desolation of my soul and infuses streams of feeling and warmth into my veins! I let it happen. I'm artist enough to let everything flow over me, for I can use it all. Fra Girolamo too had a friend who admired him and whom he loved . . .

Under the influence of the two brothers, now almost like his own, he had lost his former feeling of melancholy in company, he told their sister; and this he owed especially to Paul: 'I've made him a bit more literary and he's made me a bit more human. Both were necessary!' Paul, it seems, kept his distance, the 'hand of life' he extended was not often within Thomas's grasp. It may have made him more human; but, as his letter to Grautoff showed, he was no less 'literary' in his notion of their relationship. On its ups and downs he pondered long, using it, as he used everything, in copious source-notes for his work. A novella he planned, to be called, significantly, *The Loved Ones* rather than *The Lovers*, an unhappy affair with himself in the female role and almost all his ideas from her standpoint, would never be written as such. But the carefully hoarded material would be exploited: soon for *Tonio Kröger* and other stories, and over forty years later for *Doctor Faustus*. Then, as he leafed through them, he felt 'ashamed and touched at the recall of these griefs of youth', 'the relative happiness— with *profound* suffering', 'the support of irony'. 'Love cannot be more deeply experienced. But in the end I shall be able to say to myself that I've paid the penalty for it all. The trick was to be able to make artistic form of it . . .'[8] At the time such detachment was not so easy, and it may well have been a relief to set off again for Riva on 20 November.

[7] PdM 461.    [8] *Tb.* v 551.

The strict regime during his four weeks there, alternating extended walks with rowing on the lake and outlawing intellectual exercise in any form (so that even reading had to be in secret), soon began to do him good, he wrote to Carl Ehrenberg: 'we'll have a nice winter then, with lots of music, perhaps also in my flat if I can afford a piano. . . . Best wishes to you and to *Paul*, to whom I *may* write before long.' The first reviews of *The Buddenbrooks* began to arrive while he was there. But it was becoming clear that the book was not going to have an easy passage. Fischer's disquiet over the length (he had prudently limited his first printing to 1,000 only) and the cost (at 12 marks it was by no means cheap) was seemingly justified, for it was selling slowly, while reviewers no doubt found two volumes a somewhat daunting prospect.

Friends stood ready, however. Kurt Martens, himself with a novel just out, had a long essay by early December in the Berlin *Literarisches Echo*, in which he was lavish in his praise for the 'mature, assured technique', the 'intensity of feeling and flexibility' of 'the truly epic style', the 'stern objectivity' with which the most varied characters were presented, moderated only by the author's 'sympathetic smile' over life's hardness as his humour took on a tinge of bitterness. The novel, thought Martens, fulfilled all the promise of the short stories that had so far appeared under the name of Thomas Mann.[9] Grautoff, planning reviews for the *Münchner Neueste Nachrichten* and a Hamburg paper, received detailed hints from Riva, showing him exactly what the author wanted to see and virtually writing his piece for him. He was to underline the '*German* character of the book', notably in music and philosophy, thoroughly German in its whole manner and in the subject, especially in the father–son relationships through the generations, though Dickens and the Russians might have been forerunners; the hopelessness and melancholy of the end could be mentioned, 'a certain nihilistic tendency' in the writer, but the positive side, his *humour*, stressed; a sign of 'unusual energy to plan and execute such a work'; the epic tone splendidly maintained, with effective use of the leitmotif and a 'strongly dramatic element' in the dialogue.

In contrast, the December number of Fischer's house-magazine, the *Rundschau*, brought a more sobering critique from Arthur Eloesser of the lack of organization and the monotony in what he called this 'phlegmatic art': 'If Thomas Mann should one day be able to sacrifice small details to the needs of composition, he would gain a place among our best narrative writers. From the cameo genre which he commands, to the novel in the grand style which he has so promisingly attempted, is in fact more than just

---

[9] *Jb.* 3, 263 f.

a step.' Restraining his resentment, Mann wrote a reasoned reply in a letter to the publisher which he asked him to show to Eloesser: he had never imagined the book to be well composed, but organization was another matter, and monotony was not always objectionable, though he had done everything to avoid tedium, and had hoped for great effect from use of the leitmotif. As for 'phlegmatic art': had Eloesser any idea of the 'tortures of tearing impatience under which this "destiny of a task" had been completed and overcome? If it were not for this phlegmatic book, I would not now be condemned to rowing and physical exercises.'[10] But a long *feuilleton* would be coming in the Vienna *Abendpost*, he added for Fischer, and its enthusiastic author, Richard Schaukal, had told him how he was looking forward to 'four to five editions'—a dream to comfort him as he sunned himself in his boat and mused on the next tasks.[11]

Back in Munich by Christmas, and changing his apartment once again (away from the scene of the 'torture' of the novel), he found it hard to settle to these. The Savonarola drama, so many notes made for it, but not yet begun, must give way first to *Tonio Kröger*; and this, after several false starts, was proving more difficult than he thought. And with Paul again at hand, the story of *The Loved Ones* was still very much in his mind. At the 'trumpet calls' of Schaukal's article—'at last the great novel' thought lost to Germany since the earlier nineteenth century, an 'honest, German book . . . genuine, powerful, pure style . . . unparalleled mastery of presentation'—as at other praise for his talent, he could only smile in growing melancholy. These were from people who did not really know him: it all went to show 'the complete lack of human, personal affection, trust, devotion, friendship' from which he suffered and which he feared was beginning to disable his productivity. This at any rate was the burden of a long letter to Paul, who was evidently more interested in a round of Fasching festivities than in tête-à-têtes with an importunate lover.

*Where* is the one for me—far from amiable and capricious as I am, self-tormenting, sceptical, suspicious, but sensitive and quite uncommonly eager for sympathy— the one who will show his unstinting consent? *unwaveringly*? without letting himself be put off or intimidated by apparent coldness or rejections? or trying, in comfortable indifference, to explain them by saying '*I will just have to get used to him again*', but instead hold true to me, in inclination and trust? *Deep silence.* . . . I've been hideously hurt and feel in anything but the mood for dancing and masques, only utterly lonely, not understood, sunk in gloom, heavy at heart. A talk would do me good, I think, and I'd almost have said 'Come and see me', if I had been justified in assuming you *didn't* belong to all the others who find the talent highly respectable but its owner abominable.

[10] PdM 475 ff.    [11] SF *Brw.* 400 ff.

The trick was 'to turn it into artistic form'. A soothing visit from Paul two days after this outburst was immediately transformed to notes for Rudolf and Adelaide in *The Loved Ones*:

Friendship sealed. Promise of faithfulness. He signs some lines for her: 'Now and forever—yours.' Her pondering over this. . . . Very much the easy way out . . . he wants no more wavering and no more scenes. . . . He is in fact a little embarrassed . . . his carefree attitude a little disturbed.[12]

Paul, it is clear, was not making him less literary. Thomas's passion and his sensitivity over real or imagined rebuffs were deeply felt, there is no doubt; but it was none the less remarkable how ready he was to transform experience into art. (Indeed, it may not be over-fanciful to wonder whether 'life', in the shape of their impossible relationship, was not being lived in the interests of literature, the scenes provoked, even, in order to experiment with the result from the novelist's standpoint.)

Though the winter had not produced much work, so Thomas wrote to Martens in March, only emotional experience, his conscience was relieved by the observations which had filled his notebook. Heartening too was a perceptive review of *The Buddenbrooks* in March: Thomas Mann, wrote Rilke in the *Bremer Tageblatt*, was a name that 'must undoubtedly be noted', a chronicler and yet also a poet in enlivening the 'distinguished objectivity' of a book entirely free from authorial pretentiousness. 'It is an act of reverence to life, which is good and just, simply by happening.' Mann did not forget Rilke's approval, even though they met only once, briefly, after the First World War. But what remained in his mind forty years later from the review was the other's stress on the *deaths* in the story, the religious bent, that sense of 'the cross, death, and the grave' which, he thought, marked their affinity at that time: 'in my case . . . probably more masculine and musical, even though I'm not Tom the rhymer'.[13]

He made little progress on *Tonio Kröger* during the summer months, though Paul had left Munich in May and it was a long time before they met again. The autobiographical parts of the story had not been difficult (schooldays, his love for Armin Martens in Tonio's for Hans Hansen and his uncertainties over his sexuality, the near-arrest in Lübeck and the journey to Denmark), but the central theme of conflict between 'literature' and 'life', in Tonio's discussions with the Russian artist Lisaweta Iwanovna—his own problem now—was hard to express, because still unresolved. Writing to wish Paul success with his exhibition in Stuttgart, he said he had been working too:

that is, I waver and torture myself, in sometimes scarcely bearable fashion, with doubts, hesitations, insufficiencies and the hypersensibility of my artistic con-

---

[12] *Nb.* 7, 57 f.     [13] *AM Brw.* 321.

science. Such a tragic conjunction is probably rare, so much gnawing ambition with such nervous indolence, so much passion . . . with such heaviness.

The feeling was strong of being an outsider, unsuccessful in both homo-erotic and more normal relationships, with life passing him by and leaving him no more than a somewhat precious dilettante, a mere littérateur, lacking determination for the career on which he had embarked and from which, at last, money was coming in (the novel, reported Fischer, was proving not only a literary but also a publishing success, and he could already offer him 1,000 marks on account). 'We, the lonely, solitary, disinherited of life' long only for 'the normal, decent, amiable . . . for life in all its seductive banality', he wrote now in *The Hungry Souls*, a short psychological study, as he called it. The piece, reflecting actual experience at a theatre-ball and his exclusion from the normal life of Paul Ehrenberg, and with an ending (an encounter with a destitute and really hungry social outcast) which he dismissed himself as inconsequential and trivial, made a bridge between *Tristan* and *Tonio Kröger*, and helped with the more subtle elaboration of the latter. But it was the sentence 'another kind of love is required' that would be the most significant, and that in a more literal sense.

In a spirit of restlessness, not easily explained, he planned yet another move, to a small apartment in the Konrad Strasse in Schwabing, taking temporary quarters in September in a nearby pension and booking another stay for October in the sanatorium in Riva until it would be ready. No summer break, he wrote to Paul: the food in places like Starnberg, attract-ive though they were, was so 'stolid', 'I have a right to comfort, damn it, and if I can afford it, so much the better. In Riva everything is fine, and I'm sure to benefit.' Expatiating on Wagner performances in Munich (including, as always, *Tristan*), he deplored the new custom of no curtain-calls: 'too much dignity is unartistic . . . I at least have enough of the artist, actor, entertainer, clown, in me to feel: *there must be applause*'. He was to have ample opportunity in the years to come to indulge this appetite for acclaim.

In a six-week stay in Riva he had still not completed *Tonio Kröger*: 'difficile', he wrote to Martens, asking if he might dedicate it to him, 'I'm working . . . but carefully and even more line-by-line than usual.' Fischer now had the rest of the volume of stories in proof, so there was some urgency to add this final piece. In the leisurely atmosphere of the sana-torium and with most of the morning spent on the lake (often lazing rather than rowing), he managed to tinker with the manuscript for only an hour or so each day; but it was finished soon after his return to Munich in November, and the volume of six novellas came out by February 1903, with *Kröger* published simultaneously in the *Rundschau*. Still generous with dedications, he inscribed each separately: *Tristan* to Carl Ehrenberg 'for many a harmonious hour'—*not* to Holitscher! who was remembered with *The Way to the Churchyard*; *The Wardrobe* to his sister Carla; *Little Lizzy* to Schaukal; *Gladius Dei* to Mary Smith; and *Tonio Kröger* to Martens (who appeared as 'Karl' rather than 'Kurt', a regrettable misprint which slipped by and had to be corrected in the later editions).

And now—at last—the laurel crown was no longer a dream. At the end of 1902, as the small first edition of *The Buddenbrooks* neared sell-out, Fischer reprinted in a single volume, at less than half the previous price: cautiously still, a run of only 2,000, but this was soon exhausted, and the novel began its remarkable rise to a success foreseen least of all by its author. By the end of 1903, it had passed the 10,000 mark, and three years later reached 37,000. 'Favourable press notices, even in foreign journals, multiplied. . . . I was plunged into a whirl of success. . . . My mail increased, money streamed in, my picture was in all the illustrated papers, a hundred pens busied themselves with the product of my shy solitude, the world embraced me with praise and good wishes.' Such a reception, then as on later occasions, aroused, he claimed, mixed feelings of scepticism and gratitude: in 1903, it seems likely that gratitude predominated. For he was now established as a successful and respected man of letters, his ambition, and above all his financial independence, had been achieved. Till now his income from the Senator's estate-trustee had been less than 200 marks a month, and he had made little from journal contributions, while his royalties from the first edition of the novel came to only 2,400 marks in 1902. From the further editions, Fischer's 20 per cent rate yielded around 13,000 a year from 1903 on, a relatively substantial income. His right to comfort and a well-found life-style, which were always his prime consideration, were assured from now on; at the same time, with the prudence instilled by his upbringing, he could put money by, and also meet the demands of others. Here, it must be said, he was ever generous, as far as prudence allowed, notably in the case of Heinrich, whose much greater productivity and, as many thought, equal talent had not yet been comparably rewarded.

Thus freed from day-to-day worries, he could pursue his work at the slow pace which was his way. 'My head is almost turned by all the high expectations I seem to have aroused,' he had written to a favourable critic in December 1902. 'Well, if my health, which is somewhat uncertain, doesn't fail me, I think I can still promise . . . all kinds of remarkable things.'[14] Further public appearances played their part in building up his new-found popularity. In Munich, at the end of November, he had read *Tristan*, and in February 1903 he paid his first visit to Berlin, for two

[14] Br. iii, 442.

readings: in the Lessing Society, where he gave *The Way to the Churchyard*, while Wassermann read an excerpt from a novel, and the following evening, alone, at the invitation of the Berlin Press Club, for *Tonio Kröger*. The *Berliner Tageblatt* thought neither him nor Wassermann a 'great elocutionist', voices too low and expression spoiled by the endeavour to avoid over-emphasis, but did note the 'Simplicissimus smile round the keen eyes' of 'the thoroughly North German Thomas Mann', the nuance in his cadences, 'somewhere between rapture and roguishness'. In the Press Club, however, his performance seems to have been more effective: 'such splendid dry humour', wrote the *Lokalanzeiger*, 'such a penetrating gift of observation, that one would gladly have heard more'. He was indeed asked again, and promised to return to Berlin in the autumn. Hedwig Fischer, his publisher's wife, hearing him for the first time, was quite carried away by the 'unforgettable evening'. Recordings in later years of such readings illustrate vividly his virtuosity in maintaining, as he once said, 'clarity and total "speakability" ' in his texts: the drawbacks of his style on the printed page—over-long sentences, and humour often obscure or contrived—seem to show to positive advantage. But it took the advent of the microphone to overcome his inaudibility. Reserved among people, he could project his personality best on the podium in front of them: spoken 'direct from the manuscript, my lectures and stories are five times better and more gripping, more winning and enthralling, than when they are simply read'.

Rare among the voices of acclaim was any word of appreciation from Lübeck. *The Buddenbrooks*, in spite of a quite favourable early notice in one obscure paper, had aroused considerable exasperation among the city's notables with its 'betrayal' of his home; the gentle humour was felt to be mockery, the tone patronizing, and the appreciation of such as Ida Boy-Ed was scorned. An enthusiastic defence of his friend by Grautoff in the Lübeck *Eisenbahn-Zeitung* during 1903 did not seem to have much effect. Sales there, largely under the counter, were, however, not insubstantial, the game among gossipy readers being to decipher the originals behind the characters and draw up a solution to this *roman à clef*. His true attitude to his home city he had tried to represent in *Tonio Kröger*, he said in April 1903, and he could only wish it were read in Lübeck: 'perhaps then they would gain a less repellent idea of me than hitherto'. His relations there, it seems, were unperturbed, even Aunt Elisabeth, who commented good-humouredly that she had surely not been such a 'silly goose' as the Tony Buddenbrook her nephew had portrayed; later in life she came to be almost proud of figuring in such a successful book. Her brother Friedrich (Uncle Friedel), though outwardly incensed to find himself as the ne'er-do-well Christian and later protesting to Thomas against this 'fouling of one's own nest', was sufficiently flattered to introduce himself to strangers as Christian Buddenbrook.

Anyone who had read the earlier short stories, with their often un-pleasant themes, could well have seen the author as cynical, heartless, even inhuman, a picture which the detached, ironical tone of *The Buddenbrooks* chronicle would have done little to dispel and which had in fact not failed to draw adverse comment. *Tonio Kröger*, in the three years since the first notes from his 1899 journey to Denmark, had developed into a conscious attempt to show himself in a more attractive light. But it was more. In taking his alter ego through childhood and schooldays like his own, through the intellectual conflict between sophisticated literary endeavour, leading to detachment and inhumanity, and normal life 'in its seductive banality', and through emotional experiences exactly his own, he was writing a franker autobiography than his readers were immediately likely to realize. In Tonio's nostalgia for the north, where he discovers that his 'bourgeois love for the human, the living, the ordinary' may be the secret to 'turn the littérateur into a true writer'—'in it there is longing, and sad envy, and just a touch of contempt, and a whole world of innocent delight'— Thomas Mann had gone a long way to writing the Paul Ehrenberg complex out of his system. The trick, once again, had been to turn it into artistic form: this time into a 'prose-ballad . . . played on the home-made instru-ment of the big novel', his use of the leitmotif no longer purely descriptive but 'elevated from the mechanical to the musical'. It was not surprising that later he frequently declared it his favourite among his works, and was pleased to find it always appreciated by young people.

It was certainly a success from the start, and in separate editions was well past the hundred thousand during his lifetime. But not long after its first appearance, he expressed to Martens a doubt whether he had not sacrificed credibility to rhetoric in this confession of a love for life, which 'in its clarity and directness verges on the inartistic'. Martens, however, like others, was ignorant of the deeper implications of the Paul Ehrenberg affair. That, though Thomas's Schwabing existence kept him in frequent contact with Carl Ehrenberg and he corresponded at length with Paul, was now safely relegated to further lengthy notes for *The Loved Ones*, and in the interests, as was very soon to be evident, of the new kind of love he knew to be necessary.

2

*'If you knew what miracles and wild fables I have been letting myself dream . . .'*　　　　　　　　　　(TM, August 1903)

'I'm bored with Italy to the point of despising it!' Thomas Mann had said, in the voice of Tonio Kröger. 'It's a long time since I felt at home there. The land of art! . . . I renounce it. All that *bellezza* gets on my nerves.' The story marked the beginning of a clear divergence between the brothers. While Heinrich, more the Latin, continued to see in Italy his spiritual home and an exotic source for his work, Thomas had declared himself thoroughly 'Nordic' in temperament and outlook. In the south, Tonio Kröger, of mixed northern and southern parentage like them, had dipped into the carnal adventures that Heinrich described so vividly, but in the end nostalgia for the north, and a somewhat prudish revulsion—'perhaps something inside him inherited from his father'—had triumphed. In a review-essay in March 1903 on a recent novel by a woman writer, Thomas highlighted the contrast between its gentle 'feminine ideal of art' and the 'bombast imported here in recent years from the fair land of Italy'—a veiled dig perhaps at Heinrich's latest effort, a blockbuster novel-trilogy *The Goddesses*, published at the end of 1902, heavily erotic and his strongest bid yet for success. It was some time before Heinrich saw this review, but he did not forget it.

It was doubtless irksome for him that both *The Goddesses* and his next novel, *The Hunt for Love*, finished during the summer of 1903, signally failed to rival the success of *The Buddenbrooks*, especially in terms of the money, which for him, as he noted for a reply to Thomas's critique of *The Hunt*, was the *only* effect he craved: 'if I stop [writing], I'm done for'. Altogether too much sex, his brother had complained, a surfeit of breasts, thighs, flesh. True eroticism lay, not in such explicit descriptions, but in poetry, in 'the unnamed which lends everything its awe and sweet attraction, its secret'. In saying this, he averred, he was far from acting the Savonarola; a moralist was the opposite of a preacher of morals—'I'm entirely Nietzschean in this point.' But during that summer, he noted in himself a feeling of antagonism, almost 'hatred' towards Heinrich: in comparison, 'I am a weak-spirited plebeian, *but* equipped with much more yearning for power. Not for nothing is Savonarola my hero. . . . I hate those most who, through the feelings they arouse in me, draw attention to my weaknesses.'[15] Though he was careful not to reveal this to his brother—on the contrary telling him over the end of the year 'we both feel happiest when we're friends', Heinrich was still so much his superior in 'distinction, emotional purity, and clarity'—their difference remained, as a smouldering fuse to explode a decade later.

During that summer of 1903 the family, except for Julia, now married, had been briefly reunited. While Thomas began his work on the Savonarola, now to be called *Fiorenza*—slowly, in uncertainty over the unaccustomed form of drama, to which he feared his philosophical mono-

[15] *Nb.* 7, 83.

logues would be ill suited—both Carla and Heinrich returned to Munich for a while. He planned to remain in Germany to finish *The Hunt for Love* before returning to Florence, while Carla, after a disappointing stage début in Zwickau, was waiting for a new engagement in Düsseldorf in the autumn, from which she had higher hopes. She was beautiful enough, wrote Thomas later, but without any great native talent, and his concern over the Bohemian life she was leading was undoubtedly reinforced when he recognized her as the heroine of Heinrich's over-sexed novel. Now, he spent much time with her; and their mother, as he reported to Paul, gave an enjoyable soirée—with Carla, his two brothers, Carl, and assorted guests, including a half-dotty baroness—in her temporary home before leaving for the country. She had decided to take young Viktor from school, where he was doing badly and showing more interest in farming than learning, to Polling near Weilheim, south-west of Munich, for the rest of the year. Here both Thomas and Heinrich spent some summer weeks with her: though complaining of stomach troubles, Thomas found it a tolerable stay, with 'shady garden, good cycling, solid food, smell of manure, etc.'— though, as Martens found after Thomas had visited him at the Tegernsee, he was never in fact an enthusiast for country life as such, a keen walker and cyclist but finding anything robust and rustic either repugnant or a source of amusement.[16] The fraternal differences will not have been in evidence in Polling: Heinrich was deep in the finishing touches to his novel, and did not share Thomas's compulsive urge to give family readings from work in progress, while neither would have liked to cloud their mother's inordinate pride in her sons' distinction (at every opportunity, she was making herself known to booksellers and pressing them to order and display their books).

It was soon after his return to Munich in August that Thomas found himself plunged into dreams, night and day, 'wild fables', of a happiness that might one day be his—a happiness that, to judge from the notes he had been making for the theme of *The Loved Ones*, the querulous and unsatisfactory relationship between his Rudolf and Adelaide (read Paul and Thomas) could never bring. One of the high points of a week-long Wagner festival was an evening reception, attended by all of Munich's musical and literary world, and it was here, apparently, that the wild dream suddenly took hold. 'What a fool I am!'—he noted for a letter to Grautoff—'who'd do better to sit down and produce something good, instead of indulging in such magical fairy-tales. But never mind! One must already be something, even to reach such dreams . . .' Seeing there the well-known Alfred Pringsheim, wealthy mathematics professor and prominent Wagner enthusiast, with his wife and family, he had been suddenly seized by the idea

[16] *Jb.* 4, 255.

that the daughter Katia, just 20, attractive and clever, could one day make the ideal companion for the new life he was beginning. At concerts and in the opera he had many times observed the family and, like the rest of Munich, knew all about them: their grand house in the Arcis Strasse, a centre of attraction for the literary, musical, and artistic community, where Hedwig Pringsheim presided in graceful elegance at her receptions; the beautifully displayed collections of silver and majolica in which Alfred Pringsheim had invested his inherited wealth; the standing he had achieved at the university through his scholarly papers and his talent as a lecturer; and his early connection with Wagner, often a guest in Bayreuth and one of the first to sponsor the building of the Festspielhaus. For Thomas Mann to see himself as a successful suitor for Katia was a dream, perhaps: but why should it not be fulfilled? He was now an established writer of some repute; if not yet of means comparable with that of the Pringsheims, then well on the way there, and finding himself more and more welcomed into the social circles in which they moved.

At all events, it was a dream that took increasing hold as he resumed his work, and it was significant that very soon after this he set down his first ideas for a novel to be called *Royal Highness*. As a child, he had played at being a prince: now his new-found fame had lent him a comparable status—that of the artist, always being recognized and under observation, as Tonio Kröger had said, with that royal yet embarrassed look which marked him out from the mass. A prince, who must have a princess . . . This is not to say that he emulated a life of royal magnificence: his standard was thoroughly bourgeois, to be 'of good manners, well-dressed, cultivatedly modest', as he had been pleased to find Richard Schaukal when they first met. But he was beginning to lead, as he wrote about this time, 'a symbolic, a representative existence', discovering that he had 'a certain princely talent for representation'—ironically meant, no doubt, but none the less an accurate statement of that attention to outward show which would mark the rest of his life, and lead many people later, as he admitted now, to find him cold and reserved: 'it may be because one loses the taste for personal communication when one is accustomed to symbolic expression, i.e. through works of art'.

On a brief visit to Carla in Düsseldorf early in October he had enjoyed his first stay in a luxury hotel, its décor and service impressive enough to yield detailed notes for the royal story. An important part of the outward show was the public appearance, and at the end of the month he had embarked on a more ambitious tour of readings, in Königsberg, and in Berlin for the promised repeat of *Tonio Kröger*. There he was welcomed again by Fischer, and this time, as befitted his growing success (sales of the novel now approaching 13,000 and a second edition of *Tristan* about to appear) was introduced to personalities of great importance for him.

Foremost among them, one evening at the Fischers, was Gerhart Hauptmann, the older writer whose works had been familiar to him since his schooldays and who had by now become the greatest star in the publisher's firmament. 'Meeting him was an experience of the first order,' he wrote with his thanks: 'I only wish I had been able to give him a happier idea of myself . . . he, the victorious, will have gained an impression of confusion, struggle, nervousness, over-exhaustion—and that would not be far out. But perhaps he also felt the good in me: he is fundamentally good by nature.' If the other guests were disappointed in him, too bad: he would hope to compensate later by the work that was to come, less uninteresting than his 'moustachioed personality'. The modesty was somewhat forced, and though no doubt he really was overawed by the older Hauptmann, he seems now to have been far from suffering from such a lack of self-confidence.

For the moment, the main work to come, *Royal Highness* and *Fiorenza*, was being held up by interim pieces, for there were constant requests for journal contributions. The days were gone when he had to seek publishers: now they sought him, were prepared to accept whatever he cared to send, and, as he said to Fischer in December, accepting his royalties for a further 3,000 copies of the novel, he could always use money. By then, he had sent off to the Vienna *Neue Freie Presse* the 'sketch' *The Child Prodigy*, and was preparing for the *Rundschau* another, *A Gleam*, as well as the essay-review for a Berlin journal of the latest book by Gabriele Reuter, the novelist and women's rights enthusiast whom he had met and liked in Berlin. The second sketch, based on an anecdote he had had from Martens, was openly interim: the narrator's brief pause between 'Florence of the old days' and 'perhaps a royal castle', while 'strange, dimly glimmering things are in the process of finding their place'. That the story was a variant on the *Loved Ones* theme showed how far he had distanced himself now from the Paul Ehrenberg relationship, the ironic tone in sharp contrast to the earnestness of his notes for Rudolf and Adelaide. Both pieces were written shamelessly for the money, he confessed to Heinrich, and he took little pride in either (with reason, it must be said); and writing to him again in January 1904, he announced his intention of making an end to such 'dissipation' and reverting to more serious things. That Fischer should have hailed *The Child Prodigy* as the work of a master was what always happened: 'I work . . . without the least satisfaction, send in the stuff in deepest despair, then come the letters, the money, the praise. . . . All enjoy it—except me. . . . But perhaps that's the way it should be.' The satirical line of *The Child Prodigy* did indeed prove popular at public readings, in December in Munich and later, of all places, in Lübeck. An invitation there, from a newly founded literary society, he had heard from Ida Boy-Ed, was in the wind; but he was still wary of the city's hostile and uncomprehending atmosphere, and told her he preferred to wait a year, by which time he might hope to be seen as a son of whom they need not be ashamed.

The lengthy January letter was an attempt, not always very coherent, at reconciliation with Heinrich after his scathing remarks on *The Hunt for Love*: but to mention the money and the praise which even the pot-boiler works brought him was hardly the best tactic to this end. Nor was it diplomatic to report that he lunched twice a week now with Julia and her husband 'Jof' Löhr—epitome of the bourgeois ménage Heinrich so detested—with the conversation purportedly showing in what high esteem Heinrich was held. (A significant factor in the Löhrs' lack of sympathy for Heinrich was the pillorying of Munich society in *The Hunt*, which as a *roman à clef* put *The Buddenbrooks* in the shade and highly embarrassed banker Löhr, among other worthy citizens.) Heinrich seems all the same to have been mollified; but when in February he sent Thomas his next work, *Fulvia*, a novella of the Risorgimento, the fulsome compliments he received were followed by a critique of the liberal idea of freedom, showing clearly how far their philosophies diverged. For Thomas, freedom was 'a moral, spiritual, idea, synonymous with "honesty". Some critics call this my "coldness of heart". But for political freedom I've absolutely no interest. . . . Simply that so much blood has flowed for the idea means it has for me something uncomfortably *unfree* about it, something positively medieval.' The lines were being drawn, not only between the brothers, but also within the family, to the mounting worry of their mother: on the one hand, Heinrich and Carla, bohemians and non-conformist at heart, with success, despite great effort, still eluding them; on the other, Thomas and Julia, by the world's standards eminently successful and more than content to find their place in the established order.

Driving home the difference, Thomas continued to describe his 'new role as famous man', the acclaim for his Munich reading, the extent and variety of his correspondence, and the social invitations—in particular, to the Pringsheim mansion, where, after several visits, he had been invited to a grand ball. 'At this large gathering, literature and art were well represented: for the first time . . . I was in high society and had to show myself off in the most exhausting fashion. People walked around me, watched me, had themselves presented, listened to what I had to say. I believe I didn't do too badly.' And he had got to know, at last, the daughter of the house, 'Katia (that's her name), a wonder, something indescribably rare and costly, a being whose existence alone outweighs the cultural activity of fifteen writers or thirty artists. . . . Intoxication: but this time, if I take action, one that can have immeasurable consequences'—his dream could become reality if the will was there. He was clearly delighted with the impression he had made; and his admiration for the Pringsheim ambience knew no bounds, the distinguished father, the mother a beauty 'worthy of Lenbach' (the famous portrait-artist), Katia's twin brother, Klaus, a musician, pleasant, cultivated, with 'North German manners'. 'No thought of Jewishness among these people; one detects nothing but culture.' And a dinner invitation was in prospect:

nothing at all has happened. . . . it's all in my imagination, but too bold, too new and colourful, too marvellously adventurous for me to want to banish it. I see the *possibility*, and am in a fever, can think of nothing else. The boy in the fairy-tale had a great fall and gained a princess for his wife. And (throwing out my chest) I am more than a fairy-tale boy! It's all so fearfully complicated that I'd give a lot to be able to talk it over quietly with you. But I say right away: it's idle to ask whether it will lead to my 'happiness'. Do I aspire to happiness? To life, rather; and *with it* probably 'to my work'. And further: I'm not afraid of wealth. I've never worked from hunger . . . have already more money than I know how to use. . . . Whether I warm my feet of an evening at an oil-stove or a marble fireplace is irrelevant to the degree of my comfort . . . But all this is much too premature. We have to wait on events, and it's probably no use asking for advice, for I'm letting myself be carried along by them. . . . What will happen? From the purely practical point of view, I have the impression . . . that I would be welcome to the family. I'm a Christian, from good family, have achievements which such people know how to appreciate. The outcome? Probably nil. But is not the possibility itself a disconcerting experience?

For Heinrich, in spite of his goodwill and affection for his brother, this story of upward mobility into the social sphere to which he felt such aversion cannot have made very enjoyable reading. And one can imagine how galling he found the rather supercilious tone of the final words, which described how his publisher, Albert Langen, approaching 'almost subserviently' to be introduced for the first time to his ex-employee Thomas Mann at the ball, had been loftily advised to hold on to his Heinrich: '*one* day he *will* have a great success', at which Langen had protested he had absolutely no intention of dropping him—so 'you can rest quite easy'. The loss of Heinrich's end of the correspondence at this time leaves a tantalizing gap in our knowledge of their relationship. However much the master of psychology in his stories, Thomas was certainly showing a singular naïvety in his handling of this important problem in his own life—a reflection once again of his basically egotistic character. By no means as self-assured as his behaviour seemed to indicate and his success to warrant, he still needed his elder's support and advice—yet seemed incapable of striking the right note to get it.

With the wooing of Katia, however, it was another story: here he pursued his objective with patient determination and not a little skill. On the road to realization of that first 'wild fairy-tale', he was moved by a variety of feelings. First and foremost, the powerful attraction of her beauty and character, arousing a real love he had never before experienced for the opposite sex, and the growing confirmation of his first impression, that here, in background as in intelligence, was the ideal companion for the life of a writer of standing. Half-acknowledged and undoubtedly not without influence was the wealth she would bring with her to their union: he could profess disdain for riches, but in fact greatly preferred the marble fireplace to the oil-stove for his comfort. An ideal match, therefore, which would have the added advantage of concealment for the homo-erotic tendencies he could not openly indulge and which could find expression only in his work. (Part of Katia's attraction, indeed, may have been the tomboyish character she had developed amid a houseful of brothers.) She was not, however, to be swept off her feet overnight by his attentions. Bright and, after a home education, already one of the rare female students at the university, where she was reading physics with Röntgen and mathematics with her father, keen on tennis and cycling, she did not feel at all ready to abandon this happily independent life for an early marriage, even though her studies were pursued mainly to please her father. Thomas was not the only one to be courting the 'Princess', as people called her, but she was not prepared to take any seriously. Her father, though tolerably impressed by the young writer and finding common ground with him in their enthusiasm for Wagner, was reserved, and clearly not yet inclined to lose his only daughter; if and when it came to that, he would have preferred an academic for her husband. Hedwig Pringsheim, however, had smiled on his suit from the start, and was delighted to hear from her bookseller that the author of *The Buddenbrooks* was well on the way to becoming as great a novelist as Gottfried Keller; as he pursued Katia, in person and in letters, it was on her mother's benevolent influence that he played. While the three older brothers good-humouredly called him 'the liverish cavalry-captain', so pale and slim, so correctly elegant in his moustache and general bearing, twin Klaus entered into the game as an eager Cupid, always ready to preserve the proprieties in arranging discreet rendezvous and looking the other way.

'No thought of Jewishness among these people . . . nothing but culture.' The remark to Heinrich is the only indication we have that the thought had even entered his head. Though anti-Semitism was never far below the surface in the Germany of the time, and Alfred Pringsheim had had to wait several years before promotion to a full professorship, Munich generally paid little attention to racial origins, and had accepted the Jewish immigrant from foreign parts (Berlin) as an asset to its cultural life. He had long since abandoned the religion of his father, mine-owner and railway magnate of Upper Silesia, while his wife, also of Jewish stock, had been brought up in the Protestant faith adopted by her grandparents early in the nineteenth century. Her mother, Hedwig Dohm, was one of the earliest advocates of women's rights ('human rights have no sex!') and became adored grandmother 'Miemchen' to the Pringsheim children. They for their part had absolutely no feeling of being Jewish, and when, as was inevitable, the 'well-known Jewish question' came up during their schooldays, their mother took pains to explain the importance of tolerance. So it was to remain, until the uglier days after the First World War and the rise of National Socialism.

At the end of March, Thomas wrote to Heinrich that an idea of spending two weeks together in Riva in April looked doubtful, for the 'great affair' of his life was near a decision. After many vicissitudes, in which he had suffered quite a lot, he felt things could not be going better. 'Normally of a truly Indian passivity, I've shown unbelievable initiative in word and deed, and at good moments am full of confidence.' Katia, briefly hospital-bound for a minor operation, had been sent flowers, with the approval of her mother, who always smiled encouragingly when he spoke simply of 'Katia'. But he often feared that his imagination was outrunning reality. Work, of course, was out of the question, the peace and quiet required was lacking: 'ah, life, life!'

Reality was not yet in fact taking on the roseate hue of his imagination. Katia continued to keep him at arm's length; tête-à-têtes, even with Klaus's help, were hard to arrange; and to his appealing letters the constant response was evasion. Sometimes she took mocking refuge behind what she called her father's 'tigerish' disapproval—a disapproval which he himself, as he told her, failed to discern in the father's kind and correct behaviour towards him. Nerves and (as always) stomach suffered accordingly; after a 'big discussion' with her early in April, he decided that, if wait he must, then Riva after all would bring much-needed relief, and he left soon after to spend three weeks there, rowing, cycling, breathing good air. 'You should not let me wait again like this, Katia,' he wrote. 'Waiting is frightful. One should not confirm fate in its unpleasant habit of letting good things come only when one has become quite apathetic, just from the suspense, and can hardly enjoy them any more.' Jealous of her studies, he said he thoroughly approved of a little neglect there (for if his suit was to succeed, she would anyway have to abandon them).

Returning to Munich, he moved once again, this time to a third-floor apartment in the Ainmiller Strasse. The break had given him new impetus, and on 16 May there was a 'second big discussion' with Katia: she may have relented enough to set a date on her answer, for in his notebook he wrote 'from Thursday 19 May began the great waiting period'. He awoke from morning dreams full of longing for her, and his letters lost their slightly formal, literary tone, to take on that of the impatient lover. She was a vivid image before him, almost always as he had seen her, through his opera-glass, in the concert-hall, before they were acquainted: 'the silver shawl round your shoulders, your black hair, the pearly pallor of your face, the way you tried to hide your awareness of people's eyes on you'. She must know, he wrote, how his life hitherto had been far from a happy one, that even the acclaim of the outside world could bring him no self-assurance; only one thing could cure him—happiness

through you, my clever, sweet, kind, beloved little queen! . . . What I beg from you, hope for, long for, is trust, unquestioning devotion to me against a world, against even myself, is something like faith, in short—is *love*. . . . Be my affirmation, my perfection, my redeemer, my—wife! . . . Ah Katia! between the inexpressible delight of those seconds in the dusky garden when I felt your sweet, sweet little head against my cheek, and the sadness unto death when I left you today (my birthday!)—what a fearful difference! That is no reproach. It may be weakness, but I have no reproaches for you. Only love! Only love!

He was bound by powerful chains, he told Martens, refusing an excursion: much sorrow was his lot, but there were also brief intervals of great happiness; and as it had to be 'K. P.' that he had chosen to love and marry, he could not expect everything to go smoothly. To insist would only get a refusal; to withdraw in a huff would be tasteless. In the end all must be well, he averred.

As his pleas began to move Katia, he pursued his advantage: what was this talk of inability to be what he expected of her? 'But I love you, for God's sake, don't you understand what that means? What more is there to wait for and to "be"?' To talk seriously of not being worthy of him—worthy!—when after every meeting he asked himself anxiously whether *he* was worthy, whether he was not 'too clumsy, too unworldly, too much the "poet" '. 'And you, saying it's going too fast, gone too fast! Do you realize that, since the day I told you plainly how much I love you, two whole months have gone past?'

It was no time to get on with *Fiorenza*; but—being, as he noted later for himself, 'not a writer, but a poet who also made a composition of his own life'[17]—he artfully composed now a new story, as a 'harmless tribute' to Katia's mother. The novella, *At the Prophet's*, described in accurate and humorous detail their meeting on Good Friday, while Katia was in hospital,

[17] *Nb.* 7, 112.

at one of Ludwig Derleth's ceremonious 'evenings', a reading in his absence of his 'Proclamations'. Derleth, talented poet, was well known and popular with Munich's literary and artistic world, including the Pringsheims, where his obsession with Napoleon made him an interesting guest for Hedwig. For him too Katia was always the 'Princess'. As 'Daniel' in the story he is faithfully portrayed, likewise the dozen or so devotees, all recognizable as Munich personalities, assembled that evening to hear the 'Proclamations'— 'sermons, parables, theses, laws, visions, prophecies, summons like orders of the day'. The autobiographical framework is set by the writer—with 'stiff hat and well-trimmed moustache', knowing no one, 'from another sphere, here only by chance', with 'a certain relationship to life and a book read in bourgeois circles'—and the wealthy lady, flatteringly drawn, who 'esteems his books'. She suggests he show his sympathy for her daughter 'Sonja', unable to attend, with a flower: '"Thanks! I will!"' . . . A flower? A bunch! A whole bouquet! . . . And he felt that he had a certain relationship to life . . .' Showing Hedwig the story before its publication made a useful tactic in his campaign. And the writer's reaction to all this 'genius', as he sits on the floor seeking relief for his aching back and manfully suppressing visions of a ham roll, is not without interest: 'in this Daniel all the preconditions are there—solitude, freedom, intellectual passion, splendid outlook, belief in himself, even the proximity to crime and madness. What's missing? Perhaps humanity? A little feeling, longing, love? But this is a totally improvised hypothesis,' he tells the wealthy lady, as he sends his greetings to 'Sonja'. His own genius lay rather in a supreme capacity for taking pains (which Samuel Butler, an author not included in his wide reading, thought might be more fitly described as a capacity for getting its possessors into trouble of all kinds): but for the moment, this was less important than the 'relationship to life' he was seeking—and for that he needed Katia's love.

In July, outside forces took charge. Alfred Pringsheim fell seriously ill, and his wife and Katia accompanied him to Bad Kissingen for some weeks; then, after a short stay in Switzerland, while the three older brothers embarked on an extended cycling-tour of Europe, the twins were to be sent to relations on the Baltic. It would be an indefinite separation. Their last few days together had been wonderful, but the parting was torture for Thomas, and still without result. As long as a decision was not demanded, she was carefree; pressed, she looked at him 'like a hunted deer' and was quite incapable of making one. At the train, while thoughtful Klaus took his time seeing to the luggage, she was cautious in admitting sadness, but the long pressure of her hand, her gaze only for him as the train drew out, gave him comfort. He was in despair, he told Martens. He had gone so far as to consult a neurologist, who confirmed his suspicion that such *Angst* over a decision was a pathological condition, and recommended even more careful and diplomatic handling if there was to be hope of an engagement. But until she returned, that was empty advice. He was due for a reading in Göttingen on 21 July, and wanted to see the Bayreuth *Parsifal* later: 'but I'd give that up if instead I could see her here for a quarter of an hour'. Six weeks then with his mother in Utting, on the Ammersee, might get him back to his work: 'how happy, how strong and enterprising I could feel if she had given me some assurance when she left! You can't imagine how much I love this creature. She is in my dreams every night . . . I've experienced too much of her to be able to give up.'

What could not be cured must be endured, and others saw no sign of the lovelorn swain as he went about his affairs. The occasion with the Göttingen Literary Society was, he thought, highly successful: audience quiet as mice, a dinner afterwards with the local academics, best of all the speech by one of them in his honour—'a bit exaggerated, but when it happens to one for the first time it's a quite remarkable feeling', as he wrote to Ida Boy-Ed from Utting—and a session afterwards over Liebfraumilch with some students. (There would be many more such speeches during his life, and he never failed to enjoy the feeling, especially when praise came from academic circles.) Gratifying too was the expected invitation from Lübeck for the end of October, which he had accepted, waiving any fee, for, as he told Ida Boy-Ed, he hoped the inviting literary society was the 'real one': if it turned out to be some obscure revival with no authoritative members to guarantee a welcome, he would withdraw. He did not want people saying his heart was so set on coming that he would accept *any* invitation.

From Utting frequent letters went off to Katia, full of self-analysis and assurances designed to banish her doubts and hesitations (many passages he copied later for his notebook, continuing to make a composition of his own life and using them as material for *Royal Highness*—fortunately, for the notebook survived but the original letters, like Katia's to him, were lost). 'Never were you more in my thoughts than during these days! . . . I am seized by a burning sense of wonder, a tenderness wells up for which there are no words, no similes. And you? and you?' Till now, for him love had always meant a mixture of longing and contempt, the ironic love of Tonio Kröger for life, for the commonplace, 'sad, mocking, hopeless. And now? A being, sweet as the world—*and* good, *and* out of the ordinary, *and* capable (even if not perhaps so inclined) of responding to me with spirit and goodness: something absolutely and indescribably new! . . . my first and only *happy* love . . .' And even to Katia, he would transcribe from other

letters a phrase he thought telling, like that he had written to the friendly
critic Lublinski and was also quoting to Ida Boy-Ed, on his alleged 'coldness' and 'pretence':

not more than five or six people in Germany understand what irony actually is: that
it need not mean just 'coldness of heart', but a kind of intellectual breeding,
discipline, 'bearing', artistic dignity (and other things too), never occurs to the
fools. As to 'pretence', those of us who have learned pointed expression and
economical use of their resources have made themselves suspect to the majority of
good people and bad musicians. I'm amazed that Richard Wagner is not declared
an ice-cold humbug for making the *Liebestod* the end of the act . . .

What Katia made of this self-justification is not recorded: but it was
important to him that she should not join those who accused him of cold-
heartedness. Was he 'cold'? he asked her. She must know that he believed
in their union 'as one believes in oneself and the future. . . . But you, who
do not have this same simple feeling as I, still in doubt and oppressed by
misgivings . . .' Two or three days in Munich without her had seemed an
eternity, yet now he could manage almost three months in tolerably good
spirits. 'Man is a hardy vertebrate!'

How far he was concerned by the potential conflict between his
homoerotic impulses and the normal sex-life ahead, is difficult to gauge. 'I
may not confide in her *completely*, though,' he noted for himself about this
time. 'She is not equal to my affliction, to my torments. But without this gap
between us I would probably love her less. I do not love what is equal to
me, or even that which merely understands me.' Another note was an
indication perhaps of heterosexual experiment: 'After sexual evacuation:
quiet, useful thoughts, the artistic peace of disinterestedness.'[18] It was not
until some years later that Katia would become aware of his ambivalence.

As *Fiorenza* slowly reached the end of its second act in Utting, he
described to her too the difficulty he was finding in his work: it had never
'bubbled over' like that of the dilettante and the easily satisfied, 'who do not
live under the pressure and discipline of talent', that 'critical knowledge of
the ideal' essential for the creation and stimulation of ability; for the
'greatest and those least readily satisfied, the most rigorous scourge'.
Flaubert's words—'mon livre me fait beaucoup de douleurs'—always
seemed a comfort.

The separation was to be less than three months, for both were back in
Munich by September. Why do we suit each other so well? he wrote:
'because you belong neither to bourgeoisie nor Junkerdom, because you are
something extraordinary in your way—because you are, as I understand
the word, a *princess*. And I, who have always—now you may laugh, but you

[18] *Nb.* 7, 112, 110.

must understand me!—seen in myself a prince, I have quite definitely found in you my predestined bride and life's companion . . .' There must be an end to this intermediate state, he pleaded: and when she took him to her room to show him her books (in all propriety) he finally gained his point. 'That you—immortal words—"showed me your books". . . . You astonishing, disturbingly sweet, disturbingly severe creature . . .' On 3 October, they were engaged, 'the crowning moment of my life, without which everything I have otherwise achieved would be worthless to me'. Any doubts remaining—scruples of conscience, 'the artist's moral and ascetic mistrust of "happiness" ', as he wrote to Ida Boy-Ed—were of little account against his love for Katia.

Her parents, even her father, approved—he had no option, for Katia was now 21. Among those who did not was the critic Alfred Kerr: he, it turned out, had seen Katia at the Baltic resort, had formally proposed and been almost laughingly refused, and was furious now to find himself supplanted by one who had already earned his literary animosity. He neglected no opportunity for polemic against Thomas Mann in later years. Paul Ehrenberg was apparently startled and put out by the news; but Thomas reassured him that after the wedding the wheel of their friendship would soon be rolling again; Paul was married himself within the year. The pace moved now abruptly from lento to prestissimo, with the social rounds entailed by the engagement and a new urgency for the completion of *Fiorenza*, which he had rather rashly promised to Fischer by November; and the appearances in Berlin and Lübeck had to be put off for a month. He took Katia to meet his mother, now living in Augsburg with Viktor, who recalled much later how astounded he had been to find this academic paragon an unbespectacled and fashionably dressed beauty (that she won his mother's heart at first sight, and that there was never any trace of mother-in-law jealousy, seems, however, doubtful, to judge from Julia's later remarks).

With all the calls on his time, work on the drama was difficult; an extract was duly read to the Pringsheims, to murmurs of praise, but it was still a torso when he left for Berlin, accompanied by Hedwig and Katia for his formal introduction to the family there. For the reading in Herwarth Walden's Arts Club he added to *The Child Prodigy*, *A Gleam*, and a chapter from *Tonio Kröger*, a short foretaste of *Fiorenza*, but Fischer had to wait a long time for more than this. Katia recalled her fit of the giggles at the peculiar grumbling tone of Walden's cello as he played a piece specially composed in honour of the speaker; but she and her mother were doubtless duly impressed at his reception. Lübeck he dealt with alone. It was his first public return, and he stayed with Ida Boy-Ed; he read *The Child Prodigy* and an extract from *Fiorenza*, not always audibly enough, to a large and on the whole appreciative audience, from whom he solemnly received a triumphal garland. At a reception afterwards he spoke of the 'novel of his life': the significant turning-point of his engagement, the whole new chapter about to begin, 'conceived in ecstasy and now to be constructed with love, art, and faithfulness'. He was greatly amused by the remark in one press report about the 'superior comportment' lent him by his fame: but being thus looked up to by a 'poor little worm of a reporter' was none the less welcome.

Altogether, the 'virtuoso tour' was a sign of how far he had come in the few years since *The Buddenbrooks*: organizers prepared to change their programme at short notice to suit his convenience, the unpleasant repercussions of the novel in his home city apparently vanished, audiences ready to listen to anything from his pen, even the less than gripping prose of the *Fiorenza* draft. And, back in Berlin, he found his new standing quite up to the social demands of his introduction. At a dinner in honour of the happy couple, he met Maximilian Harden for the first time, editor of *Die Zukunft*, who had published his novella *Hungry Souls* two years before; the parents of Alfred Pringsheim, making him most welcome, presented him with a costly gold watch; even Katia's grandmother, Hedwig Dohm, though she could not, on feminist principle, approve of an independent young woman throwing away the prospect of a doctorate, and let Thomas know he was nothing less than a despoiler of women's rights, could not conceal a certain benevolence in her bright grey eyes. The acquaintance with 'Miemchen', he wrote later, remained one of the most memorable of his life.

Towards Christmas, as the preparations for a wedding in February began, he made good the long silence which these exciting months had imposed on his correspondence with Heinrich. It was partly, he said, to assure him that he had not forgotten the 'not entirely simple problem of our relationship', that he was not oblivious of all else but his own happiness; but mainly to plead that the new existence ahead in the land of Cockaigne which Heinrich had pilloried so bitterly was not all it seemed. For what was happiness?

I have never taken [it] for something light and carefree, but always for something as serious, arduous, and severe as life itself . . . I have not 'won' it, it has not simply 'come my way'—I have *submitted* myself to it: from a kind of sense of duty, of morality, of inborn imperative. . . . 'Happiness' is a service . . . and I stress that, not because I assume anything like envy in you, but suspect that on the contrary you may be looking on my new existence with some contempt. Don't do that. I haven't made it easier for myself. Happiness, *my* happiness, is to a far higher degree experience, emotion, recognition, torment, too near to sorrow, for it to be dangerous in the long run to my art. . . . Life, life! It remains an affliction. And like that it will probably with time bring me to a few good books.

And he went on to describe what the new existence entailed, his gain in worldliness symbolized now by a light-grey waistcoat with silver buttons to his tail-suit. It had been a constant 'standing to attention, and often enough all the "happiness" comes down to setting one's teeth'. There had been the emotional stress of the courtship, 'the engagement—no joke either, believe me', the effort to get used to the new family, the social duties, all these new people, 'showing myself off, behaving. . . . and every day the fruitless and enervating ecstasies customary with this absurd engagement-period'. He was so exhausted that he was thinking seriously of taking off for a time to Polling in January, to do nothing but work and breathe some 'unerotic air'. It was a great pity that Heinrich would not be there for Christmas or joining the 'singular constellation' he had put together for a dinner at the Pringsheims: their mother, the Löhrs, Viktor, and Grautoff; but he must not miss the wedding, which would be an easygoing affair, not even a church service, which Katia did not want. Meanwhile he begged for a few lines of welcome to his sister-in-law to be.

All this seems as unconvincing for us as it was, no doubt, for his brother. 'Submitted' himself to happiness, not 'won' it? Was not his exhaustion the result of the single-minded effort he had put into winning the bride he wanted and the new existence of wealth and social standing that, for all his protests, he knew was so eminently suitable? Heinrich may have envied his literary success, but he was the last person to envy him the new life, for which he felt strong aversion, if not contempt. Early in January he received a long gossipy letter from their mother. She was appalled at no church service: if these people were Protestants, they should show it at such a turning-point in Katia's life, but the worst was that the girl herself, in agreement with her father, who was of no religion, had refused. She made no bones, however nice Katia was to her, of her doubts about these 'ultra-modern' folk who did not even send New Year's cards or reply to congratulatory letters. If all turned out well for Thomas, so much the better for them all; if not, she would be prepared and not surprised. 'All this money means coldness, demands, hard heads . . . I think so often of what Papa would have thought. Lula was a little upset, when I told her my doubts and my worry about Thomas, she believes in Katia's love for him, oh God let it be so! How many other dear and less spoilt girls would have loved him truly and faithfully and cared for him!'[19] Heinrich was at all events not disposed to return from Italy, where he was held not only by a burst of productivity, but also by a love-affair of his own, with the beautiful Ines Schmied, a would-be actress and singer, which for the moment remained a secret from the family.

[19] JM 134 ff.

Carla, in mid-season at a small theatre in the most distant provincial corner of Germany, near Kattowitz in Silesia, would also be absent: to Grautoff's suggestion that she write a jolly poem for the occasion, she replied bitterly that comedy was not indicated in her present situation, where meningitis and typhus was rife. From her and Heinrich came a joint wedding-present of a porcelain coffee-service. Their mother's gift appealed to Thomas's sense of family piety: a set of the Mann silver cutlery, made up with new items, and a dozen new silver-handled knives in identical Empire style, all contained in a leather-bound canteen, converted from the old red-velvet case which had once held the family papers, and completed by a silver-plate tray in the lid. This, it turned out, would be for daily use: for from the Berlin Pringsheims came a complete silver service for twenty-four (with unbelievable things, '*those* people must have money!') But she sent him off as decently equipped as she could into the new sphere she felt was so radically different from her own.[20]

'All this money': the Pringsheims spared nothing to see their daughter's new life well found. The father took charge personally of the complete furnishing of a seven-room third-floor apartment at 2 Franz-Joseph Strasse, including telephone and a splendid baby-grand, to be ready for the couple after the wedding on 11 February 1905. Julia Mann was greatly impressed, especially by the chandeliers and the *two* water-closets; but she warned Thomas not to let himself be given *everything*, for he would hardly feel himself master in his own home if he had bought nothing himself. In the end, however, only a few Empire chairs were allowed suitable from his last bachelor lodging, which he vacated at the end of January, moving into a nearby pension. Meanwhile, for better or worse, he finished *Fiorenza* in a quiet few days in Polling, and sent off the manuscript to Fischer. To hear that it was considered 'something very choice' was satisfying; but he himself still thought his assembly of philosophical dialogues, with little dramatic appeal, an artistic failure, a hybrid, and the attempt to 'infuse an intellectual construction with life' a fiasco—a judgement which its subsequent career on stage, nearly always needing cuts and adaptations, certainly justified. It was published in two numbers of the *Neue Rundschau* in the summer and in book form in the following September.

The ceremony on 11 February took place in the Marienplatz registry office. (Though Katia claimed to recall, in old age, that there had also been a ceremony in the Lukaskirche on the Isar, her memory seems, strangely, to have been at fault.) The wedding breakfast in the Arcis Straße included the families and a few friends only; on the groom's side there was only Grautoff. The speeches were brief, and Thomas himself wisely chose to

[20] JM 143, 137.

make what was undoubtedly the shortest of his life, raising his glass quite simply to propose the healths of his new relations by their family nicknames. And then it was over: he could hardly believe he had succeeded in 'tearing a daughter from her sorrowing parents' to make her his wife and 'carry her off into the blue'—not very far, it is true, for their brief honeymoon was spent in Zurich and Lucerne, before they returned to the new apartment in Munich on 23 February.

In the Zurich Hôtel Baur au Lac they lived in princely state, as he could not resist reporting to Heinrich: 'Lunch' and 'Dîner', black tie in the evenings, liveried staff running to open doors. But 'happiness', he still stressed to his brother, remained elusive: despite all assurances of the benefits of marriage for health, he was off colour, and both he and Katia apparently consulted doctors while there. His conscience was bad in this life of ease, and he often longed, so he claimed, for a more monastic and spiritual life. Katia for her part is reported to have been advised, in view of her delicate constitution, not to have children for three or four years. If this is indeed so, neither she nor Thomas paid any attention. 'I married only because I wanted children,' Katia said not long before her death;[21] her constitution, through a very long and fertile life, was on the whole to prove anything but delicate. And Thomas was eager for a son. Late one evening, a month or so after their return to Munich, he ended a letter to a friend: 'the marriage-bed waits. It's not certain whether the prince is already on the way, one must stir oneself.'[22] There is no doubt that he passed this first real test of heterosexuality, for Katia's pregnancy was soon confirmed.

## 3

### *'I am tied, a golden ball on each foot'* (TM, June 1906)

Thomas Mann's life, as in later years he often liked to remark, seemed to progress in round numbers and tend to a neatness which, if not always factually quite correct, could readily be eased to fit (as with his birth, at the three-quarter century, which he preferred to place exactly at noon). A harmless favour from the gods, the phenomenon was always good for a smile in his frequent autobiographical revelations—humour, he insisted against his critics, was an essential aspect, if not the main justification, of his existence. His marriage now, at age 30 and in the fifth year of the new century, was not an occasion to which he drew attention in this way: yet it was a significant round number in the progression. At 25, he had completed the work that assured his fame; now, at 30, he had transformed his

---

[21] GM *Erinn.* 18.    [22] N 05/2.

life, with a marriage that was by any standard a glittering success, to secure for himself the standing he coveted, the happiness which, for all his protestations, was exactly what he needed, and the solid bourgeois base which had always been his goal. 'Wealth is really a good thing, say what you like,' as he wrote, only half in jest, in September after a stay in Berlin with Katia's aunt Else Rosenberg and her businessman husband: 'I am artist enough, corruptible enough, to be enchanted by it.'[23]

Surprising in this respect, however, considering the Mann-Buddenbrook tradition, is that there is no record of any of the financial arrangements which might have been expected to accompany the marriage. The Manns (and the Buddenbrooks) had always set great store by the provision of fitting dowries for the daughters of the family, and a good deal of space was taken up in the family records, both in fact and in fiction, by such arrangements. With the Pringsheims, apparently, it was otherwise. The wedding presents had been lavish, the Professor more than generous in furnishing the apartment, and he is reported to have given the couple financial support during the first years of their marriage. But there is nowhere any mention of a dowry, apart from a reference in 1912 to an income of Katia's, seemingly small. The rent for their apartment in the Franz-Joseph Strasse had to be met from this and the income Mann could generate from his work and public appearances. His royalties from Fischer, as *The Buddenbrooks* soared into yet more editions, made a good basis: but it was important now to get back to real productivity as soon as possible. He already had extensive notes for two stories based on his experience—the novel of *The Loved Ones* (which he was now calling *Maya*, the symbol from Buddhism of life's illusory nature) and *Royal Highness*, which he thought of as a longer novella—besides a number of other ideas. The sooner regular work could start, the better.

It took little time to settle into their new domain. He may or may not have felt himself master in his own home when he found the apartment fitted out so completely by his father-in-law—a slight testiness is apparent in his note of a talk with Alfred Pringsheim about the ready-made arrangements in his study, which included a new writing-desk and everything else the Professor thought suitable. But there is no doubt of his welcome for its vast new built-in bookcase, where he could at last begin to set up a systematic library instead of the haphazard collection he had so far assembled (Fischer was always pleased to accommodate him in this). Katia found her own situation little changed, for the apartment was near enough to her old home for a daily visit. One drawback was the stairway climb to their third floor, and this she came to feel more and more as her pregnancy advanced. Once up there, however, the outlook over the park of the Prince

---

[23] *Br. OG-BE* 156.

Leopold Palace was more than rewarding. The centre of the city was in easy reach, on foot or by a short tram-ride. This would be their home for nearly six years.

By mid-March they were sufficiently well installed for work to start at the new desk; but the works already planned had to take second place to a commissioned task. The Schiller centenary on 9 May that year was to be commemorated in a special number of *Simplicissimus*, and it was natural that Mann should be asked for a contribution. Schiller had been his admired model ever since his schooldays ('the very best reading he could have!' as the teacher at the Katharineum had urged), and Tonio Kröger's enthusiasm for *Don Carlos* had been his own. For this special occasion, his idea was not the usual formal critical essay, but a study of an episode in Schiller's life, a *biographie romancée* of one of the many 'anxious hours', as Carlyle called them, in the creation of *Wallenstein*. He prepared himself thoroughly, though largely from secondary sources, with the meticulous note-taking that was his method; and he succeeded admirably in assimilating and transforming his material, with some freedom, into a work of art. The secret lay in the fact that the third-person narrative (in which neither author nor work are actually named) relating Schiller's apparent failure to find the dramatic form he seeks for his vast material, his despair as everything—framework, language—seems false and quite unsuited to the stage, was in fact autobiography: a reflection of Mann's own efforts to finish *Fiorenza*. Many of the key lines are taken straight from his letters to Katia and from the drama itself; in everything—Schiller's desperate effort, his physical complaints, his young wife—the story mirrors his own struggles over the drama. The difference was that Schiller was great enough to conquer ('ambition speaks: is the suffering to be in vain? it must make me great!'), that despite the difficulties, he succeeded. He himself, he knew, had failed to do so in his *Fiorenza*: but perhaps his vivid portrayal of Schiller's *Weary Hour*, based on his own struggle, made some amends. As to *Fiorenza*, he was amused to find, some months after publication in the *Rundschau*, that it had registered a slight claim to fame in a Berlin fashion shop's creation named after it, a two-piece, at 75 marks, much more expensive than another christened after Frank Wedekind's play *Hidalla*.

He had begun now as he meant to go on, establishing the daily routine which would see him through the rest of his life: the morning devoted to the desk, a rest after lunch, the afternoon and evening for letters and the demands of an increasingly social life. And Katia began gradually to assume the important role of partner in the Thomas Mann enterprise: a sensitive listener to his reading from work in progress, and not only seeing to the essential household tasks and the servants, but also taking over the management of his business affairs; for although careful in money matters, he was, to say the least, inadequately equipped to deal with the complicated matters of royalties and fees.

*Royal Highness* he had already started, but instead of continuing, or making a beginning with *Maya*, he conceived now a novella on another aspect of his experience: the impressions of wealth, and Jewishness, in the new milieu to which he had been introduced. This 'Tiergarten novella', as he called it (the Tiergarten district of Berlin being where Katia's aunt Else Rosenberg lived), was a venturesome excursion into the mores of the wealthy assimilated Berlin Jews of whose life he was now part. The motif is Wagnerian: an incestuous encounter between the twins Sieglinde and Siegmund, lightly based on Katia and her twin brother, Klaus, after a *Walküre* performance and shortly before Sieglinde's arranged marriage with the Protestant von Beckerath, a dullard 'of good family', the Hunding of Wagner's tale and deceived like Hunding in this way. His final title was to be *The Blood of the Walsungs*. The whole story, with no direct mention of Jews or Jewishness, reflected the Pringsheim-Rosenberg affluent way of life. He and Katia cut short an August holiday at Zoppot, on the Baltic coast, when the weather turned, and fled to spend the final week in Berlin with the Rosenbergs, which gave him further opportunity for useful observation. 'The contradictory tendency to asceticism on the one hand and luxury on the other', he wrote afterwards to Ida Boy-Ed, 'is probably part and parcel of the modern psyche, to be seen on the grand scale in Richard Wagner.'

Finishing the novella after their return to Munich, he was aware that he was treading on dangerous ground. For all his delicate handling of the subject and care to camouflage the characters, it was much closer to home than the historical theme of *The Buddenbrooks*. By way of covering himself, he sought for the closing lines a suggestion from Alfred Pringsheim for a suitable Yiddish expression for the gulling of Beckerath—and having got it, found his father-in-law quite uninterested in the actual content of the story. As a further precaution, he read the whole text to Hedwig Pringsheim and Katia's brother Klaus, and was pleased to find they could see no objections. This seemed sufficient 'clearance' for him to send it off to Oscar Bie for the *Rundschau*'s January number, and he thought no more about it—for on 9 November Katia's time had arrived, and she gave birth, after a very long and difficult labour, to their first child, a well-formed little daughter, whom they would name Erika.

It was a fearful time, 'which I'll not forget for the rest of my life: but now all is idyll and peace, and the child at her mother's breast, herself still like a sweet child, is a sight to transfigure and sanctify the atrocious agonies of the birth'. He had had an idea of life, and of death, but this introduction to the mystery of birth was a powerful shock. He had wanted a boy, he confessed to Heinrich ten days later, and still did: a boy would somehow seem a continuation of himself, a new beginning.

Well, that can still come. And perhaps a daughter will bring me psychologically closer to the 'other' sex, of which, although I'm now a husband, I still know nothing. . . . She is to be called Erika, as her mother wants, and promises to be very pretty. At brief moments I think I can see just a little Jewishness in her, and each time I'm greatly amused.

This brought him to his real reason for writing, for in the meantime the 'Jewishness' in the *Walsungs* story, specifically in the very expression suggested by Alfred Pringsheim for the final words, had met with a strong objection from the *Rundschau* editor. With reason, Bie felt Siegmund's words of contempt for Beckerath ('we've *beganeffed* [tricked] him—the *goy!*') quite out of keeping with the discreet and highly indirect treatment of Jewishness in what had gone before, and demanded a change. It was a fair point, and Thomas was inclined to meet it. To close less forcefully with, say, 'And Beckerath?—Well, he ought to be grateful to us. He'll lead a less trivial life from now on', would meet the case, and also be more fitting if, as he planned, the novella appeared in book form, accompanied by *Royal Highness*. His brother's urgent advice, and if possible a better suggestion, would be welcome. As was to be expected, Heinrich, who never shunned such shock-effects, urged him not to give way: 'to sacrifice typicality to propriety is kitsch'. As was equally to be expected, Thomas did give way— for the *Rundschau* publication only, he assured Heinrich; in book form he would restore his original version. And again he thought no more of it, as he set off early in December on another reading-tour to Prague, Dresden, and Breslau (Katia, now up and about, had to make the best of such an early desertion, and he, it seems, had been more concerned about his own health than hers, with massage and electrical treatment for his 'nervous dyspepsia'). But the general problem of real life used for literary purposes, the *roman à clef* as literature, was very much to the fore in his mind: *The Buddenbrooks* had been cited as support in a Lübeck libel suit against an author of such a novel, and he had been moved to a public protest in a Lübeck paper, planning to follow up with a more general essay on the subject after his return.

Heinrich would probably make mock of his continual travels, he wrote, but there was no help for it: 'I enjoy the showing-off, and the change of air gets me every time out of the intellectual stagnation I'm prone to.' This short tour showed him again the value of practice: while he 'sweated' in Prague and probably cut a poor figure, in Dresden he had better command of the hall, and at the final reading in Breslau, though tired, he felt confident of success. Between tours, however, one tended to forget it all; at two further performances in Basle, now booked for the end of January, his stage fright would probably return. But Prague, he told Heinrich, and the journey through the area of the Seven Years War, had encouraged him to a project already dreamed of: a novel about Frederick the Great. On his visits to Berlin he had been twice to Potsdam and Sans-Souci, had read several biographies of Frederick, including Carlyle's, and developed an 'excited faith' in the project, as more worthy of him now. He had all the material ready for *Maya*, but felt he lacked the patience for the three years' drudgery any such modern novel of city life would take, and *Royal Highness* must of course come first, before he lost touch with the theme. A 'Frederick' would be different: a subject of dignity, for which he could find the endurance needed, and promising pride in achievement. The Schiller study and *Fiorenza*, he felt, had shown his qualifications for the historical, his talent for finding the right tone in the portrayal of heroism. This mood of feverish exultation was not to last; but, as with *Maya* and so much else, the material gathered would not be wasted.

Returning from Breslau on 15 December he had a brusque reminder that public performance also meant public exposure of his private life. Gossip was abroad in Munich that he had 'fearfully compromised' his new family by writing an anti-Semitic novella in revenge for 'humiliations' suffered at their hands, and the tale lost nothing in fanciful embroidery: gun in hand, the enraged father-in-law was said to have compelled him to have the novella withdrawn. There was no other course open in the face of such rumours, and he wired at once to Fischer to reprint the *Rundschau* number without it. It emerged that waste sheets of the first printing were then thriftily used by the publisher as packaging for books sent to Munich, where a curious bookseller's assistant, having read this interesting text, had been unable to keep the matter to himself, and gossip had done the rest. Withdrawal robbed the eager chatterers of their scandal; but it took some time for Hedwig and Klaus Pringsheim, red-faced over their earlier approval of the story, to overcome the Professor's righteous fury over the incident. 'Well, the piece wasn't all that good,' Thomas commented to his brother

and the worthwhile part, the milieu description, can probably be used elsewhere. All the same, I can't escape a feeling of lack of freedom, which oppresses me sorely in my hypochondriacal moments, and you will probably call me a cowardly bourgeois. . . . The main disappointment, when I am anyway so slow in production, is to be forced from discretion to suppress the careful work of many a long week.

Even as late as February, Fischers were still apparently using the withdrawn sheets for packaging, and the publisher received a strong protest from his author: 'this *won't do*. . . . You wouldn't believe the inordinate desire here to read this story. If you want me undisturbed by all the stupidity and malevolence around me, now I'm in such an exposed personal position here, please take care to avoid any more such carelessness . . .' What remained of the sheets must either be sent to him or carefully destroyed.[24] To make up for the absence of any new acclaim, he had been glad to hear that *Fiorenza* had reached a second edition, which for a drama, as Fischer remarked, was equivalent to ten of a novel. Reviews were, to say the least, reserved. Some, however, were urging a stage production, which he thought a doubtful proposition at this point: if *The Blood of the Walsungs* was thought anti-Semitic, then *Fiorenza* might be considered anti-clerical, and it was too tender a plant to survive being set among party squabbles.

In the meantime, he had completed and published, in a Munich paper in February, his planned 'manifesto' on the subject close to his heart: the extent to which an author may use real life in his creations. In the Lübeck libel case, the prosecution had cited *The Buddenbrooks* in the same breath as a notorious *roman-à-clef* of 1903, which had earned its author, one Lieutenant Bilse, cashiering and six months' jail, and which, banned, had become a byword for the genre. To have his own work, and in his home city too, branded as a 'novel à la Bilse', had been more than Mann could bear, and in his earlier 'Postscript' to the trial (which the prosecution had lost) he had scorned the defence line that any similarity to living persons had been unconscious: in *The Buddenbrooks*, on the contrary, he had 'looked with full consciousness at the realities', and to stick the Bilse label on every work in which this had happened would be to condemn whole libraries of world literature, foremost among them Goethe's *Werther*. Far be it from him to compare himself with Goethe: but if asked to which he felt himself more closely akin, Goethe or Bilse, that 'impure pamphletist', he would answer—without megalomania (!)—'Goethe'. In his novel he had rendered his native city as much honour as ever his father the Senator had done, by portraying a world and giving in it of himself: what mattered the identifications of actual people? Now, in his article 'Bilse and I', he developed, in unusually forceful terms, the principle of freedom for every artist to make use of real life in his work.

Goethe, Turgenev, Shakespeare: did they not all portray real people, were not all their best works based on reality rather than invention? The 'manifesto' was a bid for recognition in Lübeck of his true worth, and staked his claim—not without a touch of megalomania—to be associated with the greatest in literature. But, more important, it set out clearly the

[24] SF *Brw.* 405.

method he would continue to follow in all his work: the montage technique of using the data at hand in real life (his own and others'), regardless of the actual persons concerned, and converting it into art. Yet the people he would portray would show no one but himself: 'not you, never, take comfort, only myself, myself'. That this scarcely explained, or was comparable with, the way Goethe or Shakespeare, or for that matter the best of his contemporaries, such as Hauptmann, had gone about most of their works, he did not allow to affect his argument, the vehemence of which showed how deeply his experience so far (in the novel, in *Tristan*, and most recently with *The Blood of the Walsungs*) had gone home. The thesis was important enough to him to warrant publication later in the year of the article in brochure form, where, in a foreword, he emphasized it still further: the artist-egoist, 'raising his own heart as a monstrance', discovers he speaks for many others, and by being representative in this way achieves 'a small kind of greatness', 'the austere happiness of princes and poets'.[25] The phrase would one day mark the close of his *Royal Highness*.

Heinrich, he wrote, could afford to scoff at him as a 'cowardly bourgeois', for he was 'absolute': 'I have deigned to give myself a constitution'—by which ironically majestic turn he meant his marriage and 'bourgeois compromise', but also his aspiration to the representative, 'Royal Highness' character that was to set him, as the true artist, apart from his brother. (The artist, he wrote later, is like the prince, in that he leads a representative life: his high obligation to form is equivalent to etiquette for the prince.)[26] Heinrich's novel *Professor Unrat*, published early in 1905 and destined, especially when filmed as *The Blue Angel*, to become his most successful work, Thomas had written off as 'artistic entertainment', 'the most . . . frivolous stuff to appear in Germany for a long time'; 'I consider it immoral, from fear of the torment of idleness, to write one bad book after the other.'[27] But he had been careful to keep the criticism, in a note headed 'Anti-Heinrich', to himself: in part from family solidarity, doubtless, but mainly because of his strong need still for his brother's support. Heinrich, however contemptuous he may have been of his bourgeois life-style, certainly did not fail him in this, notably entering the lists with a polemic on his behalf in March, when Richard Schaukal, once a friend of them both, had strongly criticized *Fiorenza* as 'hack-work', 'frostily cold', and its author as decadent, 'literary to the core'. The long accounts Thomas sent Heinrich of his 'representative' life, however, and of his persistent success even with a productivity never approaching his brother's, will not have failed to underline the difference between them. Among his enthusiastic ideas for the 'Frederick', he had mentioned the 'counter-figure' of the hero's brother, the

[25] Matter i, 66    [26] Br. i, 67.    [27] Nb. 7, 115.

Prince of Prussia; but a brief sentence, emphasizing how the fraternal problem was always a stimulating theme for him, was as far as he was prepared to go for the moment in spelling out their divergence. The news of Heinrich's involvement with Ines Schmied prompted the hope that marriage might now lend warmth to his life also, and be reflected in his work: one day Heinrich too might acquire that 'constitution' of which he was so proud. To marry a singer might bring a life of uncertainty and movement: attractive though that was, and however much Thomas feared stagnation for himself from bourgeois comfort, he felt Heinrich had always longed for a more settled life. He himself was at any rate tied, 'a golden ball on each foot': and he probably knew in his heart that that was not the destiny awaiting Heinrich.

These early months of 1906 found him irresolute in his work, and—as often happened at such times—more than usually preoccupied with his health. He felt too ill to counter the Schaukal attack, which could have been expected to arouse all his polemical skill, and was all the more grateful for Heinrich's effective response—the avenging big brother, just like when they were boys. He had worked a little at *Royal Highness*, turned then to extensive notes for the 'Frederick', but bemoaned his lack of real industry and his inability to get a move on, his way of working 'nothing more than a constant hesitation'. Plans for a health-giving sea-voyage with Katia, or a visit to Venice, were considered and discarded, for a new pregnancy made these inadvisable. He decided to travel alone and, after a reading engagement in Dresden on 1 May, to reserve for a three-week cure at the sanatorium of the Weißer Hirsch nearby, where Samuel Fischer was a regular among many other notable patients (Rilke had stayed there just a year earlier), and where he hoped the celebrated Doctor Lahmann would be able to do something for his condition. But it was in vain. The manuscript of *Royal Highness* (which had a narrow escape in a minor railway-accident on his journey there) was continued for a page or two, but the stay was anything but a cure. Returning via Berlin, where Fischer wanted to show him the new house he had just built, he arrived home dead tired and was soon once more a prey at intervals to the abdominal pains, depression, 'neurasthenia', he had complained of before. Detailing his symptoms to Heinrich, he wrote that he was concealing from Katia how exhausted and played out he felt. He would have been better off without wife and dependants, he confessed: the thought tormented him that it had been a mistake to let himself be tied. But enough of such talk, 'which is probably only to draw attention to oneself'; he hoped a stay in Oberammergau in the summer would see him right again.

Certainly it was in his character to draw attention to himself—the 'manifesto' of 'Bilse and I' was sufficient evidence of this as far as his literary work was concerned. It is hard to judge, however, whether the constant complaints of his health in his letters, both during the present crisis and later, came from a *malade imaginaire* or from one who was truly ill, and if there was illness, whether it was psychosomatic. Worry and over-excitement never failed to bring on a 'failure of the nerves, affecting muscles and heart and threatening the reflective powers', as his diary noted once; and he remained a lifelong hypochondriac, daily concerned with the minor ups and downs of health, and keeping a well-stocked medicine cabinet of digestive specifics, tranquillizers, and sleeping-pills always to hand. The fact that 'attacks' seem to have coincided with periods of stress—in 1906 the stress not of overwork, but of inability to settle to work—might point to a psychosomatic cause. At all events, the preoccupation with his physical condition had an undoubted effect on his work, making it even slower and contributing to that constant hesitation of which he now complained.

Hopes of regaining his *élan* and finally getting down to *Royal Highness* he pinned on the summer stay in Oberammergau. Closing up the Munich apartment, he rented a villa there from June to September, and slowly settled to a daily routine of work, with a happiness he thought he had lost, as he wrote to Fischer: 'there's no doubt that, notwithstanding all my Indian passivity, I'm basically an industrious fellow. Work is hard, and often enough a joyless and tedious picking-around. But *not* to work—that's hell. . . . *Royal Highness* is a tender, delicate affair, that needs care in production, but must aim at *lustre* if it is one day to appear in the *Rundschau*.'[28] He saw it still as a novella, and managed only 'a couple of not bad chapters' before they returned to Munich; but by then, the concept was already turning to novel length. He had long since decided on the names Klaus Heinrich for his prince: on 18 November, this time after trouble-free labour, Katia gave birth to a real Klaus Heinrich, the son he had wanted—'Klaus' after her twin brother, 'Heinrich' after his uncle, and 'Thomas' after his father (little Erika, unable to get her tongue round 'Klaus', called him 'Eissi', a name which his father in future would always use for his son).

Peaceful months followed, in so far as the babies allowed. Katia was blissfully happy with them, and content to lead a quiet life; Thomas, commented her mother in March, was a 'real whinger', who could not stand much disturbance.[29] But sitting apart in his study, and with his health apparently restored, he could have been expected to make progress at last with the novel, not to mention with a new idea, a novella on the confessions of a confidence man, which had already found its way into his notebook. Early in 1907, however, came one of those requests beloved of the literary journals, for his views on 'the theatre'—did he believe in the

---

[28] SF *Brw*. 406.      [29] Wiedem. 26.

cultural value of the contemporary theatre, to what extent did he owe to the theatre his own development?—and he yielded to the temptation to interrupt his painfully slow 'music-making' in epic prose in favour of (as he thought) a brief excursion. The theme was timely, for in spite of his disparagement of *Fiorenza*, he had become keen to see its worth justified on stage, and after many efforts to interest producers it was promised soon for a première in Frankfurt. Though well aware that he should not waste his effort on such side-production, instead of a brief reply to the journal, he gave free rein to his admittedly 'unfortunate propensity to the polemical' in a lengthy essay disparaging the artistic pretensions of the theatre. 'Reasoning, arguing, composing', he spent weeks on the task, with a passionate dedication he had never found in his 'music-making'.

His aim was to distinguish between 'theatre'—a world in itself which he recalled enjoying in his boyhood visits to the Tivoli and *Lohengrin*—and 'drama', a literary genre, certainly, but undeserving of the pre-eminence awarded it by aesthetic presumption. As a presentation of reality, drama fell far below the epic novel, which could express its essence not only through characters and dialogue, but also through circumstances and description, giving the rounded picture which actors could never provide. In classical drama and that of Racine, he argued (perhaps with an eye to his *Fiorenza*), action was off-stage, it was the language, not the plot, that mattered. Wagner, spellbinder though he might be, was unthinkable outside the theatre, where the production was all and the text, the 'book', merely subsidiary. Though writing 'against the theatre, against the drama almost', he was far from despising it, aimed rather to praise it—as something 'happily anachronistic', cultural remains, as it were, standing almost outside modern civilization, for which the representative artistic expression was far more the psychological, European novel, of which he felt himself 'the son and servant'. (At the end of his life, by then a confirmed film-buff, he took a similar view of the sound-film: a self-confessed 'industry', but as art much closer than drama to the novel, and a genre with great hope for the future.)[30]

He loved to spread himself in this way, knew that he would never be able to renounce the pleasure of such divagations from his main road in spite of the time and nervous energy they cost. Odd, he reflected, how sharply polemical he became when offering generalities: was it the result of long study of Nietzsche, or a trait born in him?[31] The essay was hardly what the journal had expected, and to his dismay nearly a year was to pass before it appeared. When it was done, however, he took off in May with Katia on their first journey abroad together, on what was to be the first of many

---

[30] *Br.* iii, 411.     [31] O7/40.

visits to Venice. The news that the première of *Fiorenza* was due on 11 May they did not allow to disturb their bathing on the Lido, and they travelled to Frankfurt only on 22 May, to attend the sixth and last performance. It was pleasant to find it by no means as impossible as almost everyone had expected: whether or not 'dramatic', the production had shown it could gain life on the stage.

It was time, after these diversions, to get back to work. In June they once more closed up the apartment and took a villa at Seeshaupt, on the Starnberger See south-west of Munich; and once more he tried to settle to daily toil. Yet again there came a distraction, in the shape of a request by the Bonn Literary Society for a contribution to a special number of its journal; and he could not resist. This time at less length, he enlarged on work in progress—or rather, work *instead* of progress on the interrupted novel: a frank exposé of his *Essay on the Theatre* and the weeks of struggle it had cost him. He added an aside on the *Fiorenza* performance, a 'remarkable personal experience' of theatre, and ended by expatiating on the careful slowness of his real production on the novel, of which he would betray for the moment little more than the title, but for which the *Rundschau* would still have to wait awhile.

Every morning a step, a 'passage'—that happens to be my way . . . not timidity or laziness, but an extraordinarily lively sense of responsibility that demands perfect freshness, so that after the second hour of work I would rather not undertake any important sentence. But which sentence is 'important' . . . ? Does one ever know beforehand whether a sentence or fragment of a sentence may not be destined to recur, as motif, parenthesis, symbol, quotation, reference? and a sentence that is to be heard twice must have something to it . . . a certain elevation and symbolic mood to make it worthy of being sounded again. Thus every passage becomes a 'passage', every adjective a decision, and it is clear that working in this way one cannot shake pages out of one's sleeve. . . . My watchword is: set the teeth and take one slow step at a time, exercise patience, idle through half the day, go to sleep, and wait to see whether things may not flow better next day, with the mind rested. To bring to a conclusion anything of fair size . . . given the way I work, requires patience, or rather, obstinacy, stubbornness, discipline, subjugation of the will that is almost unimaginable and . . . stretches the nerves to screaming-point. . . . Belief in it becomes artificial, a reflex action . . . and ultimately one asks oneself whether all the struggle is in any way proportionate to the dignity and importance of the aim. The outcome must tell—this time, too.

It was an honest confession of the doubts that still lay behind his assurance before the public—but also of the manner in which he found his way to prose of the highest quality: not from a flow of inspiration, but in careful, step-by-step progress to the artistry which gained him his place among the classics of modern times. It was remarkable indeed that a literary society, numbering among its members Hugo von Hofmannsthal, Hermann Hesse, and Richard Dehmel, should have eagerly welcomed so purely personal a contribution. In it, to be sure, was the self-centredness characteristic of him, the need always to show and explain himself, not only in letters and in *Schriftstellerei*, mere literary activity like this, but also in the creative writing—*Dichtung*, or, as he liked to call it, his *Musizieren*—that did slowly emerge. A request for an autobiographical sketch for the December number of the *Literarisches Echo* in Berlin produced an even more personal piece: a light-hearted and ironic account of school failure and a misspent youth, even sinking as low as editing *Simplicissimus*, which, instead of bringing him to the gutter, had made him a child of fortune, with a princess for a wife, two promising children, and a life of every modern comfort, at his appearance applauded everywhere on triumphal tours and asked for his autograph. Astounding, he admitted, that society should so reward a veritable charlatan who really deserved nothing but its contempt.

Fischer was understandably impatient now to see the long-awaited successor-novel to *The Buddenbrooks*. In October he called to confirm the royalties he envisaged for the book that was not yet even half done and had already been several times announced as a forthcoming attraction: on receipt of manuscript, 6,000 marks for the *Rundschau* publication and an immediate advance of 10,000 for the book. Splendid prospects indeed, with which he doubtless hoped to spur progress. If so, he was to be disappointed: for though Thomas wrote yet another announcement for the December *Rundschau* of his 'fairy-tale of form and yearning, of representation and life, of Highness and happiness', it took more than another year to reach print. Admittedly, *The Buddenbrooks* had by then nearly reached the 50,000 mark; but it said much for the publisher's confidence and assessment of reader potential that he was prepared to plan a first edition of 10,000 of what was evidently a very different successor. Over the years, he came to accustom himself to Mann's productive tempo—and his patience never went unrewarded.

Thomas Mann *cunctator*, obstinately proceeding one pace at a time to bring his novel to a conclusion—the apologia for such long-drawn-out creativity was not exactly a true bill to describe *Royal Highness* during 1907 and the following year. In Seeshaupt, and after their return to Munich for the winter, though usually at the desk every morning, he was far from spending all his time on the search for the right 'passages', the 'important' sentences, the readier flow. Quite apart from the constant social and public demands, other temptation to set the work aside was never lacking. While still in Seeshaupt, for instance, he was one of a hundred prominent personalities asked for their views on the 'Solution to the Jewish Question' (that is, on the Zionist movement). He duly took time for a careful reply, writing as an artist who, though sometimes falsely labelled as Jewish, was of sufficiently mixed origin to be free of racism and to call himself a philo-Semite, and for whom a Zionist exodus would seem an unmitigated misfortune for Europe. The problem, he wrote, was psychological: the Jew, like the artist, was an exceptional being, all the contrasts and complications of his existence—free thought and revolutionary tendencies combined with longing for assimilation, cynicism and sentimentality, sharpness and melancholy, not least an irritating superiority in the walks of life open to him—were evidence of his singularity. And singularity was the artist's life-blood; he himself could see only his brothers in those 'who, the people feel compelled to stress, are after all "human beings too"'. The 'Question' would one day resolve itself, simply by the assimilation and 'Europeanization' of the Jews, of which there were already signs in the emancipation of their young people and the increasing incidence of mixed marriages. (This was a widely held view at the time, but he also spoke from his own experience: how could anyone foresee what a fearfully different 'solution' would be attempted within the coming thirty years?)

Towards the end of the year, again, he involved himself in the preparations and casting for a single Munich performance of *Fiorenza*, which he welcomed, but not without misgivings at the risk of a flop so close to home. He was against Heinrich's idea of Carla for the only female role, doubting whether the 'experimental character' of the whole affair could stand such an additional experiment (she was in any case engaged now in Alsace and could not easily have accepted). When the event was finally fixed for December, he attended both the dress rehearsal and the performance, and took a number of curtain calls, which for some reviewers showed the 'literary and social standing' he enjoyed in Munich and marked the evening as a *succès d'estime* for him—as man and novelist, for he had not the 'slightest talent as a dramatist'.[32] There were many more positive comments; but one attacked the drama as anti-Catholic, even anti-Christian, an accusation he took trouble to rebut in a letter to a Catholic paper. Far from lauding the Renaissance or its 'dechristianized' representatives, his dialogues made the true hero, not Lorenzo de' Medici, but Savonarola, one of the 'most passionate and most radical of all Christians'.

That he should think this letter worth reprinting in a 1922 volume of collected essays and occasional pieces, and was still commenting on *Fiorenza* in the last year of his life, showed the high value he himself set on a work in a genre he never again attempted. The *succès d'estime* in Decem-

---

[32] *Jb*. 4, 187.

ber 1907, however, was unmistakable; still in its glow, he could not resist an invitation for January to be one of a group of authors in Munich giving readings from their work—'I'm fairly well endowed with princely feelings . . . without the courage for active aloofness.'[33] In the extract he read from the still-unfinished *Royal Highness*, his by now well-known ironic approach once again drew acclaim.

By this time the pressure was on from Fischer, publication in the *Rundschau* was now scheduled for the three final numbers of 1908, and he could allow himself no more such diversions. He had reached the love-story, brought Prince Klaus Heinrich together with his American heiress, but confessed there were still great difficulties of composition. A week spent in February with his mother in Polling, with a two-hour stint every morning, brought him forward; but his tale was still taking more space and time than he had foreseen, in the event delaying publication until the following spring.

Heinrich's letters from Rome awakened dreams of a return there, with Katia. To see it again after ten years would afford him satisfaction, he thought, for after all he had now made something of himself, and could hope the next decade would see a corresponding advance: 'I often think that, if my body holds out, I shall feel at my best between 50 and 60.' Heinrich came to Munich in April to introduce Ines Schmied to the family—a surprise for his mother—and they decided on two weeks all together in Venice in May, where Carla too could join them. It was not an entirely happy stay, and it is unlikely Thomas could do much work, for Ines was a creature of moods and already disdainful of Heinrich's relations, none of whom she could stand, least of all Thomas. Back in Munich he found regular application more than tedious, and longed for what was now becoming the annual summer break out of town.

This time it was to a rented villa with a shady garden in Bad Tölz, a resort on the Isar south of the city. The air suited him well there, and quite soon after their arrival he heard of a reasonably priced plot coming available, with view on to river, village, and mountains: they made a quick decision to buy, for why rent each year when they could own? more especially as their third child was now expected, and a regular summer residence would be ideal for the larger family. Though it meant a mortgage, his royalty income was now more than adequate, and no further aid from the Pringsheims was needed. By the end of their stay in September, building had begun, and the roof was on the 'Landhaus Thomas Mann' before the end of the year. It was a decision they did not regret. (As Viktor Mann later remarked, Thomas alone of the Senator's three sons

---

[33] *Jb.* 4, 186.

continued the family tradition of house ownership; Bad Tölz was only the first of many residences he was to build and occupy.) Heinrich was spending the summer in Riva, while Ines, watchful of convention, since they were not yet married, stayed in and around Munich; she called on his mother at Polling in June, and a little later, at Thomas's invitation, came to Tölz for the day. The Mann relations were becoming more and more of a nightmare to her, she confessed, and Tölz was no idyll, with Thomas 'so cold, so indifferent . . . in the background that sober country-side, devoid of all poetry . . . a bit of woods here, a touch of meadows there'.[34]

The enchanting fairy-story was at last nearing its 'operatic end' when Thomas and Katia returned to Munich, but distractions continued to hold up its completion. In November he left for a reading-engagement in Vienna, with a chapter from the torso. During the the short stay he met the popular novelist Arthur Schnitzler, but enjoyed most a half-day visit to Hugo von Hofmannsthal in Rodaun, the second poet, after Hauptmann, to make a deep personal impression on him. Hauptmann had something of the priest about him, but the other was a 'prince', exactly the type to attract him at this point. Thanking him later for a Christmas gift of his poems, he promised in return his novel, in its perhaps 'impossible' form but in the hope that its description of the princely existence might find sympathy.[35] Christmas then intervened, with all its distractions, and, in need of ready cash for presents, he dashed off, for a Vienna paper, an account in novella form of the railway accident three years earlier which had come close to destroying his *Royal Highness* notes and part-manuscript: trash, as he described it to Heinrich, but worthwhile for the 300 marks. Though Fischer began publication of the novel in the January number of the *Rundschau*, the final words were not actually written until 13 February 1909. Readers wanting a new Thomas Mann book that year would have to wait until October: Fischer could only temporize in March with a new edition of the early *Friedemann* stories complemented by *Hungry Souls* and *The Railway Accident*.

Two years before, Mann had said he was aiming, in *Royal Highness*, at 'something like an allegory . . . a jest with deeper meaning—yet with some-thing personal and new in it'.[36] In a way it was as directly personal as *The Buddenbrooks*: the parallels with, and allusions to, his own experience are thick on the ground, the autobiographical touches unmistakable, notably in the prince's courtship of his princess and her wealthy father's financial rescue of the realm, but also in countless detailed incidents of the story. That he had portrayed his own 'princess' in Imma, the young American

---

[34] Qu. *Brw. HM* 379     [35] *Brw. Aut.* 198.     [36] 07/40.

heiress, was no secret; but there would be no contemporary keys circulating to the characters in his allegory, and few then would realize just how
much of himself lay in this counterpart to *Tonio Kröger*. The serial publication before its appearance in book form proved a disadvantage: after so
long an interval, for his second novel to be read first in this form meant
inevitably that it would be regarded as lightweight. Even a friend like Kurt
Martens saw in it no more than a 'harmless love-story', a descent from the
heights down to the 'lowlands of optimism'.[37] That in fact it *was* lightweight
he admitted himself, at the end of his life ('true, it has charm, but the
Germans don't know what to do with charm');[38] but he was disappointed
that its deeper meaning seemed to have escaped most readers—the conversion of a life of mere representation and pretence to one of reality through
the force of love; the prince, like the artist, though seemingly cold and
remote, achieving through love an 'austere happiness' in true service to the
community, and symbolizing a spiritual turn away from individualism to
democracy. This, of course, was early in the 1950s, against a background
very different from that of 1910. At the time he insisted that to see in the
book a work of social criticism was to misunderstand it: the 'democratic'
was only one of its aspects, he told Kurt Martens, and although the idea of
democracy seemed to be gaining ground among the practitioners of *belles-
lettres*, his own future production would have not the slightest connection
with it.

That he should miss his aim like this was probably due to the fact that he
had taken such an unconscionably long time over the work, extending it far
beyond his original plan, with the result that the light touch the story
needed was weighed down with elaborate trappings and a surfeit of
'Thomas Mann' style and irony. As always, he had taken immense trouble
to get his facts right for the scene in his imaginary grand dukedom: a
suitably named Dr Printz, apparently with experience of court and diplomatic life, had been happy to inform him on state financing and supply
minutiae of etiquette and procedure, notably where foreign visitors were
concerned, and he had amassed quantities of news clippings and notes
from his reading. Well and good: but when the wealth of detail was larded
with the ever-recurring 'important sentence' as leitmotifs for each character, including the dog, the product became far too intellectual to have wide
appeal. To Hermann Hesse, in a perceptive review, this undoubtedly great
artist seemed indeed a 'mistrustful intellectual', with 'the gifts, but not the
naïvety, of a Balzac or a Dickens', feeling his 'great talent more as an
isolating peculiarity than as a proud distinction . . . seeking to distance
himself from the reader by treating him ironically'.

[37] *Jb.* 4, 191.    [38] Berlin 127.

4

*'That difficult and passionate sport called artistic work'*
(TM, September 1910)

The initially indifferent reception of *Royal Highness*, both in its serial and in its later book form, did not disturb him unduly. As he continued the comfortable life assured by his not inconsiderable royalties, the eminence he had achieved seemed unaffected: looked up to as almost a classic, his opinion sought on every kind of topic, his support claimed for countless beginners, readings from his work eagerly welcomed, he was a literary celebrity whose progress was closely followed. The seriousness with which he regarded this position showed itself not only in his increasing correspondence but also in his own attitude to his literary existence, as he spoke now of *Royal Highness*, in true textbook style, as the end of a period, with a new one about to begin. But whereas in earlier days his thoughts at such times had always been of new creative work, now the essay, *Schriftstellerei*, seemed of equal importance. In March 1909 he told Heinrich that he had two irons in the fire: an essay on 'all kinds of contemporary issues', and a novella, connecting in a way with *Royal Highness*, as he put it, but offering a different atmosphere—in other words, the confidence-man theme he had long had in mind—and with something of an 'eighteenth-century' touch about it. That he should list his projects in this order did indeed mark a new period. Where before the essay had been occasional, in both senses, from now on it would be an important second string to his bow, and literary criticism and public pronouncement on topics of the day were to figure almost as large as the *Dichtung*, the creative writing on which his renown should truly rest.

On 27 March 1909 Thomas and Katia's third child was born, another son. Katia's labour was again long and painful, and a forceps delivery was only just avoided. Thomas found the child rather like 'Mucki', as he called Erika, 'slim and somewhat Chinese-looking'. He was given the names of Gottfried Angelus Thomas: Angelus was the name of a playmate of Erika's in Bad Tölz, and Katia had promised her an Angelus of her own, so that was the name he went by. But for the nanny he was 'Gelus', and when he was old enough to speak, 'Golo' was the nearest he could manage—so Golo he remained. While Katia was soon restored, it was a time of stress for the paterfamilias, resulting in the inevitable gastric disturbances and a loss of the vitality he needed if his 'new period' was to get under way. He decided on a stricter cure than that offered by Riva, and in May spent three weeks in the well-known sanatorium of Dr Bircher-Benner above Zurich, where vegetarian fare, early rising and retiring, and gardening brought a rapid recovery. In July 'Landhaus Thomas Mann' was ready for the family, and they stayed until October, through a rainy summer, during which he worked at his essay project on 'contemporary issues'; but though he kept at it for the rest of the year, it was never completed.

Disturbing too, however, had been a quarrel among the larger family circle. By this time, Heinrich had reluctantly broken off the engagement with Ines Schmied, on her insistence that they were not suited to each other; but he had passed on to Thomas her moans at her treatment by the Manns, especially over a snub from his sister Julia, in the forceful style that characterized his novels—no doubt laying the blame for her change of mind on his relatives. Thomas felt compelled to try to stop this molehill from becoming a mountain, above all to try—almost as though he had taken the Senator's place—to save the family from the fatal split that had long threatened, with himself and 'Lula' on one side and Heinrich and Carla on the other. 'Remember Beckergrube 52!' he wrote to his brother in April: 'all else is secondary'. While to some extent sharing Heinrich's contempt for their sister's bourgeois existence with her 'mean little husband', he was ready to understand and excuse her attitude to Ines, just as he could wish Carla well in her efforts for success on the stage even though aware of her only-modest talent. Each of the sisters, he felt, was 'one of us', and family solidarity must be preserved. Little more was to be heard of the temperamental Ines: she has had a poor press, as the woman who refused to marry Heinrich Mann and who dared to criticize his more eminent brother.

Despite Thomas's efforts, the divide in the family persisted, to culminate a few years later in a long-lasting feud between the brothers. For the moment, however, their relations were still good, Thomas's respect for Heinrich still that of his royal prince in the novel: 'neither good fortune nor the people's love will ever stop me being your brother'. He had tried earlier, unsuccessfully, to arrange serial publication of Heinrich's novel *The Little Town* in the *Rundschau*, and, with Katia, now pregnant once again, they spent three weeks together on the French Riviera after leaving Tölz. (Her mother, left with the three children, found the prospect of a fourth in the coming summer 'a little hasty for the delicate little woman', but wisely held her tongue.)[39] Towards the end of the year, conscious that the literary success of Heinrich's *Little Town* had not been matched by its sales, Thomas offered his brother a share in 'the economic fruits of *Royal Highness*' if he was short of a few thousand marks, and Heinrich was glad to accept the loan. Even though he was able soon afterwards to conclude a contract with another publisher, securing a small but annual income, the comparison with Thomas's financial success, with so relatively small and slow a production, no doubt continued to rankle.

[39] Wiedem. 33.

The contrast between their works had already been marked since Heinrich's first novel, *In the Land of Cockaigne*, published just before *The Buddenbrooks*, and in its obsession with the erotic and its savage satire on Berlin's *nouveau riche* society a world apart from Thomas's treatment. Heinrich was a tirelessly productive writer, subject to more powerful and conflicting emotions (and to more real illness) than his steadier brother. With both, their travels and experiences, and their mixed racial origin, were reflected in their work; there had been much of Carla and himself in Heinrich's *Hunt for Love*, but, as Thomas had complained, it held altogether too much sex. In his style, Heinrich was addicted more to sarcasm than to the gentler irony of the other, and was more impatient, less attentive to precision and neatness of style; and while both tended to caricature their subjects and emphasize the grotesque, with Heinrich this had often been carried to excess, notably in *The Blue Angel*. Here probably lay the reason for his relative lack of recognition.

The notes were accumulating, Thomas told him in January 1910, for the memoirs of confidence-man Felix Krull, probably to be his strangest work yet: 'I'm often surprised at what I'm fishing out of myself.' The project for the 'Frederick the Great' novel he had laid aside, attractive though it was—40 was the right age to tackle that, he thought, and as it turned out, that was exactly when he did turn to it again (in 1915), under admittedly very different circumstances. The basic story of Krull had been suggested by the memoirs of Manolescu, *A Prince of Thieves*, which he had seen five years earlier, but his notes clearly show how he planned to flesh it out with experiences of his own. Inveterate play-actor himself in his childhood days, he felt at home with the psychology of the deceiver: but the story-line was slow to develop, and he seized, as so often before in such a predicament, on any distractions that offered before finally putting pen to paper.

A scurrilous and anti-Semitic attack, published in January, on Samuel Lublinski—the critic whose welcome for *The Buddenbrooks* and later judgement of Thomas Mann as 'plainly the most significant novelist of the time' he remembered with gratitude—aroused his anger, and instead of joining a large number of other writers in a public protest, he was moved to publish a counterblast of his own. In it, he fell on the author, a Dr Theodor Lessing (a Jew himself and author of an *Introduction to Modern Philosophy* to which Mann had paid graceful tribute) in one of the most violent polemics he ever penned: ridiculing in detail his criticisms of Lublinski, rebutting his lies, and ending with a mordant personal attack on him as a man. 'Not with the foil, but the cane,' as he wrote to Lublinski, sending him a copy, for personal considerations were in play here too: Lessing had once been an admirer of Carla's, though never backward in deriding her performance on the boards, and formerly a frequent guest of the Pringsheims. The adversary telegraphed a challenge to a duel, which he did not follow up, but issued two further public retorts. Mann's final response in April was calculated to draw a line under the affair. Lessing, however, republished the whole in a separate brochure, with added embroideries on the decadent, dandyish young Lübecker he had met in Munich; a sharp letter from Alfred Pringsheim got him to withdraw and destroy it, but copies were already in circulation. Lessing's animosity persisted for many years afterwards.

The irritation of such a controversy did not make application any easier to *The Confessions of Felix Krull, Thief and Swindler*, as he had now decided to entitle it. Stung by Lessing's professed contempt for the 'littérateur', he spread himself in an essay on the mistrust shown the writer generally and his poor social standing in Germany, in contrast to France, with a plea for his recognition, not necessarily with more money, but at least with the official honours often awarded to artists and musicians: 'Whether these good things are salutary for genius . . . is a moot point; but there is no doubt that the realization of the dream of a "German Academy" would increase respect for the language, encourage recognition of the intellect, and raise the social position of the writer.'[40] Though this remained apparently unpublished, he would himself have no cause later for complaint at such neglect (even if the later history of the literary section of the Prussian Academy showed slight realization of the lofty aims).

The summer stay in Tölz had to be deferred, for in June their fourth child was expected, and preparations had to be made for a move in the autumn to the bigger Munich apartment they would now need. On 7 June 1910 Katia was delivered of another girl, whom they named Monika: by far the prettiest baby of them all, Katia thought. Thomas fervently hoped it would be their last, for such fertility was verging on the absurd, and the doctors agreed that Katia's constitution had suffered enough. The distraction did not prevent the long-planned start on *Krull*; and a month later, just before they left for Tölz, the father was unable to resist treating his family to a reading of most of the first chapter of this 'combination of frivolity and morality, of scepticism and passion', as he called it to Lublinski—a work which, though it was destined to remain incomplete, would rank among his most popular.

But hardly were they ensconced once again in the country house when his mother telephoned from Polling to say Carla was dead—her grief-stricken words only a hint that it was suicide—and he went at once. Carla, just 29, had at last hoped to break out of a bohemian existence, in which she was pursued by men more than by good parts, with her engagement to a wealthy young man in Alsace; but she had been troubled by anonymous

[40] Matter i. 173.

letters and finally by the accusation of her fiancé, visiting her in Polling, that she was deceiving him. Locking herself in her room, she had taken a massive dose of the cyanide she had long had by her. 'Je t'aime,' ran the note she left: '*une fois* je t'ai trompé, mais je t'aime.' The shock for Thomas was severe, not only because it was the first death in the family since that of his father, but also because it seemed to him a defection by 'one of us', a betrayal of the family solidarity he had tried to preserve. Could she have imagined the effect it would have on them all, he wrote later to Paul Ehrenberg, she would not have done it: but life had to continue, 'and as long as one is not also lying in a rectangular, black hole in the ground, interlaced with tree roots, one must go along with it a little'.[41] Heinrich, who returned from Italy to Munich only after the burial there, knew her better, understood how she had longed for the stability of real life, away from the tinsel pretence of the stage world, where her innocence had been so cruelly treated (and he would soon write an effective drama, *Actress*, picturing her life and fate). Neither brother could escape a certain feeling of guilt; and for Heinrich his bitterness served only to deepen the rift between him and Julia, whose insensitivity to Carla's struggle he could never forgive. Their mother was shattered, and never really recovered from the blow. Twenty years later, Thomas, in a dry account still betraying coolness over Carla's lack of thought for the others, could take a more sympathetic view: his own 'reality', of literary achievement, wife, children, and home, even if outwardly benign, was in its way of the same stuff as the Polling tragedy, a like breach of faith, 'for all reality is deadly earnest, and it is morality itself that, one with life, forbids us be true to the innocence of youth'.[42]

At the time, it was hard, he claimed, to turn back without loathing to the 'difficult and passionate sport called artistic work'; but although progress on *Krull* lingered, he was able to publish part of the opening chapter at the turn of the year. Before August was out, he completed a long essay on Fontane, his penetrating assessment of a great predecessor reflecting much of his own method and experience. The move to the larger and more expensive apartment on 1 October—in fact two adjoining each other in the Mauerkircher Strasse, in the newly developed Herzog Park area—took a full week, and he returned alone to Tölz for the rest of the month in an attempt to master the 'near-torture' of the manuscript of his unusual novel. Parodying the autobiographies of the eighteenth century, including Goethe's *Dichtung und Wahrheit*, it was becoming an increasingly difficult balancing act, and he was doubtful whether the tone could be sustained at novel length.

[41] *Br*. iii, 88.      [42] xi 121.

But when he returned to Munich, the following months brought other demands on his time. Increased household costs—with four servants now, and a higher rent—were making Katia's allowance inadequate, and he needed more immediate earnings. Requests for reading-tours and journal contributions were welcome, therefore. In November, he read from *Krull* in Weimar at the invitation of an old school-friend, a count who was now court chamberlain there (he found with some satisfaction that his impressions coincided exactly with his intuitions of princely life in *Royal Highness*); in January 1911 he made an extended tour of the Rhineland, Ruhr, and Westphalia. Before Christmas he had completed a short story, based on his schooldays, for the Vienna *Neue Freie Presse* (though for some reason that journal did not take it, and it appeared only in February in Germany); a brief review of a much earlier edition of Chamisso's *Peter Schlemihl* served for the Christmas number of the Berlin *Tageblatt* (and prompted Fischer, concerned to keep his author in the limelight, to ask for an introduction to his own forthcoming Chamisso edition). In the meantime, important musical occasions were not to be missed. In September he had attended the rehearsal for the first performance of Mahler's Eighth Symphony and, meeting the composer, felt that for the first time he had encountered a truly great man; later, in February, he saw Strauss's *Rosenkavalier*, not without irritation at the drowning of the words by the over-insistent music. It was scarcely surprising that *Krull* should move forward with a slowness which he blamed on a temporary nervous exhaustion.

As the doctors had foreseen, Katia's health was also not of the best, and in May 1911, joined by Heinrich, they set off for the Dalmatian coast—for Thomas, less of a holiday than a change of work, for he had already in mind a novella to release him for a while from the impasse with *Krull*. His first notion had been to portray a hopeless love-affair of Goethe's at 74 (though the actual events were somewhat confused in his mind), an absurd passion for a seventeen-year-old girl: 'the odious, yet beautiful, grotesque, and moving story' of a crisis which came near to destroying him in his Olympian existence but which he was able to sublimate in the splendid Marienbader Elegy. His own 'modest epic stage', however, was not yet ready to be the scene for a Goethe, he felt; and he had begun to envisage a more modern hero for the theme of an apparently well-established life destroyed by the 'wild god Eros-Dionysos', by the onrush of 'passion that drives to distraction and destroys dignity'.

They stayed first on the island of Brioni, but found this a mistake: the weather was indifferent, there was no decent beach, and they found tedious the almost entirely Austrian company in the hotel, not least in their deference to an archduchess, mother of the future Emperor Karl, whose

regular late entry and early rising at meals had everyone standing respectfully. While there they read of the death of Gustav Mahler, landing in
Europe on his return from a tour in America. Mann was greatly moved and,
clipping the obituary notice and portrait, decided to adopt the stern features (and later, the Christian name) of this admired artist for his hero,
whose story had yet to be devised. After ten days, they abandoned Brioni to
take ship for Venice, where the already familiar surroundings of the Grand
Hôtel des Bains on the Lido came as welcome relief, and they stayed until
the beginning of June. It had been a most marvellous holiday, as he
said after their return to Munich. They were both, it seemed, restored; on
the Lido beach he had written a long-promised article on Wagner for the
Bayreuth number of the Vienna journal *Der Merker*; and above all,
the incidents of the journey and stay were to form themselves into the
bones of the novella, as those in Denmark long before had done for *Tonio
Kröger*: the background for *Death in Venice*.

Both the brief Wagner article—diplomatically admitting how the composer's magic could still spellbind him, but critical of his outdated grandi-
ose theories—and the longer essay on Chamisso for Fischer, which he now
completed in Bad Tölz as they began their summer stay, made in their
different ways preludes to the story taking shape in his mind. In predicting
a neo-classical, post-Wagnerian art for the twentieth century—stern and
serene, no longer seeking greatness in baroque exaggeration or beauty in
intoxication—he was foreshadowing the aesthetic moralist in his protagonist, the writer Aschenbach. Chamisso's Schlemihl, the man with no
shadow, he saw not as the man without roots, but as the man lacking
the solid foundation of bourgeois existence which the author, once the
story was behind him, was yet able to acquire, as he himself had done. As
he began *Death in Venice* and lent Aschenbach so much of himself and of
his own work and life, both these strands were woven in: the search for a
new classicism, in hard application on the brink of exhaustion, and the
achievement of honours and dignity in an apparently solid bourgeois
existence.

This was the background, and to Aschenbach he could even ascribe
works he himself was never to write—a prose-epic of the life of Frederick
the Great, the novel *Maya*, the essay on 'Intellect and Art'. For the action of
the story itself, nothing needed to be invented, the experiences of the
journey stood ready-made to hand, requiring only minor adaptations—
the strange figure at the Munich cemetery, the disappointment of Brioni,
the repulsive ageing 'queen' on their gloomy ship from Pola to Venice, the
suspect gondolier, the muddle with the luggage on departure (Heinrich's,
in fact, not his own), the cholera outbreak (actually in Palermo, only
rumoured in Venice), the sinister singer. Even the irruption of passion into
Aschenbach's dignified life, in the form of homosexual rather than hetero-

sexual love, reflected his own intense infatuation, at a distance, with a godlike Polish boy (who in real life did not carry the name he gave him of Tadzio, but who many years later confirmed that he, as well as his boisterous friend 'Jaschu', had indeed been there that summer).

*Death in Venice* would be the first of Thomas Mann's works with such explicit, though indirect, expression for his innate homosexuality. He was able, as he wrote later, not only to find that 'equilibrium between sensuality and morality' ideally realized in Goethe's novel *Elective Affinities* (which he said he reread no less than five times while writing the novella), but also, in the description of Aschenbach's case, to express that 'puritanical, bourgeois' nature, 'Protestant and not Greek', which was so deeply a part of his own: 'our fundamentally mistrustful, pessimistic view of passion as such and in general'. Passion that drives to distraction and destroys dignity, he averred, was really the subject-matter of his story. But the way he told it, in a skilful combination of symbolism and realism—the Greek element, from a world which regarded homosexuality as normal, ever more insistently present to Aschenbach as Tadzio personifies Eros, but repudiated by his puritan, Protestant nature—reflected the ambivalence within himself. (It was the nearest he ever came to public revelation of his tendency to inversion; and even to the young Bonn academic Ernst Bertram—himself homosexual—with whom he had been in correspondence since 1910 and whose friendship was to last many years, it was never articulated, though without doubt it formed a bond in their relationship.)

As, in July, he began the singular tale, he had envisaged a rapid improvisation only, a brief interlude in the work on *Krull*. But as always, the thing developed a will of its own; and it took him a full year to complete. The time was not only a function of the difficulty of what he was finding 'a quite impossible' concept, and of devising the necessarily tragic end. Katia's health was not as restored as they had hoped, and with a slight but obstinate fever and chronic cough she had to spend part of September in the mountains; by March 1912, the doctors—perhaps over-eager—had diagnosed early-stage tuberculosis, and after an unavailing stay in a local sanatorium, she had repaired to a highly recommended one in Davos, where a cure looked likely to take six months. With the novella still unfinished, and alone with the children, though admittedly well provided with domestic staff, Thomas realized for the first time how much he had come to rely on her, to keep at bay the mundane matters of daily life so that he could devote himself untroubled to his work.

His expenses were rising, and although short reading-tours to Belgium and North Germany had doubtless helped, he had been constrained in February to press Heinrich for at least part repayment of his loan—with only moderate success, however, and soon he was raising his fees for readings. After a month-long visit to Davos in May, he moved out to Tölz with the children, whom his mother was only too glad to come and look after, and at last was able to bring the story to a conclusion. It was not before time, for the *Neue Rundschau* had already announced it, and with Fischer's agreement a non-trade limited luxury edition with the Hyperion Press was also planned. *Death in Venice* finally appeared in the October and November numbers of the *Rundschau*, and in the limited edition before the end of the year; that in book form with Fischer followed in 1913, reaching printings of 18,000 by the end of the year and arousing the widest literary reverberations of any of his works so far. Relatively short, it is still justly regarded as one of his finest, and in more recent years the problematic theme has inspired dramatic adaptations both in film, by Visconti, and in opera, by Benjamin Britten.

A homo-erotic disposition was neither rare nor unmentionable in Wilhelmine Germany, enjoyed indeed a certain vogue in artistic-intellectual circles under the banner of the poet Stefan George, with his cult of Platonic love. Mann's theme for *Death in Venice*, therefore—which he regarded as the most serious, because the most personal, work he had written since *The Buddenbrooks*, and where, in the euphoria of completion, he felt he had been completely successful—was not of itself likely to arouse Grundyish reactions. Yet, once it had appeared, doubts set in, and he took trouble, then and later, to stress to friends its essential morality. He was relieved to find that the reviews, with a few exceptions, were positive, with serious discussion of its literary rather than social qualities, and that, as he had hoped, he seemed to have overcome the reproach often levelled at *Royal Highness* of lowered standards in his work, of 'a descent to the lowlands of optimism'. Perhaps mercifully, he does not seem to have seen D. H. Lawrence's general critique, in 1913, of his work, which concentrated on *Tonio Kröger* and *Death in Venice* and found this middle-aged author (Lawrence apparently thought he was in his fifties) a victim of the German 'craving for form', 'a last too-sick disciple' of Flaubert in his 'stale' expression of the conflict between life and art: 'Thomas Mann is old—and we are young. Germany does not feel very young to me.'[43] It was gratifying to learn of indications that a Nobel Prize might be in the offing; but Mann thought the world and the Nobel Committee would need more from him before such a decision could be justified.

He fully intended, after this intermezzo, to return to his confidence-man Felix Krull; but to recapture the comic tone, the touch of parody, proved hard. And he had been disturbed by a careless production by Reinhardt of *Fiorenza* in Berlin in January 1913, much cut and neglecting the all-important dialogue in favour of gesture and show, and attracting a more

---

[43] *Blue Review* (n.d.) 260, 265.

than usually destructive critique from Kerr. This 'poisonous howling', as he called it in disgust, made him revive briefly the idea of the novella he had attributed to 'my late friend Gustav von Aschenbach'—*A Study in Abjection*, to combine the detestable characters of Kerr and Lessing. But it was never written, nor did he get far with *Krull*, for there were other preoccupations.

Foremost was the imminence of yet another move. Having the country house in Tölz meant spending each summer there and missing stays by the sea that would have been welcome; the town apartments were no longer adequate for the children, growing fast, who needed a garden; and soon after Katia's return in September 1912 from Davos they had decided to reconnoitre in the area of the Herzog Park, which ran along the east bank of the river and whose newly developing area offered building-plots. In February 1913 one was bought, and an architect commissioned for their new villa at No. 1 Poschinger Strasse, in a street leading down from their Mauerkircher Strasse towards the Isar. The site was directly at the riverbank, in what was virtually a wilderness area and where settlers were still few. For the much larger mortgage, he was optimistic no doubt over his income from *Death in Venice* (but also probably dependent on support from his father-in-law, for the purchase was in Katia's name). The enterprise took longer than he expected, however, and his hopes for a quick sale of the Tölz house, and a visit to the Baltic for the summer holiday, were vain: the building was in hand, and the children made excited visits to the site to see progress, but Tölz would still have to be their summer home. During June he and Katia left for what he felt was a well-deserved holiday of three weeks in Viareggio; by July they were back in Tölz, where, instead of settling to *Krull*, he began—yet again—something new.

The idea sprang from his visit to Davos during Katia's stay in the somewhat luxurious Waldsanatorium there the previous year. She had written him lively letters almost daily, with her impressions of the life in that segregated world—the doctors and nurses, her fellow patients, often eccentric and with morals less than strict, the occasional organized outings; and his own observations during his month in its rarefied atmosphere had given him much to occupy and amuse him. It was a close-run thing when the doctor, called to advise on the feverish catarrh he inevitably contracted at the unaccustomed height of 5,000 feet, said he found a spot on the lung and, scenting profit, suggested he remain for six months' treatment. As he said later, he preferred instead to return home and write something about the danger to young people of the lengthy cures in this timeless, isolated milieu, tempting them away from, and soon making them unfit for, life in the real world outside. Katia's letters and what she told him on her return had updated the sanatorium gossip. Now, a year later, he once more laid *Krull* aside, and turned to a novella on the theme, which, as he said, looked like developing into a kind of humorous counterpoint to *Death in Venice*, reducing to comedy its fascination with death, and equally envisaged as no more than a brief interlude to the novel. By September, he had decided on his hero, the young engineering student Hans Castorp, from a Hanseatic background like his own; the title would be 'The Enchanted Mountain'; and the remaining characters stood, so to speak, ready.

Fischer's *Rundschau*, ever eager to promote his author, announced it already in December (erroneously as 'The Sorcerer's Apprentice', by which time he had changed his title to 'The Magic Mountain'.) For months still he persisted in calling it a novella, though experience should have taught him how such works tended to grow; and, though the basic concept remained, he began to find it more difficult than anticipated. (What he could not foresee at this point, of course, was the violent interruption the year 1914 was to bring, and the inordinate time-span the novel into which the work was developing would occupy.) The turn of the year brought severe depression and fatigue, as his cares seemed to multiply—Katia and little Klaus with bronchial troubles, the load of debts and mortgages, Uncle Friedrich's public (and late) protest at the 'caricature' of his family in *The Buddenbrooks*—bringing him to the point almost of despair. Heinrich's capacity to portray and castigate the evils of the time he contrasted with his own lack of any intellectual or political orientation, his innate sympathy with death: his whole interest focused in decay and ruling out any hope for progress. 'I am past it, I think, and should probably never have become a writer,' he had written to him in November. 'The Buddenbrooks was a bourgeois book, with no further meaning for the twentieth century. Tonio Kröger was merely maudlin, Royal Highness frivolous, Death in Venice half-educated and false.' But a heartening reply from his brother shook him out of this mood, and restored the will to work.

The completion of the new house was due by the end of the year, and while waiting, the family was now living mainly in Tölz. Thomas, with an eye to his financial difficulties, had arranged a heavy programme of readings for November and December, in Stuttgart, Vienna, and Budapest, to be followed in January by a tour in Switzerland; later that month he appeared in Frankfurt and Munich. But meanwhile Katia, after some unavailing weeks of cure at Merano, had been recommended once again to mountain air, and, after a family Christmas celebrated at the Pringsheims', departed for the Swiss resort of Arosa on 4 January 1914. Thomas was left alone to see to the move the following day with the children to Poschinger Straße, and Katia did not see the new quarters until her return from Arosa in May. With all this movement, he could only hope to get back soon to his 'novella': the start was pretty good, he wrote to Heinrich in January, and his new study certainly splendid. For the moment, however, there had been too much on his plate, and although a brief visit to Katia's sanatorium in

Arosa undoubtedly yielded helpful impressions, the winter months could show little progress on *The Magic Mountain*.

In terms of public relations, on the other hand, they brought positive advance. His readings included not only well-known material, but also fragments of *Krull* as a foretaste of what was to come; in Hungary, where his work was already familiar in translation, he was royally entertained and enthusiastically interviewed, the brief stay including even a visit to parliament, and his performances drew almost reverent reviews. To his Munich programme in January he had added for the first time an extract from the new work barely begun: and the 'fascinating personality' of Thomas Mann, as one paper had it after his reading in the Galerie Caspari, was impressing itself more and more widely. As he established himself at No. 1 Poschinger Strasse, he will undoubtedly have felt its distinguished character no less than fitting for so prominent and representative a figure.

Fronting on the river, in a large garden surrounded by a stone wall, the house was indeed a *maison de maître*, a worthy successor to those of his forebears, though with nothing of Lübeck in its design: here lived, one would have thought, a successful businessman, not a writer. The ground floor was raised, with a perron on the river-front leading into a three-windowed room, projecting in semi-circular form, over which were built balconies for the first floor, with their (separate) bedrooms and the children's domain, and the second, for the moment empty. The main entrance, at the back, led to a large panelled hall, where stood the stuffed bear from his parents' house proffering a tray for visiting-cards, and the main staircase. The salon, with grand piano and Katia's library, and the dining-room lay to either side; a lift linked the dining-room with the kitchen and servants' quarters below. Through the hall was his study—the best room in the house, naturally, leading on to the garden steps—with his desk, high bookcases, a side desk for books in use, and embellished with the chandeliers from the Beckergrube house, sofas and the Empire chairs, and the Lenbach portrait of Katia as a child. The telephone, to him always an abominable instrument, was based below, and put through to Katia's room when she was in, but never to the study during his morning working hours. In the evenings, recalled Erika, when the green velvet curtains at the high windows were drawn, the French window closed, and the double doors open to the hall, he never failed to remark delightedly on the 'thoroughly seigneurial prospect'. It would be their home for nigh on twenty years. At this time, it was virtually the last house in Munich, but there were a few neighbours a little further in, and Bruno Walter in particular, then musical director of the Munich Opera, and his family became lifelong friends.

He was glad to be relieved of the duties of supervision such a household required by Katia's return in May, when he could turn again to his accustomed careful but regular work on the 'Davos novella'. It was developing to a 'vigorous length', he told a friend in June, and he was barely half-way: the thing had a great number of facets, and he set great hopes on it.[44] That Europe was in crisis had not escaped him: but that the upheaval of war was imminent, he seems, like most ordinary people, to have had little suspicion.

[44] *DüD.* i, 452.

# III

‒‒ 〓◊〓 ‒‒

# THE MAGIC MOUNTAIN—
# AND NON-POLITICAL
# REFLECTIONS
# 1914–1924

‒‒ 〓◊〓 ‒‒

'The problem of my brother is ... the hardest of my existence'
(TM, February 1917)

1

*'Must one not be grateful for the totally unexpected experience of
such great events?'* (TM, August 1914)

In his fortieth year, Thomas Mann had established a congenial routine in a
life of prosperity and—as far as his hypochondria would allow—well-
being, regulated by the love of order and discipline that was natural to him.
Rising sharp at eight, and taking early coffee with Katia, he would greet the
children already taking their breakfast in the upstairs hall, and descend for
his own in the dining-room, shutting himself then in his study to resume
work on the current major project from nine to noon or twelve-thirty.
Here, as the household knew, he was never on any account to be disturbed.
A page or a page and a half was the usual product, rarely more, but very
rarely less: 'give us this day our daily page' was his watchword, he told
Bertram, as the manuscript of *The Magic Mountain* accumulated. Cigarettes
in moderation accompanied his work. Then he would set out for his daily
walk, with the dog, pondering on his work and preparing for the next steps,
and sometimes meeting the children on their way home from school, to
return punctually for lunch with the family at one-thirty.

He was neither gourmet nor gourmand, and (unlike his forebears)
shunned heavy meals: his main interest was in a good soup and a tasty
dessert. His knowledge of wines was superficial, and alcohol in general

failed to tempt him, certainly never at work (though he confessed to some exceptions in earlier years—brandy grog had helped him to write *The Wardrobe*, a glass of champagne the Schiller story). At most, an occasional glass of beer with lunch and a small brandy afterwards, taken with Katia in the study, with his first cigar of the day, before he turned to the lighter work of the afternoon—reading on the sofa and making notes—and then settled to at least an hour of sleep, a rest he hated to be deprived of. The remainder of the afternoon was devoted to lighter tasks, what he called, with Goethe, 'the demands of the day'—his copious correspondence, proof-correcting, or journal contributions; now he was prepared to tolerate interruptions, visitors, even telephone calls if unavoidable. Occasionally before dinner another short walk; after dinner, often a reading of the latest work completed, to the family and any visitors on hand, and perhaps some music (though for the moment there was no gramophone, later to become a passion); more reading if they were alone, and bed at midnight with a book.

He liked to emphasize the dogged nature of such a working routine, which he had admired in Schopenhauer, and to say, with Baudelaire, 'inspiration is without doubt the sister of daily toil'. The point became almost legendary, the many times that curious interviewers sought to embellish their texts, or literary journals to describe his working methods. In essence, however, it was the routine he held to all his life, whether now in Munich and in the Tölz 'Landhaus', or on the frequent journeys he undertook later: scarcely a day would pass without the morning stint of application, even if it meant working in a hotel room or on a beach (provided always he could have some sort of roof over his head). And, in the early months of 1914, as he wrote later, he 'would have staked house and home' on the proposition that he and his peaceable world would not see war in Europe.[1]

For the children, he was naturally a more remote figure than their mother. 'Mielein', as they called her, though leaving their regime largely to the nannies, was at hand for story-reading, or an outing to pick berries in the Tölz woods; he was 'Pielein', then 'Papale', and went finally under the name of 'The Magician', the sorcerer demanding quiet for the spells that seemed to set the literary atmosphere of the house. He lacked Mielein's *savoir-faire* in their everyday affairs, but could impress them with certain talents, like the ability to whip up white of egg in a saucer to perfect stiffness, or sprinkle them expertly with the garden hose, or enliven their walks in Tölz with improvised fairy-stories. For their 'ocean liner' game in the garden there, he was the captain, his study the bridge, seldom showing

---

[1] xii 184.

himself but in absolute charge of the ship. Against Mielein's orders, there was always the possibility of rebellion, wrote Klaus: but the Magician's decisions were final. Sundays in Munich meant always a long walk with him to lunch with their Pringsheim grandparents: for the children, in spite of their fear of breaking something in that grand house, an exciting day, with games that were 'special' to the Arcis Strasse garden, but for their father something of a chore, not least because he had to miss his afternoon's rest.

In Tölz, in that summer of 1914, the Löhrs had taken a house nearby, and Klaus and Erika were in their garden with the three girl cousins rehearsing a play—'Pandora's Box', with their own text and home-made costumes—when word came that a war had broken out (Germany's declaration against Russia). Berlin would be set on fire by the French, said know-all cousin Eva: more important to eight-year-old Klaus was whether this far-off event would put paid to their stage plans, and he and Erika ran off to find their parents. Folding up the blankets from his afternoon rest on the veranda, their father looked out towards the mountains and said, portentously: 'Now I suppose there'll soon be a fiery sword appearing in the heavens. If the old man were still alive—no need for him to do anything, but just be there at Yasnaya Polyana—it would not have happened, not have *dared* to happen.'[2] But Tolstoy was dead, and Pandora's box was open. It was not a moment to ask him about the play.

Two days before, under the 'fearful pressure of reality' in the report of mobilization, he had remained optimistic, he said: too much of a 'civilian cast of mind' to believe the monstrous possible—but who could tell what madness might seize Europe when once carried away? This to Heinrich, who was on holiday in Nice after completing his *Man of Straw*, a bitterly satirical novel on Kaiser Wilhelm's Germany: deeply worried by the news, and particularly by the assassination of Jaurès on 31 July, which he saw as making war with France inevitable, he returned at the last moment to Germany. Viktor, at 24 already called up, married his young fiancée, Nelly Kilian, in haste on 2 August, and both Thomas and Heinrich, as well as their mother, were able to bid him goodbye before he left for the front. Of Katia's four brothers, Heinz was already in the cavalry, the scientist Peter, attending a British Association meeting in Australia, was interned there for the duration, but neither Erik, the eldest, nor her twin, Klaus, was yet militarily involved. Thomas, in the older reserve age-groups not yet called up, returned for the moment to Tölz to await events; Heinrich remained for a month in Upper Bavaria, but married on 12 August the Prague actress Mimi Kanová, whom he had met in Berlin the year before during rehearsals

[2] PdM 976.

for one of his plays and with whom he had been living on and off in Munich. (After Ines Schmied, there had been a sceptical attitude towards Heinrich's 'failed fiancées', as Katia put it, and Thomas remarked on his sometimes curious taste: but by and large they were well-disposed towards Mimi.)

The brothers' reactions to the war were beginning to take different lines. Thomas, though expecting a ruinous change in his material situation, felt an intense curiosity to witness the great events to come, gratitude even for such an unexpected opportunity, and the 'deepest sympathy for this hated . . . Germany which, even if it has not so far held "civilization" as the highest good, is at least ready to destroy the vilest police-state in the world' (meaning Russia). Writing thus on 7 August to Heinrich, he seemed to have no notion of how repugnant such a line would be to his brother, who was deeply depressed at the invasion of Belgium and the attack on his beloved France. Heinrich was also worried over the abrupt termination of the serial publication of *Man of Straw*. The novel, which, despite its aggressive criticism of conditions in imperial Germany, had been welcomed by Thomas, had been running since January in an illustrated weekly: if it were to continue, the publisher, sensibly, feared censorship difficulties. The Russian serial version in St Petersburg went on uninterrupted, of course, and the book itself appeared there in 1915, but that could now bring no money in. For Thomas, the pre-war world had seemed ripe for decay, he wrote to Fischer towards the end of August, and his *Magic Mountain* would show the inevitability of catastrophe, with the outbreak of war giving him the solution he wanted for the novel—war and the victory of 'German culture' as the instruments of salvation.[3] To him, *Man of Straw* seemed a similar portrayal, and he had little idea yet how much more down-to-earth, pessimistic, and 'unpatriotic', indeed revolutionary, his brother's thoughts were.

He was insensible too to Heinrich's financial plight, as he reviewed his own apparently dire situation. The Tölz 'Landhaus' was unsellable for the time being, his father-in-law's support had been halved, and he was earning nothing: hearing that Heinrich was due for a small legacy, he asked him in September for repayment of the 2,000 marks he was owed, and brushed aside his protests and his pessimism over his literary prospects. Heinrich, after all, had no children and few commitments, at the worst he had only to economize, and that he too was doing—'within the framework unfortunately set for us' (a framework he was clearly not about to change if he could help it, and the risk to which in fact he grossly exaggerated). 'Can you really believe that, in this great, fundamentally just, indeed solemn war, German culture should be so brought down as to reject permanently

[3] *DüD.* i, 454.

your talent?' Heinrich promised to do what he could—which for the moment was nothing, as the legacy was not paid until three years later.

But this was a dialogue of the deaf. While Heinrich's hopes were already pinned on a quite different flowering of German culture, in a republic to be built on the ruins of a defeated empire, Thomas held firmly to the conventionally patriotic line, which he was emphatically affirming in an essay just completed, 'Thoughts in the War'. In it, he saw the conflict as an honourable defence of 'German' values (Lutheran, romantic) against the insults being hurled from all sides at his Fatherland, and hailed it as 'purification and liberation' from the corruption of peacetime 'civilization'. In this high-flown rhetoric he was at one with the fervent chorus of his writing colleagues—Hauptmann, Dehmel among them—most, like himself, with little more than a literary knowledge of the enemy countries. He contrasted imperial Germany's 'social' state, progressive and modern, with that of its adversaries, a 'lawyer's parliamentarism which in its moments of enthusiasm still threshes the straw of 1789' and which must fail in its aim of 'democratizing' and 'educating' Germany to its own level of so-called civilization. It was nothing short of blasphemy to wish to see German culture disappear from the face of the earth 'in favour of *humanité* and *raison*, still less of cant'.

Among those who rejected such a line was Wilhelm Herzog, whose anti-militarist monthly *Forum* had begun four months before the war with essays by Romain Rolland, Heinrich Mann, and Frank Wedekind (and even a reprint of *The Child Prodigy*, the novella by Thomas Mann, whom he greatly admired): when he read 'Thoughts in the War', in Heinrich's company, they were pained and horrified to see such errors 'from so well-balanced a spirit', and in his December issue he wrote a sharp polemic against this 'false doctrine, manicured in literary form, of the German soul'.[4] Whether Heinrich in fact saw or wrote to his brother at this time, we do not know, but there is no doubt of the profound breach between them from now on. Many years later, Heinrich's wife, Mimi, recalled the last argument between them: her husband's quiet forecast that Germany would lose the war and that the fall of the monarchy must follow, and Thomas's abrupt departure.

Thomas had returned meanwhile to Munich, and, as was his duty, reported to the military, to find that the medical officer, bowing subserviently before such a famous name, decided at once he should be left in peace. Miserable, he claimed, to have to stay home when all were sacrificing themselves for Germany, he had struggled hard; but army service would have been a nonsense, 'head, stomach, and nerves would have stood it only a for a few days, and I'd only be a burden'.[5] Richard Dehmel,

---

[4] üPdM 1007.      [5] Franke 22.

we may note, though twelve years older, had not hesitated to volunteer, and later, from the trenches, wrote him an enthusiastic welcome for the essay. His reply, confessing still to a certain shame, expressed satisfaction that his journalistic effort at least to put his brain in the service of the cause had not been entirely superfluous. But qualms over his exemption do not seem to have troubled him long; and, far too stimulated by events to resume work on his novel, he continued his service to the cause now with a longer essay.

'Germany today is Frederick the Great,' he had written in the 'Thoughts': 'This is his battle . . . which we have to fight once again', against a similar European coalition 'formed in hatred'. 'Frederick and the Great Coalition: An Outline for the Day and the Hour', which he completed by the end of the year and which was published in January 1915, developed this parallel between the Seven Years War and that of 1914 (rather speciously comparing Frederick's invasion of neutral Saxony with that now of Belgium), but in a less polemical style and with insights on Frederick the man more suited to the novel he had long prepared but never written, relinquishing it instead to Gustav von Aschenbach. (Fifteen years later, long after his views had radically changed, he still reckoned this essay among his best; and, much later still, in its 'strange mixture of critical discretion and hotheaded patriotic allusion',[6] as deserving a place in his collected prose pieces of five decades.)

Though he was not a signatory to the October 1914 manifesto of ninety-three professors, writers, and artists, in self-righteous protest against Rolland's allegations of German brutality in the occupation of Belgium, its burden of total solidarity with emperor and government exactly expressed his own feelings. In April 1915 he embarked on more journalism, in reply to an enquiry by the Swedish daily *Svenska Dagbladet* on Germany and the world war. Germany, he argued, so far from wanting war, had been *forced* to want it, and the question of who had started was irrelevant, for none could deny that Europe's pre-war condition was untenable. Germany had welcomed the war because it was the harbinger of her 'Third Reich', that 'synthesis of power and intellect' she had dreamed of, which was leading her out of the Bismarck era to a new epoch of political education, to 'humanity and freedom'. If she were defeated, she could not rest until restored to her present position: peace could be found only in her 'self-assertion and self-fulfilment. . . . At all events Germany will stand, decisively proved and recognized, and the peoples will have to live with her.'

He had been proud enough of his Frederick essay to want to see it published in more permanent form. Fischer had demurred, fearing that its

[6]  xi 697.

emphasis on the Prussian King's ruthless character, which many in Germany too had already criticized, would be misused by foreign propaganda; and Thomas for his part admitted that its glorification of Prussia might argue against wider dissemination. But the idea now of a slim volume sandwiching it between 'Thoughts in the War' and the *Dagbladet* contribution appealed to the publisher, and this appeared in June 1915. It made popular reading among the military, Thomas averred: and perhaps it may indeed have helped morale, now that trench warfare had succeeded the first furious advance on the western front. But both admirers and detractors of Frederick—both patriots, and radicals like Heinrich and Herzog or the *émigrés* in Zurich preaching brotherhood—joined from their different standpoints in sharply criticizing his view in the essay, which drew more attention than the more ephemeral and chauvinistic pieces surrounding it.

By this time he had turned back to *The Magic Mountain* (referring to it now, for the first time, as a novel); but in May and June every member of the family, with the sole exception of himself, was stricken by appendicitis. Successive operations in a distant clinic saw Golo, Monika, and Erika safely through, and Katia at the end of June: but with Klaus, admitted during May, there were serious complications, including peritonitis, making altogether four operations necessary, until his life, it seemed, hung by a thread. Although his mother was only just up herself from her operation, it was her devotion, Klaus was later convinced, that alone had pulled him back from death: when the doctors had given up hope, in desperation she rubbed him from head to foot with eau-de-cologne, and overnight there came the turn. Living virtually on the tram between house and clinic, the worried father could do little work on the novel. In addition there was doubt whether the army would continue to leave him free, though this cloud was apparently lifted during his time with the family in Tölz, to which they repaired early in August as soon as 'Eissi'—out of danger, but thin and wasted—could be moved.

The war, now a year old, had in fact brought more uncertainty into Mann's work plans than he had at first realized. While its outbreak, as he had immediately said, would make the perfect ending to the novel, this in itself had started only as an interlude to the work on *Krull*, of which he reckoned barely a third was written and to which he must return as soon as the other was done. Yet, with head and heart so preoccupied with events, he felt he should not continue spinning the 'fable' before he had fully and conscientiously said his say on the burning problems of the hour. He had done another, shorter article of 'Thoughts in the War' on 1 August, rehashing the earlier theme and with nothing new. Now, as he said in a letter in September, he felt the need to embark on a fuller critical and political essay, a personal analysis of the conflict of 'culture' against 'civilization', describing his notion of the future—nothing less than the social reorganization of Europe, of which the West was incapable and which must be Germany's mission, for he held it superstition to regard Western ideas, 'world liberalism', as the key to progress. Sickened by the 'political lawyers' of France, the 'democratic doctrinaires and tyrannical schoolmasters of revolution', he had parted for ever 'from those friends of the Entente within Germany, our radical littérateurs . . . all those literary politicians who . . . today, believe me! are bitterly disappointed that the Franco-English invasion simply will not materialize'.[7]

There can be little doubt that Heinrich, though nowhere named, was foremost among the targets of this invective. But it is also clear that Thomas felt the unburdening of himself in such an extensive essay was in fact an inescapable preliminary to the artistic working-out of his concept for the novel. It had to remain a pre-war story, and even if the figure of Settembrini, the 'civilization littérateur' *par excellence* who had already made his appearance in the draft, would embody many of his current ideas, their full expression required separate development. Whether by design or not, he had been absent from his brother's lecture in Munich, on 18 June, on Émile Zola: for Heinrich, Zola was the poet standing four-square a part of life, a 'democratic leader', 'conscious genius of a democracy', and he had chosen him as his subject because 'we, and the others, even now, have remained Europeans and must learn from each other'.[8] He was expanding the theme in a lengthy essay for *Die Weissen Blätter*, edited by the like-minded René Schickele, where it appeared in November; but this too Thomas did not see until the turn of the year. With the gulf between them now, he was perhaps unsurprised, but certainly sickened to find its burden directed almost as much against himself as against Germany. By this time he was already deep in his own work, on diametrically opposed lines, his *Reflections of a Non-Political Man*. Though it was obviously beginning to develop far beyond essay length, he did not yet foresee that it would take him most of the war years to complete, to stand then almost as a monument to bygone ideas.

2

*'War moans, special sighs, longsufferings of understanding'*
(*Joyce*, Finnegans Wake)

Through this second winter of war—with shortages, particularly of fuel, beginning to make themselves felt on the home front—Mann held stub-

---

[7] *Amann Br.* 33.     [8] PdM 1031.

bornly, often almost desperately, to the task on which he had set his priority. It was a matter of conscience for him, its literary value of indifference, as he said towards the end of the year, and would probably turn out enjoyable only to those truly sympathetic to his life and efforts. He read widely in historical and political literature, excerpting at length the passages which suited his line, and was absorbed especially by Dostoevsky and his interpreter Merezhkovsky, as well as by Tolstoy. In correspondence and on his visits, Ernst Bertram became his constant confidant. From his academic background Bertram was ever ready with quotations and instances, to bolster or set right the argument of the sometimes rambling dissertation, particularly where Nietzsche was concerned, on whom he was preparing a book of his own, and to make good the gaps in his friend's knowledge of German literature. At the end of January, he listened to the draft passage on the 'civilization littérateur', which showed all too clearly the intemperate fury sparked by Heinrich's Zola essay. Neither brother actually mentioned the name of the other, but the personal allusions in both works were unmistakable, and Bertram was concerned to urge Thomas to moderate the sweeping invective he was pouring out against Heinrich.

Yet, for all this help, he was beginning to weaken in his resolve, and he declared in February that he was at a loss to know what he was really about. Impossible to publish, the *Reflections* seemed nothing more than a statement of the inner crisis induced in him by the times, and 'useless as an aid for others to clarity, which is after all the task of the writer'.[9] From a young Austrian, Paul Amann, with whom he had been in correspondence and who had heard from the start of his ideas for the essay, he received an article on Romain Rolland; and, in spite of his own criticism of Rolland's *Au-dessus de la mêlée* as self-deception, he found ideas beginning to dawn which were far removed from those of his vehement polemic. He was tired of the hatred, the accusations, excessively weary of the 'war', he wrote to Amann on 25 February, 'profoundly inclined to gentleness, to peace, even to penitence': it would finally be realized that there could be no 'victory' for either of the parties, and that there was in fact a common will to the renewal and rebirth of Europe, the only basis for reconciliation. 'I can feel something of the Europe to come: an exhausted Europe, but full of youthful hope, sensitive, refined, and blessed by common suffering ... undoctrinaire, undogmatic, for all the earlier antitheses and slogans will be obsolete.' He was not stupid enough, he said in March, to deny that the democratization, politicization of Germany—in short, all that might be called her 'de-Germanization'—was inevitable: but that was far from believing it

[9] PdM 1074.

desirable.[10] Reason might make him a democrat; but his feelings, rather a conservative.

What good, then, to continue with the 'long monologue'? In such a mood, small wonder that he should fall ill, with a high fever and influenza, followed, hardly was he up, by erysipelas. To reread *Anna Karenina* proved the best road to health ('I recall what a support it was as I worked at *The Buddenbrooks*'); and during the Easter holidays at Tölz he found renewed vigour for his 'monster' of a book—for book it was becoming, no longer an essay that might appear in the *Rundschau* and thus at least bring some income. Whatever his milder thoughts on democracy and reconciliation, he was too deeply into his subject, and the antitheses, not least that with his brother, burned too sharply in his mind for him to abandon the project now. But returning to Munich in September, he had to confess that the summer months in Tölz had been anything but conducive to work, and that he longed to return to something 'three-dimensional', to real epic composition, instead of this wearying grind at 'direct speech' which was not normally his concern. And he was by no means finished. Much still remained to be said, he told Bertram: on the aesthete and the politician, the Jacobins, politics and art, irony, humanity and freedom, democracy, conservatism as opposition—to the scorn of the literati and doubtless the boredom of the public. It would be 'a bulky book for a few friends, like you'.

As the third winter of the war began, he declared himself still confident of the German cause, though admitting the worsening military situation and the unlikelihood of peace offers from the Entente. Katia no longer shared his confidence, as the children noticed; but she and they loyally strove to lighten the burden of the increasing shortages in rations and clothing. Thomas never remarked how the family were economizing on their sugar ration so that he should not go short: take some, he would urge a guest at tea, they always had plenty. Katia was daily out early on her cycle in the hunt for new sources of eggs or other rarities, and did not hesitate to tap the black market if necessary. Klaus, hearing once of a shop in the suburbs where eggs were to be had, queued with Erika for hours in the cold, started back holding the booty in his cap—then dropped them from his frozen hands before they reached home. 'Never again has the world seemed to me so cold, so unbelievably hard and cruel.' Sunday lunch was still at the Pringsheims, but the former lavish menu was reduced now to an emaciated bird, some kind of heron with a penetrating oily flavour, and an awful pink ersatz pudding—and they had to bring along their own bread.

Their father too was no longer the same. Tense and preoccupied now,

---

[10] *Düd* i, 636.

stern of look, often letting his beard grow for weeks on end, he seemed tired after the morning's work, which to Klaus was evidently something abstract, more mysterious than one of the Magician's tales. To visitors asking after his new work, he replied in slight embarrassment it was just a book, and had to do with the war. He presided gloomily at meals, and not seldom there were sudden outbursts of anger, mostly directed at Klaus but also reducing Golo, who could not bear scenes, to tears. After lunch, he would retire again to his study, closing the door firmly, and clearly even less to be disturbed than usual. At home, he wore what he called his 'service jacket', a Russian-style battle-dress tunic, a field-grey rig chosen perhaps to reinforce to himself the notion that he too, even if not in the front line, was playing his part in the conflict. In November 1916, with a suitable medical certificate, he had survived a further examination without being called up, but continued uneasy and not without a certain guilty feeling over his exemption, which he expected, if the war continued, might yet be reversed.

'The times are impetuous, and I am slow,' he told Bertram: in the *Reflections* he had to settle accounts, in his exhaustive and pedantic way, and was getting old and tired in the process. He had admitted that his inability to keep his thoughts on a tight rein, the *'furor* of wanting to say everything', was a dangerous weakness; and it was clear that the task he had imposed on himself had many months still to run, with every passing day increasing the risk that the final result would be obsolete, overtaken by events. There was no help for it, however; he had to hold out—even though interruptions by other work were not unwelcome, not least as an interim source of income. Successful public readings from *Krull* in the autumn, in Munich, Breslau, and Berlin, and an essay, 'Music in Munich', devoted to his friend and neighbour Bruno Walter in January 1917, brought him back briefly to the world of creativity and music, where he felt more truly at home: the only sphere, he thought, in which 'German solidarity and synthesis' was expressed, never in intellectual life or politics. A similar theme had appeared in an essay on Eichendorff's *Taugenichts*, for the November *Rundschau*: treating the ne'er-do-well miller's son with his violin, the artist and genius, as an 'exemplary German' in the 'humane moderation of his being'.[11] Yet all these apparent diversions were closely bound up with the theses for the *Reflections* which were his constant preoccupation, as was his December review of a new edition of Carlyle's *Frederick the Great*.

Heinrich meanwhile had found his totally different course rewarding. Not that, in the by now widely known fraternal controversy, adherents

[11] PdM 1091.

were exactly swarming around him, nor was there yet in Germany an overwhelming ground-swell of democratic or republican feeling, still less a powerful revolutionary movement, that might accord with his views. But the courage of his Zola essay had found many sympathizers, and it had proved a turning-point in his literary career. In 1916 his scattered works were taken up by the young avant-garde publisher Kurt Wolff and reissued in a ten-volume collected edition which achieved sales so far unheard-of for him. Wolff also prepared a private printing of *Man of Straw*, for which, of course, the times were hardly yet favourable, sending the ten copies to a very select readership, including Mechtilde Lichnowsky, wife of the pre-war ambassador to London (whose vain efforts for peace were later to be gratefully recalled by the British Foreign Secretary). The author's biggest success, however, came in February 1917, when his drama *Madame Legros* was premièred simultaneously in Lübeck and Munich, followed by productions on many other stages—so many, in fact, that one Berlin paper nicknamed it 'Madame Engros'.

The story was a simple one—a brave woman's successful fight, single-handed, to secure the freedom of an unjustly imprisoned Bastille prisoner; and writing it in 1913, with, of course, no premonition of the European war which was soon to follow, Heinrich had expressed his admiration for the initial idealism of the French Revolution. Now, amid increasing war-weariness and a ferment of political speculation when the Kaiser was promising electoral reform, the emphasis on the humanitarian beginnings of the Revolution in France struck a chord: 'at last we can look one another in the eyes again', said one spectator.[12] In Berlin, after its production there in April, Heinrich found himself pressed by no less a person than the president of the National Bank to put his dramatic talent at the service of the German revolution, and heard Prince Lichnowsky's forecast of Germany's military defeat.

For Thomas, who had read and praised the play in 1913, but did not now attend a performance, its apotheosis of such French idealism was thoroughly anti-German, and yet one of 'those profoundly German things of which one never knows, and never will know, whether to despair or to be glad'. To him, Germany's destiny seemed symbolized and personified in himself and his brother, and their personal relationship 'the fundamental, at any rate the hardest problem', of his existence. He could not grudge Heinrich his success when he himself, so long fortune's favourite, had produced little recently: but he could not forgive the political passion and injustice towards Germany's cause in the war which had led his brother to treat his *Thoughts in the War* as a provocation, and to seal their break with the Zola essay. The 'civilization' and 'justice' lauded in *Madame Legros* went

---

[12] *Zeitalter* 226.

deeply against the grain of the conservative nationalism to which he still firmly held: 'justice' there was merely a political outcry, 'a fanfare leading to bloody deeds', aggressive and conscienceless, 'fundamentally *unjust*'.[13] It was one further mark of the radical littérateur, the 'Entente enthusiast', whose dogmatic obstinacy he had castigated in the chapter of the 'non-political' *Reflections* provoked by Heinrich's Zola essay and who now, with his magic formula 'democracy', figured largely in the chapter 'Politics' he had embarked on.

The critical events early in 1917—Germany's January declaration of unrestricted submarine warfare, bringing America into the war in April, the Tsar's abdication in March, and Lenin's arrival in Petrograd in April—found surprisingly little echo in his letters, his notes, and the *Reflections*. He had no idea of the inevitability of Germany's defeat once the Allies' material superiority was assured with America at their side; he still apparently hoped that submarine warfare would bring England to her knees by the summer; and seemed to regard the upheaval in Russia, after his lengthy reading in Tolstoy and Dostoevsky, in purely literary terms, with little appreciation of the political implications, even if it held up some prospect for peace. And he continued with his interminable soliloquy, though often feeling like 'crawling up the wall' in his impatience to become an artist again: 'these years are just as lost to me as if I were in the army'.[14]

Completing now the long section 'Politics', he felt the coming summer might at last see the end. The original idea of publishing the whole in the *Rundschau*, before its appearance as a book, had long been out of the question; even his offer of the chapter 'Contemplation'—largely autobiographical, on his relationship to the three 'great Germans' Schopenhauer, Wagner, and Nietzsche—had at first been found unsuitable, on political grounds and as 'too European'. It finally appeared in the March 1917 number, however, and the fee was certainly welcome, as had been those for an extract on 'Art and Politics' in a Munich paper in February and for his reading, in Berlin the previous November, of the *Taugenichts* review, which he had now worked into the general argument of the *Reflections*. To this extent, the world gained an idea of what he had been about over these long months; and he drew some sharp criticism with his thesis of resistance to the 'civilization littérateur' and to a politicization of the musical atmosphere of Germany, in which alone, he argued, her national solidarity could be found. As he turned now to the chapter on 'Virtue' and developed this theme further—citing *Fiorenza* as a 'satire on the democratization of the artistic', inveighing once more against 'democratic wisdom's famous equation, reason = virtue = happiness'[15]—it was for music in Germany that he reserved his praise.

[13] *Nb.* 12, 301.    [14] *DüD.* i, 646 f.    [15] xii 382, 397.

In Munich, in June, Bruno Walter had presented the première of Hans Pfitzner's opera *Palestrina*, and Mann's enthusiasm was such that he attended three performances and invited the composer to Poschinger Strasse. His long article on the experience for the *Rundschau*, taken virtually intact into the *Reflections*, emphasized Pfitzner's words to him that evening, contrasting the *Meistersinger*, as 'the apotheosis of the new', with *Palestrina*, in which the whole trend was towards the past, towards 'sympathy with death'. Pfitzner's formulation was a surprise, for it caught a major thematic element of the still-unfinished *Magic Mountain*: there his hero Hans Castorp, held in the Davos sanatorium by an 'unvirtuous sympathy with death' and pinned in the cross-fire between the progressive littérateur Settembrini and the arch-reactionary advocate of anti-reason Naphta, would be faced with the choice between duty to life and the fascination of decay. As he had written to Amann in March, it was remarkable how, before the war, the political problems in the *Reflections* had already been in his mind: he had embarked on them precisely because he wanted to avoid an 'intellectually impossible overloading' of the novel.

The summer of 1917 was to be the family's last in Bad Tölz. By July Thomas had managed to sell the house, at what he thought the reasonable price of 55,000 marks, but it was agreed he could use it till the end of the Summer, thereafter the better pieces of its furniture would serve nicely to complement that of Poschinger Strasse. Bertram devoted his vacation to Tölz, providing useful comments and quotations and making an indispensable auditor for the latest drafts of what the children, with whom he was a popular visitor, called 'this mysterious book'. Its seemingly endless stream Mann thought had been tolerably dammed by August; and, amid plans for an extended reading-tour early in 1918, it seemed he would soon be able to dispatch the 'monster' to the publisher. Indeed, after his reading of an extract in Munich in December, a senior civil servant urged immediate publication of a book so important in the present situation; but his own feeling was that, as a purely personal document, it should wait for peacetime, and in any case it had still to be provided with a suitable preamble.

Peace did indeed seem to be approaching. April had seen the first major strikes in Germany, and although the generals had been encouraged by the failure of the Entente offensives and the resounding defeat of the Italians at Caporetto, and had secured the resignation in July of Bethmann-Hollweg as Chancellor, the Reichstag had given its approval to a resolution for a peace without annexations. And in November, after the Bolshevik revolution, Lenin let it be known that he sought immediate peace. Following the mood of the times, in December the liberal *Berliner Tageblatt* sought the views of writers and scholars on the prospects for a 'world peace', and devoted much space in a Christmas number to their contributions, including one from Heinrich Mann, 'Life—not Destruction!', in which he urged democracy as the only way. Thomas, perhaps deliberately, sent in his own later, entitled 'World Peace', with a question-mark, and it was published on 27 December, with an editorial disclaimer: for he repudiated any such faith in politics, in socialism and the 'république démocratique, sociale et universelle'. Quoting Dehmel ('a little kindness between individuals is better than all love for humanity'), he looked forward to a time when, cleansed of politics, he could once more contemplate life and humanity, when the peoples could 'live together in dignity and honour behind peacefully assured frontiers in the exchange of their finest qualities: the handsome Englishman, the polished Frenchman, the humane Russian, the German with his deeper understanding'.

This, so Heinrich thought, seemed directly addressed to himself; and he was moved to write to his brother on 30 December in an attempt at the reconciliation he felt long overdue.

All your work I have followed in the best of wills to understand and sympathize with it. The contrariness of your nature I was familiar with of old: your extreme position over the war, if it surprised you yourself, for me was not unexpected. But the knowledge did not stop me from often caring for your work . . . repeatedly praising and defending it in public, and in your moments of despair comforting you as a younger brother. And when all this was not reciprocated, I was not discouraged. I knew that for your own assurance you needed self-restraint, even the opposition of others—and so your attacks on me too . . . were never much trouble to get over. Only once did I reply, when it was no longer a matter of personalities or intellectual obstinacy, but of the most general emergency and danger. My 'Zola' was a protest against those who were . . . thrusting themselves forward with harmful intent. Not just against you, but against a whole legion. But today, instead of a legion, there remain only a few despairing souls.

He had never acted out of hatred for his brother, and he hoped for a hearing for his assurance that Thomas need never think of him as an enemy.

It was a generous gesture; but it drew a bitter response. On the point of leaving for his reading-tour, Thomas professed himself unable to write an adequate reply, and doubted in fact whether it was worthwhile to try once more to compress the 'intellectual torment' of the past two years into a letter which must of necessity turn out much longer than his brother's. He nevertheless did so, at considerable length and in terms which ruled out any reconciliation. He was ready to believe Heinrich felt no hatred for him. But as he said, their views of the world, so totally at odds, were bound to lend a personal colour to everything; and he returned to the attack on the *Zola*, that 'glittering but shoddy effort', with its 'truly French malevolence, calumnies, slanders'.

That my conduct over the war has been 'extreme', is an untruth. Yours has, to the point of becoming completely detestable. But I haven't suffered and struggled for two years, abandoned my fondest plans, condemned myself to total artistic silence, searched my heart . . . to let myself be persuaded by a letter which—understand-ably—breathes triumph, regards me in far-fetched argument as leading a handful of 'despairing souls', and ends by finding no reason for me to look on you as an enemy—a letter every line of which is dictated by self-satisfaction and self-right-eousness—just to fall sobbing on your breast. What lies behind me was the work of a galley-slave: but I owe to it the consciousness that I stand now less helpless against your zealous vapourings than at the time when they could draw blood. You and your kind may call me a parasite. The truth, *my* truth, is that I'm not. . . . Stifter wrote in a letter: 'My books are not simply poetic works, but—as moral revelations, as examples in disciplined seriousness of human dignity—have a value which will endure longer than the poetic.' I have a right to say this with him, and thousands whom I have helped to live—even without reciting the *contrat social*, one hand on the heart, the other in the air—*recognize* that right.

Not you. You can't see the ethos and the right of my life, for you are my brother. Why did no one else, neither Hauptmann, nor Dehmel . . . nor the preventive-war advocate Harden (whom you now honour with admiring visits) see the invective of the 'Zola' article as directed against them? Why was all its tearing polemic aimed at me? Our fraternal experience of the world compelled you to it. To the same Dehmel, who sent me from the trenches thanks and congratulations for my first war-article, you can now offer . . . the warmest sympathy, and he can accept it; for, although you are very different spirits, you aren't brothers, and so you can both live.—Let the tragedy of our brotherly relationship fulfil itself.

Pain? That's all right. One becomes hard and insensible. After Carla died and you broke for ever with Lula, separation for the rest of this life on earth is nothing new in our community. I didn't make this life. I abominate it. We must live it as best we can.

Farewell.

No letter of Thomas Mann's, among the many thousands left to us, shows more patently than this his self-centredness. After three and a half years of the most destructive war Europe had ever seen, its casualties rising to millions, he could think only of his art, of his own 'galley-slave' suffering and heart-searchings, and persisted in what even he must by now have realized could be no more than a rearguard action against the impending defeat of his reactionary ideas. Heinrich wrote, but did not send, a reply: silence seemed the only course against this rejection of his outstretched hand, and there was no further communication between them until four years had passed. It is hardly likely that his reply, had it been sent, would have made any difference. Despite its conciliatory tone, his shrewd assess-ments of his brother's faults—the 'raging passion' for his own ego, the total lack of respect for what he thought beneath his level, his incapacity ever to appreciate the true seriousness of another's life, the 'insignificant extras representing the "people"' in his work—would scarcely have dented the carapace of Thomas's complacency, and served only to provoke further polemic between them, which Heinrich preferred to avoid, to the extent of leaving the *Reflections* unread. 'I don't believe that victory in any cause is worth speaking of,' he wrote in his draft reply, 'when people are going to their destruction. . . . I don't know whether anyone can "help his fellow man to live": I only hope our literature doesn't help him to die!' With *Madame Legros* he had been the first to bring to the tormented some trust in a better future: 'but you, who find my attitude completely detestable, will *deo volente* have another forty years to test yourself, if not to assert yourself. The time will come, I hope, when you see human beings, not shadows, and then see also me.' That time would be long in coming. Thomas, it must be said, had behaved deplorably. Even after their later reconciliation, he never specifically retracted what he had said, and a superficially polite relationship continued to conceal his fundamental antipathy towards Heinrich.

The reading-tour in January 1918 served to restore his self-confidence after this passage of arms, though its start in Essen, after a visit to Strasburg, was not exactly auspicious. The local journal was disappointed with his reading in the Krupp Hall, from the first chapter of the *Magic Mountain* manuscript: the poet turned out an 'ineffably superior' aristocrat, and his work a tedious account devoid of any action. 'Thomas Mann . . . plays the fool, plays "psychology" . . . but wears royal ermine.' The *Krull* extract which followed was the 'most attractive part of the evening—but by then . . . the hall was already very empty.'[16] His next appointment, on 9 January in occupied Brussels, was more satisfying. Though his train was late, and the *Child Prodigy* novella had to be read in his absence, he was in time to attend most of the following production by the garrison theatre of the third act of *Fiorenza*. It was flattering to be invited to lunch the following day with the city governor and his officers, all wearing ('Heaven knows for what services') the Iron Cross first class, as well as later to receive a letter from one addressing him as 'comrade-in-arms': at any rate, worthy of mention, not entirely flippantly, in the brief account of his wartime 'service with the pen' in his 1930 'Sketch of my Life'—'in truth, my war was as hard as these gentlemen's'. The remainder of the programme—*The Child Prodigy*, the Schiller novella, and extracts from *Krull* and *Royal Highness* in Hamburg, Rostock, and Lübeck—passed successfully enough, and he was able to visit Fischer in Berlin on the return journey, to find him optimistic over publication of the *Reflections* despite paper-rationing.

Only the foreword remained to be finalized, it seemed, for this 'unparalleled ragout, a thing of no genre';[17] but there too he did not hesitate to

---

[16] *Essener Volkszeitung*, (?8) Jan. 1918.     [17] *Amann Br.* 59.

spread himself, and it was not until 12 March that he could ask Bertram to come and hear the finished product. Even then, he could not resist an addition to the chapter 'On Faith', provoked by the funeral of Frank Wedekind, who had just died. For there the funeral oration was to be spoken by none other than Heinrich. No greeting or word passed between them; immediately after it, Thomas and Katia jumped into the taxi he had providently kept waiting; and no sooner home, he dashed off an insertion on the attitude of the despised littérateur at such a solemn moment. For that creature, religion was 'duty to the intellect': 'and we know what he understands by that'—literature, politics, and with that, democracy. 'After I had had to listen to this unctuous counterfeiting of ideas by a free-thinking Sunday preacher, this attempt to claim for politics a soul search-ing in the last moments for salvation, I clapped on my top hat and went home.' Including this final bitter outburst against his brother, the vast manuscript—not much shorter than that of *The Buddenbrooks*—was sent off to Fischer on 16 March. But only after Mann had pulled strings (prob-ably with the civil servant who had pressed in Munich for immediate publication) could the necessary paper-allowance be secured, and even then six months passed, and the war was almost over, before the book appeared.

It is hard to avoid the conclusion that the precious paper might have been put to better use in the Germany of 1918. As had often happened before (and often would again) he had embarked, as he thought, on a short piece of work—in this instance, to clear his mind in the face of important events, before returning to the novel already started—and, eager to leave nothing unsaid, had found it develop a momentum of its own, the end seemingly never in sight. Looking back twelve years later, he was right to call it 'a directionless struggle through the undergrowth'. The result, de-spite manful efforts to lend it shape, was a rambling collection of 'explo-rations, explications, expectorations' on the times, giving vent to his 'irritability' in the face of the current trend towards a democracy he ab-horred, and with its load of quotations and instances confessedly verging on the pedantic. Though even before publication he was claiming to have already distanced himself from it, and his political outlook would not be long in changing, the convictions he had expressed were deeply held at the time he had begun the work; and it was almost specious to assert, after the Second World War, that his concern had only ever been 'to defend hu-manity'. Towards the end of his life, indeed, during the 'cold war', he could venture the unlikely assertion that 'the criticism of Western democracy in the *Reflections* will outlive all my later benevolent political utterances'.[18] We have reason to be grateful, it is true, for what these 500 pages reveal: the

[18] *AM Brw.* 750.

self-importance dominant in his character, the pseudo-academic assessment of the influence of Schopenhauer, Nietzsche, Wagner on his work,
the deep-seated conflict between the brothers, above all this early and
mistaken treatment of the German problem which would prove critical for
his later career. But the *Reflections* make a corner of the collected works
which few of Mann's admirers today will find the courage to visit or, if they
do, to struggle through the convolutions, no matter how elegantly expressed, of its dated rhetoric.

His own feeling, once the 'monstrosity' was out of his hands, was one of
immense relief. He was released at last from the long monologue of 'direct
speech', to return to the 'three-dimensional'. Even in the midst of the
preamble to the monologue, his thoughts had been turning to the next
steps for the novel: but he felt time was required to find his way back, and
instead began a kind of practice-run with a harmless 'idyll'—the story of his
dog Bauschan, the companion of his daily walk along the Isar. Relief no
doubt too for the family, that the incubus had been lifted. For Katia was
heavily pregnant yet again. Her mother had been greatly concerned, for
Katia was past her thirty-fifth birthday, and the doctor, she wrote to a
friend, had shaken his head over this 'venturesome experiment' after an
eight-year interval: 'as someone said, Thomas Mann is more fruitful in
producing children than books'.[19] But the birth on 24 April was entirely
normal and trouble-free, and he was delighted to report to all his friends
the arrival of a splendid daughter, Elisabeth Veronika. She became at once
his special darling, none of the others had awakened such a feeling of
tenderness as 'Lisa', or 'Medi', as they came to call her: it seemed to go hand
in hand with the increasing joy in nature he found in describing the scene
of his walks with Bauschan. 'Is it just the passage of time, making me more
generally cheerful—or the harshness of these times disposing me more to
*love*?'[20] Bertram, who had seen him through the travail of the *Reflections*,
was the obvious choice for a godfather at the christening planned for
September—if only to recompense him for the work now beginning with
the galley proofs, daily packets of which already began to arrive in May. His
friend, who had already relieved him at drafting the announcement Fischer
wanted for the book, set willingly to work; ideas flowed between them for
corrections and additions; but within a month all the galleys had been sent
off to the publisher. Thomas had been happy to leave him a free hand, not
only for checking the innumerable quotations, but also for the extensive
editing needed for his repetitious text; their work was then resumed on the
page-proofs as they began to come in.

Had he known that the previous summer in the Tölz house was to bring
another child, he would doubtless have delayed selling it, for now they had

---

[19] Wiedem. 36.     [20] *Br. OG-BE* 194.

to rent somewhere else suitable for Katia's convalescence and the customary break which, whatever the difficulties or the food shortages, there was
no question of missing. In March Ludendorff's great offensive in the west
had given him sleepless nights in the tense expectation of final victory, and
for him, like many others, the peace terms imposed on the Bolsheviks at
Brest-Litovsk revived confidence in Germany's ability to prevail. But he had
to recognize that his confidence was misplaced. By the time they set off for
Abwinkl, on the Tegernsee, in July, he was full of forebodings for his
country's future—not least because of the constant talk of 'democracy', of
which people's disorderly behaviour on the trains gave distasteful promise
('oh yes, one will have to love them very much').

But, like the children, he was not disappointed by the change from Tölz.
The rented house, with garden going down to the lake and its own boat-
house, gave ample space for the Mann caravanserai, with separate rooms
for all, including a cook, a maid, and the nanny newly recruited for the
baby, and even a study for his work on the proofs and on 'Bauschan'. Food
was shorter even than in Munich, but there was plenty of milk, as well as
Katia's hoard of honey, her husband's favourite nourishment—for he and
the baby of course had priority. Erika, Klaus, and Golo were delighted to
fish for roach to add to the rations, and even snails were collected and
cooked. There was a sad disappointment when the cream they had carefully skimmed off and stored in the cellar, as a surprise for their mother's
birthday on 24 July, was found to have drowned a mouse; but their joy was
the rowing-boat, the only means of transport to the village on the opposite
side, and they were enthusiastic oarsmen—in Klaus's case with disastrous
consequences for the seat of his ersatz trousers.

Even Thomas, normally happier by the sea than among inland lakes and
mountains, took pleasure in the surrounding nature. He climbed one day
with Katia to the summit of the neighbouring Hirschberg, to overnight at
the hut and admire the sunrise—the only venture of this kind in his life. He
read deeply in Stifter, admiring his observation of natural events, and
hoped he would be able to match his incomparable narrative effect when he
returned to *The Magic Mountain*—a hope superbly fulfilled in the description of Hans Castorp's stranding in a heavy snowfall. For the moment, his
interest was confined to the milder scene of the banks of the Isar, in 'A Man
and his Dog', for which, in his pedantic way, he was seeking to remedy his
ignorance of tree and plant names, and which was progressing slowly. In its
way, it would be a pendant to the *Reflections*: people could be helped to live
'even without social attitudinizing, without the urge and the rhetorical
talent for setting the world to rights'.[21] The fifteen or twenty pages

---

[21] N 18/60 Korr.

originally planned for these harmless observations were steadily swelling: as he said, to lend interest to such an insignificant theme demanded precision, and that took space. In the end, if a trifle ponderous, it proved one of his most effective lighter pieces. Publication was to be in a limited edition, with illustrations by his friend the Munich artist Emil Preetorius, and the proceeds donated to the German Writers' Support Fund.

The war news was depressing, with the new Allied offensive in the west and the arrival of American troops; the thought of a surrender of Alsace-Lorraine as the road to peace appalled him, and he foresaw, correctly, that that would make another war inevitable. But as he returned with the family to Munich early in September, he seems still not to have recognized that Germany had no hope of continuing the war, or realized that Austria's capitulation was impending, and remained detached, almost encapsulated in his own private world. For better or worse, the *Reflections* would soon be out, and he persisted in his rearguard stance against the new generation of writers, those expressionists and activists appearing not only in Kurt Wolff's publications but also in the *Rundschau*: a 'crocodile brood' of radical intellectuals joining Heinrich in the ranks of the despised littérateurs, a school or clique with nothing but politics in their mind. In his heart he protested still against a democratic levelling of Germany, clung to the 'romanticism' of the monarchy—and was profoundly shocked when on 30 September the Kaiser decreed a wider participation in government 'by men enjoying the confidence of the people'. The day before, the Reichstag under the new Chancellor, Prince Max of Baden, had decided to sue at once for an armistice; Wilson's 'Fourteen Points' became known early in October; the clamour for the Kaiser's departure increased, his reluctance to agree not only obscuring the significance of the constitutional change but also pro-ducing a surge of extreme left-wing pressure. Mann, in spite of all he had written, was apparently little moved: 'Three cheers for the President of the world!' he wrote to Bertram on 10 October. But—'as long as the Kaiser is still there, romantic Germany has not been completely wiped out'.

That small ray of comfort was soon to be extinguished. Yet he, surprising though it seemed after the vehemence of the *Reflections*, maintained his detachment. Disgusted at the 'humbug' in the exchange of notes between Wilson and Germany, his only wish the selfish one not to be plunged into poverty himself, he seemed concerned only with his own affairs: finishing 'A Man and his Dog'; congratulating Bertram on his appointment to Bonn University after the appearance of his *Nietzsche*; awaiting in impatience the first reviews and comments on his own book, which Bertram's had beaten to the post; and arranging for Elisabeth's christening, which, after postponements, took place quietly on 23 October. His great-grandfather's silver bowl was in evidence for the baptism (and already thought of as a motif for *The Magic Mountain*, symbolic of history and death). It was the fifth of such ceremonies for him, but this one left a deeper impression than the others, for he regarded her in a way as his first child. In his diary he had asked himself what the future might hold for his growing brood, and in particular how his elder boy would turn out. Klaus had been discovered one night lying stark naked on his bed, the light on—a combination of the play of puberty with his tendency to sleep-walking? 'Someone like me, of course, "ought" not to bring children into the world.' Katia was now pregnant yet again, but strenuously resisted her doctor's recommendation of an abortion in view of her weakened condition. Thomas was resigned: whether six or five children made little difference, the chance for them of an inheritance in the post-war world was probably illusory, and the only objection he himself could see, apart from Katia's health, was prejudice to his delight in little Elisabeth, his one child among all the rest.[22]

For her, he began now to sketch out a prose draft for a poem, to keep the world and its problems at bay, as he had done with 'A Man and his Dog', until the time should come when he could settle again to the novel. The prose devoted to Bauschan had often tended to slip into hexameters, the measure to which German so readily lends itself, and it was this form that he decided to adopt for his 'Song of the Child'. He told no one of his project, not even Katia, until the draft was finished in December and he felt, after lengthy reading in Goethe and very conscious of his shortcomings as a versifier, prepared enough to make a hesitant start in the unaccustomed medium. 'Am I a poet?' he had written before the end of the year

> or was, now and then? I know not. In France
> I would not be called one. There they sensibly draw the distinction,
> On one side the rhyme-smith, on t'other the man whose speech is
>     direct.
> One's called a poet, the other an author perhaps, or a stylist,
> A writer—in truth, his talent's not held in lower esteem,
> Only as poet he cannot appear, for he doesn't turn verses.
>
> ·     ·     ·     ·     ·     ·     ·     ·     ·     ·
>
> Remained just a writer, a spinner of prose tales?
> Were you never to feel yourself poet, the poet the book would define?
> Your life sealed thus, attested by fate?—But no, let us see!
> One cadence I know—that favourite both of the Greeks and the
>     Germans—
> Its tone-fall so moderate, observant, cheerful and honestly upright,
> Set on mid-course between paean and words of good sense, at once
> Both festive and sober. For depiction of passion, the exploration

---

[22] *Tb.* i, 11, 17 f.

Of inmost recesses, with subtlest distinction, far from well suited.
But to mirror in sensuous grace the outer world's sunny attractions
In all their ramifications, its numbers most justly adapted.

> . . . . . . . . . . . .

Grant me then, Muse, just once, this joyously measured expression
For public acclaim! The hour is here, the occasion most splendid!
For I will say and sing of the child, my newest arrival,
Who came to a father no longer so young, in times of the hardest.
May that which ne'er yet welled up from soul-depths or sprang from
   great danger
Be called forth by fatherly feeling—and make me a *metrical poet.*

Metrical certainly: but scarcely worthy of the name poet, as he admitted to himself during the three months the labour took him, sticking gamely to his last but despairing at his meagre daily output in comparison with Goethe's.

Meanwhile, towards the end of October, the first copies of the *Reflections* arrived. They had borne the burden together, he wrote in graceful tribute in Katia's copy, he out of need and defiance, but she out of love: his conscience over what she had suffered through the long years could be relieved only by a lasting gratitude. It was his hope, he had said earlier to Kurt Martens, that it would be seen not so much as a book which tried to lead and convince, but rather as a novel in which a 'consciously experienced destiny' was recorded and thus already inwardly overcome and put aside. Now it had appeared, with nothing in it that he regretted and much indeed that seemed to be borne out by events, it could stand as a historical document, and he refused to make any changes for the second edition which was needed before the end of the year. As he feared, however, the Heinrich controversy central to the argument did not fail to hold the critics' attention. The collapse of the monarchy and the end of censorship had given the green light for Kurt Wolff to publish Heinrich's *Man of Straw*, which came out shortly afterwards and within a few months had reached the 100,000 mark—far outstripping the *Reflections*, though that, despite its difficult character, was quickly sold out in the first edition of 6,000.

To compare and contrast the brothers was a temptation few reviewers could resist, and it was in vain that Thomas remonstrated with Ida Boy-Ed, for example, against naming names and bringing the personal element into the discussion. Even Bertram, who did not, as Thomas had hoped, publish an immediate review, but only much later devoted a lecture to the book, made the fraternal dispute his centre-piece (showing himself more royalist than the king in vitriolic attacks on Heinrich). And Amann, from whom Thomas had expected friendlier words, sharply criticized the extremes of the 'family polemic' in this 'chauvinistic work of art', and demanded a fairer assessment of Heinrich. It was natural that the book should be reviewed mainly in right-wing journals and be largely ignored by the liberal Left, but really friendly words were few. Kurt Martens foresaw that for some time to come Thomas Mann would remain an outcast in the wilderness of intellectual isolation.

The tide of events was meantime lapping closer. By early November the situation had become increasingly chaotic, with sporadic revolutionary movements, prompted by fear of the consequences of a continuation of the war as the armistice negotiations dragged out, not only in disintegrating Austria-Hungary, but also in Germany, against the interim government of Prince Max. In Munich on 3 November, at a vast gathering on the Theresienwiese, the left-wing socialist Kurt Eisner, just released from detention for his anti-war agitation, called for a popular regime to proclaim peace together with the new Austrian republic. Four days later he led a mob from a similarly enormous demonstration to seize control of the city's garrisons, with little bloodshed but much firing, and proclaimed a Bavarian republic under a provisional Council of Workers, Soldiers, and Peasants. This was enough to decide the fate of the Bismarckian Reich: no longer in control, the government resigned on 9 November, Prince Max announcing that the Kaiser and Crown Prince relinquished their rights to the throne and naming the social democrat leader, Friedrich Ebert, as Chancellor. A Constituent Assembly was to determine what form the new state would take: a republic was not specifically indicated. But later that day Philip Scheidemann, the second-ranking social democrat, ended a mass demonstration in front of the Reichstag by crying: 'The Hohenzollerns have abdicated! Long live the great German Republic!' The Kaiser bowed to the inevitable and fled to Holland.

Amid the uncertainty, Mann's placid way of life seemed little disturbed, at most by the occasional interruption of mail deliveries and fuel shortages. As he continued with his draft for the poem, his diary marked a thoroughly normal round: he noted events as far as he was able to follow them, not without some acid comments on the almost exclusively Jewish leadership of the Munich revolution and its dictatorship character, but awaited the outcome with resignation, even 'fairly cold-blooded and not without a certain sympathy'. 'Revolutions come only when they find no further resistance . . . and that in itself shows they are natural and justified'—a surprising admission perhaps from the author of the *Reflections*, but he comforted himself in noting that conservative elements were not excluded. In events in France and the ebbing of hostility towards Germany he discerned signs of a new brotherhood between the nations, and found in himself a 'cosmopolitan goodwill' towards the new world that was beginning: 'it will not be hostile towards me, nor I towards it'. From his house, shots continued to be heard, the armistice terms seemed monstrous, there were reports of executions (might not he too, after his stand during the war, find himself before the firing-squad?); but order seemed maintained, he continued his daily walks with Bauschan, a man was quietly tidying up the Poschinger Strasse garden for the winter. He felt a 'thoroughly conciliatory and positive attitude towards the social republic of Germany' which was developing in comforting contrast to the 'bourgeois plutocracy' of the West. But he was not interested enough to attend the bizarre revolutionary festival held in the National Theatre on 17 November, where among the audience the literary and artistic world of Munich heard Eisner (that 'little long-bearded Jewish man', reported Mann's friends) hail Beethoven's *Egmont* overture as the signal for a new mankind. Although disturbed, as November wore on, over the Council's communist tendencies and the apparent drift towards mob rule and anarchy *à la russe*, he could not help feeling that the future belonged to the idea of socialism, or even communism.

With such notions germinating, it was irritating to be reminded of the past in the report of a Council speech by Heinrich glorying in the victory of republican virtue—'when will he have had enough?' Though he signed Dehmel's protest in December against the amputation of German territory under the peace terms, it was not without reservations over its tone. For the time being, in sharp contrast to Heinrich, he remained in public, if not in conversation with his friends, a non-political man, avoiding any direct involvement. Careful in his club to keep out of a discussion on war guilt, he was in fact far more interested there in the sight of an elegant and attractive young man: an 'impression of the kind I've not had for a long time', sufficient to arouse erotic fantasies that disturbed his sleep.


### 3

*'So, in later years, one's active life becomes that of a bustling businessman'*                                        (TM, September 1922)

The war may have ended in débâcle for his country, but Thomas Mann himself had little to complain of. Though he can hardly be said to have enjoyed the long struggle to finish the *Reflections*, and their reception on publication had been, to say the least, mixed, his standing was unimpaired, and before Christmas he heard with satisfaction of his award of the 'prize of honour' of the Nietzsche Archive in Weimar, sharing it with Bertram's *Nietzsche* and another book. Altogether, his war service with the pen had been well rewarded. In November 1918 new editions of *The Buddenbrooks* and *The Child Prodigy* had brought him around 35,000 marks, and Katia, his careful bookkeeper, reckoned the year's income as close to 90,000. For the first peacetime Christmas Eve in Poschinger Strasse, elaborate gifts were naturally hard to come by, but the table in front of the tree was still well-laden, and he was touched to receive from Katia photographs of each of the children, that of Klaus, in a black velvet suit, particularly appealing: 'a joy to have such a handsome boy as my son'. For Lisa, wearing her first dress and shoes, Bertram had sent a delightful crib with wax figures; Monika and Golo, by special request, had each a separate small tree. There was turkey and a dessert, Mosel and a sweet wine, with Christmas pastries to follow, and the children sang Christmas songs to Erika's piano. Few signs here, and in the festive, if quiet, family occasions which followed, of the austerity to which the outside world of Munich was condemned: shops unlighted and their displays cleared against looting; food shortages; little or no heat for the theatres or concert halls; few papers but floods of leaflets; and the city full of apocalyptic rumours.

On Christmas morning, after a visit from the Löhrs— the banker gloom-ily forecasting civil war and anarchy— the family took the tram to Katia's parents in Arcis Strasse, for a rich lunch of almost pre-war standard. (As he watched the butler, now back at his post, Thomas thought how greatly manservants were to be preferred over the maids with whom he was surrounded: but this was a change in her household which Katia, sensibly perhaps, never countenanced.) Next day they were joined by the Löhrs, with their daughters, and Viktor, who had returned unscathed from his army service, for a lunch of goose with chocolate dessert. His brother's music-hall improvisations on the piano and his niece's stumbling Beethoven performance left Thomas nervous and irritated, and he was relieved when the family invasion was at an end. These nights he was sleeping badly, disturbed too by the baby's suffering with a painful ear-infection, but work on his versifying continued each day, and as he took the little one in his arms to calm her and watched her treatment by the doctor, it was with half an ear for the hexameters in which the incident would be captured. He closed his diary for the year in the hope that he could bring the poem satisfactorily to an end without spending too much more time on it: for his thoughts had already returned to the novel, with plans for recasting its opening chapters. The incessant gun-fire to be heard at midnight on New Year's Eve he could only trust was in celebration.

He had been out and about on his normal occasions, rarely missing his daily walk, and still with a wide circle of old friends—the writer Bruno Frank, Martens, Bertram, and especially the Herzog Park neighbours Bruno Walter and the Hallgarten family. But he remained aloof from the new political sphere, hearing only at second hand of the salons in which Heinrich and other now prominent personalities were to be seen. He had

confessed to himself, towards the end of December, what a 'lonely, detached, moody, strange, melancholy existence' he was leading: 'H's life, on
the contrary, is now very sunny.' The bitterness towards his brother had
not softened. An extract from *Man of Straw* in the paper he thought
vulgarly written, with nothing human, nothing artistic about it—'but all
reports say it's selling like hot cakes'.[23] Before the elections to the National
Assembly in January, both contributed their views on the new Germany to
the social democratic *Vorwärts*: Heinrich in three lines ('the intellectual
renewal of Germany . . . is made easier by the revolution. We walk at last
hand in hand with the state'), but Thomas, as ever, at greater length. He
argued that while the 'social people's state' was appropriate and thoroughly
logical in Germany's development, for survival it needed an admixture of
the bourgeois 'spirit of morality': a pure workers' republic, the dictatorship
of the proletariat, would be barbarism.[24] It was the first public sign that he
was abandoning the reactionary rearguard position of the *Reflections*: but
he was far from ready yet to walk hand in hand with the state, still less with
his brother.

In January Klaus and Erika revived their passion for amateur dramatics
which had been so abruptly stifled in 1914. With their friend Ricki
Hallgarten and others from the Herzog Park clique they founded the
ambitiously named 'Amateur League of German Players', and on 12
January—election day for the Bavarian parliament—gave their first performance in the Mann home, an obscure piece by Schiller's friend Körner.
Entrance was free, but the hat was passed round by Golo as usher, in
evening dress and somewhat piqued at having no stage role. A benevolent
audience found the production a success; and a lengthy critique by Thomas
Mann (the only theatre review he ever wrote, and later piously preserved in
the collected works) was the first entry in their new 'actors' book'. It was by
no means the last, for their venture continued at intervals well into 1922,
with altogether eight productions, including Lessing's *Minna von Barnhelm*,
Molière's *Médecin malgré lui*, and *As You Like It*. Golo graduated to the stage
in *Minna*, heavily made up as a lady in mourning, and for Bruno Walter,
whose daughters figured among the players, his performance stole the
show with his idea for frivolous emphasis of her cleavage by a pronounced
vertical charcoal line. The actors' book accumulated pseudonymous contributions from Walter, the Pringsheims, the novelist Josef Ponten, and many
others. Both Klaus and Erika were now all enthusiasm for a stage career:
but while Klaus was a comparative failure in these early attempts (his
mother firmly said he had no talent, and his father criticized his tendency
to speak with his back to the audience), and soon gave up in favour of

[23] *Tb.* 119, 114.    [24] PdM ii, 34.

writing, Erika as Viola in *As You Like It* showed much more promise, and her ambition would one day be realized.

The Bavarian elections, like those to the National Assembly, had resulted in a landslide in favour of the moderate bourgeois parties and the Majority Socialists—in Munich, a humiliating defeat for the Independents. As Eisner walked to the Landtag building on 21 February to tender his resignation, he was shot and killed by a young nobleman, Count Arco-Valley; in revenge, a member of the Revolutionary Workers' Council entered parliament and gravely wounded the Majority Socialist leader Erich Auer; and the shots were the signal for a tumultuous new wave of violence and chaos in the city. Public transport and newspapers were suspended for some days, a curfew came into force, and Mann had to rely on the telephone for such news as he could get. Though it was mostly rumour—of looting, house searches, arms for the workers—the pressure seemed undoubtedly mounting towards the overthrow of the hesitating parliamentary regime by a Soviet-style republican government. It was a development which he felt would not be unwelcome: for the author of the *Reflections*, Germany needed to be freed from the 'politics' he despised—by which he still meant Western-type parliamentary democracy—and guided to an authoritarian state which 'Soviets', if they kept out extremists like Erich Mühsam, might well provide. Such was the burden of his denial of a press report, early in March, that he had turned his wartime coat and joined the Independent Socialists: neither they nor any other party had his allegiance, he protested, Germany had to find 'something new *in politicis*', for which the Councils, 'developed to corporate representation', would probably play an important role—but he was far from advocating class rule, and least of all 'expecting salvation from the proletariat'.[25] To himself, however, in his new-found sympathy for the 'healthy, human, national, anti-Entente, *anti-political*' elements in the cause of the Left, he admitted that the report had not really been so absurd.

In April, after the government had prudently removed to Bamberg, the first Soviet Republic was proclaimed, 'under as strange a band of tribunes as had been seen since the days of the Paris Commune'[26]—among others the anarchist philosopher Gustav Landauer and the expressionist playwright Ernst Toller (who as a young student, Mann recalled, had once provided them with eggs). Within days it was superseded by the second, under the communist Eugen Leviné, who proclaimed the dictatorship of the proletariat and began recruitment of a Red Guard for its defence while he hoped for a link with the communist regimes in Austria and Hungary. These proved shortlived; and in Germany, a large force of Reichswehr ordered south by Ebert, joining with local 'free corps', cleared Augsburg of

---

[25] Matter iii, 12.     [26] Gordon Craig, *Germany 1866–1945* (Oxford: OUP, 1978), 411.

'Reds' and entered Munich on 1 May. The Republic collapsed, after minimal resistance but not before subsequent indiscriminate firing by the 'Whites', provoked by barbarous killing of hostages, had caused over a thousand people to lose their lives.

In these turbulent months, it was business as usual for Thomas Mann, to judge from his lengthy diary-entries. There is much comment on the events, but in the absence of hard information it is mostly superficial, as he turns this way and that in his attitude to the leftward trend and finally admits to a welcome for the return of more conservative order, the city in comforting military aspect and the blue-and-white flag over the Residence. His main preoccupation was with his work, with daily application regardless of the uproar, in the final effort to finish his 'Song of the Child' and prepare for its publication, and the return at last, on Easter Sunday, to the novel; continuing his correspondence as far as the irregular postal service allowed; a public reading in town on 2 April. The revolutionary turmoil and the gun-fire seems to have remained sufficiently remote from Poschinger Strasse to permit such detachment. Although he followed his brother-in-law's advice to accumulate a cash reserve before the 'Soviet' clamp on bank withdrawals, he had been relaxed enough to invest 10,000 marks (a considerable sum at that time) in a *pied-à-terre* at Feldafing on the Starnbergersee early in March. Thoughts of a move out of Munich, perhaps a return to Lübeck, did not last.

Not only was the world thus kept at bay: he himself stuck stubbornly to his daily routine as far as he could, making sure that family needs took second place to his own, and irritable when Katia criticized his butter consumption, or argued with him over his ambivalent attitude to communism, or Klaus tormented Golo to tears. Despite his sympathy for Katia in another difficult labour (they had recruited the best doctors and the leading midwife—who travelled to her duties by taxi—but it had again to be a forceps delivery), the happy outcome with the arrival of his third son, Michael, on Easter Monday left him little moved: three of each sex gave a satisfying symmetry, but none could bring the joy he found in Lisa. (All his children, in fact, for all his affection for them, seem to have remained marginal to his firmly dedicated life—left largely to their own devices, their admiration welcome, but their needs little understood.) Spending a week by himself in Feldafing later in May, a lone Tonio Kröger again for the first time for many years, he pondered on the pros and cons of family life and solitude. For him the decisive consideration, he felt, was that he could shelter in bourgeois life yet avoid becoming a bourgeois: 'if one has depth, the difference between solitude and non-solitude is not great, merely external'.[27] Keeping his family to some extent at arm's length, he contrived that

[27] *Tb.* i, 247.

there should in fact be no significant difference: but whether in the process he avoided becoming a bourgeois, is doubtful.

With the restoration of order, the non-political man began to give public voice to his changing attitude, though in diary and correspondence there were still frequent echoes of his earlier fulminations. On 8 April he added his signature to a published 'Appeal against Arrogance' from the leading literary and artistic luminaries of Munich. Non-party, and concerned only 'for the inward and outward recovery of our people', the appeal—to the 'bourgeoisie from which we are sprung'—was to resist any feelings of triumph, any attempt to apportion guilt for the recent atrocities, and to recognize that its destiny lay with the 'working people', using its knowledge and experience in a common cause to achieve a new social order. The long list of signatories included Preetorius, Rilke, Bruno Walter, and— Heinrich Mann. It was the first political document to be subscribed by the brothers jointly; but it did not bring them together. The report of Heinrich's speech at the Eisner memorial ceremony—'fallen as a martyr to truth'—had sickened Thomas; and in two short commentaries, published in Berlin papers a few weeks later, flaying the Carthaginian peace-terms of Versailles and the role of that 'venomous old man' Clemenceau as the grave-digger of Western culture, he could not resist a shot at his old foes the 'civilization littérateurs' of Germany: in the face of such terms even they, he had heard, were taken aback by the spirit in which Western 'democracy' had entered into and conducted the war.

But in June he refused Martens an article on the political scene: his priority must be to concentrate on his novels, with an eye to getting out his collected works by the time he was 50. And, as he said in a letter in July, a certain fatalism was indicated (he had just been deep in Spengler, 'a great find'). If the allied victory and Anglo-Saxon world-domination should mark the end of Western culture, that could be lived with; the German spirit would survive, if only in a nostalgic, romantic form; and such a world must not be allowed to disturb those, in Bruckner's words, whose life work was 'composition', quite enough for the nerves. For he was now back with the draft for *The Magic Mountain*. Taking out the bundle of manuscript and notes—unopened for four years—just before Easter, he had overcome his first doubts whether the undertaking was now obsolete: it had to be completed, as a 'story of the old times' which had come to an end with the war, like Heinrich's *Man of Straw*, and which displayed similar, if less astringent, elements of satire. Even if both it and the tale of Felix Krull (still very much in mind) had become 'historical long before done', they remained a daily task to be elaborated and finished off.

And with history in mind, rather than simply resuming where he had left off, he had tried to recast the first chapter, starting Hans Castorp's story much further back in time in his relationship with his grandfather, a Hamburg senator (and bringing in the cherished motif of the silver christening-bowl). It proved a more difficult process than he had imagined: for he must have exact details of such a worthy, his formal dress as senator, whether he should be bearded or not. It was not until June, with the aid of a contemporary print and guidance from a knowledgeable neighbour, that he felt he had a satisfactory picture of the figure, but then was still trying to find how to convey the pre-war atmosphere, Castorp's 'moral and intellectual indifference, his lack of faith, his absence of prospects' before the journey to Davos. Once that hurdle had been overcome, and the whole draft had been painstakingly revised and written out anew—the only way to get all the threads back in hand—he was free in July to continue the narrative (though still not satisfied with the Hamburg chapter, which remained a long time unresolved).

But progress during the rest of the year was slow, for the 'demands of the day' had resumed in established peacetime fashion. An article in May on post-war literature, a speech in June at Pfitzner's fiftieth-birthday celebration, an article in July on Gottfried Keller for the *Neue Zürcher Zeitung* (with welcome hard-currency fee) were followed by readings in Munich in September, Nuremberg in November, and Vienna in December, the last taking on an almost official character, in the State Chancellery, and followed by satisfying performances of *Fiorenza*, at which the author was much in demand. Austrian bureaucratic requirements, including even a body-search at customs, and the difficult post-war railway conditions, made the journey exceptionally irksome, and his stay was costly. He had protested against the absurdity of letting himself be chased around the world, when all he wanted was quiet and stability: but Vienna's enthusiastic reception more than compensated for the pressures in its appeal to his vanity, already agreeably boosted in July with the award by Bonn University of an honorary doctorate.

It was the pattern which he had long followed, and which would continue for the rest of his life. Work on the current project, at his deliberate pace, would always be even more protracted by his unfailing care to keep himself before the public eye, with readings, lectures, formal appearances of all kinds, and interviews, rarely refused (one Danish journalist, in November 1921, reverently called his reception an 'audience'); essays and articles, pre-prints from work still unfinished; occasional pieces sometimes on the most trivial of subjects—all highly time-consuming and often exhausting, but gaining for him a status which his main literary output alone would probably never have secured. His name and prestige brought an ever-increasing flood of visitors, correspondents pressing their manuscripts on him, admirers, 'followers and even disciples'. In 1919, at 44, his contract with Fischer renewed for a further six years at a royalty rate of 25 per cent, he was well enough off to afford the time and cost of trips like that to Vienna (the end-of-year statement showed an income of over 100,000 marks); and although he protested at being constantly kept away from his main task, he had reason to be well content with the results of his public-relations exercises. True, prices were steadily rising, the mark worth less and less, as he noticed himself and as not infrequent complaints from Katia over their household costs reminded him. By November he could see the strain for her was beginning to tell, and he resolved on a more intensive programme of reading-tours in the coming years to increase their income.

The comfortable life he had established for himself, however, was never seriously affected, and when money was to hand, he spent it. For Christmas, there were presents on a pre-war scale—goose, Mosel and French champagne; the celebrations were clouded for him only by worry over his faithful Bauschan, under the vet for a serious distemper, and having to be put down in January. Readings planned for the coming February demanded a new suit and the refurbishing of his overcoat: that this would use up the fees in advance seemed not to concern him. Similarly, during the summer, he had had no hesitation in accepting Fischer's invitation to join him and his wife for a holiday up at Glücksburg, on the Baltic coast, near the Danish border. Having to leave Katia and the children at home (they could holiday by themselves later) was no bar to his enjoyment of the three-week stay, in an area hardly touched by the war, which he had last seen as a boy. 'A thousand boyhood feelings', 'the air, the smells, the colours, the speech, the human types—Tonio Kröger, Tonio Kröger', combined with the good food and a lively social life, even swimming, to make it a delightful and refreshing interlude. To register for the first time as 'Doctor Thomas Mann', at his Berlin hotel on the return journey, was uncommonly gratifying. Spending three weeks without adding a line to the manuscript had been an entirely acceptable sacrifice.

There had been an 'experience' too in Glücksburg, a young man to admire (at a distance, of course, scarcely even eye contact): exactly as he pictured Hans Castorp and reminding him of his boyish love for Armin Martens. Once again, it seemed a renewal of springtime, disturbing his sleep; and the impression was revived on his return by a touching letter of congratulation on the doctorate from Paul Ehrenberg: there too he had found 'something like a happy love'. In his 'ideal marriage' with Katia, as her brother now described it, such thoughts were confined to his diary, though she was not unaware of his sexual ambivalence: their 'rencontres', if hardly frequent, gave him in fact some concern, for there must be

*top*
1. View of Lübeck, nineteenth century.
*above left*
2. Johann Siegmund Mann the Elder,
great-grandfather.

*above right*
3. Johann Siegmund Mann the Younger,
grandfather.

*left*
4. Elisabeth Mann, née Marty, grandmother.

*above left*
5. Johann Ludwig Bruhns, grandfather.
*above right*
6. Maria Bruhns-da Silva, grandmother.

*left*
7. Thomas Heinrich and Julia Mann, parents.
*above*
8. Julia Mann with children Heinrich, Thomas, and Julia, *c.*1879.

9. Katharineum School, 1890: TM (*front row left*), Armin Martens
(*second from right, second row from top*).

10. TM's sister Julia, 1900

11. TM's sister Carla, *c.*1894.

12. Hedwig Pringsheim and Katia, *c*.1900.

13. Heinrich and TM, 1902.

14. Katia Pringsheim shortly before marriage, 1905.

15. Thomas and Katia Mann, with Klaus, Erika, and baby Golo, at 'Landhaus Thomas Mann', Bad Tölz, 1909.

16. Katia and children, early 1920s. (*Left to right*) Elisabeth, Golo, Monika, Klaus, Michael, Erika.

17. TM at his desk in Poschinger Strasse, Munich.

18. *Die Quelle*, oil painting by Ludwig von Hofmann, purchased by TM in
1914 and for many years hanging opposite his desk.

19. Klaus and Erika Mann, *c*.1930.

*below left*
20. Erika Mann and Pamela Wedekind.
*below right*
21. TM's fiftieth birthday, 1925. (*Left to right*) Arthur Eloesser, Mimi Kanová, TM, Golo, Erika, Monika, Katia, Heinrich, Klaus, unknown.

22.  Nazi Burning of the Books, Berlin, 10 May 1933.

23.  Erika and Wystan Auden, 1935.

24.  Klaus and Erika in Spain during the Civil
War, 1938.

no question of further pregnancy. Occasional escapes alone to Feldafing may have helped towards the restraint which was all her doctor could recommend.

The small house there had been built by his friend Georg Richter, art historian and collector and patron of bibliophile editions, whose proposal that they should share the costs and the use Mann had welcomed. Two rooms were at his disposal, with the services of the housekeeper, and he found this 'mousehole', as he called it, a conveniently isolated and not uncomfortable refuge for quiet work. His cash contribution, he thought, was entirely on a business basis, though Katia had had her doubts as to its wisdom, and he had stipulated that his capital be withdrawable at six months' notice, in case of a later need for his own country place. As it turned out, Richter did not use the 10,000 marks, and when galloping inflation set in three years later gaily fished out of his safe the same notes, by that time no more than museum pieces, to return to him, without any thought of making good the loss. Financially, it was far from a good bargain. Their friendship, however, was not affected, it seems, and Richter, already another jolly uncle for the children, was his choice for godfather to Michael. The advantages of Feldafing far outweighed any misgivings, and his frequent stays there, for weeks at a time in the autumn of 1919 and during the following year, were highly favourable to progress on the novel. Best of all was Richter's newly installed gramophone, with an extensive collection of records, including opera with Caruso and Melba—an irresistible attraction. Thomas's passion for the instrument grew, as he confessed, almost to a vice: and recorded music became at once an important motif for his text and a stimulus in its composition. Where musical form in *The Buddenbrooks* had expressed itself merely in Wagnerian self-quotation and leitmotif, *The Magic Mountain* he began to conceive as a symphonic construction in the contrapuntal interweaving of its themes.

The work proceeded at two levels: on the one, an eager search for factual information, especially the accumulation of 'physiological notes'; on the other, an attempt to achieve a structure which would raise his narrative above mere realism and be seen as so doing (a stylistic quality he had missed in Hesse's novel *Demian*). At both levels, there was immense scope for his unfailing tendency to spread himself, and, as he later admitted, the draft proved 'as adaptable as a sponge in its ability to expand'.[28] In February he arranged for himself an X-ray demonstration in the local hospital, viewing, absorbed, the skeleton of his hand on the screen, and in May noted with interest that the doctor at Katia's medical examination set no

[28] xiii 107 f.

store by temperature readings, in contrast to his semi-fictional doctor at Davos, who attributed crucial importance to the patient's chart. Early the following year, during a reading-tour in Switzerland, he was all eyes as he revisited the 'long since spiritualized reality' of his scene; shortly afterwards, in Coburg, he had the privilege of donning a white smock to attend two minor operations, and of touring the hospital. There was thus no lack of factual material, and in one way or another it was all exploited. Nor was he backward that year, when he came to the dialogue in French between Hans Castorp and Clawdia Chauchat, in seeking from friends their advice and corrections.

The structural composition, however, posed a bigger problem. His original concept of a short novel, a humorous treatment of fascination with death, was developing into a more than full-length *Bildungsroman*—the 'education' of Hans Castorp, in his isolation on the mountain—and a *Zeitroman*, in the conflict of ideas in pre-war Germany as expressed by the dialectic between Settembrini and Naphta. And although he had thought, with the *Reflections*, to avoid overloading the novel with philosophical ratiocination, the changes in his ideas since then were leading him into thickets almost as impenetrable. Settembrini, Italian, Freemason, still the prototype of the abominated 'civilization littérateur', was yet taking on the qualities almost of a humanist, proclaiming that 'all human dignity, human respect, and self-respect' and all politics were inseparably linked to literature; Naphta, on the other hand, who could have stood as a noble representative of the German soul, appeared as an East European Jew, a reactionary admirer of the Middle Ages, a Jesuit with communist ideas. In their debates, each was to contribute to the education of Hans Castorp, 'typical average German of pre-war days': but the problems of those times were now looked at in the new light of post-war revolution and the restoration of Germany's innate conservatism, for Thomas Mann the saving grace to make democracy tolerable. And still the other themes, 'fine threads and motifs', to be held together—the atmosphere in the clinic of hectic pleasure-seeking in the face of illness and death, the sexual tension in Castorp's attraction to the temptress Clawdia.

It is not be wondered at that during 1920 and the following years he found himself at times in despair at whether to persist in the effort. 'The uselessness and lack of resonance' of his work came over him; he felt reluctant to continue with 'no light, no faith'; like the *Reflections*, the work was becoming a monstrosity, a 'crazy book' which he began to doubt could ever be readable. In April 1920, as he sat alone in Feldafing, it seemed to him that both *The Magic Mountain* and *Krull* were mere diversions in comparison with the real novel he should be writing: a 'book of life' from the great story of his own family, of Heinrich and himself, Lula and Carla, with Vikko as light relief; his mother 'very human'; the Pringsheims. It could make 'an epic à la Tolstoy', and one day, so he dreamed, in the decade between 50 and 60, he might find the strength. Such an autobiographical sequel to *The Buddenbrooks*, its figures more openly revealed, would certainly have been a delicate undertaking, and it remained a dream.

He held stubbornly to the present task, however, in spite of increasingly frequent interruptions. One of his difficulties in progressing with the novel was his own political uncertainty. He was ready to assert, in an interview in May 1920, that, although the pronounced conservatism of his *Reflections* was essentially unchanged, it now took a more liberal form, ready to meet the justified social demands of all classes of society. He was beginning to move away from the pessimism of Spengler, and democracy in the shape of the Weimar Republic, it seemed, was now acceptable to him—provided it was kept on moderate lines by a leavening of conservatism, and excesses avoided both of Bolshevism and of such right-wing adventures as the short-lived Kapp *putsch* that March. The centralized German state envisaged in the Weimar constitution, however, he considered a mistake. Its future must lie on federal lines, particularly when it was joined by Austria, a development forbidden by Versailles but to his mind greatly to be desired and one day inevitable, as he said in two short articles later in the year. Briefly attracted by the writings of the conservative thinker Hermann, Count Keyserling, and his project for a 'School of Wisdom' in Darmstadt, he had spent fully two weeks over Christmas 1919 on an essay in the form of an open letter to him, 'Clarifications', a pendant to the *Reflections*; but it soon became clear to him that he had moved on from there. To socialism as such he was by no means averse but, as he said in September 1920, did not believe in its internationalism: 'the fact remains that the human can be realized only in the national'. Such a form of nationalism was a long way from his earlier line, and indeed from that of most conservatives in Germany at this time, notably the academics and in particular those in Bonn, for whom the *Reflections* had doubtless been a major factor in the award of his doctorate and who to a man were firmly in the right-wing German nationalist camp.

His ideas were still far from settled, however, and these changes did not yet moderate the deep-rooted antipathy he felt for his brother. In February, at a reading by Martens, finding himself seated just behind Heinrich, he moved ostentatiously further back, and escaped promptly at the end to avoid him. News from Julia of Mimi's serious illness in Prague brought him only a certain *schadenfreude*. There was no question of his attending the elaborate fiftieth-birthday celebrations organized in April 1921 by Kurt Wolff; Heinrich, he wrote to his brother's close friend Ludwig Ewers, could be a satisfied man, 'reconciled with the world and even with his country, who perhaps will now . . . prefer your friendship to that of those Jewish-radical errand-boys and town criers of his'. After the formal breach occasioned by the Zola essay, Heinrich would have had little respect for him had he accepted his offer of reconciliation: 'in the end, a rift like ours should be held in honour, and no attempt made to take away its deadly serious accent. Separated, we are perhaps *more* brothers, one to the other, than we would be dining together at a festive board.'[29]

To outsiders, he could explain their antagonism in lofty terms—the Nordic-Protestant element in himself as opposed to the Roman-Catholic in Heinrich, his own ethical individualism against his brother's socialism, his emphasis more on conscience, Heinrich's on the activistic will, the antithesis running through their every relationship. There was much truth in this, of course; but many of his diary entries through 1920 and 1921 indicate a less philosophical and more ill-natured attitude. Heinrich's misfortune with his wife's illness is the occasion almost for glee, while the 'fanfare and gloria' of the fiftieth-birthday celebrations prompt the sneering comment 'what a level of satisfaction with the world he must have reached'. Indirect word from Sweden in May 1921, that he himself may be next in line for the Nobel Prize, emphasizes for him the rivalry with his brother—'if I get it, it will be said it should have gone to Heinrich, and if it's he, then I couldn't bear it'. And any chance encounters, if they cannot be avoided, are the occasion of bitter comment.

True, this was often because of the recurrent crises in progress with the novel—reflected then also, as usual, in complaints over his health and in irritability with the rest of the family. At the frequent contacts with the Löhrs, he had little sympathy for his sister's unhappiness, and only contempt for her extra-marital affairs. Like his mother, he clearly felt both Heinrich and Viktor had married beneath them, and was far from taken with such unsuitable sisters-in-law, no matter that Heinrich's Mimi was for the time being not in evidence; Viktor's Nelly he found a 'frightful' table-companion. During 1920 and the following year, there were outbursts of anger over the children's noise, and he joined Katia in scolding Klaus for his 'slackness and self-satisfaction'. It was one's duty, he noted in his diary, not to spare oneself such unpleasant emotional outbreaks: but they were also by way of compensating for the overwhelming attraction he felt to the boy's adolescent beauty, as he came on him in the bath or lying naked on his bed.

It seemed entirely natural that he should fall in love with his son. But he was far from clear on his own sexual orientation. In July 1920, evidently after an unsuccessful 'rencontre' with Katia, he noted

---

[29] Qu. *Brw. HM* 394 f.

it can hardly be actual impotence, but more the usual confusion and unreliability of my 'sex life'. Without doubt, there's a nervous weakness resulting from desires which tend towards the other side. How would it be if it were a boy there? At all events, it wouldn't be sensible to let myself be depressed by a failure for which the reasons aren't new to me. . . . negligence, caprice, indifference, self-assurance . . . are the best 'cures'. . . . Tonight we are off to Feldafing. I got my working things together after breakfast . . .

Katia, it seems, did not stay long there with him, and on the return journey he noted his pleasure in a short talk with a young man sharing his compartment: 'it looks as though I have finally done with the female side?' But such experiences, often recurring in these and later years, were clearly never more than fascination at a distance, sidelong glances sometimes returned, brown-armed gardeners observed from his study-window: he never discovered what it would be like 'if a boy were there'.

This had emerged in a letter written shortly before to a reader querying the apparently negative attitude to homosexuality in *Death in Venice*. The homo-erotic, he said, was 'a feeling I hold in honour, because it almost inevitably—at any rate, much more inevitably than with the "normal"—has *intellect*. I would not wish you—and others—to be left with the impression that I deny it or, as far as it is accessible to me (and I may say it is almost compulsive with me), would even wish to disown it.' The law of polarity did not always hold good, the male did not necessarily have to be attracted by the female, and experience showed that homosexuality did not always mean effeminacy (who would maintain that Michelangelo or Frederick the Great were effeminate?) Culturally it was as neutral as the other, everything depended on the individual, and the degenerate instincts of a Ludwig II of Bavaria were more than counterbalanced by the stern discipline and dignity of a Stefan George. He himself, by instinct and conviction a family man both as son and father, loving his children and most of all the little daughter he idolized, found the problem of eroticism and of beauty decided in the relationship between life and intellect—two worlds with a mutual longing, as he had written in the *Reflections*, their relationship 'highly delicate, difficult, exciting, painful, charged with eroticism and irony', but not erotic in the sense of 'sexual polarity . . . there can be no union between them, only the brief, intoxicating illusion of union and understanding, an eternal tension never resolved'. Could there be a clearer self-betrayal? he asked. Clearer perhaps, we may think: this was scarcely a 'coming out' in the modern sense, and not many readers of the *Reflections* at the time can have marked these words as a personal confession. But the analysis indicates plainly enough the dichotomy in his nature which would persist to the end of his days. In his diary, while this letter was still on the stocks, he noted: 'In love with Klaus these days'—and thought of writing a 'father and son' novella. That was not pursued: but it was thus that the mild aberrations of the bourgeois family-man would always look for sublimation in literary art.

And his art, his work in all its various senses (the novels, the journalism, the public appearances) remained pre-eminent for him. It is quite clear, from the very full diary which has survived from 1919 to the end of 1921, that, although he was certainly much concerned over his sex-life, it was not a problem to override all others. He had in fact a remarkable capacity for separating out the different strands of his life, ordering his day and his programme to accommodate their needs. His gratitude to Katia for her understanding of his ambivalence is evident; and though this would never change, he had no difficulty in submerging its faint demands, as he pursued with vigour the busy public life their budget required, and restricting to expression in his work the feelings of sensuality which were occasionally aroused ('the *Magic Mountain* will be the most sensual thing I've written, but in cool style', he noted in March 1920).

His diary entry for New Year's Eve 1920 recorded hopefully that 1921, one way or the other, would see the novel's end, and he had in fact made substantial progress during the year. But there had been—and would continue to be—too many interruptions for this hope to be realized: readings in Regensburg and Augsburg in the spring, in Munich in the autumn; a summer holiday divided between Garmisch, with Fischer, and Polling to see his mother; a comprehensive tour through the Rhineland in November, including a seminar at Bonn University (interesting to note that, to the students in that seat of German nationalism, he was at pains to stress his own 'idealistic individualism' and to urge on them a sense of their country's European responsibility); in December, some days' work in Berlin as adviser to a committee on, of all things, spelling-reform—surprising, as he thought to himself, in view of his own old-fashioned practices. The 'frightful turmoil' of the reading-tours continued unabated in the New Year, with appearances in no fewer than ten cities during three weeks in Switzerland, followed almost at once by ten intensive days in eastern Germany in February. Inflation steadily increasing, the income from such activities was becoming more and more urgent. There were servant problems; the house, he had noted in May 1920, was beginning to take on an uncared-for look, even as household expenses mounted alarmingly; and their tax for the year, 'even if we conceal a lot', would amount to 20,000 marks. He was raising his fee for a reading to a minimum of 1,000, but travel costs were rising too. Hard currency was therefore all the more attractive: he was only too glad to accept invitations to revisit Basle and Zurich in November, and a dollar cheque from the *Dial* in New York for a translation of the long-forgotten novella *Little Lizzy* was doubly welcome.

Between all this, he was much in demand for articles and contributions: on the twenty-fifth anniversary of the *Simplicissimus*, awakening memories of his work there over twenty years ago; on Ludwig Hardt, the popular public reader, and the Austrian writer Peter Altenberg, who had died in 1919; on the 'cosmopolitan enterprise' of the Insel Verlag in their 'Pandora' and 'Biblioteca mundi' series; an introduction to an anthology of Russian literature; a somewhat flippant piece on 'Intellect and Money', where he acknowledged, despite his insouciance over money matters, the personal debt he owed from his earliest years to the capitalist system; on Kurt Martens's autobiography, and many other, less engaging topics. All these, though each relatively quickly disposed of, together took much time from his main task. More difficult was a contribution on 'The Jewish Question' for Efraim Frisch's *Neuer Merkur*, which he drafted in October 1921 but later, after objections from Katia and attempts to abbreviate it, withdrew entirely: for his treatment revealed the 'autobiographical radicalism to which I am inclined', and although he stressed how much he owed in his career to the people who had been his discoverers, publishers, producers, and best critics, and ended with a fervent plea against the absurdity and injustice of seeking in the Jews a scapegoat for the world's ills, there were enough disparaging remarks in his draft to make its appearance anything but advisable amid the then mounting wave of anti-Semitism in Germany. He refused Keyserling's invitation to write on the poet Rabindranath Tagore, however, for whom a special week in Darmstadt was impending: the sage's Indian pacifism, 'anaemic humanity and principled gentleness' had always seemed antipathetic, and the impression he made of a 'fine old English dame' at his later lecture in Munich in June did not dispel the feeling ('I pushed my wife forward "who speaks English better than I". He probably did not know who I was . . .').

By that time there were larger preoccupations. Fischer had long had in mind the publication of a 'collected works' edition, and as a start they had agreed on a volume of his essays and shorter pieces and an abbreviated version of the *Reflections*. Both demanded much work and correspondence: for the essay volume in particular, to be entitled 'Dissertation and Response', the texts had to be retrieved, sometimes from others, and the more controversial pieces such as 'Bilse and I' revised, and although the cuts in the *Reflections* were left largely to Fischer's own staff, careful thought was required before he could give his imprimatur.

In June, however, Mann had received the first proofs of the essay collection, and could turn in earnest to the next major task—a lecture due in Lübeck in September, and yet another distraction from work on the novel. The occasion was a 'Nordic Week', designed to promote German–Scandinavian relations; but, after briefly considering Knut Hamsun, he had settled on 'Goethe and Tolstoy'—a far from obviously relevant theme. Since April he had been reading and rereading deeply in both and in a mass of relevant literature, making copious pencil-notes and excerpts, and thereby developing far too wide a range of ideas and too great a larding of quotations to arrive at a talk of acceptable length and concentration. Once started, pen in hand, in June, he did indeed find his draft much too ambitious, and decided to restrict himself to his subjects' ideas on education. What he had already written, however, was by no means cast aside, but carefully kept in reserve: for he foresaw good use for it later.

The Lübeck appointment gave the opportunity for a late summer holiday with Katia beforehand. Household cares and influenza had greatly affected her over the past two years, and although she had been able to spend two months in Oberstdorf in the Allgäu the previous autumn (the house-keys in charge of the capable Erika), she was now badly in need of a break. So rooms were arranged from early August in Timmendorf, on the familiar Baltic coast. A card to the children reflected their mood of relaxation: 'we often think how you'd enjoy it . . . but you'd find the water icy compared with the Starnberger'; 'whipped cream every day', added Katia; and there was a postscript from godfather Bertram, who had joined them for a time. They spent a week visiting Katia's cousins on the island of Sylt, bathing enthusiastically in the powerful 'predatory' breakers and 'splendid carpets of foam', wandering over the strange dune-filled landscape. It was not all relaxation, however, for his lecture still had to be brought to final form, and the last touches were added just before they reached Lübeck on 2 September. Here they were met and put up by Ida Boy-Ed—ageing now, but always glad to welcome the distinguished colleague whose early efforts she had done so much to encourage.

Their week there passed with honours which he felt highly gratifying to enjoy in his birthplace. The lecture, given to a packed house on 4 September, went off successfully. Hitherto his public appearances had been confined to readings from his works, and at this he had developed considerable expertise and often a winning manner; but actual speeches had been rare and only to a restricted circle. A talk before a large public, and of such length (it must have taken at least an hour and a half), was a début for him, needing a new technique even though written out and read, and it was not surprising that its composition had taken so long. It was the forerunner of many others, both in form and content: the first of a series of public utterances, as opposed to essays, on the problem of Germany and its position in the post-war world with which he was to become increasingly preoccupied.

The theme of education he had chosen for this occasion arose directly from the concept of *Bildungsroman* for *The Magic Mountain*, and showed how the autobiographical in an artist's work (by implication, also his own) inevitably led him to become an educator, however differently this tendency might show itself in his examples of Goethe and Tolstoy. But in touching on the wider problem of Europe's future—the apparent crumbling of its classical foundations in revolutionary Russia and the question whether this might prove Germany's case too—and in his phraseology, which often echoed that of the *Reflections*, he revealed a political outlook typical of German conservatives of the time, with an antipathy towards purely Western humanism and stressing the 'great possibilities of understanding' between the German and the Russian spirit. Events of the coming few years would change his view, and lead him to a much revised 'Goethe and Tolstoy' for his second collection of essays in 1925, subtitling it 'Fragments on the Problem of Humanity'. For the moment, he could enjoy its success at repeat performances in Berlin, where he drew an audience of 1,000, in Munich, and on a brief but exhausting further visit to Zurich in the university *Aula* in November.

There was a little time, after their return home, for some attention to the novel, particularly during a week alone in Feldafing; but the effort of the Zurich trip had left a certain depression, and only during November did he regain his 'joy in life, in the icy-grey winter mornings, in work'. His money-making activities had been worthwhile, it seemed—income for the year, he noted with satisfaction, amounted to 300,000 marks—but there was to be no relaxation of effort: he shuddered at the thought of the tour of Prague, Brno, Vienna, and Budapest already scheduled for the coming January, and it was evident that the hopes, briefly revived, of finishing the novel over the winter were vain.

4

*'The Magic Mountain made the same impression on me as the view of Mont Blanc: I felt no desire to live with it'*

(*Graham Greene*)

Katia was to accompany him on the tour, for which he was already well-armed with the 'Goethe and Tolstoy' lecture and his usual repertoire of novellas and *Magic Mountain* extracts, so that no further preparation was needed. The journey began badly, with long train-delays and an unforeseen overnight stop on the way to Prague: but in the end it turned out splendidly. In Vienna in particular the reception for them was 'overwhelming', their quarters 'princely, with no charge'; even the visit of a hotel thief, who got away with Thomas's watch, pearl cuff-links, and some leather items but—apparently disturbed—failed to secure Katia's jewellery, was taken in good part and duly noted for possible use in *Felix Krull*. Interviews were not lacking, and in Budapest, where they stayed with the wealthy banker father of Georg Lukács, in the same house as Béla Bartók, the morning appointments had to be organized like a dentist's, so high had become the standing of this doyen of German letters since his last visit in 1913. After their return, towards the end of January, there came disturbing news: following influenza, Heinrich fell seriously ill with peritonitis, and with fears of lung and heart complications his position remained very dangerous for a few days. Greatly moved, Thomas enquired daily of his progress, with words of sympathy which evidently touched his brother, and at the end of the month, the danger over, sent flowers with a note: 'Difficult days lie behind us, but now we're over the hill and will travel better—together, if your heart says the same as mine.'

The breach was—apparently—healed at last. Heinrich sent his thanks, in the hope that now, however their opinions might differ, they would 'never lose one another again'. But Thomas, as he wrote to Bertram, had no illusions over the delicate nature and difficulty of this new relationship.

A decent, human *modus vivendi* is all that can be expected. Actual friendship is hardly conceivable. The memorials of our dispute still stand: by the way, I am assured that he has never read the *Reflections*—which is good, and yet not good, for it means he has no idea of what I went through. My heart turns over when I hear that after reading some sentences in the *Berliner Tageblatt*, in which I spoke of those who preach God's love and hate their brothers, he sat down and wept. But for me the years of struggle . . . left no time for tears. Of that, and of how time made a man of me, how I developed and learned to become an aid and guide for others too—of all that, he knows nothing. Perhaps he will feel it somehow, when we meet again. For the moment he may not see anyone.

They say he has softened, become kindlier over these years. It's impossible that his views should not have suffered some correction. There may have been a certain development bringing us nearer each other: that is my feeling when I consider that my own prevailing thoughts at the moment are of a new, personal fulfilment of the idea of humanity—as opposed, of course, to the humanitarian world of Rousseau.[30]

The sober assessment, after the bitterness that had prevailed for so many years, was scarcely surprising; and, as time would show, more than that polite *modus vivendi* could never be possible between them, even though the gradual *rapprochement* in their views which Thomas thought to discern soon gained pace.

The 'idea of humanity' (he did not yet call it 'humanism') was to be his theme in a speech on 1 March, in the Frankfurt Opera House before a *Magic Flute* performance, during the Goethe week there to mark the ninetieth anniversary of the poet's death. It was a grand occasion, opened by President Ebert in person and with a speech also by Gerhart Hauptmann.

[30] *EB Br.* 107 f.

Thomas Mann, with admirable and, for him, unusual brevity, developed the idea, from his 'Goethe and Tolstoy', of autobiography as education, as shown in Goethe's *Wilhelm Meister*—'boldly human experiments with the social question, the problem . . . of internal politics. But from Goethe, not from Rousseau and his forerunners, we have also the notion of external politics . . . of the unity of Europe and the West.' The European idea in Goethe, unlike that preached by 'radical internationalism', was a 'cosmopolitanism of sympathetic assimilation and unpremeditated humanity', which might with some justice be called German, but was to be found in all countries, offering better prospects of international brotherhood than any 'activist programme of pacifism'. An effusive professorial introduction hailed Mann not only as heir to the prose style of Goethe, Stifter, and Fontane, and as 'representative German author', but also as 'teacher of the nation and guide to its youth'.[31]

He was by no means averse to assuming the mantle of *praeceptor Germaniae et dux juventutis*. The essay form—a 'critical monitoring of my life'—he had felt to be a necessary part of his literary production: to extend it now, in the shape of public speech on matters of moment in the cultural and political sphere, seemed equally important. It was in keeping with the position he had reached, and a continuation of his *Reflections*, in a more direct and less diffuse form than the ponderous tome issued in 1918, his political ideas maturing slowly as he went along. The notion of humanity he sketched at this point was politically still something of a vague dream, a world in which 'the individual and the social, the aristocratic and the democratic, need not necessarily be opposed, but should grow organically together, one from the other': to infuse life into this idea he felt was 'the most important task for the German spirit'.[32] Giving the 'Goethe and Tolstoy' lecture again, to a crowded house on his first visit to Heidelberg in July, he was impressed by the 'youthful intellectuality' in the romantic surroundings, and especially by a group of Swedish girl students from whom he received a rapturous welcome: here he felt himself indeed a guide for youth, even if it seemed mainly Nordic.

The political crisis in Germany, however, had by this time greatly sharpened. The immense burden of war reparations imposed by the Allies, and the consequent acceleration of inflation, had led to the country's virtual bankruptcy; and while an atmosphere of crisis had been endemic throughout the three years of the Republic, there was a severe shock now at the assassination by young nationalist zealots in June of Walther Rathenau. An efficient wartime organizer of military materials supply, Rathenau had sacrificed his business interests to the service of the new regime; as Minister of Reconstruction he had been a staunch advocate of fulfilment of the

---

[31] *Frankfurt a. M. Nachrichten*, 29 Feb. 1922.     [32] 22/28.

reparations demands; and after his recent appointment as Foreign Minister had signed the Rapallo Treaty with the Soviet Union. In his policies, and as a Jew, he was a natural target for the hatred of *völkisch* extremists. For Thomas Mann it was dismaying and painful to note the 'benighted minds of these barbarians', as he wrote on 8 July to Bertram, 'the distortion in the German countenance', 'the perils of history in the way it obscures with false analogies the uniqueness of the situation and leads certain young people astray into mad acts'. He was far from abjuring the arguments of his *Reflections* and expecting from the young

enthusiasm for ideas, like socialism and democracy, they have long since inwardly discarded; but mechanical reaction I've already called sentimental coarseness, and the new humanity may after all flourish no worse on the soil of democracy than on that of the old Germany. . . . As if 'the Republic' were not still the German Reich, which today in fact is placed in the hands of each one of us, to a much greater extent than when historical forces which had degenerated into banal theatricality were enthroned over it—and that precisely is democracy.

And he determined now to use a speech to be made in Berlin, on the occasion of Hauptmann's sixtieth birthday in October, as a manifesto for the Republic, an address not only to the conscience of his country's youth—'trying to make the Republic palatable to them' by stressing its links with German romanticism—but to the nation as a whole; and it was sketched out during a few weeks in August at Ahlbeck, on the Baltic coast.

With the inflation, his own financial position gave increasing cause for concern. At Easter Klaus and Erika had been sent to the Bergschule in Hochwaldhausen, a boarding-school, progressive and co-educational, where they proved difficult to handle but for their part had justifiable complaints about the teaching, and by the summer had asked to be withdrawn; the fees had been a substantial load for an already strained budget. His introduction in August to the American editor of *The Dial* and their agreement for him to contribute a series of 'German Letters' at 25 dollars a time came as manna from heaven—both now, when the dollar was worth nearly 500 marks, and during 1923, when it rapidly climbed to billions. 'Without foreign cash, life would be impossible for a family like mine,' he wrote to Fischer on 1 September, 'so like everyone else I'm taking care to get some. I go to Holland in October, later probably to Sweden and even Spain, and have become correspondent for an American journal. . . . My big essay "On the German Republic" . . . goes off to the Rundschau today. Let me know the impression it makes on you and your circle—and give me a decent fee!'[33] He was turning again to the novel, but the other work would obviously hold it up, and he hoped for Fischer's patience.

[33] SF *Brw.* 418.

That his first 'German Letter' was to appear translated into the tongue of Emerson and Whitman, and read by so 'admirable a species of mankind' as the Americans, enveloped him, he wrote, in a 'heartening whiff of humanity'; and as his introduction to what became a lengthy and disparaging review of Spengler's *Decline of the West*, he stressed the new-found democratic and republican trend in his country. 'Today we may call ourselves republicans in a sense deeper and more important than the constitutional, if we say that republicanism means a sense of responsibility'—for this too had undoubtedly deepened and broadened in Germany despite superficial signs of a paltry frivolity. A main plank in his speech on 13 October, in the Berlin Beethovensaal was the essence of the Republic as individual responsibility: the first public statement from such a known conservative of support for the new state form, and recognized as such in the wide and very mixed press-coverage it received. 'Self-contradiction in person,' wrote Hermann Bahr in Vienna, 'but therein precisely the most German German of the time'; 'Mann overboard', said another paper, while the socialist *Vorwärts* slated his vanity in attempting to arouse in his hearers an enthusiasm for the Republic he did not himself feel. It doubtless seemed to many a sensational recantation, wrote *The Living Age* in Boston later: 'his auditors were mainly university men who presumably expected a very different message'.

Yet, as has rightly been pointed out, his new standpoint, however exemplary as a conservative's change of heart, was still 'only a first groping towards realities'.[34] While he tried to distinguish between true German romanticism, as a foundation for democracy, and its perversion in the 'sentimental obscurantism' which ended in political acts of terror like the murder of Rathenau, his statement was weakened by a mass of literary allusion and lengthy, often far-fetched, quotations from Novalis and Walt Whitman—still much in the style of the *Reflections*. Even well-disposed listeners to the speech, as the Berlin *Die Zeit* commented, found it hard to follow, not least because he was reading from a manuscript. It would be some years yet before he gained clarity and assurance in a new political view, even though much later he could justifiably date his conversion to an anti-fascist stand from this important, and at the time courageous, speech. Its text appeared in the special Hauptmann number of the *Rundschau* in November; for separate publication later as a brochure, however, he felt it necessary to write a foreword, in reply to the 'stupid handling' by his many critics: a protest that 'I may have changed my thoughts—but not my opinions'. In praising the Republic, he claimed, the author of the *Reflections* was firmly continuing the sense of that book, namely the cause of German

[34] Reed 293.

humanity, and was quite prepared, having been castigated then as reactionary, to be called now a Jacobin. 'I thought I might be of some little
assistance through this minor action, which became an action precisely
because it was I, the notorious and deep-dyed *Bürger*, who undertook it.'
He had defined the Republic, not as something already existing, but as
something still to be created, and had tried to breathe into this 'unhappy
constitutional form' some soul and life.[35]

The speech made the start of an extensive tour of northern Germany and
Holland, lasting till the end of October, with readings from *The Magic
Mountain* and *Krull* and a repeat of his 'Goethe and Tolstoy' in Amsterdam.
Holland had certainly been a land worth seeing, he wrote to Bertram
after his return home on 3 November, but he was 'glad to be back in
Germany: all that satiety and lack of damage gets on our nerves'. For
his final appearance, in Frankfurt, he had had the biggest public ever:
'2,500 people, a moving sight from the podium'. Klaus, now at Paul
Geheeb's Odenwaldschule at Heppenheim, but still a difficult pupil, had
been able to meet him in Darmstadt, and found him genial and ready with
generous pocket-money.

He could tell Bertram he had had enough of the world, but already an
active programme in the quest for hard currency as well as marks was
planned for 1923—Switzerland again in January, Vienna thereafter, then
Spain, in between a number of appearances in Germany—and it would be
quite a trick to gain the concentration he needed to complete the novel. To
what extent he succeeded in adding to it in the short time before leaving for
Switzerland is not clear. There was new material to hand, however, in the
shape of two spiritualist seances, organized just before Christmas and early
in the New Year by the Munich doctor and parapsychologist Baron von
Schrenck-Notzing, which he attended with great interest, and which promised a marvellous incident for his narrative. His enthusiastic accounts of
the usual table-turning, handkerchief-lifting, bell-ringing, typewriting,
tambourines, even materializations—'telekinetic phenomena, whose genu-
ineness I find impossible to contest'—not only regaled the family at dinner
but were also recorded more soberly in detailed reports to Schrenck-
Notzing; prepared later in essay form, 'with humour, but with conviction',[36]
the experience yielded some of his most successful public readings. Katia,
'a "mathematical mind", certainly did not accept all this', daughter Monika
recalled in later years, 'but she accepted his *belief*, as she never failed to do
when profound tact towards him was needed'.[37] He worked his 'occult
experiences' in some detail into *The Magic Mountain*, to add yet another
chapter before its long-delayed end, which Fischer—ever-optimistic—had
announced at the end of the year.

---

[35] xi 809–11.     [36] 23/28.     [37] MM *Erinn.* 25.

The Swiss tour in January 1923, with Katia, was pleasant but brief, for she was alarmed by the ever-steeper fall of the mark, now 20,000 to the dollar, and anxious to be home. For him, however, the hectic round continued: 'Goethe and Tolstoy' repeated in Tübingen at the end of the month; a reading from the novel in Dresden soon after (where the fee of 40,000 marks would have brought him nothing had he not had private accommodation); Berlin then, to negotiate on the filming of *The Buddenbrooks*, for which welcome hard cash from the foreign rights was already on the table, and more in prospect, to compensate for the 'witless and sentimental cinema drama' he expected to result. It was a continual interruption to the current work, impossible in between such distractions, he told Bertram, to recover the regular and tedious application a work like *The Magic Mountain* required. Such a task could only be achieved 'against the times', which favoured nothing but articles, manifestos, improvis-ations—like the 'Occult Experiences', which he was shortly to 'produce' in Augsburg. The French occupation of the Ruhr aroused his fury, cutting as it did across all the good intentions and the dreams, like his own, of a new humanity: 'it's as though Germany is regarded outside not as a republic like any other, but as a leaderless land . . . with which one can do what one likes'. But the many interviews he anticipated on his forthcoming journeys to Vienna and Hungary, and of course the next 'German Letter', would give him ample chance for comment.

Before he set off again, however, he had the sad duty of burying his mother. At 71 and ill, the remains of her inheritance incomprehensibly lost in the inflation, the Frau Senator had stayed a while with them during the autumn, insisting on paying for her keep but with banknotes long since worthless; still weak when she left to stay for the winter in an inn at Wessling, near Munich, she had soon needed a nurse; and on 10 March the phone call came that she was not expected to last the night. Thomas was summoned back from Feldafing, where he had been spending a few days, and Golo, who had to meet him at the station, later remembered his bad mood—as much, apparently, at the disturbance to his work as over its occasion. Heinrich joined him to drive down to Wessling; but it was to him, rather than to Heinrich, that fell all the arrangements for the funeral and her interment next to Carla in the Munich cemetery. Of the children, Klaus being at boarding-school, only Erika attended (and told the younger ones, not without some pride, how she had seen not only their father, but also both uncles all in tears). His mother's passing had moved Thomas deeply, but there was little time for mourning: within two weeks he was off on his next tour to Austria, Hungary, and Czechoslovakia.

Vienna had been his first appointment, but he had accepted a last-minute invitation from Stefan Zweig to speak on the way in Salzburg; and here 'Goethe and Tolstoy' brought high praise from the press for the 'strong and upright spirit, affirmed by the manful support for the German Republic with which he took his place at Gerhart Hauptmann's side as a leader of the nation'. In Vienna, Budapest, and Prague, however, he renounced the pedagogical in favour of the occult, his experiences holding his audiences with outstanding effect, and reserved any political comments for the many interviews sought. These, as he had anticipated, gave him ample scope to castigate the extremists and set Germany's hopes in the victory of a middle line founded on democracy. In Vienna came the first question to him on Adolf Hitler (Munich leader of the radical right-wing National Socialist Party since 1921): he pointed out the confusion of 'all these putschists'— virulently anti-French, yet working for the destruction of Germany, which was the fundamental aim of French imperialism[38]—but discounted the apparent support for them from Ludendorff and Hindenburg. Both in Hungary and in Germany, he said in Budapest, the people were divided: 'on one side, the nationalists, on the other the European humanists, and in both countries the opposing views are clear-cut as never before'—in both, the swastika appearing as the symbol of the 'barbarians'. (One thing he did not mention, commented his interviewer: 'while in Hungary the nationalistic Scythians are gaining over the European humanists, the German swastika gentry's bid for power is—for the moment—vain'.)[39]

The Spanish journey, on which he embarked with Katia soon after his return from Prague in April, was more for pleasure than for business, though his by now standard repertoire could attract good audiences in the German schools of Diego de León and Madrid, where he was received by the Infanta Isabella. He had felt a deep antipathy, 'a truly shuddering revulsion', against seeking a French visa in the current situation (though he was on good terms with his admirer and translator Félix Bertaux, and would soon be asking him to credit the fee for a French version of *Death in Venice* to his recently opened Swiss account), and they decided on a complicated journey by sea: outward, Genoa to Barcelona, return from Santander via Plymouth to Hamburg on the Hapag liner *Toledo*, in which they were shown all due deference. The month in this, for him, quite new country was a well-filled touristic experience, and gave him, as he told Bertram, the element of old Spain which he sought and to which he had lent 'a humorously concealed role in the starched ruff of Hans Castorp's grandfather' in the novel. Not Catalonia, or Andalusia and the Alhambra— 'whose spirit I find more congenial in the hints of Venice or Toledo than in its full deployment'—but the classic Spain of Castile, 'the granite and stony plain from Madrid to the Escorial and the Guadarrama', Toledo, the journey to Segovia, and not least the art of El Greco. He had 'dragged along'

---

[38] *Fr./Antw.* 59.        [39] *Ungarn* 324.

the manuscript of the novel, but there was no time to devote to it until their return towards the end of May, when the distractions came at last to an end. For the summer at least he himself planned no more travel; Katia and the younger children would have a holiday at the Ammersee, while Erika and Klaus would make a walking-tour of Thuringia.

The education of the teenagers, and especially of Klaus, had been far from problem-free. After the failure of the Bergschule, Erika had rejoined the local secondary school, where she stayed until her matriculation in 1924; but the experiment of the Odenwaldschule for Klaus—a pioneer establishment of highly progressive ideas, the emphasis on students' free-dom to 'find themselves'—was not proving a happy one. Already by March he had asked to be withdrawn after the Easter holidays, and his father, loath to exert parental authority, had had to ask Geheeb to interview and persuade him. This succeeded, and there was hope Klaus would complete his studies there and ready himself, as his father put it, for a career related to his literary ambitions, for he had long been writing, both verse and prose; but he was too impatient to stay the course. Before the summer holidays, he had his parents' agreement to leave, and in June tried to explain himself in a letter to the principal, with whom he was on the best of terms: grateful for the 'good and fruitful weeks since Easter' and the way he had been left so much to himself, 'enjoying the solitude which for me is a *precondition for life*', he was still convinced that he was in the wrong place. 'I can't create here in the way I feel I could elsewhere. . . . Admittedly, where I *would* feel entirely at home—God knows. I am betraying no small part of myself when I tell you: everywhere I shall be—an alien. A person of my sort is, always and everywhere, completely alone . . .'[40]

In fact, the beard-and-sandal, back-to-nature regime of such a com-munity was not to the boy's taste; more actively homosexual than his father had ever been, he sought the wilder life of the city; and the confession to Geheeb was revealing of the existential crisis that would haunt and eventu-ally destroy him. Private tuition back in Munich was arranged; but he skipped most of it in a dissipated life, and in the end did not complete the final examination—which Erika took the following year only to please the parents, barely scraping through (after all, neither their father nor uncle Heinrich had achieved that distinction). Instead of walking in Thuringia that summer of 1923, they absconded to the more attractive world of Berlin's night-spots, and it was the capital which both thought would hold their future. For Klaus, a compromise solution was found: he was to spend a year near Heidelberg in the home of the poet Alexander von Bernus—anthroposophist and homoeopathy enthusiast—to try to clear his mind

---

[40] KlM *Br. Antw.* 14 f.

and decide on what he wanted to do. Here at least he settled to serious writing, completing several novellas and sending articles to Berlin journals which, coming from the son of the famous writer, were readily accepted—with, of course, the disadvantage, in an ever-jealous literary world, of critical accusations that he was merely exploiting his father's name. For all his undoubted talent as a writer, he would never be able to emerge fully from the shadow of his famous parent.

That leader of German youth, unable to give his own son the guidance he needed, found his duty lay on the wider scene. In June he was asked to speak at a remembrance ceremony for Rathenau, organized in Berlin by an association of republican students. The reactions to his earlier speech had taught him that the appeal to 'German romanticism' was not the way to convert young people to support for the Republic, and this time he adduced Goethe rather than Novalis to make his case: *Wilhelm Meister* as the precursor of German progress 'from the subjective towards the objective, the political, towards republicanism'. And he warned against the dangers of 'anti-humanity', whose most evident effects were to be seen now in Bolshevism, Italian fascism, and the reactionary trends in Hungary and France. 'Germany's republican youth realizes that humanity is the idea of the future, the idea to which Europe must strive, with which it must be animated and in which must lie its life—if it wants to survive.'

His next two 'German Letters' for the Americans, written during the summer, were less political, and devoted rather to the cultural scene; but he stressed Munich's tradition of popular democracy in conservative form as opposed to the socialist north, even though it might be the city of the swastika, 'that symbol of *völkisch* obstinacy and an ethnic aristocratism, whose behaviour is certainly anything but aristocratic and has nothing to do with the feudalism of pre-war Prussia'. (His unflattering incidental notices of Arnolt Bronnen's play *Parricide* and the young Bertolt Brecht's *In the Jungle of the Cities*, the latter interrupted by stink-bombs from a hostile audience in Munich, were an unwitting foretaste of his own future, for one day a Thomas Mann performance would suffer similar treatment, organized by no less than Arnolt Bronnen.) The threat to the traditional theatre posed by the cinema received some passing mention; and in September he saw the *Buddenbrooks* film, condemning it as a stupid effort even if a technical success, at the Berlin première, but concluding that it was so remote from the original that the sales of the book would not be affected. With the years, though rarely enthusiastic over films from his own work, he would develop an almost consuming passion for the cinema; and indeed, towards the end of 1923, prepared an outline script for a film of *Tristan and Isolde* in the production of which his brother Viktor was to be concerned—as he wrote later, marking the return, technically and materially developed, of the old morality-play to the vast audiences for so popular a medium.

The *Magic Mountain* manuscript was meanwhile accumulating, and he thought he had the end of the 'monster' in sight. A holiday in October with Katia in Bolzano, however, turned out to provide new inspiration: at last he had found the original he needed for his Mynheer Peeperkorn, with whom Clawdia Chauchat returns to the sanatorium and who dominates its se- cluded world with his powerful personality. For in their hotel were Gerhart Hauptmann and his wife, with whom they made a congenial foursome. In daily contact, keeping pace—if somewhat reluctantly—with the older col- league's consumption of chilled wine, listening to his stammering, often illogical-seeming discourse, observing his distinguished bearing as they returned to the hotel to the respectful smiles of the staff, he saw at once: 'This is the man!' To draw his Peeperkorn after this model, though it risked attracting the wrath of Hauptmann's admirers, even of the great man himself, was an irresistible temptation. The conclusion of the novel had still to be written, but Fischer was already going ahead with printing what was available, his editor finding it 'splendid', and the hope was that the spring could see publication. But the author was not about to change his ways: commitments as public performer, pundit, journalist were firmly pursued, while those to his major work as author had to take their turn. Further readings were due almost immediately, in Lübeck, Kiel, and Berlin, and writing thereafter in January 1924 to Fischer he confessed that though he could register daily progress on the book, 'curious . . . *sui generis* one may well say', it was still proving hard to finish, and he had more bookings to fulfil in the coming months. Consolingly, however, he added that it would make a 'mighty complement' to the ten-volume collected works, which were continuing steadily with Fischer, and he would provide a further volume of essays and speeches to round the collection off by the coming Christmas.[41]

The American connection, if hardly liberally rewarded, had been a vital element in his budget. In November the end of the inflation through the introduction of the Rentenmark had greatly reduced the need for dollars; but he was concerned to exploit the name he had begun to make for himself in the United States, so far more that of an advocate of republicanism (his theme in an essay 'Five Years of Democracy in Germany' for the New York journal *Current History* in July) than of a successful author. The publisher Alfred A. Knopf in New York had secured from Fischer in 1921 the translation rights for *The Buddenbrooks* and for a further work annually thereafter: now, in April 1924, Mann received his first copies of *The*

[41] SF *Brw.* 421 f.

*Buddenbrooks* in English. He was freer with his praise to Helen Lowe-Porter, the translator, than his rather limited knowledge of the language warranted—though for the time being hesitating to meet her request to be appointed his exclusive translator. The American reviews which followed were not entirely encouraging: Nunnally Johnson found it almost unbearably long, astounded that it should have had fifty editions in Germany, when six copies of such a tome would indicate a 'rare patience in a nation'; but Robert Lovett praised the beauty and eloquence of which Thomas Mann was a master, and Ludwig Lewisohn (better able to judge the 'on the whole adequate translation') thought it a very great book, 'a first-rate work of art'.

In France, unsurprisingly, *The Buddenbrooks* found no favour yet with a publisher: the first Mann translation appeared there now in the shape of *Tonio Kröger*—'a masterpiece', said one reviewer, 'though written by a German'. Franco-German hostility was clearly not yet a thing of the past; and although, as Mann said, his inclinations were beginning to take a Westernized turn—'if only in the interest of German balance'[42]—as he prepared to accept an invitation to Holland for early May, to be followed by a visit to England as guest of the newly formed PEN Club, there was again no question of travelling via France. Family problems were evidently of less concern for the moment. Before joining him on the tour, Katia had taken a six-week cure at Davos in February, leaving the younger children alone with her husband but in capable hands; Michael, already showing signs of great musical talent, received his first instrument on his fifth birthday in April. Klaus was packed off to the Bernus estate near Heidelberg; Erika, the *Abitur* behind her, was now firmly decided on a stage career, and her father, despite misgivings over her insistence on a start in Berlin, gave her her head. They would visit her there after returning to Hamburg from England by sea, and there were plans for a July holiday with all the family at Hiddensee, the small Baltic island off Rügen.

In Holland, and particularly on this first visit to England, it was the theme of Europe that held him. In a brief speech to the Amsterdam Literary Circle on 3 May, among an assembly of 'European-minded writers', he noted with approval the city's ties with its historic-aristocratic past, but also its readiness not to remain backward-looking, but to raise its head into the freedom of the 'modern, life-loving and democratic idea', the idea that was needed for Europe's moral recovery. In London, as guest of honour at the PEN Club, he was warmly greeted by Galsworthy; and, in spite of a lone protest by one member against this 'pro-German' function, felt himself the object of 'the most emphatic demonstrations' of the desire for cultural reconciliation. His American-born translator's husband, Avery Lowe, was

[42] Bl. 7, 10.

their guide to the city and then to Oxford, where Lowe was reader in palaeography. Writing to Helen Lowe-Porter after their return home, he marked Oxford as the high point of their journey: 'to breathe the air of English humanism—a specially noble variety of this (if Tolstoy is to be believed) vanishing spirit'—had been a truly magical experience. To her, his thoroughly correct appearance, in dark pin-stripe suit, seemed like that of a businessman, and his manner rather dry and stiff, though kindly. He had obviously been pleased to make her acquaintance, but, as correspondence in 1925 indicated, after Knopf had shown interest in *The Magic Mountain*, he expressed doubts over her suitability for its translation, recommending George Scheffauer instead, who he thought had done well with his version of the Bauschan story; and it was only after Knopf's insistence that Lowe-Porter achieved her ambition of becoming his permanent translator (not always, as many critics have pointed out, entirely successfully in an admittedly very difficult task).[43]

Before the summer holiday in July, he was fascinated to be asked to give a radio talk, from the Frankfurt station, his first venture before the impersonal microphone—as time would show, a medium which suited him well. When the family finally assembled at Kloster on Hiddensee, their quarters in the pension 'House by the Sea' became an 'enormous summer camp' for no fewer than nine, for Klaus had invited Wedekind's daughter Pamela to join them. A long-standing Munich friend of Erika and Klaus, she was already well into a stage career, and Klaus—apparently in all seriousness—had proposed they should become engaged: discovered by the press, this naturally made headlines, and though his father dismissed it now as a childish escapade (they were both still under 17), they did not abandon the idea for another year or more, in spite of Klaus's increasingly overt homosexual life. Gerhart Hauptmann and his wife were spending their usual summer holiday in the same lodgings, and of their many evenings together Thomas long remembered the first reading of his he had heard, from the *Till Eugenspiegel* still in manuscript. With some reluctance, he was persuaded to make his own contribution, from the manuscript of *The Magic Mountain*: no need for hesitation, said Hauptmann, 'in my father's house are many mansions'. The adults of the Mann family were entertained to a wine cup in the Hauptmann rooms, among many distinguished guests, and Erika was astounded at the drunken gaiety of them all—except, of course, her father, who in fact was busy thinking how to exploit the scene for his narrative.

The crowded, 'primitive and exorbitantly expensive' conditions at Kloster had no effect on his ability to work. But after two weeks there he moved camp to Bansin, further east on the mainland coast, a decision

---

[43] Cf. David Luke, introd. to *Thomas Mann: Selected Stories* (Penguin, 1993).

which he justified on the children's account but which was more likely due to his own need for a little more comfort. There, all of them, especially he himself, were enjoying themselves so much that he extended the stay to 25 August, moving again to nearby Ahlbeck. 'Even that won't see *The Magic Mountain* absolutely finished!' he wrote to Bertram. 'But what remains is steadily reducing, for I never work more smoothly and more productively than after my morning devotions in the sea.' There was, naturally, no holiday from the demands of the day. Little persuasion was needed for him to speak in Stralsund on 11 August, on the fifth anniversary of the Weimar constitution, nor did he hesitate to respond to the Chicago *Daily Tribune*'s futile question 'What books of other authors would you have liked to have written?'—none, he said, his only wish was to have made a better job of his own. When the company broke up, Erika returned to Berlin, where, though still taking voice-training lessons, she had been engaged for small parts with the Max Reinhardt ensemble, and soon progressed to more important roles. Klaus too finally made it to the capital, launched, as he hoped, on a literary career when Heinrich helped him to a post as theatre critic for the *12-Uhr-Blatt*. Relying on their parents' support, however, they could both look on Berlin more as an adventure than as the start of a serious career.

In the weeks that followed the return to Munich at the end of August, Thomas Mann settled with determination to the final spurt on the novel. The duel scene between Naphta and Settembrini was quickly finished: yet the closing chapter, the last days of Hans Castorp's seven years on the mountain and his departure for the war, posed problems. 'The brain-pan feels as though numbed,' he wrote to Erika. It was almost as if he was reluctant to let the final pages of this 'fearful brute' of a book leave his hands for the impatiently waiting printer. But on 28 September they were done and dispatched, his 'triumph of obstinacy' marked by a celebration with the faithful Bertram. Since most of the text had already been set, publication of the two volumes could be expected in November—over twelve years since Katia's stay in Davos and the germination of the idea. Fischer was hugely relieved to have the manuscript at last to hand, and advance orders were encouraging enough to make a first printing of 20,000.

Mann had spoken earlier of a new period in his production, and this was amply justified by the novel which had taken so long to emerge. From the straightforward narratives of his earlier novellas and *The Buddenbrooks*, he had moved through the psychological study of *Death in Venice* to a more contemplative approach: still in the tradition of the *Bildungsroman*, showing the maturing of the character of the average young man Hans Castorp in the isolated world of the sanatorium, but with an eloquent and complex commentary on its futile and introverted life, by inference on the whole of pre-war civilization—'the swan-song', as he wrote later, 'of that form of existence. Perhaps it is almost a law, that epic portrayals should mark the close of a way of life, for it to disappear after them.'[44] His treatment of dialogues and characters displayed the irony that had always marked his work, and his love for detail was as unrestrained as ever, carried at times to Proustian lengths; but the post-war years in which he finally completed the novel, while his own political ideas were changing, had coloured the end-result, for by implication it argues for a humane, enlightened democracy. In these senses, it did indeed mark a significant turning-point in his work, and he was disappointed, when the time came for his Nobel Prize, to find it awarded specifically for *The Buddenbrooks*, without mention of what had come since.

Few present-day authors, however eminent and sales-worthy, could expect their publisher's indulgence for such apparently dilatory production. Fischer, however, was well aware of the abiding worth of Thomas Mann's work, as well as of his value to himself. On several occasions in recent years he had not been over-pleased to see the appearance of special editions with other publishers of certain of the works, sometimes with his permission but sometimes not (the latest now a *Tristan* with Reclam); and during September, responding to Mann's request (perhaps at Katia's prompting) for a revised and improved contract, took some trouble to point out the advantages for him of an exclusive relationship between them. The new contract he offered was certainly generous: for every new work, a premium above royalties of 3,000 marks, starting with *The Magic Mountain*, for which it would exceptionally be raised to 5,000, and the promised second volume of essays; alongside the collected works in ten volumes, a second edition in 1925 to be sold complete and boxed, the royalty to be decided when the essay volume was to hand; in addition to a monthly royalty-instalment of 2,000 marks, advance payment of 30 per cent of the total due, beginning with *The Magic Mountain*; and running quarterly statements. After hinting gently that speeding up his production would naturally improve the royalty prospects, he added that there had already been advances of 6,000 marks on *The Magic Mountain*, so there could be no question of interest being lost; and he hoped the contract could be regarded as a fresh start—'I do what I can.'

Mann had every reason to be pleased with the offer, and was more than usually confident of a good reception for the new work, excerpts from which he planned to use for some readings in November. But he felt he had earned a rest first, and in October took a few weeks in Italy, at Sestri Levante, where Katia and the youngest children, and Bertram for a time,

[44] xiii 153.

were able to join him. The choice of place seems to have been made on impulse, but it will not have escaped him that it was once again one of Hauptmann's favourite haunts: at any rate, he hastened to send him a greeting-card, clearly keen to lose no opportunity of securing his goodwill, and doubtless in some anxiety over his reception of the Peeperkorn episode when he came to read the book. That trouble might lie ahead over the caricature was brought home to him when, after part of the episode had been read at his first appearance in Munich early in November, to general acclaim, an artist who had been a visitor at Hiddensee said he had had no difficulty in recognizing the original. As it was to be his text for the tour now planned, through Stuttgart, Freiburg, Dresden, and finally Berlin, he was greatly concerned whether others, especially in the capital, where Hauptmann had many friends, might seize on the resemblance and criticize the impiety of drawing so grotesque a figure.

For the moment, he need not have worried: he found the halls half-empty till he reached Berlin, and although there the reception was better and he had many curtain-calls, in the wide press-coverage there was no particular comment on Peeperkorn. Praise for his 'fabulous technique', his artistic manipulation of irony, was modulated only by criticism of the pretentious manner in his familiar predilection for the leitmotif, with the risk of wearying the hearer, and of his occasional inaudibility. The socialist *Vorwärts*, ever ready to carp at the Thomas Mann whose changed political stance was not to its liking, sneered at these 'picture postcards' of the author's magic mountain. Hauptmann himself—not present, and not yet through reading the whole—was unstinting in his praise to Fischer: 'my opinion, from the sample Thomas Mann read to us', he wrote on 26 November, 'is now thoroughly confirmed . . . if the work continues like this . . . it will rank among the few masterpieces of the genre'. By January, however, he had reached the end, and his fury knew no bounds at Mann's shameless collection of personal details as 'rags to clothe his Peeperkorn puppet', using his 'approach to me as a guest' to make an observation-post for Hans Castorp. Fischer (also worried as he read the book for the first time) did his best to calm the storm, but was the target for a bombardment of complaints from Hauptmann: 'Look at it how you like, Peeperkorn points to me, and the fact is that it's a disparagement. I'd be inclined even to see in it Freudian complexes.' In a letter drafted but probably not sent, Hauptmann went so far as to say that Mann had never meant anything to him, had 'never interested' him.[45] But he was finally prepared to close the file and forget it, and indeed played his part, along with Mann, in putting a stop to a public protest one of his friends was about to launch. In the coming years, an easy, if not cordial, relationship would be restored.

[45] SF *Brw.* 253, 257, 255.

The first reviews, as 1925 drew to a close, were respectful in admiration for a characteristic Mann work, but not without some adverse remarks on its length. For Felix Salten, Mann's somewhat condescending attitude towards his creations was nevertheless that of a 'sovereign', and the big dialogues to be compared with Fontane's. The most welcome comments came in letters: from the novelist Annette Kolb, who would have liked it a thousand pages longer—he had never yet shown such mastery, 'what a heart!'; from Jakob Wassermann, who—reading it, so to speak, at the source, on a sanatorium bed in Davos—found it a 'stupefying achievement', 'a crystallization of all the intellectual events of the past twenty years', an entirely new form of novel.[46]

The heaviest criticism, after the turn of the year, was from overseas. For twenty-five years, wrote *Books Abroad* in America, Thomas Mann had held the unique position of an accepted classic, but there was little doubt that this, 'enshrouding his every word in an oracular impressiveness, has encouraged him to etherealize his magnificent talent to the point of—dullness'; the writing was superb, the characterization delicate, but his preoccupation with things of the mind and 'minute description of complicated emotions provoke a doubt of his creative artistry. One sighs as one contemplates the pages ahead . . .' The London *Times Literary Supplement*, while considering it hardly likely to be a very popular novel, 'at least outside Germany', allowed it was a document of considerable importance to students of Central European life and thought. Edwin Muir, however, writing later in the *Nation & Athenaeum*, compared him favourably with Proust and Joyce, and found the book astonishing in its fullness, its most difficult passages and chapters the most fascinating.

There was no doubt of its success in Germany, however, and by Christmas, Fischer had printed a further 10,000, in spite of the relatively high price. A Hungarian translation appeared promptly, and versions in Dutch and Swedish were not slow to follow. Meanwhile a lecture-tour in Denmark during December, as guest of the German Minister at the Copenhagen legation, continued the author's triumphal progress. 'He has reached the summit of his fame,' commented Hedwig Pringsheim to her friend Dagny Björnson, 'his position not only in literature but also in the world is brilliant, and Katia can sun herself in the glamour. . . . They've just acquired a car and built themselves a garage . . .'[47] He had been amused, but no doubt also flattered, to see that autumn an article by Yeats in the *Dial* mentioning a report that the Nobel Prize would probably go to himself or to 'Herr Mann the distinguished novelist', and conceding that Mann was 'in every way' much the more fitted. It was not the first of such speculations, and there were to be more over the coming years.

---

[46] *Brw. Aut.* 268, 482 ff.    [47] Wiedem. 47 f.

# IV

## INVOLVEMENT OF A LATTER-DAY GOETHE 1925–1932

'He is an official, an official of art, with all the precision, care, and pedantry that was long the best tradition of the Prussian state'
(Ferdinand Lion)

### 1

*'It was the fault of the man that he was imbued too strongly with self-consciousness. He could do a great thing or two. . . . He could sacrifice all that he had to duty. . . . But he could not forget to pay a tribute to himself for the greatness of his own actions'*
(*Anthony Trollope,* The Last Chronicle of Barset)

As the long haul for *The Magic Mountain* was drawing to an end, Thomas Mann had said he would not be embarking on another such effort of composition for a long time to come, and would turn his attention again to the novella. Though an offhand remark which suited the letter he was writing, this was typical—for all his major efforts were first thought of as short stories, only later developing their own momentum. A novella certainly was soon in his mind, prompted by the behaviour of young people, and in particular his own children, in the difficult but heady days of the inflation in Germany; before January was out, part was ready for a reading in Marburg, and he would complete it in time for the June 1925 issue of the *Rundschau*, under the title 'Disorder and Early Sorrow'. But he had already formed 'shadowy plans' for something which would prove to be more substantial and which he was not yet prepared to reveal to others: to retell the Bible story of Joseph and his brothers, that 'charming myth' which Goethe himself had once said was too short and simply begged to be developed. In January he had begun to figure out how to meet the expense of a visit to Egypt, as an entry into what he would call 'my mystical-humorous aquarium'. With *The Magic Mountain* approaching its fiftieth thousand, cost was not really a problem, for his royalties were accumulating most encouragingly; but an invitation from the Stinnes Line to a March Mediterranean cruise which would include Egypt was naturally a more welcome solution.

The second volume of essays had first to be cleared away. The 'Goethe and Tolstoy' and 'German Republic' speeches were the major items, and he took some trouble to rework and extend the first in line with his changed political position, strengthening the appeal to a European humanism as the necessary counter to the right-wing extremism which was disturbingly on the increase. Reviews of *The Magic Mountain*, still mixed, continued to occupy him, though its sales were unaffected. What most incensed him were reproaches for its lack of composition, after all his years of sitting at the loom 'like an oriental carpet-maker'. Much was made of the excessive length: but Schnitzler, like Annette Kolb, told him he would gladly have read more, even four volumes, in this style. The *New York Times* in January, though admiring the original display of such a wealth of learning, was painfully aware that Mann's 'plastic creative power, the . . . joy in the solid figures of red-blooded men, has been absorbed by a very strong intellectuality', and found a certain frigidity in his mode of presentation. (The cool American reception, however, did not deter Knopf from plans for a translation, for which he insisted, against Mann's doubts, on retaining Helen Lowe-Porter.) In medical circles there began a vigorous debate, which would last a long time and in which both doctors and patients had their say over the ironic treatment of the sanatorium and its staff. None could fault his medical facts, however, and one of the main critics later admitted that his strictures had been mere niggling in the face of the supreme achievement of the novel.

The cornerstone of the new European humanism Mann advocated must be an improvement in Franco-German relations, as he came to realize in working on the revised 'Goethe and Tolstoy' essay. Before leaving on the March cruise, he developed part of it in a text on the theme of 'Germany and Democracy' for the Paris journal *L'Europe nouvelle*, where it appeared under the title 'L'Esprit de l'Allemagne et son avenir entre la mystique slave et la latinité occidentale'. The article stressed the danger for Germany's development towards democracy of Poincaré's aggressive chauvinism, which could only foster its equivalent in Germany. The Dawes Plan of the previous year, scaling down the reparations obligations, and Foreign Minister Stresemann's preparations for the Locarno Pact as an international guarantee of the status quo in the West, were moves in the right direction; and Thomas Mann—avowedly unwilling to intervene in day-to-day politics—was ready later to make a small contribution towards a *rapprochement* with France by accepting an invitation to Paris for early in 1926. But he was more alert than most to the risk for democracy in Hindenburg's candidacy for president after Ebert's death in February, and intervened with a widely publicized but vain appeal before the election in April, which the old marshal won by a narrow margin. By the time that risk became clear, it was too late.

The cruise, begun in familiar Venice on 3 March, appealed to Mann's love of the good life (Katia, it seems, was not included in the invitation). Aboard the Stinnes Line *General San Martin*, 6,500 tons, the doctor's cabin vacated for him, he found every comfort, enjoying his hot sea-water bath, the excellent food, and most especially the formality of dressing for dinner. Inevitably, an article on the tour took shape before the trip ended. In it, he underplayed his praise, for fear of the 'social provocation' that might be given by any impression of an orgy of post-war capitalists: there was something in that, he admitted, but then again here was a German vessel, with a salutary atmosphere of Hamburg seriousness and cleanliness, amid the exotica, and he took care to ackowledge Stinnes's enterprise. On this strangest tour of inspection he had ever experienced, his personal objective was Egypt: from Port Said down to Cairo, with all its flies and pestering souvenir-sellers; the museum with some of the Tutankhamun treasures; the pyramids of Giza; then the sleeper journey down to Luxor and the Valley of the Kings at Karnak, where the mummy of Amenophis IV, hidden through the ages, lay bared in 'shaming indiscretion' to public view. 'The East has become mine,' he wrote—how deeply he penetrated would later, much later, be clear from his version of the Joseph story. After Constantinople and Athens, and with the weather an increasingly cold contrast to Egypt, he began to weary of the voyage, and instead of continuing to Spain and Genoa, left the ship at Naples to return home.

As his fiftieth birthday approached, he was resting on laurels aready won: for lectures, he had only to recycle existing material; the plan for a 'Joseph' as his next big work was still embryonic. *Disorder and Early Sorrow* was rapidly finished off during May. It was a cameo straight from life, himself as the academic father looking on in benevolent bewilderment as his two older children, clearly recognizable as Erika and Klaus, take over the house for a mildly bohemian party with their friends. Significantly or not, his two middle children, Golo and Monika, do not appear, but Elisabeth and Michael are unmistakable as the little ones Ellie and Snapper: Michael in an accurate portrayal of his quaint looks and outbursts of temper, but his favourite Elisabeth drawn with a moving sentimentality rarely to be found in Mann—the memory as he holds her in his arms of the birth of the 'little miracle', 'love at first sight, love everlasting' but a 'not quite disinterested, not quite unexceptionable love'. The whole episode, with the young people's private jargon and casually ironic manner, the extraordinarily unisex dress, the so-called dancing now the rage, is recounted in the gently humorous tone that had pervaded *The Magic Mountain*, but without its philosophical overlay. Michael was not best pleased to read it in later years, and Klaus, though his comments are not recorded, must certainly have been less than appreciative of the 'paternal envy' of a steadier and more promising young man among the guests.

In a sense the story was already outdated, for Erika and Klaus were now beginning to make their mark as adults on stage and page. Klaus, though footloose and off in March on a tour of London and Paris, had finished a drama, *Anja and Esther*, which he had plans to produce; when he had returned, his volume of novellas, *The Threshold of Life*, was already in print. In these, he inevitably followed the well-trodden family path of ill-concealed autobiography. His father, indeed, found it necessary to apologize to Paul Geheeb for the 'scurrilous' caricature of the former headmaster it contained, and to send his excuses for the artistic naïvety of this 'obviously so immature beginner' in abandoning reality for the grotesque.[1] To Erika, in Berlin, he wrote that though the stories were remarkable, there was a thoroughgoing father-complex here. He had himself, meanwhile, been busy making amends for his comparable, if more subtle, offence against Hauptmann with his Peeperkorn, and when Hauptmann visited Munich early in May, for the dress rehearsal of his festival piece for the inauguration of the German Museum, made sure to drive him in the new car: 'we shook hands a lot, and all is now well again', he told Erika.

Soon after this, he visited Italy, attending an international culture week in Florence as German representative and using his 'Goethe and Tolstoy' as his contribution. In an interview, he brought the Mann family solidarity to the fore—a 'dynasty' of writers, himself, Heinrich, and now his eighteen-year-old son with a new book showing the 'colourful, passionate, penetrating style' with which the younger generation sought distinction. An extract from the 'Goethe and Tolstoy' also served for a lecture at the Vienna PEN Club on 2 June, and for a short speech at the banquet his theme was Austria, 'problem-child of life' like his hero Hans Castorp. An interviewer, describing him alongside Hauptmann and Heinrich Mann as the great representative of present-day Germany, elicited some political comments: his hope that, despite the feared tension, Hindenburg's election as President could yet bring a certain adjustment, and his insistence on the necess-

---

[1] 25/78.

ity of a United States of Europe, 'probably in some federalistic form'.[2] An
excellent performance of *Fiorenza* in the Concordia rounded off the four-
day visit.

The fiftieth birthday then, on 6 June, was an occasion which few of his
colleagues wanted to miss, and the published tributes were many and
lavish. Even the London *Observer* took note of this literary life 'of so much
thought and so little output' in which Mann had rediscovered Germany to
the Germans. At a ceremony in Munich's old Town Hall, following a dull
and surprisingly critical introduction from a professor and some banal
words from the mayor, he gave a brief speech expressing appropriate
modesty over his 'fragmentary, inadequate work, not free from dross'; his
belief, acquired the hard way, that he could represent something for his
people and his country; and his desire that posterity might say of his work
'it is friendly to life, although it knows of death'. (Thomas Mann seems to
have a slight horror of fame, commented the *Hamburger Fremdenblatt*:
thinks more of the 'Crucify him!' than of the 'Hosannah!') Tired after the
Vienna trip, he was not on his best form here; but Heinrich saved the
occasion by words which moved him greatly, recalling their childhood
birthdays. The next afternoon his reading from *Felix Krull* in the
Residenztheater was followed by the strains of Mozart and a choir, he was
surrounded by flower-bearing girls, and had to duck away from the prof-
fered silver laurel-wreath.

His modesty was not entirely assumed; but there is no doubt of the
gratification he drew from the flood of spoken and written tributes, from
Hofmannsthal, Wassermann, Pfitzner, and many others, occupying him for
a week in diligent acknowledgements (so many that for the less important
he had recourse for the first time to a printed card). Hauptmann was
fulsome over his ascent from *The Buddenbrooks* to *The Magic Mountain*: 'he
is a poet, the apparent dryness and prosaic form does not hide this'. Others
stressed rather his representative character, the 'genius of responsibility'
(Stefan Zweig), the writer like Goethe with attributes of the tribune (Josef
Ponten). Ludwig Lewisohn, who had seen him in Vienna, later drew a not
unflattering portrait for the New York *Nation* of his thoughtful, measured,
calm, uncondescending manner, 'neither eager for praise nor impatient of
it, nor unkindly towards the adulation of fools', one who might easily be
mistaken for a man of business. Fischer, whose good wishes came in the
form of a silver cigarette-case, had also commissioned a portrait of him
from the prominent artist Max Liebermann, a form of flattery to which he
was never averse, and he was not slow to suggest a first sitting in Berlin for
October, on his way back from another birthday celebration in Lübeck.

[2] *Fr./Antw.* 70.

And, once again, there was mention of a coming Nobel Prize, this time in the Stockholm *Dagens Nyheter*.

With it all, he began to feel a certain discontent over the 'solemn misunderstanding, the dizziness of fame, and the shallowness of those who serve it to us'.[3] There was an inclination now to abandon the demands of the world and the day and settle to real work after the constant movements of the past few years. As well as the Joseph story, he had ideas on other historical themes—Luther and Erasmus, perhaps, or Philip II of Spain, costume pieces, as he put it; *Krull* too still waited to be finished. But there was some truth in his blithe confession that he lacked discipline, smoked too much, and could not 'say No to life'[4]—at any rate, in this latter respect, for there was no relaxing of his journalistic efforts in the months that followed, no matter how Katia tried to ward off telephone enquirers, nor of the travel he claimed to be weary of.

In July and August he spent some time on a contribution to Keyserling's book on marriage: an essay in letter form, 'Marriage in Transition', touching on the problems in the post-war world of free love, easier divorce, women's emancipation, the increasing outward similarity between the sexes, and homo-eroticism, and adducing his own experience, in both life and work, in subtler terms than in his 1920 letter on *Death in Venice*. Shaw had refused to contribute ('no man dare write the truth about marriage while his wife lives!'); Katia, however, is not likely to have been surprised, or perturbed, by her husband's philosophical approach. In August they spent a week in Salzburg, for the Festspiele, driving now instead of going by train, with a smart and efficient new chauffeur, and calling in on Wassermann in Alt-Aussee. There were performances of Donizetti's *Don Pasquale*, under Bruno Walter, of Vollmöller's *Miracle* and Hofmannsthal's *Das Salzburger große Welttheater* (their baroque allegory humbug for the Anglo-Saxons' benefit, he thought).

Proofs for the essay volume awaited him on return, and he had on the stocks a light-hearted piece on his attitude to cosmopolitanism: incompetent, he said, in any language other than his own, his happiest and most fruitful experiences with that spirit had been 'internally German', with the Europeanism of Goethe, Schopenhauer, and Nietzsche, to the point where a French critic could now speak of his thought as that of a 'European moralist'.[5] There followed a few weeks' holiday in September with Katia and the youngest children, at Ischia: African almost in the heat and the sand, marvellous grapes and figs, and, apart from sleep disturbed by fleas, a thoroughly refreshing interlude. In October he was off to Lübeck, where *Fiorenza* was performed for his birthday, and then Berlin, where he read

---

[3] *Br.* i, 242.    [4] *Bl.* 7, 11.    [5] x 191.

twice from *Disorder* and duly sat for Liebermann. Immediately thereafter came the première of Klaus's *Anja and Esther* in Munich; and readings were scheduled in January in four cities on his way to Paris. When would there be time, he wondered, for preparation of the Joseph?

It was nothing new for the literary businessman to have so many simultaneous commitments, reluctant as he was to refuse the constant invitations his position brought: that he could find it possible to compartmentalize them and not lose sight of the longer-term projects, was all the more remarkable. Inability to say no, the tolerance for the adulation of fools which Lewisohn had noted, had also enlarged his acquaintance with numbers of young admirers, often desperate hangers-on as they sought his aid and advice: his over-kindly letters were not calculated to keep them at bay, or away from his home. Ida Herz, for example, a spinster bookseller's assistant whom he had met in Nuremberg, had had her admiration rewarded by an invitation to tea in January 1925, and was not dismayed to find herself the butt of his often sarcastic humour; she longed to be his secretary, but had to be content with a commission in July to catalogue his library, on which she worked until September; later he helped to get her a post as archivist with Fischer in Berlin. Over the years to come, he was glad of her aid whenever he needed books, special writing-paper or the like, and pleased by the Thomas Mann archive, including a very full collection of press-cuttings, which she assembled. But despite Katia's sympathy for her, he refused any direct financial aid, and successfully managed to space the visits and support the persistent attentions of this 'hysterical old maid'.[6] 'Die Herz' became something of a family joke; the temptation years later to use her, with heavy irony, as the model for a character in his *Doctor Faustus*, was irresistible, and she was indulgent enough to feel flattered; but to read his acid comments in the posthumously published diaries for 1933 and onwards was a grievous hurt for one who had thought herself a welcome acolyte.

Less easy to resist was the writer Josef Ponten, Mann's junior by eight years, whose first long novel in 1918 he had been unwary enough to praise in too fulsome terms and who had become a prolific correspondent. After moving to Munich in 1920, Ponten had thrust himself forward with invitations to his Schwabing home, which were naturally returned, until he was a regular *habitué* of Poschinger Strasse; his eager reading-aloud from his manuscripts, however, was not a welcome experience for Mann, who preferred to present his own. By now, the other's almost 'pathological fixation' on him had become a burden: but a sharp reproof in April—there must be an end to 'this constant comparison with me, measuring yourself

[6] *Tb.* iii, 85.

against me'—had availed little. Ponten contrived to speak his piece (on Katia, rather than Thomas) at the Munich fiftieth-birthday celebration; and if there were fewer exchanges of visits, there was no slackening in those of letters, where Mann's polite diligence rarely failed him, no matter what he really thought of his correspondent (like the Irish driver in Shaw's *John Bull's other Island*, 'he'd say whatever was the least trouble to himself and the pleasantest to you').

For the Munich Kammerspiele première of his *Anja and Esther* on 20 October, Klaus had the enthusiastic support of the actor Gustaf Gründgens, who recruited Erika together with Pamela Wedekind for the title-roles, insisted on himself and Klaus appearing too, and took over the production for the later performance in Hamburg. The prominent, not to say notorious, cast, and the lesbian theme (which reflected Erika's current passion for Pamela), ensured a *succès de scandale* and on the whole not unreceptive audiences for the 'ridiculous sexual play', as Klaus had called it to Pamela when he first sent her the text. It did not escape the critics' lash, however, many of whom remarked unfavourably on the dynastic succession; and his father, who saw the second Munich performance and was ready despite many objections to admit in it a 'certain youthful, over-youthful charm', was himself a target for both published attacks and anonymous letters. For a beginner's play, he wrote to Erika on her birthday, it was nothing like as bad as most people seemed to find it, and he was delighted to hear praise for her own promise as an actress. A *Simplicissimus* cartoon in December showed a young Klaus looking over his shoulder with the words: 'You know Papa, the genius never has one as a son— so you're no genius.' In the following March, when *Anja and Esther* had been produced in Vienna, Papa took the trouble to write and squash the rumour that he found his son's work 'immoral': he was not a nun, and the future of the talented nineteen-year-old was 'a question of character and destiny'.[7] A Fasching newspaper spoof meanwhile carried the advertisement 'For sale by Thomas Mann, very cheap: a well-preserved conservative philosophy . . . and a father's cane, scarcely used, exchange possible for a Jacobin cap in good condition, with adjustable cockade . . .'

Young people's work was judged in the light of how far they were ready for a new war of revenge, he thought, in the 'quagmire' that was Munich. And as he prepared himself in January 1926 for the tour that would bring him to Paris, he was fully aware that its leading paper, the *Neueste Nachrichten*, would 'sooner bite out its tongue' than announce a German lecture in the enemy camp.[8] His appearance there was at the invitation of the Carnegie Foundation for International Peace (though he privately

[7] 26/30.
[8] To Georg Hirschfeld, 4 Jan. 1926 (Hartung & Karl auction cat. 31, 1981).

claimed to have accepted only after some resistance, and under a certain political and national pressure,[9] there can be little doubt that he welcomed the honour). As it happened, he arrived with Katia on 20 January hard on the heels of Einstein and of the critic Alfred Kerr, his old foe, who was still there. Reactions against a German speaker in the Boulevard Saint-Germain were more pronounced here than they had been at the London PEN Club function. There had been disturbances at Kerr's lecture the previous day, and the organizers judged it prudent to produce Mann's in a smaller room, restricting the audience to at most 150, and to limit the press attendance. His speech, presenting himself as a typical German, urging Europe's need for Franco-German understanding and mutual sympathy, and subtly correcting the antithesis 'culture–civilization' from his *Reflections*, drew warm applause from the select audience, which included the German ambassador, Sorbonne and Strasburg professors of German, and the literary historian Charles Du Bos. The scenes over the strict controls at the entrance naturally produced hostile reactions in the next day's headlines—'Thomas Mann Speaks Behind Closed Doors', 'Snub to German Right-Wing Press', 'Newspapermen Excluded'; but there was praise from *Le Matin* and the *Journal des Débats*—and some relief that he had not come with a plea for revision of the Versailles treaty.

The handling of the press had been far from clever, and the tight schedule arranged allowed no time for him to set things right by interviews, for immediately following came a formal dinner at the embassy. Guests included Ministers Daladier and Painlevé and the Secretary-General for Foreign Affairs, the Austrian ambassador, Benjamin Crémieux of the Cercle littéraire international—and Kerr, and a large representative crowd was received afterwards for coffee. The next day some impromptu words (never his forte) were expected at a meeting of the 'Union pour la vérité', and later he attended a gathering of Du Bos's 'Union intellectuelle française'. At each, and in the many discussions during the rest of the week, before they boarded the Orient Express back to Munich on 28 January— with Edmond Jaloux, Bertaux, Fabre-Luce, Jules Romains, Mauriac, and a host of other personalities—he was struck by the goodwill of the French, their understanding for his development since the *Reflections*, and the general enthusiasm for *rapprochement*.

That this was not so general, on either side of the Rhine, became apparent, both soon after his return and in the years to come. Hanns Johst, a notorious reactionary, referring to him disparagingly as 'Kerr's young man', enlarged on how both had disgraced themselves; the Paris *Annales*, admitting the virtue of his visit after all his insults to France in the

---

[9] To Hedda Eulenberg, 7. Jan. 1926 (photocopy in Thomas Mann Collection, University Library, Düsseldorf).

*Reflections*, raked over old coals in asking whether Thomas Mann—'though a Jew [!] the most German of Germans'—had perhaps been mistaken for the author of the Zola essay, his brother. He had already decided, in view of the criticism over the publicity arrangements, to set the record straight by writing a detailed account of his tour, which was published in the May *Rundschau* and later as a book; but Johst's article seemed to call for a specific reply. He was right in insisting thus publicly on the value of Franco-German understanding, as would soon be clear from the increasingly violent right-wing and Nazi campaign against the man 'kowtowing' to Paris.[10] In April he began to note in Ernst Bertram how 'professorial chauvinism' was gaining the upper hand.[11] In his *Paris Account*, presenting what he had seen and heard in its best light, there was one passage which seems, curiously, to have escaped notice. In a discussion on democracy with Painlevé, he wrote, 'I said what everybody thinks, that these days it is in a way rather a hindrance. ... What Europe needs today is an enlightened dictatorship.' It was not a remark he may have cared to recall as the lines were drawn in the final days of the Weimar Republic.

He and Katia had both returned with influenza, and though his cleared up readily, Katia's persisted as a lung affection, for which the doctors later recommended, as usual, mountain air. Davos, after the stir created by *The Magic Mountain*, was hardly indicated, and they settled for Arosa in May. There her condition was slow to improve; for his part, he found the darkness of the incessant snowstorms, the coughing and gramophone-playing neighbours a superfluous *Magic Mountain* replay. The year was running away fast, with still no start on the *Joseph*, as occasional pieces continued to take up his time and a major speech had to be prepared for 5 June on the occasion of Lübeck's seven hundredth anniversary. Katia would stay on in Arosa, in the hope of more relief, and not accompany him there. Inexorably, he noted as he prepared for departure, there came the demands of the world on one 'stupid enough to possess a public conscience and thus arouse the misconception that he was born to be a preceptor'.[12] But it was a role he was not inclined to abandon, and there was no refusing a reading to students in Zurich from *Disorder and Early Sorrow*, between the final touches to his Lübeck contribution.

His idea was to celebrate the free city as an 'intellectual way of life': to present its burghers, not in the political sense as bourgeois, as mere capitalists, but as truly German in their defence of world citizenship and the principles of humanity and in their staunch readiness to meet the tide of change and revolution—with his own experience and work, from *The Buddenbrooks* to *The Magic Mountain*, as his text. The burghers proved only

---

[10] *Berliner Nachtausgabe*, 6 Feb. 1928.     [11] 26/45.     [12] Br. i, 255.

too ready to take pride in reminiscences of a famous son in this rather flattering form—the reminiscences of the narrator of 'actually only one story, that of his emancipation, not to the bourgeois or the Marxist, but to the artist, to art soaring to irony and freedom'. He watched with interest the medieval torchlight parade through the old city, 'laden with history and hardly any longer capable of surviving', and was touched by the Senate's award of the honorary title of professor. That he still felt he had to send a reminder for payment of his 1,000-mark lecture-fee showed how firmly on the ground were the feet of the soaring artist: there was careful calculation for his budget as he continued during the year to meet the inexorable demands of the world, even while assembling notes and impressions for the start on the Joseph story.

Katia returned from Arosa at the end of June, in time for a new episode in the less than conventional life of their eldest child. Erika, on an impulse like Klaus's with Pamela Wedekind, had suddenly decided on marriage with Gustaf Gründgens, and the civil ceremony was fixed for 24 July, with her father and Katia's twin brother as witnesses. Gründgens, now producer with the Hamburg Kammerspiele, made a good figure, and to Thomas he seemed sympathetic and a highly talented artist; but in the marriage, though a step further than Klaus could take with Pamela (soon to marry the playwright Carl Sternheim), there was a good measure of play-acting, for Gründgens also was a homosexual. Conflicts were inevitable, and it was not destined to last beyond three years.

In August, a magazine carried an article by Klaus: 'The New Parents', and alongside it 'The New Children, a Conversation with Thomas Mann' (in fact, with both), their portraits appearing on facing pages. 'Mr Thomas Mann (who is he?) looks worriedly at his famous son (who doesn't know him?)' was Bert Brecht's sarcastic comment. 'If statistically there have been fewer parricides recently . . . that is no ground for comfort. We might find, for instance, that our eye falls longingly on our sons!'[13] Public attention to the Mann father–son relationship, however, was becoming something of an irritant for Klaus, in his feeling that, no matter what his progress as an author, he could never emerge from the Magician's shadow. For his father too it was publicity he could do without, as he tried to concentrate on his ever-deepening preliminary research for the Joseph story.

They had decided on a holiday from the end of August with the other children on the Italian coast at Forte dei Marmi, near Viareggio. It would be at most four weeks, he told Bertram: he would really sooner stay in Munich, but was looking forward to the sea and the south, the sight of

[13] *Das Tage-Buch* 33/1926, 1202 f. (quoted cat. 4, Buchhandlung Matthias Loidl, Unterreit, 1990).

southern people, useful for his '*idée fixe*', which in spite of dogged work he was not yet ready to start on. 'It is frightful how little one knows and how much one would have to know. How long did it take in 1400 BC to travel from Hebron to the Delta? Imagine having to tell about a time when the land of Atlantis probably still existed! I shall fail—or in the end take the thing very lightly, I think.' Visual impressions, however, played as important a role as the historical and mythological delving. On a visit in October to Golo at the Salem School, a glimpse of his new friend, a boy of Spanish origin, made him ask for photographs, finding here a model for his young Joseph; and indeed his first impulse to write the story had been the sight of a series of illustrations to it by an artist friend in Munich.

In the intense heat of their Italian stay, he had to be busy on more incidental work: a foreword to a German edition of Conrad's *Secret Agent*, and an article dealing with as yet unknown younger writers, in which he was concerned to play down the alleged gulf between the generations. Minor offensive incidents and the atmosphere of xenophobia under fascism were depressing, though he found the people themselves as friendly as ever and secure from the inflated influence of the Duce. A truly European level, he felt, could be found only in the French and the Germans (including the Austrians): the English, and even more the Italians, were not up to it.[14] (These negative impressions of Mussolini's fascism would find their way into a later story, *Mario and the Magician*.) In Germany itself, he said in an interview after his return, there were encouraging signs of a regeneration of its traditional culture, against the iconoclastic tendencies of Russian Bolshevism and Italian fascism, in the proliferation of book clubs and theatre organizations—and in the sales of books with literary qualifications like his *Magic Mountain*, which to his own surprise was now reaching the eightieth thousand in spite of its high price.[15] The optimism here was belied by his forceful line at a well-attended meeting in Munich on 30 November, where he joined his brother and artists and musicians in a demonstration against the city's growing reputation as a seat of political reaction, and urging the restoration of its tradition as a true centre of culture. It was time, he said, to abandon the inadequate cliché of southern *Gemüt*, of feeling, as opposed to northern *Verstand*, of reason: Rathenau's murder was also an expression of *Gemüt*, in its craziest form, and 'if one day Europe destroys itself, that too will be a suicide out of deepest feeling. Alas, we are almost at the point where anyone showing traces of intelligence is immediately branded as a Jew and thus finished off.' Whatever the irrationalists and mystics might say, intelligence was today the highest human value, a truth

[14] *Brw. Aut.* 216.     [15] *Fr./Antw.* 100.

underlined by the award of the Nobel Prize to Bernard Shaw.[16] The explosion of applause these words drew was deceptive: the latter-day *Kulturkampf* was beginning in earnest, and Munich's future as the capital of the National Socialist movement was already in the making.

Moves to organize a literature section in the Prussian Academy for the Arts in Berlin occupied much of his time towards the end of the year. He had long argued for some such official recognition of the writer's standing, and, against the misgivings of colleagues like Hofmannsthal, George, and Hauptmann, he put a strong case for seizing this 'historic' opportunity to develop from the Prussian a truly German Academy, on the lines of the French. Essential above all, he felt, was to extend its membership over the whole German-speaking area, and he welcomed the initial election of Hesse (long a Swiss citizen) and the Austrians Schnitzler, Franz Werfel, and Wassermann, alongside himself, his brother, poet and essayist Oskar Loerke, and novelist Ricarda Huch. At the first meeting in Berlin, on 18 November, it was not by chance that he should be called upon to speak, he wrote later: 'more than any other writer, perhaps, I had had very personal experience of the necessity today to move from the metaphysical and individual into the social sphere'. There was a powerful and secret attraction for the artist in such a 'union of the daemonic with the official, of solitude and adventurousness with social representation'.[17] The combination was part of the conscious patterning of his life on that of Goethe, which would only gain with the years.

Through the final months of the year he did not neglect his public readings—in Hamburg, Cologne, Heidelberg—and in October exchanged the lectern for the microphone, to show a new aspect of the Mann dynasty: a forty-five-minute radio session with Erika in Berlin, reading himself from his Conrad essay before she gave an extract from *The Magic Mountain*. Her stage career had been advancing well, with successes in Shaw's *St Joan* and *Androcles and the Lion*; and though his amusement over Klaus's new book, *Kindernovelle*, was tinged with a few doubts, he was proud and indulgent of them both. As Christmas drew near, he could at last start on his prologue to *Joseph*, glad to be writing again, he told Erika: 'a kind of essayistic or humorous pseudo-scientific foundation-laying I'm amusing myself with. . . . It is something new and at the same time intellectually remarkable, in which meaning and existence, myth and reality are interwoven in these people, with Joseph a kind of mythical con man.' A welcome gift from Bertram was a genealogy of legends, confirming his idea of Joseph as a 'Tammuz–Osiris–Adonis–Dionysos figure'—'which need not go to prove that he never really lived'. The attraction for him was the treat-

---

[16] x 224 f.        [17] xi 136.

ment of tradition as a timeless mystery, the experience of oneself as myth—but in light and humorous vein, without elevated gestures or religious fervour.

## 2
*'The secret and almost noiseless adventures in life are the greatest'*
(*TM, 19 October 1927*)

Probing the bottomless well of the past—but 'not much deeper than three thousand years, and what is that compared to the unfathomable?'—to prepare for 'the myth made flesh' in the story of Joseph, gradually brought home to him the lengths to which this 'novella' would finally have to stretch. The prologue, which appropriately or not he entitled 'Descent into Hell', already began over Christmas and January to spread itself in a way which to most writers might have seemed alarming: for him, there was nothing but delight in accumulating page after page, at last back to the epic narration that was his strength. The demands of the world and of the day, however, did not relax, and, though never losing sight of his objective, he would have to accept long gaps in its production.

Why did he allow himself to be so often distracted? With the regular income from his contract with Fischer, and the growing royalties from new and foreign editions, he was now anything but financially pressed; fees from public appearances and journalism had become icing on the cake, no longer the bread-and-butter of earlier years. That he could not bring himself to abstain sprang, certainly, from an urge to achieve an ever more comfortable life-style, till it verged on the princely: and here a streak of vanity played its part. More important was probably the obligation to maintain his pre-eminent position in the world of letters in Germany, and in the world beyond, certificated by the invitations to London and Paris and now by one for March to Warsaw. It was not surprising to find him a member of Rotary and always ready to oblige with a talk in the Munich club or at other European branches. He had kept up, though at longer intervals, his series of 'German Letters' for the *Dial*, for while the dollars were no longer so vital as during the inflation, it seemed prudent to keep his name before the public in America too. In Germany, seeking writers' views on the most diverse of topics was in great vogue, and he never failed to respond. Though he would often complain at the time and effort thus diverted from the main task, it was an obligation he never sought to evade—just as no letter remained unanswered, no matter that his study thereby became more an office than a work-bench for creation. The position he had now reached, not entirely involuntarily, of guide and philosopher for his nation and its youth, also brought its responsibilities, in the form of occasional speeches and essays.

To balance all these burdens required careful programming, with the method of compartmentalization at which he had become adept; it would never have been possible without Katia's support, but it also needed judiciously spaced holidays, either with her and the family, or alone. Thus, in the early months of 1927, the *Joseph* laid aside, he was busy with the editorship he had undertaken, with George Scheffauer, of a series 'The World's Novels', with a publisher other than Fischer: a general introduction from him was required for the first (Hugh Walpole's *Portrait of a Red-Haired Man*), and he devoted much time to the continuing work of selection. The Berlin *Literarische Welt* sought, and obtained, a New Year message for Germany's 'intellectually productive youth', in which he again minimized the generation gap: there should be no opposition between the young and the old, only between the intellectuals and the non-intellectuals, between the natural liberalism of the mind, in which salvation lay, and the fanatical terrorism of the barbarians. He listened approvingly to Hofmannsthal's lecture at Munich University on 10 January, with its emphasis on 'conservative revolution'—a notion he himself would elaborate a year later in an essay on 'Culture and Socialism', 'a pact between the conservative idea of culture and revolutionary social thought, between Greece and Moscow'. In pursuit of the humanistic ideal, he was ready to lend support wherever reaction loomed and regardless of party politics—later in the year, for example, in public protests against the imprisonment of Ernst Toller and of Max Hölz (the bourgeoisie's 'panic-stricken fear of revolution'), and now in a letter to the communist Red Aid against the government's threat to close one of their orphanages. This was Heinrich Vogeler's former home in Worpswede, and the demand was for the artist's murals, idealistically portraying world salvation through the proletarian revolution, to be replaced by products of a more acceptable ideology. But at the end of January he escaped for a fortnight with Katia to Ettal, near Oberammergau, taking the Joseph manuscript with him and enjoying a 'fairly industrious' winter break, away from the social life of Munich.

He was increasingly uneasy at the growth of right-wing persuasions, whether in their extreme Nazi and *völkisch* manifestations or in the milder arguments of the 'cultural struggle' in Munich; and later in the year he tried to exert his influence, though with little effect, to bring the *Neueste Nachrichten* to a more liberal editorial policy. He had been surprised at Bertram's refusal of the offer of a professorship in Munich, which he had strongly canvassed: his friend's preference for Cologne, where reactionary tendencies were even stronger, marked a growing estrangement between them. In his 'German Letter' for the *Dial*, published in April, he denounced in 'our—how shall I put it—fascist epoch' a general trend to anti-idealism which looked likely to be the spirit of the Germany of 1930, and was typified in one kind of youth 'which reckons to have done for all time with the concept of humanity and has embroidered the swastika of joyous brutalization on its flag'.[18]

In Warsaw for a week, at the invitation of the Polish PEN Club, he found his reception both more cordial and more official in character than in London, Amsterdam, or Paris: lavish hospitality and a ceremony worthy almost of a head of state. A large PEN Club delegation awaited him at the station on 8 March, and, following a grand banquet that evening—the guests a spectrum of the capital's literary, social, and diplomatic world—there were lengthy speeches of welcome, in French, Polish, and German, for 'le Maître Thomas Mann... un des plus grands citoyens de cette république des lettres pour laquelle il n'est point de frontières', 'le plus grand écrivain de l'Allemagne contemporaine et un grand Européen'.[19] In his brief reply, he stressed that Germany, like Poland, amid the tensions of the post-war world, stood as mediator between West and East: 'the dream of humanity lives on in that west–east problem, as it did once in the conflict between the Nordic north and the south of classical antiquity... Our central position borders on both east and west... and our freedom is a reservation against extreme and militant alternatives, its crowning aim the victory of the humane.' It was flattering to be entertained during the days that followed by Prince Radziwill, leader of the Conservative Party, and Count Branicki at his country seat. He was invited by the German chargé d'affaires; met Pilsudski's adjutant and was impressed to hear of the marshal's non-militarist views; visited the university library at Cracow and the German seminar of Warsaw University; and gave his formal lecture, an extract, 'Freedom and Distinction', from his 'Goethe and Tolstoy', to a crowded house. Seen off by the State Secretary for Foreign Affairs, he left with the impression, as he wrote later, of an honest respect and gratitude for a German culture 'eagerly seizing the human opportunity of maintaining its position against political difficulties and contradictions'.[20]

On his return, critics began to make themselves heard, both in the press and in letters, over his co-editorship of the 'World's Novels' series. Demeaning, thought Rudolf Binding, that an author of his standing should actually write such a foreword *for money*; the Literature Section of the Academy, in its campaign against undue foreign invasion of German letters, complained that of his first six selections none was German (this in fact still applied to the first eighteen). Mann could justly argue that suitable

---

[18] x 679 f.
[19] Hans-Ulrich Lindken (ed.), *Das magische Dreieck* ... (1992), 160, 165.
[20] xi 406 f., 133.

candidates were hard to find in Germany among those for whom the rights were free, but that some were in mind; if his search proved vain, he wrote in a public reply in May, or if the level of quality suffered, he was ready to withdraw his name. But the criticism irked, and by June he was already preparing to give up the ungrateful task, on the pretext of his distance from the co-editor in Berlin. A sunnier prospect was a filming of *Royal Highness*. The silent version in 1923 of *The Buddenbrooks* had been a disappointment, but *Royal Highness* he thought would be far better in a medium which, as he had said in a Warsaw interview, was more suited to novels than to dramas, and for which his sympathy was growing, especially after seeing the excellent Russian film of Gorky's *Mother* in Berlin. He had encouraged the writer Erich Ebermayer to prepare the script, and an exposé was ready by April, but preliminary discussions with film people from Berlin were apparently not encouraging.

On 10 May 1927, his sister Julia committed suicide—how, is no longer certain, but according to Klaus by hanging herself. Returning the day after from a week in the Rhineland and readings in Essen and Heidelberg, Thomas was deeply shaken—not so much by this loss of a near relation whose way of life had long since become antipathetic, but (as Golo over-heard him say to Katia) because this sudden death was like a bolt of lightning striking perilously close to himself. Whether or not he had felt his sister, like Goethe's Cornelia, as a 'female alter ego, not made to make a wife',[21] he was pale and drawn at the funeral, and only too glad to find his prepared speech replaced by tactful words from the pastor who had bap-tized her children. Julia's marriage in 1900 had been one of convenience, without love ('there shouldn't be too much idealism in these things,' the still-single and worldly-wise Thomas had remarked at the time to Paul Ehrenberg: 'all respect to love, but you get further without it'.)[22] To her stolid husband, fifteen years her senior, she had borne three daughters; but happiness with a series of lovers had eluded her, and there had been a growing addiction to morphine, which she had begun to take long before Löhr's death in 1922, as the only way to make his sexual demands on her tolerable.

In his will, her father the Senator had not unwisely judged her lively temperament as needing 'strict supervision' and to be held in check—an instruction which his widow, in the new life in Munich, had made little effort to follow, largely leaving her and the younger Carla to lead their own lives (and Thomas said later that Julia and Heinrich were probably the least loved of her five children). Now, despite their different ways of life, both sisters had ended in suicide: Thomas had proved no more of a support to

---

[21] ii 654.     [22] *Br.* iii, 425 f.

the elder than Heinrich had been to the younger. Their mother's loving care, he wrote later, had seemingly fitted her sons for life better than her daughters. The news of Julia's death, said Klaus in his autobiography, left him at the time fairly unmoved, he had never made much of this aunt: 'later, however, I have often thought of her with compassion'—a thought which his father would not have found surprising, for he saw much of Julia in Klaus.[23] At the funeral Heinrich remarked to Alfred Pringsheim that for his sister, 'convention incarnate', keeping up appearances had been all-important, and that had been her downfall; for Golo, writing much later, it was much more the awful contrast between her 'super-bourgeois public life and her secret existence'.[24]

That he was cold and unfeeling was a reproach often made against Thomas Mann during his life. To all appearances now, the loss of his sister in so tragic a way left him little moved; even later he gave no sign of emotion in his references to it; and the episode made no disturbance in the tenor of his existence—in vain his avowed intention, in June, of cutting down his tours as 'wandering rhapsodist' in the months to come. That he felt more deeply than he showed, however, may have been indicated by another brief escape during July, this time alone, to the mountains at Kreuth, a quiet spa south of the Tegernsee which had been one of his parents' favourites. At all events, it gave him time for reflection and to find relief in the 'fun' of completing the prologue to *Joseph*. The attack on the story proper now needed much further study: he was already seeking advice and help from the Munich Egyptologist Wilhelm Spiegelberg and from Rabbi Jakob Horowitz to elaborate the groundwork for this 'novellistic realization', which, as he wrote to the American publisher at the turn of the year, was still very much a thing of the distant future, though he thought it would be not without interest for the American reader. (Knopf, though thinking his German expression 'Jahr und Tag' meant 'a year', resigned himself with appropriate caution to a much longer time before the translator would be able to begin work.)

For their summer holiday Thomas and Katia had chosen the North Sea instead of the Baltic, and they spent four weeks in August and September with the three younger children at Kampen, on the island of Sylt in the Heligoland Bight. It was beautiful, but the climate rugged, and at the start he found himself unable even to read, let alone write. Ernst Bertram, though pressed, preferred visiting his relations to joining the Manns on Sylt in what Thomas described as its 'refreshing melancholy'—the reflection probably of yet another of those erotic experiences at a distance which recurred through his life, an attraction to a fellow guest, Klaus Heuser, the

---

[23] *Der Wendepunkt*, quoted Krüll 253.      [24] GM *Erinn.* 221.

seventeen-year-old son of a Düsseldorf professor. He took care to note their address, had the boy to stay in Munich soon after their return, and would later contrive to see him on several visits to the family in Düsseldorf.

It had been deeply moving for him, as he noted some years afterwards in his diary, to find that even at 52 he was not immune to such attraction, and to feel in it even more fulfilment than in the juvenile emotion for Armin Martens and that later for Paul Ehrenberg: by all normal standards, 'it was my last passion—and it was the happiest'.[25] On his return, as he settled to the preparation of a lecture on Kleist's comedy *Amphitryon*, to be given in Munich in October at a ceremony in commemoration of the poet's hundred and fiftieth anniversary, his introductory words were directly written with Klaus Heuser in mind:

What is loyalty? It is love without seeing, the victory over detested forgetfulness. We see a countenance which we love, and then . . . are parted from it. . . . all the pain of parting is but sorrow at the certainty that we will forget. The sensual imagination, our ability to remember, is weaker than we would like to believe. We will see no more, but never cease to love. There remains only the certainty that every new meeting . . . will once again renew . . . our love . . . love that may speak as though it were still alive, because it is sure to regain life, immediately and as by a law, once it sees its object.

It made a perfect lead-in to his treatment of *Amphitryon*—a play which he had loved, then forgotten, but now, after reading it again, proceeded to analyse anew, in the manner of the Sainte-Beuve Germany had never had. But his greatest pleasure came from this concealed avowal for Klaus Heuser, now a house-guest and among the audience in the Schauspielhaus on 10 October, as he wrote soon after to Erika and his own Klaus, who were well aware of his penchant.

The two had embarked on 6 October on their own adventure, a jaunt to see the world, beginning with America, where Klaus had an offer from the publisher of his short story 'The Fifth Child' (the *Kindernovelle*) for lectures which promised to develop into a regular tour. It was something of an escape for both: Erika from her marriage with Gründgens ('one of those queer modern unions', wrote Hedwig Pringsheim, 'where it would take the Holy Ghost itself to grant me the joys of being a great-grandmother');[26] Klaus from nagging critical attacks on his 'impotent' attempts to rival his father, and from his unsustainable engagement with Pamela Wedekind, who had anyway now firmly decided to marry Carl Sternheim. With commissions for articles, and an armful of introductions, they arrived with considerable éclat in New York, presenting themselves as 'the literary Mann

---

[25] *Tb.* ii, 185.     [26] Wiedem. 50.

twins' and acclaimed by the papers as 'full of Continental wit and sophis-tication'. Though the lecture tour as such evaporated, there were sufficient dates, journalistic advances, and hospitality to keep them going, for a visit to the west coast and back to New York. (Professor Hermann Weigand, the Thomas Mann admirer and interpreter of his work, was one to open his house to them.) Finally, thanks to artful telegraphic appeals to Germany (even including their father's publisher in Berlin, but at all costs not the parents themselves), they managed a return to California and the home-ward journey through Honolulu to Japan and China and across Soviet Russia.

Their first carefree cable home on arrival in America had roused their father to address to New York an equally light-hearted letter. Quoting the annoying remark of actor Albert Bassermann's wife—'these children, Pamela, Klaus, Erika, are sinning against the names of their fathers'—he described the 'adventure' of the other Klaus's stay and his affection for him. 'I call him *Du*, and at our goodbyes, to his express approval, held him to my heart. Eissi is required to withdraw voluntarily and not disturb my [magic] circles. I'm already old and famous, why should you be the only sinners?' Klaus Heuser had written to say with what a heavy heart he had gone home after the two weeks in Munich, the happiest of his life; and it had made something of a high point to the visit to have him hear the passages in which he had been not without influence. 'The secret and almost noiseless adventures in life are the greatest.' (With Klaus Heuser, the adventure had in reality been so secret that, neither then nor at their later brief encounters, did the young man remark anything of it. For Mann, however, it was clearly another of those experiences in which he could fancy himself a lover, in retrospect recall kisses which never took place, and feel lasting gratitude for an 'unhoped-for fulfilment' which was in fact purely imaginary.)

'May all go well for you, with no disappointments!' he had added to his own Klaus and Erika. 'We are off tomorrow to Berlin, a week only . . . and in between, readings in Stettin and Frankfurt an der Oder, because they are highly paid. This year again the remarkably obstinate rumour, started by the Swedish press, that I am to get the Nobel Prize . . .'[27] Hearing that Ferdinand Bruckner's play *Illness of Youth*, to be premièred in Berlin, which depicted the promiscuous and disillusioned life of young students, actually had Klaus by name in one of the roles, he took the trouble to protest to the author and urge him to depersonalize the text, so as not to expose his absent son to malicious laughter and pander to the sensation-seeking of the

---

[27] EM *Br. Antw.* i, 17 f.

mob. Whether this stout defence of the dynasty succeeded is not clear: the play had already been produced in Hamburg and Vienna, and Erika would appear in it with some success in Frankfurt two years later. To her and Klaus he now pooh-poohed the idea of any embarrassment from their antics over in America. At Christmas he wrote to Hofmannsthal, whose son was also visiting Hollywood, how funny it was to gain vicarious experience of the world through one's children, and disclaimed any personal longing to see America. Soon afterwards he received a financially tempting offer for an extensive lecture-tour there for 1929, but in the end found his commitments in Europe were too great. It would be some years yet before he made the crossing for the first time, under very different circumstances.

The weeks he had spent on the *Amphitryon* lecture, an 'absorption in love', had not been wasted, he wrote later, for there were 'all kinds of subterranean connections' with the *Joseph*, and 'love is never uneconomic'. There too myth and reality were closely interwoven, and in the apparently separate compartments of his work there was nevertheless a certain continuity, even though the main thrust might seem to suffer. His studies, the consultations with Egyptologist and Rabbi, continued between the usual lecture commitments; and asked by an Austrian interviewer in December whether this was turning him into an orientalist, he conceded with some amusement that Professor Spiegelberg thought he had the makings of one. 'And yet you find the time to give lectures in many German cities, even in Paris!' marvelled the journalist.[28] He had given a reading of the Joseph prologue early in November in Munich, somewhat embarrassed to find Spiegelberg in the audience, and there had been an extensive tour covering Karlsruhe, Wiesbaden, Aachen, Krefeld—and Düsseldorf, where he had the opportunity of seeing Klaus Heuser again.

He found time too for political questions. The December interview not only ranged widely over his work and plans, but was a chance to stress that his Paris journey had been in the interest of European understanding; Coudenhove-Kalergi's 'Paneuropa' idea attracted him, though he felt it a mistake to exclude Russia and England; and he was strongly in favour of a union between Germany and Austria, which he saw as a natural and necessary development. Replying in December to the question 'Should Germany pursue a colonial policy?', he argued that imperialist colonialism was a thing of the past, self-determination was now everywhere the watchword, and Europe could no longer decently present itself as a bringer of blessings in the process of enriching itself. Germany should, however, insist on equality of opportunity to draw her raw materials from foreign colonies and mandated territories. And in the essay 'Culture and

[28] *Fr./Antw.* 119.

Socialism', written at the turn of the year and published in the *Prussian Yearbooks* in 1928, he defined the problem for Germany: was the social idea, in his country's traditional and conservative spirit, to be interpreted in a cultural or a political sense? There should be a fusion of the socialist idea of society with the more conservative idea of German culture, the 'pact between Greece and Moscow', a meeting of minds between Marx and Hölderlin.

In January 1928, in an interview with Louis Durieux (the son of the French consul-general in Munich), he pursued his theme of Franco-German *rapprochement*, the two Continental powers whose concerns were remote from England's splendid isolation and tended in the same direction. Stressing the anti-chauvinistic trend among young authors in Germany, like Arnold Zweig and Fritz von Unruh, he remarked on the attraction for German readers in the analytical thought and psychological sensibility of the work of Valéry and of Gide, whose *Faux-monnayeurs* he characterized as one of his favourite books. This drew a virulent attack in the *Berliner Nachtausgabe* of 6 February (the anonymous author apparently thinking Mann had paid another visit to Paris), with banner headlines: 'Thomas Mann's Kowtow to Paris—The Advocate of Traitors to the Fatherland and Slanderer of his people.' He was justifiably furious, and replied at once with an open letter to the *Literarische Welt*, in a closely argued polemic against the 'hollow, unproven, worthless, hired patriotism of party and street' from people who 'have never done other than bring shame to their country, have driven it to its ruin, and if allowed would do the same tomorrow';[29] but the hostile refrain was later taken up by others from the right-wing press, notably the Nazi *Völkischer Beobachter*.

A somewhat different controversy was stirred up that summer by a Munich journalist's mordant critique of his change of stance in the abbreviated post-war edition of the *Reflections*. After increasingly sharp letters had been exchanged, and published, in which Mann ascribed the hostility to his refusal to collaborate with the journal, and made clear his antipathy for its politics, a pamphlet appeared with the whole polemic—including unauthorized publication of other letters of his, in one of which he had incautiously made a disparaging remark on the overblown Munich reception for the first aviators to fly the Atlantic east to west. Taken up also in Berlin, and with his threats of legal action, the affair led to rumours that he intended, in disgust, to move away from Munich. In the autumn, the Heidelberg city authorities did in fact invite him to make his new home there, but he declined the 'honour', saying that Munich was more sensible than its press. Interviewed in December, he categorically denied any ru-

[29]  xi 767.

mour of a move: he had no thought whatever of yielding to the pressures of 'a certain clique' and letting himself be driven from the marvellously beautiful city where he had made his home. All the same, the 'organized bestiality' of its press and the demonstration of the impotence of 'reason and goodwill against obstinacy and hatred' had left him depressed.[30]

There were to be many similar assaults on his position over the years to come. But for the moment the sedate, almost statesmanlike career of this 'sincere and winning man of the world, professor and doctor *honoris causa*',[31] as one interviewer found him, proceeded from success to success, even though no major work had seen the light for four years. In January, at a Berlin meeting of the Literature Section of the Academy welcoming new members, his colleagues had been eager to have a reading from him (and accepted his characteristic proposal that the occasion should be given a 'noble' and ceremonious air, with evening dress and refreshments). During the year, *The Magic Mountain* marked its 100,000, in an elegant limited edition, full leather, with a portrait by Olaf Gulbransson, and all the narrative works were reissued in a three-volume thin-paper production. By his journalism his name was constantly before the public, while through interviews the whole world knew of his ideas for the *Joseph*, though his remarks were still general thoughts rather than a firm outline of his plan; and interest was maintained by the publication of the prologue in the December 1927 number of the *Rundschau*. Both he and Fischer had every reason to be satisfied with the finances of their association, and he could afford to continue the work at the same leisurely pace. (If he was regarded by many as a bad German, as he said, he was certainly very German in his andante tempo.)[32]

Even his rounds with readings (now exclusively from the early chapters of the *Joseph*) could be rather more spaced, and it was only after a long April car-tour with Katia through Switzerland and the south of France that he began again, appearing in May in Frankfurt, Cologne, and Düsseldorf, while the next major circuit, to Vienna and Switzerland, would not be until the autumn. A new, more luxurious automobile was bought in June, and in August came their month's holiday, once again at the North Sea on Sylt. Before leaving for Vienna, he was invited (who could be surprised at the choice?) to give the celebratory address on 1 October at the centenary of the Reclam publishing house in Leipzig. To his introductory words he lent a personal note by recalling the earlier centenary of another business-house, at which he had stood, a silent and uncertain fourteen-year-old, watching the celebration of his father's firm in Lübeck. At the lectern

---

[30] *Fr./Antw.* 141; 28/120.    [31] *Fr./Antw.* 134.    [32] 28/86.

now, in elegant cravat and frock-coat every inch the statesman of literature, he traced the 'peculiar threads of fate' linking for him that anniversary of trade with the present one of culture: his family novel, after two generations a German classic, perhaps one day to find its way into the admirable conspectus of world literature in the little paperbacks of the 'Reclam Universal Library'.

For his readings from the *Joseph* in early November in Vienna, Basle, and Lucerne, and on a December tour of the Rhineland, Hamburg and Lübeck, Magdeburg and Berlin, he prepared a short introduction, explaining his aim of retelling the story as it had, or might have, actually happened. Rachel's handsome first-born, though situated in time around 1400 BC, during the reign in Egypt of Amenhotep III and IV, was nevertheless to feel himself actually the great-grandson of the Abraham who had lived 800 years earlier, in the time of Hammurabi the lawgiver. It posed a 'diverting difficulty', he said, to tell of people 'who do not know exactly who they are'—people whose consciousness was based much less on a clear distinction of their existence here and now, between past and future, 'than on their identity with a mythical type'. Thus his theme was 'myth as the timeless ever-present', the idea of repetition, 'an obedient succession on well-worn mythical paths'; and he had begun with the story of the forefathers—told not chronologically but in the associative folk-memories recalled by father Jacob, who combined piety with a touch of divine cunning, while his favourite son would later bring off the dazzling confidence-trick of adapting his personality and his Hebrew monotheism to the Tammuz–Osiris pattern of Pharaoh Echnaton's religion. It was the fullest public exposé he had yet given of the project, still barely begun, which would extend over many years and end as a tetralogy appearing volume by volume, of which *The Tales of Jacob* formed only the first—not a novel in the usual sense, but an 'unfashionably long-winded work' requiring an 'obstinate patience'. The learning he had accumulated, in his desire for exactitude, was worn reasonably lightly, and he contrived to avoid what he called to his listeners the 'archaeological brocade' so seductive to writers of historical novels.[33] A further extract from *The Tales of Jacob*, which appeared in the *Rundschau* for January 1929, now exhausted the possibilities of such previews, and his readers too would need much patience as they awaited the sequel. But the apparent welcome for these published foretastes allayed any fears that the German public might not be inclined to breathe, in Goethe's words, 'the air of the patriarchs', and encouraged him to continue.[34]

---

[33] xi 626 ff.    [34] 28/190.

3

*'Humanism is humiliated or dead. Consequence: we must establish
it anew'*                                        (TM, 26 June 1930)

Though he hardly foresaw how long in fact it would take him to complete
the *Joseph*, Mann was not inclined to undertake any longer work to interrupt it, even when earlier ideas were recalled. Thus, in Berlin in December
1928, when Fischer asked him to consider a biography of Erasmus, and
together with Stefan Zweig to undertake the general editorship of a series
of which this would be part, he did no more than take serious note for later,
in spite of his abiding interest in Reformation themes. (It may have been
the idea of such a collaboration which did not appeal: though always
personally polite towards Zweig, and esteeming his humanism, he was not
one of the many admirers of his work, and was perhaps even jealous of a
phenomenal productivity achieving a success which rivalled his own.)
Other diversions from the main task continued, however, some ephemeral,
but some more demanding. During a few days' retreat to Ettal early in
January 1929, he settled to the completion of a speech for the bicentennial
Lessing celebration in the Academy in February—and on his return to
Munich, with careful economy, used much of what had had to be omitted
from the overlong text for a short article in the *Berliner Tageblatt*, journal
of the anti-idealistic, *völkisch* tendency he detested, on the eighteenth-
century rationalist's true significance for today. Two months later, after a
spell at the *Joseph*, he was busy on an essay on Freud, to be given as a
lecture to the Munich Democratic Students' Club in May: 'Freud's position
in Modern Intellectual History'.

In these various expositions, he was pursuing in effect a political line,
developing from the given literary and intellectual themes the necessity for
a rational and democratic approach to the new humanism he sought to
encourage. To the Academy in Berlin he presented Lessing's historic and
seemingly outmoded enlightenment as vital for modern times, to counter
the anti-idealism current in morality and politics: 'In Lessing's spirit and
name, it is time to transcend every kind of fascism, and achieve that union
of reason and blood which alone could deserve the name of full humanity.'
His belief in humanity and its 'coming time of manhood', he argued—
against the expected hostility of the *Berliner Tageblatt*'s readers—could be
called 'odious optimism', but today 'there reigns only an odious pessimism,
at least in politics, the determining factor of the epoch'. The main purpose
of his Freud lecture, he wrote to Charles Du Bos, was to highlight psychoanalysis as the only phenomenon of modern anti-rationalism which did not
lend itself to reactionary misuse. (Freud, 'as one of your oldest readers',
sent him his thanks for this defence against any reproach of reactionary

mysticism, and especially for placing him in the context of German thought, 'I who had imagined I was a foreign body for that nation.')[35] To a correspondent in May, he confirmed his aversion to the 'modish prostration before the irrational which, in political terms, reveals itself as "*völkisch* soul".' Far from any desire to sow confusion, he said that autumn, his political utterances were simply a record of his own personal development, with no claim to set a trend or seek a following, but in the conviction that it had a certain 'representative' sense in the national context.[36] In the deepening rift between Left and Right in the Weimar Republic, however, his sympathy for the Left was clear, as he did not hesitate to confirm in a message to the socialist *Reichsbanner* for the tenth anniversary of the constitution in August, describing the progress of his ideas from a romantic concept of community to that of a socialist form of society.

Between whiles he had been able to add to the manuscript of the *Joseph*, but the pile mounted only slowly, and by the end of May a certain fatigue had set in. He reluctantly refused an invitation from the Vienna PEN Club, and settled on a three-week cure with Katia at Bad Gastein in June in order to be fit for the next public commitment—the opening speech at the Heidelberg Festival, where both he and Hauptmann were to be honoured. Golo was now a student there, and he hoped also to see Erika, for whom he tried to obtain a Festival role. She was in Munich at the moment, enjoying the role of the queen in Schiller's *Don Carlos*, and it was to her he wrote on his birthday with his thanks to all the children for their wishes: 'The inquisitive spa-crowd on the promenade is killing me, and the whole thing is constricting. But the waters are definitely effective, for they make me remarkably tired and sleepy, so we can hope for the best. . . . No question of work, letter-writing uses up all the morning hours I might spend on it. But I am reading a lot . . .' They had already decided, once the Heidelberg assignment was over on 20 July, to take their summer holiday at the resort of Rauschen, near Königsberg (the later Kaliningrad) in East Prussia, where the Goethe Society had several times asked for his visit and was ready to arrange their rooms; and while he might complain of the Gastein crowd's attentions, he was quite prepared to make the plan public when the local paper asked him for a contribution to their supplement extolling the attractions of the area. To see East Prussia for the first time would fill a gap in his education, he wrote, and his visit would be something of a demonstration against the prejudices of those who regarded it as a backwater, to which the vital flow of German life only trickled.[37]

They spent most of August at Rauschen, with Elisabeth and Michael, and the stay was all he had hoped for. It was not practical to take the materials

---

[35] *DüD.* ii, 361.    [36] 29/73; 29/174.    [37] 26/86 Korr.

for *Joseph* and the already cumbersome manuscript along, but, since a holiday without work was inconceivable, the mornings on the beach, with the children playing on the sand, were spent in drawing up for Fischer suggestions for a further collection of his essays and shorter pieces, and in sketching out a new novella, *Mario and the Magician*, the idea for which went back to their stay three summers earlier in Forte dei Marmi. Like *Death in Venice*, the story was entirely based on fact: they had stayed in such a hotel and had actually witnessed the 'magician's' performance of conjuring and hypnotism, but the tragic outcome must be credited to Erika, who, when she first heard the tale, had been amazed that the disgusting charlatan had not been shot. The experience of the sinister and unsettling atmosphere of fascist Italy found full expression, and the theme has figured in a number of operatic productions in recent times. Although, as Mann said later, it would be going too far to see in the figure of Cipolla simply a Mussolini in disguise, he was clear on the ethical lesson he had tried to draw: a warning against human degradation and the willing submission to the power of dictators and 'leaders' disturbingly on the increase in Europe.[38] It is tempting to read into the magician's mysteriously deformed appearance and his hypnotic power of mass suggestion, as one critic with hindsight has done, a satanic combination of Adolf Hitler and Joseph Goebbels: that much was scarcely in the author's mind at the time, but he certainly regarded the work as his 'first act of war' against the fascist trend.[39]

Nazi influence would soon be sharply to the fore in East Prussia, but for the moment the presence of Thomas Mann was warmly welcomed in Königsberg; and before he left he gave a reading from *Joseph* to the Goethe Society. The high point of the stay, however, was a visit to the nearby Memel area, ceded by Russia under Brest-Litovsk but since taken over by Lithuania. On a brief stay in Nidden (Nida), they were fascinated by the fantastic world of the 'Kurische Nehrung', the strip of land between the sweet-water lake of the Haff and the rolling Baltic open as far as Sweden: a country of sand-dunes reminiscent of the Sahara, but with pine and birch woods sheltering a colony of elks, placid monsters which the children soon learned to approach. The friendly fisher-folk, speaking a German strongly influenced by Slavonic and Lithuanian, and the unusual attractions of land and sea here, awakened once more Thomas Mann's urge to build, and the first steps to acquire some land were taken on the spot. After their return, Katia pursued the project with characteristic energy, and all was arranged by correspondence: a 99-year lease on 'Mother-in-law's Hill' and a contract with an architect's firm to build and fit out a simple wooden

---

[38] 41/233.    [39] Jürgen Kolbe, 1987; 47/158.

holiday-house in the local style, with reed-thatched roof, the traditional crossed horses' heads on the gable, and brown-wood furniture. Finance was more than assured by a new popular edition of *The Buddenbrooks*, from which Fischer promised him 125,000 marks in instalments between October and the following July. The house comprised only bedrooms, living-dining area, and verandah, but had, of course, a small separate first-floor study for the master. When the time came for their 1930 vacation, all was ready, and for three years the Thomas Mann house, or 'Uncle Tom's Cabin', as some locals dubbed it—the first visitor's home to be built in the area—was to make their summer retreat. Katia said later that it was his first exposure to the primitive life: but contemporary photographs indicate a fair measure of comfort, and he was not entirely ironic in referring to it as his 'country seat'.[40]

Resuming work on the *Joseph* in the autumn, he resisted as far as he could other claims on his time, and declined to visit Erlangen to receive the Platen Society medal: 'one thing follows another, the months and years go by, and one has the worrying feeling, through pure weakness and indulgence of the world's demands, of never getting down to one's real work'.[41] But on 12 November 1929 came word from Stockholm of a call on his time that could not be refused: the award of the Nobel Prize for literature, the first to a German author since Hauptmann's in 1912. Though this did not find him unprepared, in view of his frequent mention as a candidate, and his feeling that it must one day come to him, he had never pushed his own name forward in the many discussions of recent years. His only surprise was that the award singled out *The Buddenbrooks* as his achievement, 'ever more firmly recognized over the years as one of present-day literature's classics', rather than his work as a whole, and particularly his progress to *The Magic Mountain*, which he felt should surely have also been taken into account.

To some voices criticizing the selection in place of the naturalist playwright Arno Holz, who had just died, he was firm in asserting his own prior claim to the distinction, and in refusing any direct aid now for Holz's widow. The money was not designed for welfare purposes, he said, but for the material support of the writer, especially when engaged through years of no income 'on a great work without practical prospects, as I am now, and to free me from worry for myself and my family'.[42] Such Pharisaism, from one whose income now had rarely been better and who could safely count on the practical prospects of the current 'great work', however long it took to complete, is disappointing to note. He did promise to contribute to support-funds for needy writers, a route by which Frau Holz might be

[40] 30/124.      [41] 29/164.      [42] 29/193.

helped: how far the promise was fulfilled is not recorded. To judge by his autobiographical sketch, written soon afterwards, not far: he was faced with the choice—so ran the disingenuous plea there—of playing 'either the hard-hearted disciple of Mammon or the weakminded idiot who throws away money intended for other purposes'. There seems no doubt that the cash inflow of some 200,000 marks for the most part found personal use, apart from a few donations and the settlement of the pressing debts of Erika and Klaus. Heinrich's congratulatory broadcast was perhaps not without a note of envy: 'the Nobel Prize . . . puts an anyway successful writer among the wealthy. That is as it should be. . . . Literature remains, as always, a power; and since power understandably finds expression in money, so money falls to it.'[43]

The news of the award brought him an enormous mail, and in replies later to many of the congratulatory letters, if he felt his printed card of thanks inadequate, he adopted a deprecatory tone: 'I'm not the man to let something like Stockholm go to my head! . . . the absurd risk of vanity could come only with retirement. Work keeps one modest.' But the dozens of interviews for the German and the world press and the celebratory evenings which followed were not unwelcome. He had to appear twice in Munich, and to a reading-tour already planned in the Rhineland at the end of November was added a ceremony in Bonn University's auditorium maximum, where the floor threatened to collapse under the students' enthusiastic stamping. The few weeks before he set off with Katia in December for Stockholm were thus heavily occupied, and it was to be almost Christmas Eve before they could reach safe haven again in Munich.

Arriving in the Swedish capital on 9 December, they were received by representatives of the Swedish Academy, the German Society, and the German-Swedish Union, and after a press conference and a reception at the German embassy he gave a reading at the Union from *The Buddenbrooks* and *Joseph*. The ceremonial presentation by King Gustav Adolf V on 10 December, where he was in company with the other prize-winners, including Louis de Broglie (physics) and Sir Frederic Hopkins (medicine), was followed by the traditional banquet in the Konserthus. In his brief speech he expressed due modesty in the face of the overwhelmingly dramatic effect of the occasion on the normally placid existence of the narrative writer, and sought to see in the honour which had fallen 'more or less by chance' to his name a tribute, renewed after long years, to the spirit of Germany and the German people: 'You can scarcely imagine the receptive sensibility of such a sign of world sympathy for this injured and much misunderstood people.' Germany, despite the unfavourable conditions of

---

[43] Quoted Krüll 325.

the past fifteen years, had held to a European point of honour: politically, by avoiding anarchy, and intellectually, by combining the Eastern principle of suffering with the Western principle of form in her artistic production. The following day there was a lunch at the Rotary Club, and dinner given by the King, at which previous prize-winners, including Selma Lagerlöf, were also present; on 12 December he gave a further reading in the German-Swedish Union. More invitations awaited him in Copenhagen, with a speech in his honour by the German ambassador Ulrich von Hassell (to be executed in 1944 for his part in the July plot against Hitler), then in Berlin, where there was a reception by the PEN Club and he gave a short broadcast, before the final return to Munich.

Interviewed in Hamburg, he had described as his most welcome impression in Sweden a regard and sympathetic understanding for Germany which was now even more evident than during the war, and it was natural that in his speech he should have struck the patriotic note he would have avoided at home. As his Mario novella would show, he made no secret of his antipathy for the fascism of Italy, and was firmly against any similar regime for Germany. Certainly, Europe's diversity made generalization inadvisable, and the road to the unity of the Continent would be long and complicated; but he was optimistic for the future. His New Year's message to a Hamburg paper deplored the foreign therapies constantly commended for the treatment of the 'German psyche'—'fascism and Americanism . . . are both equally impossible, equally useless, both can be preached only by people who have no idea of Germany and of Europe's spiritual condition'—and he put his hopes on the younger generation.[44]

The events of the year to come were not to justify even this qualified optimism. The advent in February of a National Socialist regime in Thuringia, under the subsequently notorious Wilhelm Frick, he could not let pass unremarked: but in an open letter still expressed the hope that this was a transient episode only. In January he spent ten days in Ettal, occupied with the brief curriculum vitae asked for by the Nobel Committee, but also preparing a fuller 'Sketch of my Life' for publication in Germany—a premature and provisional account only, he wrote after its appearance in the *Rundschau* for June, for he had in mind one day to write a full autobiography. 1930, as he could not resist mentioning, was another of those round numbers in his career, this time marking his silver wedding, and he concluded the sketch with a graceful tribute to Katia, through 'this difficult life, demanding much patience, but fragile and an easy prey to fatigue, which I would not have known how to sustain without the sensible, brave, and tenderly energetic support of my extraordinary companion'. When the

---

[44] N 29/17.

day came on 11 February, and the Pringsheims gave an opulent dinner for the family in Arcis Strasse, Viktor recalled to everyone's enjoyment his brother's speech at the wedding—the shortest ever heard from him.

Worries over the political situation in Germany, with steeply rising unemployment and sharpening right–left controversy, and the world economic crisis since the New York stock-market crash in October 1929, could soon be left behind for a while. The closing words of the autobiographical sketch mentioned preparations for 'a journey which will take me to the sites of my new novel, to Egypt and Palestine. There I hope to find the heavens and much of mankind unchanged after 3,500 years.' This second, two-month 'inspection tour'—'the longest and most significant journey of my life'—was doubtless expensive, but undeniably in the interest of 'the great work' and so in his view a justifiable use for the prize money. It began on 14 February, taking them via Genoa to Alexandria and Cairo, then by steamer up the Nile as far as Aswan and Nubia. They revisited Luxor on the way back to Cairo, and then made their way to Palestine; but a severe amoebic dysentery Katia caught in Cairo, to which he too then succumbed, restricted them largely to Jerusalem, though he was able to visit one of the nearby kibbutzim and make a sortie to Tel-Aviv. Much of their time was spent perforce in the German hospital in Jerusalem, and though, under the good care of an Arab doctor, they were sufficiently restored to take ship from Haifa for Trieste early in April, Katia continued to suffer until June.

In spite of this set-back, Mann had found the visual impressions of the scenes of his story, so little changed after three and a half millennia, of inestimable value for the background he needed. But he was alive too to the modern situation of Palestine and the immense achievements of the Jewish settlers. In an interview for the *Palestine Bulletin* he spoke freely of his sympathy for the Zionist movement, though careful to stress the need for tolerance towards the indigenous Arabs, whose historical links and rights to the land must not be neglected. If the hot-headed impatience of the Zionist vision could be restrained, there should be nothing to prevent coexistence in friendship. In its aims and ideals it seemed to him similar to the nineteenth-century romantic movement in Germany, stimulated by the same desire for self-liberation. Later, however, he averred that Zionism could not be the overall solution to the problem of the '16 million Jews' of the world (now an increasingly burning issue, as anti-Semitism in Germany grew in stridency): Jews in Europe and America should be able happily to remain well-assimilated citizens of their countries while fully retaining their traditional beliefs.[45]

---

[45] Letter of 22 Aug. 1930 (photocopy in Thomas Mann Collection, University Library, Düsseldorf).

News of the completion of the house in Nidden awaited them on return, and they began plans for a long summer vacation there. The political outlook in Germany was far from bright. Brüning, with President Hindenburg's support appointed Chancellor in March, had taken the line that the only answer to the problems of the depression, unemployment, and the sharpening political divisions was fiscal reform, pushed through, if necessary, by emergency decree; when the Reichstag resisted, it was dissolved in July, new elections being fixed for 14 September, and the financial programme was put into effect under presidential authority. With the best of intentions, Brüning thereby opened the first breach in the Weimar constitution, preparing the way for more ruthless men who would soon shove him aside and complete the destruction of democratic government in Germany.

It is not likely that Thomas Mann appreciated such a prospect during the summer, but he was certainly greatly disturbed by the growing political polarization. In June, in an interview with Manfred George of the *Neue Leipziger Zeitung*, the journalist instanced his recent experience of Oberammergau and Mann's of the Zionist experiment as examples of a world impregnated with 'beliefs and credulous faiths' of all kinds, and cited the two great political movements of fascism and communism as equally founded on mass belief. Mann, however, roundly denounced these as mere surrogates for a true faith. Neither offered a meaning for life, and were not likely to endure, though communism had played a part in awakening mankind's social conscience: 'I am against every one-sided movement, because of my need for balance.'[46] In July he was ready to lend his name publicly to a campaign in a Vienna paper against racist theory (which in the so-called Aryan doctrine was a major demagogic plank in the Nazi programme). But his chief preoccupation was the moral rather than the political aspect: the need for that synthesis of intellect and life which alone could be creative, as he remarked in the interview, at the risk of being called an old-fashioned nineteenth-century liberal. In a letter in May, he said art today was 'in the hands of malevolent philistines and militarists, who when they say "soul" mean gas warfare and are greatly vexed when we do not fall into the trap of this confusion'.[47]

It was a sentence he was to use later verbatim in a talk to the Rotary Club in The Hague on the writer's position—the very day before the new Reichstag elections, for which it had little relevance. The election campaign was marked by considerable violence, particularly at the big Nazi and communist meetings and in the conflicting demonstrations, and resulted in a major advance for the Nazis, who polled over 6 million votes, eight times

[46] *Fr./Antw.* 163 f.     [47] *Br.* i, 301.

their 1928 level. But Mann still put his hopes in the commonsense of the German people, and looked on this now powerful National Socialist German Workers' Party as 'a colossus with feet of clay'. Bertram, venturing to call on him soon afterwards, was dismayed by his fulminations against Hitler, the Führer of a movement for 'Reich, power, and freedom', in which he (Bertram) thought to see the realization of Stefan George's aesthetic ideals. Mann had just returned from the lecture in The Hague and a reading in Geneva from *Joseph* while the League of Nations was meeting, and in an interview for the *Schweizer Illustrierte* had underlined the obligation on the artist and writer to help stem the tide of unreason: he must not stand aside in silence when the world was trying to solve the greatest of all problems— how to keep man from being his fellow man's worst enemy. Bertram wondered what George would make of that. He himself, already seduced by the promise of the Nazi movement, and with no eyes for its brutality and nihilism, was clearly now set on a political path fundamentally opposed to Thomas Mann's, though their friendly relationship continued.

During August, in his retreat with the family at Nidden, Mann had seen nothing of the election campaign. He had taken the *Joseph* manuscript with him, resisted invitations, and worked steadily through the mornings; the rest of the day was devoted to Elisabeth and Michael, reading and sometimes painting for them and taking them rowing on the Haff by moonlight. The house was everything they had hoped for, and its compara- tive isolation from the village well chosen, for Nidden had become a popular resort for Berliners, copies of *The Buddenbrooks* were stacked in the bookshop, and the local children eagerly offered photographs of Thomas Mann for sale along with their baskets of berries or fish: it was as well to be at a distance from the curious and avoid offering them photo-opportunities in bathing-costume or nautical rig of cap and blazer. They celebrated Alfred Pringsheim's eightieth birthday there, with a firework display rarely seen in those parts, and the old man hugely enjoyed a climb over the dunes. With them too for part of the time was Hans Reisiger, the writer, nine years younger than Thomas and a friend since just after his marriage. 'Reisi' was a favourite with all the children, sporty, a great teller of tales, a thoroughly outgoing and natural companion, without the usual grown-up's conde- scension. Though an industrious worker, notably on translations from the English, he had more than a touch of the bohemian, and it was this which may have appealed to their father, for whom, as Golo noted, he became a sort of court jester. 'Papa is always so gay with Mr Reisiger,' said Elisabeth. He was at any rate one of the few friends with whom he seemed really to relax, and now and later was always a welcome guest.

It was a mercy that the month in Nidden could bring good progress on the main work, for the rest of the year was fully occupied with other things.

By October, between the excursions to The Hague and Geneva, he could write 'finis' to *The Tales of Jacob*, and the new volume of essays (*Demands of the Day*, with his speeches and essays of the past five years) had been published. It was more than time then to raise his voice once more on the political scene as the new Reichstag opened in Berlin, amid scenes of unprecedented violence, the Nazis demonstrating their street power and breaking up Jewish-owned department stores. On 17 October, in the Beethovensaal in Berlin, he rose to give what he called a 'German Address: A Call to Reason'—a warning against the danger of National Socialism and a call for a union of conservative and social democratic forces against it. His presence had been the signal for the Nazis to pack the hall with their supporters, organized by Arnolt Bronnen, who concealed himself behind dark glasses, and as his speech progressed it was more and more difficult to make himself heard above the heckling and catcalls. He continued man-fully, and Erika and Klaus, who were present, were proud of his courage; but he was finally obliged to bring his drowned-out remarks to an accelerando close (much to the relief of Fischer's wife, in the front row, who had whispered 'Stop as soon as possible!'). The angry words of his opponents threatened to lead to blows when he left the platform, but Bruno Walter and his wife were able to smuggle him from the ante-room through to the neighbouring Philharmonic Hall and out by a side exit, where Walter had prudently left his car.

'Nazis as a party I hold to be a mischief which will soon pass,' he said in an interview three days later: they were distinguished from the fascists of Italy by their utter lack of intellectuality. 'I cannot stand Mussolini either, but he is a demigod compared with Herr Hitler. At least he knows some-thing of the world.'[48] Non-party himself, his faith was in the democratic Republic: for that reason he had urged co-operation between freedom-loving conservatives and the social democrats, and welcomed the re-elec-tion of a socialist President of the Reichstag. It was his firm conviction that for the foreseeable future the German people were far too sensible to admit of political anarchy. Though he would allow, much later, that at that time a conservative-socialist alliance could have been no more than an empty dream, he still had no regrets over his attempt to bring it into being; and in fact this was his first direct intervention in the world of active politics. Heinrich apparently drafted a manifesto for such an alliance, but neither he nor Thomas, who tried in vain to enlist Hauptmann in the cause against the 'shame of Nazi mob rule', could register any success. At this point, Thomas was ready to welcome any support against Nazism, even from the Catholic Church, or from communism, 'which after all is somehow on the intellec-

[48] *Fr./Antw.* 173.

tual search for justice and happiness'. (For some years a member of the society of 'Friends of the New Russia', he told Ida Herz, he had been receiving interesting material on a country 'about whose great social experiment one can never know too much, whether or not one is in sympathy with communism'.)[49]

At the end of November came a highly attractive proposal from the publisher Droemer: a commission for a book on Goethe, in time for the centenary in 1932, in an edition of one million, for which he would receive 200,000 marks, half on signature of contract and half on delivery of manuscript. Informing Fischer, as he was obliged to do, he confessed it somehow went against his nature to write to order for a specific deadline of this kind. There were, however, good arguments in favour. An extensive work on Goethe certainly belonged in his 'inner programme', however much it might set back the *Joseph*, and he never allowed such longer diversions to prevent him from holding 'tooth and nail' to his main objective; it might also be that the public would receive such a book next year more favourably than the first volume of the *Joseph* (a delicate reference to the anti-Semitism now rampant); finally, it seemed the translation rights would fall to him, and he might secure better terms for an English version than from Knopf's standing contract with Fischer. In short, he was more than half inclined to do it, and sought from Fischer either his consent or an alternative proposal in similar terms from his side. The latter, understandably, proved the case, and Gottfried Bermann, Fischer's son-in-law, who was now in the process of taking over the management from the old man, drafted a detailed contract with much the same offer. Droemer was obliged to look elsewhere; the prospect, however, of a long interruption in the *Joseph* production, only to have two similar works competing then in the centenary year, reawakened Mann's reluctance; and in the end neither publisher carried out the project. It was a remarkable illustration, however, of the sums he was in a position to expect for his work at this time, and of his (and Katia's) sharp attention to financial advantage.

Progress towards the development of the Literature Section of the Prussian Academy into a national 'Academy', on the lines of the French, had been anything but promising in the four years since the founding of the Literature Section in Berlin. Behind the public discussion there had been internal dissension, often merely over trivial procedural questions, notably on whether those elected should be entitled or even required to add 'Member of the Academy' to their names. But as 1930 drew to a close, a deeper division became increasingly clear, not only between those for and against the national as opposed to the Prussian concept, but also between right and left in the political sense. In November, Hermann Hesse an-

---

[49] 30/165, 30/179.

nounced his resignation, feeling, as he said, that 'when the next war came' such an academy was likely to provide many of the prominent people whose lies on behalf of the state would once more mislead the people, as in 1914. At special meetings during December the Berlin members (Döblin, Walter von Molo, Oskar Loerke, and others) secured a majority vote, including those of Thomas and Heinrich Mann, for a motion to suspend the original statutes and start again, resulting in the resignation in January of the more right-wing members Wilhelm Schäfer, Erwin Kolbenheyer, and Emil Strauss. Thomas Mann held definite views on the future role of the Literature Section, and was prepared to spend time on letters about it to those concerned, but not to the point of interrupting his plans for work— or for a winter holiday with Katia in St. Moritz; the extraordinary general meeting held in Berlin on 27 January, at which his brother, who had now moved to the capital, was elected chairman, had to proceed without him. He was encouraged by the communiqué then issued, but the following months of intrigue and endless discussion on the revised statutes were disappointing: the darkening political horizon in Germany made him feel the matter was becoming academic indeed, though he continued to be active as far as possible and later in the year attempted, without success, to persuade Hesse to withdraw his resignation.

He resisted interruptions, where he could, to the already less than steady application to the *Joseph* task. To an invitation in March to appear at a function for Freud, he pleaded inescapable commitments elsewhere and the need at his age to husband his resources, taking comfort, however, in the knowledge that he had already had the opportunity of a public tribute to that 'great scholar'.[50] The commitments were another visit to Paris, for the launch in May of the French edition of *The Magic Mountain*, and before that Berlin at the end of March, for Heinrich's sixtieth birthday, to be marked by the usual speeches at a celebration in the Academy. Though with his brother there was now a certain solidarity in matters political, their personal relationship was still no more than the 'decent, human *modus vivendi*' he had foreseen at the time of their reconciliation in 1922. It was clear, from his review in December 1930 of the latest novel, that strong reservations concerning Heinrich's artistic worth persisted: ending the review with the word 'genius' did not abate his forthright criticism of the breathless tempo and jargon-ridden style that, for him, had as little appeal as in the earlier works.

There was nothing of this, of course, in his *laudatio* on the great occasion in Berlin. His speech there became, as might be expected, an essay for separate publication, which he could entitle 'The German Writer's Profession in our Times'. Combining the personal with the general, recalling

[50] Letter of 19 Mar. 1931, addressee unknown (in private ownership).

their childhood amid Lübeck's 'Gothic with a touch of Latinity', and the fulfilment since of their early literary ambitions, each now covered with honours, his concern was to counter the anti-humanism of incipient fascism by stressing the essentially Germanic quality of his brother's contribution to literature, as a 'classical representative of German-Mediterranean artistry'. 'Un-German? oh yes, the Gallic cultural element colouring the timbre of your work is un-German ... un-German for those who would exclude once and for all as unbecoming to the notion of the German ... clarity, brio ... critical spirit, colourfulness, sensual spirituality, psychological instinct, artistic delicatesse.' That should be a reason for satisfaction and cause for pride, not regarded as national treachery: 'the question of what ... can be German, and the place your work will take in German cultural history, will not be decided by those who today presume to administer the by no means simple concept of what is German'. It was a handsome tribute, recalling too Heinrich's earlier triumphs, such as his enthusiastic welcome in Paris as the representative of Germany at the Victor Hugo commemoration.

In describing the 'European-German-Latin synthesis' typified in his brother's work, he was taking a similar line to that of his earlier talk in The Hague—the writer's task to offer the alternative of reason and intellectual honesty to the barbarism of Nazism and other fascist movements in Europe—and on his way to Paris in May he repeated that speech in the Conservatoire in Strasburg. The stay in Paris, where he gave an extract from the Goethe and Tolstoy essay and the Freud lecture, and talks after his return to republican students in Erlangen and Nuremberg, seemed to encourage faith in the success of such an idealistic approach. He met André Gide for the first time in Paris, and when Gide visited Munich in July was impressed by his 'astonishing understanding' for the aims of the *Joseph*. The encounter then with other literary notables in Geneva (Paul Valéry, Gilbert Murray, Karel Čapek, Salvador de Madariaga among them), at a session of the League of Nations Commission for Literature and the Arts, gave heartening sign of a truly Europe-wide humanism.

The home front, however, showed a different and more disturbing face. The establishment in Munich of a Council for World Peace, in which the Manns' neighbour Constance Hallgarten was prominent, provoked the Nazi *Völkischer Beobachter* to a violent attack on 'wealthy Jewesses of pacifism and salon Bolshevism, Bavarian Princesses on the signboard of the Bogenhausen ghetto'; and the Council became a popular target for abuse in other extremist papers, jeering at the 'Valkyrie ride' of these 'purest of the pure ... Vicki Baum, Frau Gerhart Hauptmann, Frau Thomas Mann ...'[51]

----

[51] Häntzschel 313 ff.

During the Manns' summer months in Nidden, they found a Nazi youth-camp had been established not far away, on German territory, the harsh commands for paramilitary training and the patriotic songs carrying over on the wind to 'Uncle Tom's Cabin'. Klaus, who was there, recalled seeing some of the hundreds of youngsters, under training apparently as glider-pilots, tramping along the beach or sporting rowdily on the dunes or in the sea, their shirts, sweaters, even bathing-costumes, prominently emblazoned with the swastika. His father was relaxed enough to accord a lengthy interview to Carmel Haden Guest, for *John O'London's Weekly*, enlarging professorially on his career and work; but he seized the opportunity to characterize Nazism as 'a mushroom growth without roots' and its so-called revolutionary programme, based on Hitler's absurd *Mein Kampf*, an aberration in no way comparable with that of social democracy and the philosophy of Marx's 'epoch-making' *Das Kapital*. As for communism, he believed that in spite of the wide support for the party, nothing short of some great catastrophe could lead Germany along that road, and even then the German version would be very different from the Russian.[52]

But the detachment becoming to a Nobel Prize winner was getting harder to sustain. A particular irritation, while he was at Nidden, was an article in the Paris *Nouvelles littéraires* on a recently issued French version of the long-forgotten *Blood of the Walsungs*, raking up once more the gossip over the withdrawal of that story of incest from publication in Germany—at father-in-law's pistol-point, of course—twenty years earlier. 'Sang réservé: Histoire d'une nouvelle' was not the first disparaging comment in France: a review had already attacked the immorality of a story which the author had never thought fit to publish in his own country—erroneous, this, for in fact it had appeared in German as long ago as 1921. He was concerned over his good name in France, for there had been encouraging first reports of sales for *La Montagne magique*, though not all reviews had been favourable: so a firm rebuttal was dispatched to Martin Du Gard, editor of the *Nouvelles*, setting out the true facts on the work and its history. He sent it also for publication in the Berlin *Literarische Welt*, for the affair had not escaped the notice of the extremist press in Germany, where it made another welcome stick with which to beat Thomas Mann: an article the previous October had sharply attacked this portrayal of incest in French as 'intellectual uncleanness in the face of the German public', sheer 'greed for profit'.[53]

His outspoken attitude towards Nazism was provoking almost an orchestrated campaign against him, which, as the year advanced, began to tell. Normally generous, over-generous perhaps, with his time for visitors,

---

[52] *Fr./Antw.* 178.    [53] *Jb.* 3, 66.

he was now more ungracious. When Ida Herz brought him her problems in September, hoping for sage words of advice, she had to return unsatisfied, and her proposal for his portrait by an artist friend was brusquely rejected, as no more likely to sell than one of any other citizen. He had reached the limit of his capabilities where financial help was concerned, he told one young supplicant in November, and recommendations to publishers were useless in the present economic crisis. The constant inflow of manuscripts for his assessment, usually received with kindness if not always given his full attention, was somehow becoming a more and more unwelcome load; and though in fact recommendations to publishers still came from his pen in a steady stream, his judgement seemed often off-course. To return Elias Canetti's *Die Blendung* (*Auto da Fé*) unread in November was a particularly glaring error, and a hard blow for the young author, who had expected not just approval but something more like enthusiasm for his pessimistic 'human comedy of madmen'.

His ill-humour, unquestionably, sprang from dismay at the rising tide of nationalism over Europe, the 'melancholy episode now sweeping darkly' over the Continent, as he put it to Croce. On a visit to Golo in Heidelberg in November, Erika told her brother that the old man was even thinking of moving to Switzerland, convinced he was on the Nazi arrest list. The talk around Munich was of nothing but the coming 'Third Reich', found Klaus; his father was morose over the situation, with the thought he might be obliged to leave Germany. Worries over money too seemed suddenly to have arisen: he had earned only 1,200 marks in the last three months, said Erika, 'not even a tenth of what he's used to'. Such pessimism was premature, for by December a new source of income was in the offing with a new book-club edition of *The Magic Mountain*, from which a tidy sum would be due, and he had probably already taken the precaution of crediting his Swiss bank-account with part of the Nobel Prize award. At all events, the Christmas celebrations in Munich, with all the family there, showed no sign of belt-tightening, and his present of the latest model of radiogramophone, with special loudspeaker, was a delight.

But the gloom persisted into the New Year, with the inevitable effect on his health, to the point of making him take to his bed over most of the holiday. In the remarkable progress of Michael's musical talent he had seemed to take little pride or pleasure, and for Golo the interminable family meals were cheerless, lightened only when Erika made her appearance. His father's unseasonable message to Bertram on 27 December spoke of the successive 'waves of blood' he expected to pass over Germany: 'believe me, the days of your "universities" too are numbered, and in the end it won't much matter—the whole thing won't much matter, but what will we have to endure!' In a letter early in January, answering the despair of an unknown admirer in Frankfurt, he attributed the uncertainty of the times to the transition from the bourgeois epoch, for him the home of the intellect, to something new, with unforeseeable dangerous cataracts ahead for 'the flood now carrying us'. The nineteenth-century bourgeois national idea was now dead, or rather transformed to evil with the Nazis' success in giving it a false revolutionary colour in the eyes of young people.[54]

4

*'The decisive thing for me is that any direct involvement in political affairs is to the highest degree repulsive, and that I cannot possibly regard it as my mission'* (TM, March 1932)

Whatever his private gloom, in public Thomas Mann continued to declare his opposition to the Nazis, sometimes with an optimism which events were to prove unwarranted. Culture had nothing to expect from these people, he said in an interview at the end of the year, and he did not believe they would take over the helm, for there were powerful contrary forces: not only Marxism, but Catholicism, which could prove a bulwark against the 'assault of barbarism'. Today's events were typical of Germany's destiny: the German was called to politics, but was not born to it, he was and remained a non-political animal—like Hamlet 'called to action but born to thought, study, and analysis'.[55] He did not hesitate in January 1932 to give open support to the protest against the Reichsgericht's iniquitous judgement in the case of Carl von Ossietzky, editor of the left-wing *Weltbühne*—'not a judgement in the strict sense of the word, but a political act designed to conceal the aversion of certain powers and interests to any public control'. In his comments, it is true, whether sought by interviewers or in spontaneous articles, he often took more of a philosophical than a directly political approach, and he had no desire or intention to enter the political lists in active combat. To stay thus *au-dessus de la mêlée* was not to the taste of Erika, whose stage appearances were beginning to be boycotted and who wanted to see action. Her vigorous speech at a women's pacifist meeting in Munich in January drew the fire of the Nazi press in violent terms, not only against these 'Bolshevist furies', 'hysterical women, mannish and blasé', but against the family as a whole, vilified as a veritable 'Munich scandal, to be liquidated too when the time comes'.[56]

The head of the family had more than enough to do with his preparations for an extended 'Goethe journey' in the centenary year: Switzerland at the end of February, Prague and Vienna in March, then Berlin, and Weimar for

[54] 32/3.    [55] *Fr./Antw.* 182 f.    [56] Häntzschel 321; *Pfeff.* 8.

the culminating celebration. He planned two speeches, 'Goethe's Career as Writer' and 'Goethe as Representative of the Bourgeois Epoch'—the latter primarily for the foreign audiences—and it was essential to escape from the tensions in Germany if they were to be ready in time. So most of February was spent in St. Moritz, where Erika showed her talents as editor in reducing his prolixity to bearable lengths, before the first appearance in Berne at the end of the month. In both, the treatment of his 'father-imago' left no doubt that he saw himself as a Goethe successor: 'only from his own substance and being, from a certain family experience then . . . can someone like me speak of Goethe—and why deny a recognition, a right to confidence which reaches beyond the personal to the national!'[57] His sense of 'a certain mythical succession, a following in the footsteps', was very lively, and found expression in both these speeches, he wrote later that year: with Stifter, he could say 'I am no Goethe, but I am of his family.' They were not the occasions for political reflection or analysis, but, as he said in a chatty account of his tour to the Munich Rotary Club in April, the international respect shown for Germany's greatest poet made this a year of honour for her people and culture. 'The German is all too ready to think himself despised, and poison his soul with the thought. There is very little reason for this, and even Goethe, who, God knows, had much to find fault with in his Germans . . . still never ceased to believe in our imperishability and our future. . . . We are anything but despised. At most, we are feared. But in Goethe, mankind's favourite, we are also loved.'[58]

These soothing words were spoken after events in Germany which belied them and of which, on his journey, he had learned only from press reports, with little idea of the intrigues behind. Hindenburg had hoped to extend his term as President and avoid the certain turmoil an election would bring; but Chancellor Brüning had failed to secure the other parties' agreement, notably that of the Nazis, and the old marshal found himself obliged to run against not only the former corporal Hitler but also the communist Ernst Thälmann. The first vote was held on 13 March (the Manns' early train for Prague that day preventing them from casting their ballots), and for Hindenburg it was humiliating to find almost half the nation against him. Though he had an easy lead in the April run-off, with 19 million votes to Hitler's 13 million and Thälmann's 3.7 million, this was thanks only to centre and socialist support offsetting the defection of many of his former admirers to the Nazi camp; and his irrational resentment against Brüning, fostered by the machinations of Schleicher, was to have significant consequences. Interviewed in Prague on 15 March, Thomas Mann was optimistic, greatly relieved by the result, and confident in the healthy instinct of

---

[57] ix 297 f.          [58] xiii 75.

the German people: time had been gained to await more favourable economic circumstances, but whatever happened, the German workers would never accept the abolition of the Weimar constitution or the loss of the social achievements of the Republic. To the press in Vienna, before his Goethe speech in the Hofburg, he expatiated on political influence on literature, as entirely natural in the post-war era, but warned of the danger in the reactionary anti-humanism of the Nazi idea, for all its insignificance as literature. In Hitler, the only Austrian characteristic he could see was his anti-Semitism: indeed, there was nothing truly Germanic about him, and to hear this man from Bohemia preaching racial purity was almost comic. His apparent success was merely cheap demagogy, agitation which widened the gulf between Germany and the rest of the world and raised the spectre of a new war. 'In a word—admittedly a strong one—I would characterize the influence of the non-Austrian Hitler as: criminal.'[59] This was indeed strong stuff, which would not be forgotten by the Nazis.

The demands of his tour, however, were exacting enough to divert him from political concerns. In Berlin on 18 March, in the Prussian Academy, he was duly conscious of the honour of speaking to a select audience of 300, 'the still-remaining intellectual élite of Berlin', including the French ambassador François-Poncet, and impressed by the musical framework arranged, with chorales by Zelter and other contemporaries of Goethe. Weimar, which followed, was more disappointing. It was faintly amusing, in this centre of Hitlerism, to see the juxtaposition of the swastika culture with the due adulation for Goethe and touristic exploitation of Germany's classical past. The organizational arrangements, however, were less than pleasing. He had complained beforehand at the bad seats offered him for the theatre performances, and still more at having to pay for Katia's seat at his speech. While these shortcomings were no doubt made good, when the time came for him to appear in the Stadthalle, with the talk on Goethe's career as writer, the late hour arranged resulted in a mass exodus of his listeners towards the end, to catch the performance of *Egmont*, and he felt cheated of the success he deserved. Listening later to former academician Kolbenheyer, as he denied Goethe world citizenship and claimed *Iphigenie* as a thoroughly *völkisch* German work, was not calculated to improve his mood. Even the award of the Goethe medal at a subsequent ceremony, attended by Brüning and Defence Minister Groener, was offset for him by failure actually to meet and talk with these dignitaries, for he had not been introduced and did not feel he could push himself forward (he was not to know that two months later both would be out of office). But further performances in May in Nuremberg, Frankfurt am Main at the dedication

---

[59] *Fr./Antw.* 186–8.

of the extension to the Goethe Museum, and finally in June to a large audience in Munich University, restored him. There the many young people showed themselves 'passionately smitten', he told Bertram: 'do with Germany what you like—people of my sort will never be alone'.

By that time, the uproar caused by Brüning's decree banning Hitler's Storm Troops and SS, his black-uniformed élite, but exempting the socialist Reichsbanner had led to Hindenburg's demand for the resignation of his cabinet. State elections in April had made the Nazis the strongest party in all the diets except Bavaria: and Papen, urged on the President by Schleicher as replacement Chancellor, hoped to secure Hitler's support, and subservience, by reversing the decree and promising new elections to the Reichstag. But this was an open invitation to murder, in Thälmann's words, for the brawls then provoked by the brown-shirted Storm Troopers (SA) throughout the country became regular battles in which thousands were injured and hundreds killed. Papen's response was to depose the Prussian government, as no longer capable of maintaining order—a coup which ended the old dualism between Prussia and the Reich, and, he hoped, deprived Hitler of important resources which a Nazi government there could have used against the Reich. The result of the Reichstag elections on 31 July, raising the number of Nazi seats from 107 to 230, emboldened Hitler to demand the chancellorship for himself: furious at Papen's refusal and the dressing-down Hindenburg gave him, he forced new Reichstag elections in November, at which his party's vote was greatly reduced and which led many to believe he had lost his chances for good.

Thomas Mann, meanwhile, anxious now to return to his real work on the *Joseph*, had retreated early in July to Nidden, alone apart from Reisiger, then joined after two weeks by the family. He was, of course, disturbed by the Nazi advance and at seeing Germany 'reduced to the concept these blockheads make of it! what absurdity!';[60] but he had as yet no notion that the beautiful summer—praiseworthy as far as nature was concerned, if not in what the Germans were making of it, as he wrote to Ida Herz—would be their last there. The first two volumes of *Joseph* completed, he was turning to the next, *Joseph in Egypt*, encouraged by Fischer's compliments on the work so far and his acceptance of an extract from *The Young Joseph* for the autumn *Rundschau*. A sharp controversy with the publisher earlier in the year, following his refusal after all to allow the profitable book-club edition of *The Magic Mountain*, had been more or less satisfactorily resolved, with lower terms for that and with financial proposals to meet what Mann regarded as indispensable to survive the long gestation-period without reducing his accustomed standard of living; and he was no longer bitter

---

[60] *Brw. Aut.* 254.

over what had seemed arbitrary decisions on his prospects. They were still arguing over the book publication of *Joseph*, Fischer being inclined to release the volumes already finished, while Mann felt it better, in the current political mood, to withhold them until the whole work was ready; but at least the way was clear to continue, and progress was good, even though overshadowed by politics. It was no pleasure to live and work in Germany these days, he told himself and others, but one must never forget that amid the din of *völkisch* mythology there was another, better tradition.

The Nazi-provoked mayhem of July, however, which spread to nearby Königsberg at the end of the month, with attacks on socialist and communist deputies and the deposed Prussian government president, called him once again to public action, and at the request of the *Berliner Tageblatt* he sent a courageously outspoken article in protest. 'Will these shameful deeds of blood . . . finally open our eyes to the true nature of this disease among the people, this mish-mash of hysteria and mouldering romanticism which . . . is the caricature and degradation of everything that is German?' We have had enough, he cried, of this poisoning of the atmosphere by the 'boasts and threats of the Nazi press and the half-idiotic slavering of so-called Führers who call for heads, hangings, food for the ravens, and nights of the long knives'. Among the millions attracted by the 'false Messiah' there must be many of good faith, who should be ashamed of such rubbish and ready to lend support to the firm measures taken by the Reich government to 'root out this barbaric degeneration of the German soul'. But he warned of the dangers of over-eager submission to a rule 'above party', and demanded the long-overdue establishment of a true social republic as the only course for the future.[61] The journal, fearful of Nazi attacks and a possible ban, felt compelled to weaken the more extreme passages—a depressing experience, as he wrote to Fischer: better to remain silent, if one's accustomed freedom of expression was to be thwarted.

He soon felt the 'breath of hatred'[62] against him: stones were thrown at the house, and a partly burned copy of *The Buddenbrooks* was found by the hedge. He carefully kept the charred remains, he told Hesse later, 'as witness one day to the mood of the German people in 1932', and was not deterred from his scheduled public appearances—readings in Königsberg on 3 September before they left, and Elbing the following day, finally a talk in Lübeck on the homeward journey, at the four-hundredth anniversary of his school. His equanimity seemed undisturbed, and their life in Munich was resumed, untouched by the economic crisis. There were still five servants, including an unnecessary nanny for Elisabeth and Michael, as Golo noted on his visits: good food and drink, two cars, journeys in every comfort, a prosperity assured by the Nobel Prize funds and the *Magic Mountain* income. If not flaunted, it was certainly unconcealed, and likely to make him even more hated among the growing number of his political opponents: for an industrialist, it might pass, but not for a writer, especially one now accounted as left wing.[63] Equanimity became almost complacency: Goebbels in the *Angriff* might rant as he liked against him as a 'writing mongrel of Indian, negro, Moorish blood' who should be forbidden to call himself German, but 'I go so far as to count myself one of that intellectual company of Europe alongside which the "German master race" has become a very indifferent club'[64]—the European company whose meetings in the Geneva Standing Commission for Arts and Letters he celebrated in a contribution to the *Neue Zürcher Zeitung* in October.

A public programme almost as full as ever lay ahead: rounding off the Goethe year in November with a repeat of the 'Career as Writer' talk in Essen, then an extended tour in the New Year with a lecture on Wagner, the fiftieth anniversary of whose death was due in February, beginning in Munich and continuing to Amsterdam, Brussels, and Paris. Before the lengthy preparation this would need could begin, however, there was another engagement, in October in Vienna. It would mark an important difference from his usual aesthetic approach, for he had been invited to speak before a specifically working-class audience at Ottakring, in one of the housing estates established by the socialist administration, and he welcomed the chance of showing where his political sympathies lay. It was the first time, he told his enthusiastic hearers, that he, bourgeois born and bred, stood before socialist workers, a situation not only characterizing the times they were living in, but also marking an epoch in his personal life and his intellectual development. His message was couched in typical Mannian prose, with much on culture and civilization, intellect and life, the artist and the bourgeois, humanism and reaction. But the occasion was something new and moving for him—to be able to show these 'modest people assailed by a triumphant reactionary trend that they are not abandoned'— and an unmistakable affirmation of his political position.

To his friend Bertram, whom he visited in Cologne after the Essen talk in November just after the new Reichstag elections, that stance is unlikely to have appealed; and though their friendship was never broken off, they were to meet only once more before Thomas Mann died. The advent of Hauptmann's seventieth birthday made a lighter interlude: Mann wrote a gently ironic tribute in the November *Rundschau*, and his address to his colleague at the ceremony in the Munich National Theatre on 11 December celebrated the fusion of Lutheran religiosity and joy of life characterizing

---

[63] GM *Erinn.* 430 f.       [64] 32/127.

the work of a man psychologically placed, as Nietzsche had said of Goethe, between the pietistic and the Greek. For Hauptmann, Munich was only one stage in a somewhat bewildering tour, and in his impromptu reply, as diffuse and incoherent as ever Peeperkorn's had been in *The Magic Mountain*, he seemed not quite sure which city he was in. The high point for the Manns, however, as Katia wrote to Hedwig Fischer, was their afternoon visit to him in his hotel: visibly relieved that the official affairs were done with, and amid floods of champagne, he kept them there till six, in a truly Peeperkorn orgy, and it was satisfying to find any lingering shadow from that novelistic liberty now thoroughly expunged. By then, the political shadows too seemed to be lifting, with the set-back for Hitler in the elections and the appointment of Schleicher, a general but still a reasonable and socially responsible man, as Chancellor in place of Papen. Thomas Mann, though still the target for letters of hatred and abuse, could feel the worst of the madness was over.

# V

# THE HESITANT *ÉMIGRÉ*
# 1933–1936

'Colourful the web of lies
That holds our great Reich firm entwined.

. . . . . .

Lie just once, you're not believed,
Lie all the time, you cannot fail'
(Die Pfeffermühle, 1934)

1

*'A relapse into darkest barbarism. I'll never yield, but sooner die
than come to terms with it'*       (TM, 3 April 1933)

The worst was by no means over. Schleicher, something of an unwilling
Chancellor, had thought to exploit the impatience of Hitler's party-follow-
ers for action appropriate to their strength by encouraging a mass defection
from the apparently hesitant Führer—Gregor Strasser, head of the party
administration, had intimated he was ready for a break—and aiming for an
army-labour coalition. Neither idea bore fruit. Hitler profited from
Strasser's temporary absence to abolish his position and set up a new
central party office under Rudolf Hess which would assure him of united
support; the army, for its part, though fundamentally opposed to involvement in politics, was by no means unsympathetic to National Socialism. On
23 January 1933 Schleicher was forced to admit to Hindenburg he had
failed to secure a new majority, and his request for Reichstag dissolution,
new elections, and a renewed ban on the Nazi and communist party-
organizations was refused by the President, who wanted Papen back to
form a new government. Papen recognized that to be strong enough this
must have the Nazis' support, but hoped to restrain them by forming a
coalition cabinet, to which he obtained Hindenburg's agreement on 30
January: Hitler as Chancellor, himself as Vice-Chancellor, Blomberg Defence Minister, Hugenberg of the National Party Minister of Economics,

and only two other Nazis—Frick for the Interior and Goering (still significantly Prussian Minister of the Interior) as Minister without portfolio. The hopes of this constellation, designed to 'box in' Hitler and give him the shadow without the substance of power, would soon be seen to be vain.

Thomas Mann was meanwhile busy with his own concerns, and as yet scarcely conceiving that these changes could really affect them, or that the Republic could be doomed. His programme for the Wagner lecture-tour stood firm: first at Munich University on 10 February, three days later in the Concertgebouw Amsterdam, followed by Brussels at the PEN Club and then Paris, and for both these latter needing a French version, which Félix Bertaux had undertaken for him. This meant an intensive month of January for its preparation—in the knowledge that, in view of his lifelong preoccupation with Wagner, it would first take the form of a full essay, from which a suitable lecture must then be excerpted. But it was not possible to remain aloof from the political mêlée. Months earlier, following his Vienna socialist declaration, he had agreed to attend a meeting in Berlin on 15 January and give one of his 'active speeches', as the organizer put it, lending his authority to the 'moral necessity' of socialism. Feeling now overloaded, and suffering into the bargain from flu, he telegraphed a refusal early in January, suggesting his brother instead. The postponement to March then suggested he could not accept, for by then he planned the three-week rest in Arosa which the doctor had ordered after his tour; but he sent a long letter, a manifesto almost, setting out his ideas, which could be read at the meeting, and turned to the intensive labour needed for the Wagner essay.

These two efforts, though he could not know it at the time, would be his last works written on German soil. The 'Socialist Confession', as it came to be known, in much a repetition of his Vienna speech, was an even clearer declaration:

socialism is nothing other than the decision duty requires, no longer to hide one's head in the sand of loftier ideas from those more pressing of material things, but to rally to the side of those who strive to give the world a meaning—the meaning of humanity. In that sense, I am a socialist. And I am a democrat, in the simple and general sense of believing in the imperishability of ideas that seem to me unshakeably linked with every feeling of humanity—that of freedom, for example, declared today to be obsolete and destined for the scrap-heap of history. . . . Social and democratic Germany, I am deeply convinced, may be confident that the present constellation is but transitory, and that the future is hers. The fury of nationalist passion is no more than a late and final flare-up of a fire already burnt down, a dying reignition mistaking itself for a new blaze of life. All the facts of life, of economic, technical, and intellectual development, bear witness that the future lies on the road the peoples have long since decided to take, the road to the social world of unity, freedom, and peace.

Had he been able to attend the meeting in person, however, it was unlikely he would have had the chance to speak these words. From his first day as Chancellor on 30 January, Hitler, far from being boxed in, showed clearly in his speeches that he was determined on absolute power, with new policies which Frick concisely characterized as 'the will and the strength to act'. He placated the commanders of the Reichswehr by persuading them that their own interests were best served by an authoritarian state leadership; and meanwhile assured himself of the forces outside their control, the police. Goering ordered the use of the Storm Troops and SS as police auxiliaries, thus ensuring that opposition assemblies could be ruthlessly broken up. A sweeping decree of 4 February authorized the prohibition of all newspapers and meetings deemed against the state or its officials. With this, the whole of the communist press was eliminated and severe restrictions placed on that of the SPD and Centre. When a congress of artists and intellectuals to advocate 'Free Speech' attempted to assemble in the Kroll Opera House on 19 February, on the same day as the socialist meeting planned in the Volksbühne, both were dispersed, and only a part of Mann's letter could be read out.

He heard from Heinrich on the eve of his first Wagner lecture on 10 February: his brother, whose attendance at the congress had been announced without his consent, and who had therefore refused to go, had presided earlier in the month at fruitless discussions in the Academy on a possible demonstrative declaration against 'cultural reaction', and he trusted Thomas would agree with him on the uselessness of such gestures. In the face of events, there was no doubt he did. His Vienna speech, written on 4 February, was out of date and inadequate; much more needed to be said now; but at nearly 60, he was not disposed to enter the lists in 'a ruinous political battle' while trying to fulfil his real tasks. 'True, the day may come when nothing remains but to cast everything aside and mount the barricades. But for the moment, one still prays the cup may pass.'[1] In fact, after the lecture, as he prepared to leave for Amsterdam the next day with Katia, they seriously discussed once again whether it was time to quit Munich and the hostile atmosphere of their country for more favourable climes elsewhere in the German-speaking world. Katia was in favour: but he was not to be persuaded, it would look as though he was abandoning Germany and would be a disastrous discouragement for so many others. His tour would go ahead, and after it, their three weeks in Arosa. Their joint passport was due to expire on 3 April, but by then they would be back.

---

[1] 33/26.

Erika, however, had not been prepared to sit back inactive. On 1 January she had opened, with her friend the character actress Therese Giehse, a literary-political cabaret in the intimate Munich theatre 'Bonbonnière', right next to the Nazi haunt the Hofbräuhaus. She was her own compère and wrote most of the texts herself; Klaus, however, also contributed to the venturesome anti-Nazi satire. The well-chosen title 'The Peppermill' (Die Pfeffermühle) was their father's idea, a fact which soon became public knowledge, the *Neue Zürcher Zeitung* notice calling it in fact 'a Mann family enterprise'.[2] From the première, which all the Manns and their friends attended, it had scored an immediate success, playing to full houses, and thoroughly in tune with Munich's Fasching mood: the proprietor was enthusiastic enough to extend the booking to the end of February. Even the press reports, with the exception naturally of the *Völkischer Beobachter*, were favourable. Quite an adventure in the Germany of that time, recalled Klaus later, and the success of its daring they thought a good sign for the future. As they opened again with a new programme on 1 February, Hitler was giving his inauguration speech in the Hofbräuhaus next door: but Erika noted that Frick had denied himself the pleasure of listening to his Führer in favour of the 'Peppermill', scribbling furiously—names no doubt for his blacklist. Her determination to do all she could in the struggle against Hitler carried Klaus along, despite his more defeatist frame of mind: in his diary of 19 February, his private thoughts were of 'nothing but the wish to die'. Had he poison handy, he would not hesitate—if it were not for Erika and his mother. 'But I'm more and more certain that E's death would mean mine as well, that then even work would not hold me back. . . . Death *can* only be regarded as deliverance . . .'[3] But the family, least of all his parents, already away, knew nothing of that.

Ten days before their departure, the full Wagner essay had been sent to Fischer, who planned to publish it in the April *Rundschau* and later that month in book form, and agreed to the author's request for an unusually generous fee ('on no account do I want to arouse your discontent'). He too longed to get away from the 'disagreeable things happening here'; but his hopes of a meeting somewhere in the south were unlikely to be fulfilled, Mann had replied—he must get to Arosa after the tour, and then return to work on the *Joseph* with renewed vigour. It was clear he would be in need of the rest in Switzerland: in the short time remaining, his text had to be condensed by at least two-thirds for the first reading of the lecture ('cutting into my own flesh', as he wrote to Bertaux)[4] and he would not have long to practise the French version for Brussels and Paris.

[2] PdM ii, 100.    [3] KlM *Tb.* i, 118.    [4] PdM ii, 106.

The auditorium maximum of Munich University on 10 February was well filled to hear his presentation of 'The Sorrows and Grandeur of Richard Wagner'; and although not all the leading personalities of the city were to be seen among the 500 listeners, he was well pleased with its success and the applause. Here at least, unlike in Berlin, there was no disturbance, Munich still presented a civilized face, and the press notices— the *Völkischer Beobachter* always excepted—were well-disposed. What his actual words were, in excerpt from the much longer written piece, we do not know. He said later that, for what was after all a celebratory occasion, he had avoided the more literary form of the essay and necessarily omitted many of its psychological insights; and it seems doubtful that, in the current climate, if he used its passages on Wagner's contradictory roman-ticism in matters political, he will have included its warning against the simplistic claiming of him as a hero of German nationalism. For the rest, what he wrote was a skilfully worked compendium of his earlier publica-tions and views on Wagner, as the epigraph he chose, from Maurice Barrès ('il y a là mes blâmes, mes éloges et tout ce que j'ai dit'), clearly showed: from the essay on the theatre of 1908 and his extensive notes of 1909–10 for the 'Literature' essay never completed, through the 'Coming to Terms with Wagner' of 1911 and the 1918 *Reflections*, to his 'Ibsen and Wagner' of 1928.

As he continued on his journey, repeating the lecture as scheduled—13 February in Amsterdam, the next day to the Brussels PEN Club in the Palais des Beaux-Arts, followed by a reception at the German embassy, and finally in two appearances in Paris on 17 and 18 February—there were further ominous developments in Germany, of which he learned only on the sudden arrival of Heinrich in Paris a few days later. His brother had been among the signatories of a call for co-operation between communists and socialists in the new Reichstag elections ordered by Hitler for 5 March; the Nazi Prussian Minister for Culture had demanded, and secured, from the compliant members, Heinrich's immediate removal as president of the Literature Section of the Academy; a violent press-campaign against him had followed, a watch was placed on his house, and he wisely decided to leave Germany at once, unobtrusively drawing what cash he could from the bank and taking a train via Frankfurt and Strasburg for Paris. With the news he brought of unbelievable conditions at home, Thomas had to agree that they were well-advised to stay away—at least for the time being, which was anyway his plan, and he and Katia went on down to Arosa on 24 February. Other nations, after all, had survived similar experiences; he would await developments. Heinrich, expecting confiscation of his house and assets in Berlin, was less sanguine, and decided to move down to Nice to continue with the novel he had begun, hoping Nelly Kröger, whom he planned to make his second wife, could join him there later. With a little saved in Switzerland, his head was for the moment above water.

With increasing persecution and intimidation of the Left, and Joseph Goebbels's mastery of propaganda, especially through the radio, now under state control, Hitler hoped for a resounding success in the elections. The burning-down of the Reichstag building, on 27 February—whether by the half-witted Dutch vagrant van der Lubbe, who was tried and executed for the crime, or, as seems more probable, by a special SS unit—served to ensure the elimination of the major opposition, the communists, through the arrest the following day of all their leading officials and members, along with many intellectuals who had roused Nazi wrath. President Hindenburg, persuaded that a communist revolution had been imminent, was induced at noon to sign a fateful emergency decree, inaugurating the policy which would be the corner-stone of the National Socialist state: arrest on suspicion, imprisonment without trial or right of hearing, and all the horrors of the concentration camps.

Yet Hitler's party fell far short of absolute triumph on 5 March, though retaining with its allies a majority: the Centre and socialists came close to their usual number of seats, and even the communists won eighty-one. But the opposition's lack of will, unsurprising in the spate of arrests and street violence which followed, and the displacement of legally constituted governments in many of the *Länder* by Reich commissioners, induced a growing fatalism. In Arosa, Katia had passed a sleepless night, realizing instinctively that they would not be able to return; only a good deal later did this sink in for her husband, in constant agitation and violent emotion, as he began to face the possibility of exile. In Bavaria, the moderate Held government had been replaced by a *Reichsstatthalter*, none other than Von Epp, former leader of the Free Corps which helped crush the 1919 Soviet Republic: but Thomas Mann could not believe Bavaria would not stay as it was—'the rule of law in some form and a half-way decent way of life will be restored in a short space of time'.[5] He had done his best to avert disaster; if fate disposed otherwise, he would return quietly to Germany, where he belonged, and henceforth devote himself exclusively to his writing, distancing himself entirely from politics.

Elisabeth, now 15 and on holiday, had joined them in Arosa, for the skiing; Michael was still at his boarding-school, Monika at her music studies in Florence, and Golo, after his doctorate in Heidelberg, in Göttingen on a course for a teaching qualification. Erika and Klaus, preparing their planned transfer of the 'Peppermill' on 1 April to a larger Schwabing venue, had taken a break in Lenzerheide, not far from Arosa;

[5] *Bl.* 18, 12.

but, uneasy, they returned to Munich, and were met by the chauffeur in a highly nervous state, saying they must keep away from Poschinger Strasse, where the brownshirts were after them (as later became clear, his nervousness was understandable, for he had long been a spy for the Nazis, reporting on his employers). There was obviously no question of their parents moving back as planned on 11 March. A number of Munich friends wrote the same, as did Gottfried Bermann from Berlin, veiling his warning as a former doctor: 'at this point in your treatment, a sensitive constitution like yours could be exposed to unexpected attacks. Such a danger to your health, if at all possible, must be avoided.' Their bags stood ready packed as Erika and Klaus insisted urgently, but at first vainly, in a guarded telephone-call to their father, on the awful weather in Munich, the great disorder with the house being spring-cleaned. They finally had to speak out directly: 'Stay in Switzerland! You would not be safe here.'[6] Erika returned to them on 13 March, bringing with her the *Joseph* manuscript and material; Klaus left the same evening for Paris, and their cabaret colleague Therese Giehse for the Tyrol, abandoning everything to escape. Day by day came news of fresh arrests, and Thomas Mann was at last convinced. They briefly thought of a return by Katia alone, to see to the house, but abandoned the idea, in view of the risk. It was a joy through these days to have his two favourite children, Erika and Elisabeth, about him.

Though almost in despair over how to adapt their life, and still hoping for at least a brief return-visit to arrange his affairs for an orderly emigration to Switzerland, he had to face the prospect of an exile of years, if not for ever. Beginning a new diary on 15 March, he told himself the change was a 'necessity that, for all the sclerosis of my 58 years, I find good intellectually, and welcome': it was the opportunity to divest his life at one stroke of all the representative activities it had brought over the years, out of 'social good nature, "duty", "vanity", whatever . . . and live henceforth in complete composure for myself'. Resigning his chairmanship of the Bavarian Writers Union was the mark of this decision; and a few days later he sent in his resignation from the Academy in response to its request for a declaration of loyalty 'in recognition of the changed historical situation' (though he refused the 'yes or no' answer demanded, stating that he had no intention of working against the government, would continue his service to German culture, and was henceforth abandoning any form of public life).

Such apparently firm steps masked the uncertainty he faced—where to settle, how to ensure renewal of their passport, the risk of confiscation of property and blocking of funds in Germany, the future of the three children, and, of course, of Katia's parents, still there—with the infinitely

[6] PdM ii, 122, 124.

depressing daily news of the steady move towards dictatorship and speculation, rumour-fed, of worse to come. He saw the new masters as 'occupying powers', executing an 'internal Versailles more horrible than the
external . . . 49 per cent of the German people no less relentlessly treated,
no less humiliated . . . than post-war Germany then'.[7] Moving temporarily
to a rented chalet in Lenzerheide, they dispatched Elisabeth back to school
in Munich on 17 March, and Golo was told to return home and run the
house, where one faithful maid remained, Klaus and Erika being now, as
Katia put it, 'otherwise engaged'. A friend returning to Munich was charged
with trying to renew their passport and see to the sending of some clothing
and funds, but it seemed there were bureaucratic delays, and results hung
fire, though some money could be transferred. 'A queer experience, having
your country, when you happen to be abroad, running away from you,
irrecoverably.'

Golo found his uncle Viktor accommodating himself to the new regime,
drawing advantage from the dismissal of Jewish colleagues in the bank to
gain promotion and exchange his modest house for a more elegant one in
Schwabing. A rumour that Erika was now in the Dachau concentration
camp was being gleefully spread in Munich, with acid comments on the
Mann family's insolence ('why did they think themselves better than us?').[8]
Her later account of a daring return incognito to Poschinger Strasse, to
scoop up the papers her father needed and bring them out stowed with the
oily tools under the car seat, which has entered into both family and
literary legend, owed more to her talent for story-telling and dramatic effect
than to the truth. In fact, she remained in Switzerland, and having already
fetched Therese Giehse from the Tyrol, began plans to reopen the cabaret
in Zurich and find a suitable lodging for the parents somewhere there,
meanwhile installing them in a Lugano hotel on 24 March. With the
reported imminence of stricter exit-controls from Germany, Katia longed
to have Elisabeth out, and was immensely relieved when Golo telephoned
from Zurich on 2 April to report their safe arrival. Golo, having secured the
new political-clearance certificate required, was now able to pass freely,
and made several more journeys to and from Munich during April. Young
Michael was also now with them, whether brought out by Golo or travelling on his own is not clear. The energetic Erika drove off to meet Klaus in
Aigue-Belle in the south of France, an area already a haven for many of the
refugees, and persuaded him to come back with her for a short time.

Knowing the family was thus in what, for the moment, passed for safety
did not serve to allay Thomas Mann's gnawing worries over his future. An
attempt towards the end of March to resume work on the *Joseph* was in

[7] Ibid. 118; *Tb.* ii, 9.     [8] GM *Erinn.* 510 f.

vain, the disturbance to his routine had been too great, and there were recurrent crises of despair, irresolution, a fear of losing his balanced outlook, all reflected in a constant need for tranquillizers. His daily 'work' was no more than at the diary, important to him in such times, and at his correspondence, which still included much with Germany. Katia, as always, succeeded in calming him; but the discussions, with the family and the many exiles in Switzerland, on where best to find a half-way congenial existence, were never-ending, against the darkening background of the news from Germany. On 23 March, Hitler had succeeded, by the elimination of the communists, prevention of many of the socialists from attending, and intimidation of the Centre, in pushing through the Reichstag the final establishment of his effective dictatorship: the Enabling Act to dispense with constitutional forms and limitations and thus free him to mould the government and social system as he pleased. On 1 April, the day of publication of the Wagner essay in the *Rundschau*, began a regular boycott of Jews and Jewish enterprises.

The possible effect of this on the Fischer Verlag was a major concern for Thomas Mann. He was dependent on their agreed monthly remittance of 1,000 marks against royalties, which for the moment continued uninterrupted, together with any foreign-rights income accruing, the latter, as Bermann told him, being impossible to credit to him direct without transgressing the new currency-regulations. To speak out 'to the American nation' against the persecution of the Jews, as he was now urged to do by Lewisohn in Paris, would mean the confiscation of all his German assets, Golo and the Pringsheims taken as hostages or worse, the banning of his books and the loss of his German readership. He was firm in his determination not to return to 'darkest barbarism', as he wrote to Viktor on leave in Bolzano. Publicly, however, he must keep silent, so that quiet efforts could be made to ensure the safety of the Pringsheims, the recovery from Munich of such effects as could be got out, and above all the renewal of his and Katia's passport, expiring on 3 April, for which Katia found in the Zurich consulate-general a polite but firm refusal.

He had also just remembered important material left in the key-safe in Poschinger Strasse: family documents, but especially—a far more personal worry—all his diaries, going back fifty years, which none of the family had ever been allowed to see and which must not fall into other hands. Golo was sent the key and told what to select, pack in a suitcase, and send to Lugano: 'I count on your discretion not yourself to read [the diaries]',[9] an instruction Golo faithfully obeyed. The chauffeur, noticing his precautions over packing the material and suspecting it had political significance,

[9] PdM ii, 134.

volunteered to take the case for dispatch by rail freight on 10 April—and came under suspicion of having passed it to his Nazi spymasters. For when Golo made another visit to Switzerland on 14 April with further essential material for the *Joseph* his father had asked for, and profiting from the mark allowance to bring out some cash for him, the case had still not arrived, and his concern can be imagined. Meanwhile Golo had found a reliable Munich lawyer, Valentin Heins, to take care of the Mann affairs, in particular the passport renewal; and he was duly instructed on 18 April. In these early days of the Nazi regime, the step might have seemed an all-too-trusting faith in the rule of law; but surprisingly it proved not without some success, even though Heins's stewardship of papers, including some important manuscripts which came later into his care, was never beyond doubt.

Viktor Mann was one example among the host of ordinary people who, if not initially enthusiastic nor later taking out party membership, were nevertheless carried along by the wave of fervour for the 'movement' which appeared to promise so much. More significant was the number of the great and the good who did more than just acquiesce. Early in March, before the elections, 300 professors had issued a call for support of the National Socialists; on 21 March, their voice was heard in a declaration by the Universities' Union hailing the *Machtübernahme* as a 'rebirth of the German people', linking the great names of the academic tradition with the new 'reform' in education on nationalist lines and its emphasis on military and labour training. The change, and the extent to which he would now be shunned, was brought home to Thomas Mann when Ernst Bertram, taking a holiday in nearby Locarno, pointedly avoided calling on him, despite their continuing friendly correspondence. 'That was not pleasant,' he wrote to him months later, 'but I know your moral fibre was never very great. Strong enough now, it seems, to approve and glorify what to me is fundamentally repulsive and at the same time to invite me warmly to make common cause. . . . I wish you well in your *völkisch* glasshouse, shielded from reality by a brutality so little suited to you!'

A more severe shock was the sudden appearance on 16 April in the Munich *Neueste Nachrichten* of a 'Protest of the Richard Wagner City' against the 'calumny' in his Wagner lecture and his effrontery in posing with it abroad as a 'representative of German culture'. Among the forty-five signatories, headed by Hitler's publisher Max Amann but followed alphabetically by names of standing in Munich's artistic, academic, and governmental life, including Richard Strauss, appeared many whom he had hitherto thought sympathetic to him—notably Pfitzner and Hans Knappertsbusch, who in the culmination of a long-standing campaign against the 'racially undesirable' Bruno Walter had now replaced him as musical director of the Opera. The originator (he suspected Pfitzner, who had long admired Hitler, but it was almost certainly Knappertsbusch) had waited two months since the lecture—presumably to make sure the 'national uprising' was firmly in place—and not many of the signatories had actually heard it in Munich, when it had been acclaimed. Yet the text of the 'Protest' made no mention of the complete essay, long since in print in Germany, which developed his ideas at greater length.

He was stirred to an immediate and dignified response, which he sent to a number of papers in Germany and Austria and which (Nazi control of the press being as yet far from complete) appeared in several, though, as he expected, not in the *Neueste Nachrichten*. The lecture, reflecting the passion for Wagner's work which had run through his whole life, he wrote, had been everywhere well received, and the German envoys abroad had all expressed their gratitude for his service to the German name: the 'Protest' was a total misunderstanding and did him bitter injustice. 'Only a complete ignorance of the role which Wagner's gigantic work has always played in my life and my own work could have led them to take part in this iniquitous action against a German writer. I sincerely beg the silent friends of my work in Germany not to be led astray into doubting my devotion to German culture and tradition, and to them.'[10]

This Munich demonstration was the beginning of his 'national excommunication', showing, 'plain and clear, that I am to be proscribed'; and his somewhat hesitant reluctance to return to Germany now became a firm resolve. Privately, he gave vent to his 'disgust and loathing' for the political and moral condition to which his country had been brought, the regime's 'inferior, pathologically murderous assault on the intellect . . . its whole being . . . nothing but hatred, resentment, revenge, meanness'.[11] But there was nothing of this in his first public statement, in the Wagner affair, its circumspect terms a clear indication that it was the safeguarding of his personal position and his German readership that primarily concerned him. He was prepared to reply, but not to attack. It would be going too far to say, with a later critic, that it was not the fate of others, not the fate of democracy, but only what was done to him personally, that determined his attitude. But his words now—'I am convinced that a German revolution which casts someone like me out of the country cannot be quite in order'— showed how his mind lay. Later, he noted in his diary, when he had 'liquidated' his affairs at home, he would certainly write something against the new barbarism; for the moment, seemingly, the reaction against Jewishness would be acceptable, if it were not for 'the Germans' stupid tendency' to treat him personally the same way. Klaus, writing to Golo, felt their father's public caution, his 'obsequious' behaviour, repugnant: 'I have

[10]  xi 785 ff.
[11]  *Tb.* ii, 52; to Max Mohr, 21 Apr. 1933 (Stargardt auction cat. 599, 1972).

sensed and known from the start that for us nothing, *nothing*, can be expected from these people in power'; but he understood the dilemma of a man who felt himself somehow responsible for his country, and was incapable of living without it. Golo himself thought the Wagner reply spineless, a little too pleading: better if it had never been written.[12]

When he came with Heins at the end of April to meet his parents at Rohrschach, not far from the German frontier, bringing more suitcases of effects, his news was far from good. He had succeeded in drawing and hiding 60,000 marks in cash, but had found any further withdrawals blocked. The house had been searched by the SA, luckily without their finding the cash; the Manns' cars, which it had been hoped to bring out, had been confiscated; and the chauffeur had brazenly admitted his Nazi sympathies. Thomas Mann had nightmares at the thought of Gestapo agents turning over his diaries: 'they'll publish extracts in the *Völkischer Beobachter*, they'll ruin everything and me too'. He had already arranged with the loyal Ida Herz for the discreet removal and dispatch to a Swiss accommodation address of two-thirds of his library. They decided now to maintain the fiction—or indeed the possibility, who could tell?—of a return to Munich by officially retaining the house: rent it out, with a room or two reserved for the maid, and divide the remaining household-effects, shipping what was possible and leaving the rest, including the valuable manuscripts of all his earlier works, in the care of Heins. Golo, it was clear, must get out as soon as possible. Heins would meanwhile continue his efforts to recover the stolen case from the Gestapo, renew the passport, and find tenants. But the biggest worry remained the missing diaries, the fundamental 'assault on the secrets of my life', which, to his mind, could have fatal results.

Returning with Heins, and finding his own car too then appropriated by the SA, Golo spent most of May in Berlin, where Monika had also made her way from Italy. He was able to arrange with Ambassador François-Poncet for the successful export of the 60,000 marks by French diplomatic bag to Paris; but attempts at the banks to withdraw further cash were fruitless, in spite of the pretext of a 'dowry' of 100,000 marks for Monika in a letter which his father doubtless rather enjoyed writing, in thorough Buddenbrook style, bidding her ensure its investment in gilt-edged and sensible inheritance arrangements. She left for Paris soon after, Golo following at the end of May, to join the parents in the south of France near Sanary, between Marseilles and Toulon.

Klaus and Erika, installed in Bandol, had already taken Michael and Elisabeth there, and Thomas and Katia, after a reconnaissance of Basle, had

---

[12] GM *Erinn.* 536, 517; KlM *Br. Antw.* 87.

arrived on 6 May. Their expired passport gave no trouble at the French border (the blessing of an internationally known name, at a time when *émigrés* with no papers were normally finding frontiers barred to them). Though Mann's preference was for a German-speaking area, there was a prospect here of a congenial and cheaper lodging, if only temporary: somewhere where he could finally install himself in peace and quiet and find the atmosphere for work. The area, not yet fashionable, now housed a number of the exiled, mostly Jewish: Walter Hasenclever and Walter Benjamin had already discovered Bandol, and others were in and around Sanary—Lion Feuchtwanger, Julius Meier-Graefe—while brother Heinrich, now earning his keep with articles for the local press, was not far away in Nice. Centring on the home of René Schickele (for whom in 1914 Thomas Mann the chauvinist had been an 'arch-swine'), the circle that year attracted a host of more temporary visitors: the novelist Hermann Kesten, the writer and critic Ludwig Marcuse, the avant-garde impresario Erwin Piscator, Arnold Zweig before his emigration to Palestine; Aldous Huxley was to be seen, and Paul Valéry. First impressions were admittedly far from favourable: everything seemed 'shabby, unsteady, and not up to my life-style'. But the arrival at last of the suitcase from Munich—held up in fact by the German border police, who had removed papers about his finances but mercifully left the diaries untouched—lifted a great weight from his mind. A house was eventually found near Sanary, and they moved in on 12 June. 'La Tranquille' was their first place to call 'home' since the disaster struck, not big enough to house the entire family, but offering him a study with a verandah, and in surroundings on which, long afterwards, he could look back with pleasure—the climate magically light and even in midsummer unoppressive thanks to the mistral.

There was relief certainly in recovering here a certain stability and something of the routine essential to his way of life and work. He had already added a few lines to the *Joseph*, but with indifferent success, and now, taking out the materials which had reached him, tried to resume. His financial situation, unlike that of most of the other exiles, was relatively good: during June a handsome Peugeot convertible, going at 13,000 francs, replaced the cars lost in Munich, and the sale of German mortgage bonds held in his Swiss bank, even at a nominal 60 per cent loss, brought his capital there to some 200,000 Swiss francs. 'I was pleased at the thought that that represents a million French . . . "illegal", of course, but I'm forced to this more and more the longer I stay out of the country—and what illegality on the part of those who have started to rob me. I'm anyway throwing them half my fortune and the house.'[13]

---

[13] *Tb.* ii, 114.

The complaint at how much he had lost by staying out of Germany was one that would frequently recur, no matter that with what remained to him he had every chance of resuming his usual life-style and was incomparably better off than most of his fellow exiles—a fact which not seldom aroused their resentment, despite their regard for him as the leading representative of the 'true' Germany. Certainly, he had a large family to provide for, even if the older children could well make their own way now. Klaus had already begun work with the new *émigré* publishing-house of Querido in Amsterdam, and was busy with the project of a German-language monthly which, though avowedly literary, could fulfil a political aim in raising the flag of freedom against the oppression at home. For Erika, working on a book for children and with plenty of other plans, he need have few worries, and Golo could have some confidence in seeking an academic post. Even so, the three continued to rely on his support, while the two youngest had still to finish their education, and Monika her studies in Florence. There was money enough, however; and as their entry to France had shown, his lack of a valid travel-document was no cause for concern.

And yet: during that summer in Sanary, there was worry enough. He had not yet come fully to terms with the break from Germany. However great his inner determination never to compromise with the new regime, the fact remained that the Fischer Verlag was carrying on apparently unmolested, and there was every prospect for publication soon of the first two volumes of the *Joseph*, so that his overriding aim of preserving his German readership could be satisfied. Bermann, however, was strongly arguing the risk they both ran in this respect if he remained abroad and put himself in what was now an illegal position (a German citizen failing to comply with a summons to return could now be deprived of his or her citizenship). He assured him that in Berlin, regardless of the 'local measures' in Munich, which had no approval from the government, there was no official black mark on his file, and he could see nothing to prevent his return. In the April/May 'blacklists' of books to be banned from public libraries—'asphalt literature', 'anti-German' and 'subversive Jewish' works—nothing by Thomas Mann had figured, except his two pro-Republic essays; nor had his books been among those ceremoniously consigned to the flames in the infamous *auto-da-fé* organized by the Nazis on 10 May in the main university cities (in Cologne, indeed, Bertram, who still hoped for his friend's return, took some pride in ensuring their exclusion, even though he was far from condemning the shameful proceedings themselves).

Decisive for Mann, however, still in his dilemma, was the Wagner affair, from which the waves continued to reach him and which he could not regard as a purely 'local measure'. He had been sufficiently heartened by strong support from Willi Schuh, music critic of the *Neue Zürcher Zeitung*, to disregard the further protests this aroused in the German press; but after an article in July by Pfitzner he felt compelled to an unambiguous declaration against the way the denunciation had led to his virtual 'expulsion' from Germany, his 'national excommunication'. (Pfitzner had justified his presence among the signatories, not because of what Mann had said about Wagner—permissible certainly 'among artists of rank'—but because he had said it *outside Germany* with all the authority of his world prominence.) His lengthy draft-reply aroused much discussion when read to the circle of exiles in Sanary, disappointing Erika in particular with its 'melancholy tone of conciliation', and he conceded privately the paradoxical situation he was provoking: if it appeared, as he hoped, in the *Rundschau*, the mild way in which he set out the facts still left the door open for his return—which he would then refuse. In the event, the *Rundschau* was too cautious to publish it; at the end of July, resigned, he finally made clear to both Bermann and the old Samuel Fischer that a return was out of the question. There were situations, he wrote to Fischer, which forced even so conciliatory a person as himself to declare his position, and his intellectual honour, as well as family reasons and his physical safety, forbade it. 'You all are carefully considering the undoubtedly ominous consequences which refusal of your advice will entail for me. I do so too, I assure you. But I also consider more clearly than you those . . . which following it could bring, and my decision is final. . . . I am sacrificing much; but that will make it easier for me to justify it to the world, as I plan to do when I must, in moderate but clear terms.'[14] Meanwhile, Fischer would be glad to hear, he was back at regular work on the next part of the *Joseph*, and was reading the proofs of the first volume, which he looked forward to seeing published.

This all sounded decisive enough: but his decision had been taken only in private, and it would still be a long time before he felt the moment had come to declare himself publicly. Even when the confiscation of the house in August and his formal notification to the authorities of removal from Munich seemed to have set a final seal on his excommunication, he remained silent. It was a silence much criticized by his fellow exiles, in France, Switzerland, and England, who felt, with some justification, that the voice of the best-known of all German writers was badly needed in the propaganda war they were waging against Hitler. (It has been a matter for reproach too by not a few later critics, who saw it as a defection from duty to the true Germany which was to survive Hitlerism.) He himself felt he had to find a 'thoughtful way', as he noted in his diary early in September, between the 'often hysterical wounded feelings of *émigré* journalists' and

---

[14] SF *Brw.* 449.

the submissiveness of those writers, like Rudolf Binding and Gottfried Benn, who had remained in Germany to work with the 'rebuilding' movement;[15] and he was still in serious doubt how best to act.

Paramount, however, was to do nothing which would jeopardize the publication of the first *Joseph* volume, *The Tales of Jacob*. During August, he had felt resigned enough to ask Fischer's to relinquish it to the Amsterdam firm of Querido, but was persuaded against by Bermann's highly optimistic forecast for its future, quoting the big advance-orders already received and the continuing excellent sales-figures for his other books. Its transfer abroad would effectively lose his readers in Germany and render his future income problematic—as well as strike a near-mortal blow for the publisher who had fostered his work from the start and could not fairly be asked to give up his star performer. Silence was therefore politic, both now and when the book came out. He was faced, however, with an immediate problem over Klaus's monthly journal *Die Sammlung*.

The first number appeared in September, 'under the patronage of André Gide, Aldous Huxley, Heinrich Mann'. By no means confined to the purely literary, which had been his father's understanding, it plainly announced, in Klaus's editorial, its 'political mission' to leave no room for doubt 'where we, the editors, and our contributors stand'—which was abundantly clear from the contents. Thomas Mann's name, as he had earlier agreed for the prospectus, appeared among the long international list (from Max Brod, Cocteau, Döblin, Sinclair Lewis, and Mencken, to Rolland, Joseph Roth, Schickele, and Stefan Zweig) of contributors now and to come. The understandably nervous Bermann at once protested to him over Klaus's 'irresponsible behaviour'—the German authorities would not hesitate to take 'rigorous measures' against the German authors cited— and begged him to withdraw his name, at the same time pressing Schickele and Döblin, also Fischer authors, to do the same. With some reluctance, he compromised with a weak telegram 'can only confirm that character of first number . . . does not correspond to original programme', which he later amplified in writing to the logical conclusion that his name was to be considered removed.[16] Schickele, who had a novel ready and stood to lose heavily, and Döblin (from solidarity, rather, for his latest book was anyway appearing with Querido), were more forceful in their disclaimers. Stefan Zweig, who had promised Klaus an extract from his *Erasmus* study—a 'veiled self-portrait' in showing the humanist similarly trapped between rival forces of extremism—and who feared the same risks to his own publisher's position, felt compelled also to withdraw his name.

[15] *Tb.* ii, 167.    [16] *Urteil* 208.

These actions had the desired effect. In October, the 'Reich Office for the Promotion of German Literature', which had fulminated against these authors' collaboration with *émigré* journals in their propaganda war on the new Germany, withdrew its accusation of 'intellectual treason' and accepted their intention to abstain from political statements abroad—though still condemning their attitude. But the defections were a shattering blow for Klaus, who had felt no little pride in what he thought a great achievement, and he was bitter against the cowardice which he saw behind it all. His father's argument, that the likely success of the *Tales of Jacob* (it was due out early in October) would represent 'a more striking victory over those in power than a whole bunch of *émigré* polemics',[17] was hardly convincing for him. He had never particularly liked Bermann, and protested vigorously directly to him against the personal insults which he heard had accompanied the political criticism.

Erika too was incensed over what she saw as a ploy by the publisher simply to avoid trouble for himself in Germany, as she wrote to Klaus: 'the whole thing is as I prophesied months ago to our father—the false step of staying with Fischer . . . sows mischief, contradictions, and untenability all along the line where you can no longer distinguish the personal from the political'.[18] From Zurich, where she had begun preparations for the opening of her 'Peppermill' cabaret, she addressed a sharp letter to her father, the very day after his move with the family on 27 September to Switzerland, to the house she had found for them in Küsnacht, overlooking the Zurich lake. Weeks before, as they were deciding on the move, Katia, to his irritation, had indicated that Golo too, like the others, was longing for a public declaration from him against Hitler's Germany: but she had fully agreed with him that with the novel about to appear he must at all costs avoid queering the publisher's pitch. The older children's opposition was disturbing, certainly, and he took pains over a soothing letter to reach Erika at her dress rehearsal for the 'Peppermill' opening on 30 September. But he was definite in his determination to distance himself from the polemics and the 'execrations of the *émigré* press', as he called them, and to preserve his works for his readers in Germany as long as he could—an aim amply fulfilled by the success of the novel, of which the first printing of 10,000 was sold out in a week. Was this to be thrown away? he wrote to Schickele: 'materially I get nothing from it, the royalties are confiscated, and with Querido in this respect I would have fared more securely and better. But the non-material interest remains.'[19] (He had, however, already sought and obtained Bermann's agreement to a Swiss book-club edition— the royalty from which would more than cover a half-year's rent for the

[17] KlM *Br. Antw.* 134.     [18] PdM ii, 223.     [19] *TM Stud.* x, 42.

Küsnacht house—while loyally protesting his refusal of other 'significant offers' he had received from abroad.)[20]

The new quarters in the Schiedhalden Strasse in Küsnacht went a long way to restoring his equanimity. He was back in a German-speaking environment, even if still a little too close for comfort to the frontier, in an elegant house which offered the prospect of restoring the comfortable patrician life-style of Munich after the barely tolerable standard of French housing. Küsnacht, wrote Heinrich early in October, was 'the best possible substitute for your Munich environment', and he thoroughly approved of the decision to continue publishing within Germany: 'if I could, I'd do exactly the same myself, i.e. carry on the fight against those in power from within'. Within two months, much of the Poschinger Strasse furniture and household equipment, consigned cunningly via cover addresses, and the books sent by Ida Herz, had arrived (the renown of Thomas Mann ensuring that no customs duty was charged), and it was like a dream to see his study as if by magic set up again as it always had been, down to the smallest details. Two of their Munich maidservants followed soon after; the four bathrooms were well served with hot water; a new Fiat car graced the garage.

Thoughts of what had been lost, nevertheless, were still disquieting, as hopes flickered, then faded, between the conflicting decisions of Munich and Berlin over the possible recovery of his assets. The familiar possessions seemed to confirm the reality of permanent exile, and from time to time doubts would well up whether he had taken the right course: after all, if he returned, there would be no need to behave like Hauptmann or Richard Strauss, one could maintain a 'severe isolation abjuring any prominence', and there would be friends enough. Still, the elegant new surroundings, with guests coming and going as before, gave a comforting impression of an unchanged way of life. There was indeed a certain enjoyment in showing visitors from 'inside' that he had not been reduced to the poverty-stricken existence of the typical *émigré*; and he could take pride in the knowledge that the Munich authorities had been unable to 'prevent us from living in a fine house in freedom'. Even a journalist from the Nazi rag *The SA Man*, two years later, inspecting from the outside the 'very imposing villa in which the "poor" emigrant Thomas Mann manages to lead his contemplative life', could not deny his 'admiration for the discriminating taste of the owner'.[21] Though Mann already had thoughts of building a place of his own, such a move needed a cautious approach at Swiss prices, and the Küsnacht house was to remain their home for nearly five years.

[20] *GBF Brw.* 46.    [21] Sprecher 39.

2

> *'Better far to quit one's land for ever*
> *Than under sway of breed so infantine*
> *To tolerate the yoke of blind mob-hate'* (Platen)

The Swiss authorities showed an engagingly forthcoming attitude to the famous foreign writer who had arrived without valid papers, but evidently adequate funds, at a time when 'undesirable foreigners' risked being smartly thrust back over the frontier or, if allowed to stay, subjected to severe restrictions. Any questions he had for officialdom were answered amiably and helpfully, and his contributions to the Swiss press and, later, his pronouncedly political statements, which from others would have been grounds for deportation, were overlooked. He had every reason to be grateful, as he said in a broadcast in December 1934, for the way the path to a new home had been smoothed for him, the 'generous complaisance' of the authorities and the 'friendly sympathy' of the Swiss public, of which the ovation following his reading from *Joseph* in Zurich University on 8 November 1933 was a comforting manifestation. Yet all was not sweetness and light. He spoke during the war of 'the stigma, often hardly noticeable, but none the less unmistakeable, which attached to us *émigrés*'.[22] Klaus recalled the suspicion in the approach of the Swiss during the thirties—not because the newcomers were Germans, but because they had left Germany: 'a decent person stands by his country, no matter what the government; whoever is against the legitimate power, becomes suspect. . . . And did not Hitler represent the legitimate power? Yes indeed, most thought.'[23] And of course Nazi sympathizers were not lacking. Threats from 'swastika types' began to be heard even before the opening of the 'Peppermill', and the audiences arriving for performances during October were the target for insults; the allusive satire of Erika's pieces had to be discreet enough to suit Swiss neutral sentiments; and the cabaret's tours which followed in 1934, despite undoubted popularity and full houses, were not without serious incident, resulting once in police protection for her and the Küsnacht house. A year later, after a ban in three cantons, the permit for Zurich was not renewed.

All this, however, cast no more than a faint shadow on the Mann family's existence in exile. The two youngest children settled happily into their new life: accepted for the 'Free' (but fee-paying) *Gymnasium*, they were also able to pursue music studies at the Conservatoire, Elisabeth for piano and Michael for violin. For the moment they were the only two living permanently with the parents, but all were reunited for Christmas 1933, together with Reisiger from Austria and Erika's 'Peppermill' colleague Therese

---

[22] xi 975.    [23] Quoted Sprecher 42.

Giehse—an occasion just as of old. Golo came from Saint-Cloud, where he had obtained a teaching-post in October, Monika from Florence, and Klaus—alone representing the *émigré* type vilified by the Nazis press, and still restive under his father's 'cowardice'—from his commuter existence between the European capitals (he had homosexual friends in each, but his visits to Zurich were mainly to secure a morphine-based prescription to satisfy his increasing drug-addiction).

Thomas Mann himself, settled now in a life and surroundings closely resembling those of Munich, could resume the orderly routine essential for him: the morning devoted to painstaking progress on the third volume of the *Joseph* novel; then his walk and his usual rest; and the remainder of the day occupied with correspondence or coping with the steady stream of visitors, admirers, journalists—their stays, as ever, sternly regulated by Katia. His dependence on her, if anything greater now than before, had been brought home to him by her illness in November (a growth in the womb, fortunately benign but requiring rest): it was 'the signal for a restriction in my activity in future', he noted with concern, and 'very worrying, for everything is founded on her vigour'. The locals—at that time Küsnacht was little more than a village of a few thousand—showed typical reserve towards this foreign family, well-known though it might be, and sometimes resentment over Katia's peremptory manner ('I am Frau Thomas Mann!' as she pushed her way forward in shops).[24] For his part, he had little interest in their affairs, for he was content enough now, and felt sufficiently at home, to pursue his own: 'if one is from Lübeck, it makes no particular difference whether one lives in Munich or Zurich'.[25]

During the latter half of 1933 there came two official communications from the Reich which seemed to finalize his break: a demand, now that Germany had ostentatiously left the League of Nations, that he should resign his membership of the League's Commission for Literature and the Arts, and another, via the publishers, for his signed undertaking to join and abide by the rules of the 'Reichsverband Deutscher Schriftsteller'. This was now the official writers' organization, under the presidency of Hans Friedrich Blunck, the nationalistic novelist, and, as with all the professions, designed to ensure *Gleichschaltung* under full Nazi control. With neither was he prepared to comply: but the second, while the *Joseph* publication was in preparation, caused great concern for Bermann and Suhrkamp at Fischer's. They succeeded in temporizing, with his arguments that he continued to regard himself as belonging to German literature and wished for nothing better than to maintain his link with Germany and his readers there; that for him, as an honorary member of the former Writers' Union,

[24] Ibid. 53.    [25] *EB Br.* 186.

now absorbed into the new organization, there was no need of any further formality; and that to press for such 'impossible undertakings' would simply have the effect of driving him into the '*émigrés*' camp'. He had not much hope this would succeed, expected in fact the extract from the second volume due to appear in the January 1934 *Rundschau* to be his 'literary swan-song for Germany'—but still refused to sign the form required. A compromise, however, was found, by inscribing him as a member among the Germans 'resident abroad' who need not sign[26]—an indication, doubtless, that the Reich was not yet willing to lose the prestige of his name.

Bermann Fischer, as he was now styled after his marriage to Samuel Fischer's daughter Brigitte, could therefore go ahead with volume two, *The Young Joseph*, long ready and its printing already in hand. It was published separately in 1934, announcing altogether four volumes for the complete work. For the third, Mann had estimated another two years (in December, he noted with satisfaction that Conrad reckoned thirty lines as a good day's average, though admittedly one he himself was not reaching); the fourth must lie even more distant. But for the moment, his readership in Germany remained secured, and he was not concerned over the impression this might give of collaboration with the Reich.

Through all this, his mood had fluctuated between optimism and hopelessness. To Schickele, at the end of November, he had surmised that before very long they would be able to live in Germany again, 'in two or three years or so, maybe even sooner', and agreed with him that 'the older, better, higher Germany can do no other than . . . seek an indirect effect, a kind of cellular creation. . . . There is no other way.'[27] Yet on New Year's Eve his diary lamented the condition of his nerves and spirits, making work impossible—'fatigue, intellectual lassitude, ennui, which, if it showed, would have a dubious look'—and the news next day of the death of his old friend and contemporary Wassermann greatly depressed him, making him wonder how long he himself still had. Though he had often smiled over Wassermann's work, which was not without a 'certain empty pomp', he wrote to Schickele, 'I also saw he had more narrative sap in him than I': the 'stinking idiocy' of the German press, however, dismissing him as one of the most esteemed writers of the old 'November Germany' but of no significance for the literature of the new, read like an 'obituary for us all'.[28]

At the same time, to hear of the huge success of Erika's new 'Peppermill' programme, premièred in Zurich on New Year's Day, and continuing to packed houses, came as a great lift to his low spirits. He had more pleasure

---

[26] PdM ii, 257.    [27] TM *Stud.* x, 48.    [28] Ibid. 51.

from that than over any praise he might earn for the novel, he wrote to both Hesse and Bertram: it was the 'abdication of his age, creeping in, imperceptibly and painlessly, in favour of the young people'. To write to Bertram at all, indeed, whose last letter trying to explain the glories of the new Germany had been lying unanswered since November, was, he felt, a sure sign that he was regaining his 'nervous strength'; and in firm but friendly terms he made his position clear, at the start of 'Year II', as he put it. He was his own man, and had no contact at all with the German *émigrés* scattered over the world, who were entirely lacking in intellectual or political unity. 'If the right appreciation of the attraction and dignity of your Reich is not yet to be found everywhere in the world, that is no fault or merit on the part of these people, who are completely without influence', and he urged Bertram to make this point firmly with his Nazi friends.

No, I see the new Germany . . . not through any distorting medium, but, as I always do, through my own eyes. I know its thoughts and works, the way it speaks and writes, its German language bogus in every sense, its moral and intellectual level proclaimed with astonishing frankness—and that is enough. That that level is sometimes an embarrassment to you too, I am firmly convinced, however vigorously you may deny it.

If they should meet again ('but will you risk a turn in the open air?'), his attitude in their discussion of the 'landslide of the century' would be that of Goethe's in Napoleonic times: 'My friend, I too believe in Germany's future.' And he went on to detail the family news, to describe his hope for Swiss naturalization and his wish to be buried in Switzerland, like Stefan George, and his extensive reading-tour round the country due early in February—which would include a few repetitions of the Wagner lecture that had been so applauded, almost a year ago, in Munich on the eve of their fateful departure.

For one always acutely conscious of the turn of the calendar's leaves, there were melancholy reminders of such anniversaries almost daily during February, especially as the tightly scheduled reading-tour drew to a close and they prepared for a break once again in Arosa. In the diary he had begun twelve months earlier—'a comfort and aid' through trials which had aged him and Katia more than just the year—it was with mixed feelings that he noted how Arosa would 'close the circle exactly': a return to where 'our exile began . . . and the thread of our former life was snapped off'. Yet his new life seemed to have settled nearly into the old routine, as he resumed daily toil on the manuscript, and his correspondence brought encouraging offers for Scandinavian editions of the first *Joseph* volume. He could be content with the standard of living he had found—'my bath, my car, a fine study, good meals'—and renewing the rental of the Küsnacht house freed him from worries over another move in the foreseeable future. Through Heins, he had paid the heavy tax demanded of Germans who had moved abroad, and still hoped this would effect the release of his remaining Munich property; but the passport renewal hung fire, the Zurich consul-general confirming he had no authority and nearly provoking him to forget politeness with his close questions about Erika and her 'imprudence'.

After Christmas, Reisiger had stayed on, in indecision over his own future as they watched Austria's lapse into its own form of fascism and the suppression by Dollfuss of the social democratic uprising in Vienna—freeing his hand, as he claimed, to combat the Nazism of Germany, but more likely acting as its forerunner. Though Mann realized his friend was something of a parasite, Reisiger still made a welcome companion and confidant, who would be much missed when they left for Arosa. With him, he could discuss the crippling inhibitions he felt over expressing his protests against the 'German crime': how he could hardly bear even to mention the name of Adolf Hitler, still less to write about the horrors of the concentration camps; how he needed 'artistic freedom, distance, gaining of time'; his inclination just to let the world go its way. His thoughts returned now to the earlier notion of a novella on the Faust theme: 'such a free symbol for the condition and the fate of Europe would perhaps be not only happier, but also more correct and appropriate than a discursive and judgemental personal statement'.[29] That idea, as Hitler's world went its way unchecked from 'historic' success to success, would take a long time before taking shape as Thomas Mann's most significant pronouncement on the German tragedy. For the moment, any form of dialogue with Germany was impossible, as he wrote from Arosa early in March to Schickele, and he confessed a 'certain lack of interest in politics in the face of the current brutal nonsense' there. 'My rejection of the German state totalitarianism, founded on crimes, lies, and humbug, I make clear by living and remaining outside, and the world may take note'—a world which showed every sign of accommodating itself to Hitler and little inclination to listen to the protests of embittered *émigrés*.[30]

In Arosa, however, where he spent nearly three weeks with Katia, he was beset by recurrent nervous crises, preventing any real progress with the novel. Though he put this down to the height and the constant föhn, it came in fact from a persistent uncertainty in his own mind. He felt a deep-seated rejection of the 'martyrdom' which had been thrust upon him: as he recalled Gottfried Benn's remark once, that Thomas Mann's house in Munich had 'truly something Goethean about it', the loss of that Olympian existence seemed 'a serious stylistic fault' in his life, a gross error of fate,

[29] *Tb.* ii, 320 f.      [30] *TM Stud.* x, 57.

with which he was unable to come to terms, and the impossibility of ever putting this right was 'eating at my heart'. Back in Küsnacht on 16 March, he found it strange how the thought of a return to Germany was constantly recurring, although for the moment such a move was quite out of the question: the notion of reaching some kind of peaceable arrangement if he could only frame a suitable letter to the authorities. It did not last long, as he conned the reports from Germany of conditions there, noted the obsequious behaviour of the academics towards their Führer, the politicized Nazi directives on school tuition and training for the medical profession, and saw the 'whole fraudulent chaos of Nazism' symbolized in absurd hotchpotch on the millions of medals to be issued on May Day—Goethe, Reich eagle, swastika, and Moscow emblems of sickle and hammer. And he began to consider a rewrite of the *Reflections of a Non-Political Man*, that 'personal and relentless disputation in book form on German affairs' which he would have (one day) to produce and which of course would mean a definitive break until the end of the regime, 'i.e. probably to the end of my days'.[31]

Writing to Bertram about the fate of books he still had on loan from him in Munich (if their release from the Gestapo's hands could be secured, they would be returned), he alluded to how much calmer he was now than a year earlier. Taking as his motto Lucan's line from the *Pharsalia* (the gods are pleased by a victorious cause, but Cato by one that was conquered), he expressed his doubts whether the form of victory this time could be pleasing even to the gods. He was not surprised to hear in April the verdict of one of Bertram's students on his tutor: 'the most obstinate and bigoted of all Nazi professors, insufferable, impossible'.[32] A return visit on 21 March to Basle, where he repeated his Wagner lecture, served to overcome any further wavering of contentment with the new life in exile, and it was pleasing to find the first copies of *The Young Joseph* awaiting him back in Küsnacht. In particular, he was at pains during April firmly to counter Bermann's criticism of Erika's continuing exposure with the 'Peppermill' as damaging to his own—and the publisher's—prospects in Germany: it was too much to demand that he should disavow his family to kowtow to this 'shameful regime of injustice', and he categorically refused to attempt any 'attack on the moral freedom of my children' merely to secure outward advantage for himself.[33] But it would be some time yet before he could bring himself to the inevitable public statement of his position, in book form or otherwise: for his priority was still the long-considered letter to the Interior Ministry, in a final bid for the passport renewal and the release of his remaining Munich assets.

---

[31] Ibid. 61.    [32] *Tb. ii*, 401.    [33] SF *Brw.* 456 f.

How far he realized this would be a forlorn hope is not clear: but he took many days during April over the drafting. The result was a lengthy statement of the position into which the year's events and the illegal confiscations by the Munich authorities had forced him, factual and—probably sensibly, in view of its uncertain reception—free of exaggerated polemic. For a writer, he argued, whose whole work did honour to Germany and who was regarded abroad as the representative, not of any political system, but of its very spirit, to be compelled to live apparently disowned by his country was unjust and absurd. His continuing antipathy for the National Socialist ideology he would not deny; but now that history had apparently given its judgement, he had remained silent, and would adhere to the resolve stated with his resignation from the Academy, namely to abjure any further official activity and devote himself in complete retirement to completing his life's work. That must now perforce be outside the boundaries of Germany—whatever the difficulties, for one nearing 60, in being cut off thus from his accustomed way of life. But the unexpected exile, with his position now regularized under the new Reich laws, he regarded simply as an 'episode ordained by fate, a leave of absence, so to speak, from the community, for an indefinite but measured period', while hoping to continue in contact with his readers at home and refusing publication in German elsewhere. And he ended with a plea for the return of passport and assets confiscated—less for the practical reasons than for the spiritual, 'for . . . it would mean a falsification of my natural destiny to live in unhappy dissension with my country, and I feel that in the eyes of the world such a situation could be of no benefit to the honour of Germany either'.[34]

While he was still completing this, a new perspective opened. Blanche Knopf, his American publisher's wife, who was visiting Europe, arrived with a cable from her husband: the English version of *The Tales of Jacob* was to appear in New York on his fifty-ninth birthday, and Knopf proposed he should attend the celebration dinner planned for the day and stay for a week, offering to meet his costs and half those for Katia. They accepted at once, though realizing it might be a strain for Katia; by 1 May Knopf had cabled arrangements for sea crossings; and they found the American consulate agreeably forthcoming, with a certificate of identity to serve as their travel document, and the French making no difficulty over a visa for transit via Paris. It would cause surprise and anger in Munich, he thought with some pleasure, when they saw him free to get as far as America even though passportless. The letter to the ministry was meanwhile sent on its way, and the few weeks remaining before their departure were well enough filled to

[34] xiii 96–106.

banish any concern over the response (none was in fact ever received): a welcome reunion with Bruno Walter after his Zurich concert, and—perhaps for the last time, he felt—with the old Samuel Fischer, then visiting Switzerland; two more lectures, repetitions of *Goethe's Career as Writer*, in Basle and Zurich; preparation of his after-dinner speech for New York; and steady work on the manuscript of the *Joseph*, which he planned to take along. It was disturbing, when he received from New York advance copies of the first volume, to find it entitled *Joseph and his Brothers*, with no indication that more was to follow (the London edition with Secker would have the correct title); but to him Helen Lowe-Porter's translation seemed well done.

Katia was in fact fully recovered from her previous indisposition, and any strain from their maiden voyage to the United States was more likely to fall on him. Just before their departure for Arosa the doctor had confirmed the menopause, and she was fully reconciled, as she put it to her husband, to this ending of the 'magic of spring'. He had been deeply affected by the revelation, which, with the realization of how life was passing, aroused a gamut of emotions, from 'gentle compassion to abysmal dread of death and panic-stricken horror'. Against this, there was growing sensuous pleasure in the little everyday amenities of his life, and he had thought how the praise of comfort and the senses must be one of the themes for the Faust novella he had in mind.

He was prompted now to musing on his own sexuality, as he searched his old notebooks and diaries for an Elizabeth Barrett Browning quotation to use in his New York speech, and became immersed in what he had written nearly thirty years earlier in the fervour of his relationship with Paul Ehrenberg, transcending the many other homo-erotic attractions before and since. Once only, he reflected, in that 'central emotional experience of the heart at 25', had such passion been granted him and happiness in the fulfilment of actually enfolding the loved one in his arms. 'That is no doubt humanly fitting, and thanks to this normality I can regard my life as more integrated into the natural order of things than through marriage and children.'[35] Strangely, the day before this was written, Klaus in Amsterdam entered a laconic note in his own diary: 'dreamed about the Magician's secret homosexual life', adding 'relationship with Kruse'[36] (Werner Kruse was one of the musicians in the 'Peppermill' ensemble during 1934). The fiction of dream? or fact? We can no longer say; but certainly Thomas Mann continued as susceptible as ever to the attraction of the young male figure. On his midday walk at the end of April, the sight of a gardener, stripped to the waist for work, so moved him with its 'normal, everyday,

---

[35] *Tb.* ii, 338, 412.      [36] KlM *Tb.* ii, 32.

and natural "beauty", the breast, the swelling of the biceps', that he pondered at length afterwards on the 'unreal, illusory, aesthetic nature' of his tendency, erotic but seemingly seeking only to look and admire, neither reason nor the senses desiring fulfilment.

On 18 May they took the train for Paris, where Golo met them, and the following day boarded the *Volendam* in Boulogne, bound for New York. The Dutch steamer was relatively slow, but fairly empty, with excellent food, and comfortable enough—like a first-class sanatorium cut off from the world. He passed the time, rather than taking up the manuscript again, in making notes of his impressions of the voyage and in varied reading: *The Golden Ass*, Plutarch, Jean Giono, above all finishing *Don Quixote*, which he had been dipping into over the previous weeks, and which showed a pleasing emphasis on humour as a vital element of the epic, suiting his conception of the *Joseph*. Their table companions, however, they found uncongenial, of a 'particularly low intellectual level', as he noted, and, like the captain, apparently quite unaware who he was. This was satisfyingly put right, however, when the Statue of Liberty was sighted, early on 29 May, and a tender put out with Knopf and a pack of journalists aboard, so that the other passengers could be duly impressed by the throng of interviewers gathered on deck to see the great man. He confessed later to a certain stage-fright, after this new encounter with a truly open sea, over his first appearance on the American scene: but at least his nervousness over the adequacy of his temporary document to cope with the rumoured strict immigration-controls proved happily unfounded, and though the customs took a close look at the *Joseph* manuscript for any subversive material, they made no trouble.

Knopf exploited to the full the publicity opportunities, extending the visit to ten days and efficiently organizing a very crowded programme, with lavish hospitality. Their room on the twenty-fourth floor of the Savoy Plaza was filled with flowers, and the first day was crammed with further interviews, before a dinner in the evening to which Mencken, Willa Cather, and Henry Seidel Canby were invited. There followed a reception in the New York PEN Club, a lunch with the editor of the *Nation*, a lecture (once again Goethe) to the German Department at Yale, a mercifully quiet weekend with the Knopfs out of town, and a dinner in the Authors' Club, before the high point of his birthday: lunch with the editors of the *New York Times*, and the 'Testimonial Dinner' in the Plaza. With his limited command of English, there were bound to be communication difficulties, but he held his own under the strain of question and answer, and, having taken the precaution of sending the text of his dinner address in advance for translation, had time to study and practise it. The 300 guests, headed by Mayor

La Guardia, and including Sinclair Lewis, his wife Dorothy Thompson, Canby, Willa Cather, and professors from Yale and Princeton, seemed impressed, to judge by their applause, not least when he succeeded in blowing out the fifty-nine candles on the gigantic cake.

Knopf had every reason for satisfaction with the success of his enterprise; while for Mann, feeling he had played his own part quite well, it was a boon to see the 'harvest of so much sympathy, sown and waxing with the years, especially when the harvest at home has been destroyed by hail'.[37] He was able, before leaving, to express his thanks to a wider public in a brief radio-address, with his belief that, despite the current wave of unreason and inhumanity and the grave economic difficulties in the world, the 'manly peaceableness' of the American nation was on a better road to restore mankind's dignity in a new humanism than could be taken on the ancient continent of Europe. Their luxury cabin on the larger *Rotterdam*, when they sailed on 9 June, was filled with flowers and gifts of fruit, books, and cigars; and he had particularly appreciated the present from Knopf of a Sibelius symphony recording. The whole 'splendid spree', as he called it later to Heinrich, had cost him a month's working time, but he would not have missed the impressions of America, however superficial: the democratic intentions behind Roosevelt's admittedly dictatorial regime, New York's amalgam of races, languages, and types well represented by La Guardia, the Italian half-Jew with an adopted son from Sweden. 'It is the only true world city, a humanly free country, and could, I believe, absorb even us . . . One could become an American, and maybe one should.'[38]

The crossing was rougher this time, but speedier, and the *Rotterdam*, though older than the *Volendam* and coal-fired, reached her home port via Plymouth and Boulogne in nine days. It was gratifying to find himself recognized by the more international company on board, indeed almost too well-known for comfort: for his consent to give a short talk to a group of Yale and Vassar students, at which a larger audience, including the captain, assembled, seemed the signal for all and sundry afterwards to get into conversation. He would have preferred to land in Boulogne, since they had the French visa, but decided to continue to Rotterdam in order to meet Klaus, which entailed a disconcerting delay on arrival, before a two-day permit to stay could be obtained. Klaus was as helpful as ever, though depressed by the suicide in Paris of one of his close friends. The onward rail-journey via Brussels, where they met Katia's brother Peter, now in a university post there, and Strasburg, in a comfortable sleeper, was uneventful; but at Basle came a new complication, for the re-entry visa now

[37] *EB Br.* 184.    [38] *Jb.* 1, 174.

required for Switzerland was secured as an exceptional case only after higher-level argument and production of his French recommendation and League of Nations certificate. At Zurich they were met by Erika and the two youngest, and driven at last back to Küsnacht.

It proved by no means easy to return to his interrupted routine. Katia's parents arrived the following day for a two-week stay—though their house in Munich had been sequestrated, in order to tear it down and replace it with a pretentious construction in the new Nazi style, they had apparently been left personally unmolested and free to travel; and, as often before, he found them irritating at close quarters, Hedwig Pringsheim particularly now with her professed objectivity, even tolerance, towards the regime, reports of whose excesses she dismissed as propaganda. Michael, now learning the viola and doing well, was proving unamenable to discipline, reacting insolently to any kind of correction; while Monika was asking again to come home from Italy, a proposal to which Katia was reluctant to agree. Events meanwhile—notably Hitler's meeting with Mussolini and the insecurity of Austria's situation between the two—and the danger of a 'European explosion' evoked in discussions with Klaus, Erika, and Golo, had been unsettling enough to make them think, briefly, of abandoning the 'mousetrap' of Switzerland for the south of France again. Schickele had in fact long been urging such a move, stressing how much cheaper life there would be. But the idea seemed to lose any urgency in the comfort of Küsnacht and with an invitation to Venice at the end of July for an international arts congress, a journey for which he would now have the added security of a Swiss identity-card.

He continued, however, to be disturbed over the 'mindless nervousness' in Germany—the apparent confusion there over Papen's outspoken criticism of the regime, and Hitler's ruthless and bloody suppression on 30 June of the so-called 'Röhm putsch', eliminating opposition, real or imagined, among old and new fighters of the Storm Troops. In the familiar surroundings of the Hôtel des Bains and the Lido, when they arrived in the Venice which always seemed like another Lübeck, 'a second homeland magically transformed into the oriental',[39] his pleasure quickly faded in the useless deliberations of the congress sessions—'a mockery and a disgrace' (not least perhaps because, though ready to speak, he was not called upon). This dissatisfaction, coupled with the intolerable heat and finally the news of the Nazis' murder of the Austrian Chancellor Dollfuss on 25 July, led him to cut short the stay.

The Austrian developments, with Mussolini's partial mobilization in apparent resistance to Hitler, provoked more long discussions with Golo,

[39] 36/121.

home for the vacation, and Erika. Was this the beginning of the end for the regime, he wondered, a *finis Germaniae* even? The new *élan* in Protestant Germany had shown itself as degenerate, based on lies and brutality, and its making of history as 'the most miserable error ever committed by a leading nation', ending in 'a worse hangover than that which had emerged from 1914'. 'We shall see,' he had said, as he reminded Bertram: 'but have we begun to see? No, for your eyes are held closed by blood-stained hands, and you are only too willing to accept the "protection"'. History indeed had perhaps assigned the Germans the role that Goethe had once found fitting for them: to be condemned in the world of the future, like the Jews, to dissolution in a diaspora. The thought was premature, of course (though one to which he would return in the apocalypse to come): but he felt once more the time was at hand to speak his mind. Why not a thoroughgoing open letter to the London *Times*?—'to urge the world, and especially cautious England, to make an end with the disgraceful regime in Berlin. . . . This may truly be the right moment.' ('If only he *would* do it!' commented Klaus,[40] hearing the idea and pressing, as always, for action.) He began a draft at once with excerpts from his 1933 diary, for it was natural for him that such a statement, as with the wartime *Reflections*, demanded a thorough 'settlement of accounts, both personal and general', and, unlike his brother, he was incapable of dashing off such a political piece without his usual meticulous, quasi-academic preparation.

Any notion of the regime's imminent collapse, however, was quickly dispelled with the assumption of full power by Hitler on 4 August, combining the offices of President and Reich Chancellor following Hindenburg's death. Though dismayed by this unexpected stabilization of a power he had thought wavering—'unhappy land! unhappy Europe!'[41]—Mann persisted with his plan. He felt a permanent crisis of conscience, which prevented him from devoting himself to his work, the 'game, sublime though it may be', of the novel, before he had expressed all the sorrow, hatred, and contempt for his country that oppressed him. 'The moment could soon come when I would regret continuing to bide my time in silence.'[42] It was awkward now, of course, that outspoken criticism of a head of state, as Hitler, however illegally, had now become, was no longer possible, even in the foreign press. But he continued his draft 'with a certain eagerness and angry enthusiasm', though not yet clear as to its form, regardless, as he wrote to Schickele, of the final break it must entail with Germany—'this is what I want, and I'd also rather my books were outside now'.[43] It was encouraging to hear from Stefan Zweig, whose *Erasmus* he had at first criticized but on further reading found acceptable in its implied analogy

[40] KlM *Tb.* ii, 45.    [41] N 34/13.    [42] *Br.* i, 369 f.    [43] *TM Stud.* x, 74.

between the anti-humanist and irrational excesses of Luther and Hitler, that he fully agreed the time had come for the 'politicum', as he was now calling it.

The burst of enthusiasm did not last long, however. In growing doubt whether it was worthwhile trying to 'defend the world against the German basilisk', and uncertain how and where he could publish, he decided after ten days of work to lay the draft aside. Better to await further developments and then perhaps, 'in a new moment of passion', come out with a brief incisive utterance—a decision which Reisiger too, independently, recommended. What was so far on paper, of course, was carefully preserved, and he continued in fact with diary excerpts, press cuttings, and further notes, to be used in the fullness of time. But instead then of returning to the *Joseph*, which had been entirely abandoned all this time, he began a temporary diversion with something more neutral, one of those highly personal accounts he always enjoyed, based on the sea journey to America—*Voyage with Don Quixote*. This he thought could make a *feuilleton* for the *Neue Zürcher Zeitung*, as well as a useful complement to a new volume of essays Bermann was planning to issue.

He continued with it until October, finishing during a fortnight's holiday in Lugano. He had been ashamed at times to be spending himself in so trivial a pursuit, instead of completing the 'politicum': as Schickele argued, even if publication was deferred, that would strike a decisive blow on behalf of the *émigrés*. Reading the typed copy of the lighter piece before despatch to the NZZ, he was not very happy with it, and had to confess to himself that it had probably been written only that he might at least get *something* done. Though privately unadmitted, the importance of not disturbing his chances of further publication in Germany will also have contributed to the faint-heartedness over his 'politicum': the Fischer concern was continuing as before, and there was the essay volume to come, *Sorrows and Greatness of the Masters*, though he had some doubts (since it would include the notorious Wagner essay) of its suitability for the new Germany. He could not know it, but in the Foreign Affairs Ministry at this time there was strong resistance to the Interior Ministry's demand to deprive him of his citizenship. 'Thomas Mann is considered [abroad] as one of the most eminent representatives of German writing,' wrote the Foreign Affairs Ministry, 'and cultural defamation is one of the most important and dangerous methods of anti-German—and especially Jewish—propaganda [to which] depriving Mann of his citizenship would undoubtedly give a strong boost. . . . It would not be in the interests of the Reich [by such a move] to drive him into the camp of the anti-German agitators.'[44] Thus both parties, for different reasons, stayed their hands, and

---

[44] Stahlb. 236 f.

Mann for his part was to wait a long time yet before making his decisive move.

There was no such hesitation on either side in the case of Klaus, of course, who had never made any secret of his anti-Nazi stance and fully expected the loss of his citizenship, which followed on 1 November. Having meanwhile obtained a Dutch stateless passport, he attended the Soviet Writers' Congress in Moscow during August, which attracted mostly the communists and extreme left-wingers among the *émigrés*. The 1,500 roubles due to his father on account of royalties were unexportable, so he used them on a couple of *objets d'art* and assistance to a sick colleague there. Golo had presumably acquired French temporary papers for his post at Saint-Cloud. Erika—possibly still with her German passport, though this is not clear—continued her tours with the 'Peppermill', and was particularly successful with the reopening in Zurich on 3 November, though murmurings in the press and Nazi-inspired demonstrations, with barracking and even tear-gas once in the auditorium, were on the increase, and permits for performances in other cantons were withheld. In Davos in particular, the home of the leader of the Swiss National Socialist party and with many German residents and tourists, the local council pronounced firmly in December against a permit, recalling incidentally that since *The Magic Mountain* their community had 'no special duty of gratitude towards the Mann family'.[45]

This, mercifully, was not the general attitude of Switzerland to the Manns, however; and Thomas, though depressed over developments there often painfully similar to the fascist rise in Germany, found no obstacles to his own, less controversial activities during the final months of 1934. In October his radio talk, 'Greeting to Switzerland', expressing thanks for his reception, brought much approving mail, and he could publish in the *Basler Nachrichten* an *in memoriam* on the death of Samuel Fischer; in November the *Don Quixote* appeared in the *NZZ*, and he spoke to a large audience at the European Union meeting in Basle; in Küsnacht on 2 December he gave a reading from *Joseph* to a youth club in the local gymnasium. Officially too he continued to be well treated. On 23 November the Swiss Federal Justice and Police Department issued a new identity-card, valid till August 1935, specifically authorizing his residence in Küsnacht and his 'activity as independent writer' (for Katia, however, forbidding any gainful occupation).

The news, as they were returning from Lugano in October, of the passing of Samuel Fischer, his publisher and friend of almost four decades, could not fail to affect him deeply. 'A part of my life, and a sizeable part of the life of Germany,' he noted in his diary, 'accompanies to the grave the little Jew

[45] *Pfeff.* 116.

who was blessed of fortune and a kind of genius.' 'I lose a friend, for whom I shall keep a grateful affection till the end of my own life,' he telegraphed the widow; and in his letter to her later wrote: 'Between us there was a cheerful warmth such as I have rarely experienced in my relationships . . . our characters suited each other, and I always felt that I was the born author for him and he my born publisher.' That had been perhaps the strongest factor compelling loyalty to the firm through these early years of the Third Reich, and, though there was never a similar warmth between him and Gottfried Bermann Fischer, it would continue to keep him faithful through the vicissitudes to come.

3

*'For the rest, I lack nothing I need to bring my life and work to a conclusion'*                    (TM, December 1935)

'Year II' had certainly not been without its difficulties for the Führer, but he had emerged apparently stronger than ever, and the immense propaganda effort already under way for the plebiscite in the Saar in January 1935 showed every sign of securing the reincorporation of the area into the Reich. For Thomas Mann, his defaulting from political commitment had left an unpleasant taste of failure, and although he had resumed daily work on the *Joseph* it was sometimes not without a sense of hopelessness. There had been, too, the inevitable effect on his health. From October, he had followed the advice of a Basle doctor to rest more, rising later before continuing his work; but in a life of outwardly even tenor a nervous tension and general fatigue persisted. Over Christmas, celebrated as usual with all the children (save for Monika), Reisiger, and Therese Giehse, it was scarcely helpful to hear a spirited argument between Erika and Katia over his passive political attitude, 'or rather non-attitude', as Klaus called it.

As always, however, the presence of Reisiger seemed to soothe, and progress on the manuscript was steady, even if he acknowledged to himself his fatal tendency to admit, even welcome, interruptions. A lecture tour to Prague, Brno, Vienna, and Budapest was already planned for January; and he agreed with Knopf to prepare for his 1936 list a collected edition of the short stories as the contractually required annual volume in English, for the next *Joseph* would clearly not be ready by then. Financially, as Katia had shown him earlier in December, their situation was still quite favour-able, with an annual budget only two-thirds of what it had been in Munich, but well covered by income and needing no significant inroads into capital. When they set off by train in wintry conditions for Prague on 19 January, he was still far from himself, either mentally or physically, and the result of the Saar plebiscite a few days before—a 90 per cent vote for Germany, even though probably not for Hitler, he thought—had hardly been reassuring. But the resumption in this way of the representational existence which had always been so satisfying, however taxing the tour might be, did much to restore him.

Erika was already in Prague, where the 'Peppermill' had just opened, once again to 'delirious success', as he was glad to learn from the *Prager Tagblatt* before their arrival on 20 January, and they were able to see her briefly before that evening's show. Their welcome in Prague was as deferential and well provided for as it had been three years earlier, with a flower-decked suite in the same Hotel Esplanade and a car from his Czech publisher at their disposal. The first assignment was a broadcast the following afternoon in a German-language programme: a 'Greeting to Prague', affirming his commitment to the understanding between peoples and cultures typified in the multiracial democracies of Switzerland and Czechoslovakia, but also expressing gratitude for the enthusiastic reception of his works in Czech translation. Erika and Therese Giehse joined them that evening for the caviare and champagne now traditional in celebration of the cabaret's success.

In the unavoidable interviews which followed, he took care to say nothing about Germany—not surprising, wrote the left-wing *Rote Fahne*, since he was continuing to publish his work there. But this did not prevent the embassy from reporting to Berlin the scandalized reaction in pro-German circles against any interview at all with the hostile press in Prague, nor hold back the correspondent of the *Völkischer Beobachter* from snide comment on the decadent aspect of this *soigné* 'honorary *émigré*, honorary because his emigration was voluntary and not compulsory', and on his boast that his works were passport enough for him. For his appearance on 22 January to a big audience in the Urania, he had chosen to repeat the Wagner lecture, which was encouragingly well received and applauded at length, to many curtain calls. Next day was filled with visits, book-signing, and autographs, and responding briefly to an invitation from students, before they boarded the train for Brno, where the one-night stand was equally crowded.

In one interview, however, he had been less cautious. The article 'Thomas Mann and Jewry', which appeared in the *Jüdisches Volksblatt* after his departure from Prague—expressing his concern over the fate of Jews in Germany, his rejection of anti-Semitism, his personal debt to Jews for the early recognition and support of his work, and finally his welcome for the bravery of the Zionist experiment—was in fact, he later claimed in a letter to the editor, a distortion of his actual words on anti-Semitism. It was painful for him to have to make such a *démenti*, as he wrote thereafter to the author of the article, but he had to maintain his position if his works were still to be published in Germany: 'When I want to break with Germany, then I'll do it myself, and not through an interviewer.'[46] The article nevertheless made useful ammunition for the Gestapo's renewed efforts that summer to have his citizenship withdrawn.

After Brno came Vienna, then two days in Budapest, as guests of the writer Lajos Hatvány, during which Mann was as splendidly entertained as on his previous visit. In both cities the Wagner lecture was equally applauded, and in Budapest the receptions, press conferences, lunch and dinner invitations made an even more hectic programme than in Prague. Nothing like such a press of autograph-hunters, he was told, had been seen there since the early days of the popular actor Moïssi. He was particularly amused by a polyphoto series of action shots taken during his lecture, surprising him by the lively performance they showed. In his interview for the *Pester Lloyd* he stressed his confidence that a fundamental humanism in all countries would before long conquer the trend to the inhuman ideology of totalitarianism: he felt more affinity now for his Settembrini than for Naphta, 'perhaps because I have more sympathy and understanding for people and less for the preaching of the irrational'. Returning to Vienna, he chose for a second performance readings from the *Joseph* manuscript and from the story of Bauschan the dog, once again to a packed and attentive house.

Already in Prague Erika had been astonished at his ability to stand the pressure, but he had not felt particularly tired; and in Vienna now, before they took the train to return on 30 January, his diary recorded a 'certain biological satisfaction' over his endurance, and the impression that he would reach Küsnacht in better form than when he had left. There can be no doubt of the stimulus for him in this return to centre stage and the prominence he felt his due. 'The manifestations I found everywhere of sympathy for my existence are of course a boon for the nerves,' he noted; and the favourable reception for the *Joseph* extracts had also restored his confidence that there was a charm in what he was writing, however tedious its length. Further invitations—for a similar tour, this time as far as Poland, Romania, and Yugoslavia, and to repeat the Wagner lecture during the August Salzburg Festspiele—completed the favourable impressions of a journey more gratifying even than the many he had made in earlier years. Approaching 60, he had found 'a new resplendence for my existence, evidently more brilliant and valued more highly by the public than those of the Kolbenheyers and Pontens'—even if this might be a lonely eminence, and he must recognize that much of the respect accorded him had been for the survivor of a past 'higher epoch'.[47]

[46] *Fr./Antw.* 208.     [47] *Tb.* iii, 23–5.

Many in Prague and Vienna had urged him to settle there rather than Switzerland, but it was an idea which could hold little appeal, not merely because he was so well ensconced in Küsnacht, but also because he was firmly convinced that a war was inevitable (a conviction that was soon reinforced by Hitler's provocative introduction of conscription in March). However self-satisfied he may have felt at surviving the demands of the tour, he was not about to plunge directly into a routine of work before a suitable break, though a page or two was added to the manuscript, and a two-week holiday with Katia was imediately arranged in Chantarella, near St. Moritz. Here they celebrated their thirtieth wedding anniversary on 11 February, and, as he could not fail to note, the second of their departure from Germany. They enjoyed seeing Bruno Walter and his wife, who were in the same hotel; but the stay was not a success, Katia caught a severe cold, and they fell out over her well-meant attempt, without consulting him, to lure him into a reception in the hotel organized by an admirer—not normally something he would evade, but in this instance provoking him to pack at once for departure and sulk all through the five-hour return-journey to Küsnacht. Erika was due back from Prague the following day, and it would be good for Katia, he felt, to have the children again and no longer be alone with him.

New commitments were meanwhile looming. He was asked to give a talk on 'The Education of Modern Man' at a Nice meeting in April of the League of Nations Arts and Letters Committee—'fine education! my talk will be nothing but a polemic', as he wrote to Schickele, whom he hoped to see, as well as his own brother, on the visit. Its thesis, under the title 'Europe Beware!', was the urgent need for a 'militant humanism' to counter the 'collectivist intoxication' of young people, their empty-headed enjoyment of mass marches singing 'a mixture of degraded folk-songs and leading articles'.[48] As he completed his draft towards the end of March, however, he was dismayed by a call from Bermann Fischer, counselling strongly against the trip: it would be highly counter-productive, said the publisher, at a moment when he was negotiating permission to transfer the Fischer Verlag abroad, Mann's own position looked likely to be satisfactorily resolved, and the essay volume was on the point of appearing. Bermann so far knew nothing about the draft speech, the undiplomatic form of which had already aroused objections in Geneva. It was clear that to proceed could have disastrous effects, both for Fischer's and for himself. He therefore decided, most unwillingly, to cancel his appearance in Nice, alleging health grounds, tone down the text which would be read for him, and ask Geneva to ensure it had only a limited distribution. He was conscious, he wrote to Heinrich, that to deliver personally what he had written would make

[48] xii 779, 769.

difficulties for the League, quite apart from prejudicing his publisher's hopes of survival. He and Katia would, all the same, plan a private visit to Nice later, during May perhaps.[49]

Such a visit would now have to be brief, for during all this had come an invitation from Harvard, offering him an honorary doctorate of letters on Commencement Day 20 June, the jubilee of the university's foundation, provided he could attend in person. It was an offer he must not fail to accept, for it would be an important political gesture towards Germany, 'both the hostile and the friendly'. Harvard was not only the most prominent university in America, but also the one which had coolly declined to accept funds for a scholarship offered by Hitler's foreign-press chief, 'Putzi' Hanfstaengl—a great offence for the Nazi government, which had thereupon refused to send any representative to the jubilee. Their anger, as he told Heinrich, would be all the greater when they learned he was to attend.

The agreement Bermann was making with the Propaganda Ministry was for the transfer abroad of all the firm's 'undesirable' or banned authors, with the stocks of their works, and certain of the firm's assets, on condition that the Fischer family—the widow Hedwig Fischer being now sole owner after her husband's death—sold off the remainder to reliable (i.e. non-Jewish) investors. This was now being arranged with Peter Suhrkamp, the 'Aryan' member of the firm, who raised the necessary finance for the purchase and would take over the management of what was left. The final setting-up of the new S. Fischer Verlag under Suhrkamp was to take well over a year. Though in financial terms it acquired over two-thirds of the assets, the part to be transferred was qualitatively rather more valuable: of the significant authors, only Hauptmann, Hesse, and Manfred Hausmann remained with Suhrkamp, while Bermann took the rights for Döblin, Hofmannsthal, Annette Kolb, Thomas Mann, and Schnitzler. Bermann had meanwhile concluded a merger with Heinemann's in London, but his hope to set up his new house in Switzerland met resistance from publishers there, who contrived the refusal of the Swiss authorities; his plan then to set up in Vienna was thought too risky by Heinemann's, who withdrew from the merger, and the final result was the establishment, on 1 May 1936, of the independent Bermann Fischer Verlag in Vienna, where Thomas Mann's works would from now on appear. The essay volume *Sorrows and Greatness of the Masters* was to be his last published under the Third Reich by the old Fischer Verlag.

This metamorphosis was of vital importance for him, and not merely financially, though that was an aspect he never lost sight of: what counted

[49] *Jb.* 1, 184.

was the preservation of his *œuvre* in German, if not in his homeland then somewhere outside. But the long process and the complications of the manœuvres required aroused often contradictory feelings. At the end of March, in revulsion against the unspeakable behaviour in Germany, he had been moved for a brief moment to long for the final severance of his links, expecting, even hoping, then that this would finish him with Fischer and the essay volume would not appear. Second and, as it seemed, wiser thoughts had then prevailed, with the realization that this might spell the end for the firm itself, and he had 'saved Bermann once again' with his decision to abandon the Nice appearance.[50] He had perhaps an exaggerated sense of his own importance, but there is no doubt that for the publisher the retention of the Thomas Mann rights was a major consideration. He kept Mann closely informed, over this and the following year, of progress towards the establishment of his house abroad.

For the moment, however, the uncertainty had its effect on his author's work. A brief holiday in Nice would help, Mann felt, but the thought of the forthcoming sixtieth-birthday celebrations in Zurich, where a fitting ceremony was being planned, and of the visit then to Harvard, was unsettling. 'When will the *Joseph* be finished? I don't like to think of it.' Conditions at home over Easter were not exactly helpful: not only were the Pringsheims visiting once more, and Monika, who never got on with Katia, but also Ida Herz, pressing to accompany him on his walks and as importunate as ever in her admiration. He contrived to maintain his good humour, but resolved never again to encourage the 'hysterical old maid'. Nevertheless, when he could be alone (and his hours at the desk, if not always on walks, remained sacrosanct), *Joseph* was not lost sight of; and he even toyed again with the idea of a 'politicum', in a different form, a 'memorandum' to the German people, to explain the hostility of the rest of the world and warn them 'in warm and truthful manner against appearing as enemies of the human race.' With the Stresa conference, and then the League in Geneva, condemning Hitler's surprise revelation in March of Germany's new air force and of his expansion of the Reichswehr in defiance of Versailles, and the recent Nazi kidnap from Zurich of a prominent *émigré*, this was perhaps the right moment. His Munich lawyer, however, continued to report hopes of success in freeing his assets there, and once again he held back from upsetting them. Indeed, the young writer Joachim Maass when he called was surprised to hear his calm 'epic objectivity', even humour, in describing what was happening to his former possessions—how he was actually being sued for accidental damage to his confiscated car in the hands of a drunken SA man.

[50] 35/62.

The break in Nice was for barely a week, but he made sure that it would be a real restorative, for himself at least if not for Katia, who was kept busy on secretarial work for much of the time. They travelled comfortably by car to Geneva, stopping in Ouchy, near Lausanne, to see Ferdinand Lion, the Alsatian writer who had emigrated to Switzerland in 1933 and was presently engaged on a biography of the master; then by night train to Nice. Heinrich was at the station to meet them—older-looking, without a beard, but the moustache now white—and they spent much time with him and his wife-to-be during their stay. It was their first meeting with Nelly Kröger, a great contrast to the first wife, the actress Mimi Kanová, on whom they had called in Prague: Nelly was a Lübecker of little intellectual capacity, and Thomas found her 'common' (an impression which was to last). Klaus was also in Nice—thinner and reportedly still using morphine, though in moderation—and stayed some days before he left for the Barcelona PEN Congress. He worked with his mother on a translation and on the transcript of an extract from the *Joseph* due for publication in Prague and Basle journals, while his father relaxed, enjoying his rest, his meals, and the return to the Gitanes cigarettes which had been his favourites in Sanary. There were calls on Schickele and the former editor of the *Berliner Tageblatt*, Theodor Wolff, where many of the *émigrés* were invited and a general air of optimism seemed to prevail, and there was a visit to the faded elegance of Monte Carlo. Heinrich was visibly moved as he saw them off again on the sleeper to Geneva on 20 May. Lunch next day in the Schweizerhof in Berne was followed by a satisfactory call on the Ministry of Foreign Affairs, where an eager 'well-read' official was pleased to arrange for a new travel-document.

Such a refreshing interlude could have meant a new start for his work, but for the imminence of 'festivities in two continents', he wrote to Lion, causing 'agitation and confusion'. The ceremony in Zurich was to be on 26 May, in advance of the actual birthday, in the Corso Theatre, with speeches followed by a performance of the third act of *Fiorenza*. He had therefore to get down at once to preparing his own offering, for a 'cultural demonstration' which—unusually for him—he expected to prove even more painful and absurd, as he had said earlier to Lion, than that for his fiftieth in Munich. 'Where then should the honours and celebrations come from, anyway? Better without them. . . . People think I put up a good show, but inwardly I suffer indescribably.'[51] Tributes from colleagues had already begun to arrive, and he feared, with reason in the event, that his birthday mail would be nigh impossible to deal with.

But he held his own when the day came, and was in fact not displeased with the harmonious proceedings that Sunday morning: the theatre flower-

---

[51] Sprecher 162.

bedecked, every seat taken, an immediate ovation from the audience when he entered his box. A musical prelude was followed by Robert Faesi's brief words of gratitude from the Swiss for his presence on their own soil, in an area where he could still hear, if in a harsher form, the native tongue he commanded in so masterly a fashion; and after presentation of the city's gift, a portfolio of lithographs, he took the stage himself. Whether or no his praise of eastern Switzerland—no foreign land, but a 'homeland for a German of my kind'—as an 'ancient seat of German culture', 'a piece of Germany' beyond her frontiers, and 'one of the indispensable fragments of the Germanic where this merges into the European', was quite what his hearers may have expected, it did not affect their long-lasting applause. The heavily cut third act of *Fiorenza* then, despite what he thought a 'provincial' cast, seemed moderately successful in conveying something of the ideas of the play. Katia had arranged for a lunch at home in Küsnacht, to which Faesi and the more prominent guests were invited, together with Stefan Zweig, whose princely gift from his autograph collection of a Goethe quatrain gave Mann immense pleasure.

The children now began to assemble for the celebration *en famille* on 6 June, which Reisiger and Therese Giehse as usual were to join; and the ten days passed quietly, in beautiful early summer weather—not without some attention to the manuscript, but his time taken up more and more with correspondence as the congratulations and published tributes began to pile up, to reach a climax with literally hundreds of letters and telegrams on the day. It was heartening to receive so many from Germany itself, some from Labour Service camps, showing that even now 'fine reserves of decency and the will to freedom' were not lacking,[52] and especially to hear after so many years from Kurt Martens in Dresden, who he had thought had died long since. He had the impression that the world's picture of him had changed from that of ten years earlier: 'the accents are more ceremonious, more purely honorific, a kind of security, of immortalization has set in'. Hesitatingly and half-unwillingly in these troubled times, the world had come, he felt, to acquiesce in the permanent character of his life and work.[53] He was particularly moved when Bermann, arriving on his birthday, presented him with a casket containing the collected handwritten tributes of ninety or more authors, colleagues great and small, and famous contemporaries of many nations, including some of the 'inner emigration' and even Gerhart Hauptmann. 'Has this difficult life been worth it after all, then, and better, greater than my worried modesty would credit?'

'Official' Germany remained silent, surprisingly perhaps considering the still not uniformly hostile view of him in high quarters there: there had been news on 29 May of Frick's decision for the time being not to withdraw

---

[52] 35/142.     [53] *Tb.* iii, 114.

his citizenship and to restore his Munich possessions, provided he maintained his 'reserve'. In renewed optimism, he had at once thought of a move to another house nearby large enough to take the additional furniture, and, in the interests of 'reserve', taken care to demand the excision of the political passages from an interview to be published in Switzerland on 6 June. But the flicker of hope soon faded. Klaus noted too that there had been no congratulatory messages from the 'real emigration'—by which he doubtless meant the more extreme representatives, mostly centred in France, who, like him, were bitter over his father's stubborn reluctance to take a clear political stand. In Küsnacht now, tension between him (with Erika) and Bermann was to be expected, though the publisher was at this moment discussing with their father possible future arrangements if he set up in Switzerland. (It might have upset Klaus even more, had he known that in this event his father was not ruling out the possibility of transferring to another publisher in Germany.)

Whatever the prevailing view of Thomas Mann in Berlin, there was no doubt over that taken of his daughter. Erika's name figured now on the fourth list issued on 8 June of those to be stripped of their German citizenship (the reason in her case, according to the bureaucratic record, being the 'Peppermill'). Visiting Klaus in Holland, she astonished one of his English friends, the novelist Christopher Isherwood, with a proposal for a marriage of convenience to give her a British passport, after which she would leave him well alone. Isherwood demurred, chiefly, and ironically, because Heinz, his current lover, was a stateless German exile not eligible for such a luxury, but also because he was loath to give any impression he might be trying to pass as a heterosexual, even for the noblest motive; and he suggested instead another of their circle, the poet Wystan Auden. Klaus immediately wired Auden in England, who, though he had never yet met her, replied he would be delighted, and she flew to England on 12 June, where the marriage took place three days later. 'I didn't see her till the ceremony,' Auden wrote to Stephen Spender, 'and perhaps I shall never see her again. But she is very nice.' It was a generous gesture on his part, even if he was not likely ever to be looking for a wife in the real sense; and in fact from this purely pro forma union there developed later a very cordial relationship between him and all the Mann family. Erika held firmly to her British passport till the end of her life.

The birthday once over, there remained only a few days before the departure for America. It was impossible yet even to read, let alone answer, all the messages, but they would be taken along, and, as before, a printed card of thanks was put in hand for the less important replies. Passage had been booked on the French liner *Lafayette* from Le Havre, and Thomas, Katia, and Golo set off by train to Paris on 10 June, to enjoy a quiet foursome dinner with Annette Kolb, before Golo left to return to Saint-Cloud and they for Le Havre the following morning. The voyage passed quietly, with avoidance of most shipboard entertainments, except the cinema, for which he was a ready fan, with a predilection for American rather than French offerings. The arrival of a radio-telegram from England, with 'all love from Mrs Auden', was noted but evoked no comment in his diary. He did nothing on the manuscript, the daily writing-time being taken up with the task of birthday acknowledgements, some in letter form but mostly with brief additions to the printed cards, of which nearly 200 accumulated for mailing in America. The translation of his Goethe lecture, prepared for possible use during the stay, he found badly done, over-long, and hard to enunciate, and was relieved to learn from Knopf on arrival in New York on 19 June that his only public commitment was to be the Harvard ceremony the following day.

After interviews on board, Knopf, as before, took care of everything efficiently on landing, and drove them to his Fifth Avenue office, where a stack of post awaited them, then to the train for Boston. There were invitations to stay with Hendrik Van Loon, at his house in Connecticut, from Sinclair Lewis and Dorothy Thompson (whose anti-Nazi reports, as foreign correspondent in Berlin, had led to her deportation the year before). The Harvard visit was brief but impressive: after a comfortable night in President Conant's house, they found an audience of 6,000 gathered in the morning in a great marquee for the jubilee celebration and degree ceremonies, at which Mann and Einstein, in full academic fig, were greeted with thunderous applause as they formed up for their doctorates. After a grand buffet-lunch, and further speeches by the president of the Harvard alumni association, the Governor, and the Agriculture Minister Henry Wallace, they had a quiet evening with the Conants, toured some of the university institutions the following morning, then left by train for Stamford *en route* for Van Loon's house in Riverside. After a few days there would come the visit to the Sinclair Lewises. Van Loon, Dutch-born author of best-selling works of biography and science, ever ready with assistance for German refugees, was a genial host, and happy to leave the Manns largely to their own devices, while arranging a succession of luncheon and dinner guests who might interest them: writers, publishers, literary agents, and a selection of the neighbours. These occasions Mann found over-protracted and tiring, but with a table at his disposal during the day, he was able to pursue something of his normal routine during the cool, though humid, summer days in Connecticut, with a walk most days, much correspondence, and even adding some pages to the manuscript.

Their plans had to be changed, by higher command, when an invitation arrived to dine at the White House on 29 June. The visit to the Lewises was abandoned, but Dorothy Thompson was able to tell him at the Van Loons of her admiration for the *Joseph*, and of the book she was planning on him (but never completed), for which she left a list of questions. The President's invitation, for obvious political reasons, was purely private, and the arrangements for Washington were handled by Anthony Muto, the chief of the White House press-photographer corps: a flight from New York on 28 June (their first ever, and not without some excitement); a tour of the city that evening, 'extraordinarily beautiful', its perspectives reminding him of Paris; elegant rooms in the Mayflower Hotel; a lively session of Congress the following morning, with introduction to the Speaker and lunch in the members' restaurant; then a visit to Mount Vernon before the time came for Muto to bring them to the White House, where they were welcomed by the First Lady.

They found only two or three other guests when they entered the dining-room, where Franklin Roosevelt, in velvet smoking-jacket, awaited them in his wheelchair. In the quiet conversation, in English of course, over what Mann thought only a moderate dinner, the President impressed with his shrewdness and the self-willed determination which, with his New Deal, had made him so many enemies. He did not conceal his contempt for Congress and especially for the short life of French administrations, contrasting his own position as both leader of government and head of state, unassailable for four years, 'they can't get me out'. Coffee was followed by an over-long movie-show and a tour of the apartments, before Eleanor Roosevelt gave the sign for departure. Mann had been left with the impression of a ruler of authoritarian outlook but deserving of admiration, of which he left no doubt in an interview in New York. Whatever the dictatorial aspects of the Roosevelt regime, he wrote to Bermann later, its foes were mainly among the wealthy, and it stood after all 'in the service of freedom and democracy: it would probably be worse for America if he were to fail'. The following day, after an interview with the *Washington Post*, an excursion with Muto into the hills brought welcome relief from the near-tropical heat of the capital before their return flight to New York on 1 July.

It was as well that only a few days remained before they sailed, for the inevitable reaction against 'letting the world lead him by the nose' had set in. Knopf did his best to entertain them, with visits to friends; books were signed and dispatched from his office to their earlier hosts, including a copy of the two *Joseph* volumes to the 'most gracious First Lady'. The German hotel-manager and his wife were ready guides for the formalities connected with sailing, for errands and shopping, and Independence Day was spent in the country. But he found it hard to overcome a certain depression, longed for his escape from the oppressive climate, to which he attributed a touch of rheumatism in the right arm, and it was an immense relief when the Knopfs drove them to the pier on 6 July for the midnight sailing of the *Berengaria*. He had had enough, more than enough, of the whirl, and his longing for solitude and rest was 'like physical thirst'.

The luxury voyage and rejuvenating sea-air soon restored him. It was well worth the high fare, he thought, their cabin lofty, meals of the highest quality, caviare always on the menu, a whole lobster for Katia whenever she wanted. They would be in Cherbourg in six days, and planned to travel as directly as possible via Paris to Zurich and Küsnacht. The Pringsheims awaited them for the celebration of Hedwig's eightieth birthday, and he would settle at once to work, finishing the current chapter and revising what was so far done for the third *Joseph* volume. The signs of Europe's hopeless 'demoralization and madness' in the press reports during their absence would be firmly put out of his mind: Hitler's major diplomatic triumph, and England's shame, in the Anglo-German accord, allowing him 35 per cent of the British naval strength and parity in U-boats; the imminent Italian intervention in Abyssinia. In Paris, at Golo's suggestion, they spent the evening of their arrival with Félix Bertaux out in Sèvres, before taking the night train from the Gare de l'Est, and were back in Küsnacht early on 13 July.

Resuming work was not as easy as he had thought. Order had first to be restored after the journey, a pile of accumulated mail, with many more birthday messages, sorted and dealt with; the usual stream of visitors set in—publishers, colleagues, Ferdinand Lion busy on his book, the English translator Helen Lowe-Porter; Klaus, Erika, Monika, and Golo arrived to stay, if only briefly; and soon he had to prepare for his scheduled appearance at the Salzburg Festspiele. Hedwig Pringsheim brought word of the death of his school-friend Otto Grautoff, the confidant of his boyhood passions and of his aspirations as a writer, with whom he had long since lost touch: it was saddening, but he could not feel much sympathy for the loss of one who, not content to be a satellite to his own star, had tried ineffectually to emulate him. With her also came a letter from the lawyer on his Munich affairs, seemingly close to an unfavourable conclusion, with nettling, sometimes absurd, details: his books in translation had been handed over to the Munich city library; others left with a friend were appropriated personally by an official; and there was an impertinent demand for 5,000 marks to cover administrative costs. (It was not to be long before the citizenship issue would come to the fore again, largely because of the interviews in America, some of which, for all his caution, had put stronger words in his mouth than he had actually used.)

The Küsnacht routine was gradually picked up, and by the end of July he was working well again; but it was impossible to ignore the clouds over Europe and the increasing strength and stability of Hitler's regime, as he read the press, listened to visitors' stories from Germany, or twiddled the dials of the excellent new wireless that had been the family's birthday present. Radio Moscow's prophetic talk of the few years remaining before the next war, which would begin once Mussolini had achieved his African conquest, confirmed his own thoughts: he might have a few years still to finish the *Joseph*, and—who could tell?—perhaps four years, the duration of the First World War, might yet see the reportedly growing opposition to the Nazis in Germany bring them down. As he recorded this over-optimistic note on 9 August, it was ironic to hear that Rudolf Binding proposed to come to Zurich to explain the absence of any official German recognition of his birthday: the man who, having taken office in the Literature Section of the Academy with some enthusiasm for the Nazi 'revolution', had yet, illogically, striven to maintain contacts with his exiled colleagues. His proposal that the German Academy, as it was now called, should send appropriate greetings to Mann, perhaps even a delegation of honour, had been rejected flat by Frick, he now explained over a *café-crème* in Zurich. 'Irony, insolence, or foolishness?' noted Mann. 'I took note, with thanks.' And he continued his work on the *Joseph* for the few days remaining before setting off with Katia by car for Austria.

*En route* to Salzburg, he had an engagement in Bad Gastein on 20 August, for a reading from the current *Joseph* manuscript: well-attended, but a *succès d'estime* only, he thought, if perhaps with a touch of understanding for his text. On arrival in Salzburg the next day, he was on at once, giving his Wagner lecture that evening, to a good reception. A reading in the Mozarteum later in the week, again from the *Joseph* manuscript, was the only commitment thereafter, and they were free to enjoy the Festspiele productions—Reinhardt's open-air performance of Goethe's *Faust*, followed by a late supper with him at Leopoldskron; a concert under Toscanini, and *Fidelio*, with Lotte Lehmann; Verdi's *Falstaff*; a splendid *Don Giovanni* under Bruno Walter. There was time for visits to Bruno Frank and wife, over from London for the summer, and Carl Zuckmayer at nearby Henndorf, for quiet talks too with Toscanini and, of course, Bruno Walter; but the press of journalists and many other less familiar acquaintances made it all more tiring than he had expected.

Once back in Küsnacht on 29 August, he immediately returned to work on the manuscript. By early October it had reached over thirteen hundred pages, and the first part was in type, with Katia, Golo, even Michael co-opted for collation work (the days were gone when handwritten copy would suffice for the printer, and a typescript was urgently required for a start on the English and French translations). The typist's very fast progress spurred him to productivity, and he ventured to hope that the coming winter, with avoidance of further travels, might bring the end in sight—of the third volume, for it was abundantly clear that there would now have to be a fourth to complete the work. For all that, his routine was not entirely undisturbed. Ida Herz suddenly appeared on their doorstep during September, following renewed anti-Semitic demonstrations after the promulgation of the infamous Nuremberg Laws, which removed the last civil rights of the Jews. She needed a refuge, and money, and his hope for her early return home and an end to the burdensome visit was frustrated, for she stayed for weeks before going on to Geneva and finally taking up illegal employment with the Zurich publisher Emil Oprecht in October. He was concerned too about Klaus: finances had finally run out for his *Sammlung* journal, the last number appearing in August, and he too needed support as he wandered to Budapest and then Vienna; in Küsnacht in November, he was evidently far gone in morphine addiction.

Pondering his own situation, Mann found it amusing that, with his intellectual powers, a few degrees more vitality might have made him a great genius; and memories of his passion for Klaus Heuser, 'last variation of a love which will probably never again revive', 'at 50 happy and rewarded—but then all over', brought to mind the contrast with Goethe's erotic drive till well over 70, 'always girls'. 'But in my case the inhibitions are probably more powerful, and fatigue sets in earlier, quite apart from the difference in vitality.' A brief unexpected visit then from Heuser, still boyish at 24, was a coincidence which he treated with reserve, grateful for his presence but with no outward demonstration of affection.

Meanwhile it had become increasingly clear that, despite his denials of words attributed to him in the American interviews, his German citizenship was once more at risk and that little hope remained of recovery of the Munich assets. The authorities, however, both there and in Berlin, seemed in no hurry to take a decision, and towards the end of the year the Gestapo was still interrogating one of the maids in Munich. In one way, he almost looked forward to the inevitable final break (certainly Katia was relieved for the moment not to have to face an influx of more household effects), and he longed for the finalization of the Fischer emigration to give him independence. 'Had it been left to my decision, I would probably not have left Germany,' he wrote at the end of September. 'Now I thank God daily that I did. A good writing-desk, a good safety-razor, good food, a well-polished little car—what more can one need . . .' 'Despite my age, and in the face of a hundred hostile circumstances, I have a work to see through, and can genuinely claim the right to a modicum of cool self-protection.'[54] At the same time, he shied from any step himself which might precipitate the severance, and insisted it was still too early for him take the public stand

[54] 35/177, 35/176.

which so many urged upon him. His record of opposition to the new absolutism, as he wrote to an American critic, the sacrifices he had made in order to remain in freedom outside the borders of the Reich, were clear enough demonstration of his position, without need for polemic. He had stopped publication of a Salzburg interview in which he had speculated ('quietly and with difficulty, as though trying to convince himself', the journalist had written) on the West's need for a true 'Third Reich' synthesizing the Christian with the pagan ancient world, a theme obviously wide-open to misinterpretation: when the time came to give his views on German events, he would do so directly himself, not in the 'provisional, premature, and inadequate' form of an interview.[55] But his recommendation in October of Carl von Ossietzky, the left-wing Berlin journalist three years now in a concentration camp, for the Nobel Peace Prize, underlining with heavy irony how this would confirm Hitler's constant assurances of his peaceful intentions, would not have escaped notice in Berlin.

He was filled with disgust for the 'swamp of stupidity and meanness' that was Germany now, as he listened to a radio recording of the Führer's Reichstag speech on 15 September, the voice of the 'abominable demagogue' announcing the Nuremberg Laws; read the absurd racist chatter about Germany's 'rebirth'; and watched the preparations for the 1936 Olympic Games in Berlin developing into a monster advertising-campaign for the Reich. His aversion still found expression only in private: but as Christmas approached, he felt the time for silence was fast running out. That it was their third in exile left him quite unmoved: he did not miss the remaining possessions very much, was far happier to be out of his homeland, and basically lacked nothing he needed to bring life and work to a conclusion. 'External events once more coincide with my work, as they did in the war, of which today's situation is very reminiscent.' And through the usual celebrations he added his daily page to the manuscript.

4

*'After three years of hesitation, I have let my conscience and my
firm conviction speak. My words will not fail to impress'*
(*TM 31 January 1936*)

'Around 1940, you'll be standing in Zurich station, asking in a voice trembling with emotion for a single to Munich,' wrote a Swiss friend with his New Year greetings for 1936. Strangely enough, he replied, Heinrich had also prophesied 1940 would mark the end of Europe's 'period of fascist

[55] *Fr./Antw.* 220; 35/156.

unreason'—but a return among 'those desecrated people, well, I really don't know'.[56] The coming year did not promise much change, and he would be content if it showed the end of the current *Joseph* volume and a start on a novella about Goethe which he planned as his next undertaking. During January the first proofs began to arrive of *Joseph in Egypt*, as he had now decided to entitle the third volume of the enormous work: the fourth and final (but when would that be done?) would be called *Joseph the Provider*. Bermann himself had meantime been in London to pursue the negotiations with Heinemann's, and Mann—taking the usual January holiday with Katia in Arosa—was delighted to hear the news of his projected English-Swiss set-up, with more than adequate capital.

On 11 January, however, there had come a virulent attack, in the Paris *émigré* journal *Das Neue Tage-Buch*, against the publisher and the good relations he seemed to enjoy with the Reich authorities. While his authors, Thomas Mann at their head, were the target of all possible harassment, there had never been any adverse comment from Goebbels, or even in the notorious anti-Semitic *Stürmer*, on Bermann or the firm, which had ensured for itself a curiously privileged position, with Bermann one of the regime's 'pet Jews' (there was mention of a 1933 Fischer publication with a printed dedication to no less than Hermann Goering). He was apparently now able openly to arrange for a convenient emigration, if not to Switzerland then to Austria: and the article questioned whether either country would welcome the establishment of an enterprise so clearly hand in glove with the Berlin Propaganda Ministry.[57] On Bermann's excited phone-call from London, Mann agreed to publish in the *Neue Zürcher Zeitung*, jointly with Hesse and Annette Kolb, a protest, from their knowledge of the true facts, against this 'wholly unjust' criticism of the firm's conduct and slander of Bermann himself. He also wrote directly on the same lines to its author, Schwarzschild, editor of the Paris *Tage-Buch*, though conceding that he and the others had 'regretted and condemned' Bermann's failure to emigrate earlier—a statement that, in his own case, was, to say the least, economical with the truth. The public argument continued, Schwarzschild insisting that Bermann's attempt now to set up abroad could only damage the limited chances of survival for the existing *émigré* firms, while if he remained, he was likely to publish only what was acceptable to the Reich: Thomas Mann must not continue to lend his name and prestige to such an enterprise, but declare his error and identify himself firmly with the true *émigrés*.

For Mann himself, the most painful result was the passionate criticism his action provoked from his own daughter. Erika was quick to condemn

---

[56] *Tb.* iii, 233; A & N 691.      [57] *Urteil* 259 f.

what she considered an attack by her father on the *émigrés* as a group and their fight for freedom, apparently preparing an open break with them when his place should be firmly at their side. He would probably take her letter badly, she wrote, but she was prepared for that. He seemed ready to make every sacrifice in the interest of Bermann and his house: if it meant he had to sacrifice her too, 'slowly but surely', then so be it, 'sad and fearful' though this would be for her. The threat of such a rift with the favourite among his children came as a profound shock, and it took him some time, during their last few days in Arosa, to prepare—'for her and posterity'—a long reply to ward it off if he could, his difficulty sharpened by the arrival of a letter from Klaus supporting Erika's views. Katia meanwhile wrote in an attempt to pour oil on the troubled waters: 'apart from me and Medi [as they called Elisabeth], you are the only one he really cares for, and your letter caused him much grief and pain'. She had forecast to him the trouble and unpleasantness this action would arouse, but had not expected Erika's understandable disapproval to lead her to such a break; 'and for me too, who am after all his accessory, it is very hard'.

He realized, her father finally wrote, after setting out the facts and arguments, that Erika had always nourished a latent opposition to the way he had conducted himself since 1933, and it was this which had erupted in her present distress: but it took two to make a quarrel, and his feeling for her would not allow him to be the other. 'When I think how often you have laughed and cried when I read you something of my work, your declaration seems rather improbable. You are far too much my child Eri, even in your anger against me . . . and that too is an offspring of mine, the objectivization, so to speak, of my own scruples and doubts.' And he repeated his usual refrain: he was far from being against people like Schwarzschild, but by keeping himself out of the general run of *émigré* polemic he had not wasted the possibility of exerting a real moral influence—when the time came. 'I form a reserve which one day can be useful.' He had in fact interrupted the *Joseph* for months in the preparation of a 'politicum', but had then returned to the novel, for the time was not yet ripe, and patience was still needed. 'There is little use in rousing the world against the horrors as long as the Germans in themselves are not thoroughly done with them . . .'

Whatever he thought, however, the time was close at hand when he would be compelled to abandon his reserve position and nail his colours to the mast. Three days later, on 26 January, just before their departure from Arosa, there appeared in the *Neue Zürcher Zeitung* an article by the *feuilleton* editor Eduard Korrodi, remonstrating sharply against Schwarzschild's reply to Thomas Mann in which he had claimed that German literature virtually in its entirety was now to be found in the emigration. This 'absurdity', thrown in the teeth of none other than the author of *The Buddenbrooks* because his works could still appear in Germany, was nothing less than 'ghetto madness' on the part of some *émigrés* who identified German literature with the work of a few Jewish authors. Not so, wrote Korrodi: its true representatives had remained in Germany, not a single *Dichter* was to be found in the emigration, which consisted first and foremost of the 'novel industry and a few real novelists of ability'. He was sarcastic over the blinkered outlook which had no eyes for Gerhart Hauptmann, Ricarda Huch, and the many others still in Germany, no thought for Switzerland or Austria, could see only the publishers Querido and De Lange in Amsterdam. Such an attitude would be a triumph for the Nazis, for whose propaganda Jewish control of literature had always been a key contention. 'We can understand that there are respected writers in emigration who would prefer not to belong to this German literature, for which hatred is more welcome than striving for truth and justice.'[58] The implication was plain that Thomas Mann was one such respected writer.

The brief *feuilleton* was scarcely a bombshell for the world at large, preoccupied with matters of greater moment (the Franco-Soviet pact, Germany's threat to remilitarize the Rhineland): it certainly landed as one, however, in the camp of the exiles. Klaus, with Fritz Landshoff of Querido, telegraphed his father the same day, urging a reply to the article 'however and wherever you can. This time it's really a matter of life and death for us all.' For Thomas Mann, Korrodi's denigration of the *émigrés*, and his open attempt to separate him from their company, came as nothing less than a challenge to declare where he stood. He began at once to plan an open letter to Korrodi in reply, and on return to Küsnacht asked Katia to begin the draft for him. It took him five days, conscious as he was of the significance of this decisive step after three years of hesitation.

Quietly but firmly, he rebutted the article's arguments. It was natural, seeing the rampant anti-Semitism of the Nazis, that Jewish authors should figure largely among the exiles, but there were many non-Jewish among them (such as himself and his brother, and Schickele), and they were far from being only novelists, for were not Bert Brecht and Johannes Becher poets, *Dichter* in the true sense? And even so, was not the novel the commanding genre of today's literature, the 'representative and preponderant literary work of art'? Korrodi himself had recognized this in his earlier comments on Wassermann, and indeed noted how the German novel had developed to European status thanks to the international component of Jewishness. But Heinrich and Thomas Mann, who were not Jews, had also contributed to this development, perhaps because of the tinge in their blood of the Latin and the Swiss. 'German hatred of Jews,

---

[58] *Urteil* 266 f.

or that shown by those presently in power, is . . . a hatred not of Jews, or not of them alone, but of Europe . . . of the Christian and classical foundations of Western culture . . . it is the attempt (symbolized in the withdrawal from the League of Nations) to shake off the ties of civilization, bringing the threat of a fearful alienation, pregnant with calamity, of the country of Goethe from the rest of the world.' He concluded with a powerful statement of his personal conviction that nothing good, either for Germany or the world, could possibly come from the present German government: 'this conviction has led me to avoid the country in whose intellectual tradition I am more deeply rooted than those who have been hesitating for three years whether to dare openly to withdraw my citizenship. . . . I am sure that I have acted rightly, towards my contemporaries and before posterity, to rally to those inspired by the words of a truly noble German poet:

> "But he whose inmost heart despises evil
> Must one day face an exile from his home
> When evil's honoured there by a folk of slaves.
> Better far to quit one's land for ever
> Than under sway of breed so infantine
> To tolerate the yoke of blind mob hate".'

He had often before, in private, quoted these lines from Platen. His emotion as he penned them now, at the close of this public declaration, which in its personal challenge to the Reich would put an end to the continuing ambiguity of his position, provoked a violent nervous reaction: was he truly acting from personal conviction, or had he been forced by outside influences into this momentous step? Once it was done, however, and personally delivered to the *Neue Zürcher*, his composure was restored. Korrodi had compelled him to declare himself: but it was a 'welcome obligation'. He was satisfied that he had let his 'conscience and firm conviction speak', he noted in his diary: 'my words will not fail to impress'. The number of approving telephone-calls he received on its publication on 3 February, including one from a historian in Berlin, increased his satisfaction at having dealt 'the vile regime a blow of undoubted severity', and he was ready for the vengeance that would follow: the final loss of the rest of his assets in Germany, a ban on his books, his citizenship withdrawn. 'Either there will be war, or in a few years' time conditions in Germany that once more permit distribution of my books,' he wrote to Hesse, who, though understanding, had deplored his action. 'I shall continue with my work as before, and leave it to time to confirm my prophecy that nothing good can come from National Socialism. But my conscience would not have been easy . . . had I not made that prophecy.'

His statement may not have come as the severe blow that he thought, with his natural self-importance, for a government that had weightier affairs on its mind—Hitler's orders for the occupation of the Rhineland were issued on 3 March—but the case of Thomas Mann certainly confronted it with a problem. There were few enough stars still remaining in Germany's cultural firmament, and while Mann figured among them, in however dubious a shape, the Reich authorities were not keen to take steps that would exclude him for good, in spite of strongly worded minutes from the Gestapo to the Interior Ministry. As with Richard Strauss, who had insisted in 1935 on naming his Jewish librettist, Stefan Zweig, at the première of his new opera *The Silent Woman*, it took time before party doctrine overcame the expediency of prestige and propaganda. Strauss had secured Hitler's personal permission for the première, but his stubborn loyalty to Zweig brought him the enmity of the party zealots; his opera was banned after two further performances, and in the end he was forced to resign his post as president of the Reichsmusikkammer. It was not until nearly a year later, in December 1936, that Mann was stripped of his citizenship, along with Katia and the four other children. The grounds cited were his continued appearance in demonstrations of 'international organizations, mostly under Jewish influence, whose hostility to Germany is well-known', and specifically his declaration in the *Neue Zürcher* of solidarity with the emigration, accompanied by 'violent insults to the Reich'. By then, however, in expectation of the manœuvre, he had accepted Czech nationality, and in a press statement could show how the Reich's action was juridically meaningless. More important, continuing steadily with his work, he had finished *Joseph in Egypt*, and it could be published by the new Bermann Fischer Verlag, Bermann having the same month received final authorization for the transfer to Vienna of part of the former firm, the rest remaining as the S. Fischer Verlag in Germany, in the 'Aryan' hands of Suhrkamp.

Mann may have overestimated the effect of his statement on the Nazi authorities, but its value for the morale of the exiles was unquestionable. Erika of course found it splendid—'now he has put everything right, and stands unambiguously in the clear'—and for Klaus his 'proud provocation' of the Nazis was a triumph. Letters from all quarters spoke of the lifting of depression and the new courage his words had brought, and it was moving for him to find the welcome these 'few simple and obvious words' had evoked.[59] Many wanted him to continue the good work, with further articles, and as he read the newspapers, his earlier idea of a letter to the London *Times* often recurred: but he decided against. He had shot his bolt,

[59] *Amann Br.* 62.

the world did not want to know, and there was no point in exposing himself further. The admiration many felt for the courage of his action was to some extent, perhaps, misplaced, for he had acted from a position of relatively great security, and it had in fact cost him nothing that would not anyway have been lost in due course. But there is no denying its significant moral effect upon the exiles, and he could justifiably feel the reserve he represented had been brought to bear at the right time to 'stiffen the backbone of the emigration'.

It had also stiffened his own, increasing his contempt for those, like the minor novelist Erich Ebermayer, who, while considering themselves emigrants in spirit, nevertheless stayed in Germany and managed successfully to continue their work there. Ebermayer, a homosexual and a friend of Klaus and of Stefan Zweig, had scripted a popular film, with Emil Jannings, which Mann saw now in Zurich and found very good (noting the predilection now in German films for 'boys' bodies naked to the waist'); but he was disgusted, when Ebermayer came to lunch the next day, to hear this 'insignificant wretch' talk of nothing but its success with Goebbels and Hitler. All the same, while he continued with the *Joseph*, the apparent inevitability of war made him think of removal to a place of greater safety: in Arosa he had already considered with Katia the advisability of a more peripheral area like Copenhagen, 'cheap, civilized, near the Baltic, and surely safe from invasion'—a naïve notion, as events would, of course, show. Much depended on what citizenship he could acquire when, as was now certain, his German one was revoked. In March, Bruno Walter, whose sixtieth birthday he had just celebrated in a contribution to a Vienna publication, was looking into his prospects for Austrian citizenship; but Mann needed first to know whether this was dependent on residence in Vienna, a move of which Bermann was naturally much in favour. While corresponding with Knopf over the introduction to the *Stories of Three Decades* collection, he had sought advice too on American naturalization. This, as Knopf doubtless explained, was far from easy; but the idea began to grow of a move to America, in his depression over Hitler's continued successes and the apparent lack, particularly in England, of any will to oppose him. 'If this goes on, in fifteen years this Germany will control Europe.' Writing to Van Loon in March, he said his next visit to the States would probably mark a final farewell to Europe: 'conditions on our continent are such that it has long made the purest sense to leave it and turn to yours, which has decidedly more hope and future than ours'.[60]

*Joseph in Egypt* was now not far from its conclusion, but more interruptions lay ahead. Freud's eightieth birthday was due in May, and Mann had

[60] 36/68.

already joined in Heinrich Meng's preparations for a congratulatory address, accompanied by personal tributes, which he was to present; he had revised Zweig's draft and recommended Rolland, James Joyce, Virginia Woolf, and Gide for the committee to organize the many contributors. His plan now was for a celebratory lecture himself, in the course of a two-week tour which would take him to Brno and Prague as well as Vienna. At first unwelcome, the task of its preparation gradually roused his enthusiasm as he began to feel his theme of 'Freud and the Future' need after all not take him far from that of the novel, and he was satisfied with the result when he completed it just before leaving with Katia for Vienna on 6 May. For as always his approach was personal and autobiographical: his celebration of Freud's work—which he saw as the scientific validation of a field long since opened up in philosophy and literature, by Novalis, Nietzsche, Kierkegaard, Schopenhauer—turned largely on his own use of psychoanalytical insights, from *Little Herr Friedemann* and *Tonio Kröger* on to *Joseph and his Brothers* with its motif of myth continually relived. 'The Joseph of the novel is an artist, a player on the unconscious with his *imitatio dei*, and my feeling of expectancy and joy in the future is inexpressible as I surrender to . . . this epic encounter between psychology and myth, which is also a festive meeting of literary composition and psychoanalysis.' 'Myth' might have been more appropriate for his title, but as he had it, he was expressing his own involuntary association with the name of Freud, who would be honoured as 'the pathfinder to a humanism of the future': standing in 'a bolder, freer, more joyous, artistically more mature relationship to the powers of the underworld, the unconscious, the Id, than is granted to today's humanity, as it struggles in neurotic *Angst* and its accompanying hatred'.

He called on the old man at his Vienna home on the morning of 8 May, bringing him the collection of international tributes, and also a copy of his lecture, for Freud was too ailing to hear it that evening or attend the later banquet in his honour. After lunch with the Walters and Alma Mahler-Werfel, an audience with Chancellor Schuschnigg, who had intimated he was ready to grant Mann immediate Austrian citizenship, proved unproductive, for the condition was maintained that he should move to Vienna, and this he was still not inclined to find acceptable. The reception for his lecture he later recalled as decidedly one of the most enthusiastic of his long career at the lectern, the applause overwhelming. If some of the faithful may have been disconcerted to hear that Freud's ideas had been anticipated by Nietzsche and Schopenhauer, this was not the case with Freud's wife and daughter Anna, who pleaded for a repeat performance for Freud himself at home; and that he promised, when he returned after a Budapest visit planned for June.

The talk was similarly successful in Brno and Prague, where he arrived on 10 May; but the highlight was a long private lunch with President Beneš and his wife at the Hradčany Palace. Mann found Beneš sympathetic and intelligent, and was struck by his optimism over the political situation: he spoke not only of the superior wisdom of Britain's 'civilized' policy towards Germany (he had, it seemed, just talked to Chamberlain), but also of the loyalty to the Czech state of the Sudeten German minority. Though he admitted it was unwelcome to see one of their leaders as a deputy in the Reichstag, he appeared convinced of Hitler's peaceful intentions, and pooh-poohed the idea that the Nazis were agitating for the Austrian anschluss. Mann thought this showed little knowledge of the spirit of Nazism, telling him that it 'recognized only two principles: lies and force. His reply was that it had none at all—which I suppose is also an opinion to be wel-comed.'[61] It was an interview he would not forget, when Beneš's confidence was shown to be vastly misplaced.

As before, in both Prague and Vienna, where he briefly returned on the way home, he was constantly pressed to make his home in one or the other, and in Vienna he actually viewed a number of possible properties; but for the moment his inclination was still to remain in Switzerland. He had been sparing with interviews, only in Prague speaking of his solidarity now with 'that emigration which is fighting for a better Germany'. In Vienna he restricted himself to the Freud theme, but also enlarged on his personal plans, as he was never loath to do: the final touches to the third volume of *Joseph*, to appear in the autumn, a reading from it in Vienna in June on his way to Budapest for a meeting of the League Committee for Intellectual Co-operation, and in September his first visit to South America for the PEN Club Congress in Buenos Aires, with a stop in Rio de Janeiro, his mother's birthplace. And then? a fourth volume to conclude the *Joseph* story, but first, two quite different interludes: a novella about Goethe in Weimar, and a Nietzsche essay as a counterpart to that on Wagner.

He probably had little idea himself how long-term these projects would turn out to be, but once back in Küsnacht on 14 May soon abandoned the plan to visit the 'notoriously uninteresting' Buenos Aires. The preparation of yet another address, and an absence of eight or ten weeks, even with all expenses paid, seemed out of the question, and he preferred to think, after Budapest, of a shorter summer break somewhere in France. Once his Budapest address had been dictated, he turned back to the now high-pressure work on the final chapters of *Joseph in Egypt*, confident that he could soon complete it once the next interruption was over. The manu-script accompanied him to Budapest, where he arrived with Katia on 6

---

[61] *Tb.* iii, 301.

June, and he was able to keep up the work to some extent, between the lively social commitments and meetings with prominent colleagues— Valéry, Madariaga, Čapek among them. It gave him some enjoyment, from his now more assured position, to cast a pebble into the calm waters of academic deliberation at the League Committee sessions, with a call in his 'Humaniora and Humanism' for a militant democracy to resist the 'murderers of freedom'. The contrast with the other, rather timid, speeches brought lengthy applause and an enthusiastic embrace from Karel Čapek; but it was far from welcome in official quarters in Hungary, where sympathies for fascism were growing and the presence of a prominent exile from Nazi Germany was viewed with suspicion. It also earned a protest from the German legation to the Hungarian Interior Ministry over the excessive press attention he was receiving: amusing, he thought, to find official Germany complaining of press interest in the only German taking part in a meeting of European intellectuals. A repeat of the Freud lecture before he left, however, was well received.

In Vienna then, after his reading from the manuscript on 13 June, he joined the Bermanns at the Opera for the third act of *Tristan* under Bruno Walter—to find the performance disrupted by Nazi stink-bombs. Isolde, her voice quite lost, could 'make only a lovely gesture of incapacity', he reported later to Heinrich, 'and did not rise from Tristan's corpse', Walter having continued manfully, as the auditorium rapidly emptied, to the *Liebestod*. There had been simultaneous disturbances in the Burgtheater and three cinemas, he learned: 'at least one knows now what National Socialism smells like: sweaty feet to the nth degree'. This was hardly a favourable omen for a move to Vienna, which he found was now regarded here as a *fait accompli*, at one reception indeed loudly applauded. On their last day more properties were viewed, in Grinzing and on the Hohe Warte, but without their finding anything that appealed, and his doubts remained, in spite of Bermann's urging. Hitler's professed recognition soon afterwards of the independence of Austria and his 'guarantee' of non-interference could scarcely inspire confidence. Meanwhile Mann had paid his promised call on Freud, who was near to tears as he listened to his personal reading of the lecture and eagerly discussed his idea of myth constantly relived, even putting forward the thesis that Napoleon's daemonic career might have sprung from just such a replay of the Joseph legend. He embraced him warmly, and sent to his hotel a bottle of old Tokay with fruit and cakes, which made an excellent lunch for them on the train back.

Whatever the pros and cons of a move to Vienna, it was not the moment now to pursue the idea, as he embarked in July on the closing scenes of *Joseph in Egypt*, energetically enough to meet the autumn publication-deadline but without marked disturbance to his normal way of life. In anticipation of the Nietzsche essay, he found time for an excursion to Lucerne and the scene of the friendship with Wagner at Tribschen—would there one day, he wondered aloud to Katia, be a tablet on the Küsnacht house, recording his completion there of the *Joseph*, the Freud lecture, and perhaps the Nietzsche essay?—and at the end of the month they pursued Nietzsche memories with a week at Sils-Baselgia. With the news of the Franco insurrection in Spain, and Italian and German intervention in the ensuing civil war, a move from Switzerland seemed less and less re-commended, particularly as Katia could now confirm there was no financial pressure to look for a more economical life-style. And on 6 August came an important new development: a visit from Czechoslovakia and the offer of Czech citizenship with no residence strings attached. Rudolf Fleischmann, a businessman from the small town of Proseč in central Bohemia, who had already secured this for Heinrich a year earlier and was working on an application from Klaus, arrived with the formal offer from his community, and Thomas Mann did not hesitate a moment to sign the application for himself, Katia, and the two minor children, Elisabeth and Michael. There would be due discretion, he was assured, in view of his still-uncertain position in Germany. The application was approved by the Proseč council on 18 August, together with a separate one for Golo, and the two, with that for Klaus, were forwarded next day to Prague. Monika, who was still in Italy, could, it seemed, be dealt with separately later. It was a relief to have a regularization for the whole family thus in prospect, Erika being already provided with a British passport; their future movements, whatever they might be, would at least be made easier; and at this point no one could foresee the fate in store for Czechoslovakia.

On 23 August Mann celebrated at last the completion of *Joseph in Egypt*, with a champagne cup in the family circle, a jolly poem written by Erika and recited by Elisabeth, and the inevitable reading of part of the closing chapter. It had taken all the three and a half years since they left Munich, he reflected, but there had been one or two intermediate works of signifi-cance, and distractions and long pauses occasioned by the two visits to America and the abandoned 'politicum': if his health permitted, he could hope to add the fourth and final volume in much shorter order. (As he would before long be starting on yet another interlude, the novella on Goethe, the tempo of his work and the inescapable demands of the day on his time made this certain to be no more than a pious hope.) 'Alas, the tome has monstrously pedantic *longueurs*, I fear,' he wrote to Bruno Walter, 'but I think it can bring a little higher gaiety on to the scene [in Germany], much-needed there. We are packing now and will be leaving quietly by car for a rest on the Côte d'Azur . . .'

Hopes of a rest, however, were largely illusory. They drove first, with stops in Geneva and Avignon, to Saint-Cyr and Les Lecques for a week's stay, in uncertain weather, with a strong mistral, though an occasional dip was possible; there were visits to the Schickeles, and they saw a number of other exiled friends. In Aigue-Belle, where they were joined by Heinrich, and his daughter visiting from Prague, they were all unwell with a throat infection like a quinsy, which Katia in particular found hard to shake off, and by the time they reached Le Lavandou on 18 September they were both under doctor's orders. He was not sorry to start the return journey and escape the oppressive south, and rejoiced in Geneva to be back in his own sphere—and away from Heinrich's, as he had to note: a month later, during his afternoon rest, he dreamed heavily, angrily even, of his brother, in whose figure was mingled faintly that of his father. Exile, and the convergence of their political views, had clearly not overcome entirely the deep-seated antipathy between the brothers.

Reaching safe haven again in Küsnacht on 23 September, all the same, did not bring the end of their troubles. Mann was attacked immediately by an irritating erysipelas, with high fever, which confined him to bed for a few days; Katia was soon under treatment again for a recurrence of the throat infection; early in October a neuralgia developed in his left shoulder, and his regular manicurist contrived to provoke an abscess on a finger, which made writing very difficult for a week or more. The unremitting demands on the literary businessman were fulfilled as best they might, extensive correspondence dealt with, often by dictation to the long-suffering Katia, a series of dedications written in the *Joseph* volumes now out, and even one or two articles: but it was not until the end of October that he felt sufficient strength returning to make a start on his notes for the Goethe. It would have a historical base: the unexpected visit to the distinguished Privy Councillor in Weimar by his youthful flame, Charlotte Kestner, née Buff, whom he had not seen since his exposure of their relationship in his best-seller *Werther*. In the south of France Mann had been rereading Morike's *Mozart on the Journey to Prague*, which seemed to strike exactly the right note for the type of narrative he had in mind, and his thoughts had never been far from the project through the succession of bodily complaints to which he had been prey.

To some extent these will have been due to his disquiet over events in Europe. The Spanish civil war showed clearly how freedom was everywhere abused by fascist movements, and reinforced, he thought, his call for firmness on the part of the democracies, for a militant humanism to replace their feeble and outdated liberalism, for the 'enlightened dictatorship' which he had seen as necessary in the twenties. The concern of the capitalist press for France's neutrality in the Spanish hostilities, while ignoring the open intervention of Germany and Italy, he found nothing short of infamous. Now that the Soviet Union had reserved its freedom of action, Spain might well prove the flashpoint for a more general conflict, and it seemed senseless to remain in Europe, but 'one carries on from day to day towards chaos with a singular sense of fatalism'. The award in November of the Nobel Peace Prize to Hitler's prisoner Ossietzky came as one bright gleam in the darkness, 'a sign of courage and resistance in the world after all the subservience and timid retreating';[62] but it had been perplexing to read earlier of the unbelievable confessions and the death sentences in the Moscow show-trial of some of the alleged 'Trotskyite conspirators'.

There were worries at this time too over Monika and Michael. Such things mostly left him little troubled, especially where his least-favourite children were concerned, and were quickly dismissed from his mind. But when, as now, they perturbed Katia, indispensable accessory to the smooth running of his life, it was another story. Monika, now 26, had written from Florence of her unhappy love-life—of some promiscuity, it seems—and was depressed over her poor prospects for a musical career. When she returned home in October she seemed far from well, though a suspected pregnancy was not confirmed; she was something of an outsider in the household, refusing to join the usual Christmas celebrations, and a question mark remained over her future. Michael had made excellent progress with both viola and violin, giving a successful test-performance at the Conservatoire, impressing in concerts at home and with friends, and passing his May violin examination with distinction: but his outbursts of temper and his tendency to eccentric behaviour were making him so difficult to handle that an appointment with a psychiatrist was arranged—which he ignored. He and Elisabeth were given a car between them, and he moved to a room of his own in town in November; later that month it came to a stand-up row with his father, bitter over the constant trouble he was giving Katia, and she was sleepless with worry after he had stormed out and could not be found till late next evening, having spent the night with one of Hesse's sons. (He never came to terms with the problem of the relationship with his 'unapproachable' father: forty years later, as he told Golo, he still had dreams of wrestling with him.) After a visit to Paris in December it was decided that in the New Year he should continue his studies there under Galamian, and there seemed every chance that his talent would make its way. His close friendship with a Swiss school-friend of Elisabeth's, Gret Moser, was meanwhile a welcome steadying influence. The parents

[62] *Amann Br.* 65.

began to prepare themselves for a departure before long of both the younger children, Elisabeth having now passed well in her examinations. On 19 November they listened as their father took the oath in the Czech consulate and received the solemn document of naturalization.

Golo, on the other hand, who had now exchanged his post at Saint-Cloud for one in Rennes, made an exemplary son, spending all his vacations in Küsnacht, often bringing his friends, and always ready to play a part in the literary business of the house, whether in proof-reading or revision of article manuscripts. With the procedure for his own Czech citizenship completed, he decided in October to transfer to Prague, in the hope of securing an appointment there. Erika, also a frequent visitor between her many engagements, felt that the 'Peppermill', after its thousandth performance and a final tour in Luxemburg in May, had exhausted its possibilities in the uncertainties of Europe, and had determined to try her luck in America with an English-language version. To help launch her project, Reinhardt had organized a select performance in Salzburg, at Leopoldskron, in August—attractively candle-lit, because he was short of cash to meet his electricity bills—for sixteen mainly American guests, Helen Hayes and Marlene Dietrich among them. (La Dietrich's elegantly theatrical exits and entrances for constant phone-calls from New York and San Francisco fascinated the audience more, Therese Giehse thought, than the show itself, which was politely received but with little understanding.) Klaus, always to and fro (and often standing up for Michael in the family discussions), left for Holland later in August, planning to join Erika for the American experiment. They sailed for New York in September, followed soon after by a loyal though still-dubious Therese Giehse. Sponsors were found, among them Alfred Knopf; Auden helped with the translation of their texts; and by the end of the year the cast was assembled for the opening in January in a small theatre on Lexington at Forty-Second Street, the programme embellished with an enthusiastic note from Thomas Mann. (Unsurprisingly, however, the European themes and the satire were largely lost on an audience in isolationist America, which had barely yet noticed the existence of Adolf Hitler, and the brave venture proved a disappointing flop.)

By 11 November the notes for the Goethe novella had progressed to a start on the actual writing, and this now became Mann's daily task, at his customary deliberate speed. Early in December, however, there began a flood of congratulatory letters after the news of his naturalization broke, approaching that on the occasion of the Nobel Prize award and on his fiftieth and sixtieth birthdays. His only regret was that his own press announcement, agreed with the Czech authorities, was forestalled by the notice of excommunication from Berlin; but at least his position was clarified at last. 'A future Germany will not hold it against me that I parted from the present one, and will accept me again, whether I'm still alive or not.'[63] On Christmas Day, celebrated this year in a smaller circle, came a further excommunicatory notice from Germany—a curt notification from the dean of the Faculty of Philosophy at Bonn University of the annulment of his honorary doctorate—and he spent the final days of 1936 in the formulation of a firm and dignified response.

The guilty responsibility of the German universities for Germany's moral decline, he wrote, had long since destroyed for him any pleasure in the title granted him by Bonn: that from Harvard, however, remained, bestowed on him for his work, along with a very few contemporaries, to 'preserve the lofty dignity of German culture'. 'I could never have continued to live and work, would have suffocated . . . had I not been able from time to time to give frank expression to my immeasurable revulsion against the wretched events at home, the pitiable words and even more miserable deeds.' Deserved or not, his name was linked for the world with its well-loved conception of the essence of that culture, and through his work he had striven to uphold the idea of peace against the National Socialist doctrine of war that would lead only to Germany's ruin. 'It is not from bold presumption that I have spoken, but from an anxiety and torment from which your usurpers of power could not release me when they ordained that I should no longer be a German: an anguish of mind and thought which for four years has not left me for a single hour. . . . God help our darkened and misused country, and teach it to make peace with the world and with itself!'

It was an eloquent protest, more powerful than his earlier, merely literary, statement: a hard-hitting indictment of the regime's betrayal of Germany and its open preparations for war. After the appearance of the exchange as an article in Switzerland and Prague, it achieved wide distribution as a separate pamphlet, issued by the Zurich publisher Oprecht and reaching 20,000 in the course of 1937, then in translation in America and all over the world, and copied and circulated in Germany, where it even appeared in a number of camouflaged editions. To a year in which he had emerged from his silence to take his stance at the head of the exiles, his clarion call—however doubtful its influence on the course of events—made a fitting end.

[63] *A & N* 695.

# VI

+‒+ ≒◊≒ +‒+

# 'I BELIEVE IN AMERICA'
# 1937–1941

+‒+ ≒◊≒ +‒+

'In the nose, the smell of world history in flames, in the ears the
cries for help from those going under'          (TM, 1940)

1

*'Never shall I think any country in Europe to be secure whilst there
is established, in the very centre of it, a state ... founded on
principles of anarchy ... a college of armed fanatics for the
propagation of the principles of assassination, robbery, rebellion,
fraud, faction, oppression, and impiety'*     (Edmund Burke, 1791)

From his new situation as a Czech, Thomas Mann immediately initiated an
attempt, through diplomatic channels, to recover the remaining Munich
property, though there was faint hope of success after the publication of his
letter to Bonn. To have written that had made their Christmas and New
Year the happiest for a long time, he agreed with Katia, and though he was
momentarily in two minds whether publication had been entirely wise, any
remaining doubts were soon dispelled by Oprecht's rapid production of
the leaflet, the 'waves of gratitude'[1] that began to reach him from all sides,
and the report that many copies of the text were already circulating in
Germany. It was the 'manifesto of our existence', wrote one of the exiles;
'magnifico, commovente, profondo, umano', said Toscanini, and Schickele:
'it will stand one day in German textbooks!' Most encouraging perhaps was
word from a Stuttgart lawyer: 'Your letter ... has already become a form of
evening service among many circles and families. It is wonderful how the
evolution of your readers' ideas answers to your own described there.'

It was with a renewed confidence that he had started his calendar for
1937, and with a lively curiosity to see what the year would bring: but the

---

[1] *DüD.* ii, 543.

dates that soon began to fill it gave promise of interruptions to come for his Goethe interlude (to be entitled *Lotte in Weimar*), where he was already on the second chapter and continuing with, for him, uncommon *élan*. Another brief tour was immediately in prospect for January—to Prague, of course, and his adopted home-town, Proseč, where he must convey his thanks in person, followed by Budapest and Vienna again. There would have to be discussions on a project for a new journal, for which his name and assistance were needed; another visit to America some time in the spring was already in sight; and the annual winter-stay in Arosa, now almost a tradition, had to be fitted in, though there at least he would be able to continue with *Lotte*. As far as he could foresee, therefore, a typical Thomas Mann year lay ahead, with the same unremitting demands of the world on time he could ill spare from his work. But the return to the Goethe scene, with the complete change of style it required after that of the *Joseph*, was a welcome stimulus, and helped to calm his disquiet over the political tensions in Europe, as the Spanish conflict looked more and more likely to end in a fascist victory.

He set off with Katia for Prague on 8 January, and they were met by Golo and by Heinrich's daughter Leonie, spending the first evening quietly *en famille* with sister-in-law Mimi, before the heavy programme for the short stay began: calls on the Foreign and Interior Ministries, tea with President Beneš, and an official reception in Proseč. To fund the journey, he had arranged for readings, here and in the other capitals, for which he would use not only *Joseph in Egypt* but also the first chapter of the *Lotte*, with his usual concern to keep an eager public apprised of work in progress. In an interview, he expressed his pride at belonging now to a state whose political and spiritual attitudes corresponded closely to his own, and his trust that an accommodation with the German-speaking minority would be reached. Beneš received him alone for a talk of over two hours, inevitably on politics, before it was time to don evening dress for the reading in the Urania. It was a festive occasion, with an appreciative Golo among the big audience, and in a few words after his reading he emphasized his gratitude for the warmth of his reception in Prague, adding his hope that he could prove it was possible to be a good German and at the same time a good Czech.

The following day a car from the Foreign Ministry took them with Golo to Proseč, for the ceremony, if not comparable ostentation, of a local council meeting. There were speeches by the mayor and postmaster, and many of the twelve hundred inhabitants of the little town assembled outside the Town Hall. Invited then to Fleischmann's, they had to listen to addresses in three languages from a group of communists, for whom the naturalization of Thomas Mann was undoubtedly a morale-booster. There were gifts of pipes for him and Golo, and embroidered table-napkins for Katia, and a long but simple dinner, before they joined the night train for Budapest and said goodbye to their attentive son.

The invitation there for a reading-evening had come from the editors of a newly founded radical journal, with whose views his friend Baron Hatvány, his host once again, was in sympathy, and his visit was therefore strictly unofficial. The Horthy government could hardly refuse him entry, as a Czech citizen now; but they laid down that there must be no political speeches at his performance, and arranged for a heavy police presence both outside and inside the hall.[2] They also barred the young left-wing poet Attila Jószef from opening the evening with his specially written verses of greeting: the longing for words of beauty from the master in the face of an ever more menacing future. 'When will the wolfish scum turn on us? How much longer will a hall stand ready for you? . . . When you speak, our light burns still. . . . And many come just to see you, content to turn to you, the European among the Whites.'[3] It was not surprising after the official hostility that, despite his audience's evident appreciation of the *Lotte* extract, he should soon come to feel the road to Hungary was henceforth cut off for him.

They were glad to accept Hatvány's offer for his son to drive them on to Vienna on 14 January, again for a brief stay only, but with the welcome to which he was accustomed, and a large audience in the Konzerthaus for his performance that evening. The following day, before they left by the night train for Zurich, he had satisfactory discussions with Bermann, for the renewal of his contract with continuing monthly advances against royalties, and a new edition of *The Magic Mountain*; and he returned with heavy baggage of accumulated mail and books, including an excellent Tolstoy edition cheaply acquired *en route*. They were off then for a three-week stay in Arosa, where he could resume work on the *Lotte* but also, assisted by Katia, deal with his continuing massive correspondence. Much of this concerned his letter to Bonn, but some was more urgent, for the meeting needed with the sponsor and others interested in the new journal being planned.

The proposal had first reached him over the New Year. Madame Aline Mayrisch de Saint-Hubert, widow of a wealthy Luxemburg steel-magnate and already a supporter, anonymously, of individual exiles from Germany, had offered up to 30,000 Swiss francs a year, in instalments, for general assistance to the cause; and it had been concluded that the best use of this generosity would be for a mainly cultural journal rather than for yet another of the many political *émigré* organs with which the scene was

---

[2] *Ungarn* 24.    [3] Ibid. 457.

crowded enough. Ferdinand Lion was envisaged as editor, but all agreed
that the prestige of Thomas Mann's name as general overseer and occasional contributor was indispensable. A meeting was finally arranged in
Küsnacht on 13 February, after his return from Arosa, with her, Lion,
Oprecht, and others, and they decided on a bimonthly publication, the
financing remaining anonymous, under the title *Standards and Values*, for
which he would appear as overall editor and for its first issue write a
programmatic foreword. He was fully alive to the adverse effect this would
have on his work, but the project greatly appealed. Although in the course
of its three-year existence most of the day-to-day work was Lion's responsibility, he himself was effectively the centre round which it revolved,
and a valuable moderator in the inevitable conflicts between editor, contributors, and publisher; the journal, though the Swiss dramatist Konrad
Falke later signed as his co-editor, remained peculiarly his own, more
especially when Golo, returning to Switzerland in 1939, took over the
editorial chair from Lion.

The first number appeared in September/October 1937, under Oprecht's
imprint, with Thomas Mann's contribution of the first chapter of *Lotte* and
a lengthy foreword in which he justified and defended the lofty, cliché-
sounding title chosen. ' "Today," says Goethe, the artist, "what counts is
the individual's weight on the scales of humanity. All else is mere vanity." '
Their aim as artists was to combat barbarism, to keep up standards and
defend values, 'to despise philistine and trashy literature [most particu-
larly] where it masquerades in vulgar mendaciousness as revolution'. For
such an aim, they knew they had allies in all countries: but the undertaking
was launched from a German platform because of the urgent need 'to create
for the German soul, whose tradition—betrayed today at home by those
who have no right to be its spokesmen—is inalienably European and
humane, a forum where it may pursue freely and unreservedly its true
mission, and find creative expression in company with fraternal spirits in
other nations'.[4] The object, he had written to Hesse in February, hoping for
his collaboration, was to establish an arena, not for polemic, but for
constructive productivity: restorative and at the same time with an eye to
the future, 'a refuge for Germany's highest contemporary culture while the
internal interregnum there lasts'. In a sense, it made a successor to Klaus
Mann's *Sammlung*; but it was significant that Heinrich, the indefatigable
contributor to any and every anti-Nazi publication, appeared only once
here, with an essay on Nietzsche, while Klaus himself was left entirely out
in the cold.

Klaus had returned to Europe, after the collapse of the 'Peppermill'
venture in America, irresolute and trying vainly to break his morphine

⁴ xii 799, 812.

habit, and when he came to Küsnacht at the end of February noted in his diary how very strongly he once again felt his father's total coldness towards him: 'Whether benevolent or irritated (strangely "embarrassed" by the existence of a son), never interested, never concerned with me in a more serious way'—typical, he thought, of his complete lack of interest in others in general. It was a consistent line, from the novella *Disorder and Early Sorrow* to 'the present situation, where he has completely *forgotten* me in the matter of the journal. Charming comments [on my work] do not prove the contrary. He writes equally charmingly to complete strangers. A mixture of highly intelligent, almost indulgent conciliation—and icy impassivity. All this particularly accentuated where I am concerned.'[5] Talking this over with Katia later, he thought she was right in observing that his father was irritated by literary aspirations in other members of the family—Heinrich above all, but also Klaus.

Thomas Mann's was without doubt a cold nature, outwardly at least, and Klaus's accusation here of his complete lack of interest and of real feeling for others (particularly cruel in his own case, at a time when thoughts of suicide were not far below the surface) was thoroughly justified. Of his children, only Erika and Elisabeth awakened anything approaching true affection, and even the springs of genuine love for Katia—which in their courtship had welled up the more strongly in the prospect of an advantageous marriage—were soon no more than a quiet streamlet once her position as helpmeet and 'accessory' had been prescribed for her. His friends he looked on merely as the supporting cast in the drama—with which he was obsessed—of his own life and progress, to be kept up with, neglected, or discarded as the play continued: witness his diary note on hearing of Otto Grautoff's death. Even including the few who were the object of his homo-erotic advances, mostly repulsed, none of the friends—Grautoff, Kurt Martens, Georg Richter, the Munich neighbours, Ernst Bertram, Bruno Frank, Hans Reisiger, and the rest—rose to real intimacy or a more important role: as he conceded himself, it was very rare that he could get on Christian-name terms with anyone outside the family. The judgement is inescapable that he regarded others, whether family, friends, or more distant strangers, as mere appendages to his own life and work, to be handled from his Olympian height—in complaisant and conciliatory fashion certainly—only in order to exploit them for his personal convenience (and occasionally, as we have seen, to turn them into characters for his narratives).

The compliments in the 'charming' letters he could produce on other people's work often belied the real views he noted in his diary. Only the previous summer, Stefan Zweig's *The Right to Heresy: Castellio against*

---

[5] KlM *Tb*. iii, 110.

*Calvin* had struck him as 'jejune and second-rate, as usual', despite the interest of the parallel Zweig implied between sixteenth- and twentieth-century persecution. Yet he could write to him effusively a few days later on this 'sensation', 'profoundly exciting': 'for a long time I have not read a book with such eagerness or been so gripped by the material and its construction . . . congratulations!'[6] He was capable sometimes of the right encouraging words when he had not even read the manuscript a hopeful correspondent had sent. We have seen too, on a less exalted plane, how he could keep Ida Herz in play, though she was often tiresome, purely because of her dedication to his service in many minor, but to him important, matters. He was unlikely now to become less cold in his relations with others.

The coming journey to America had arisen from an invitation in January to give a series of lectures at Alvin Johnson's New School for Social Research in New York. He had been strongly urged to accept by the *émigré* publicist Prince Löwenstein, who had secured the support of a number of leading Americans, Johnson among them, for the establishment of an 'American Guild for German Cultural Freedom' in the cause of assistance to exiled intellectuals, and had in 1936 founded a 'German Academy' in New York. The aims of the Academy—no less than the reconstruction and defence of German cultural assets—were similar to those of Mann's new journal and, though not entirely satisfied with the way it had been started, he had lent his name to its presidium as well as to the committee of the Guild. Cables had meanwhile been exchanged, and after hesitation over what seemed a waste of time and a transatlantic phone-call, he finally agreed to make the trip in April if a suitable ship could be found.

Katia had urged him to accept, and there was much to be said for another visit, for Erika had remained there, determined now to further the anti-Nazi cause by methods more direct than the 'Peppermill' could ever have been. On 17 March she spoke at a mass demonstration in Madison Square Garden organized by the American Jewish Congress and attended by Mayor La Guardia, the trade-union leader John L. Lewis, and other prominent personalities. She also read to the meeting a lengthy cable from her father, congratulating her on this first appearance, in her own right but also in a sense representing him, in witness against the 'force and lies today apparently so victorious', and with his own message to 'the land of Lincoln, Whitman, and Franklin Roosevelt' of 'humanity's belief in America's mission to lead the way to peace and social justice'. For her, it was the start of a career in the United States as lecturer which she was to pursue with energy and success in the years to come.

[6] *Tb.* iii, 306; Br. i, 417.

A further persuasive argument for making the journey had been a letter early in March from Joseph Angell, an enthusiastic young graduate-student at Yale, announcing his project for a Thomas Mann Collection there, 'a "creative scholar's library" for the study of your life and work'. The promise of a lasting foundation for his posthumous fame, as well as for such academic study, was attractive: both were dear to his heart, and it would not have been like him to lose any opportunity to foster and encourage both. A meeting with Angell was clearly indicated. He had promised him suitable material, and held out the hope that Ida Herz might be willing to contribute her collection, if suitably recompensed now that she was in need in her London exile. He must, however, retain the valuable manuscripts of his major works, he said, in the interests of his numerous family, seeing that 'almost all my fortune has been sacrificed to my political convictions'.[7] Goethe, was his sidelong reflection, had received letters like Angell's: the arrival next day from Paris of an article on Thomas Mann 'L'Excommunié', describing him as 'le personnage littéraire le plus important de l'Europe'— apart from Claudel or D'Annunzio, and possibly Wells or Shaw, 'pas de figure d'artiste plus haute et plus majestueuse'—was a most satisfying tribute to his own Goethe-like standing, and confirmed his enthusiasm for the Yale project.

During the hesitations over America, a visit from Landshoff, of the Amsterdam Querido firm, brought a proposal for lectures there, and London too had been mooted. He had never been happy over the relative neglect in England of his work, and bewailed now the lack of reaction to the English edition, with a foreword by Priestley, of his declaration in the Bonn letter, on which the Labour MP Charles Trevelyan had been the only one to write to him—a reflection, he thought, of England's head-in-sand attitude towards Nazi Germany, though her hesitant start in rearmament was at last an encouraging sign. In the end, both Holland and England were ruled out as an unnecessary complication. Passages were booked on the *Normandie* from Le Havre on 8 April, there would be nearly two weeks in New York, and so practically a month away from the work which he was 'burning to get on with' and which, through all the preparations, had been making steady progress.

A new suit had to be ordered, made to measure. Trying it on at the 'London House' tailors in Zurich, he was asked by the assistant if he would like to meet Gerhart Hauptmann, who happened to be below in the shop: both parties declined the opportunity, Hauptmann remarking that their meeting would have to await 'other times'—'he's wrong there', noted Mann in his diary. A draft for his speech at the fourth-anniversary banquet of the

[7] *Philobiblon*, 34/2, (June 1990), 99, 101.

Social Research School was quickly dictated, while old material, including 'Goethe's Career as Writer', could be used as the basis for his lectures. The necessary rehearsals of the English versions with the Zurich translator, and further suit-fittings, took up much time over the Easter period; but he continued daily with *Lotte*.

His reply, just before departure, to the Soviet Writers' Union, as a contribution to their congratulatory volume on the twentieth anniversary of the USSR, set out his current political views: he was not, as often alleged, 'communistic', but simply a writer searching for truth—in opposition certainly to the 'lying world of fascist nationalism', but not necessarily against dictatorship as such, provided, like Roosevelt's, it was in the cause of freedom, justice, humanity; he had all respect for the 'mighty social experiment' of the Russian Revolution, though not unmixed with something of a shudder; and he had every hope that the new humanism now to be discerned in the anti-fascist struggle in Europe would lead to 'that social and vigorous democracy' outlined in the constitution of the Soviet Union. Gide's critical *Retour de l'URSS*—'incredible sensation'—was part of his reading on the voyage.

With the *Normandie* he had certainly made sure of a suitable ship, their first-class passage with every luxury, but sciatica began to disturb him, and developed to give unremitting pain throughout the expected turbulence of the New York stay. He earned his fee with four lectures at the New School for Social Research, ringing the changes on Goethe, Wagner, and Freud (though whether he managed the last two in English is not clear), and he learned that his speech at the anniversary banquet had brought in a donation of 100,000 dollars. There were private reading-evenings from *Lotte*, many dinners, meetings, interviews, and constant crowds of visitors; flowers, books, and mail arrived in quantity. Angell visited New York for a brief discussion on the Yale project. They spent much time with Erika, of course, and her translation was very useful for the many shorter addresses he had to improvise, notably one on 21 April at a mass meeting in memorial to the victims of fascism, which was also broadcast: the world situation and the cause of freedom, he urged, demanded now that 'the intellect shed its inherent gentleness and inertia and learn to defend itself'.[8] He was delighted by Dorothy Thompson's 'sensational' article in the *New York Times* of 14 April: 'We are glad that you are here, Thomas Mann. No nation can exile you. Yours is a larger citizenship, in no mean country.' He represented the preservation of the cultural inheritance of Germany through the dark days of National Socialism, the culture of Goethe, Nietzsche, and Wagner: 'you are of that culture, inalienably, and carry it

---

[8] xiii 642.

with you wherever you go. . . . wherever minds are sensitive, hearts generous, and spirits free—there is your home.' Robinson Jeffers, introducing a reprint of this, described him as 'a living criterion of intellectual freedom and responsibility'.

Not the least interesting, though, was an invitation to Hollywood, its promise of high reward opening a 'new perspective' for his life, and, as the return voyage began on the *Île de France* on 24 April, he had serious thoughts of entering this quite different arena, once *Lotte in Weimar* had been completed. At the moment that day seemed still far off: but after returning to Küsnacht he determined from now on to spend at least part of each year in America. Among his many interviews, one just before departure for the *Washington Post*, in which he foresaw a future democratic Germany, warned against treating fascism and communism as identical movements, and stressed that he himself was decidedly no communist—'in Russia I should be very unhappy, because I would feel circumscribed'—was to prove of great significance for his future reception in the United States, in every sense: for the interviewer was Agnes E. Meyer, the wife of the *Post*'s owner, Eugene Meyer, after reading *Joseph* a devotee of Thomas Mann, and resolved to do all in her power for him there. The standing of the *Post*, and her wide connections at high level in America, would turn out precious assets for him. The correspondence between them, beginning with a routine fan-letter and her dispatch of a copy of the interview, lasted till the end of his life.

The weeks that followed his return passed in increasing pain from the sciatica and accompanying neuralgia, which warmth, rest, and the doctor's drugs did little to relieve. Work suffered, there was none of the usual pleasure in Zurich's mild spring weather, and his irritability mounted. The daily walk became increasingly difficult, and a camp-chair had to be taken along for frequent rests before he was picked up in the car. It was a struggle to complete the promised foreword for the journal, and Lion's comment that it was the only good contribution he had had confirmed his forebodings that he would have to bear the whole burden himself. Kesten's 'tendentious and fulsome praise' of the novelist Alfred Döblin in the Paris *Neues Tage-Buch*, 'unmistakably at my expense', roused him to uncharacteristic rage: to see Döblin lauded as the creator of the German mythical epic, as if the *Joseph* did not exist, was typical of the Jewish critics who had always treated him iniquitously and now ignored his achievement by 'taking as their leader one of their own race and clique, against me the stupid goy'.[9] (The outburst was soon forgotten, and within a year he was writing to Kesten in warm appreciation of his review of *Felix Krull*, published by

---

[9] *Tb.* iv, 590 f.

Querido in its still incomplete form.) Digging out the manuscripts he had promised for Yale, he was depressed at looking backward in this way, stirring up things long laid to rest: 'life can only be lived looking forward and to the new'. He found some distraction in occasional theatre-evenings, or a cinema show: enjoying the fun of Charles Laughton's *Ruggles of Red Gap*, but not the newsreel horrors of the airship Hindenburg going up in flames in America, when he had hoped to see ceremonial pageantry for England's new king, George VI.

Both Katia and he were deeply concerned at this time over Klaus. In an effort to get off drugs, he had started treatment in a Budapest sanatorium in May; but his letters and the reports from the doctor were so disturbing that his father early in June added his own 'serious words' to a letter from Katia. They trusted, he wrote, in his good sense and courage in holding to his decision, in remaining true to his life's work, and were confident he could give up for good his 'vie facile', the too-easy path to which he had seen so many of his friends fall victim 'without being able really to respect them'. 'Today we all have much to hate, to despise, to oppose, but how is this possible, how can one insist on morality and human decency against the ranters if to their derisive cries one takes the easy road which leads to death? These days and nights must be really hard for you . . . but think of us, and see them through with courage! Life has much of joy and beauty to offer even without that false gloss [of drugs].' At last taking him seriously, Klaus may have thought: but in his diary he had noted that all those to whom he felt attracted had looked for death, and insisted now that he did have respect for them. 'To seek death is not contemptible, but wise.'[10] His father, however, following a phone call to the sanatorium by Katia and Erika, now over for a visit from America, noted impassively: 'the boy is not really all there, in a moral and self-critical sense. Suffers no authority, but forfeits the right not to suffer it.' Writing later to Hatvány, he said that with Klaus's 'loose hold on life' their hopes must rest more on his devotion to those who loved him than on his attachment 'to a world where moral effort is indeed a thankless business'.[11]

Thomas Mann's birthday-month began in what he thought the worst pain he had ever experienced. By day, sitting or lying, it was hard to find a position he could hold; his nights were poor in sleep, despite strong pain-killers, which left him listless and tired the next day. The purchase of a new car (with good trade-in, he was pleased to note, for the old Fiat), the excellent première, 'tout Zurich' in attendance, of Alban Berg's opera *Lulu*, and above all the presence of Erika, even though her stay would be short, helped him to overcome a powerful mood of self-pity. His birthday

---

[10] KlM *Br. Antw.* 724; KlM *Tb.* iii, 139.     [11] 37/107.

was exceptionally quiet, with none of the usual guests and of the children only Elisabeth and Erika. But it had been as much as he could do to add now and then a page or two to the *Lotte*, and he was driven finally to arrange for a stay at the waters of Bad Ragaz, in the hope of more effective treatment.

The thermal baths were exhausting, and he ended a month there with no noticeable improvement for the sciatica, though at his final examination the doctor stoutly promised it soon. The quiet life had brought some relief, however; with Katia in attendance some routine work had been done and many letters written; and soon after their return he was able to get back to *Lotte*, amid encouragement from enthusiastic listeners to his readings of the latest additions—Bruno Frank and his wife, as well as a larger family-circle, both Klaus and Golo being now also for a while in Küsnacht. At the end of July, though still in pain and walking with difficulty, he thought he remarked some progress, and the future began to brighten. The proofs of the first number of *Standards and Values* arrived, its content greatly to his satisfaction, and he was in correspondence with an American agent for an extended lecture-tour there in March, to cover twelve cities coast-to-coast.

America indeed had remained very much in his thoughts. He had discussed with Erika, who left on 17 July with Klaus for Paris on her way back to New York, its long-term advantages for the family, including Golo. (Klaus in fact, in better form and with many projects in mind, followed Erika to New York at the end of September.) Further letters had been exchanged with Agnes Meyer, sending her the journal foreword which she had offered to translate, and later gratefully agreeing this should appear, as 'Standards and Values', in the *Post* and other papers. She had immediately subscribed to the journal, as well as sending a generous donation, and had also suggested he should lecture in Washington. From her recommendation, in fact offer, of the *Washington Post* ('read by every official from the President down') as an influential outlet for his views, he realized the importance of this new contact, and looked forward to meeting her during his tour. He informed Angell of his plans for that, proposed he should include Yale for the inauguration of the collection, and began to sketch out some ideas for his lecture, on 'Democracy'. A letter in August from Caroline Newton, of Jamestown, Rhode Island, whom he had met briefly in Berlin in 1929, assured him of his welcome over there, and in his reply he said how often he and Katia had considered shaking off the dust of Europe in its present state and spending at least most of their time in America. She too was later to prove a useful, if sometimes tiresome, friend.

There were still moments of depression. Left alone in the house as the others saw Erika and Klaus off, his chance recall of the death of Grautoff had prompted melancholy thoughts on his present circumstances: an impasse, the beginning perhaps of a dissolution. But such moments passed quickly, as they always had. His improved health, the success of the first number of the journal, and the plans for America, made a substantial boost for his morale, as the winter approached; and *Lotte in Weimar* continued to make great strides, as he burned to get this 'improvisation' behind him so that he could turn to the final volume of the *Joseph*.

He was already aware that what he was taking on for the coming spring in America made that a very distant prospect. And to say he was 'burning' to get on with a work was in Thomas Mann parlance a very relative expression: in terms of actual writing, his remained a leisurely life, and he made no noticeable change in his customary hours of work, whether on the novel or on anything else which intervened. The comfortable Küsnacht routine continued, with no pause in the number of visitors, and plenty of time for excursions or evening entertainments, as well as for correspondence and the stream of minor commitments, notably a request for a memorial notice for Masaryk, who died in September. Three weeks with Katia at the end of that month in Locarno, in mostly rainy weather, allowed more concentration on *Lotte*, but the end was by no means yet in sight. He was often reading Nietzsche, with the essay project still in mind, and after their return to Küsnacht paid another visit to Tribschen, with its 'frightful oil-paintings', the elements of Hitlerism unmistakable, 'even if only latent and foreglimpsed'.

An invitation then to give a lecture on Wagner, on the occasion of a complete production of the *Ring* cycle in Zurich in November, thus came appositely (if inconveniently pressing in time), for this was after all a subject peculiarly his own, and it recalled his last appearance in Germany. Reading Nietzsche's 'Wagner in Bayreuth', as he started his preparation, he noted how much had been suppressed there: 'no one can write on that without writhing under the suffering it brings. How comes it that I too must take the line of piety? Delicacy and gratitude again.' 'On revient toujours,' he wrote to Zweig on 14 November, after 'working like a Trojan' to finish in time.

He made his offering two days later, in the well-filled *Aula* of the university. Much shorter than the *Sorrows and Greatness* essay of 1933, it opened with a quotation from his 1933 lecture derived from that, the personal declaration of his lifelong passion for Wagner's *œuvre*. Directed specifically to the *Ring*, and to his Swiss audience, it made much of Wagner's discovery of myth and his road to 'a new form of drama born of myth and music', but also of the close associations between the work and Zurich, the 'international city . . . and one that has always looked with favour on the innovative endeavours of the European avant-garde—and will, I hope, continue to do so'. But he did not mince his words on the mischievous abuse to which the Wagner phenomenon was subject, when he was claimed 'as the artistic prophet of a political present that would like to mirror itself in him': '*Volk* and sword and myth and Nordic hero-worship on certain lips are only despicable plagiarisms', Wagner had not 'emerged from the age of bourgeois culture in order to exchange its values for a totalitarianism that destroys mind and spirit. The German spirit signified everything to him, the German state nothing.' The political lesson was probably not quite what his hearers had expected, but there were sufficient plaudits and congratulations afterwards to leave him satisfied, and the lecture was in every way a suitable contribution later for *Standards and Values*.

He must turn now to the lecture for America. Aesthetic problems, as he wrote to Schickele, were so much more interesting than politics, and over the theme of 'The Coming Victory of Democracy' he had a momentary hesitation: did he really believe in 'democratic idealism'? or was he simply thinking himself into it, playing a part like a good actor, just because he hated fascism and Hitler? At all events, there would be no harm in reminding the world, and he pressed ahead, though he would rather have put his sermon in the mouth of a character in a novel. In spite of disturbed nights, with a painful eczema in the inner ear, by mid-December he had produced no less than forty-one pages, in the familiar urge to leave nothing unsaid: 'I'll have to leave out half the mess,' he told Erika in New York, 'a fearful waste, but once I'm turned loose there's no holding me.' Still, he was pleased with the result—a simple presentation of the case, 'a definition and at the same time an exhortation'—and admiring friends who listened to a reading agreed it must have wide distribution, in all languages.

The 'representational' Thomas Mann was now becoming more and more the publicist. To criticism that his work with *Standards and Values* was with an *émigré* journal unworthy of him, he replied firmly that his opposition to the Third Reich was of a piece with the humanist trend of his life's work as an artist. While he still avoided the more sterile polemic of the exile journalists, his essays and lectures on loftier and wider-ranging political themes were beginning to reach a wider public in printed form. Even in England, the academic journal *German Life and Letters* now reprinted the 'Standards and Values' foreword, while in France an edition of a selection of his recent writings, with part of the foreword and the Bonn letter, was prefaced by Gide. His draft for the lecture in America, in its extended form, made a special number of *Standards and Values* in January/February 1938, and in Agnes Meyer's translation would be published both in the USA and England later that year. Meanwhile in America he found 'business' of a more practical nature for him was blossoming: a foreword was requested for a condensed Schopenhauer edition in Longman's 'Living Thoughts Library' for a fee of 800 dollars, while Harvard proposed three lectures on Goethe, for 1,000. Having now prepared the lecture for the tour, and also a speech for Yale, he would be hard put to it to get all this done, and had to look forward to a year of considerable effort; as he put it to Klaus, art would have to take second place to bread, and have to wait. Erika, however, advised caution over the Longman proposal, the payment seeming to her in doubt, and before starting he demanded half in advance, over Christmas meanwhile stealing the time to add a few pages to the novel.

On New Year's Eve, he set out for himself the programme he saw ahead: the Schopenhauer essay, to be written during their usual January stay in Arosa; the three months of the whirl in America; a tour to Prague and Vienna in May or June; the summer then, perhaps at a spa somewhere, or the autumn, might bring the end of *Lotte in Weimar*. ' "Bring" is what I believe and hope for, rather than energy and activity. Time brings everything. May time be granted me!' What he did not foresee were the political upheavals that time would bring during 1938 in Central Europe, as Hitler skilfully and relentlessly pursued the programme long since set out in *Mein Kampf*, and their radical effect on the plans and life of Thomas Mann.

## 2

*'Welcome to Thomas Mann, new American citizen . . . a writer for whom wreaths are likely to be cut from trees still unplanted'*
(New York Post, 9 May 1938)

'Why don't you consider the possibilities of settling over here?' Agnes Meyer had written to Katia in December. Though she could not quite imagine Mann permanently established in America, she thought the atmosphere there might 'interfere less with his concentration on his own work'. It was something they certainly had in mind, and not for the first time, as they began to prepare for passage on the *Queen Mary* in February, but for the moment it was no more than a vague idea. He himself probably regarded the tour, on which he would see much more of the country than was so far familiar, rather as a reconnaissance than as a step to actual emigration: for that, the logistics would present formidable problems, and not only in terms of possessions, the family being still so scattered. Over Christmas, both Golo, who had been back from Prague for some time, and Michael had been with them; though Michael had been seriously ill, he had recovered well enough for Katia to leave him for Arosa, and he was to accompany them to America, to which some of his Paris instructors in chamber music had now emigrated. Golo, who had been of great assistance to his father in routine work and on the journal affairs, was working on a biography of Friedrich von Gentz (1764–1832), the political writer and translator of Edmund Burke's 'Reflections on the French Revolution': he would hold the fort in Küsnacht, and take care of Elisabeth, who, though only 19, had already had impetuous ideas of marriage (she had been attracted not only to Landshoff, but also to the *émigré* author Ignazio Silone, then in Zurich). Küsnacht also made a base for Klaus when he returned from America to Europe in January, while Monika continued her independent life in Florence, and Erika her lecture tours in America. Their father was too preoccupied with his own immediate affairs to give more than a passing attention at this stage to the idea of a move.

Arosa, where he spent three weeks during January with Katia, saw him well ahead, though by no means yet finished, with the Schopenhauer foreword, with the novel too, and he also prepared a preface for the French edition of Schickele's new novel *The Widow Bosca*. The familiar and comfortable, though wintry, surroundings were a restorative, and he compared them, with some foreboding, with those to come in America, where he would be snatched out of his accustomed world and standing up before a microphone to audiences of thousands. Agnes Meyer's intention of writing an extensive review of *Joseph in Egypt*, due to appear on his arrival, was most welcome, he told her, for it would restore the emphasis on his artistic, as opposed to his political, work: he had been driven to the latter 'purely and simply by circumstances, very much against my nature and against my will. . . . you are quite right that today perhaps, particularly in America, the political side of my existence is brought too much into the forefront.'[12] Smoothing over a clash between the temperamental Lion and the publisher Oprecht took time while he was in Arosa; and he was so irritated to learn that Ida Herz, in excitement over the possibility of a post with the Yale Mann Collection, had written, without consulting him, direct to Roosevelt about her immigration to America, that he at first refused to stand surety for her application (later softening over this, but still lukewarm in his recommendation of her to Angell).

As their stay drew to an end, however, his doubts over too much stress on his political existence began to dissipate. Sending Schickele the promised preface, he said he felt his 'Democracy' lecture would be just what was wanted in the USA, and a support for Roosevelt's policy. A trial run early in February before members of a Zurich Jewish club proved satisfactory, though his text was still in need of cuts. Now work had to be more or less laid aside in favour of preparations for the journey, which for one of his fastidiousness needed more attention than for the ordinary mortal: another

---

[12] *AM Brw.* 112.

new suit, and new full evening dress, to be ordered and fitted, and two capacious wardrobe-trunks readied for advance dispatch on 12 February. Reporting to Bermann, promising the Schopenhauer for publication in German in due course, he said it would probably have to be finished in California at the end of the tour: 'a detailed study was unavoidable—people ought not to set me on such a trail! . . . I'm sorry for you, having to do with an author who . . . always keeps you waiting interminably—when I think of the *Lotte*, and even more *Joseph IV*, my heart fails me. But what's to be done, that's how I am.'[13] For the Yale Collection, he had finally promised at least one of the major manuscripts, and prepared to take with him that of the *Joseph*, pending recovery of the *Magic Mountain* from Germany.

The news now from there was most disturbing, for it was clear that a crisis was being provoked over Austria. Just before their departure for Paris came Hitler's dramatic summons of Chancellor Schuschnigg to Berchtesgaden, where, attended by his generals and Ribbentrop, he accused him hysterically of breaches of the 1936 agreement, and browbeat him into legalizing the Austrian Nazi party. Their journey on 16 February to join the *Queen Mary* at Cherbourg, accompanied by Elisabeth and Monika as far as Paris, was under the ominous shadow of an imminent catastrophe for Austria, with Hitler evidently bent on the anschluss, and who could tell what consequences for Czechoslovakia and Switzerland. Where would their future lie: should they think of Paris, or London—or America? In this mood, as they boarded the liner, a giant building, as it seemed, and most impressive for young Michael, even damaged luggage and the mislaying (fortunately only temporary) of his case with the manuscripts seemed of little moment. The ship's newspaper next day brought brief word of Schuschnigg compelled to pardon the murderers of Dollfuss and other Nazi terrorists, of the dejection of Austrian patriots and growing panic among Catholics and Jews. (He did not yet know that Schuschnigg had been forced even to admit prominent Nazis to his government, including their leader, the notorious Seyss-Inquart, as Interior Minister.) Writing to Lion on 20 February, the day before they reached New York, he bemoaned the lack of detailed news—'for me personally, the loss of Vienna is sad enough'—and asked whether losing readers in Austria could be tolerable for the journal. Noting with Katia their thirty-third wedding anniversary, his depression prompted him to remark that he would not like to have to live over again a life in which distress and pain had predominated—not what she liked or expected to hear, of course, and, as he later admitted to himself, a meaningless judgement.

---

[13] *GBF Brw.* 141.

Docked in New York, they were delighted to be joined in their cabin by Erika, and when the interviews began, she acted as his interpreter, for he was not yet confident enough in English. He was pushed, however, to an impromptu address on deck, before a microphone, on the Austrian situation. Unsurprisingly, the journalists were even more pressing than on the previous occasion, and their questions directed to the political rather than the literary. The *New York Post* reported him confident of the survival of democracy, provided it learned to defend itself 'against murderers', but forecasting a complete nazification of Austria before Hitler then, inevitably, began his attack on Czechoslovakia—a tougher nut to crack, he thought, for it had both a strong government and a strong army. (The reporters found unsettling his tendency in his replies to turn to the interpreter rather than to the questioners; but it would be some time yet before he could venture to dispense with an intermediary.) Knopf saw to smooth landing-arrangements, taking care of all details, and installed them in the familiar rooms, filled as usual with flowers, in the Hotel Bedford, before taking them off to supper later and enthusing over the prospects for *Joseph in Egypt*, of which a copy arrived next day.

A full press conference was called in the hotel on 22 February, with Erika again interpreting. For the *Herald Tribune* the main thrust of his remarks was the failure of the democracies to stand up to Hitler ('Thomas Mann is Sorry British Bowed to Nazis'), for the *Times* his positive assessment of America's attitude ('Mann Finds US Sole Peace Hope'); and in the latter's report came the words 'Where I am, there is Germany'—later much quoted, though the context made clear that this was not as self-assertive as it sounded, for he was actually stressing that exile from the 'poisoned atmosphere in Germany' represented no loss for him: 'Where I am, there is Germany. I carry my German culture within me. I have contact with the world and I do not consider myself fallen.'[14] Agnes Meyer attended, and afterwards had the longed-for privilege of a personal meeting, at which she heard his Yale address and he her draft essay-review of *Joseph*.

The three days before he was due in New Haven were programmed efficiently, thanks to Knopf and Erika, with more interviews, sessions with photographers, visitors, discussions with the publisher, the lecture-tour agent, and Joseph Angell in preparation for the exhibition opening at Yale he was looking forward to. There was time, however, for quiet meals with Erika and Michael, and to enjoy the Kaufman/Hart comedy *You Can't Take it with You*. They took supper with the Meyers, and he was invited to dine with the bibliophile banker Frank Altschul, later chairman of the Yale

---

[14] *AM Brw.* 833 f.

Library Associates, in an assembly of professors and scholars joined by Angell and Dorothy Thompson. Angell's naïvety he found embarrassing, and was glad he had already refused his invitation to stay, preferring one from Professor Weigand, a long-time admirer whose Thomas Mann studies he had appreciated; but on arrival in New Haven on 25 February they lunched with the young man, together with Knopf and his wife, the translator Helen Lowe-Porter, and Caroline Newton.

In the afternoon a large audience had gathered to listen to his words and see the Thomas Mann Collection. Naïve Angell certainly was, and, as would later appear, not very practical in application; but the successful initiative for the Collection was nevertheless a remarkable achievement on the part of one who was not even on the faculty and faced a lack of enthusiasm in at least one of its members. In his address, Mann probably did not exaggerate when he said the occasion would remain the most memorable of his tour. In not over-modest words, he expressed his appreciation of this tribute to 'the life of an artist, no more no less, with its weaknesses, follies, and blunders together with its more blessed moments of higher, purer, and just achievement': he hoped the collection of his books, manuscripts, drafts, letters, and memorabilia might provide for friends of literature, and especially students, a review of 'a life born with the impulse to crystallize itself in word, picture, thought, to wrest the permanent from the transitory, form from chaos'.[15] (As it turned out, his hope of adding The Magic Mountain manuscript, for which he intended to ask 5,000 dollars, was vain: impossible to recover from Germany, it was almost certainly destroyed in the bombing of Munich towards the end of the Second World War. The Yale Collection contains, however, a number of substantial early drafts discarded during his revision of the text—as Angell said, the only preserved instance in his work of such large-scale revision and rejection.)

He was clearly flattered by the elaboration of this shrine to his fame in the form of a Thomas Mann research centre in a leading American university; in addition, as he had said earlier, it was one more action 'directed more or less demonstratively against the Germany of today'. No less flattering, if in manner less imposing, was his next assignment: a visit the following day to the small Wesleyan University at Middletown, Connecticut, not far from Weigand's home in Bethany. Here, to a group of advanced students, he spoke impromptu in German on Wagner, answered questions, and listened to their contributions on The Buddenbrooks and The Magic Mountain, the discussion which followed continuing over beer and cheese. Returning then to New York, he felt that, in their different ways,

[15] xi 459.

these two functions had made a highly satisfying start to the visit, before they set out with Erika on 28 February by train for Chicago, and the lecture tour proper could begin.

The programme, instead of a steady progression westwards, envisaged first a swing through Illinois and Michigan, a brief return to New York, taking in Washington, and only then the main road west via Philadelphia, and Chicago again, to Kansas City, Tulsa, Salt Lake City, San Francisco, and Los Angeles. All travel being by train, this made for a very tiring itinerary, but he stood it well, though both stimulants and sleeping-pills were often necessary; and he profited from the long hours before the first performance in Chicago to rehearse the lecture with Erika. Throughout, her assistance was invaluable, not only with the numberless interviews, but also in preparing the adaptations to his text made necessary by events in Europe. The unopposed march of German troops into Austria on 12 March, Hitler's proclamation next day of the anschluss with the Reich, and his immediate opening of an intense propaganda campaign against Czechoslovakia, demanding a similar 'return' of the Sudeten German lands, cast a deep shadow over the tour. Before it was over Thomas Mann had determined to stay in the United States. The return itinerary east then included not only visits to Champaign-Urbana, Illinois, to receive the Cardinal Newman award 'for services to literature', but also additional lectures in Cleveland and Toronto, from where he and Katia could formally apply for immigration and citizenship. Offers of honorary doctorates and of accommodation left him in no doubt of their welcome as residents.

His audiences in Chicago and Ann Arbor were large and attentive, though the applause seemed restrained, probably, as Erika said, because of the impersonal nature of his text. Back in New York he spoke on Goethe in Brooklyn and gave the 'Democracy' lecture in the Town Hall; but it was only thereafter that his real success began. The tour as a whole, as he wrote later to Klaus, was a triumph, and he felt he had well earned the fee of 15,000 dollars (even if the agent was to cream off 25 per cent). Knopf, who accompanied them on part of the journey, could report sales of *Joseph in Egypt* reaching 9,000 by the time they left Kansas City on 15 March. In Washington, where they stayed in the Meyers' elegant town-house, their hostess gave a big reception, with many notables and diplomats, after Mann's lecture in Constitution Hall; in Philadelphia, where he first learned of the anschluss during an interview and adapted the start of his text accordingly, the Opera House was packed to hear him, and the 'grand evening' served to lighten somewhat his deep depression over Austria; at each stop the days were filled with entertainments, invitations, and inspection tours. The culmination was his performance on 1 April, before an audience of 7,000 in the Los Angeles Shrine Auditorium: afterwards with

Bruno Frank and his wife, as Agnes Meyer's daughter reported, he was 'incredibly happy and human and even sprightly . . . he had never had such receptions before the American tour, and the one here topped them all. He wasn't tired at all, and talked and talked . . . '[16]

In interviews he was forthcoming. Early in March, in Detroit, he had left no doubt of his 'indescribable feeling of freedom' in America and his confidence in her ability to defend it. In Tulsa, after the anschluss, he did not conceal his misgivings over the future in Europe—Austria would not be the end of the expansion aims of a Hitler 'mad with power', and Czechoslovakia and Hungary would be next on the list—but he was still convinced that the madness of fascism and Nazism would not last against the ideals of democracy. The *Los Angeles Times* headed its interview of 24 March 'Duplicity Laid to Great Britain': the British, he said, had from the beginning of Hitler's rise been playing with him, a group 'now represented by Chamberlain' regarding him as a bulwark against any left-wing trend in Europe.

It was in Salt Lake City, on 21 March, that he reached the conclusion that, whether there was war or not, a return to Switzerland was increasingly inadvisable. Writing to Agnes Meyer, he said that following the fearful events in Austria his earlier idea of settling in America had now become a firm decision: 'Europe is no longer a place for one like me, and quite apart from all my psychological resistance, Switzerland would no longer offer me even physical safety.' Deciding therefore to stay, they planned, subject to developments in the coming weeks, to send Erika back alone to Küsnacht to see to everything there. It was luck again, he noted in his diary, that they were 'outside', and he must trust in that luck continuing, have confidence, as he put it, that 'the individual character of my life will always assert itself and come through'. Amid the attractions then of California—blue skies, palm-trees, tasteful residences, and above all the surrounding movie-world, where there was already talk of a film of *Joseph*—the plan took shape. After the San Francisco lecture, they would spend the whole of April in Hollywood, before returning to New York via Cleveland; he and Katia would then accept Caroline Newton's invitation to spend the summer in her country-house in Jamestown, west of Newport, Rhode Island, leaving Erika to return to Küsnacht and send Golo and Elisabeth over to America to join them.

That it would fall to others to see to the nuts and bolts was never a consideration to disturb him. While he rested, Erika and Katia at once saw to a month's rental of a charming bungalow annexed to the Beverley Wilshire Hotel; when the time came, the task of winding up their affairs in

---

[16] AM Brw. 838.

Küsnacht could be left to Erika; he need think only of buying new clothes and having books and his summer things sent over. Whatever happened, he could be assured that his own comfort would not suffer. Meanwhile he could make good use of the month's respite in the pleasant surroundings of Hollywood to resume work: immediately on moving into the bungalow he turned his thoughts again to the Schopenhauer essay and the final stages of *Lotte in Weimar*.

His confidence in his personal star of good fortune was unshaken, but that did not mean their plans for the future were now firm. Katia, though entirely in favour of their immigration, the papers for which Erika had now started work on, was understandably reluctant to set a conclusion to Küsnacht by remote control, and discussion continued whether they should not after all revisit there themselves before the summer was out. Nor did it mean he was no longer greatly depressed at the situation in Germany and the seemingly unstoppable advance of the Greater German Reich, or any the less worried over the outcome for Europe, though he was increasingly resigned over England's obvious indifference. Hedwig Pringsheim's letter from Munich at the end of March, reporting the swastika flag waving gaily over 'a certain little house' in Poschinger Strasse, now a home to encourage fertility among Nazi mothers,[17] was a melancholy reminder of conditions over there. Detailed news on Austria was hard to come by, but Mann was personally concerned over a report of Reisiger's arrest, fortunately soon followed by word of his release. There were many suicides, the plight of the Jews was evident, and the number of refugees ever increasing. He spoke on 31 March at a hundred-dollar dinner for refugee aid given by the film magnate Jack Warner, which produced 'colossal' sums, and his Los Angeles lecture on 1 April was followed by a moving appeal by Erika which also raised a large amount for the Austrian refugees. Within a few days, the work which he resumed, at the standard page or two a day, was interwoven with an essay promised for the magazine *Cosmopolitan*, based on his diary entries for 1933–4, as a specifically anti-Hitler tract for the times. The editor found it unsuitable, but its ironic sketch of Hitler was extracted for separate publication in *Esquire*, and in German in the Paris *Das Neue Tage-Buch*, a year later. 'Brother Hitler' was the only piece, as he wrote later, in which he ever dealt directly with that revolting figure, 'irony keeping in check the indescribable disgust I had always felt for him'. He continued too his financial support for the American Guild for German Cultural Freedom, which offered stipends for refugee writers.

Though he was naturally concerned about Bermann Fischer and his family in Vienna, and cabled to Hedwig Fischer in Rapallo to enquire, the

---

[17] Wiedem. 3.

probable total confiscation of the firm in Vienna and loss of his last publisher in the German area seems to have left him less troubled than might have been expected. Bermann, on learning of the imminent arrival of German troops, had acted at once on 13 March, packing the bare necessities, his Stradivarius, and a few essential papers, and entrained with his wife and children for the Italian border—ironically enough passing the Vienna ticket-barrier with the German passports they still had, while they saw travellers with Austrian papers detained. Leaving the children with Hedwig Fischer in Rapallo, they went on to Zurich, where he had maintained a separate Swiss firm for the remaining rights, which he planned somehow to continue to exploit. They had barely escaped the visit of the SS, and lost not only their personal possessions, but also the whole stock of books and all the files and business papers when the firm was put under a Nazi commissar, attempts later by a Swiss friend to secure their release proving ineffectual.

One of his first ideas had been to reopen as an *émigré* house in Sweden, in collaboration with Bonnier in Stockholm. In a telegram to Mann, however, he also mentioned a possible similar collaborative venture in America, and this Mann decisively rejected: much as he wanted his work to be sustained in its German form and not be totally eclipsed by translations, he was convinced that only an established American publisher could succeed in that, and he would personally recommend his friend to abandon publishing in favour of a return to his original career as a doctor. This was a dose of cold water for Bermann, who was confident that he had succeeded, against attacks from both sides, in keeping alive an effective German enterprise in emigration, and he was not prepared to give up the struggle to continue it, in whatever form could be found: he was ready to come over for a discussion with Knopf should he be interested. Mann maintained his reservations, stressing how his own position (it had been mainly his name, after all, which had enabled the Vienna enterprise to continue) had suffered from Bermann's sometimes ambiguous conduct and poor publicity-methods. In an exchange of cables and letter-telegrams during May, after Bermann had announced a new start in Stockholm for June (and asked when he could expect to see *Lotte in Weimar*), Mann went so far as to refuse any future link with the firm—a unilateral annulment of his contract which the other pleaded strongly he should abandon, more especially in view of the close collaboration planned with the two *émigré* firms in Amsterdam, ensuring joint coverage of the whole German-speaking market, with distribution also in America. In June, Mann finally yielded to his arguments, and from then on the Bermann Fischer Verlag in Stockholm became his German-language publishers, their relations restored though still not without occasional asperities.

All this was while he was settling into his congenial new life: 'America is exceedingly good to me,' as he wrote to Klaus. No sooner arrived in Hollywood, he was invited by Ernst Lubitsch to the Paramount studios, the place packed, as it seemed, with idle screen-writers (many were recruited among the refugees, but in most cases the task was ill-suited to their talents). During April he made long inspection tours of the Disney, MGM, and Fox studios, fascinated by the 'trick world' of the vast permanent sets, watching Peter Lorre in action, and seeing child star Shirley Temple at her lessons in a mobile home. It was highly gratifying to hear MGM's virtual promise of the *Joseph* film, with Robert Montgomery billed for the lead, from which he might expect vast sums (surprisingly, after a private viewing of *Night Must Fall*, he thought Montgomery, if too heavily built, psycho-logically suited for the role, though it is hard to see what 'definite Joseph elements' he can have distinguished in that thriller).[18] He 'fairly wallowed' in the movie sphere, amid constant invitations to film shows, dinners, and lavish evenings with people who of course were often of German or Austrian origin—like Lubitsch himself, at whose house he was charmed by Madeleine Carroll, and Lorre, whose embrace of Katia on one occasion was so violently emotional that he gave her a love-bite on the arm.

It was not surprising that California remained for him the most attractive corner of the States, though promising avenues for a future elsewhere had already begun to open up, notably, thanks to Agnes Meyer, the possibility of a position at Princeton, which he planned to visit as soon as he could. A letter from Lion pleading for his return to Zurich was reminiscent of those he had received from Bermann in the first year of exile, and he himself was surprised how little tempted he felt (one of the brighter aspects of his decision, he thought, was that he never need see the temperamental Lion again). His intention was for the whole family to settle in America, except for Monika, who had now taken the oath for her Czech citizenship, with Klaus as witness, at the Zurich consulate and would stay in Florence. For him and Katia the 'first papers' for immigration had been drawn up by the time the return journey east began at the end of the month: to Chicago, for the Cardinal Newman award at Urbana, then Cleveland, where he repeated the 'Democracy' lecture and Erika left them for an assignment of her own. Toronto came immediately after, where a large audience in the Massey Hall applauded 'the lean, austere Nobel Prize winner who relinquished country, home, and property for an ideal'. His presence there, however, was prima-rily for the formal presentation of 'first papers' and the necessary documen-tation at the US consulate, whereupon they could return as certified applicants for naturalization—for which a further five years' residence

[18] *Tb.* iv, 207 f.

would then be required. Golo had meanwhile started the same procedure for himself.

Klaus, also still in Küsnacht, had reported a rumour in the Czech press, possibly Nazi-inspired, of his father's intention, and urged all possible discretion in view of the understandable sensitivity of the Czechs at the present juncture. But discretion in America over such a newsworthy item was impossible with the close public interest in Thomas Mann, and in fact, in an interview with the *Cleveland Plain Dealer* on 2 May, he revealed it. Immediately on their return to New York on 5 May a cable was dispatched to President Beneš, to offset any embarrassment, in which he expressed his continuing deep sympathy with the Republic and his gratitude for the protection it had offered him in his 'homeless' condition, and assured him he would remain a Czech citizen even if in time American citizenship was also granted him. A few days later the *New York Post* headlined its 'Welcome to the New American Citizen' over an article expressing the honour at receiving 'this discard from Nazi Germany': 'America is fortunately and unexpectedly enriched.' His final lecture of the tour was in Carnegie Hall on 6 May, but there were several other appearances scheduled, one a dinner in his honour at the Hotel Astor given by the Committee for Christian German Refugees: for this he needed Erika's help once again to prepare his speech, in which he pointed out the persecution of Christianity in Germany and the consonance of its ideals with those of democracy. On 8 May they visited Princeton, forming excellent impressions of conditions there should a firm offer materialize, returning then for the Astor dinner, at which Dorothy Thompson presented him with a 'Golden Book of Remembrance' with hand-written tributes from a large number of prominent Americans.

The gift shortly afterwards of an American flag from an admirer seemed a symbol of the general goodwill towards him, and to Lion he made clear he was determined not to return to 'a Europe where the shameful deed against Austria' had been possible (though, if circumstances allowed, a visit to Switzerland might not be ruled out). He believed in America, he wrote, where he had been received in honour and friendship, and where he hoped to find a post at some university which could offer enough to live on and at the same time leave him time to pursue his own work. (Both Harvard and Princeton had been possibilities, though, as he wrote to Klaus, he had some misgivings over a 'scholarly atmosphere': 'I'd really prefer the movie mob.')[19] A plan for a visit to Küsnacht, which Katia continued to press for, had indeed by now begun to take shape: the situation in Europe, with Czech mobilization showing firm resistance to Hitler's propaganda cam-

[19] KlM *Br. Antw.* 351.

paign, looked more hopeful, and a war, this year at least, seemed unlikely. Michael wanted in any case to return to Paris for a summer course with Galamian; Erika had already arrived there and was planning to go on with Klaus to Spain as correspondents on the Civil War. Their own dates could not yet be decided, the Princeton offer being still in embryo as they prepared the transfer in the last week of May to Caroline Newton's house by the sea in Rhode Island. There, having now finished the Schopenhauer essay, he hoped to return to *Lotte in Weimar*.

It made a tolerably comfortable staging-post, with a servant provided, and at first gave a welcome tranquillity, as soon as their over-eager hostess left them to themselves, and as far as the constant sound of the foghorn, bellowing 'like a sick cow', allowed. His desk was soon ready, and he prepared for work. The day after their arrival came the firm offer from Princeton of 6,000 dollars for a year's attachment to the university in the coming academic year, with a commitment for only four lectures. The compass needle now made a definite swing in that direction, and after some reflection he sent his acceptance, with his thanks for the honour. The stay in Jamestown would be only for a month, as Mrs Newton planned to return herself at the end of June and he could not face remaining under one roof with such a chatterbox. Equally unappealing would be a long visit to Agnes Meyer at her 'château' of Mount Kisco near New York, even if, as she suggested, he used it merely as a base of operations. The intervening months until October must therefore see a serious search for accommodation in Princeton, and then the visit to Europe, and Katia began enquiries for a suitable passage towards the end of June. True, Klaus wrote to his mother from Küsnacht that their longing to see the 'decayed continent' again was stupid, and listed all the well-known drawbacks of Switzerland: but it was obviously sensible to see personally to the winding-up, and he felt happy at the thought of driving once more up to the house in the Schiedhalden Strasse, where all six children would be temporarily assembled.

There were unsettling reports of alarm and agitation in Czechoslovakia over his decision to emigrate (and, though he did not yet know it, Schwarzschild in Paris had publicly accused him of 'disloyalty to Europe'). But any lingering doubts were soon dismissed, and shortly afterwards, accepting honorary membership of a 'Free Czech' committee, he stressed again that settling in America did not mean relinquishing his Czech citizenship. In fact, however, this was required under American regulations, and he wrote explaining the situation to President Beneš and to the commune of Proseč.

Though Caroline Newton had provided him with a welcome complete Goethe edition, and the library at Newport was at his disposal, the few weeks in Jamestown saw only intermittent progress with the novel. A life so buried in 'nature', and plagued by insects to boot, was never really to his taste, nor apparently did the 'extraordinarily stimulating' aphrodisiac of the sea air have the effect that might once have been expected. There were occasional visitors, including the film agent, to his retreat: but he soon began to find this existence boring and monotonous. On 1 June he had travelled up to New York to receive his honorary doctorate from Columbia University, following Dorothy Thompson to the tribune in cap and gown to great applause, especially when his immigration was mentioned. A further similar ceremony was scheduled at the Yale commencement on 21 June, and their booking for Europe was made for two days later. After Katia's unsatisfactory search in Princeton for accommodation, however, they decided to defer the sailing (about which he himself was still in two minds) until 29 June, to allow them time to look together for a suitable house and also for a brief stay with Agnes Meyer, which he felt he could not refuse in view of all her help, and whose house at Mount Kisco would indeed make a base for the things not needed for New York and Zurich.

The complicated arrangements were finally worked out, and having dispatched the heavy luggage to New York they drove direct from Jamestown to New Haven on 21 June for the lengthy ceremonial at Yale next day. In his *laudatio*, the Orator laid stress on the Nobel Prize winner's restoration of his country's renown for the novel as an art form, and his sacrifice now in writing political speeches instead, convinced that the world danger to liberty made this the right course. Honorary degrees were awarded also to John Buchan, Governor-General of Canada, and Serge Koussevitzky, the celebrated conductor of the Boston Symphony, but Mann was pleased to find the greatest applause for himself and Walt Disney. Back that evening in New York, they took a drive through Harlem and witnessed the frantic jubilation over Joe Louis's sensational knock-out victory in the first round over the German heavyweight Max Schmeling (who had received a premature cable of victory from the Führer). A day then of sorting and packing books—one of the few administrative chores which he did not leave entirely to the indefatigable Katia—was followed by a survey of properties with the agent in Princeton. The owners of one of their choice called off next day—'childish business-methods', he commented crossly—but there was another, better possibility, though the owners, an English couple, readers of his, were still hesitating between rental or sale. A further visit would have to be made from Mount Kisco, for where they were picked up by Agnes Meyer's limousine, after further packing and repacking in the New York heat, on 26 June.

In these cooler surroundings, of 'park, quiet, wealth, and comfort', he learned the full extent of her help over the Princeton appointment.

Through her personal efforts, budget difficulties for the university had been solved by a grant from the Rockefeller Foundation and assistance from other organizations and individuals whom she approached. There was every possibility of extension beyond the year if he so wished, the post would be relatively undemanding on his time, and it seemed clear that he need have no financial worries in America (though both these assumptions proved over-optimistic in the event). She was ready to have them driven next day to Princeton, where the deal was made at once to take the 'noble' furnished house they had seen in Stockton Street.

Secluded behind a brick wall and with mature pines and a dogwood, elegant and practical, it was more than ample for their needs (pure early Victorian, thought Annette Kolb on a visit later). There were fine bedrooms (one to himself), a large library, vast reception rooms, and a separate studio already marked as his study, with the indispensable couch, while servants as well as a caretaker and a washerwoman would be available. They took it for a year, at a favourable rental, the owners hoping the famous occupant would improve its sale prospects, perhaps even buy it himself. Undoubtedly, he thought, an improvement in living-standards over Küsnacht. 'I set great store on always falling upstairs,' as he wrote later,[20] and here, as so often in his life, his luck had held.

The knowledge that this new home would be waiting on their return was a mighty relief, especially for Katia, when they embarked on the *Washington* two days later; but he himself was momentarily downcast, as he turned his diary page to July and began yet another three months of travel. How much he had gone through, how much started, since their departure from Küsnacht! 'If I could only believe in the sense and the fruitfulness of it all. Much achieved, and yet nothing actually done, unless in terms of "life".' Since the 1920s, it is true, the demands of life had more and more encroached on those of his work. No morning passed which did not see him at a desk, wherever he might find himself. Yet so much of the day was spent pursuing with enthusiasm the interests of Thomas Mann the public figure, the leading representative of German letters, that not even his morning's customary stint on the current work could always proceed undisturbed by considerations of the next extraneous undertaking—a further essay, his ever-increasing correspondence, another appearance on a podium somewhere. And on the wide-ranging tours he rarely refused, readings from his work had been increasingly supplanted by lectures and speeches, as the rise of Nazism drew him into the political sphere, to the point where—as the Yale Orator had said—he was now sacrificing his true vocation to the fight for freedom. To some extent too he was sacrificing it

[20] *Bl.* 10, 71.

(as with the Schopenhauer essay) for the sake of immediate income: not strictly necessary in his comparatively affluent exile, though of the six children only Erika was as yet fully independent of his support, but still as he saw it essential for maintaining the life-style he was used to.

After the four months in America, *Lotte in Weimar*, first conceived as a brief interlude in the saga of Joseph, had become a major work, and was not yet near its end; and while looking forward to seeing the Zurich friends again, he could not suppress a certain dread of Europe in its new form, and horror over the way his life was slipping away. He might have been encouraged had he seen, in the July number of the journal *New Literature*, how the Nazis still thought it necessary to devote effort to counteracting his influence: the editorial slated him as 'a dead man' now, yet constantly exploited by the foreign press for anti-German purposes, and an article condemned his work as interested only in 'weaknesses, perversions, decline, or dissolution'.[21]

At all events, as they landed in Le Havre on 6 July, and went on directly through Paris to Basle, from where Golo and Elisabeth drove them to Küsnacht, his equanimity was restored. His arrival was a demonstration, as he wrote, of his determination not to abandon Europe, and he thought now of making an annual visit: once settled back in Küsnacht, indeed, they spent some time in a vain search for a *pied-à-terre* in Switzerland which might serve after the house was given up. Erika and Klaus returned from their adventures in Spain full of admiration for the bravery of the Republicans in their armed struggle against Franco—the one place where fascism was being actively opposed, in the face of the one-sided 'non-intervention' policy of Britain and France. He had little inclination, he told Ida Herz, to visit England—though clearly the disastrous political attitude there counted for less than English indifference towards his work, when he considered that *Joseph in Egypt* had sold 20,000 in America; and he refused an invitation to attend the 'Rassemblement universel pour la Paix' on 20 July in Paris, to be chaired by Robert Cecil, though sending a warm message of solidarity with the Spanish people's exemplary defence of freedom and undoubted moral victory.

It was like a dream to be back in the familiar surroundings. But it was to be all too brief, for the packers were due to begin work at the end of August; and the load of correspondence, discharged with his usual diligence, made for some dissatisfaction over what was little more than an interim period in his work. He continued well with *Lotte* during July, but it had then to be interrupted for the many other calls on his time. Another foreword was required for *Standards and Values*, as its second year opened (with Oprecht

---

[21] Quoted cat. 4, Buchhandlung Matthias Loidl, Überreit, 1990.

it was agreed that Golo should before long take over as editor); at the end of August he read and assessed—mostly adversely—no fewer than seven novels submitted for a prize award from the American Guild for German Cultural Freedom. Preparation too must not be delayed for his first Princeton lecture, on Goethe's *Faust*, and during a week at Sils-Baselgia in August he made a start. Much time had to be spent on correspondence with Bermann: the plans for the 'Forum Books', to include one of his novellas, to be published jointly by Bermann Fischer, Querido, and De Lange; his own next publication, a volume of the political essays and speeches; aid for the Austrian author Robert Musil, for which he enlisted Aline Mayrisch and the Guild in America, as well as guaranteeing a modest contribution from himself if Musil could reach America; and not least, his complaints over poor distribution of his books and lack of accounting for his royalties. For the essay volume the title *Achtung, Europa!* was agreed, some transcripts prepared, and the 'Brother Hitler' essay now readied to complement the rest.

With Heinrich, who came to stay towards the end of August, and with Zurich friends, there were long discussions on the worsening situation in Europe, as Hitler's pressure on Czechoslovakia increased, and it appeared that little country was to be 'coldly sacrificed' when the London *Times* advocated the cession of the Sudeten German lands. He sent for publication in Prague his congratulations on the twentieth anniversary of the Republic, the state whose 'fight for freedom has a significance far beyond its own fate'. With Erika he wrote in support of a group in Paris, striving to overcome disunity among the *émigré* opposition, a circular letter, urging combined effort to bring down Hitler as the only way to avoid war, or, if it came, to end it before Germany was destroyed. Even as his bookshelves were emptied, his study gradually stripped, along with the rest of their own furniture in the house, and they awaited the big lift-van which would transport it all to Princeton, he continued as busy as ever: dictation of letters, corrections for the Schopenhauer and the essay volume, and further work on the Princeton lecture; a contribution to Clifton Fadiman's forthcoming anthology of personal philosophies of the eminent, with a restatement of his faith in humanism. A brief speech had also to be prepared for a ceremony planned by his many well-wishers, in the Zurich Schauspielhaus, on 13 September just before their departure. In this preface to a reading from *Lotte*, he recalled his unforgettable five years spent among the free community of Switzerland, exemplary for the Europe of the future—a speech made under the shadow of an ultimatum from the Sudeten German leader, the Czech government's desperate efforts for a negotiated settlement, the British Prime Minister's preparation for his conciliatory attendance on Hitler at Berchtesgaden, and the fear of war.

Katia, as may be imagined, was exhausted when the time came for the night train for Paris next day. In his own terms, he himself had worked hard (even on the last morning he wrote on at the lecture): but she had had to bear the main burden of what was after all their first complete house-move in thirty years of marriage. Such effort in his service he usually took for granted, but for once what it had involved dawned on him, and as she rested he personally carried up to her room some ham and red wine for their final meal. The whole family, save for Monika, who was returning to Florence, were assembled in Paris for the final farewells: Elisabeth was to accompany them on the *New Amsterdam* from Boulogne, Golo to return to Zurich, where he would in due course take over the journal editorship, and Klaus to sail separately for America, while Erika remained for the time being in Paris until she sent or brought Michael across. A morning was spent in conference with the exile group, Heinrich also attending, to draft the appeal for unity. In Thomas Mann's view, as the Czech crisis deepened, this was an unproductive activity, with a preponderance of communist voices and no representatives of the Protestant and bourgeois-democratic opposition, and he was glad to leave the final effort to Erika. He could protest that he was not abandoning Europe; but his departure now undoubtedly marked a significant break, and once on board ship on 17 September his one concern was to turn aside from the disastrous situation he was leaving behind and to concentrate on the 'personal and intellectual'. After two days, he found he could work again, and even sleep at night without benefit of pills. 'I need serenity, and to be aware of my privileged position. Helpless hatred must not be my line,' he noted, as the news began to come through of Czechoslovakia left to stand alone, 'one of the most shameful events in history'.[22] Whatever might come, he was determined to survive.

Though, immediately on his arrival in New York, billed as main speaker at a gigantic mass meeting in Madison Square Garden, amid tremendous demonstrations for Hitler's downfall and hopes that the Czechs would fight, he was greatly troubled by what little he could learn of events, and his mood was one of resignation. His concern was with his own affairs, and he continued work on the lecture in his hotel room until it was time to move into their new home in Princeton, on 28 September—exactly 'five and a half years since the loss of my German existence and I made the first entries in this diary'. It was the very day of the announcement of the emergency Four Power conference in Munich, at which Hitler then, supported by Mussolini, triumphantly secured everything he had demanded, and Czechoslovakia lost a third of her population, her most important indus-

[22] *Tb.* iv, 291.

trial areas, and her only effective means of self-defence. By skilful exploitation of the pacifist longings of the British and French, and with the
sacrifice, in Chamberlain's words, of that 'far-away country of which we
know little', Hitler had registered yet another successful step in the fulfilment of his programme. But at least war had been averted. As the Manns
settled in at Stockton Street—provisionally, till the arrival of the lift-van,
and not without complaints by the master over defects in the house,
though a servant couple stood ready—his first thought, amid his depression and disgust over the Munich disaster, was that Michael and Erika
might soon now be expected to join them.

His objective was to persist in his life and work as he had always done,
regardless of the path 'history' had taken—'so swinish a road of lies and
baseness that no one need be ashamed of refusing to follow it'.[23] In physical
terms, this was possible when the van and the rest of their effects arrived
early in October, and he could re-create his study, set up and arrange his
desk, to the last detail in exactly the form it had had in Munich and
Küsnacht, and resume the accustomed daily routine. Against the flood now
of invitations for lectures, dinners, contributions, reviews, and the like, he
could and did stand as firm as was decently possible, pleading poor health
and overburden of work. Mentally, it was not so easy. His Faust lecture was
now ready, but somehow simply to take up the novel again seemed impossible yet, however much he tried to distance himself from events: and he put
it off for the moment in favour of an essay setting out the bitter truth on the
'peace' which had been achieved. 'This Peace', which both Bermann and
Knopf brought out before the end of the year, would make the right
foreword too for the essay volume: a statement to meet the demands of a
critical moment in Europe's history, setting an updated framework for the
rest of the now more historical pieces, and pillorying the treachery of that
'Papen redivivus' Neville Chamberlain, who, in 'one of the filthiest dramas
ever performed', had surrendered the mastery of Europe to Adolf Hitler
when there had been a chance of bringing him to a fall.

With that, he had said his say, aware that the public to read it in German
would now be even more limited. It remained for him now to cultivate his
own garden, in the comfortable American sphere for which fortune had
spared him. Significantly, though he had prepared an introductory speech
for the reception in New York of ex-President Beneš's brother, he had not
attended to deliver it. He did, it is true, take what action he could to assist
those in danger, such as the members of the Thomas Mann Society in
Prague, whose urgent case for visas he pleaded direct with Secretary of
State Cordell Hull at the end of October; and at a 'Book and Author

[23] *Br.* ii, 58.

Luncheon' organized by the *Herald Tribune* in New York on 9 November, an invitation he could not refuse, he recalled the 'drama in which European statesmen who still call themselves democratic consciously and deliberately manœuvred to save fascism from its approaching fall', and he reiterated America's task 'to preserve and cherish the cultural inheritance of the Western world'.[24]

But the extent to which he was now trying to close his mind to Europe's crisis was shown by his lack of reaction to the sensational news that broke next day: the infamous *Kristallnacht* of widespread organized pogroms in Germany and Austria, in revenge for the murder, by a young Jewish *émigré*, of a German embassy official in Paris, with the systematic destruction of almost all synagogues and over 7,000 Jewish-owned businesses, and the arrest of more than 30,000 Jews. Sol Liptzin vividly recalls his visit to Stockton Street on 11 November, with one of his students, to seek Mann's views on these ghastly events, and how taken aback they were by his unemotional remarks. Measuring his words as if from a rostrum, the lofty Lübeck patrician considered that for Germany—which he described in his familiar phrase as the meeting-point of Viking civilization and Graeco-Roman classical culture, of Western rationalism and Eastern mysticism—the horror was really no more than a temporary aberration, and he seemed loath to be too critical.

That he had suffered greatly under the successive strokes of the anschluss and the Munich agreement, there is no doubt. But, as he wrote to Bermann, he had to try 'in a certain phlegmatic egoism' to put all that behind him in order to concentrate on maintaining his own work—'as far as the demands that this country in its naïve eagerness makes on me will allow'. When he did yield to those demands, it was in a philosophical rather than a directly political vein. Thus in November, at Dorothy Thompson's urging, he undertook the draft of a manifesto, to be signed by eminent representatives of the 'moral and intellectual world', against injustice and the rule of force (though, discouraged by controversy aroused by its premature disclosure, he abandoned the attempt at the end of the year). His lecture commitment was 'loyally acquitted' at the end of November, but apart from a talk at a German-American function in New York, he continued to refuse the many other invitations; and through that month and December worked daily and steadily at the novel. His correspondence, however, especially with exiles seeking his help, had by now reached almost unmanageable proportions: for that in English, he had welcome volunteer help from Molly Shenstone, wife of a Canadian professor at Princeton, but the German was now far beyond what Katia could handle

---

[24] *Tb.* iv, 891, 893.

alone. With some reluctance, therefore, he yielded to her proposal for a part-time secretary, and Hans Meisel, recently arrived in America, who had translated Sinclair Lewis's novel *It Can't Happen Here* for Querido, was recruited—to continue in the job, not always to the satisfaction of his employer, until 1940.

In the preparations for Christmas in America, so unforeseen a year ago, they had the comfort that the whole family, with the exception of Monika, would once again be there. Golo, of military age, had had some difficulties in extricating himself from the demands of his Czech citizenship, but these were finally overcome, and he arrived in Princeton on 23 December. For Michael and Elisabeth, it had been possible, with Agnes Meyer's help, to put formal immigration in motion via Toronto, though this would take time, while Michael's Swiss fiancée, Gret Moser, reaching New York on 7 November, had been rescued from Ellis Island by Erika two weeks later. Both Klaus and Erika had been actively engaged in lecture tours (not without occasional criticism for their 'communistic' line), and were completing a book together, *Escape to Life*, a kind of 'Who's Who' of the German emigration; both would be in Princeton for Christmas, if only briefly. But it would be a quieter celebration than those in Europe, with fewer outside visitors. As the day approached, the post-bag swelling and gifts beginning to pile up, a wreath on the door, coloured lights on the outside steps, and the Christmas tree erected, Thomas Mann continued his daily routine: but the presence of the children seems to have given him more pleasure than in previous years, as he showed them with justifiable pride the new home, listened to their song before the Christmas Eve present-giving, and on Christmas Day treated them to a reading of a chapter of *Lotte in Weimar*. Though not yet finished, that had been his consolation through a year of tribulation. 'I should devote myself entirely to it, if I could be allowed,' he wrote to Schickele on New Year's Eve: 'but now I've had to leave it again to prepare the lecture with which I am soon to start my travels again; I am calling it "The Problem of Freedom" . . .'[25]

3

*'For countries ruled by despots, there is no salvation but in ruin'*
*(Schiller)*

Over Christmas 1938, in a letter for Klaus and Erika which might serve as introduction to their *Escape to Life*, he welcomed this 'book of solidarity' with the emigration: 'not only in pride and suffering, but also in guilt', the

---

[25] *TM Stud.* x, 131.

guilt of the intellectuals in the Weimar Republic who had not looked to the preservation of freedom while there was still time. 'We were unfledged then in the practice of freedom, politically very young and inexperienced.' It was the right moment, he wrote, for such a book, to draw the attention of an 'immeasurably threatened world' to the true inner life of the German people, and awaken sympathy for the exiles, with vivid portraits illustrating the 'rich individual value and content of the German emigration'. Of his own solidarity, in contrast with his apparently equivocal stance in the first three years of exile, there was now no doubt, as so many asking and securing his help could testify. In January, for the poet Karl Wolfskehl, who had reached New Zealand from Italy and needed a testimonial to assist his immigration, the name of Thomas Mann worked 'like a magic key'.[26] Whether this was so with all the many others for whom he sought aid is doubtful: but he spent much time in the effort, both in individual cases— like that of Felix Salten, the author of *Bambi*, about whom he wrote to Walt Disney, or the writer Julius Bab, still in Germany—and generally, as over the British plan for resettlement of German *émigrés* in Southern Rhodesia, on which he interceded with Colonial Secretary Malcolm Macdonald. As Annette Kolb wrote from Paris, his existence was more than a great consolation: it was a refuge.

Personal intercessions in the cause of refugee aid would remain a significant part now of his business activity, and the will to help was there: but in the early months of 1939 it was discharged, as it were, with his left hand, amid frequent moments of depression over an inability to recover productivity in what should be his real work. The physical effects of the unaccustomed climate in this distant transplantation took their toll, and he sometimes felt homesick for Switzerland, where life had seemed better. By the middle of January, he had finished the 'Problem of Freedom' lecture for the tour due to start in March—resolved, as he noted, not to embark on anything of this kind for another year at least, and not entirely happy with its perhaps excessively pedagogic tone. Tracing the historical beginnings of democracy and its development from a one-time revolutionary movement to its present form as the most conservative power on earth, he stressed that the freedom it celebrated must now be fought for and defended against the current nihilism: true freedom must not include the freedom to destroy democracy.

For this, as for the Princeton lectures on Wagner and Freud he gave in January and February, he could make good use of earlier material, recycling and adapting like a true academic. But they made greater inroads on his time than he had expected, and although well content with the recep-

[26] *Brw. Aut.* 533.

tion of the Freud, after which the renewal of his appointment seemed likely, he found it difficult to return to the novel. The social obligations of his professorial position at the university, and the constant stream of visitors (including Wystan Auden in January, who, with Isherwood, had just arrived, and with Erika had been received at the White House), made life at Stockton Street as busy as it had ever been in Munich and Küsnacht: though this was never unwelcome to him, it was not conducive to steady work. He gave two successful performances of the 'Freedom' lecture towards the end of February, in New York to a large audience in the Opera House and in New Jersey at a high school; but his inner unease was reflected in a troublesome outbreak of shingles immediately afterwards. It was not surprising that with his advancing years he should experience such problems of adaptation, he wrote to Hedwig Fischer, who had succeeded in leaving Berlin to join her daughter and son-in-law in January in Stockholm: 'what work I've done—and it's not a little—has come only after hard struggle, and now the irritation has culminated in a minor but real illness'.[27]

Big changes were impending now in the lives of the children. Elisabeth, her earlier girlish passions forgotten, announced that she planned to marry the Italian writer and historian Giuseppe Borgese, who from anti-fascist convictions had remained in America since 1931, and was now a professor at Chicago University. They had occasionally met at Princeton and in New York, and though she was not yet quite 21 and he over thirty years older, it appeared their minds were made up. Monika too had plans for marriage, to the thirty-five-year-old Hungarian art-historian Jenö Lányi with whom she was now in London, and the wedding took place there in March. Finally, Michael and Gret Moser were wed in New York on 6 March—a discreet affair, with no family present, for they had already been living together, and had deferred marriage till after their formal immigration in order not to put Gret's Swiss citizenship at risk; but they came on to Princeton that night. (It would not be the last time that Gret's common sense, for she was three years older, was to restrain the more impulsive Michael.) All this affected Katia much more than her husband, who maintained a sovereign detachment in the pursuit of his own affairs, though he lifted his champagne glass with the others to the health of the young couple before starting to pack for his own departure with Katia.

The shingles attack had scarcely yielded to treatment when they started on 7 March for the first assignment of the tour proper in Boston. Erika, as his practised secretary and assistant, accompanied them. As before, her services were invaluable at interviews, press conferences, and the questions after his talks, as also with important adaptations to his text *en route*: for while they were in Chicago, on 16 March, German troops marched into Prague; at the end of the month, at Portland, there was news of the surrender of Madrid to the Franco forces; and in Beverley Hills on 5 April, of the Italian occupation of Albania. The events lent his somewhat philosophical treatment of the problem of freedom an actuality which, if not entirely unforeseen, was none the less gravely disturbing. His feeling was that, though the crisis would probably once again pass without a major war, that would not be long following, possibly before the year was out: but England's craven policy of appeasement could well herald just as 'peaceful' a nazification of western Europe as that of the east, and he was full of revulsion against the 'filthy romanticism' of the celebrations of the 'Holy German Empire' amid the wave of persecutions and suicides in Prague. In Chicago he talked for two hours with ex-President Beneš, with sympathy for his misplaced confidence in the Munich agreement, but still convinced that greater firmness might have saved Czechoslovakia. In an interview in St Louis on 18 March, he forecast that Hitler's annexations would continue until the pro-fascist clique in England, led by that 'very stupid man Chamberlain', gave way to a government more in keeping with her traditional imperialism—which would mean war: 'the world's hope for peace rests on the United States and Russia'.[28]

The tour progressed with the publicity and well-filled auditoriums to which he was by now accustomed, and he withstood well the strain of the long train-journeys, incessant interviews and photography sessions, and nine performances of the lecture over the first three weeks. In Beverley Hills, which they reached on 1 April, staying in the familiar hotel-bungalow before taking the *Super Chief* back for Chicago a week later, he enjoyed being among the 'movie mob' again: several times in the comfortable projection-rooms of the MGM and Warner studios, he saw Garbo in *Queen Christina*, Hitchcock's *The Lady Vanishes*, and after a lunch at Warners, Edward G. Robinson in *Confessions of a Nazi Spy*. He was particularly impressed by Dieterle's *Juarez*, with Paul Muni, which he thought a great distinction for the Hollywood industry. California once again delighted them: its 'slight foolishness is outweighed by the manifold charm of its natural surroundings and life', he wrote to Agnes Meyer, 'might it yet be the place for us to build a home?' The stay was not all relaxation, however, for a speech was required on 5 April at a banquet organized by the Committee for Christian German Refugees. For this his draft of the manifesto that had been proposed by Dorothy Thompson came in useful: in spite of careful preparation with Erika of the English version, his performance was by no

[28] Fr./Antw. 242.

means free of mistakes, but was still warmly acclaimed by the 300 guests, the *crème de la crème* of Hollywood. Erika followed with an address of her own, and over 3,000 dollars was raised for refugee aid.

In Chicago Erika left them, to return to New York in preparation for a lecture tour of her own. For her father, another appearance was due, at a large meeting again arranged by the Committee for Christian German Refugees. From there it was on by night train to Washington, for a few days' stay with the Meyers at their Crescent Place mansion. After a Bruno Walter concert in Constitution Hall on the evening of their arrival, Agnes Meyer took him out next day to their country place in Virginia, romantically situated overlooking the Potomac valley, as an opportunity to go through with him the introduction of her planned book ('my psychological history of Thomas Mann', as she called it—destined not to be completed): he no doubt strove to temper her judgement of his 'coldness' and lack of spontaneity in relationships with others.

Washington high society was open to him, at a dinner-party of her own and a soirée given by the retired diplomat and art-collector Robert Bliss in Dumbarton Oaks. On 15 April he was invited to share the table of honour with Roosevelt, Cordell Hull, and senators at the annual dinner of the 'Gridiron', the exclusive journalists' and politicians' club, where the traditional 'roasting' of the prominent figures of the day in satirical songs and sketches gave him much quiet amusement, not least when he reflected, as the *Post*'s report noted next day, how impossible this kind of thing was under the German dictatorship. His admiration and respect was renewed for the President as he entered with humour into the spirit of the occasion, and he was impressed by his courageous demeanour in spite of his disability. There had been much discussion over his message to Hitler and Mussolini, just published, asking if they would give guarantees of non-aggression against thirty-one specified countries: a mistaken initiative, in Mann's view (for who could envisage Hitler as member of a peaceful world?), and a double-edged instrument, of value in American internal politics perhaps, but allowing the 'monster . . . and his secret helpers' an undeserved respite.[29]

As he reached home in Princeton on 18 April, his warm thanks to Agnes Meyer and her husband (who had promised a subsidy of 2,000 dollars for the uncertain finances of *Standards and Values*) were genuinely felt—though it is hard to imagine so shrewd a woman, however dazzled by the admired author, swallowing his effusive description of her draft Thomas Mann study ('delicate and helpfully interpretative effort of a noble feminine spirit') as the high point of his tour.[30] For better or worse, that was at last

[29] *TM Stud.* x, 132.    [30] *AM Brw.* 153.

over, except for a final appearance due on 25 April in the Lyric Opera House in Baltimore; but his hopes of a steady resumption of work on the *Lotte*, now not far off conclusion, were frustrated by the ever-increasing literary, political, and social demands laid upon him, and by the burden of correspondence, even though he left that largely to his three secretarial assistants and scarcely touched it himself now unless he recognized the handwriting.

The conscientious discharge of his academic duties was a priority. In April and May, immediately after Baltimore, he gave two lectures to ad-vanced students, and an introduction to *The Magic Mountain*; a reading of the first chapter of *Lotte* for teachers of German; and with Einstein on 19 May a talk to theologians in the university chapel, with an abbreviated form of the 'Freedom' lecture. Three more honorary doctorates were offered, at Rutgers University, Princeton, and Hobart College in Geneva, New York State; and between times there came an extraordinary International PEN Congress (a 'World Congress of Writers', Germany not participating) on 9 May, on the occasion of the World's Fair in New York, followed by a further visit there for the opening of the Soviet Pavilion on 17 May and a dinner of the American Booksellers' Association the same night. Except for the Soviet occasion, for him merely an *acte de présence*, seated next to a Red Army colonel at the ambassadors' table, all these required the appropriate speech. It could not and must not continue like this, he wrote on 11 May, and said he was seriously thinking of withdrawing into private life and moving to California to write the fourth *Joseph* volume.[31] The idea was attractive, despite the financial uncertainty it would involve; and when on 16 May President Dodds offered him renewal of the Princeton appointment for the spring semester 1940, at a stipend of 3,000 dollars, he hesitated for some weeks before finally accepting. 'I'll have cards printed next year, to say I'm a literary man and must get on with my writing,' he told Agnes Meyer towards the end of the month.

But, with the world situation as it was, it was clearly impossible for him to abrogate the politically prominent position he had reached, no matter where he chose to live in America. What was more, as renewed attempts at appeasement looked likely, he felt it imperative to do everything possible to encourage the resistance to the regime within Germany which, he was convinced, must surely exist. During May he conceived a plan for the infiltration there, both clandestine and through the post, of a score of brochures, to be written by emigrant scholars, authors, theologians, and artists over the coming twelve months, making a non-political appeal to the German people's better instincts. Financial support was promised, from a committee headed by Frank Kingdon, President of Newark University, for printing at least 5,000 copies each time, which could be confidently expected to circulate as widely as his own letter to Bonn University was reported to be doing. He wrote first to his brother outlining the plan and seeking his support: 'Only if—should [war] not be avoided—the Germans *before the defeat* refuse to follow the regime, can we hope for a peace which does not contain the seeds of a new war. The Germans must be brought to reason, and who is to do it, if we remain silent?' And in similar terms later in the month he sought the collaboration of a range of colleagues and friends: Bruno and Leonhard Frank, René Schickele, Fritz von Unruh, Franz Werfel, and Stefan Zweig; Lotte Lehmann, Max Reinhardt, Wilhelm Dieterle; the physicists James Franck and Erwin Schrödinger (though not Einstein), and the theologian Paul Tillich; on the political front, Ludwig Renn and Hermann Rauschning. War, however, was closer than he knew—the Führer, following the venturesome, and to him infuriating, Anglo-French guarantee to Poland on 31 March, had already given orders to the Wehrmacht to start planning for the destruction of that country—and in the event there was no time to develop this essentially long-term project.

Mann himself, as the end of his Princeton commitments approached, had in any case decided on summer holidays—'hopefully with plenty of work'—in Switzerland and Sweden (where the next PEN Congress was due in September), and had booked passages for 6 June to Le Havre, with Katia and Erika, on the *Île de France*. Announcing this to Agnes Meyer on 20 May, he outlined the difficult budgetary situation for *Standards and Values*, with the likely deficit for the year around 3,000 dollars, and he made bold to ask—successfully—if Eugene would make good his promise of 2,000 with a cheque he could take with him.

The three weeks before departure still held a heavy work-load: apart from the doctorate ceremony at Hobart College, he was due with Erika at the Congress of American Writers in Carnegie Hall on 2 June, with speeches to be prepared for both, and his social calendar was as well filled with visitors as ever. Questions from his other potential biographer, Caroline Newton, had to be dealt with as politely as possible (as with Agnes Meyer, her work never saw the light of day); his old friend Georg Richter, recently arrived in America, turned up to discuss his plans for a university post—a strange reminder of the old days in Munich, when they had shared the Feldafing chalet, and though of an age with him, looking an old man. At the Carnegie Hall congress, speaking in his capacity as honorary president of the German-American Writers' Association, and recalling the death of Karel Čapek and the recent suicide in New York of Ernst Toller, his message was one of confidence that Hitler's so-called nationalist revolution could not last. Urgent among the pile of correspondence to be cleared before leaving was a letter to Rudolf Olden, co-founder of the exiled German PEN Club in England and concerned to assist Robert Musil's settling there: he sent a testimonial in the warmest terms, praising Musil's novel *The Man without Qualities*, still probably little known in England, as 'without doubt the greatest prose, ranking with the most eminent our age has to offer, a book which . . . the future will hold in high honour'. Two new assignments however, as he told Agnes Meyer, promised a welcome return to his proper sphere from that of the political pundit—forewords to a new Random House edition of Tolstoy's *Anna Karenina* and Knopf's reprint of his own *Royal Highness*—and, having detailed Meisel to prepare suitable excerpts, he planned to complete them during the break in Europe, as well as hoping for decisive progress with *Lotte in Weimar*.

A cable from Katia's parents in Munich on 4 June made them think again about their itinerary. At last about to secure authorization to emigrate, the Pringsheims feared it might be withdrawn if it became known the Manns were awaiting them in Switzerland. This, coupled with the uncertain situation and the likelihood of renewed crisis in the early autumn, seemed to rule out a stay there, and during the crossing he decided to await events first in Holland. At Plymouth, where they called on 12 June, there was further news. The Reich, instead of merely confiscating all the Pringsheims' wealth and possessions, had seized the chance to acquire useful foreign currency, and arranged an auction of their main asset, the priceless majolica collection, through Sothebys in London, from the proceeds of which only a quarter would be released to them with their passports; the first part had gone under the hammer a few days earlier, and the second was to follow in July. (The final result was only £5,000 for the Pringsheims; but instead of recognizing their luck compared with the many Jewish emigrants deported penniless, Thomas Mann could still, after six years of Nazi rule, be shocked by the illegality of such a 'gangster deal'.) It seemed all the more important to stay away from Switzerland until the money was actually paid over, so as not to provoke any hitch in their eventual emigration: and Noordwijk on Holland's North Sea coast was fixed as their first staging-post.

*En route*, in Paris, Katia had to busy herself over the visas needed for both Belgium and Holland: for the latter, with their passports from a country no longer in existence, all they could obtain was a letter of recommendation from the Dutch ambassador. Heinrich surprised them with a phone call, and with Erika they were able to spend two evenings with him before leaving Paris on 15 June. (To a young *émigré* student, who had heard one of Heinrich's lectures about this time, he looked like a cross between a French provincial and a suburban German dentist, far removed from the revolutionary model of his writings: sentimental, and in exaggerated optimism over the opposition to Hitler mistaking his desires for accomplished fact.)[32] In the atmosphere of crisis, the leave-taking from Heinrich before their departure was moving, for Erika at least, if not for her father. To be encumbered with over twenty pieces of luggage did not make for easy travel, but the frontiers were passed without hindrance, and by the evening of 16 June they were installed in the pension Huis ter Duin in Noordwijk.

The stay here lasted seven weeks, until news came from London of the payment to the Pringsheims and a transfer to Zurich could be considered. From the start, Mann had been irritated by having to miss out Switzerland, deflected from what had been intended as a restful holiday after the efforts in America: and Noordwijk made an uneasy interlude. True, the sea air had its usual tonic effect, and he settled to work at once, scribbling daily in a covered beach-chair like those of the Baltic coast and dealing with the promised forewords for Random House and Knopf in short order before getting back to the final chapters of *Lotte*. But he found it hard to get used to the changeable climate, and in understandable nervousness over the uncertain political situation, as German pressure over Danzig and Poland increased, his health suffered. Erika's departure at the end of June for Amsterdam, Paris, and Switzerland left him particularly depressed, and her telephoned news soon after, that according to a high Nazi official the opening of hostilities was fixed for the beginning of August, made him decide, though sceptical, on provisional reservations for an American sailing then. There were problems with *Standards and Values*: Lion made difficulties over his future collaboration after Golo, due in Zurich in August, took over the editorial chair, and the finances were still uncertain in spite of Meyer's cheque.

Nevertheless, with the excellent mail and telephone communications, a typing-agency recruited in Amsterdam, many visitors, including Knopf and Bermann, and a rented car which Katia piloted with skill through the hordes of cyclists, the Thomas Mann enterprise was proceeding much as usual, his daily round in the accustomed groove. With Bermann a further volume of his earlier pieces was even under discussion; journalists and photographers came for the inevitable interview. In The Hague he visited the Mauritshuis gallery, with its Rembrandts, and lunched with the Dutch writer Menno ter Braak, friend of Klaus and one-time contributor to his *Sammlung*, who arranged a reception for him for the end of July; the German-born Dutch artist Paul Citroen made sketches of him as he worked on the beach.

Klaus's novel of *émigré* life *The Volcano* arrived, and he read it carefully, at first with some resistance, but then with increasing enjoyment and pride:

[32] Hartmut Weill, letter of 6–14 June 1939 from Paris to a friend in Zurich.

with it, as he wrote to him, the son who had long been disparaged as a lightweight, hanging to his father's coat-tails, had incontestably proved himself as an independent talent. (To hear this was all the more satisfying, Klaus replied from California, when he considered how in the past his father's glance had been anxious and sometimes scornful.) There were moments of despondency, but he managed to regain confidence in his daily stretch on the *Lotte*, and in hopes that Bermann, who already had the earlier parts in print, might be able to bring it out in October he began the penultimate chapter with a will towards the end of July. By that time, there had been signs of *détente*, though he was disgusted at the defeatist outlook of the French over Danzig and fully expected more appeasement and another 'betrayal' by the West.

The August booking for America was abandoned, and after further hesitation he decided to carry on to Zurich as planned, to spend a fortnight there before crossing to London, where they could see Monika and her husband, and thence to Sweden, in good time for the September PEN Congress. Arrangements were in hand with the Oprechts for the reception of the Pringsheims in Zurich; if all went well it might be possible to return there after Sweden to see them before the return to America—the 'new homeland, for which we have the "first papers" and where I am honorary doctor at no fewer than six universities', as he wrote before leaving to Karl Kerényi, the Budapest philologist and theologian who had been a useful adviser on the mythology for *Joseph*. 'Those are pleasant anchors they've had me sink there—though I'm not really capable of striking roots there and do not even want to.' Meanwhile, he said, Noordwijk had left him 'quite remarkably rested after the efforts of the American winter'.[33]

There was hardly a break in his work: the morning before they took the night train via Strasburg for Basle, he was in his beach chair as usual, and two days later, on 7 August, in luxury quarters at the Waldhotel Dolder above Zurich, back at a desk. Zurich was all he had looked forward to, with friendly welcomes from the pharmacist and pedicurist, and the hairdresser who remembered him well, the city beflagged for the Swiss National Exhibition, shopping-trips for all the things they seemed to lack in America, and above all satisfactory medical examinations with doctors in whom he put greater trust than in the Americans. Golo met them on arrival, and produced an excellent outline for the next number of the journal; Erika, who had been in Arosa, came to visit with Therese Giehse; and Oprecht saw to evening entertainment and an excursion to Lucerne to call on Bruno Walter, there for the Festspiele. A visit to Küsnacht could not be omitted, the now empty house in the Schiedhalden Strasse bringing

---

[33] *KK Brw.* 90.

nostalgic reminders of the work accomplished there. They again pursued the idea of acquiring a *pied-à-terre* for the future, but the owner of a promising plot at Zumikon, outside the city, proved unwilling to sell, and no more was achieved. Though tension was unabated in the political situation, with Burckhardt, the League Commissioner for Danzig, summoned on 11 August to the Führer at Berchtesgaden, he doubted whether Hitler was really bent on war, and saw no reason to change their plans. Having sent luggage in advance to Sweden, therefore, where Bermann had already arranged accommodation, they joined a Swissair flight for London via Basle on 18 August.

Here they were met by Monika and her husband, who saw to their modest entertainment during the few days' stay. Lányi had made a good impression when they met the year before in Küsnacht, and the couple were well-suited and happy enough, though he and Katia felt somewhat disturbed over Monika's fragile appearance. They enjoyed a day's outing with them to Hampton Court, meals in restaurants or at their flat, a visit to the British Museum, and a performance at the Globe Theatre of *The Importance of Being Earnest*. Ida Herz, of course, did not fail to make contact, and they strolled with her through the parks, to Buckingham Palace, Trafalgar Square, and the Parliament area; there were visits to Katia's cousins, now settled in London after an eventful emigration. He had hoped to call on Harold Nicolson, the diplomat and writer with whom he had corresponded since his favourable review of Klaus and Erika's *Escape to Life* ('this amazing family' was a remark he was not likely to forget): apparently this proved impossible, but he wrote later from Sweden to Nicolson asking for his support for Monika and her husband in the event of war.

It was not a time for work—even less so when the sensational news broke, on 22 August, of the Nazi–Soviet pact just negotiated in Moscow by Ribbentrop. The unexpected *coup* left him as bewildered as everyone else, with no knowledge of what had actually been agreed: though it seemed to bring war nearer, Poland remained firm. He continued confident that Hitler would still not risk it and, if anything, found more shattering the private news that Bruno Walter's younger daughter had been shot dead by her husband in Basle. Erika and Golo would represent the family at the funeral. (Only later, it seems, did he realize the effect of the pact on the anti-fascist cause, with the immediate volte-face of communist parties over the world to treat Germany and the USSR as allied against the 'militarist-imperialist' powers England and France; and he withdrew his name from the German-American Writers' Association when it took this party line.) Next day, seen off by the Lányis and Ida Herz, they were on the way to Tilbury, to join the *Suecia* for Göteborg, where they took the train for Stockholm.

Speculating in ignorance, he was still clear in his own mind that any-thing was preferable to yet another unopposed aggression and another 'Munich agreement', which, according to reports, was expected in Ger-many. 'War is what I want, *because* its consequences are unforeseeable and it will make an end, probably in Germany too, to the present situation.' Erika joined them from Holland on 30 August; Michael, who had been attending a summer course in Belgium and had visited them in Noordwijk, was now with his wife in London, and so was Monika. In the last days of August, in quiet luxury out at Saltsjöbaden and royally entertained by the Bermanns and the Swedish publisher Bonnier, he continued to doubt it would come to war, even when the PEN Congress was postponed indefi-nitely and there was mobilization on all sides. In cautious words at a press conference on 31 August he said the horrors of the next war were unimaginable, yet his personal hope was that avoiding it would not be at the unacceptable cost of ensuring the survival of a regime whose only *raison d'être* was war—if that was to endure, 'Europe will never have peace. This regime . . . has the idea of war as its basis . . .'[34] The greater part of the interview, however, was taken up with his purely personal affairs—the life in Princeton, his recent work, with details on *Lotte in Weimar*, and the plans to continue with *Joseph* on their return on 12 September. Readers of the *Dagens Nyheter* next morning will have found little interest in all this after news of the bombardment of Warsaw and the devastating German assault on Poland.

Awaiting events, Thomas Mann quietly resumed his work. He and Katia were fetched by city car for lunch and a tour of the Town Hall with the mayor; Bert Brecht, not a favourite compatriot, who had moved on from Denmark, with Helene Weigel, was also among the guests. With Erika, they bought a radio and listened to Hitler's speech in the Reichstag; next day, they tuned to London to hear Chamberlain's ultimatum, and read the world reactions. 'Now at last they are talking our language, Hitler is called a madman. It's late, late! . . . I think much on the forecasts in my letter to Bonn . . .' With the expiry of the British ultimatum, on 3 September, both England and France were at war with Germany, and they began enquiries for the return to America, now of course extremely difficult. In the end, a ship from England seemed the only chance, and their departure for London was arranged by air from Malmö on 9 September. Erika took care of everything, while he added for Bermann last touches to the seven chapters of *Lotte* so far completed, and with Katia attended a final dinner given by Prince Wilhelm for those PEN members who had reached Stockholm, including H. G. Wells. For the flight from Malmö they had to abandon

[34] *Fr./Antw.* 247.

most of their luggage, and it was left with Bermann to be forwarded later to Princeton.

An unusually thorough customs examination awaited them at London airport, particularly of his material in German, with a manuscript arousing natural suspicion, but at least his name was well-known. After the long bus-ride, through magnificent summer weather and in a weekend atmosphere, to the city already ringed with anti-aircraft balloons, they were in time for the Waterloo–Southampton train that evening. The English papers, reporting the cold rejection of Goering's offers of peace, showed encouraging firmness of government and people; unopposed leaflet-dropping flights had been made over Germany, and though French troops were already fighting in the Saar, it seemed to him that the West was hoping to escape blood-letting by a war of attrition. In Southampton, with the delay in arrival of the SS *Washington* for which they were finally booked, a long wait was in store, time which they used to make good their needs for the journey. As in London, gas-masks hung on everyone's shoulders, and feverish air-defence preparations were in train, with trenches and sandbags everywhere. They were in touch with Michael, who had followed his violin teacher to Wales and apparently thought of trying for a passage from Holland to America; what the Lányis' hopes and plans were, is not clear. (Both couples were still in England a month later.)

When the *Washington* was finally announced for 12 September, they moved to the docks, only to wait for hours in a long line of passengers until Erika, pleading her father's illness, succeeded in jumping the queue, piloted him aboard, and sat him down in an already overfilled saloon until she and Katia had seen to their accommodation. First class was at last arranged, once his contacts with the management were known, but this made little difference for a highly uncomfortable passage in the crowded ship. The line had risen to the emergency, with improvised sleeping-quarters and separation of the sexes (a concentration camp, commented his neighbour). Though the restaurants kept up normal appearances and the food was as excellent as usual, there was too little water for baths, it was impossible to be alone, and he found the cost had gone up by at least 1,000 dollars ('but if it means the grave for Hitler, I really shan't mind').

In such conditions, the six-day crossing was a torment for one so used to his comfort. Still, he held obstinately to his purpose, scribbling on in his deck-chair every morning at the *Lotte*; and, with good meals and sleeping-pills, contrived to maintain his 'calm and confidence in my destiny', as he noted in his only diary-entry, 'though more and more aware how incalculable, both in time and outcome, is the process that has begun and whose end I can't be certain of surviving'. (The supreme egoism here is as remarkable as the blinkered application to his work.) Telegrams had been sent to

advise of their arrival in New York on 19 September, and they were met by
Caroline Newton, and Meisel with the car to drive them direct to
Princeton, while Erika stayed in New York. He was back in his 'emergency
home', perhaps for the rest of his life if, as all seemed persuaded, the war
was to last a decade: but it was a relief to have regained base, and the decks
were cleared at once for work, to meet his commitment to Bermann of
sending the last two chapters of *Lotte* by October. Katia was meanwhile
relieved to hear that her parents had reached Zurich at the end of September and with attention from Golo and Oprecht were finally installed in
safety.

During their journey, Russia too had entered Poland, giving her a common frontier with Germany, and the Polish government was now in exile,
though Warsaw still held out. 'What I expect and hope for is Germany as
a theatre of war between Russia and the West, a communist revolution, and
with it Hitler's destruction. [But] finally all I want is the end of the regime,
with sore affliction for that guilty country.' That was a distant prospect, and
the beginning of a 'long-drawn-out catastrophe' was not the time, he felt,
for appeals from an exile to which Hitler's Germans, in their enthusiasm for
war, were unlikely to listen. Even a new introduction to the wartime
*Standards and Values* was hard to write; and though interviews could not be
avoided, he was glad that major lectures would not be due from him for
some time to come. In periods of depression in Noordwijk, indeed, he had
resolved on no further repetition of the grand lecture-tour which had
become an annual event: now, however, his vigour restored and progress
rapid with the completion of *Lotte*, it was not long before plans for another
tour, once again with 'The Problem of Freedom', began to form.

On 26 October he could write 'finis' to *Lotte*. It was not much to show,
he reflected, for thirty-seven months of work, but still an achievement,
considering what else had intervened in its slow gestation: the essays on
Schopenhauer, Faust, Wagner; 'Achtung, Europa!'; the major lectures on
democracy and freedom. In it, he had attempted an original approach to the
great predecessor with whom he had long felt an almost mythical identifi-
cation: a new portrait of intimacy, gaiety, a familiarity with greatness
relieved by a touch of 'democratic irony'.[35] By skilful montage, from the
factual framework and the plentiful recorded conversations and writings of
Goethe, he had yielded a picture which, if with minor anachronisms, was
none the less 'true' of the artistic egoist who, like himself, ruthlessly
exploited all those around him for the demands of his work. For English
readers, the more comprehensible title 'The Beloved Returns' was chosen:
for the action, such as it is, hangs on a series of meetings between Lotte and

[35] *Tb.* iv, 493.

those now in Goethe's entourage (Riemer, his assistant; August, his son; Schopenhauer's sister Adele), her attendance as one of his guests at lunch, and finally an (imaginary) second meeting, in which he admits his guilt towards those he has sacrificed to his art. Moths drawn to the candle-flame, no doubt—but his candle consumes itself as well as them to produce light, she realizes, and she can leave in a spirit of conciliation.

For want of a better term, Mann had called it a novel, but felt 'intellectual comedy' more apt, or even a monograph in dialogue form. It was written for a German public at the moment non-existent, but one day to return; and, by using, adapting, or inventing Goethe's words in a long communion with himself, he had contrived to give vent to his own obstinate Germanness, against the resistance of his present-day countrymen, and his deep antipathy towards them:

That they don't know the attraction of truth is regrettable, that they welcome vapourings, intoxication, and every berserk excess, repulsive—that they fall willing victims to any ecstatic rogue who can arouse their lowest instincts. . . . They think they are Germany, but it is I who am Germany, and if it were to be exterminated root and branch, it would endure in me. Behave how you like to fend me off—I still stand for you. But . . . I am born for reconciliation rather than for tragedy . . . universal humanity . . . for Germanness is freedom, education, universality, and love—that they don't know this, does not alter it . . .[36]

He was encouraged to hear later that anti-Nazis, from copies smuggled during the war into Germany, extracted the more virulent passages and circulated them under the camouflaged title of 'Goethe's Conversations with Riemer' (and it was something of a compliment, after the war, to find them quoted as Goethe's by Sir Hartley Shawcross prosecuting at the Nuremberg trials: correcting this, he could still vouch for the fact that, even if Goethe had not actually spoken them, he could easily have done so, so that in a higher sense Shawcross had been justified). The quotations continued to be reproduced and cited, however, and it was not until 1949 that the riddle was solved in Germany.

'For Tommy it was a great joy to be able to work so intensively,' wrote Katia to Bermann, detailing the arrangements for sending the final chapters both by sea and the new Clipper air route, 'and I must almost be sorry that this task is over. But once a few minor journalistic things have been dealt with, he hopes very soon to be deep in the last "Joseph" volume.' He himself had told Agnes Meyer, just before finishing, 'the next morning, if I know me, the first lines of *Joseph IV* will be on paper'. In earlier, less pressing times, such an immediate new start had been possible: but not now. For one thing, much more than a little journalism was on the

[36] ii 657 f.

immediate programme for November and December: a reading at Columbia University, New York, two lectures at Princeton and another at Wagner
College, Staten Island; and more would be required for Princeton in the
months to come. In new-found admiration for England's firm stand—
despite the lack yet of any substantial action against Hitler—he was moved
too to pen 'This War', 'an energetic pro-British piece, from the heart and
from conviction'.[37] Between times, yet another diversion from the *Joseph*
(or, as he half-admitted, another excuse for putting it off) suggested
itself—a novella on an Indian theme, even deeper in the world of mythology, which he had noted years before, and this was started on New Year's
Day, as he began to ready himself for the lecture tour now planned to take
place shortly.

So the last months of the year were well filled, but in his usual routine
and comforted by a new dog, the gift of Caroline Newton, and without any
feeling of pressure or haste. As Klaus wrote to Golo, in Küsnacht on one of
his brief visits at the end of November, their father, still slightly tanned
from the stay in Holland, and having finished *Lotte* more quickly than had
been hoped, was plagued but at the same time entertained by a host of
admirers; their mother, 'plunging from one political excitement to another'
and irritated now by the tour agent, now by the maid Lucy, was still
'resistant, agreeable, and alert'. Elisabeth was about to enter the 'holy state
of matrimony—let's hope that goes well, at the moment she is flirting
shamelessly with Hermann Broch . . .' And he described Erika's current
lecture-tour in the Midwest, his own just finished, for which his theme had
mostly been 'After Hitler—What?', and his hopes of returning to Europe in
the spring.[38]

The church wedding for Elisabeth and Borgese took place on 23 November, for Katia the first proper occasion with any of her children—and for
Thomas, seeing this daughter, always his favourite among the youngest, in
white, touching almost to tears. Of the family, Erika and Klaus at least
could attend, and Auden arrived later, producing for each guest at the
dinner next day a copy of an 'Epithalamion' specially written for the
occasion (though he did not receive the payment he half expected for his
work). Elisabeth had married her anti-fascist professor, Thomas reported
to Heinrich, (who had meanwhile married his Nelly Kröger): 'at 57 he
won't have thought of ever winning so much youth. But the child wanted
it, and got her way. He is an intelligent, pleasant, and very well-preserved
man . . . a convinced American, and although Medi knows Italian and he
German, they speak only English among themselves.'[39] To his mind the
union represented a gratifying counter-axis to that of Hitler and Mussolini.

[37] *Br.* ii, 130.     [38] KlM *Br. Antw.* 400.     [39] *Brw. HM* 276 f.

Their residence would be in Chicago, of course, so he and Katia would now be alone in the big house at Stockton Street. That was a condition which he himself, after the family had reassembled, as far as this was possible, over Christmas and had all left again by the end of the month, did not find unwelcome. Solitude was conducive to 'invention and planning', he felt, as he contemplated with foreboding the fateful year to come, even if the novella he was now ready to start looked more and more like mere amusement, and he could only hope it would be worthy of him.

He had completed 'This War' just before Christmas. Since the democracies were at war, all was 'forgiven and forgotten', he was wholeheartedly with them, he wrote on Boxing Day.[40] Later, to Gilbert Murray, he said it was supposed to be an appeal to the decent elements in Germany, 'a futile endeavour, I am afraid, but I [had] to make the attempt'—true enough, as it turned out, for Bermann in his continuing collaboration with the Amsterdam firms had it printed there, and most of the stocks were destroyed after the German invasion. *Lotte in Weimar* had been similarly produced, but the stocks prudently removed to Stockholm (though the outbreak of the Russo-Finnish war in November had made Bermann wonder how long Sweden itself could last). The sight of his first copies just at Christmas gave much pleasure, and, as he said in his congratulations to the publisher, caused Borgese to reflect on civilization's powers of resistance shown in the production at this time of a German book in so immaculate a form. 'I told him . . . that you are indestructible, and if after Berlin and Vienna, Stockholm too were to go, you would continue just as distinguished production in London or New York or New Zealand, and bring out my next novel too in the finest form.' Thanking Stefan Zweig, now in exile in London, for his enthusiastic letter, he admitted that, considering in the old days such a book's first printing would have been 100,000, he could not avoid 'a slight displeasure over Hitler'—but today's 10,000 would have more value. 'Do you see Harold Nicolson? If so . . . tell him with what sympathy I read his political writings. My favourite sentence from his pen is: "The German character is one of the finest and most inconvenient developments of human nature." '[41]

The 'amusement' of the Indian fantasy—*The Transposed Heads*, as he was to entitle it—took hold in the New Year. It was his first approach to 'the French surrealist sphere' of Cocteau,[42] which had long attracted him in its exuberant contrast with the naturalism of, say, Tolstoy, and by the time he started for the lecture tour on 22 January he had the first twenty pages of the story on paper. On 10 January Michael and his wife, already pregnant, arrived from England in New York, and were met by Katia. Neither the

---

[40] 39/535.      [41] *GBF Brw.* 253; Br. ii, 130.      [42] *Tb.* v, 16.

severe cold she caught from the long wait on the pier, nor a subsequent disturbing haemorrhage, which needed cauterization of the womb, deterred her from accompanying him on the tour. This time, however, Erika would not be along: she had returned from a lecture tour also with a cold and fever, and other assignments lay ahead for her.

The journey, for which he would mainly use the 'Freedom' lecture suitably updated, was actually in two parts: first, New York, Canada, and Toledo, Ohio, then in February further afield, largely in cities where he had not yet appeared. In New York on the morning of 22 January, at the Town Hall, he read his Princeton introduction to *The Magic Mountain* to a large and attentive audience, relaxing in the evening at an enjoyable performance of Lillian Hellman's long-running *The Little Foxes*, and profited from Caroline Newton's aid next day to rehearse the English version of a pro-British excerpt from 'This War', to be inserted in the 'Freedom' lecture in Ottawa. It was a new experience to find the thermometer there at thirty below, but they withstood the cold well. In the out-of-town Hotel Château Lourdes the talk was apparently well received, though the room was only three parts full, and it was gratifying to be approached by the new American ambassador with an invitation to lunch next day, after their signature of the Governor-General's book. To Toledo the train journey, with a long break in Detroit, was tiring, but gave time to study his adaptation of the lecture, and in spite of his fatigue he carried it off well, even with an added after-lunch speech, unexpected and impromptu, which was also broadcast, and was followed by endless book-signing. *The Transposed Heads* was very much in his mind throughout, and he determined to carry it on both now and during the second part of the tour. It started to present problems during the week in Princeton, however. Leaving for New York on 6 February, to entrain for the first appearance in Delaware, Ohio, he was dissatisfied with the tedium of his latest additions and, with a recurrence of his inner-ear eczema, was not in best form.

They were seen off from New York by Erika, Klaus, and Michael and his wife—the latter, in view of her condition, to come down now to live in the Princeton house. At the Wesleyan University in Delaware the audience for his lecture included many young people, with questions to be answered, and at the simple entertainment next day he found the conversation heavy going. From there they travelled via Chicago to Dubuque, Iowa, where yet another honour awaited him: this time, instead of an honorary doctorate, the highly exceptional nomination as honorary rector of the University, and his 'Freedom' lecture was hailed in the local press as worthy of the famous debates at the American Constitutional Congress of Philadelphia in 1787. The investiture ceremony, for which he wore a gold-trimmed robe, impressed him immensely, he felt he had carried himself well, and was particularly struck by the international character of the students. But here again the pressure of eager hospitality next day, in the predominantly Presbyterian atmosphere, was a burden, and for all his gratitude he was relieved to regain the sleeper for Chicago, where they could have two days' rest in a comfortable hotel and enjoy the company of Elisabeth and her husband. With the efficient postal communications of those days, a stack of letters from Princeton and Europe awaited him there—saddest of all, one from Schickele, written two weeks before his death, of which they had had news before leaving, the loss of yet another among the friends who shared his exile.

From Chicago there followed a close-packed itinerary: the State College in Ames, Iowa; the University of Minnesota in Minneapolis; the High School in Topeka, Kansas; the Southern Methodist University of Dallas, Texas, with a further performance in Houston; and finally, on 26 February, the State College for Women in Denton, Texas. Audiences were sometimes several thousand, but sometimes disappointing, and it was hard to tell whether his hosts' assurances of satisfaction were genuine. A few days' break between Houston and Denton was possible in San Antonio, and by then he felt half-way content with his performance, better and more successful anyway than those of his colleagues Stefan Zweig and Emil Ludwig, who were also on lecture tours about this time. Memorable for him in Minneapolis was word from a young American student of the German Department who had been under Ernst Bertram in Cologne: his old friend had been removed for a time from his professorial chair, then more or less reinstated, but from the student's report seemed 'overfull of pity for me— though it is I who have chosen the better course. Plan to get a copy of *Lotte* to him through Dutch travellers.'[43] The ear was giving him increasing pain, and on 27 February it was with great relief that he started the long train-journey back to New York and Princeton. As so often before, he resolved to avoid any further time-wasting tours of this kind and, with the highly uncertain war news, was in pessimistic mood over how to order the years that might remain to him, to find the strength to finish the *Joseph* after the superfluous digression with the novella.

Throughout these last months, despite numerous invitations, he had been scrupulous to avoid involvement in purely American affairs, pleading that he was not yet an American citizen, but in his adapted lectures he had gone as far as he could in trying to explain the situation in Europe and the difference between neutrality and isolation. It had been painful, however, to note an anti-British tendency among those he met, not in any wish that Hitler might emerge victorious, but rather that 'poor Germany' should not

[43] *Tb.* v 29.

suffer too greatly at the end under any new Versailles treaty. The March visit of deputy Foreign Minister Sumner Welles to the dictators showed, he thought, a naïve faith in their international credibility and disastrous ignorance of their character. He resigned in April from the American Guild for Cultural Freedom, when it argued against the Allied war-aim of the total destruction of Germany: in this 'world civil war' he could never condone a softer line. To the Austrian poet Felix Braun, who had emigrated to England, he wrote almost enviously that he should be living in a country at war against Hitler ('for us, the atmosphere of neutrality goes all too often against the grain').[44] But where he could put in his word in acceptable terms, he did, notably in a broadcast on 9 March from New York, on behalf of the United Jewish Appeal for Refugees, emphasizing the danger for democracy of anti-Semitism ('I am a Gentile [but] I know from bitter experience that the flames in which the Jew burns will not stop at his stake, but will lap the surrounding houses.')[45]

Continuing with his Princeton commitments during March, April, and May—a long lecture 'On Myself', given several times, repeats of the *Magic Mountain* introduction, and a new talk on 'The Art of the Novel'—he felt growing discontent, even boredom, with this rather dilettantish occupation. These offerings for the students were actually more for their professors, but neither had much understanding for them; and, as he told Agnes Meyer on 22 March, he did not feel he would accept any prolongation of his appointment. 'For the fourth Joseph, which ought to be done by my seventieth birthday (or if possible a few years earlier) I must be quite free.' He mentioned a summer break in Beverley Hills, where Michael and Gret were now installed and their first grandchild was expected: in fact, within a few days, he returned with more interest to the earlier idea of a permanent move to California, perhaps to Santa Monica, and plans were formed for a transfer in the summer vacation. That ideal climate would provide the right background for the final *Joseph* volume. Tributes and distinctions continued to flow in: in April, *Books Abroad* classed him with Proust, Joyce, and Aldous Huxley among the authors of the 'most distinguished literary work of the post-1918 period', and he was made honorary president of the Whitman Society. Later he chaired a meeting of a 'Committee on Europe', organized by Borgese and attended by, among others, Gaetano Salvemini, with a view to a declaration, 'The City of Man', affirming faith in America as a democratic world-power and arguing for a decisive anti-fascist front there. For early June, there was an invitation to give the Phi-Beta-Kappa address at Swarthmore College Commencement.

But the war news was more than unsettling. With the successful German operation that month against Denmark and Norway, though not without

[44] 40/172.     [45] xiii 494.

substantial naval losses, and the imminence of a general offensive against the Low Countries and France, he and Katia were greatly worried over the safety of Golo and the Pringsheims, still in Zurich, and of Monika and her husband, for whom he had already tried, without success, to obtain a suitable post in America. In May, after the full-scale campaign against the West had begun, he secured through Cordell Hull, and with Agnes Meyer's intervention with the State Department, American protection for Golo and the promise of a visa if he travelled via Lisbon, but learned by telephone on 16 May that he intended to go to France to volunteer for military service there—a step of which he could not but approve, whatever the dangers and even if events made it look useless. For the Lányis, after the fall of France, he started attempts for a passage to Canada.

At first despondent over the disaster in France, he rightly saw in the British mood after Dunkirk and Churchill's splendid speech of defiance a gleam of hope that the German victory would not last, and—in public at least—shared his faith in the power of the New World to save and liberate the Old. In an interview on 7 June for the New York German-language paper *Aufbau*, he saw his new country not just as a refuge for himself and his like, but as 'the future towards which we can all work together . . . the preservation and stewardship of the West's cultural inheritance has passed to America'.[46] In private, all the same, he confessed he had long since lost such faith. America was 'undermined, ripe like the rest of civilization for a fall', and very possibly might not offer security for much longer: like all the capitalist countries, the United States had facilitated Germany's war and Japan's campaign against China. 'What will be the end for me personally in this confusion?' He had doubts over Roosevelt's reserved attitude, and though seeing encouragement in America's rearmament programme, felt that only a declaration of war could clear the air. But it was not for foreigners, however well-intentioned, to sound warning of the dangers; and he went ahead with the plans for California, at least for the summer, when a suitable house was on offer for rental at Brentwood, near Hollywood.

4

*'If it were not for my games with world mythology, I would probably not be able to see the misery through'*
(TM 5 June 1941)

For the move, a handsome new Buick was acquired—'dark blue, with radio, heating and every comfort'—so that John and Lucy Long, the servant couple, could drive this over to Brentwood with additional luggage and the

---

[46] *Fr./Antw.* 258 f.

dog, while he and Katia went by train. Summer tenants were arranged for the Stockton Street house, and their own effects packed suitably for later dispatch if required. The Meyers had offered a few days' stay at Mount Kisco before their final departure from New York on 1 July. All was thus in place for a transfer, in the comfortable style he had come to expect, to where he could hope 'occasionally to gain the illusion of non-involvement'.[47]

During June, certainly, such an illusion was far from his mind. France's betrayal, the replay of the capitulation drama in the railway coach at Compiègne, with French and German roles reversed, the prospect of full collaboration of French fascism with Hitler and then of a completely totalitarian Europe, were appalling. On the personal front, attempts to find out what had happened to Golo and Heinrich, and to the many friends among the refugee writers in France, bore only vague fruit. He played an active part, however, in the establishment of Frank Kingdon's Emergency Rescue Committee, which began to collect information on the endangered anti-fascist intellectuals, to campaign for private donations, and to press for the grant of emergency US visas. For Golo, with Agnes Meyer's help, there was a possibility of a Brazilian visa, when they finally learned he was at liberty in the unoccupied south of France. Heartening at least was Britain's stand and the apparent solidarity of her empire: if she could only hold out, even till the autumn, while America rearmed, Hitler must be lost. America's attitude was disquieting, however. The Meyers, like most of their compatriots, seemed to have no serious understanding of the danger, little real sympathy for England, and to be interested only in American internal affairs, notably now the presidential election due in November (Eugene had been attending the Convention where Wendell Willkie was nominated as the Republican candidate to stand against Roosevelt). During the month of preparation for the journey, a few pages were nevertheless added now and then to *The Transposed Heads*, from which he read an extract for Agnes Meyer's somewhat over-effusive appreciation before he and Katia left for the train from New York.

For so experienced a rail traveller, and with a short break in Chicago, where they of course saw the Borgeses, this was a familiar trip, with no problems, and leisure to think further on the development of *The Transposed Heads*, but with an anxious eye for what could be gleaned from papers or radio on the European situation. At Chicago, they were joined by Erika and Klaus, who were to accompany them on the Streamliner to Los Angeles on 3 July. The moving strains on the club car radio of 'God Save the King' from Canada helped to outweigh his depression over con-

[47] 40/367.

ditions in France. If England could stand and hold, they would be 'the greatest people of the world': as he noted later, it was the first time Hitler had faced a people united against him, fighting alone but not for themselves alone, and whether he invaded or not, he would be lost. But England must be aided.

Arriving in Los Angeles early on 5 July, they were met by his old friend Bruno Frank, who had been established in Beverley Hills since 1937 as one of the few successful script-writers for MGM, and had secured the Brentwood house for them, at 441 Rockingham Street. He drove them later in the day out there to see the owner, and they were quickly installed. The two-storey house among the attractive hills was spacious and elegant, with a swimming-pool, and he did not regret the high rental. He had his own room, to serve both as bedroom and study, and within forty-eight hours was at work: to finish the 'Indian jest' as quickly as possible and turn to the *Joseph*, for which all the material had, of course, accompanied him, in surroundings where the groves of palm-trees seemed a reminder of Egyptian temple halls. To think of embarking on an epic in German, a work only for a distant future, he owned, had a touch of arrogance, with world history in flames and the ears filled with the cries for help of those about to perish: but he held to his purpose, devoting his mornings firmly to his work and only the rest of the day to such efforts as were possible to answer those cries.

As Klaus said, it seemed a matter of course for the whole German emigration to turn to him, 'like a nation which looked on him as their ambassador', and the house on Rockingham Street rapidly became a lifeline for those in danger in the occupied countries as well as in England. He gave his personal guarantee in many cases, including that of Lion Feuchtwanger. Success rarely seemed to correspond to the effort, though, in particular in the family cases of his brother and Golo. At the end of July there had been a letter from Heinrich, who was still in Nice, reporting that Golo was interned in Nîmes, and trying to reach a French port: the continent 'is in complete disintegration', wrote Heinrich, 'only the chalk cliffs of England still stand'.[48] (His addition to the letter of a short will, leaving everything to his wife, gave Thomas the impression that he had resigned himself to ending his life in Europe.) On 28 July, *The Transposed Heads* just finished, Rockingham Street was the venue for a meeting of the California branch of the Emergency Rescue Committee, with Kingdon and a representative group of actors, artists, producers, and journalists, including Charles Boyer, Lubitsch, and Bruno Walter and his wife, and 4,500 dollars were subscribed.

[48] *Brw. HM* 284.

For the restless Erika, however, writing letters and raising funds was not enough. If British resistance remained firm, she hoped to go to England, as correspondent for the *Nation* but if possible to work for a while for the Ministry of Information there, over which she was in touch with Duff Cooper. When he cabled on 10 August that this would be 'desirable', her mind was made up. Her father was anxious and heavy-hearted over such a venture, when intensive air-attack on England was obviously to be expected. But he could applaud her brave words from New York on 19 August, before she took off for Lisbon: 'one can't play the soldier for seven years . . . only to desert when the trumpet finally sounds'; flying would be uncertain, but 'I'm a) pretty lucky, b) fairly clever—and c) resolved not to *allow* anything to happen to me'.[49] There was compensation when Golo telegraphed from Le Lavandou that he now had his visa for America, as well as for Spain and Portugal, and foresaw no great difficulty in getting out: but it was evident that, with the Vichy regime's policy of surrendering wanted persons to the Germans, this would be useless without an exit permit or other means of passing the frontier into Spain, and his father tried every channel in Washington to aid on this. From Lisbon Erika cabled for money for an agent claiming he could rescue both Heinrich and Golo, and this was sent at once by two successive Clippers at the end of August. The RAF, he was glad to hear, could find 'the time and the strength to bomb Munich, which I don't begrudge that stupid village'. The British must be helped, he had written to Agnes Meyer; 'send them destroyers! I'm giving a good example by sending them my daughter'.

Michael and Gret had made their temporary home in Carmel, an artists' colony south of San Francisco, near Monterey, where Michael had opportunities for occasional concert work and began to specialize in the viola, with a view to an orchestra appointment; on the last day of July they had telegraphed the arrival of a boy, Fridolin. Katia naturally paid them a visit, but her husband was little impressed by his new status of grandfather (in fact this first grandchild was later to be a great joy): it was curious, he thought, how truly American the boy was, with his German, Brazilian, Jewish, and Swiss ancestry. Before the end of the year, a second grandchild was due, for Elisabeth in Chicago was also pregnant. They were concerned over Erika, who had reached London just as the heavy air-attacks were beginning, and she was sorely missed. But perhaps Golo could be expected before long, and the house that seemed so empty was more supportable, now that the *Joseph* material was on the desk and he had started work again. During August, even before Erika's departure, the first lines of *Joseph the Provider* were on paper. Meanwhile it seemed sensible to think of more

[49] EM *Br. Antw.* i, 155.

permanent quarters in California, for at best England's defensive battle would be long, and the uncertainty of war would persist for years: and he began to look around for a suitable site to build a home. The wartime inflation of prices was not encouraging, but before they returned to Princeton an attractive site had been bought, in Pacific Palisades, for 6,500 dollars, and an architect commissioned for the building-plans, though there was still uncertainty over the financing. It had seven palms, and some lemon-trees— 'suddenly, Egypt and Palestine together, which can only be good for the *Joseph*', as he wrote to Ida Herz.[50]

September brought both good and bad news about the missing members of the family. Golo and Heinrich cabled from Lisbon, which they had reached after an adventurous night-crossing of the Pyrenees (on paths more suited to goats than writers of advanced age, as Heinrich observed later), to say they were awaiting a ship for the States. By the end of the month, together with a number of other refugees, including Franz and Alma Werfel, the Feuchtwangers, Alfred Polgar, and Stefan Zweig's first wife and stepchildren, they had firm passages in the Greek ship *Nea Hellas* sailing on 3 October, thanks largely to the efforts of the Emergency Rescue Committee. For Monika and her husband, however, whose emigration to Canada had been arranged, there was tragedy. They were aboard the *City of Benares*, along with several hundred refugee passengers, including many evacuated children, when it was sunk by a German U-boat on the night of 17 September; Monika, after twenty hours in the water clinging to a piece of wood, was among those saved, but her husband was drowned in the heavy seas before her eyes. The survivors were landed in Scotland; Erika was able to collect her from hospital there, in a pitiable state after the immense suffering endured and from the cold and the oil she had swallowed. Erika hoped on her recovery she could accompany or send her across later. In the end, the distressed young widow had to face another sea-crossing alone, and was expected towards the end of October. The day when Erika's cable arrived was one when Thomas Mann, imagining the condition of his frail daughter, for once could not bring himself to work.

It had been an effort, in any case, to regain enthusiasm for the theme which had not occupied him for over four years, and to return to its atmosphere. As they prepared for the journey east early in October, however, he could feel reasonably satisfied with the way he had fulfilled his plans for the summer: not only the Indian novella completed and a good start made on *Joseph the Provider*, but in addition, during September, a new version prepared of 'The Problem of Freedom' lecture with which he hoped to influence America towards abandonment of her short-sighted policy of

[50] 40/452.

isolation. Entitling it now 'War and Democracy', he made it as critical of America's conduct since 1939 as he could. 'As a German who knows his place in this fight, I refuse openly—just because I do not have my second papers—[to remain silent] in this country where, in all probability, the future of the Western world will be decided'; and he argued powerfully the case for the British 'who, while defending their own country . . . will save all of us—may it please God—from falling into slavery to a monster'. After a first performance of this in Los Angeles on 3 October he saw a symptom of hope in finding his line not just accepted, but received with applause. Whether Roosevelt or Willkie was elected in November, he felt, by the spring 'we'll have this country in the war': but while the election hung in the balance, and there were recurring fears that England would not be able to hold out, this optimistic outlook wavered.

Agnes Meyer had once again offered them a stay at Mount Kisco, and they arrived there on 11 October, in time to meet Heinrich, his wife, and Golo when their ship docked in New York two days later. It was decided that the whole party should go straight down to Princeton. Though the servants had not yet arrived, willing aid from Molly Shenstone ensured an easy reinstallation in the house which, however temporary, seemed like home. Its grandeur naturally drew the admiration of the weary travellers from Europe, and there were long discussions with them on the situation over there: how much irretrievably lost, and Germany's 'natural mission to organize Europe' ruined by the absurd fantasies of the Hitler regime; England's heroism, and the historically compromising failure of France, however understandable in the circumstances. But whatever his welcome for the guests, their presence was not permitted to disturb the resumption of the work on *Joseph*. Heinrich and his wife, at any rate, did not stay long: a year's script-writer contract with Warner Brothers was arranged (whether or not with his brother's help is unclear, but it was undoubtedly to his relief), and after a family dinner on 24 October, the circle enlarged after Erika's return, he and Nelly left for California on 1 November. Golo, of course, stayed on, and was put to work assisting with various minor commitments, while Klaus appeared from time to time from New York: he was busy preparing the first number of yet another journal, this time in English, to be called *Decision*, for which he had secured financial backers and recruited for the editorial board, among others, Somerset Maugham. On 28 October Monika was fetched from her ship in New York by Katia, and for a time a sick-room had to be arranged in the Princeton accommodation: but this too, for all her father's sympathy, made no difference to his daily round. His cold-bloodedness, despite the strong sense of family, was always marked, and in the case of Monika both he and Katia seem to have been particularly unfeeling.

It was extraordinary now, in fact, with what calm he had managed to order his day through October and find the concentration for a work so remote from the events and deep concerns of the time. Almost daily, there came requests for his presence or assistance in one cause or another: and although he firmly refused all those involving commitment in internal American affairs, especially in the presidential campaign, he was as active as ever in individual refugee cases and in the work of Kingdon's Emergency Rescue Committee. There were visits to New York: once for a short question-and-answer broadcast on CBC, and a first discussion with the British Broadcasting Corporation of their project for regular transmission of messages from him to the German people, the first of which he recorded later in the month (a day of which he made further good use, spending over an hour in the Egyptian section of the Metropolitan Museum of Art). He was there again, overnight, at the end of the month to attend the ERC's meeting in honour of those who had been saved and in celebration of its success— a celebration, as he said in his address, of a victory worthy of the name, 'a civilian Dunkirk'. Coming a few days before the election, it was the occasion for a thorough pro-British demonstration, and 11,000 or 12,000 dollars was collected.

An even bigger victory was Roosevelt's re-election for a third term on 6 November. The tension had meant a sleepless night for Mann, realizing how vital the decision was, and he had telegraphed the pundit-journalist Raymond Gram Swing to stress the importance of national unity whoever won. For him, it was 'the first joy, the first victory for more than seven years that have brought nothing but disappointment and grief', and could well decide the outcome of a war which, as Churchill had said, was likely to last till 1943. 'An appeaser clique, from whom the worst was to be expected, has been put out of action, England encouraged, the Nazi *canaille* can see their end approaching.'[51] He could not resist a telegram of congratulations to the President. But attending an American Legion ceremony in East Orange for Armistice Day, he was still surprised to find so many convinced of the pro-communist tendencies of Roosevelt's regime, and was dubious of what these people's attitude would be in war.

Readings of his 'War and Democracy' lecture had now been arranged in Chicago, to coincide, they hoped, with the arrival of Elisabeth's first child. He spoke first in Evanston, at the Northwestern University, then at the University of Chicago; but more and more days passed with no sign of an approaching birth, and the Borgeses' wedding anniversary on 23 November was celebrated uneventfully. They relaxed over the comic nonsense of Chaplin's *Great Dictator* and a production of Clarence Day's *Life with*

---

[51] *Tb.* v, 175.

318                 *'I Believe in America'*

*Father*, and watched a disappointing performance of *Salome*; he quickly completed and dispatched the second message for the BBC to broadcast. But he began to feel the visit had lasted long enough, and it was becoming tedious to listen to constant fulminations against the Vatican from Borgese, who held that the Pope was behind all the world's troubles: impatient, and doubtless to Katia's disappointment, he decided the first inspection of the tardy grandchild would have to wait, and they left for Princeton on 27 November (the baby, a fine girl, arrived two days later). He had his own priority: though he had been able to complete another chapter of the *Joseph*, he needed to be home to get the next ahead quickly, before the coming world upheavals could disturb the tone of calm humour he was finding.

And the same routine began, unperturbed, though always with a sharp eye on the news reports and noting with satisfaction the signs of growing American financial and material assistance for Britain. Almost every morning a page or two was added, his rest and the walk with the dog were rarely missed; the day was then taken up with political discussions with the frequent visitors, his heavy correspondence, or incidental work like the messages for the BBC; the evenings he often spent relaxing with music from radio or gramophone before retiring with a book. Even when sorties, to New York or New Haven, were unavoidable, his programme always allowed for time first with the manuscript. At a Yale meeting on 11 December both he and Erika joined Edgar Mowrer and others to speak for the cause of aid for Britain, and he took the opportunity of presenting for the Mann Collection the manuscript of his earlier address and a copy of Knopf's luxury edition of *The Beloved Returns*; but he kept his stay there as short as possible. On 18 December, overnight only in New York, he combined attendance at a surprise birthday-party for Blanche Knopf, where he read to applause his Christmas message to the Germans, with the actual recording of this in the BBC studio, so that it would this time bring his countrymen his own voice instead of another's reading. It was a fervent exhortation to abandon the false prophet who was leading them away from Christianity to inevitable defeat and ordering them to sing 'the bloody party anthem' instead of 'Silent Night': 'Save yourselves! Save your souls by renouncing your belief in your tyrants . . .!' The outside world would never accept Hitler's 'New Order', 'the subhuman utopia of horror': 'never will these great Christian peoples allow a peace, which after all you also long for, to be built over the grave of freedom and human dignity . . .'[52]

But, as he wrote to Agnes Meyer, he feared the Germans would continue their berserk fight for a long time yet. Mussolini's subjects (who had been

---

[52] xi 994.

surrendering in their thousands to the British in Libya) were 'more intelligent, they are simply abandoning the New Order...' Christmas in Princeton was quiet, with few guests and only four of the children, but with welcome gifts for him of new records and a silk house-jacket from Agnes Meyer. In true paterfamilias tradition, he read from the Bible—his own version, that is—to general amusement. 'This book is a harmless diversion, exactly what I need,' and it would appear one day, in times when many would without doubt stand in need of its consolation.[53] At last then, he and Katia could make their long-deferred visit to the new grandchild, Angelica Borgese, and on 28 December they were once again on the night-train for Chicago.

With him went the manuscript and the few books he needed, but he spent a restless night in the sleeper, in nervous apprehension over the never-ending and conflicting demands to which he seemed to be condemned. It was a mood that did not last, as they were met in the morning by the new mother, and settled into their familiar Hotel Windermere. To judge by his diary for that day, the sight of the baby roused little emotion— 'looks like the father' was his only comment. He was much more moved by Roosevelt's speech, which they caught in the evening on the radio—the unvarnished truth, he felt, and in powerful contrast to the stupidity of the opposition cries, in the following day's reactions, for a negotiated peace. While Katia spent more time with Elisabeth and the baby, he was back at work in the hotel room, but they enjoyed a festive champagne-dinner on New Year's Eve with the couple, joined by Erika, who had flown in from New York. A year of most difficult decision lay ahead, he noted that night. It would not see the end of the war, and the possibility that England would fall had to be faced, but even then the struggle of the Anglo-Saxon world would continue against the 'insupportable. I refrain still from expecting complete and clear satisfaction. But to hope is human.'

By 3 January 1941 they were back in Princeton, and he prepared for a busy programme. Priority was still, of course, the completion of *Joseph*: it was boring at times, but it had to be done, and as he said to Agnes Meyer later, when he thought how tedious Tolstoy had found *Anna Karenina*, the author's boredom might not be the reader's. But he planned further performances of the 'War and Democracy' lecture during the month, first in the Washington Town Hall on 12 January, and, having asked permission to call on the President, he had received an invitation to stay at the White House that and the following night, with Katia and Erika, before going on to the next assignments. This was hospitality of a high order, gratifying, naturally, to his self-esteem, but also a greatly appreciated privilege to see

---

[53] *AM Brw.* 249.

again at close quarters the statesman he regarded as the born opponent of the scoundrels in Europe.

Eleanor Roosevelt, at breakfast, was concerned over his sore throat after the lecture, and at once ordered the doctor to treat it; the first day was spent in her busy company, with invited lecturers on the refugee problem, a concert given before a large audience, and an after-dinner discussion with students. The following morning they were joined by the President, in lively talk over his coming inauguration-speech and his intention to stress the political and moral over the economic aspect. They lunched in the Senate dining-room, returned to attend the President's afternoon press conference, and, before their final dinner, took cocktails in his study, while the other guests waited downstairs and Eleanor briefed him on their concerns. A copy of the private print of 'War and Democracy' was presented, with the dedication 'To FDR, President of the United States and of a coming better world.' At dinner their host's loquacity made it hard for the other guests to get a word in on their own topics, and occasioned some delay for the First Lady's concert, planned to follow; he even came to the door to bid them farewell personally as they left to take their night train for North Carolina. Mann had found him an astonishing mixture of 'naïvety, faith, cunning, play-acting, and amiability': when one considered his power and significance, a fascinating man to be with, hard to characterize, but with an aura about him of the blessed. 'Here is a modern-style tamer of the masses, who seeks the good or at least the better,' he wrote later to Agnes Meyer, 'and who stands with us like no one else in the world. How could I not stand with him? I felt strengthened as I left. Let us hope he has more influence over the people than airman Lindbergh' (the pioneer of the west–east Atlantic flight, and a powerful advocate of American non-intervention in a war where he expected Hitler to be unbeatable).[54] In Roosevelt, he saw a 'provider' like his Joseph; and his picture of the latter, in his advance to a leading role in the Egypt of the Pharaohs, bears unmistakable traits of the American 'wheelchair Caesar'. In a later statement, Mann said he had been made aware of FDR's conviction that it was America's job to rid the world of Hitler, but that the people were as yet unprepared, and needed further education in their responsibilities: for the moment, all that could be done was to try to support the adversaries of the Third Reich.

His own plans for a settled establishment in California were meanwhile progressing, in detailed correspondence with the architect, and he hoped, after the minor lecture-tour he had undertaken in the south, all would be ready by March for their move there, to temporary quarters, till the new house could be ready. At Duke University, Durham, North Carolina he

---

[54] AM Brw. 254.

spoke on *The Magic Mountain*, but the next assignments in Georgia (At-
lanta and Athens) were occasions for a repeat of 'War and Democracy',
before returning to Princeton towards the end of January for, as he hoped,
a few quiet weeks' work. There was no more thought of non-involvement,
however. What Agnes Meyer, in her concern for his work, looked on as
regrettable excursions into mere politics, were for him, he told her, part of
his personal war, in a battle for humanity itself in which everything was at
stake—including 'the fate of my life's work, that for decades at least will not
be able to return to Germany . . . if that wretched crew should prevail
whom an indolent, cowardly, unwitting world these eight years has provided with nothing but victories'.[55] He had been able to continue his work
over those years while at the same time playing his part in the vital combat,
and he was determined to carry on in the same way, with work every
morning on *Joseph the Provider* (and, once, even a thought of what might
follow it—the long-nourished plan for a novella on the Faust theme), the
rest of the day devoted to the fight, in either public or private efforts for
those less privileged.

Thus, in New York on 22 January, he was the first speaker at a 'Union
Now' dinner organized by Clarence Streit, the advocate of federal union
between America, Britain, and the other English-speaking nations; and, as
they made ready for the transfer west, he programmed further performances of 'War and Democracy'—before leaving New York—in Denver,
Colorado *en route*, and in Los Angeles on arrival. Erika, after a Midwest
lecture-tour, was to reconnoitre a provisional rented home, in the
Brentwood-Beverley Hills area, and Katia had to bear all the burden of yet
another major move, with the additional complications of wartime restrictions, while he worked on to the very last moment as the packers were busy
around him. More funny than uncomfortable, he could say, though this
time too he was not without an occasional twinge of conscience over
Katia's evident stress. The servants John and Lucy would drive the car west,
with the dog as before, and await them in California.

Early in March, his mood became gloomier, with news of likely German
successes in the Balkans, and he had doubts over the Lend-Lease bill now
passed by the Senate, which he thought would take too long to bring
Britain effective help. Erika's tour was bringing her unpleasant experiences,
with threatening letters, one this time even signed; Heinrich had had phone
calls of the same type, and had asked for police surveillance. As the packers
began work, there was a bus strike in New York, and further such acts of
'sabotage' could well be expected. Altogether, conditions in America
seemed only too reminiscent of the Germany of 1932. But the mood soon

[55] Ibid. 253.

passed when the day came for departure from Stockton Street and a journey which would become yet another lecture-tour, if small-scale. In New York he gave 'War and Democracy', in the synagogue (with hat on, a new experience). After a break in Chicago to see the Borgeses, and Monika, who was staying with them before moving on to Michael and Gret in Carmel, he spoke in the Arts Centre at Colorado Springs, repeating his introduction to *The Magic Mountain*, and in an interview was optimistic over the war: 'if the British, with or without American help, can hold out for the coming four months, Hitler will be vanquished'. In Denver then, a half-full hall for his 'War and Democracy' (adapted as he went along) was disappointing—financially too, as his fee this time depended on the attendance—but those who came seemed receptive.

A stressful programme awaited him on arrival in Los Angeles in the evening of 26 March. He was on stage in the Wilshire Theatre within two hours, before a large audience, while Katia conferred with architect and contractor for the Pacific Palisades development, and had to contend after-wards with a great crowd of journalists, acquaintances, and autograph-seekers. Early next morning there was a flight to San Francisco for the award of his seventh honorary doctorate, this time law, at Berkeley. With time pressing, he was given a police escort to the ceremony, sirens blaring and red lights ignored—as if he were being brought back to Germany as President after Hitler's fall, was his wry comment later—and as always took great pleasure in the ritual acknowledgement of his status. After a further function in Berkeley, a lecture was due at Stanford University, Palo Alto, on 3 April, and, as the temporary home Erika had found in Pacific Palisades would not be ready till 8 April, there would also be time to visit Michael and Gret in Carmel.

At a banquet on 29 March he was received with Freemason-like cer-emony into the Berkeley chapter of the Phi-Beta-Kappa order, and in a short speech of thanks afterwards touched on the significance now of this symbol of 'philosophy as guide to life', in the face of a Germany without philosophy, morality, or religion. Would not Nietzsche turn in his grave if he could see the political perversion of his ideas of power, and if he were here, surely as an emigrant like himself, be the candidate in his place for such an honour? 'Philosophy shares the fate of democracy. It is compelled to be militant simply in the interest of self-preservation. . . . The true totali-tarianism which we offer in opposition is that of man.'[56]

The days in Berkeley they spent sightseeing in San Francisco, but were also often in the company of Katia's brother Peter Pringsheim, visiting from Chicago, who took them round the Physics Institute, with its somewhat

[56] x 366 f.

sinister installations for the splitting of the atom. The appointment on 3 April at Stanford was an 'all-university' occasion, and he presented his 'War and Democracy', again suitably adapted and well received (the new insertion of Nietzsche as a Phi-Beta-Kappa member giving particular amusement to the large audience); but it was with some relief that they left the same evening for a few days' rest, and some work on *Joseph*, at Pebble Beach, on the Monterey Peninsula, not far from Michael's home in Carmel.

Stormy weather at first spoiled their enjoyment of the magnificent view on the Gulf of Monterey, and while Katia went in some eagerness to see how the young couple were installed, he settled to work and left his call on them till the afternoon. Grandson Frido, now a spirited boy of nine months, was more attractive this time, and a walk on the beach was possible between showers. There were clearly problems, however, between Monika and her brother and his wife, and he could see difficulties ahead if she stayed on with them. The area was used to celebrity visitors, and interviews were inevitable. Michael and Gret arranged interesting entertainment for them: a lunch-party with an art enthusiast, and a musical evening at their own house, at both of which they met the poet Robinson Jeffers. Before leaving for Los Angeles on 7 April they were driven out to the west of the peninsula—the most western point of America, looking over to Asia, with splendid cypresses and the rocks alive with sea-lions.

Met by John with the Buick, they were driven to their new quarters at 740 Amalfi Drive, Pacific Palisades, not far from the western end of Sunset Boulevard. The spreading bungalow-style house, then still in country surroundings, with an ocean view from the terrace, struck him as not unpractical, if still without adequate furniture. They settled in in tolerable comfort, with enough of their things about them to give him a feeling of being at home again, and Katia could even offer Lotte Walter a bed for a few days. Thomas, of course, was back at once in the accustomed routine: while waiting to establish a study in the studio, he set up a desk in the bedroom for immediate progress with the *Joseph*, and each morning saw additions to the manuscript. Konrad Katzenellenbogen, the children's friend from Munich days, who had recently moved to California, was recruited as his secretary, easing the burden of correspondence considerably, and it seemed it was business as usual.

With the same capacity for detachment, he found it possible to concentrate on the work, keeping it resolutely apart from his concern at the dispiriting war situation in Greece and North Africa, and above all in the Atlantic, where British shipping-losses were mounting alarmingly. It was depressing to hear the radio report of Churchill's urgent appeal for American help there interspersed with commercials: 'only too characteristic. I certainly don't think Hitler will become master of the world, nor do I say the world deserves this. . . . But it will hardly have got what it deserves if he fails to become its master.' The reports of air-raid destruction in London were terrible, America's help would come too late, he thought, if it came at all, and it was sickening to read of the swastika waving over the Acropolis. There were great personal worries too over the shaky finances of Klaus's journal *Decision*, and while he did what he could to help to attract backers, he was not prepared to sign as co-editor. His optimism over the permanent home on the site he had acquired was dampened when he learned of the increased cost, now estimated at 30,000 dollars, a figure impossible at his age to amortize, and the architect was instructed to produce new plans for a maximum of 20,000. In the face of constantly rising prices, however, which made even this amount likely to be untenable, and especially in depression over Hitler's apparent successes, he began to dither over the whole project and wonder whether a return east would not after all be best. He had always, over big decisions, been prone to such vacillation, provoked often enough by very minor irritations—as now, the non-arrival of his library: 'I am patient by nature, but nothing makes me more bitter than feeling my patience abused.' But the lucky star which he liked to think ruled his destiny usually kept him to the path decided on, and so it would prove here, though only after much longer hesitation than usual.

He confided his doubts at great length to Agnes Meyer—perhaps not without a thought that she and her husband might be a source of financial help—and, from her well-informed position in Washington, she firmly scolded him for his lack of confidence, at least where the war was concerned. America was 'speeding up', important decisions were due in the near future: more was being done than he, in his relative isolation there, could know. He was a child in questions of life: 'please do not go up and down . . . when bad news comes that everyone knew was inevitable . . . you haven't the right to wear yourself out over things you cannot change'. Above all she insisted that his decision for the house was practical and wise: 'You will be able to build in a year's time with a quiet mind whether we are still at war or not.'[57] There was no indication of any possible financial help there; but during May he put the necessary mortgage in motion, cancelled again in June when the price went up by 10 per cent, and finally reinstated it at the end of the month, covering the extra amount by a cheque after being assured he could rely on the Meyers, not only for help over securing the building-materials, but also over finance. By mid-July, ground was broken, and he could see marked out the space for his future studio, 'where my books and my Munich desk will stand and I can expect

[57] AM Brw. 268 f.

to finish the *Joseph* . . .'[58] It was the fourth time he had built his own house, and he could only hope the experience would turn out better than with the others.

'Whatever you do, don't let the German refugees sit on your doorstep,' Agnes Meyer had urged him, in her concern for his work. His efforts on behalf of those far away needing help did not flag, and with the aid of his secretary (now going under the name of Konrad Kellen) his correspondence to this end continued unabated, as well as phone calls and the search for funds for the Emergency Committee, 'so as not to disappoint at least some of the hopes placed in me'. On his doorstep, of course, were a large number of refugees, including Heinrich: those closest to him well enough off, but socially time-consuming. The delayed celebration-dinner for Heinrich's seventieth birthday was given on 2 May by Salka Viertel, wife of the successful stage and film director Berthold Viertel and herself a busy script-writer, notably for Garbo's films. Her salon in Santa Monica was a focal point for the exiled German colony, and most were present—not only the writers Döblin, Feuchtwanger, Leonhard Frank, Alfred Neumann, Marcuse, but also Reinhardt and some of the movie moguls. It was the usual performance (no decade passed without it, said Frank to Salka afterwards), each brother pulling from his pocket a carefully prepared speech-essay on the other, quite ready for publication, and Feuchtwanger adding his contribution. 'We sat over the dessert and listened to German literati among themselves,' wrote Döblin.[59] Thomas took up his familiar theme of the 'world civil war' in which they stood, the cry of European unity now transformed to one for the unity of the whole world. He cited a recent article by the English poet Herbert Read, whose deep sympathy for German culture was mingled with despair—'it is as though every road taken by German poets and philosophers led to the edge of an abyss . . . which they could not withdraw from but must fall into headlong'. 'There is something about us Germans which I believe does not exist with other peoples—the suffering our great men cause us,' Nietzsche once again his example. And he ended by praising Heinrich's political foresight—a reference probably not lost on that audience, who would know well how the brothers' views had diverged in earlier years—and with the hope he would live to see the downfall of the tyrant.

Whatever Agnes Meyer thought, he could not help being affected by the ups and downs of the political and war news, or resist being drawn into public comment. After the dramatic flight of Rudolf Hess to Scotland, on 12 May, he responded at once to the London *Daily Telegraph*'s request for his views, and Erika, visiting, translated and telephoned them through: Hess

---

[58] *Brw. Aut.* 300.    [59] *DüD.* ii, 623.

was probably more sane than the rest, a relatively pure figure within that 'grotesque clique', perhaps the only true friend Hitler had ever had, and his defection was undoubtedly a terrible blow to his Führer. He spoke on 20 May at another Federal Union dinner, in Beverley Hills, urging the defeat of Hitler as still absolute priority and expressing his confidence that 'America would throw her full weight into the scale of honour'.[60] In private, however, he maintained his doubts of her capacity for war, and although encouraged by Roosevelt's important speech on 27 May, announcing a full state of emergency, was dubious whether he would be able to carry the country all the way with him. America, he told Aldous Huxley later, was simply a colonial territory thrown together from disparate elements, admittedly with great technological know-how, but, like Europe, with a fascist minority: could this be a source of salvation? 'As soon as America has her Vichy government,' he wrote sarcastically to Agnes Meyer on 20 May, 'you will be able to experience here the nicest *coopération complète* with Hitler. It's not inevitable, but I'd like you to apprehend it, or understand that it's what I fear.'[61] To such a politically sensitive and patriotic American, it was an incautious outburst, which he was quickly at pains to correct, but which reflected, if in extreme terms, his inner misgivings and depression.

If it were not for the *Joseph*, he felt, the misery would be insupportable. There at least he was continuing to progress, though conscious that his irresistible tendency to get everything in was threatening to make it over-long (towards the end of June, with several hundred pages of manuscript, he was still barely half-way towards the conclusion). Sales, and most reviews, of *The Transposed Heads* were disappointing. To add to his cares, there were problems over the scattered family during May and June. Something had to be done about Monika, Michael and Gret having finally given an ultimatum that she must go: he was not prepared to keep her long at Pacific Palisades, and accommodation in Los Angeles was hard to find, especially since she insisted on a piano. Klaus was in ever-deepening financial straits over *Decision*, and in despair over what he would do if it collapsed. Golo was looking for a teaching-appointment, but his father's reconnaissance at Pomona College, Claremont, which Angell had suggested, was unfruitful. Finally, Erika, who had spent over a month in Pacific Palisades, was attracted by another call from the London Ministry of Information and was preparing to fly over again—a resolve he could not but praise, though he would miss her presence more than any. His public face was preserved, as he continued his regular broadcast messages for the BBC (now being recorded on disc for air dispatch across), joined the committee of a 'Legion for American Unity and Action', agreed to broadcast

---

[60] *Tb.* v, 1051, 1057.     [61] *AM Brw.* 277.

in July in a series of propaganda calls for Defence Bond subscriptions, and countered, with an article 'Germany's Guilt and Mission', the pessimism of Prince Bernhard of the Netherlands, now an RAF officer. But in Hitler's bold venture of the invasion of Russia, on 21 June, he saw at first only a temporary respite for the Anglo-Saxon world until Russia was defeated, and could not share Heinrich's jubilation.

# VII

## ANGUISH OVER GERMANY
## 1941–1948

'It would well be that I'm 70 before this comes to an end'
(TM, 28 January 1942)

### 1

*'I will never return to the Germans, even if this should become
unobjectionable'* (TM, 30 March 1942)

Thomas Mann's depression persisted during July 1941. Russia, he was sure, would be defeated in this conflict, and Stalin (a blackguard, though this was not the moment to say so) would get what he deserved after trying to appease Hitler with the German-Soviet pact. His doubt was whether the time thereby gained for England and America would be enough, for they clearly needed a lot. In a telegram to the Soviet news-agency Tass at the end of June, he had expressed his hope that the attack, revealing Hitler's rediscovery of his anti-Bolshevism for the 'obscene farce' it was, would revive the idea of a united anti-fascist 'people's front' and resolve the confusion that had followed Munich and the German-Russian pact;[1] and he sent a further telegram on 17 July welcoming the British-Russian alliance just announced. Inwardly however, though hardly despairing, he was dispirited, and had begun to lose energy for his work, even one day breaking off and settling to read in the garden instead, something quite new for him. He put this down to the enervating effect of the climate, and felt relieved when, after a blood test, thyroid deficiency was diagnosed and prescribed for; but he continued to complain, to many a correspondent, at the 'vicious circle of depression and a feeling of insufficiency'. He recalled with emotion their visit in the summer of 1939 to the house in the Schiedhalden Strasse,

[1] N 41/5.

and thought how good it would be to live in Switzerland and await his death there rather than in America.

That was an idea which remained in the back of his mind, whatever his general admiration for America and some aspects of its life. Within a few days, however, he began to advance *Joseph the Provider* with renewed vigour—though forecasting at least another year before it could be concluded. He followed with enthusiasm the progress with the building, and on frequent visits to the site saw promise of the finest house and garden he had ever possessed, practical and spacious, with an ideal study and an outstanding all-round view. A busy social life occupied his afternoons and evenings through late July and August, with Bruno Walter concerts in the Hollywood Bowl, tea-parties, occasional private film-showings or other invitations from the 'movie mob' (at the house of the British actor Cedric Hardwicke, he was amused to see Alfred Hitchcock drop off and snore in his chair after dinner). Visits from Caroline Newton and Agnes Meyer— both fatiguing, not to say boring, with their biographical projects—he was able to handle diplomatically, though they probably, as he surmised, departed in some disappointment with him.

The Mann journal-enterprises *Standards and Values* and *Decision* were now at an end, or near it. Editorial, financial, and distribution difficulties had proved too great for the former in 1940, and it had folded after the end of its third year. His heart had truly been in it, but continuation had seemed impossible, Mann wrote now to Oprecht, thanking him for his assistance in Zurich to Hedwig Pringsheim after the death in July of her husband. 'But who knows whether the moment will not come one day for its resurrection. The title, well chosen when we started, will perhaps be even more timely in the era of moral and material reconstruction which has to come.' Klaus for his part was desperate over *Decision*: heavily in debt, it was on the point of collapse unless 8,000 dollars could be raised urgently, and the only hope for that, he thought, was Agnes Meyer. His father, however, who had always considered the undertaking too venturesome, was not prepared to turn to her, despite his sympathy for Klaus, and there was finally no alternative to its liquidation before many more months had passed.

During September, somewhat against the grain, he prepared a lecture to be produced on a further tour, with the customary programme across America, in October and November. He had latterly been tending, in incidental articles and pieces (such as a foreword to an edition of Pastor Niemöller's sermons), to stress the philosophical and moral rather than the political aspects of the struggle—'a kind of higher propaganda', with education as well as polemic in mind. In August, to avert any idea that his fight against Hitler had some personal political end in view, he had

firmly refused the honorary presidency of a 'German-American Council
for Liberation from Nazism', a 'Free Germany' committee of exiled politicians who hoped one day to resume the reins of power there. 'Nothing is
further from me than the role of a Masaryk. He had political faith in his
country, which is exactly what I haven't'; and it would be the height of
embarrassment to appear publicly to intercede for a people so devoid
of political nous.[2] Reassuring Agnes Meyer—busy with her study on him,
for which she proposed the high-sounding title 'The Godseeker', and
ever concerned over any distractions from his true work—he averred his
coming discourse on 'The War and the Future' would be worthy of him:
expatiating not so much on the 'devilry of Hitlerism' as on the general
problem of freedom, the need for a 'moral restoration of the idea of *justice*
out of the current crazy decline', and, as far as America was concerned,
pointing out the danger of an isolationist line. He had noted how Roosevelt,
after U-boat sinkings of American merchant ships and a conference on the
high seas with Churchill, had broadcast on 11 September what seemed
tantamount to a declaration of naval war against Germany. But it had been
followed by a virulent outburst from Lindbergh, in words worthy of the
Nazi *Völkischer Beobachter*, against the warmongering of 'the English, the
Jews, and the Roosevelt government'. Speculating on the effect of such
opposition on the American people, he felt his own words might not
be without weight in the controversy, even if the lecture tour would
be something of a Calvary (business too, however, for a few thousand
dollars would be gained, and, as father of a family, he had to have an eye
to that).

The relationship with Agnes Meyer had been giving him increasing
concern. It was vital, of course, not to put her goodwill at risk, but he was
fearful that her interest in him was becoming an obsession, with constant
psychological speculations and all the attendant implications. Throughout
his life he had been on his guard against others' attempts to get too close to
him: in her case, there seemed even a danger that she might see in Thomas
Mann the successor in her emotional life to the French writer Paul Claudel,
once, as he believed, her lover. From all points of view, that would never
do. She intended in her study, she avowed, to steer clear of the hagiography
of which the books written on Rilke by the many women in his life were
forbidding examples: in her twenties, she had personally witnessed Rodin's
contempt for his secretary ('c'est un jeune allemand qui écrit sur moi!'),
and felt the poet had transferred this humiliation later to the women of his
entourage 'as compensation and revenge'. Rilke she saw as a 'feminine
talent, the obverse of exaggerated German "masculinity"'; and Mann,

---

[2] *AM Brw.* 308.

though amused over the Rodin anecdote, did not care for the probing into his own nature her words implied.

Early in October, when the time for his departure was approaching, there came what she herself described as an 'irrational letter', full of worry over the cares she suspected his reticence concealed—to his mind a sign of her 'bad conscience'. It was high time to clear this up, for they would meet in Washington in November: and he spent several days over the concoction of what he called a *Staatsschreiben*—an 'official' letter setting out once and for all, and at great length, the truth as he wanted her to see it, on his life and character, his work and health (and his finances), in terms he could hope might leave untroubled a relationship capital for his future in America.

He had already begun with further comments on her view of Rilke: for him still a great poet whose lyric genius he admired without claiming fully to understand him, admittedly full of preciosity and a snob, but in his eyes with another important claim to renown, of which she might not be aware, in that he had written one of the earliest and best reviews of *The Buddenbrooks*. Now he turned to dismissing her apprehensions about himself. Far from being hard, as she thought, his life had been 'happy and blessed': not without tribulations, certainly, but one in which he had been able to pursue his work undisturbed. He could say, with his *Joseph*, that he was a 'glad-sorry man', the happy side of his nature able to bear much suffering but refusing to believe it would be 'too dense for his own light, or the light of God within him, to penetrate'. A 'Sunday child', therefore, with every reason to be grateful for the destiny which had always turned things well for him. In America, where her support for his work was hardly less than he had enjoyed in Germany (perhaps an understandable hyperbole here), his only care was to avoid frivolously forfeiting the position he had gained. A hard life? He was an artist, at play to entertain himself and others, and one who had chosen so essentially amusing a profession had no right to play the martyr. Politics, though certainly a dire burden, was still interesting and suspenseful, 'and if having been right makes a man happy, then I may be very happy, for I have been totally right, against my countrymen and the world of the appeasers, about where "National Socialism" would lead, and as far as one can judge, I shall also be right about the outcome'. The shape that might take left him indifferent, for *anything at all* must be preferable to Hitler. As to his health, it was the same old story— not really well, but without any serious complaint, 'and basically I believe my constitution . . . tends to patience, endurance, a long pull to carry things through to the end'.

Hence his urge to build a house, reckless perhaps, but founded on his habits and needs, his 'natural life-style'. But, if he might confess it here—

a hint in which he undoubtedly saw the crux of his long outpouring—he had often asked himself why it never occurred to a world so ready to grant him honours costing nothing to think of his practical needs, and consider providing him with a house, as a rich Swiss patron had done for Hermann Hesse. Neither a city nor a university here had had the idea, even if only to be able to say 'we have him, he is ours'. Did they think a Nobel Prize winner (who had lost that and most other assets to the Nazis) needed no help? or was it pure thoughtlessness, counting on his idealism, and with the notion that such a one should not have regard for money? 'It would of course be more just and more dignified if he didn't have to think about it.' So he was building the house himself, affordable despite his now much-reduced income: there would be no distress, but certainly inconvenience and need for great economy. Yet all that did not correspond to the reality of his existence as a whole, as opposed to the conditions of the moment. The war could not last more than four years at the most, and his works could expect renewed life in a Germany without Hitler and a liberated Europe, 'drawn in as a vacuum draws in air'. He would finish the *Joseph*; editions of the complete works were planned in German and English; and the good prospect of a high-profile Joseph film would be no little aid to refloating his ship, if one might so speak of a vessel that was not actually aground. 'In short, "I" am an enterprise that can be regarded as a good credit-risk, and does not need to be treated with nerve-racking tact'—an expression which she might ascribe to the commercial spirit that *Joseph* now personified. 'I do sometimes think that way, and the feminine intuition in your letter has loosened the checks on my tongue—which it was meant to do, as I imagine.' The ban just announced on private building had luckily come too late to interrupt his plans, though progress was slow, and they would not be in before the end of the year; a pity only that meantime they would be, as it were, paying rental twice over. To her question when *Joseph* would be finished, he could say by the coming summer at all events.

It was a skilful effort in diplomacy, but also an exposé, franker than ever before to a friend, of the Thomas Mann enterprise and its material aspects (never far from his mind, whatever the pleasure of the artist in his game). He was naturally curious, perhaps a little apprehensive over her reception of the screed, and it was reassuring to receive, after starting his tour, a brief, almost penitent-sounding interim reply with her particular gratitude for this first allusion to his financial position. 'If my intellectual efforts are at your disposal, why not then every material resource I possess?' He was to be sure to reserve some uninterrupted hours for her in Washington. He had set out with Katia on 14 October, realizing that fully six weeks would be taken up through the stations of his Calvary, but resolved to let its demands flow over him and concentrate on furthering the manuscript during the long train-journeys. In this he succeeded; and though complaining of the heat and the sometimes unsatisfactory arrangements through Austin, Texas; New Orleans; Birmingham, Alabama; and South Carolina, he could feel tolerably content, both over the effect of the lecture and with his pencilled additions to *Joseph*, by the time they reached Washington on 1 November.

This was a very brief interlude only, before he started on the second part of the tour, but long enough to hear how Agnes Meyer had put her resources to work. True, there was no sudden offer from any public or private funds of a house for the Master, which was hardly what he had expected, nor what he needed now. She had had a more appropriate idea, which pleased him far better: a sinecure at the Library of Congress, in the newly invented post of 'Consultant in Germanic Literature', with a yearly stipend of 4,800 dollars, in return for which he had merely to be at the Library's disposal for questions in that field, undertake an annual lecture there, for an additional fee of 1,000 dollars, and try to be in residence in Washington for two weeks every year. She had long been a member of the Library's Congress Trust Fund Board, handling the budget in which the 'Eugene and Agnes E. Meyer Foundation' already figured among other important private and anonymous donors, and the financing of the proposal could therefore be entirely hers. It needed the approval of the Librarian, Archibald MacLeish, but he was a close friend of hers and an admirer of Thomas Mann, and had already been of similar assistance to exiled writers with funds from the Rockefeller Foundation and the ERC: he was only too pleased later in November to finalize the appointment. For Mann it was an ideal solution. From Chicago on 3 November, his next stop, he sent Agnes Meyer his warm thanks for her 'elegantly inventive gift': 'I am artist enough to take almost more pleasure in the form you contrived for it than in its "content". Truly, this new symbolic connection with America and with Washington has something deeply satisfying for me, even apart from the associated material reassurance.' Sincere, no doubt: but he was certainly greatly interested in the material support it would bring. After seven doctor's gowns which, however prestigious, had brought no tangible reward, here at last was an honour from his new country which could banish further need for the economy he detested, and preserve the life-style to which he had always felt entitled.

He could continue the tour with a lighter heart. After Chicago, Iowa, Indianapolis, and Bloomington, Delaware—the last two occasions of a decidedly triumphal character, he thought, with large audiences—they reached New York on 7 November, where they would spend over a week.

Elisabeth was there, as well as Klaus, and Erika just back from an exciting time in England, including an adventurous Channel trip over to Calais, on which a young English pilot had been rescued. To her father's concern, she too, though far from well, was now preparing for a lecture tour, with nine appearances in ten days more strenuous and on a theme more personal than his—'Our War, our Victory, our Peace', in which she vividly recalled her vain efforts in the peace movement in Germany before the Nazi dictatorship, and urged militancy on an America which by then would be drawn into the war after the December attack on Pearl Harbour. For him, the days in New York were anything but restful, with the host of friends there, and the problem, now come to a head, of the proposed 'European PEN in America', which their London colleagues regarded as undermining the organization. Work was out of the question, and amid the distractions, he felt pessimistic over his loss of contact with the main task and what remained to be done. Commitments followed to speak in Amherst, Massachusetts, and Philadelphia, and a short visit to Princeton, mainly to discuss with Helen Lowe-Porter the *Joseph* translation.

Briefly back then in New York, he found Agnes Meyer's letter confirming the arrangements with MacLeish for the Library of Congress appointment, and stressing in particular how the annual lectures were an attempt to secure his contribution to American cultural life. That, with word of good progress on the California house, helped to dispel the nigh-despair that overcame him on tours of this kind, which he always came to consider, whatever the outward prestige, as a waste of time; and he wrote to her quickly how immensely grateful and 'indescribably happy' he felt. Only one further performance remained, at the College of the Pacific in Stockton, Sacramento on 24 November, and he and Katia journeyed directly to San Francisco, where Michael was now installed and doing well in the state Youth Orchestra, and Gret expecting her second child. The lecture at Stockton once successfully discharged, next day they were at last on the way homeward, taking with them little Frido, who, it was decided, would stay in Pacific Palisades until Christmas—a 'delightful burden', he found, for he was greatly taken with his grandson, and also, of course, a welcome one for Katia.

Though he had bemoaned his loss of contact with the work and lack of productivity on the tour, longed for a proper installation of his library, and foresaw further interruptions by incidental political commitments, the six weeks had not in fact gone by without result, and ideas for the continuation had germinated. Within a few days he was deep in the episode of Thamar, wife of Judah and Joseph's sister-in-law, which occupied him until the end of the year, developing into a lengthy short story in its own right (his picture of that 'remarkable woman, neglecting no method of inserting herself into the story of salvation',[3] not without certain characteristics of Agnes Meyer).

The official letter of his appointment with the Library of Congress arrived the day after Japan's devastating attack on the American fleet at Pearl Harbour on 7 December, and he wrote at once to MacLeish to express his gratitude and elation at being included now 'in the cultural life of this my new homeland whose citizen I shall be very soon. . . . Please accept my heartiest thanks and wishes in this grave hour which ties us still faster to this country fighting for freedom and human right.' 'God Bless America!', ended his telegram with the news to Agnes Meyer—though a letter from her just before had nettled him no little with her over-black picture of the financial demands of his children on him, and he had just written at some length to correct this: they were no real burden, were all well-intentioned and active in their own way, save only for Monika, and compared well with other young emigrants who did not even take the trouble to learn English. The salary he was to get and whatever else he could earn was for his own comfort only, not for them.

One burden he did not tell her about was his brother. Heinrich's initial contract as screen-writer had not been renewed, wholly unsuited as he was, with his background and very limited English, to make any money in America as a writer, while his books found little or no favour for translation. An appeal by Thomas to the Soviet ambassador for transfer of Russian royalties had to await the arrival of his replacement, Maxim Litvinov: after a reminder later to Litvinov, this eventually succeeded, but for the moment his brother was virtually without resources. Katia was dispatched for a discussion, and the outcome was the promise of an immediate cheque for 300 dollars, to be followed by 100 monthly, in other words a quarter of the monthly stipend from the Library, which fortunately was due to start from December. Hard, Thomas found, but he could scarcely do otherwise. In strong contrast with his brother, Heinrich saw America as a 'waste land': his first impressions on landing in New York had been 'insignificant', and he recalled his last sight of the 'incredibly beautiful' harbour of Lisbon, the intense pain of his farewell. 'Everything granted to me I had experienced in Europe, the joy and the pain of an age that was mine but also that of the many who had gone before.' In exile in America he was never to lose this feeling.[4]

America's immediate declaration of war against Japan, followed a few days later by those of Germany and Italy against the USA, brought the turning-point he had longed for, with the great majority of mankind now

[3] *Br.* ii, 230.
[4] Quoted Koopman, 'Thomas Mann in Amerika', in Begleitheft zur Ausstellung 'Thomas Mann im amerikanischen Exil 1938–1952', Universität Augsburg 1991, 3.

on the side of America and England. He had listened approvingly to
Roosevelt's dignified radio-speech, and noted how rapidly the country was
turning over to a war footing in preparation for the sacrifices, discipline,
and unity the President demanded, in a fight which must be long and hard.
On 20 December, he spoke at a mass meeting for civil defence, organized
in Santa Monica by the 'Fight for Freedom Committee' (sending afterwards
a copy of his words to Roosevelt): 'it was your, or may I say my, President
. . . the born and destined antagonist of those forces striving to destroy
freedom and human dignity', who, however dangerous a foe the Japanese
might be, had left no doubt that Hitler was the principal adversary.
'England's stand after Dunkirk is proof of what democratic and inherently
peace-loving men can accomplish even in war.' The English-speaking
peoples, with the powerful help of Russia and China, with their industrial
resources, and not least in the knowledge of having been 'chosen for the
defence of those human values established in the Bill of Rights, will not fail
to repulse this onslaught and save humanity from the fascist horror'.[5]

Though speaking as technically an 'enemy alien', as he said, he had felt
justified in his fervently American line. Like the other exiles, however, he
was well aware of the trouble such a technicality could bring in a country
newly at war, as had been shown in England and France in 1939 and 1940
by internment, or at least restrictions on movement, of almost all Germans
and Austrians, no matter how anti-Nazi their credentials. This was the case
now in principle in America too, with internment for many, especially
Japanese, and registration and movement-permits for all. After Christmas,
thanking Agnes Meyer for her magnificent gift of a silver coffee and
tea service, he asked her whether he was actually considered an enemy
alien: 'I don't mean "actually", of course! Actually I'm pretty friendly. But
technically?' She consulted Francis Biddle, the Attorney-General, and he
himself wrote to Biddle at the New Year, setting out his impeccable record
and American honours: there were no exceptions, but in his case no real
difficulties, and he was a little ashamed at complaining. Others were not
so fortunate, however, and as there seemed to be no general attempt
to remedy the injustice, he initiated in February a direct appeal to the
President, co-signed by Einstein, Toscanini, Bruno Walter, and others,
urging positive discrimination in favour of 'the victims and sworn foes of
totalitarian evil'. But it was to be a long-lasting problem for most of the
exiles.

The November and December numbers of the *New Yorker* contained
a 'Profile' of him by Janet Flanner: flatteringly entitled 'Goethe in
Hollywood', but irritating with its journalistic distortion ('every second fact

[5] xiii 717f.

wrong'), and leaving him especially indignant over the nonsensical caricature of the three 'bluestockings' Caroline Newton, Agnes Meyer, and Helen
Lowe-Porter as united in a 'cult of admiration' for him. Flanner, who from
1929 had contributed fortnightly letters to the *New Yorker* from Paris, a
flamboyant figure in Natalie Clifford Barney's salon and in her own eyes an
expert on the European scene, had interviewed him in Princeton in 1940,
as he recalled, and he had certainly been then as 'monstrously polite, stiff,
and reserved' as she portrayed him—for which his only regret now was the
politeness. The second half of the profile, which reached him on Christmas
Eve, though just as full of stupid inaccuracies and ruthlessly repeated
gossip, seemed nevertheless to leave his dignity unimpaired (an impression
no doubt reinforced by the title), and he was content to say no more.

To Eugene Meyer, with his thanks for an unexpected gift of cigars, he
reported in 'wild-grown English' on their Christmas Eve, 'with good friends
and our little grandson . . . whose presence gilds our old days'. Inviting
them to the new house-warming hoped for in the second half of January, he
could only 'pray the coast will not be evacuated, so that a[n American]
general will reside there and later possibly the Mikado'. For Christmas, the
house seemed over-full, though of the children only Golo, Monika, and
Erika could be there, with Katia's brother Peter Pringsheim. It was the
first time Mann could dandle a grandson on his knee while the tree's
candles were lit for the present-giving—and also the first time, perhaps in
consideration for little Frido, that he forbore to give a festive reading from
work in progress. No invitation went to his brother and Nelly, a coolish
note with New Year wishes seemingly sufficient now he was doing his duty
with financial support: 'let us know as soon as you feel like a visit'.

He was pleased while Erika was there to see Auden for lunch one day,
'boyish and nice as always' and a creditable performer at entertaining the
baby.[6] Erika had been taken to inspect the new premises, 'Seven Palms
House', as he called it, now taking delightful shape, and his study in
particular looking to be the best he had ever had, even if it was running
'unnervingly into the money'. He wrote and recorded two short messages
for BBC transmission, on yet another bloody Christmas in the long years of
struggle Germany was promised by her leaders, and on Hitler's order
announcing his personal assumption of military command: the inner voice
he said had prompted him should have warned of America's latent
strength, which the 'yellow brother-in-arms' had been foolish to disturb.
Such propaganda, and whatever his welcome for the ovation for Churchill
in the streets of Washington and admiration for his speeches to Congress
and the Canadian parliament, concealed his own, but modest, expectations

6 *Br.* ii, 231.

from the year to come. With the German army outside Moscow and into the Ukraine, the serious shipping-losses in the Atlantic, and the Japanese attacking the Philippines, there was certainly little room for optimism. His diary entry for New Year's Eve—usually the occasion for a portentous forecast—was subdued, simply the hope that things might 'one day improve, and finally go well', and that 1942, 'if I live', would see the completion of the *Joseph* in the new surroundings.

That at least he could get on with, and much was added to the Thamar episode before he was due for another lecture in San Francisco on 20 January. Frido came with them, to be returned to the parents he at first scarcely recognized, and his grandfather was uncommonly sad at having to go back without him. An updated version of 'War and Democracy' served for the performance, newly titled 'How to Win the Peace'. It was a fatiguing eighty minutes, followed then and afterwards by a stream of questions—'a real vice of your great nation', as he told Agnes Meyer, 'but I always extricate myself in the most amusing way by not answering the question at all, but arbitrarily talking around it . . . the people are heartily content with that, at least they seem so . . . God bless them. That wish comes from my heart.' The patronizing tone is hardly likely to have appealed to her, and goes a long way to explain her sometimes critical attitude, which so often irritated him. The long haul that lay ahead in the war was brought home to him with the report of Churchill's Commons statement later in January, and he noted, prophetically, that it could well be three more years before the end.

The final fitting-out of the new house, at 1550 San Remo Drive in Pacific Palisades, was taking longer than hoped, but in his impatience they decided to move in on 5 February, even though the study of which he already boasted was still not finished and with their furniture from Princeton on the point of arriving. The plans finally settled on had been designed primarily round his personal needs: he would have an entirely private suite, the study, with its view over avocado-groves to the sea, linked to the drawing-room by a corridor which could be shut off and from which a separate staircase led up to his bedroom. Where most of the exiles rented, he had been as determined as ever to follow the old Hanseatic tradition and build a dignified and representative dwelling of decidedly personal character: and the result here, when finally completed, entirely met his aim, surpassing even the more sumptuous Munich house. His early ideas for Colonial-type or Early American design had been overruled by the architect, who insisted that the Californian landscape called for Modern ('he was a man of strong will', commented Katia Mann later, 'so we have a modern house. We like it though'). If not as spacious as the Poschinger Strasse house, it was enough to accommodate the children on their visits;

and the wide patio with sea view, on to which the drawing-room opened, could here be used all the year round for relaxation and informal meals.

Some chaos was inevitable for a month or so, with problems when the servant couple left them, and the difficulty of getting good workmen. He set up his desk temporarily in the bedroom, finding the books he wanted as best he could from the pile which Golo and Katia were trying to set in order, and continuing phlegmatically with his accustomed routine. The house had certainly cost a great deal, but income was not unsatisfactory, with small but useful royalties for the previous year from Bermann, the first cheque from the Library covering December and January, and a repeat of 'How to Win the Peace' at the Los Angeles Rotary Club on 12 February. There was longer-term promise, he hoped, from a collection with Knopf of his major speeches and essays in English, under the title *Order of the Day*, which was to occupy much of his time over the coming months in arranging, checking, and writing a foreword. It was difficult looking over this bygone stuff, he told Helen Lowe-Porter, but in the end 'these English editions are all I have, for in German I shall certainly not appear in my lifetime'[7]—an unnecessarily gloomy view.

Disturbingly, a number of Californian publishers were reported to be pressing for the evacuation from the coast of all 'enemy aliens', and the problem for his fellow exiles was a continuing preoccupation for him. His telegram to Roosevelt and letters seeking support from notables like Upton Sinclair had perhaps not been without effect, for a 'Congressional Committee on Evacuation of Enemy Aliens' under Congressman John H. Tolan was instituted soon afterwards, to begin public hearings in Los Angeles early in March. He and Bruno Frank, as leading representatives for the Germans, attended on 7 March. Although he personally felt Frank was over-hysterical in his plea against destroying the 'frail roots' of 'foreigners who have fought against the same hideous foe as your boys', and kept his own statement and answers as low-key as possible, his friend's words undoubtedly struck the right note for the polite American inquisitors, and may have carried more weight than those of the respected doyen of the *émigrés*. At all events, the policy of wholesale evacuation was finally abandoned, and the life of the exiled Germans and Austrians, with a few exceptions, was left undisturbed by the American state-apparatus through the war years, and until—as will be seen—the anti-communist fervour of the cold war discovered a different enemy.

To the unquestioned leader of German literature in exile, the suicide of Stefan Zweig at the end of February in the remote resort of Petrópolis, near Rio de Janeiro, seemed more a dereliction of duty than the tragic despair of

---

[7] *DüD.* ii, 599.

a Jewish humanist. In a telegram to the New York journal *PM*, while paying tribute to Zweig's well-deserved world-fame and the creative understanding in his historical biographies, he laid more stress on the 'painful breach torn in the ranks of the European literary emigrants' by so regrettable a weakness, a humanity not robust enough to help him survive the darkness and live to see the dawn. He could not justify Zweig's decision, he wrote privately later, precisely because of its disheartening effect on brother exiles far worse off than he. 'He should never have granted the Nazis this triumph, and had he had a more powerful hatred and contempt for them, he would never have done it.'[8] It could hardly have been from affliction, or necessity, he told Erika at the time, and the farewell message seemed an inadequate explanation: what was this impossibility of reconstructing his life? For himself, *any* life was possible, so long as it was not under Hitler. The tragedy caused him little emotion, for he had never shared the universal admiration for Zweig as a writer. Others might think to see in it the end of 'our world', but there was nothing of his own world there: 'who wants to identify himself with liberal humanism?'[9] For one who had never failed to commemorate the passing of a colleague, even some of the least significant and in often exaggerated terms, it was a cold response. When Zweig's first wife, Friderike, took justifiable umbrage at his failure to render appropriate tribute, he cited his psychological inability at the time to give of his best, but while mourning the outstanding man still insisted on the abdication of responsibility and the concession to the 'arch-enemy' the suicide represented. Moving though it was to receive at the end of the year the enthusiastic review Zweig had written long before of *Lotte in Weimar*, he could not bring himself to contribute more than a terse note to the memorial issue of the New York *Aufbau*, or a dust-cover comment to one of the books later produced. In 1952, on the tenth anniversary, he acknowledged Zweig's humanity and generosity, and the world-wide renown he had achieved, but confessed how incomprehensible at the time he had found his outright pacifism, though events since had shown that even a 'good war' could still generate evil.

His diary through the year shows how his own support for his fellow exiles continued unwaveringly, with visa, welfare, and grant recommendations not only for friends like Ferdinand Lion, Paul Amann, or Hans Feist, but for many others such as the writers Paul Stefan and Döblin, as well as the script-writers whose initial contracts had come to an end and for whom he had helped set up a 'European Film Fund' for further aid. It also shows how closely he followed the progress of the 'good war', and how his occasional doubts over America's capacity for victory, after the early

---

[8] Letter of 30 Sept. 1942 to Georges Motschan, Thomas Mann Archiv, Zurich.
[9] *Tb. v, 400.*

reverses in the Pacific, gradually gave way to a glimmering of optimism. Reports from the Russian front were encouraging, and as he started a new notebook in April he could foresee 'decisive world events' finding their place in it—while hoping too that it would mark the end of *Joseph the Provider*, which he was determined to finish, however the war went. No problem for him of reconstructing his life in exile: by then the new house was entirely as he wanted it, his study, with the Munich desk that had miraculously followed him across the world, exactly reproducing that of happier days, and his work continuing with the same admirable detachment from day-to-day cares both personal and general.

Of personal cares, there was no lack—foremost, the irritation occasioned by Agnes Meyer's persistence in trying, as he saw it, to intrude upon, and in some way dominate, his life, until in February he felt an 'almost uncontrollable' desire to 'give this woman tyrannizing me a piece of my mind'.[10] To a point, he was himself to blame for this, not only in offering her scope for detailed discussion of his work and his lecture drafts, but also in the often over-effusive compliments and expressions of thanks which studded his letters, encouraging her to see a warmth in their relationship which he by no means felt. But to his mind now she had developed an 'oppressive fixation' on his person, desperately abandoning all her activities for the sake of her embryonic Thomas Mann study. Even the hysteria of Molly Shenstone was preferable to 'the intellectual conceit of this troublesome woman in Washington' seeking in all seriousness to enter his life. It needed all his diplomacy to combine a welcome for a visit from her with plain words resisting her 'pedagogical tyranny' and explaining the futility of her worry about the effect of outside events on his work. For many years, that had proved immune to whatever happened in the world, so long as he was granted life and freedom; and there was no need for concern over his spiritual welfare. 'It is possible to understand me, to explain me, but not to change me . . . it's not only my age that makes me an unsuitable subject for education.' When she did come at the end of March, her few days' stay at Santa Monica, where she was joined later by her husband, entailed daily mutual visits, in which he tried to pursue his point, appeasing her with readings from the Thamar episode. Her endless psychologizing over him was still quite devoid of understanding, she had no idea of 'my complete inability to relate to people, the absence of any emotional influence on my work, at least since *Tonio Kröger*'. When she left he did his best to send her off with a quieter mind, his eye always to possible help should the expenses of the new house mount too high, for which her husband, who was duly impressed by it, fortunately seemed quite ready.

[10] Ibid. 396.

It was still painful to read the effusion of gratitude which came after her departure. He resolved to practise the 'art of ignoring', but as the months went by he continued fatally inclined to confide in her at great length, and much of what he said, notably his occasional doubts over America's capacity for war, drew disconcerting reactions. He was particularly put out in August by her remarks on his nostalgic Europe-centred outlook, in a situation where he was far better off than, say, Claudel in France, and her unjustified criticism of Klaus and Golo for not yet having joined the army and sitting in safety while American boys died. This too needed, and received, a diplomatic and soothing answer. But, however stung by her words and determined from now on not to honour her with further confidences, he found it impossible to distance himself from her; and this would not be the last crisis in what for the moment seemed a 'stupid and humiliating friendship'.

By comparison, it was easy to preserve his detachment from family worries, also not lacking. Chief, perhaps, was that over his brother. He and his 'appalling wife' were somewhat grudgingly invited to dinner early in March, but following her incoherent telephone-calls soon after, Golo, sent to investigate, reported the burden her conduct was becoming for Heinrich and the desperate state of his life with her in their cramped apartment in Los Angeles. On 27 March, his seventy-first and Golo's thirty-third birthday, there was a suitable dinner-party—for Thomas sheer torment, and he could only hope the three bottles of Burgundy made it more enjoyable for his brother. By April a temporary separation was imperative, and Heinrich stayed at San Remo Drive for a few weeks, no doubt relieved by the intellectual atmosphere in its busy social life, before returning to Nelly.

Monika, provoking her father's increasing bitterness through her in-ability to make a life for herself, remained a problem as she stayed on, but he kept himself aloof, and though he pressed Katia and Erika somehow to find separate accommodation for her, she was still there, a silent boarder, until in November she decided to move to New York. Neither Klaus nor Golo, as he had pointed out to Agnes Meyer, were backward in their efforts to join the army, but neither had yet completed their naturalization, and must wait. Golo meanwhile pursued his search for a teaching-post, and was finally successful with an appointment at Olivett College, near Chicago, for which he left during September.

Klaus, though some debts for *Decision* remained to be cleared, applied for the army, was at first rejected, but after repeated applications was finally accepted in December (his naturalization, however, still hung fire, with continuing FBI investigations into denunciations of him as a homosexual and a communist, and was not finalized till a year later). He had completed his autobiography, *The Turning-Point*, written entirely in English, and dedicated to his mother and Erika. In a letter to Katia in August he apologized for saying so little about her, the only member of their 'conspicuous family' who had avoided the limelight, yet with her unique mixture of 'acute intelligence and simplicity' the one who had held it together through all its vicissitudes. He was surely heartened by the telegram from Pacific Palisades as the whole family 'read frantically': 'Dad deeply captivated, Mielein confused and touched by splendid monument which should bring creator as much glory as it brings her honour, E. greatly surprised and moved . . .' His father, once he could recover the book from the others, wrote in September with high approval, admitting his initial misgivings over the malicious comment that might be expected on such intimate confessions, but admiring the *tour de force* in an adopted language, and his decision to undertake an autobiography at so early an age before the freshness of childhood impressions had faded. 'An unusually charming, affectionately sensitive, clever, and honestly personal book', powerfully European in its portrayal of the flaws of the pre-Hitler years, and with winning portraits of his mother and even of himself, a little mysterious in his absentmindedness and 'melancholy facetiousness'.[11]

Michael and Gret were there for a while, he reported, with their second boy, Anthony, born in July, as well as Frido, and Erika had just left for another lecture-tour. 'When they are all gone, we shall be often in the cinema.' His Washington lecture was being translated, after Erika had cut it down from thirty-two to nineteen pages—'and thus it will probably remain for all time, as I loathe cut texts'. In April, discussing with Erika what a miracle it would be if America did not lose the war (she, as always, burning to see decisive action), he had thought of making an outspoken political speech in the Library of Congress in November and also on a tour of other cities beforehand. He saw, however, that this would hardly be appropriate for his début at the Library, which, as the first public acknowledgement of gratitude for his appointment, needed something loftier and more dignified, and he chose 'The Theme of the Joseph Novels' instead, forsaking the political in favour of the 'metapolitical' and entirely abandoning the idea of an additional extensive tour.

As the summer passed, in any case, his doubtful and despondent mood had begun to evaporate, with signs of a halt to the Axis victories, and increasing air-attacks on Germany itself: the news of a massive bombing of Munich in September, the explosions heard as far as Switzerland, showed that that 'imbecile site' was getting its historical deserts. His confidence was

---

[11] KlM *Br. Antw.* 486 f.

returning too in the 'virile breed' of the Americans, their masculinity tempered by 'Christianity, i.e. mercy, i.e. femininity', as against the fundamentally 'heathenish, homosexual Germans'.[12] It was a land from which the greatest things were to be expected, destined after the war to be the world's granary—and he could only trust the struggle would be over before the sacrifices it was preparing for became too great. Before he and Katia took the train on 9 November for Chicago, to stay a few days with the Borgeses before going on to Washington, the news had broken of the American landing in North Africa, following the smashing defeat of Rommel's Afrika Korps by the British at Alamein: with the Russian resistance at Stalingrad, the beginning of set-backs for German military might. Some people, if not yet Thomas Mann, started to think and talk of a turning-point in the war: Borgese, he found, watching the increasing pressure from North Africa on Italy, was already seeing himself as the future Governor of Sicily. In Washington on 16 November, where they stayed with the Meyers at Crescent Place, there was news of the naval victory over the Japanese at the Solomon Islands.

Between them, MacLeish and Agnes Meyer, to whom the German version of the lecture had been sent in advance, had done their utmost to give the Washington occasion the next evening a suitable lustre. He was to be introduced, after preliminary words from the Librarian of Congress, by Vice-President Henry Wallace; publicity had ensured a big attendance, needing the use of a second hall with relay arrangement; and she had seen to personal invitations for all the notables of official Washington—ministers, Supreme Court justices, ambassadors, and leading newspapermen—most of whom then attended a big reception afterwards at Crescent Place. Though probably not the largest audience he had addressed in America, it was certainly the most distinguished.

Wallace, clearly well briefed, paying tribute first to the enrichment for America's thought and ideals brought by the refugees from Europe, touched on Thomas Mann's effort in his work as an artist to reconcile the fundamental conflicts in human life—a problem not only of art and religion, but also of statecraft—and his developing concern over the conflict in a democracy between liberty and equality, between the extremes of anarchy and fascist dictatorship. Thus, he introduced him as democrat and statesman as well as artist: those of his hearers more interested in the political could perhaps grasp 'his inmost being . . . by remembering that he has feared for many years the undisciplined excesses of the masses of the people and yet . . . also had the courage in 1936 to speak out resolutely for republican Spain'. What he had to offer them then was in keeping with

---

[12] 42/193.

these flattering words: a highly personal account of how he had come to the mythological in the *Joseph* theme, its development, through the Nazi years and after, to what he considered a 'symbol of humanity' in its search for 'God's wisdom'—and so, in his peroration, bringing his listeners back to the critical times in which they were living. 'It is in the foolish disobedience to the spirit, or in religious terms to God's will, that we must surely seek the true cause of the storm which rages stupefyingly over us . . . but the hope may not be vain that after this war, we—or our children and grand-children—will live in a world of happier reconciliation between spirit and reality, and "win the peace". Peace has always a religious sound to it, and its meaning is a gift of God's wisdom.'[13] High-flown, perhaps, but it was clearly to the liking of such an audience, and he was well pleased with its reception ('Spiritual Unification World Hope' was the *Post*'s headline next morning). At the reception, which went on till the small hours, it was encouraging to hear Attorney-General Biddle confide his intention of eas-ing the civic restraints on the German exiles, perhaps even more his wife's admiration for the musical effect of the lecture: 'I always feel a little like a conductor.'

They stayed nearly a week at the Meyers', with the usual round of lunch- and dinner-parties, mainly of marginal interest for him, except for a stimu-lating exchange of views with Litvinov, and walks and drives through the capital, past the temporary barracks and offices springing up round the Lincoln Memorial. In the mornings he could make some attempts to add to the manuscript, but most afternoons were inevitably taken up by read-ings from it to 'Madame', whose fervent intensity became more and more burdensome, until he felt their escape to New York could not come soon enough. The return to California would not be till 7 December, for there was much routine business to be attended to in New York, as well as a visit to Helen Lowe-Porter in Princeton on the programme. Once there, however, he was still pursued by letters from Agnes, one with the excellent news that the Library, in view of the overwhelming response to his lecture, planned to publish it, but another so infuriating that he tore it up, sending a curt wire concealing his bitterness. When she and Eugene came to New York on 30 November, and they attended a Wagner concert under Toscanini together, it proved an ill-humoured meeting, and the unsatisfactory leave-taking, he thought, befitted the whole relationship with them. (Once at a safe distance, nevertheless, their correspondence resumed, with great restraint on his side. To the outside eye, such dis-sembling subservience, apparently purely in his own material interest, seems more than a little abhorrent in one of his stature, but her adulation—

---

[13] xii 667, 669.

'your noble devotion to my work', as he called it in his Christmas letter—undoubtedly met a need which few if any of his other correspondents could fill.)

Klaus, and later Erika, were in New York, as well as Monika, her future still vague, it seems, and there were many gatherings of friends, as well as meetings with Knopf and Bermann, between attention to tasks of the day: another broadcast for the BBC, a speech to be prepared for Erika to read in his absence at the Nobel anniversary dinner on 10 December. Important financially was a 1,000-dollar contract for a new assignment: a contribution, to a book to be entitled *The Ten Commandments*, which he could envisage as a 'fantasy' on the origin of the tablets of the law received by Moses, and thus in convenient continuation of the mythological imaginings of the *Joseph*, whose completion he could reckon on by the end of the year. From the hotel room he planned the busy days with his usual skill, and found time for relaxation at a Bruno Walter *Magic Flute* performance and Thornton Wilder's *The Skin of our Teeth*; but the stress of functions and visits took its toll, and by the time they gained the relief of isolation in 'roomettes' on the train for Chicago, on 7 December, he was thoroughly overtired.

Before heading for home, they were to travel to San Francisco, to hear Michael play in the Symphony Orchestra there, but mainly, if the truth were told, for the pleasure of seeing little Frido again. Perhaps unwisely, they did not take the usual few days' break between trains in Chicago, though they saw Elisabeth and Golo, and the long and tedious journey, even with plenty of time for some desultory work, and reading in preparation for the 'Moses fantasy', only added to his great fatigue. Once back in the comfort of the Pacific Palisades, he soon recovered. There were mixed feelings over the results of the month away, but on the whole he was not displeased. Certainly the Library of Congress performance had been a great success, and it was gratifying to hear from MacLeish on Christmas Eve that his appointment had been renewed, with the new title of 'Fellow', 'warmer and more intimate', he felt. The final chapter of the *Joseph* was in hand before Christmas, a more than usually quiet festival this year: only the Borgeses were there, for neither Golo, Monika, nor Erika could come, and Klaus was awaiting transfer to his induction camp at Fort Dix. On 4 January 1943, after routine visits to manicurist and barber, he 'sat down again and just as the bell rang for lunch wrote the final lines of *Joseph the Provider*, and thus of *Joseph and his Brothers*. . . . it's done, for better or worse . . . a monument much more to my own life than to art and thought, a monument of *perseverance*'.[14]

---

[14] *Tb*. v, 520.

2

*'I shall have to write one more novel before the end comes—if an*
*actual end ever comes'*                    (TM, 22 March 1943)

'I've finished with the *Joseph* more quickly than the world with fascism—
supposing that even a victory will put an end to that.' By far his longest
work, the tetralogy over the fifteen years since its first conception had
become, as he conceded, 'a monstrous curiosity, or a curious monstrosity'.
As early as 1931 he had foreseen a result more convoluted, and with more
of a will of its own, than even *The Magic Mountain*, and he was very
uncertain even then whether it would find readers. 'But what I do know is
that it gives me an infinitely pleasurable occupation.'[15] Now, as he wrote to
Knopf, he could hardly imagine how he could have survived so many hard
years without it as his companion. The laconic biblical narrative—the
brothers' jealousy of Jacob's favourite son, their disposal of him in the well,
bringing their father his blood-stained coat of many colours as proof of his
death, his rescue and transport to Egypt by the Midianites, his successful
rise to influence and power in Pharaoh's Egypt, his resistance to the
attractions of Potiphar's wife, and the final reunion with father and family
without revenge—he had seen from the start, like Goethe, as merely the
bones of a more extensive tale. But in what he admitted was 'epic pedantry',
'the fanaticism of the *ab ovo*', his *Tales of Jacob*, the first volume, had begun
by digressing deep into the story of the forefathers and father of his hero.
Extensive studies of the historical 'truth', which was in fact largely myth,
and the Palestinian and Egyptian background, lent him the ability to 'speak
the language and develop his fictions in its spirit', with a convincingly
learned veneer that was largely spurious, and to attempt a 'psychology of
myth', uniting sympathy and reason, with the ironical style which always
attracted him, in a narrative both real and humorous.

With his innate fascination with numbers, he had found amusement in
a 'certain numerological mystique' in the organization of his text—after the
prologue, seven main chapters with sections alternating between ten, five,
and seven—and he adhered to the seven-fold division for each of the
sequels. The second volume, *The Young Joseph*, had continued in the same
quasi-mythological strain, respecting the 'facts' from the Bible as though
they were scientifically established, but using his scholarly apparatus as a
cloak, 'a mask, an artistic device'.[16] These two volumes, completed before
the Nazi seizure of power, were published in Germany; Joseph's involuntary exile in the third, *Joseph in Egypt*, had coincided with the first years
of his own exile, while the fourth, *Joseph the Provider*, with his hero

[15] xi 425.    [16] Faesi 30.

successfully setting up a benevolent economic dictatorship similar to Roosevelt's, was completed during his establishment in California.

Personal experience had thus lent an unexpected contemporary symbolism to this story of the distant past. Though he was far from drawing any direct parallels, it is not a flight of fancy to see overtones of Nazism in his Egyptian scene, and in his Joseph a fictional anti-Hitler, a personality not unlike the admired President of the United States. Heinrich was one of the few early readers to notice in the social legislation of the Judaeo-Egyptian the similarity with that of Roosevelt, Churchill, Beveridge—and the Soviet Union.[17] Over the years, the stubborn determination to finish his 'comic fairy-tale of humanity' had held many moments of despair, and towards the end he had to try to correct the prolixity to which his age made him prone: but the sometimes 'soggy mass of dough' held enough raisins and spices, he felt, to make the final result tasty. For English readers, as always with Thomas Mann, the humour of which he was proud is faint, and the Joyce-like abundance of polymathic learning and over-long digressions hard to digest. For Orville Prescott, reviewing *Joseph the Provider* for the *New York Times* in 1944, his 'brilliantly brocaded tapestry', combining 'solemn Germanic pedantry' with 'an oriental luxuriance of imagery', 'an ornate . . . excess of words that never uses one where two or two hundred will do', was a 'profoundly impressive work . . . but as fiction it is stiff, pompous and . . . aggressively, soporifically dull'. Hermann Hesse, however, hearing how astounded a reader of the episode of Thamar and the 'sin of Judas' had been to find all this was actually in the Bible—from forty brief sentences there, full forty pages in Thomas Mann, without the slightest invented addition—found it a joy to see that 'poets are after all not entirely superfluous'.[18]

Now, however, early in 1943, publication of the fourth volume in English was still a long way off. Knopf had been mightily relieved to learn of its completion, and sent congratulatory champagne, but his idea of an autumn deadline would clearly be hard to meet when Helen Lowe-Porter's translation was coming on so slowly. She had told Mann in Princeton she was feeling her advancing age, and looked on this task as her last major translation, and though he urged her to do her best, he was worried at the 'catastrophe' for his finances the delay represented. In German it was to be published in Sweden, and during January Bermann had elaborate arrangements in hand for copies of the manuscript to be sent over; but, as the royalty statement for May to December 1942 had shown, receipts from such an edition would be relatively small. As before, a few copies of a

---

[17] *Brw. HM* 310.
[18] V. Michels (ed.), *Hermann Hesse in Augenzeugenberichten* (Frankfurt a. M.: Suhrkamp, 1987), 239.

mimeographed German version would be published in America to safe-guard the copyright, but the English edition would simply have to wait for the translation. Meanwhile, as he told Agnes Meyer, he was with Moses 'in the Kadesh oasis on the Sinai peninsula, dealing with a volcanic law-giver who is much less conciliatory and calm than Joseph'.

The turning-point in the war had now definitely come, at least against Germany and Italy. The Russians' brilliant encirclement of von Paulus's Sixth Army at Stalingrad in November had developed into a vast offensive, bringing the Sixth Army's surrender and the recapture in February 1943 of Rostov, Kursk, and Kharkov; in North Africa, the Americans and British made slower but steady progress. Thomas Mann, listening to Roosevelt's hope for an end before the year was out, was less inclined to such opti-mism, and Churchill's later forecast of two more years seemed to him more probable. He felt now the depression that always followed in the period between the final lines of a manuscript and its publication, the doubt whether it had turned out well and whether the work had been in vain. But with him such depression never lasted long if he had something new to turn to, 'the narcotic of production': and that was at hand in the 'Moses novella', as he was now calling it, in the realization that the 'long short story' he had in mind would probably go far beyond the concept of the publisher who had commissioned it.

He described to Agnes an interesting evening meeting with the former American ambassador to the Soviet Union, Joseph E. Davies, now assistant to Cordell Hull. The Meyers' eldest daughter, Florence, married to the well-known actor Oscar Homolka and living in Bel-Air, had invited the Manns on 9 January to join the Feuchtwangers and others to meet Davies, whose successful book *Mission to Moscow* had been published in 1941; and Mann was struck by his optimism over the Russian successes, which if they could deny Hitler the Baku oilfields would in his view write 'finis' to the German campaign. Florence's own report on the evening showed a refreshing disrespect for the master and his wife which her mother will have received with mixed feelings, to say the least: 'we asked the Thomas's *after* dinner because a) we couldn't face the idea of Katya holding forth and b) they never ask us over. . . . You should have heard Thomas and Joe mutually congratulating each other on their literary works! It was a riot. And even Katya was subdued and decent . . .'[19] So candid a view is rare to find on the force of Katia's personality, normally overshadowed by her husband.

Agnes's letters of this time have not been preserved (Mann's diary in-dicates how often he 'eliminated' those he found distasteful and dis-putatious), but from Mann's own it is evident how she was still labouring

---

[19] *AM Brw.* 962 f.

under the difficulties of maintaining a friendship which meant so much to her.

I know the coldness and discouragement that emanates from me . . . you of course realize that the uneasy atmosphere with which I surrounded Goethe in the novel, to the point of comedy, was self-discipline and self-mockery. But that I can laugh at myself is after all a human trait, isn't it? And I am conscious of something else too: I know I have a lively, indeed very strong, capacity for gratitude. Let me believe that these two qualities are enough to base a friendship on!

Goethe, he said, also liked to repeat the biblical words of the tongues of angels as no more than a tinkling cymbal without love: 'I would despair if I had to admit that I have no love in me. And since I do *not* despair, must or should you despair over me?'[20] The time he could find to devote to such lengthy outpourings was a measure of his self-interest as much in the narcissistic as in the purely material sense.

   The Borgeses' extended their Christmas stay well into March—the husband's vehemence, obstinacy in argument, and oppressive Italian patriotism becoming a burden for Thomas, while for Katia Elisabeth's attachment to the parental home seemed excessive. But it had been harmonious; little Angelica ('Gogoi', as she called herself, or sometimes 'Borgelica'), if not as enchanting as Frido, was a droll companion; and Mann's work could go on as usual. Between minor commitments—an additional broadcast for the BBC on ten years of National Socialism, a lecture in Los Angeles—by the middle of February over fifty pages had accumulated of *The Tables of the Law*, and in three more weeks, with nearly fifty more, this sequel to the *Joseph* was done. Writing to Klaus, in camp in Arkansas, and congratulating him on his study of Gide, he said he had finished so rapidly that he need no longer feel envious of his son's readier pen: after a big work, he always liked something of this kind that gave no trouble. In his methodical way, he at once packed away all the *Joseph* material, and turned his thoughts to the plan of a work on the Faust theme, which had first occurred to him some forty years earlier. Such a link with his earliest days was attractive, as he recalled Goethe's words that the happiest man was he who could tie in the end of his life with its beginning. Now, the demonic turn of history since the advent of Nazism, the apocalyptic outcome that must lie in store and that he could not but wish on an unrecalcitrant Germany, seemed to make this the right moment.

   The next few days were spent going through all his old papers and notebooks in the search for his earlier ideas on the subject, and for material, particularly in his diaries, that would now be relevant. He turned up his original notion for a novella, a few lines jotted down around 1904: 'the

[20] *AM Brw.* 454 f.

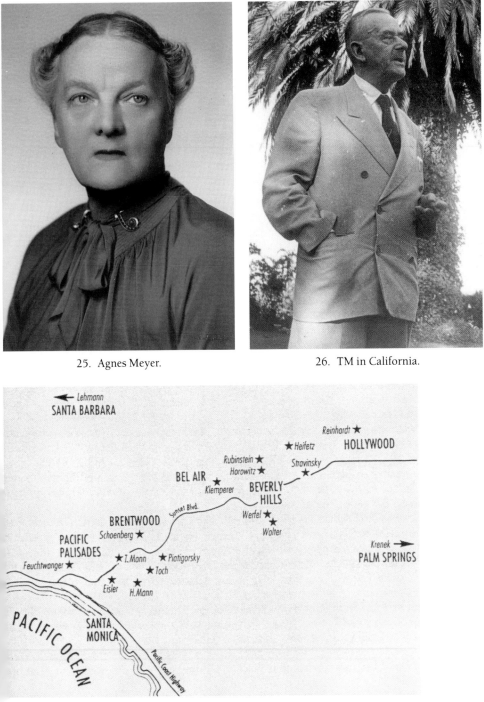

25. Agnes Meyer.

26. TM in California.

27. 'Exiles in Paradise': Hollywood/Los Angeles.

28. Thomas and Katia Mann, 1940.

29. TM reading to the family, 1940. (*Left to right*) TM, Michael, Katia, Golo,
Erika, Klaus, Elisabeth.

30. TM with Heinrich Mann on his arrival in New York, October 1940.

31. Erika as war correspondent.

32. Klaus as American soldier.

33. Gret Mann with Toni and Frido, *c*.1942.

34. TM reading to Frido and Toni, 1948.

35. Thomas and Katia Mann with grandchildren, December 1944. (*Left to right*) TM (*standing*), Borgese, Frido, Katia, Angelica and Domenica Borgese, Elisabeth Mann-Borgese, Gret Mann with Toni, Michael Mann.

36. Katia, Erika, and Elisabeth Mann-Borgese with TM leaving Billings hospital, Chicago, April 1946.

37. Erika, Katia, and TM in Pacific Palisades, 1951.

*top left*
38. TM, Katia, and Erika boarding plane for Europe, 16 May 1949.

*top right*
39. TM in Weimar, 1949.

*above left*
40. Heinrich Mann in Santa Monica, 1950.

*above right*
41. Thomas and Katia Mann in Sorrento, *en route* to Taormina, February 1954.

*op left*
2. TM at desk, 1954.

*op right*
3. Katia Mann at the grave.

*bove left*
4. Elisabeth Mann-Borgese in the 1970s.

*bove right*
5. Monika Mann in Capri, 1986.

*top left*
46. Last photograph of Michael Mann, 1970.

*top right*
47. Erika in the 1960s.

*above left*
48. Golo Mann in the 1970s.

*above right*
49. Katia at the TM centenary in Kilchberg, 1975, aged 93.

syphilitic artist: as Dr Faust and in bond to the Devil. The disease has the effect of intoxication, stimulus, inspiration: in ecstatic enthusiasm he can create wonderful works of genius, the Devil guides his hand. But finally the Devil comes to claim him: paralysis . . .'[21] Transported back then, as he delved further, to the Paul Ehrenberg and *Tonio Kröger* time, the Munich days, his other unrealized plans for novels—*The Loved Ones* and *Maya*— and all the emotions of old loves and heartaches which he had thought to overcome by turning them into art, but which had lingered as a 'basic unhappiness' beneath his astonishing success, he realized for the first time what it meant to be without the *Joseph* work, 'the task which was always beside and before me through the whole decade'. With the Moses 'sequel' too finished off, the comfortable feeling was lost of dogged application to an accustomed task. 'Will I find the strength for new conceptions? Is the theme not already exhausted? And if not—can I find the mood for it?' And his hesitation lingered, even as he began to reread the *Gesta Romanorum*, the familiar book of medieval legends, and took up Stevenson's *Jekyll and Hyde*, or a book on *Nietzsche and Women*.

In his awareness of the need to combine the pathological (Nietzsche-syphilis) with the legendary (Faustus), he was strangely timid over the project, whose difficulties seemed insurmountable, and he began to feel he had so far always drawn back from it because he felt it would be his last. Katia's idea of a continuation of *Felix Krull*, which so many of his readers had pressed for, was an interesting and not unattractive alternative— resuming where he had left off over thirty years earlier to begin *Death in Venice*, and treating all his work since, including the *Joseph*, as simply a vast interpolation. Would not that project be even better to bring his life full circle—at 68, continuing where he interrupted it at 32, once more 'under the spell of Goethean parody' in a fully satisfying theme which had never been lost to sight through the years? For it, stacks of material were to hand, though some had been left behind in Munich, and he began to picture all this brought forward to replace that for the *Joseph*. To complete this 'caprice' would show a certain defiance, self-loyalty, 'mockingly superior endurance' after the tribulations his life had brought: and there was much to be said for building on an existing foundation. In *Time* magazine, appropriately enough, an article on his *Joseph* lecture juxtaposed pictures of Thomas Mann and Goethe, 'partly malicious but respectful'. Listening to a speech from Churchill, forecasting two more years of war, he felt clear that before the end came he would have to write another novel, whatever its theme, but as the weeks went by was still dull in spirit and 'unsure of my productive future', as well as occasionally overtaken by doubt over the

[21] *Nb.* 7, 155.

whole point of the war. (The reports now reaching America of wholesale slaughter of the Jews seemed to encounter at least indifference, often outright approval, and he mused grimly that there could be no further idea of a 'people's war'; it was simply a battle between imperialisms.)

Taking out the packet of *Krull* material on 10 April, with the ideas he had noted for its continuation, he thought how akin it was, in the protagonist's isolation and solitude, to the Faust theme, and finally convinced himself that the latter, however difficult of realization, must be the right one to tackle. From now on, all his study was directed towards it—earlier Faust stories, a history of music, Luther's letters, Dürer's prints, other books on the German Middle Ages—for the conception of his Faustian artist was of a musician and composer and former theological student, and his career, through temptation to final relapse into Nietzschean madness, as an allegory of the irrationalism of Hitlerite Germany, whose 'life' was the work of the Devil. As he wrote to Klaus, now a staff-sergeant and about to depart overseas, on 27 April, it would be from the 'Maupassant-Nietzsche-Hugo Wolf etc. ambience of destiny'—

in short the theme of evil inspiration and flights of genius ending with being fetched by the Devil, i.e. paralysis. But it's also the idea of intoxicated delirium in general and its combination with anti-reason, hence also the political, the fascist, and with that the sad fate of Germany. The whole thing with old-German and Lutheran colouring (hero originally a theologian), but taking place in the Germany of yesterday and today. It will be my 'Parsifal' . . .[22]

Lacking, for the moment, were ideas for 'pregnant' characters to surround his subject, like those he had found in the sanatorium staff for *The Magic Mountain*, or in the Bible for *Joseph*. America, without historical depth, was an arid scene, and for the background he would have to rely on memories or pictures, and draw on intuition, as soon as he had a firmer idea of the entourage. Through April and May, as was his practice, he cast around for expert help in specific areas which would bear directly on his subject's life, both in wide reading and from available friends and contacts, like the theologian Paul Tillich, in exile in New York, and Bruno Walter, both of whom received detailed questionnaires on the educational methods of the early years of the century. At the same time, the notebooks and diaries yielded many ideas for characters and incidents he could use.

The arrival of Michael's two boys early in May (to stay while Gret took a job as cleaner in a tank workshop) renewed his thought of taking the charming Frido as model for the little Nepomuk Scheidewein, 'Echo', to be the delight of his hero's final years and in his tragic loss the signal for the final collapse, all of which he was already beginning to see in outline.

[22] KlM *Br. Antw.* 509 f.

Above all, he counted himself lucky on 8 May to make social contact with the Austrian composer Arnold Schönberg, now Professor of Music at California State University in Los Angeles and inventor of the modern twelve-tone system, and to find him only too pleased to continue their association. Schönberg maintained that since 1940 modern music, twelve-tone too, was allowed in Nazi Germany, to a certain extent even favoured, in spite of Nazi views on 'degenerate art'. That would have to be brought in, he noted after the long evening with him, and began to see how music's progression to atonality, in the 'iron constructivism' of twelve-tone, could be shown as representative of both Germany's and his subject's submission to a diabolical fascism.

As his notes accumulated, 200 pages of a miscellany bearing on his theme, the form of the novel became clear to him: a fictitious biography of a composer, Adrian Leverkühn, roughly his own contemporary, written two years after his tragic death by his friend Serenus Zeitblom—a mild schoolmaster of humanist leanings—during the apocalypse of Germany's defeat. By this device, he could achieve a narrative on two planes: the shattering events of a momentous life now over, recounted for posterity under the actual impact of the Allied offensives against Germany and her impending annihilation, and thus lending the whole book an atmosphere of reality. At the same time, the strong contrast between Adrian's cold genius and the innocent stolidity of Zeitblom would give scope for an essential leavening of humour. He began to write on 23 May 1943, and set this date in the modest Zeitblom's introductory paragraphs on himself and his relationship with his departed friend: a detail, as he wrote later, characteristic of the whole work, into which, as it proceeded, there would be repeated interpolations of the actual events of the war. 'I've decided to allow the war time for one more fairly extensive novel,' he had written to Ida Herz on 9 May. As it turned out, the conflict would end in Germany's collapse a year before he could complete the work, and what he was to go through, in a creation so intimately bound up with the fate of his country, would very nearly bring his own end.

As the weeks of intensive preparation came to a close, and he was set to begin, it had been unbearably irritating to receive a 'stupid' letter from Agnes Meyer, protesting against Klaus's branding of Claudel as a fascist, in his Gide book, and agonizing over a public controversy involving not only him and his father, but also MacLeish. Enclosed was a malignant letter to the *Herald Tribune* from a Smith College woman academic, with allusions to the 'cynical dislike of democracy' in Thomas Mann's 1918 *Reflections* and to a stipend of '$9,000 a year for some work in the Library of Congress that can be done in California'. He was incensed, not only by the attack on Klaus, whose treatment of Claudel had in fact been highly respectful, but also by her insensitivity in sending on such grossly inaccurate and 'insignificant blather' with accompanying hand-wringing over the unhappy situation for one to whom Claudel and he were 'equally holy'. Provoking though this was, his reaction cannot be seen as reasonable: but it was almost as though she had deliberately chosen to inflict this trouble on him at the critical moment when he was about to start on his new work. And once again, he felt it imperative to put an end to the relationship; what was more, in view of the malicious *Tribune* publicity, he must offer the Library his resignation.

Whole days were spent over a reply in strong, yet sometimes almost pathetic, terms to this 'wretched woman', a highly annoying distraction from his plans which left him nervous and sleepless and unable to concentrate on anything else. He upbraided her for her 'unconcealed disparagement and rejection' of his children, and for calling *him* to account for the only passage in Klaus's Gide book to which there could be objection—Claudel's possibly collaborationist attitude after the occupation of France.

I must suffer for it and . . . see the shattering of a friendship which was dear to me . . . to which I have devoted more thought, nervous energy, and work at the desk than to any other relationship in the world. . . . Nothing was right, nothing enough. . . . you always wanted me different from the way I am. You had not the humour, or the respect, or the discretion to take me as I am. You always wanted to educate, dominate, improve, redeem me. In vain I warned you . . . I cannot but feel your outbreak of wrath . . . is merely the eruption of a profounder disappointment . . . I had wished so much [for] balance and serenity, [for] calm, invulnerable cordiality in this relationship of ours. But now it has reached the crisis which probably threatened it from the first moment. Let us grant it and ourselves the tranquillity which alone can restore our psychological equilibrium. I at least need this, to get out of this torment and find my way back to myself and my work—it doesn't yet look as though this will be easy. . . . Full of good wishes for you and yours, I bid you a heartfelt farewell.[23]

Neither this nor his letter to MacLeish at the Library had the effect he thought he wanted. Her replies he found full of misunderstandings and stupidities (she spoke of their 'mysterious, suprapersonal affinity', the friendship for her an 'ecstasy', complained of his stony heart)—but in the end the situation between them remained as before, he could only resort to an evasive politeness to keep the distance. Nor was MacLeish, who had already written a dignified and factual reply to the *Tribune*, about to accept his resignation: his connection with the Library was one of their principal distinctions, he wrote. At the time, however, Mann felt relief at having

---

[23] *AM Brw.* 477 ff.

taken these carefully considered steps, in a 'balancing act which has stretched my nerves no little'.

For her part, Agnes was not prepared to loosen a bond in which she could reasonably feel she had much to offer him, and probably realized how much he needed her as confessor. (When Knopf shortly afterwards enquired whether she would relieve Helen Lowe-Porter at the translator's post when the time came for the new book, she readily agreed.) Looking back in October, she felt that their testing of the relationship 'to the limit in abusing each other' had cleared the air: she realized 'how really difficult it is for him to accept from any woman a relationship that is democratic not only in mind but also in heart. He is always reminding me how old he is (I think in self-defence) but actually he has more elasticity than most young people . . .'[24] At all events, there was no break in their correspondence, and by June he was reporting as calmly as before on the progress of the novel, which despite all this had advanced to the third chapter, and telling her of his amusement over a *Saturday Evening Post* article on Eugene Meyer and his wife, which described her enthusiasm for his work, and the 'tide of energy' surging through the house which appeared to overwhelm the 'shy, retiring' novelist when he came to stay.

He related too his appearance on 17 June at a protest meeting in San Francisco against the horrific persecution of the Jews in Germany. Again, an unwelcome interruption to the work, but unavoidable; and although probably ineffectual with its four-point resolution urging America and Britain to relax the rules on asylum, at least a popular and generous demonstration before an audience of 10,000, mostly non-Jews he thought. Germany's defeat was still a long way off, and he reflected in disquiet on the march of the Afrika Korps into captivity in Tunisia: a sign not of demoralization, but merely of saving men for the next war, 'and that, unless every effort is made to remove from Germany the means for it, will be with us in ten years' time'.

The grandsons' long stay came to an end in July, when they were returned to Michael in San Francisco—for Katia, with little or no help in the house, a relief, though she had taken as much pleasure in them as he had. Golo had also been with them for a month, convalescing from a difficult hernia-operation, before returning to his college post to await the call-up due soon; and with Erika also now away, on a new assignment as war correspondent in the Middle East, the house was empty again. As he worked on steadily at *Doktor Faustus* through the summer, and read Theodor Adorno's draft tract on 'The Philosophy of Modern Music', the difficulty of what he had taken on became more and more apparent: how

[24] Ibid. 973.

to contrive a fictitious picture of a musician of rank and importance, and describe his non-existent works in a contemporary musical world in which all the leading roles were taken. Leverkühn's youth, studies, and early development, as seen through the eyes of his admirer-narrator Zeitblom, were not hard to make attractive; but presenting his invention of the twelve-tone system (for which he himself had no particular enthusiasm) and its use in the creation of authentic works of art in a detestable world, would be another matter—delicate indeed, as he would find, for after all that system was of Schönberg's devising.

By August, with seven chapters done, he felt the first *élan* abating, and broke off to prepare his autumn Washington lecture. Dictating it to Katia now that Konni Kellen had been called up, he hoped that what Washington would regard as 'leftish' was sufficiently 'dusted over with conservative and traditional sugar', for he did not hesitate to stress the democracies' complicity in the rise of fascist dictatorship, nor to 'poke some fun at the bourgeois world's absurd panic over communism'.[25] To Agnes Meyer he described it as less a formal lecture than a 'high-level chat, on Germany, Wagner, Europe, the coming humanism, the similarity between our horror of social change and our ear's resistance to progress in music [but stressing] my elemental need for balance . . . I sit by instinct on the *higher* side of the heeling boat, not on that practically in the water which the conformists of the day crowd towards'.[26]

In September, however, there came renewed impetus for the novel as he launched into the important influence of Leverkühn's tutor, the Pennsylvania-born organist Kretzschmar. For that, discussions with Schönberg and listening to Adorno's critical presentation of his theory, as well as his exposition of Beethoven's last piano sonata Op. 111, gave him exactly what he needed. In the background to these endeavours— and indeed, in view of his aim for the novel as an allegory of Germany's fate, of vital concern for them—came renewed political speculation in America, as the Allied invasion of Sicily and Italy led to Italy's capitulation and Mussolini's arrest, and the question of what was finally to be done with Germany became a live issue. Early in July, a *Washington Post* article spoke of the non-party fighter against Nazism Thomas Mann as the best choice for President of a 'reborn German republic'—a thought which he himself ridiculed. 'Germany will be under a complete tutelage,' he wrote to Agnes Meyer, 'and need no head at all, only sensible local administrations'; in any case, Washington would have its word to say on the matter, and there he did not feel, as a so-called 'premature anti-fascist', he was all that welcome. 'It would only be under the greatest pressure that I could ever

25 Br. ii, 340.    26 AM Brw. 509 f.

contemplate playing a political role.' His statement to the Soviet agency Tass on the manifesto of the 'Free Germany Committee' in Moscow held the same message he had constantly repeated in his BBC broadcasts: that only a genuine renunciation of their Nazi leaders could rehabilitate the Germans.

Following a meeting on 1 August, however, of the west-coast exiles (Feuchtwanger, his brother, Marcuse, and Brecht among them) he withdrew his signature from their draft manifesto, which insisted on a sharp distinction between the Hitler regime and the German people. He maintained, to Brecht's disgust, that this was a falsely patriotic betrayal of the Allied war-effort, and that it was not up to exiles to give America advice. As far as he was concerned, no fall for the Germans, no penance, could be deep enough 'after the vicious presumption, the wild frenzy of superiority and chimeras of power this people has shown in its intoxication'. The idea, becoming fashionable, that 'nothing must happen to Germany', could never be his. He mistrusted Russian and communist aims, but paramount was his opposition to any distinction between National Socialists and Germans as a whole. What caused his 'suffering over Germany' had been the appalling fact that the leaders of her culture had either succumbed to Nazism or at least gone along with it, and *Faustus* was to be his expression of that suffering. The controversy over German responsibility, however, and whether or not to distinguish between 'good' and 'bad' Germans, continued till the end of the war and after, with frequent questioning of his democratic standpoint and pressure from well-meaning American liberals to explain himself.

Agnes Meyer, who had volunteered to translate his Washington lecture, was not afraid to criticize what she considered the weaknesses of the text she received. She thought it 'an ungenerous effort': 'you turned from the strain of . . . a great new novel to toss off a sop to everyday life'. 'What the public here expects from you is not a discussion of communism but of Germany and its possible return to human society. . . . Do you still believe in Germany or do you not? If . . . the balance of mind and spirit is important, what can Germany still contribute to [it] as a warning or a help?' And she begged him to recast it 'in a mold more worthy of your great powers and your unique world role'. He was reluctant to do so, stressing that he had deliberately made it too long so it could be adapted to the various audiences before whom he would present it, and that there would be time to discuss it when they met. She did the job, but still complained he had given no indication of Germany's cultural contributions to Western civilization, and he took care to insert a little to this effect. In the end, in fact, his text for 'The War and the Future', as used in the Library of Congress on 13 October and adapted in his later appearances, owed a good deal to her criticisms—though she exaggerated in telling Golo afterwards that he had 'revamped the whole thing'.

Her initial reaction was in fact not unjustified. After Washington, what became a two-month lecture-tour (Hunter College, New York; Boston; Manchester, New Hampshire; New Bedford; Montreal; Chicago; Lewiston, Maine; Columbia University, New York; Daylesford, Philadelphia; Cincinnati; Kansas City) was largely the presentation of recycled Thomas Mann, as he made adroit use of what was to hand, now from his new draft under various titles, now from his Joseph talk, or on one occasion impromptu. Throughout, *Faustus* was never far from his thoughts: he read extracts to friends, considered changes to the Kretzschmar chapter, read Adorno's manuscript again, and turned over the problem of inspiration for the syphilitic artist. But there was much business too, his own in discussions with Bermann and others, and also in the matter of the growing 'Free Germany' movement among the exiles, and their pressure for him to assume a leadership from which he devoutly hoped God would preserve him. At their request, he took the question up with Berle in the State Department, and was relieved when Berle advised caution in thus lending his name—a diplomatic response which he interpreted, and reported back, as the Department's aversion to anything approaching a government in exile. In a letter to the *New York Times*, on 30 November, denying rumours that he had been invited by the State Department to join or preside over a Free German Committee, he said that was a body for which he did not consider the moment opportune. His evasion was, of course, not popular among the exiles. Tillich considered he had condemned Germany to death, and Brecht sharply criticized his lack of faith in democracy, inditing bitter verses headed 'When . . . Thomas Mann granted the Americans and the English the right to punish the German people with a ten-year sentence for the crimes of the Hitler regime.' If the Russians helped that party-liner to power in Germany, Mann commented to Agnes Meyer, 'he'll do me all kinds of harm. But I've acted correctly.'

During this long absence from home in Pacific Palisades, its comfort and regular meals greatly missed, they had had the joy of seeing both Erika, back briefly from the Middle East to undertake a lecture tour of her own, and Klaus on leave from Italy. Both were due off again almost immediately, however: Erika on another war-correspondent assignment, and Klaus sailing for Casablanca on Christmas Eve under the aegis of the grandly titled Psychological Warfare Bureau (which would later mean work on the army paper *Stars and Stripes* in Italy); their farewells took place in a Kansas City hotel room, early in December, in the prospect of a long separation. Golo too was now in the army, and after his basic training found himself transferred to special duties whose nature he was somewhat perplexed about, but which turned out to be intelligence. On a few days' leave he was the only one to be able to join them for Christmas, Michael being on concert duty for the troops. On New Year's Eve, not unnaturally, Katia was in melancholy mood, missing the children and grandchildren, and hoping only that the coming year would not bring the loss of a son. Thomas, too, looking to resuming work on the novel, was more sad than hopeful that the rest of the winter, and the crucial events impending in the war, after the Teheran conference of the 'Big Three' (Roosevelt, Churchill, Stalin), might bring progress for both.

3

'Crimes have been committed which no psychology can help to excuse'                                              (TM, 11 March 1945)

On 4 January 1944 Thomas and Katia underwent the official examination for American citizenship, important, he felt, for his status there, and practical for post-war conditions, though he was a little uneasy at abandoning the Czechs in this way. The following day an alarming report appeared in the *LA Times*—'Heinrich Mann Wife a Victim of Drug Overdose': she had been hospitalized after taking it apparently under threat of prosecution for a traffic violation. It was not alarming enough to interrupt work, however, and they were content to leave a note at noon at Heinrich's apartment when they found him out. For the work on *Faustus* had been resumed—with renewed doubts whether he had not embarked for the first time on an impossible task. To treat *of* music was after all quite different from philosophizing *about* it; reading a book on Alban Berg, he was uncertain whether this would help or merely intimidate him, in his anxiety over the technical aspect; and he felt his love for music waning just when he needed it. Visiting Franz Werfel on his sick-bed and hearing his extravagant praise for the 'immortal' *Buddenbrooks*, which he had just reread in three days, made him wonder whether that one youthful book might after all be his only lasting achievement, and everything since just a tolerably interesting way of life. Not, certainly, like the *Cavalleria Rusticana* for Mascagni, perhaps more comparable with the *Freischütz* for Weber: but he had at least emulated Goethe in giving his life shape with *The Magic Mountain, Joseph, Lotte*. It was a resignation that did not last, as he renewed his contact with Adorno and discussed the work so far; but he was not contented with his progress, feeling the book had begun to slip out of control, in a fatal tendency to take on *Magic Mountain* dimensions.

His age was clearly beginning to tell, the routine of mornings on the manuscript left him indisposed afterwards to meet the many demands in other directions, and sometimes it seemed as though not much time was left for him. It was something of a shock too—salutary perhaps, when he had just heard of vast sums in prospect for the MGM film of *Joseph*—to receive in March Hesse's new novel *The Glass Bead Game*, just published in Switzerland. Here was a remarkable coincidence—a strangely similar fictitious biography, in which among amusing invented names he found himself as 'Thomas von der Trave', Master of the Game: 'a famous, widely-travelled and worldly man, conciliatory and outgoing, but in the Game of the most vigilant and ascetic strictness . . . his brilliantly-constructed, formally unsurpassable ploys showing for connoisseurs a close familiarity with the recondite problems of the game world'. Such a reminder that one was not alone in the world was disconcerting, he noted: and the similarity of the two works was startling, not to say uncanny, though he felt his own would be much sharper, more pointed in tone than the other's philosophical and religious cast.

The debate, among both the exiles and American liberals like Dorothy Thompson, continued to rage on how to treat Germany after her defeat, and how the Big Three demand for unconditional surrender was to be interpreted. With colleagues like Viertel and Feuchtwanger, he found the discussion fruitless and tedious, revealing as it did the Germans' tendency to see themselves as the centre of the world. It had always been evident that Hitler would lead to catastrophe: had they expected not to have to atone for his, and their, excesses? 'I don't take it so much to heart. It has always been a singular fate, half painful, half honourable, to be born a German.'[27] What happened to Germany was not all that important, and it was anyway far too early to talk of it. 'Advise clemency, and you will probably be horribly disowned by the Germans; advise pitilessness, and you get into a false and intolerable position towards the country whose language you write.'[28] Though intrigued to receive a request in January for an article on the subject for the London *Evening Standard*, he refused, reflecting how precarious and heavy with responsibility the task was—'and does it interest me enough? . . . What a revolutionized, proletarized, capsized, naked and destitute, disorganized, faithless, ruined rabble will have to be dealt with. . . . For a decent liberal-democratic republic, the country is lost.' Serving on the jury of a prize competition in the New York *Aufbau* for a new German national anthem was an unappealing and useless duty, for after eleven or twelve years under Hitler the people would not be in a mood for singing for a long time to come. As he read of the effects of a massive Allied air-raid, and the onrush of Russian victories in the east, he thought with dismay how Germany was always either too powerful or powerless. The

[27] 44/113.     [28] Bl. 10, 27.

expected second front in the west still looked a long way off—like most people, he had no conception of the vast preparations needed for a seaborne invasion of fortress Europe, especially with caution to minimize casualties—and in moments of pessimism during these early months of 1944 he came to feel that neither he nor those prosecuting the war would live to see its end.

Financially, he was better placed than ever. The Library of Congress appointment had been renewed for a further year, while in January the Book of the Month Club announced its provisional choice of *Joseph the Provider* for later in the year. That meant further delay in its regular publication with Knopf, but it seemed he could expect 12,000 dollars as a start, a respectable sum even after taxes. By March, in fact, Knopf was assuring him of at least 40,000 dollars, and a first printing of 35,000 of his own edition—a kind of boom in his production which seemed to him the true rapture of American prosperity. Recalling to Agnes Meyer that the Library stipend was to last only as long as he needed it, he had to confess that it was now hardly essential: however, as it had been renewed, he would use it basically for the support of his brother and other writers less well placed. He also relayed Golo's amusing account of his transfer to Washington: after a clandestine rendezvous on a street corner ('is this the car for Mrs Smith?'), he was whisked off to a country house where he was to learn to become an instructor in intelligence work—'fantastic!' (From Golo he heard her remark that his letters betrayed his aversion for her: a highly intelligent observation, he noted sardonically, considering that they were full of 'devotion, admiration, gratitude, solicitude, even gallantry'.)[29] He accepted her renunciation of the *Faustus* translation task gracefully, in secret probably with relief, and altogether his tone to her in these months was more light-hearted than he really felt in his doubts over *Faustus*—not omitting the *LA Times* front-page report of a pet canary to sing at its owner's funeral in Tacoma, which had brought him to tears of laughter, more characteristic 'than anything you can tell me of the light and dark side of American civilization'.

Erika had hoped this time for an assignment to Russia, representing the Boston *Monitor*—provoking the acid comment from Agnes Meyer that the Russians had no time for 'tourists'. But it had not materialized, and, restless as ever, she was soon back again on the lecture circuit. She stood unhesitatingly at her father's side in his attitude towards the misplaced patriotism of those exiles pressing for a 'soft peace' with the Germans, arguing powerfully, in an article for the New York *Aufbau*, against blaming only the Nazi leadership for the sins of the whole people. She found no sign, among those

[29] *Tb.* vi, 22.

fighting like lions in Hitler's cause, of the so-called 'other Germany' the advocates of a Free Germany thought to distinguish; and she pursued her case more vigorously than her father, with letters both open, to the *émigré* press, and private, to individuals who sought to further Tillich's 'Council for a Democratic Germany'. It was 'lamentable and shameful and inconceivably inappropriate' at this point to perceive a 'better Germany'. The world would be happy to see one born and flourishing—but meanwhile it 'fights on, and waits'.[30]

The American appetite for lectures of enlightenment from apparently knowledgeable pundits was insatiable, and the members of this 'amazing family', including Klaus before his induction into the army, had been tireless in meeting it, though, with the agents taking a large percentage of the fees, it was not all that profitable. For Thomas Mann the reception committees at his staging-points were always deferential: local dignitaries, of university, city, women's club or Jewish organizations, were eager to offer him hospitality, transport, and other comforts; his train reservations were in the best conditions wartime America could offer; and he found time for relaxation in cinema or theatre, at concerts or sometimes opera performances. For Erika however the criss-crossing of the continent was in rather less comfortable conditions. When in the east, he and the family were not backward in exploiting to the full Agnes Meyer's readiness to help. On his October visit, he had asked if Erika, just arriving back from her Middle East tour, might stay the night at Crescent Place to give him and Katia the opportunity to meet her; Golo was now always a welcome visitor there when his 'special duties' allowed; her limousine stood ready to collect Thomas and Katia and their usually voluminous luggage whenever they stepped off the train in the capital; and her assistance was invoked at all points where administrative or publishing hurdles were encountered, be it a re-entry permit for the non-citizens returning from Canada or the placing of an article.

Perhaps not the least amazing aspect of the family was the way they contrived to meet so often, thanks to mail communications wondrously prompt by today's standards, but with no expense spared on the telegraph—the meetings no doubt an extra load on the parents' budget, over which Katia kept a watchful eye, even in the euphoria of *Joseph the Provider* as Book of the Month. Chicago made a natural break on the east–west itinerary, so that they were frequent visitors to Elisabeth and her family, and Erika or Golo had sometimes joined them there; New York's Bedford Hotel, a favourite for other exiles too, made a temporary home for them all when they were in the east; and there were brief encounters in such

[30] EM *Br. Antw.* i, 190.

unlikely places as the Kansas City hotel in December. Meanwhile Pacific Palisades stood open whenever Erika or others of the children could reach it, like Michael's family from nearby San Francisco, or Katia's brother Peter Pringsheim. Arrangements for all this were naturally always in Katia's hands, undoubtedly a burden for her, with letters and telegrams, as she spared him the complicated details on their journeys, and the return to San Remo Drive, where she had no staff now, needing the enlistment of willing friends. He could airily quote Goethe on the 'benevolence of our contemporaries'—'there were people to fetch us from Los Angeles station, others who at once brought butter, cream, cakes, flowers to our ser-vantless home'—and turn immediately to his work. When the car was needed, Katia was the only driver unless Erika happened to be on hand, the tightened petrol rationing in March a cause for some concern in car-oriented California.

In addition, she kept a keen eye on the correspondence, taking his dictation and also replying herself to many of the less important letters, but glad now to have the more professional help two afternoons a week of an excellent secretary who had been recruited in December. Hilde Kahn, who had emigrated at 21 from Germany in 1938, was at first slightly overawed by her employers—Katia often in a red velvet tea-gown, the contrast with the striking grey head lending her an almost cardinal-like air; the kindly though distant demeanour of the Master like that of a diplomat. Her afternoons began with tea with the family, at which he was usually the last to appear, refreshed from his afternoon rest and enjoying his favourite ginger biscuits with the Earl Grey, before they adjourned for dictation. She was soon at home, however, and her work, translating where necessary into English, never failed to please the always polite 'boss', as he called himself, though it was a long time into her ten years with them before Katia could bring herself to call her Hilde. For the boss she was sometimes jokingly 'Hildegard', or—after she had met Frido and occasionally acted as baby-sitter for the little grandsons on their visits—'The Lady': 'the lady has long hair!' Frido had cried (an unusual experience for him in a family where all the women were severely Eton-cropped) 'and she has prettier legs than Grandma'.[31]

At the end of March Katia and Thomas made a two-week visit to Chicago, to see Elisabeth's second daughter, Domenica, just born. His day could continue as usual: morning work in the hotel room on *Faustus*, or another broadcast message for Germany, a rest or a walk, afternoon dic-tation of letters to Katia, then the evenings mostly with Elisabeth—natu-rally with readings from the manuscript but entailing also more submission

[31] Kahn 58.

to the depressing outpourings of Borgese. Thinner and somewhat deaf, the Italian was in bitter mood, seeing in the apparent inability of the Allies to open a second front their total failure in the war and the moral collapse of the Anglo-Saxons (absurdly at odds with the encouraging words from Roosevelt and Churchill which seemed to indicate an imminent invasion). A visit there from Golo on short leave was a relief: he was about to be transferred to London, as an intelligence desk-officer, and had meanwhile good news that his monograph on Friedrich von Gentz had been accepted by Yale University Press, opening the way, his father thought, to a successful academic career later.

After their return, there were long discussions with Erika following her article for *Aufbau* in the 'Council for a Democratic Germany' controversy. He himself, having refused his signature to the Council's manifesto, was becoming awkwardly involved after part of his 'War and the Future' lecture published in *Atlantic Monthly* had given the impression that he too favoured a 'soft peace', distinguishing between 'good Germans' and Nazis. On 17 May, Clifton Fadiman urged a *démenti* and a statement 'from the most eminent living German' to help understanding of the problem of Pan-Germanism. After long deliberation, Mann decided to refuse to take such a stand. It was not only that so intricate a subject could not be dealt with in a short press statement, he replied to Fadiman, and that his brother and many respected American liberals had signed: his main objection was the irresponsibility of German exiles in pledging themselves for a future democratic regime in a land that had now become so utterly strange to them all. Equally however, it ill became a German of his type, determined, though an American citizen, to remain loyal to the language in which he hoped to finish his life's work, 'to pose today before the world tribunal as accuser, and by his witness, possibly not uninfluential, to demand the uttermost destruction of the land of his origin'. It was for the responsible statesmen to insure against another war from Germany in ten or twenty years, and no measures taken to this effect would surprise him. 'But can you blame a German writer for not wishing to stand before his people for all time as agitator for their nemesis?'[32]

His birthday coincided, remarkably, with the news of the long-awaited invasion of Normandy, telephoned excitedly by Agnes Meyer with word of Defence Ministry satisfaction over initial successes, and received with great emotion. He found the 'form and warmth' of Eisenhower's Order of the Day highly satisfying, and followed closely the news reports, American and British. But daily work on *Faustus*, where he now reckoned, in over-optimism, he was half-way, continued uninterrupted; the typescript of the

---

[32] *Br.* ii, 367 f.

early chapters was in Hilde Kahn's capable hands; and he felt he had regained the impetus with which he had started. No opportunity for musical contacts was neglected: the Austrian composer Ernst Toch, or Stravinsky. As he had written earlier to Adorno, he was receptive to any characteristic detail which intimacy with musicians could yield him, and which could be absorbed into the work by his technique of montage, the 'compositional principle' of the book.

He had not been well, since the return from Chicago, and although when he heard of heart attacks suffered by others he had been reassured by his doctor that his own health was that of one fifteen years younger, he had grasped as usual at the prescriptions offered (he was worried too to find Katia also ailing, for 'without me things can go on, but not without her').[33] But the malaise had little effect on his progress. 'I have written something good,' he told Agnes Meyer, the critical chapters with his montage of Nietzsche's brothel experience: Adrian's infection, despite her warnings, by the prostitute whom he called by the name of the tropical butterfly Hetaera Esmeralda, and the hinted-at work of the Devil to seal his fate by carrying off two doctors before they could treat him. The news was good from western Europe, the battle for Caen a threat now to Paris; in the east, the Russians were outside Minsk; though the Germans seemed not to know how desperate their situation was, he thought the 'murderous madness' of National Socialism, whose end he had been awaiting all these years, could scarcely last more than another twelve months. It was tempting to say 'I told you so', he wrote to Erich Kahler in Princeton: 'but I prefer to quit this life in the tolerably comforting knowledge that, while [for us] all sorts of activity, not always unobjectionable from a literary viewpoint, have been possible, the most stupid and vilest activity of all could not last more than eleven years'.[34]

On 23 June came the final act for citizenship, when he and Katia took the oath before a Los Angeles judge. There was much publicity, both press and radio; with his relief at the step—necessary, and right, since they would probably remain in America—there still mingled twinges of conscience over the Czechs, and later he wrote to Beneš, now leader of the Czech government in exile in London, a skilful explanation of his reasons for seeking a home in America's 'cosmopolitan universum'. A joint cable arrived from Golo and Erika, also now in London, cheerful and with no mention of the V-1 attacks on the capital which had begun (Hitler's first 'retaliatory' rocket weapon). Klaus, with the American Fifth Army, wrote from the ruined farmhouses of Italy, cheerful too, and keen to transfer to the Normandy front; soon Michael and his family were expected for a

[33] Bl. 10, 29.    [34] Ibid. 30.

month's stay, and he could look forward to seeing little Frido again, now talking well in English and German.

Less sunny were developments in the *Atlantic Monthly* affair. In the July number a Yale professor criticized Mann's apparent plea for a 'soft peace' in near-violent terms, adducing extensive quotations from his strongly nationalist writings during the First World War: if a man of his eminence and wide culture could write thus in 1915–18, when he was 40, his readers could hardly be expected to accept his conversion now to advocacy of a benevolent distinction between the German people and their Nazi leaders, sincere though it might be. Such a misrepresentation of his development and his current views had at all costs to be put right, for he was stronger now than ever on the need for a tough stand towards a people who in blind belief in their Führer had permitted the destruction by poison-gas of over one and a half million Jews. His detailed and sometimes barbed response, 'In my Defense', was held up by hesitations from the journal's editor, and did not finally appear till the October number:

I am not one of those German émigrés who stand before their country with patriotically outstretched arms and declare nothing must happen to it—when the most unbelievable things have been done to others. [To regard] Germany as the first victim of Hitler, the first of the peoples to be violated by National Socialism, I hold as not only absurd but also unworthy. . . . I shall be unmoved by any measures the statesmen of the world deem necessary to render Germany unable to repeat its performance in a foreseeable future . . .[35]

Depressing too had been the mixed reception for *Joseph the Provider*, which had just come out. 'A modern Divine Comedy', Agnes Meyer had written; 'a masterpiece', said *Time*; but the *New Yorker* saw Thomas Mann coming 'very close to being one of the greatest living bores', and Orville Prescott in the *New York Times*, as we have seen, found the book 'soporifically dull'. To call what he considered a thoroughly popular and humorous book a 'monstrosity overladen with demanding yet inept philosophy full of unbearably Olympian attitudinizing' was the work of idiots;[36] but it was comforting to find a mention of his name in the same breath as Gide, Proust, and Joyce. Reading a book on *Finnegans Wake*, he felt there might well be the affinity the author made out between himself and Joyce, but preferred not to investigate directly: if it were there, Joyce would have expressed everything 'much better, more boldly, more splendidly'.

In his diary, for posterity perhaps, he could note his longing for an end to the painful chatter of publicity, for the cup to pass of such 'misunderstanding and ignorance of what I am'.[37] At the time, however, he could find amusement in lighter self-advertisement, as he wrote a commercial for the

[35] xiii 211f.        [36] 44/291.        [37] *Tb.* vi, 72.

Guy Lombardo radio-show confirming (falsely, all the evidence suggests) that he was an Edgeworth tobacco smoker and naming as his favourite popular song Noel Coward's 'Don't Put your Daughter on the Stage'. The household had in fact been far from gloomy during these weeks, with the charm of Frido, naughty but always forgiven, for whom he was constantly drawing pictures, and Michael's music in many string-quartet evenings. Saying goodbye to them in August was affecting, however welcome the returning quiet. During the day, that is, for in the evenings a lively social round kept him late from his bed, most often still in the musical sphere, with Toch, 'the personally so attractive' Stravinsky, and Ernst Krenek, the Austrian opera-composer and theoretician whose *Music Here and Now* had become an important source for *Faustus*.

The title for it had needed long consideration before he settled on 'Doctor Faustus: The Life of the German Composer Adrian Leverkühn, as told by a Friend'. There was a certain symbolism in the not uncommon North German name he had chosen—the hint of 'life' and 'audacity'—and euphony required a separation between *Leben* and 'Leverkühn', but the essential was to have 'German' there: for that word represented the whole conception of the book and its deepest significance, the 'unhappily demonic and tragic' fate of Germany its fundamental theme.[38] What made progress so slow was the extreme difficulty of rendering in readable narrative and dialogue his hero's avant-garde ventures, with painstaking exactitude from his own studies and consultations, yet avoiding the aridity of a theoretical treatise. At the point he had reached now this was especially important: Adrian's discovery, quite independently of the Austrian school, of the twelve-tone system. From 'Hetaera Esmeralda'—and thus as the Devil's work—he was to find in the tone row B (H in German), E, A, E, E flat (Es in German), and in composing from it a *Lied*, 'O Dearest Girl, How Bad Thou Art', the possibility of almost infinite variation by inversion, transposition, or retrogression of that series, no single tone returning unless separated by the other intermediate eleven. It was the escape from classical tonality which Schönberg had in fact invented, and, as Mann commented ruefully to Agnes Meyer, would probably put an end to their friendship.

As he had found earlier with the tutor Kretzschmar's expositions, it was not easy in the attempt to convey the theory in dialogue between Adrian and Zeitblom, and in Zeitblom's attendant commentary, to escape the manner of a musicological tract (and this, for non-specialist readers, who would find other *longueurs* too, was to make the book heavy going). But his presentation was proceeding as he had planned, the composition working

[38] *AM Brw.* 586.

out in evenly constructed chapters: no physical description of Adrian himself, only the impression of the coldness of his nature as a recurring leitmotif, yet the surrounding figures of his life drawn in elaborate detail and in many cases from life—Clarissa Rodde in Munich so exactly his own sister Carla, with her dubious stage-career and later suicide; Rüdiger Schildknapp his friend Reisiger; Kretzschmar with distinct features of Adorno; and many others still to come, like his beloved grandson Frido in the little nephew Nepomuk. If the broad lines of Adrian's life owed much to Nietzsche's, in its detail it owed even more to the author's, whether in Lübeck as Adrian's home town Kaisersaschern, in his stays in Munich or Palestrina, or in the scene of his end, still only foreshadowed, in a Bavarian village like Julia Mann's last refuge. But in these final months of 1944—as both he and Zeitblom noted the fall of Paris, the advances of the 'red flood' in the east, the Germans' blind hope in the promised miracle-weapons, and in December the alarming Rundstedt counter-offensive in the Ardennes— much remained to be done. By the end of the year he was still working on chapter XXV, the sinister account of the apparition in Palestrina, accompanied by intense cold, of the Devil in person, which would mark the actual half-way point of the final work.

By his standards, he had been working quickly and steadily, and there had been fewer interruptions. In October, however, in *Love's Labour's Lost*, Adrian's youthful composition for which Zeitblom writes the libretto, he was struck by the couplet

> Their form confounded makes most form in mirth,
> When great things labouring perish in their birth.

Here, he felt, the first line might well apply to *Joseph*, but the second certainly to *Faustus*, where, as he later remarked to Helen Lowe-Porter, he was often doubtful whether he was physically capable of labouring to the end: 'Perhaps it was too late to start a thing like this.' With the previous works, the breaks enforced by lecture preparations, though he complained of them, had usually proved beneficial in the end, despite their delaying action. Now he was apprehensive rather of the commitment he had made with his agent for a tour in January–February 1945 (which of course would have to be combined with his annual appearance in the Library of Congress), when the obvious subject, Germany and the Germans after the eleven years of Hitlerism, was far from easy to prepare for a date when the final débâcle would clearly not yet be at hand. Nevertheless, he began his notes, hesitatingly and in worsening health, with a disturbing loss of weight—until in November he decided to cancel the whole tour, relieved, in the sense that he could turn back to *Faustus*, but depressed too over his evasive truancy and the lack of self-confidence it showed. Both MacLeish and Agnes Meyer were disappointed, for they had prepared a suitable advance celebration of his seventieth birthday; but all agreed to regard it simply as a postponement till the spring. His brooding in the meantime over the catastrophic character of the Germans, uniquely combining greatness and guilt, their total lack of political sense throughout their history, shown at its most disastrous in the criminal madness of National Socialism, chimed with his purpose in the novel: to express that 'anguish over Germany' which was affecting him more deeply than his professed indifference to his country's fate seemed to indicate. He found it extraordinary that Leonhard Frank, who had heard him read from the earlier chapters, should be so ecstatic over its 'Germanness', when his personal disgust just now over everything German was growing 'immeasurably'.[39]

His picture of German behaviour, from close attention to the press and radio reports, was filled out by anecdotal information from many sources. Letters from Erika, war correspondent with the Allied Forces since D-Day and accompanying them through Paris, Brussels, and Antwerp as far as devastated Aachen, and her stories when she returned at the end of the year, were full of indicative incident; Golo wrote often to Katia from London, and Klaus from Italy, where he was now starting to contribute to *Stars and Stripes*. Golo's account in October, from a Basle paper, of the visit to Lucerne by Elsa Bruckmann, wife of the well-known Munich publisher, was particularly revealing: when her passionate condemnation of American air-attacks on children's hospitals in Germany was gently questioned, considering the Germans' own fearful mass murders of children, she protested those could not be compared—'they were *Jewish* children'. Erika, attending a meeting between Robert Murphy, Eisenhower's political adviser, and Aachen notables, made herself known to the mayor, who in some embarrassment remarked: 'oh . . . yes . . . *The Buddenbrooks* is still a good book, in spite of everything'. 'Ah, Germany, Germany!' her father commented to Agnes Meyer: 'Every sound from there, even half-way friendly, sounds ghastly, grotesque . . .' Defending their 'sacred soil' inch by inch for Hitler and Himmler, the Germans had no conception that, after all their crimes, heroics could avail them little: 'we have no idea what it will be like when a people of 70 million simply refuses to accept its defeat'. A long visit from Elisabeth and her family, who had filled the house from early October and were staying till Christmas, was no help to a lighter mood. Borgese's Latin *furioso*, his chauvinistic outbursts on the 'ruin' of Italy, as if it was entirely the fault of the Allies, were a burden for the nerves, and it was a blessing that he was often away on lecture assignments. That Borgese could receive letters from old friends in Italy aroused the pessimistic

---

[39] *Br.* ii, 397.

thought in Mann that he himself would not be likely to get the same from Germany.

At least he could now, as an American citizen, speak publicly at a Democratic fund-raising meeting in Roosevelt's campaign for a fourth term: the latter's decisive victory in November over Dewey, at such a critical time, he considered one of the most important events of these eleven years. By the end of November he had found his way back to *Faustus* again, and in December had reached the important chapter with the visitation from the Evil One, when news came from Heinrich of the suicide of his wife. An overdose of sleeping-pills had this time successfully released her, as Salka Viertel put it, from 'her fear of growing old and her vain struggle against alcohol'. When he found it convenient, he called with Katia on his brother, with appropriate sympathy, a cheque for the funeral expenses, and the promise of housing him as soon as they had room, suggesting he should meanwhile go to Salka's. Heinrich, however, shattered by the loss, preferred to remain in his own apartment. Though visiting Pacific Palisades after the funeral in Santa Monica on 20 December, he returned home at once, feeling like a ghost, as he wrote later, 'back where my thoughts are only with her', where 'we shared poverty as we had once shared prosperity. . . . I feel old since 1944, 7 December, half-past midnight, when she died in the ambulance.' As his brother noted in his diary, he was given cash to redeem pawned furniture, some wine and food—and a copy of *The Tables of the Law* as a Christmas present. 'He hasn't a cent, all his very favourable income having been taken far into the red by the unfortunate behaviour of his wife. Worry with K. about him . . .'

Heinrich, however, was apparently not invited to join the rather large party assembling for the festive season. From early December Peter Pringsheim, on leave from Chicago, had joined them; Michael and his family arrived on Christmas Day; and Erika, crossing on a troop-ship to New York, came in time for New Year's Eve in California, which marked the christening of Michael's Tonio and Angelica Borgese. Decorations arranged by Katia and Elisabeth, tree with burning candles, and a turkey dinner with champagne made the usual traditional Christmas, and there was much amusement over a recording of a recitation by Frido, reading 'like some Swiss pastor'; but the host was depressed to find himself quickly tiring, and relieved when they soon had the house to themselves again. Michael, Gret, and the boys left immediately after the christening ceremony, for Michael had received his draft papers and was due to start basic training on 6 January; the Borgeses on New Year's Day; and Erika for more lectures on 7 January, though she was often back in the following weeks, and it was arranged she should accompany them on the postponed tour in May to Washington and other cities.

For Thomas Mann, at the turn of the year, there was no need of the military's warning against over-optimism. The Ardennes counter-offensive, though finally held and by the end of January driven back, was for him a demonstration of how desperately the Germans were prepared to fight on and would never capitulate (like many others, he did not appreciate that in the face of the demand for unconditional surrender, they could hardly do otherwise). Politically, on the other hand, the Allies seemed to him to have no clear idea of what they wanted. The British handling of the civil war in liberated Greece showed how little had been learned since Spain and Munich: 'we still fear socialism much more than fascism, and since, at least for Europe, those are the only alternatives, we don't know what we want, and everything could still be lost. . . . nothing but spheres of influence, undisguised imperialism and fearfully precipitate division of the spoils'.[40] The constant conflicting arguments over what to do with Germany continued to worry him; there were further attacks in the *Atlantic Monthly* during December, and to read of the objection of one exile against any occupation of Germany was staggering. From all he had seen and heard, the Germans totally lacked any realization of the extent of their crimes—but would undoubtedly see anything that happened to *them* as a monstrous injustice: 'with them limitless self-pity goes hand-in-hand with ferocity'.

From the personal point of view, he could not complain. True, the Thomas Mann boom expected after the appearance of *Joseph the Provider* had been disappointing, and Knopf's sales were unlikely to exceed the first printing; but he accepted that he was not in the popular best-seller class of Hemingway or Werfel, and at least the net proceeds of the Book of the Month Club edition could be used, as Eugene Meyer had recommended, to reduce the mortgage on the house. His connection with the Library of Congress, where Luther Evans was taking over from MacLeish, was satis-factorily renewed, without annual stipend as he had proposed, but with a thousand-dollar fee for the annual lecture, planned now for May to lead up to the seventieth-birthday celebration.

In January, as he 'struggled peevishly and without pleasure through the thicket' of chapter XXV, 'stuffed with medicine, musicology, and theology', to get it done and make a start on his lecture, the great Russian offensives towards Berlin and to encircle East Prussia began. Further south they were already past Budapest and opening the road to Vienna; Americans and British were advancing on a broad front to the Rhine; it was clear this was the beginning of the end for Germany. In the tone of the German radio-announcers, the old 'murderous arrogance' which had raged over Europe

---

[40] *AM Brw.* 608f.

came close now to hysteria over the exhaustion of Führer and people—a tendency to self-pity and false pathos which he feared might not be without influence. Recalling Guernica, Rotterdam, Warsaw, London, and Coventry, he could not be moved by Germany's suffering now from the virus of Nazism. That was just such a mark of a pact with the Devil as the syphilis of his Adrian Leverkühn, though granting the Germans only half the twenty-four years allowed to his hero. While still deep in the elaboration of Adrian's story, as the Russians approached Breslau and the Oder, and the three leaders were meeting at Yalta to lay down what was to be done with Germany, he was asked on 5 February by the journal *Free World* for an article on the imminent collapse of the Reich—a demand which he was glad to fulfil, given that it chimed with the novel's theme.

Sympathy for Germany, he wrote, must be out of place. Her people's 'lack of any sense of evil', as his diary of 1933 had noted, was unpardonable and must be punished; it was impossible now to ask the victimized peoples of Europe or the rest of the world to draw a distinction between Nazism and the German people, and he would not come forward as advocate of a soft peace—however much he hoped that one day, through the fearful suffering, some form of existence and of statehood might be found for Germany which could favour her best attributes and make her 'a true collaborator in a brighter future for mankind'.[41] In his March broadcast he went so far as to improvise a decentralized state form as 'the best for both Germany and the world':[42] a federal system of separate *Länder*, starting from a base of small self-governing units working with the occupying powers. Germany could then still survive, and be happy without the territories in east and west it lost through the catastrophe, as a country which could 'count on the diligence of its people and on the help of the world, and for which, once the worst is over, a life of fulfilment and respect may be in store'.[43]

He felt this 'funeral oration for National Socialism' had been successfully discharged. 'One thing is certain: an end has to be made of this Reich of war and its technologized romanticism, and no measure to achieve this purpose is to be condemned.' Chapter XXV then finally completed, he could turn to the draft of his lecture, which under the title 'Germany and the Germans' would be a natural follow-on to this interlude. His countrymen's history was an illustration of how, while good could come from evil, yet evil could come from good—in their case, from that *Innerlichkeit*, the tendency to subjective introspection, which had characterized the Reformation and the romantic movement in Germany—and they might well ask why everything for them seemed to lead only to evil and catastrophe. In endeavouring to

---

[41] xii 945–50.    [42] 45/214.    [43] xiii. 743.

explain their psychology and expound their melancholy story he had to avoid coming forward as an apologist, 'for crimes have been committed which no psychology can help to excuse'.[44] But he could conclude that there were not two Germanies, a good and a bad: only one, whose best qualities, 'through the Devil's cunning, turned to evil. The bad Germany is the good gone astray, the good in misfortune, guilt, and downfall.' It was not for him to wash his hands of his country and declare himself the representative of 'the good, the noble, the just Germany', for he had all this in himself too, had undergone it all personally. 'In the end, the German catastrophe is only the paradigm of the tragedy of all mankind. The grace that Germany so badly needs is the need of us all.'[45]

The draft was quickly completed, for these were ideas that had been his constant preoccupation as he continued with *Faustus*, where the notion of grace would not be absent when he came to the end. He had made a kind of 'declaration of solidarity—not with the Nazis of course, but with Germany in her misfortune';[46] and reviewing his text on 18 March (as the Allies took Koblenz, the Russians had effected two crossings of the Oder, and Danzig was being evacuated by sea) he felt it made the best lecture he had yet offered in America. Through all this time, since January in fact, he had been far from well. Though beginning the next chapter of *Faustus* in April, he found it hard to re-establish continuity amid the distractions of events and his uncertainty over whether he could bring it off. It was evident that the war's end could be expected soon, within days even, and as he began to consider the broadcast to the Germans which would be expected from him, there came the shock of Roosevelt's death.

Refusing the request for an improvised radio-address, after telegraphing words of deep sympathy to the widow he prepared his considered reaction, for publication in *Free World* and *Aufbau*, to the sudden end of this 'heroic life', of the latterday Caesar—and shrewd politician—whom he had admired and loved and under whose aegis he had been proud to become a *civis romanus*. He used the same words at the memorial service in Santa Monica and in part for a special broadcast to Germany—adding virulent condemnation of the people, once the most cultured of the world, who could treat as the 'greatest war criminal of all time' the man who, far from being their enemy, was only the most powerful enemy of their corrupters.[47] At the same time he noted, despite the world-wide tributes, that for not a few Americans there was relief instead of sadness: after this 'end of an epoch it will not be the America we came to'. Roosevelt had raised his country above its true level, he wrote to Bermann, and he feared it would soon sink back to normal. From the successor Truman's speech to Con-

[44] *DüD.* iii, 308.     [45] xi 1146, 1148.     [46] 45/145.     [47] xii 942f., xi 1121.

gress, it seemed there would be no change in matters military—all the more, he suspected, in the civil sphere.

From Golo, who had gone forward, as an officer now, to Luxemburg and had been in the Rhineland, came his first impressions of 'liberated' Germans. The only talk was of the innocent having now to pay for the guilty ('where are the guilty? Oh, they're gone, there were never many of them . . . you see, I am a Catholic . . .'). There were a few good people too, of course, and with them his father's prestige was astonishing—though that he wrote *à contre-cœur*, 'for I don't wish to see him dragged into this hopeless business'. The most depressing impression for Thomas Mann, in these final days, was the whining appeal from those who had been so brutal in victory, for clemency and generosity in their defeat, the total lack of any condemnation of National Socialism as such. And with this, the sense of shame for him as a German at the revelations of the concentration-camp horrors, surpassing all fears, when General Patton, reaching Weimar, liberated Buchenwald and ordered the whole population to file past the crematoria and piles of corpses. 'The patriotic emigration . . . take it amiss that I find *everything* German, German history, the German spirit, involved in this catastrophe. But what else can one do?' Yet perhaps the right lesson was not 'Look, that is Germany!' but rather 'Look, that is fascism! These are the deeds it is capable of, and will be in every country that falls to it.'[48]

## 4

'*A country is not only what it does—it is also what it puts up with, what it tolerates*'

(Kurt Tucholsky to Arnold Zweig, 1934)

On 7 May 1945, the day of the unconditional surrender by Admiral Doenitz, commanding in the west after Hitler's suicide in Berlin, Thomas Mann felt anything but elation. Where was the disavowal of Nazism and the condemnation of its *deeds*? the admission that to have allowed the *Machtergreifung* was an unparalleled crime? 'the declaration of the will to return to truth, justice, and humanity?' For himself, there was a certain satisfaction at having survived. 'After the fall of France Goebbels had my death reported. . . . And if I had taken Hitler's false victory seriously to heart, I suppose I'd have had no alternative but to die. Survival meant: to be victorious. It is a victory. . . . Wrote this this morning, then continued with chapter XXVI.'[49] By holding steadfastly to his daily routine, shutting himself firmly off at the desk all morning, he was able to carry the novel

---

[48] *AM Brw.* 625.　　　[49] *Tb.* vi, 200 f.

forward. There was no doubt, however, that the stress of the turbulent events in Europe, combining as they did so intimately with the theme he was struggling to present, had begun to tell. The doctor's prescriptions had no effect on his steady loss of weight, and although a general check on 4 May and elaborate X-rays on VE Day itself, 8 May, had been satisfactory, he still felt far from well, despite the lift from a celebratory bottle of champagne. That night he made a short broadcast to Germany, for the Office of War Information, on the concentration camps and the revulsion of the outside world at the dreadful human degradation now revealed, Germany standing now as an unparalleled example of evil. Even for one who had been able to escape, and had not, like the Germans, gone about his business trying not to know even when the wind brought 'the stink of burning human flesh to his nostrils', the shame was profound. And he urged his listeners, who had not been morally stout enough to free themselves from the ghastly rule of Nazism, to treat their liberators as friends and try to see themselves as restored at last to humanity.

His words were published in the American 12th Army Group paper *Frankfurter Presse* on 10 May. But his impression of Germany in these first days was dark indeed. Gerhart Hauptmann, it seemed, could weep over the destruction by Allied air-attack of Dresden, which he had personally witnessed—but over nothing else that had happened. Golo wrote sadly over the unimaginable extent of the ruins of the cities he saw. Klaus, who had made his way as *Stars and Stripes* special correspondent over the Brenner to Bavaria, reported his 'amazing hour' with Richard Strauss in Garmisch, revealing the composer's 'moral obtuseness and callousness . . . completely lacking in the most fundamental impulses of shame and decency'. In Munich, he had visited the house in Poschinger Strasse, now bombed out and the ruins a home for a few refugees, though most of that area had been spared, in contrast to the almost total destruction of the city itself. He urged his father not to think of returning or playing any kind of political role. 'All your efforts . . . would be hopelessly wasted . . . you would be blamed for the country's well-deserved, inevitable misery. More likely than not . . . assassinated . . .'[50] The press articles by Erika, who had also seen something of ruined Germany, but was now back in California, stressed how few people admitted to being Nazis (it was the 'few' at the top who were to blame and their police state had prevented any kind of opposition) and how, along with this self-justification, there was a kind of passive resistance to the occupation. The commentator Walter Lippmann, in a *Washington Post* article, called the defeat a 'total disgrace', for no Germans had come forward, even at the last minute, 'who might claim by their resistance to

---

[50] KlM *Br. Antw.* 536, 540.

Nazism . . . to be the representatives of a better Germany'. Thomas Mann, noting the growing anti-Russian feeling in America, began even to doubt whether the promised trial of German war criminals would ever be pursued.

As the time approached for departure east, he felt more and more exhausted in spite of the doctor's reassurances, but hoped the change of air and the resumption of public appearances—always a stimulus—would restore him. Erika had meanwhile rendered her usual sterling service of ruthless abbreviation of his lecture, and when they stopped over in Chicago on 25 May he already felt his head clearing. Hearing there of a wave of suicides in Germany among the better class of Nazis—officers, professors—made him wonder whether Ernst Bertram was among them (hardly likely, he thought). In Washington on 28 May, where as usual the Meyers' home was open for them and Erika, they found a letter with birthday wishes from Golo. He had broadcast from Luxemburg the 'Concentration Camp' message—in his opinion, with the *Free World* article, one of his father's finest pieces—and, enclosing press extracts, wrote how Germany now reminded him of 1933: 'then they suddenly produced the Party badges they had hidden and had been Nazis all the time: now they have never been'.

For the lecture next evening, the introduction was by MacLeish, returning specially for the occasion. Driven from his country by a force more evil than any in history, said the former Librarian of Congress, Thomas Mann, at the pinnacle of his fame, had achieved as great a renown in the new land of which he had become a citizen, yet remained proud to be a true German, and his presence symbolized the power of the human spirit, of which he was one of the greatest interpreters, to open a future for the world after the bitter years of war. It was a tribute typical of the many articles to appear on the occasion of the seventieth birthday: Marquis Childs in the *New York Post*, for example, recalling that the new American citizen, from the same Germany that had produced the horrors of Dachau and Belsen, had finally vindicated his 1938 forecast of the 'Coming Victory of Democracy'; or the *Times* after the Waldorf-Astoria dinner in his honour given by the Nation Associates on 25 June. As at the previous lectures, his audience included Attorney-General Biddle and many others among Washington's leading figures, and at the Meyers' reception afterwards he was glad to hear the favourable response, notably from Walter Lippmann, to his view of Germany and the Germans. In a tour of the Library, it was fascinating to see original manuscripts of Johann Beissel, the eighteenth-century migrant to Pennsylvania from the Palatinate, who had founded the Ephrata sect of so-called Seventh-day Baptists and whose hymns with strange polyphonic music in a novel system of notation he had already celebrated in *Faustus* with Kretzschmar's lectures to Leverkühn and Zeitblom. He and Katia were invited with Agnes and Eugene to lunch with the noted columnist Drew Pearson, and it was interesting to hear there from Sumner Welles, Deputy Secretary of State, ideas approaching his own of a federal solution for Germany.

With the return to a public role at centre stage his feeling of exhaustion had dropped away. When they left to spend ten days in New York, on 3 June, he was able to enjoy the brisk succession of both the public and private celebrations of his birthday. Their hotel room became a flower display; letters, telegrams, and gifts flooded in. A special number of *Aufbau* on 8 June brought the exiles' tributes, from Heinrich and Klaus too, and from Erika recalling his readings to the family in Munich, Tölz, or 'Uncle Tom's Cabin' in Nidden (latterly annexed by Hermann Goering), and wishing him a world in which it might be worth getting to 80. At a musical evening at the Bermanns' in Old Greenwich, with many old friends, he heard his favourite Schubert B major trio, recalling a similar occasion in former days at Samuel Fischer's Grunewald home—the pleasure this time, however, somewhat marred when it was followed by Carl Zuckmayer's over-robust performance of his own songs, to guitar and much stamping. All three daughters had contrived to be in New York for the day: as he wrote to Klaus, 'Erika animating, warm-hearted, helpful . . . poor Moni, with wilting charm, bursting into tears as soon as we talk', and Elisabeth afraid she chattered too much to 'Herr Papale' after her fourth cocktail.

The birthday itself was quiet: lunch with the Knopfs, the evening at Bruno Walter's, when his host and the violinist Bronislaw Hubermann played Mozart for him, 'a birthday present not granted to everyone'. On 8 June he repeated the lecture at Hunter College, New York—the only other performance of the tour. After the evening function next day organized by the German-American War Bond Committee and the Tribune for Free German Literature and Art, at which he spoke briefly, he heard with interest the Dachau and Buchenwald reminiscences of the writer Heinrich Eduard Jacob and his impressions of a German people medievalized under the Nazis, the 'archaic in their soul', remarks surprisingly close to his *Faustus*. Interviews and articles succeeded each other, to the point where he could no longer bear to hear or read his name: it was a relief (so he said) to think that from now on the world would probably leave him in peace until his 'blessed end', and then at any celebration he need be represented only by a bust. All the same, he was sharp to notice whose letters were so far missing among the well-wishers—Hesse, Faesi, Korrodi—and wonder why.

Not the least impressive for him was the special number Bermann had brought out in Sweden of the *Neue Rundschau*: the journal, formerly so intimately bound up with Thomas Mann's work, now not only celebrated this important birthday with a broad international range of contributions, but marked its reappearance in freedom after a tolerated existence till October 1944 with the 'Aryan' S. Fischer Verlag under the Nazis. This 'deafening orchestral tutti of homage' he took with him for closer study when he and Katia left on 14 June for a break at a mountain-resort hotel on Lake Mohonk, on the slopes of the Catskills. There were ten days free before the 'political dinner' at the Waldorf-Astoria, and Monika came from New York to join them for part of the time. The simple Quaker-run hotel—by his standards over-primitive, with poor food and only spring water to drink, though they had brought their own aperitifs—lay in its own grounds, somewhat Victorian in aspect, like an old-fashioned European spa but with no 'cure' to offer, unless temperance counted. But even with these drawbacks the quiet stay was something of a restorative, with evening concerts, and film shows in which he noted with approval American democracy's healthy self-mockery and irreverence. Letters and telegrams continued to pour in, but there was time now to write some of the more pressing responses, and prepare his address for the Waldorf dinner. News of the death of Bruno Frank came as a profound shock: for *Aufbau* he wrote an obituary of great feeling for this old friend, recently too often neglected, who through thirty-five years had been his neighbour from Munich to California, and for whom the end of Hitlerism, it seemed, had come too late. It was moving to find the first chapter of Frank's unfinished fictitious autobiography of Chamfort as his contribution to the *Rundschau* number.

Others there were represented by similar extracts from work in progress, and not all found favour with Mann, notably Werfel's fragment from his vast futuristic novel *Star of the Unborn*. To Heinrich, however, he wrote diplomatically on the piece from him which had pride of place, from his memoirs due out soon: the touching reminiscences of their father, the documentation of the fraternal variances in their attitudes towards Germany, and the 'unique prose', in its 'intellectually lively simplicity the language of the future'. (In fact, Heinrich's was prose he never felt easy with: great, no doubt, but better followed with something from Stifter for late-night reading.)[51] As was natural for him, homage in the form of the many directly personal tributes was more welcome, especially the 'melodious' words from Klaus, 'with the American Army, Christmas 1944': the only German book in his pack *Joseph the Provider*, 'deeply and solemnly moved' as he thought of his father at 70 after the twenty eventful and chastening years since the ceremony in Munich.

[51] *Tb.* vi, 266.

During the stay he was reading Dostoevsky, a duty in preparation for an introduction promised for an anthology, but not without the feeling that that 'apocalyptic-grotesque world of suffering' was also an appropriate background to that of his *Faustus*. (He noted with approval Hermann Broch's view, in the *Rundschau*, that Dostoevsky's work prefigured the total collapse of values in the twentieth century, after which, with Joyce as with Mann, the traditional novel-form was no longer possible.) In the hotel with her parents was a young college girl, reading, as he noted, an 'American classic' called *The Magic Mountain* and, as he wandered round the 'slightly childish' parkland, with its look-outs and little towers and bridges, attracting his attention not only by the book under her arm but also by the scarlet jacket setting off her youthful charm. At the evening concert, her mother, confessing to him Cynthia's excitement over the presence of the admired author, contrived to seat them together, and they talked often during the days remaining. For this 'lipstick angel . . . with the boundless naïvety and eagerness for culture of the Americans' it was a dream of happiness to be with him. 'You like my books, and I like *you*,' he told her, but she indicated that the author too was not without attraction for her. The mild flirtation carried overtones for him of Goethe's last passion in Marienbad, very different though it was for one hardly ever thus attracted to the opposite sex. As they left for New York on 24 June, and he said how he would never forget her, 'it was always a pleasure to look at you', Cynthia's blushing delight and pride, and her shy look towards the departing car, were indeed unforgettable.[52]

Only a few days in the east now remained. Lunching on 26 June tête-à-tête with Agnes Meyer, while Katia was out with Monika, he listened with proper sympathy and vague words of comfort to 'confessions of a beautiful soul' and the lack of loyalty with which (though evidently with a certain poetic enjoyment) she still seemed to reproach herself. The dinner that evening in his honour at the Waldorf was an impressive affair. With an introduction by Robert Sherwood and prominent speakers including Supreme Court Justice Frankfurter, the exiled Spanish Prime Minister Negrin, Interior Minister Harold Ickes, and William Shirer whose 'Berlin Diary' published in 1941 had been a major documentation of the reality of Nazi Germany, it was an occasion of high politics, with Ickes in particular attacking the trend to an anti-Soviet mood. He himself, in his few words at the close which he went immediately to broadcast from the CBS studio, expressed the hope that the indication sometimes apparent of a desire to preserve fascism as a bulwark against socialism was not typical. Such was not the 'will of the American people, the people of Roosevelt', he said, 'who

[52] *Bl.* 12, 17.

do not look backward under the cloak of democracy, but forward to development and fulfilment'. If they departed today strengthened in their 'belief in America's cause, the cause of democracy, of freedom and peace', then the purpose of their meeting would have been fulfilled, and he was greatly honoured that his personal day of celebration should have been the opportunity for such encouragement.[53]

Thomas Mann, said the *New York Times*, was 'part of that lofty and intangible payment of reparations' which America had begun to receive from Germany even before the war, and millions of his new countrymen were proud he could say 'we' when he spoke of their nation. More encouraging for him, however, too long a truant from the novel, was the profound effect on a gathering of friends of an impromptu reading from the 'Devil chapter' the following evening. It seemed to him the most successful he had ever given, if admittedly from passages in which he felt surest of the still uncertain work. It was a lift to his spirits as they set off on 27 June for Chicago, where a final celebratory dinner required a short improvised address, and the tedious journey home.

In his passion for order, several days had first to be spent sorting the pile of waiting mail, and the garden incinerator was kept busy before he was organized for the necessary replies. He had then to turn to the Dostoevsky introduction, required by the end of July. There was a slight interruption for another performance of the 'Germany and the Germans' lecture, at the University of California Westwood campus; but by 20 July 'Dostoevsky— in Moderation' was finished, and he was at last free to resume work on *Faustus*. He was often together with Bruno Walter, who had now settled in Los Angeles and whose memoirs *Theme and Variations* made appropriate reading. Walter made no secret of his aversion to twelve-tone, but was excitedly enthusiastic over the approach to music in the novel, particularly the treatment of Beethoven's Op. 111 and of Beissel's exotic system (no matter, as Mann noted, that his montage included much assimilated from Adorno—like Molière, 'je prends mon bien où je le trouve').

He continued steadily day by day on the manuscript, counterpointing the grotesque and tragic incidents in Adrian's life at the time of the First World War with Zeitblom's indications of the greater catastrophe imminent, but himself closely attentive to the disturbing situation in the world now. After the Big Three conference in Potsdam, on 20 July, the reports of Japanese peace-feelers gave him hope of an end at last to the state of war 'with all its corruption', but it soon became clear that the Allies' insistence on unconditional surrender, as with Germany, ruled out any negotiated settlement. They were obviously determined on constricting the German

[53] xiii 774.

(and Japanese) peoples to inadequate space, as the agreed extension of Poland's western frontier to the Oder showed; the slightly comic account of Truman's piano performance in Potsdam highlighted the lack of any serious attempt by the three powers at a fair world settlement. Meanwhile, however, he was greatly encouraged by the Labour Party's election victory in Britain over Churchill. That was a lesson for America, he thought, where, like Heinrich, who had at last been invited for a few days, he noted a distinctly fascist trend. In a letter shortly afterwards to the *St. Louis Post-Dispatch* he wrote with approval, if some scepticism, of the planned trial of war criminals—provided it was not simply a *vae victis* festival, but a quickly discharged and formal disowning of the fascism still rampant in the world. If that was the will of the American people, 'and I believe it is, then I honour and support it with all my heart'.

What he did not yet know was that on 16 July an atomic bomb (of which he had had an inkling from Peter Pringsheim) had been successfully tested in the New Mexico desert, and that Truman had already decided it should be used to force an unconditional surrender on Japan. Of more personal concern was an invitation on the Russian-controlled Berlin radio for him to return to Germany, recalling his early warnings against Nazism and saying he was needed for the 'new spirit sweeping through Germany'. So at least he was told on 27 July by *Time* magazine, to whom he gently but firmly replied that his home was in America now: 'I am an old man, and my greatest force for good is in my writings.' Privately he said he had far too great a dread of the ruins which would face him there, both of buildings and of people.[54] There was more interest for him in an attempt at the legal recovery of at least the land under the ruins he owned in Munich, and he began enquiries to this end with the American authorities, later directly addressing Secretary of State Byrnes. The controversy over Thomas Mann's proper place in relation to post-war Germany, however, had only just begun, and more would soon be required from him than simply a statement to *Time*.

On 6 August, as he had just finished chapter XXVII, the news broke of the first atom bomb, on Hiroshima, followed three days later, as he began chapter XXVIII, by the second, on Nagasaki. He followed keenly the media revelations, noting how close-run the race had been with Germany to develop this fearfully destructive new weapon, and how much the American success had owed to German and Jewish *émigré* physicists. 'We have spent two billion dollars on the greatest scientific gamble in history,' said President Truman, '—and won.' Mann wrote later that he shared the scruples of the Vatican (for the *Osservatore romano*, this was blatant misuse

[54]  45/338.

of the 'spiritual and material gifts granted by God', and the weapon would remain as a 'temptation for posterity, which we know by bitter experience learns so little from history')—but that he none the less considered it fortunate that American physics had beaten the Nazis to it. At the time, to judge from his diary, he seemed more interested in the theory behind this march of progress, the inevitable harnessing of the inmost secrets of the universe to human purposes, if at first only for destruction.

Now, on 10 August, came a renewed appeal for his return to Germany, this time from Walter von Molo. In an open letter just published, the former colleague of the Academy, who since 1933 had lived more or less in retirement and evidently regarded himself as one of those 'inner exiles' whom Mann had held in contempt for their tacit support of the regime, now claimed to have heard and read with approval many of his utterances. With 'all the reserve imposed on us after the twelve fearful years', he pleaded with him to come and see 'the inexpressible sorrow in the faces of the many who have not collaborated in the glorification of our dark side' and who had been unable to leave the 'huge concentration camp' that had developed. 'Come soon, like a good doctor, who not only sees the effect but also seeks the cause of the disease. . . . Let us seek together, as we did before 1933, the truth . . .'[55]

It was an appeal which he found, to say the least, unreasonable—'are those twelve years supposed to have been just enjoyment?'—and moreover a highly unwelcome disturbance at this time of steady progress with *Faustus*. He found bitter amusement over the absurd exaggeration of his personal influence on the Americans in German affairs: 'if the Germans have a hard time—and what else can await them—I shall be blamed for not intervening enough. Sancta simplicitas!' The same day some Jewish visitors told him that sooner or later he would have to yield to the pressure to return, for in Germany he was regarded as a prophet. On 1 September the press reported a renewed entreaty, from 'victims of fascism' in Soviet-controlled Berlin, to 'one of the greatest and ablest sons of the German people' to take up his 'historic work' there, and he heard from Golo that the Bavarian section of the reconstituted Association of German Writers was expecting the return of its 'honoured president'. It was clear that—still determined never to return there to live, but already thinking of a European visit in 1946 which might include Germany—he would have to set out and publish his considered reasons for refusing, a document as important in a way as his statement in 1937 to Bonn University; and with reluctance he finally settled to it in the early days of September.

[55] *Urteil*, 334f.

Welcome though he must find the desire in Germany to have back not just his books but himself in person, he wrote, such appeals to one who had been forced out of his country were ill-considered and illogical. Those twelve years could not simply be wiped from the slate, as if they had never been. In terms almost as pathetic as those of von Molo, he enlarged on the tribulations of exile which 'all of you who swore loyalty to the "charismatic Führer" . . . and pursued culture under Goebbels' had never experienced. 'I don't forget that you later went through much worse . . . but you never knew the heart-asthma of exile, the uprooting, the nervous terrors of homelessness.' He could see no good reason why he should abandon the life he and his family had been fortunate enough to find in America, to return to where there might certainly be many good friends, both old and young, but just as certainly many lurking enemies. Reading by chance a Nazi publication of 1937, he had felt it would be impossible to live among people who had so long been stupefied by this opium. If there was any service he could still render, then California was as good a place as any.

Germany's fate was not of his making, and he had never ceased to worry over it, had tried indeed by his broadcasts to play his part against it. He was and would remain a German writer, and in a lecture immediately after the war's end at the Library of Congress, rejecting the idea that he represented a 'good' as against a 'bad' Germany, he had declared his solidarity with the country whose pact with the Devil, as for Faust, did not rule out eventual grace. And he believed in a future for Germany in the coming world of social humanism, the awakening of mankind to their essential unity and the dawning of a world state. He had not ceased to dream of once more feeling the soil of Europe under his feet, and planned to revisit the old continent when circumstances allowed: once there, 'I suspect that my timidity and feeling of alienation, these products of a mere twelve years, will not withstand an attraction which has longer memories . . . on its side. Auf Wiedersehen then, if God so wills!'[56]

He took over a week for the task, with much rewriting, before he was satisfied enough to send 'Why I Am Not Returning to Germany' for publication in the New York *Aufbau* and many papers in Germany. As he admitted later, he should have foreseen that over there his attempt to find a conciliatory tone and a comforting conclusion would be ignored, and the only message heard would be his refusal to return for good. Not all his readers would find his arguments convincing or acceptable, and for many the mention in particular of his fear to face the ruins, both of buildings and of people, struck a wrong note. Though he had cited his Washington lecture, and it was to be published in the *Rundschau*, he realized it would

---

[56] *Br.* ii, 440–7.

not do to make wider use of the text for popular consumption, as the American occupation authorities were proposing. There was little doubt that further distressing controversy over the case of Thomas Mann and Germany was to be expected.

In the meantime exile continued to claim its victims. On 26 August Franz Werfel had succumbed to a final heart-attack, just after completing his 'impossible adventure' *Star of the Unborn*, and pen still in hand preparing a selection of his poems for publication in California. To Mann, among her many callers, Alma Werfel, widow of Gustav Mahler and ex-wife of the Bauhaus architect Walter Gropius, said she would not be at the funeral of her third husband: 'I never go'—so comically frank an utterance that the tears which shook him at the well-attended ceremony in Beverley Hills could as well have been from laughter as from sobs. The mourners' long wait, as Bruno Walter and Lotte Lehmann played and sang on and on, was not, as they thought, for the arrival of Alma, but for the priest, whose homily she had been correcting to her taste and who, apparently, had performed a secret posthumous baptism (Werfel, though for a long time close to the Catholic faith, had not yet formally abandoned the Jewish). Bruno Frank's widow, Liesl, was among those present, evidently hurt at this overshadowing of her own loss, which she continued to mourn exaggeratedly, in Thomas Mann's view. He had organized a more intimate memorial occasion for her husband at Pacific Palisades, earlier in August, at which he had tried to strike a note of happiness rather than mourning by readings from Frank's works; but it was an effort which had not come easily, and the grander affair on which she insisted at the end of September was even more of a burden for him in his fatigued state. There were further personal losses with the deaths in New York of Beer-Hofmann and Roda-Roda.

During August and September another visit from Michael and his family helped to lighten his days, Frido outrageously spoiled and probably developing into a rascal, but still captivatingly the elfin prince who would figure as Adrian's nephew in the novel. It was disturbing, however, to hear of his brother Viktor's arrest in Munich in the course of the denazification procedures (it was alleged that he had mistreated French prisoners), and while still working on the reply to von Molo he had addressed a statement to the American Counter Intelligence Corps, with his conviction that such conduct was inconceivable and that a trial would prove his innocence.

Now, however, the inevitable reactions to his 'letter to Germany' began to appear. In an article in the New York *Neue Volkszeitung*, one of those he called the 'social democratic Nazis' among the exiles attacked his whining pontifications as a 'voice from the grave', from a Thomas Mann so concerned over his own privileged position as to forget the sufferings of others over those twelve years, and expressed bitter disappointment over the idol of former days—'or is it shame at having regarded him as one of us?' Most detestable for him, however, was an article by Frank Thiess, published just after von Molo's open letter. Thiess, though he had expressly welcomed the 1933 *Machtergreifung*, had had some of his books burned and a novel critical of totalitarianism banned in 1941: he now supported the invitation to Mann to return with a self-righteous plea on behalf of the 'inner emigration', misunderstood and unjustly condemned by those outside, whom he urged to rejoin them to help their 'misled and suffering people'.[57] 'The height of shameless falsification of the position,' Mann wrote to Golo, who had reported Erich Ebermayer too as a would-be 'inner *émigré*'. After all his efforts to maintain a decent bearing, now to be branded a coward, shirking Germany's destiny and unwilling even now to share it, was insufferable, and certainly bitter confirmation of his forebodings to von Molo of what a visit to Germany would be like for him.

He was tempted to a vigorous response to these falsely heroic stay-at-homes, who 'have learned nothing and forgotten nothing', but in the end decided he had said enough to von Molo to serve as a polite reply. It would ill become him to continue the controversy, galling though it was to see those who had never raised their voice against the impending terror representing themselves as martyrs and heroes, suffering with the Fatherland while 'we led a comfortable spectator's existence outside'. And he continued with the novel instead, secure in the conviction that his works were too thoroughly German in character for his decision to stay away to be interpreted as the act of a renegade. Attacks did not cease, however, and he accepted the BBC's proposal in November for one more address to his German listeners, which went out just before the New Year. After a forceful summary of his position, he ended by stressing how exile now was no longer as in earlier times, simply a wait to return home, but brought signs of dissolving nationalism and an advance to world unity. 'I took my German inheritance with me. But I also missed nothing of Germany's misery. . . . May I not be grudged the German universality which was already natural to me at home, and allowed to continue at the advanced post of German culture which I shall seek to hold with dignity for a few more years yet.' Today more than ever he felt himself a citizen of the world, and a European, he wrote in November: but if his wish to revisit Europe were one day granted, then a look at Germany would be 'the most natural and unavoidable thing in the world'.[58]

His correspondence had doubled since contact with Germany had resumed, but he kept it to its appointed place in his day, and there were few

[57] *Urteil* 338.   [58] 45/541.

mornings in these final months of 1945 which did not see progress with *Faustus*. There, the Germany he was portraying in the aftermath of the First World War chimed with the depressing picture he saw now, the German mentality so clearly unchanged, as reports from Manfred Hausmann, Erika, and Golo confirmed. It was quite clear to him that he would not feel one whit better back there than in 1930. Defeat and collapse, said Hausmann, had altered nothing: 'German insolence is already on top again. I feel like a foreigner among my own people.' For Mann, how they should be treated was an insoluble problem, and he was glad he did not have to solve it: 'they will never be content, and whatever is done with them is wrong', he told Agnes Meyer in December. In Lübeck, it seemed—damaged, but much less so than more important cities—there was reluctance to feed and take care of the floods of refugees from further east: no sign there of the national solidarity shown by the British, who were as badly if not worse off than the Germans.

Golo and Klaus, both out of uniform by the end of November, were remaining in Europe: Golo as a civilian employee of the US Information Service in Bad Nauheim, continuing with his radio work, but Klaus choosing civilian life proper in Rome—'frivolous, corrupt, lazy, selfish, blasé, but charming'[59]—where he started work as script-writer for part of Rossellini's film *Paisà* and began to nurse other projects in the film world there and in Austria. (Characteristically, while Golo had made sure of a post with more than adequate pay, his was more a hand-to-mouth existence, dependent on parcels of clothing and other necessaries from the family.) Erika, still a uniformed correspondent with the American forces, contributing to a variety of papers, and travelling widely through Germany, planned to stay until the spring. In articles and letters she was more disgusted than her father over the Germans in defeat—their self-pity, self-justification, denial of guilt, above all the many claims to have been 'inner *émigrés*'—and as worried as he was over the forbearance of the occupying authorities. At Nuremberg, among the hundreds of journalists covering the trials which began on 20 November, she wrote bitterly over the absence in the dock of Krupp and other big industrialists, without whose powerful aid none of the twenty-two accused Nazi leaders could ever have become war criminals. But little of her material for the London *Evening Standard* found its way into print there.

At the start of the trials, Thomas Mann wrote for United Press a brief justification of the proceedings, of which there had been much criticism on grounds of conscience and especially on the lack of a legal basis for such retroactive prosecution. This, he argued, was not a traditional criminal

59 KlM *Br. Antw.* 553.

trial, but a 'political-moral demonstration with a wide-ranging educational purpose': democracy's war aims in the fight against fascism, though seemingly obscured by naked power-politics, had remained deep in the consciousness of humanity, and their expression in this way was essential. The Nazi warmakers might not have offended against any law then existing, but their trial was for an offence against one that ought to exist—the law of peace—and would one day be established through the dawning new order: a 'highest moral authority, a world government . . . an international Bill of Rights and an overriding penal law safeguarding the rights of the individual'. Admittedly, this might take a long time, and the trial meantime be regarded as hypocritical, a legal farce, merely the victors' vengeance. But he welcomed it nevertheless, for one day it would be seen as the prologue to a new reality.[60]

He was right that it would take a long time (nearly half a century later, the problem of 'war crimes' is still unresolved, and the controversy over retroactive prosecution goes on); and to his mind, as 1945 came to a close, there were few signs of any new order, in a world where fascism had still not been eliminated, and race discrimination continued rampant. He could not well refuse his signature in December to an appeal for humanitarian aid to Germany, much as he agreed with Einstein's dismissal of such a 'campaign of tears', and shared others' doubts over how to direct such aid to the deserving, if there were no distinction between anti-Nazis and those who should bear the guilt. His personal preoccupation with the problem of Germany and the Germans was finding expression in *Faustus*, as he approached the culmination of Leverkühn's pact with the Devil—the composition of his *magnum opus*, the oratorio 'Apocalipsis cum figuris', derived from Dürer's prints, with orchestra, choruses, soloists, and a speaker. For this he imagined 'something satanically religious, demonically devout, at once stringently disciplined and criminal in effect, often a mockery of art, also reaching back to the primitive and elemental . . . abandoning bar divisions, even the order of tonalities (trombone glissandi) . . . something barely performable: ancient church modes, *a capella* choruses in untempered tuning'.

But he was at a loss in December how to proceed—had indeed reached a point of physical fatigue in which he was near despair over the whole enterprise—and was badly in need of encouragement. He decided therefore to send Adorno, who had so far heard or read only extracts, the complete typescript to the point he had reached, in the hope both of general advice and of specific help to attain a convincing presentation of so very German a work as the oratorio. Confessing his shameless technique of montage and

[60] *Tb*. vi, 832f.

borrowings to compensate for his lack of true musical scholarship—the 'musical initiation' on which Toch had congratulated him was not enough—he asked him for a few more exact details, 'one or two musical features to further the illusion', for an idea in fact of how he himself would write if he were in league with the Devil.[61]

His physical weariness, despite an untroubled daily round, was a direct result of the sustained effort on a work whose theme right from the start had moved him more deeply, and into which he was putting more of his whole life, than any other. 'I'm not surprised', he wrote to Agnes Meyer on 14 December, 'that in the year I reached the age at which my mother died my life has come to a low point—from which it may still rise, however. It's the year in fact I prophesied for my death—not literally being fulfilled, apparently, but not without some indications of it.' His heart and general condition were actually sound, and the doctor could do no more than prescribe a course of vitamin tablets to correct the continuing loss of weight. Reassured, while he awaited Adorno's comments, his work continued, up to and including their quiet Christmas, for which only Michael and his family could join them. To a *Time* correspondent, who reminded him of his 1930 forecast of only another fifteen years of life, and who found him apparently in the best of shape, he admitted this had been only the reflection of his love of order and symmetry: 'now I think I will probably live to be quite old'. On New Year's Eve, the last day of a 'monstrous year, overfilled with earth-shaking events', he noted that his seventieth birthday had nevertheless fallen midway through it: a 'charming production touch'.


5

*'A German Europe has come to nothing. . . . But Germans must feel themselves European if Europe is to be created'*
(TM, 18 April 1947)


During the first weeks of January 1946 Mann was able to have many sessions with Adorno, who was encouraging in his sympathy with the aspiring aim and his appreciation of the difficulty of the project—though his suggestions for improvements brought home to the author the weaknesses of a book he was beginning to think 'artistically unsuccessful', too serious and offering no scope for his true epic and humorous style. Adorno was benevolent too towards the way so many of his own remarks on the contemporary musical scene, in his *Philosophy of Modern Music*, had been

[61] *Br.* ii, 472.

worked into the acid comments of Mann's Devil. For the apocalypse theme of the oratorio, on which Mann was now ready to start, he felt Dürer's prints were an inadequate basis, and they agreed that Leverkühn's opus must somehow take in the whole eschatology, express the ancient human tradition developed from a long line of visionaries and built on by John of Patmos. For Mann, increasingly inclined since *Joseph* 'to see all life as a cultural product and in the form of mythical tradition',[62] this was far more to his purpose than simple and straightforward inspiration for his composer. And in the course of many meetings, then and later, Adorno's suggestions and proposals for the presentation of the music itself were invaluable, fully in accord with the essential aim: to expose Leverkühn's work 'both to the reproach of bloody barbarism and to that of bloodless intellectualism'.

By the middle of January, after much reading in Dante and the Apocrypha, he was ready to begin this critical section of the novel, and over the next six weeks worked steadily day by day to get it done. He set his face as firmly as possible against other commitments. Some were inescapable, however—in January a speech on academic freedom and a recorded radio address on Roosevelt's birthday, in February an article for Heinrich's approaching seventy-fifth birthday—and as always his enormous correspondence was not neglected. He maintained his public silence on the reactions to his refusal to return to Germany revealed in many of the letters and publications he received; but he was as concerned as the military authorities over the evident influence of the persisting Nazi mentality on American soldiers there, many now returning as admirers of Hitler, and agreed to record a broadcast to counter this corruption.

In February he toyed briefly again with the idea of a European visit, following renewed proposals for a lecture tour in May. That, he felt, ought to include Germany—for, as he told Agnes Meyer, 'if I'm ever to go there again, I must do it *soon*, otherwise the gulf will be unbridgeable'. As in previous years, it could be combined with his annual Washington assignment, for which he had tentatively planned Nietzsche as the subject. Strongly advised on all sides against Germany, however, where some thought his life might even be in danger, and absorbed with the novel, he soon abandoned the project. Viktor had reported the Munich authorities prepared to restore the Poschinger Strasse house, assuming he would spend at least a few months there every year, but he warned him to make it clear that he had no such intention. He was disgusted with the way his open letter had been received in Germany, when he had tried to find his way 'between an inadmissible apology and a denunciation of my native

[62] xi 248.

country' to a declaration of solidarity and a sharing of guilt. In the end, these people had to realize that their frenzied expulsions and persecutions after 1933 were not a trivial joke which a few kind words of invitation to return could atone for. Every word he had said, even during the war and after, had been regarded as 'ignorant babble', and taken amiss by a people 'so fine, noble, innocent, offended and over-sensitive, that there is no way of getting on with them'.

As his work proceeded, relaxing social evenings were fewer, but there was the occasional film and concert. And he found the time for a session of nearly two hours with the well-known photographer Karsh, patient over the constant short-circuits caused by his apparatus, amused to hear how Churchill, who had given him only five minutes, had for once been captured in a grimly smiling likeness without his cigar, and inordinately pleased with the results for himself.

Yet he had made a poor subject, pale of countenance and looking implausibly ethereal. For his labour on *Faustus* was against the background of still-uncertain health, with sleepless nights and a constant feeling of lassitude during the day. A new doctor towards the end of January had discovered on X-ray a spot on the lung, which needed watching, but his prescriptions for the other troubles were routine and seemingly ineffective. On 3 March, just after completing the oratorio chapters, he was laid low for two weeks with an attack of influenza, and even when partially up and about again, under the care now of a third doctor, his condition continued to fluctuate alarmingly, while he did his best to concentrate on notes for the Nietzsche lecture. New X-rays on 1 April confirmed the condition of the right lung, which the doctor rightly suspected meant an early stage of cancer: to his patient he spoke only of an abscess on the lung, which a specialist confirmed and for which he prescribed penicillin treatment. Both hesitated over a bronchoscopy, and a possible operation, in view of his age. Katia though, realizing the seriousness, cut through the discussions with admirable energy, contacted through Elisabeth the Billings Hospital in Chicago, where there was an eminent lung-surgeon, and within a week had quickly arranged the long train journey there, with ambulances to and from the stations, arriving on 13 April.

It was a sign of the state Mann had reached that he accepted all this passively. He had been more surprised than alarmed at the diagnosis, for lung trouble had been the last thing he expected—but also in a way relieved to find at last revealed the reason for the difficulties he had been labouring under these last few months. For him the blame lay entirely with the 'frightful novel and the German vexations': 'no accident', as he wrote later, 'that I fell seriously ill in the middle, it was the book itself which was taking it out of me'.[63] At the Billings he surrendered in fascination to his installation and the calm investigations and attentions: it was the first time he had seen with a patient's eye a great hospital and experienced its routine, and he was highly impressed by the contrast with the authoritarian style of German institutions which he had gently caricatured in *The Magic Mountain*. Katia was able to dictate a full anamnesis; he withstood the bronchoscopy well, in itself no light matter for one of his age; his heart was pronounced in good shape; and it was decided to proceed with the operation on 24 April.

Still unaware of the serious nature of his complaint, he was weak, and blood transfusions were needed, but he could follow the preparations with lively interest. For one who all his life had been eager to learn the names and properties of the painkillers or sedatives he was taking, it was surprising, annoying even, to be treated here with an anonymous 'little something', like a nervous child. The arrival, meanwhile, of Erika from Nuremberg was a great solace both for him and Katia, who with Elisabeth had been in constant attendance. She took charge of the flowers, and brought some gaiety to patient and staff with occasional bogus newssheets, paste-ups of words and letters from the papers with outrageous headlines like 'Eisenhower May Be Arrested on Spy Charge', 'Germany Demands Dismissal of US Government', or 'Truman Hopes to Lure Stalin to Missouri'. It was a strange experience for Mann to have the pneumothorax to collapse the lung, which he had treated so lightly in *The Magic Mountain*, applied to his own body: but he found it easy to bear, earning praise for so unusually co-operative an attitude.

That was the case too for the operation itself when the day came. It was a major intervention, with a very long incision and involving removal of a rib and two-thirds of the lung. He was in fact one of the oldest patients to have undergone this type of operation: but the surgeon's skill, coupled with his basically solid constitution, ensured a satisfactory outcome and an uneventful recovery. He had needed only one further blood transfusion during the proceedings, where for younger men two or three would have been required; and in the four weeks of recovery in the hospital he qualified in every way as a model patient. Writing to Klaus later, Katia said that if he had ever suspected cancer (and she certainly thought he had), then he had entirely repressed the notion, and fully accepted the harmless lung-abscess version, which was the story to the outside world and to friends.

Over such a critical time, the words of sympathy and the presents and flowers he received, the visits from Bermann, Caroline Newton, and Bruno Walter (who alone learned the truth), made him wonder, as he wrote later,

---

[63] *DüD* iii, 98.

how he could possibly have deserved them: how could the creative artist, obsessed with his work and almost inhuman in his concentration, ever be a congenial fellow-being for those around him? It was a speculation infernal enough to be ascribed to his Adrian Leverkühn. Through these weeks the novel in fact was never far from his thoughts, and he came to feel it had been a subconscious determination to return to finish it that had brought him successfully through this great trial so late in life. Apart from a loss of appetite, which he put down to the continuing dosage of penicillin, his progress was remarkably good, and the doctors readily agreed to his proposal for a few days' transitional convalescence in less severe surroundings, at the familiar Hotel Windermere, before entraining for Los Angeles. At a press conference before leaving the hospital he described his operation merely as a masterpiece (having been discouraged from more details, or any personal publicity for those responsible for this 'most elegant' performance). Although eager to speak, he was sensibly held in check by Erika, to save his strength, and his brief political remarks on the desirability of a *rapprochement* between Russia and the West, in the long term perhaps a world federation, were carried only by one paper. When he said that after *Faustus* he would confine himself to shorter works, Katia pointed out how little this meant: *The Magic Mountain* had, after all, started out as a short story.

By the end of May he was back in Pacific Palisades, happy and relieved, after this 'late examination, passed *cum laude*', to be among his books again, and determined to leave aside the Nietzsche lecture and concentrate on finishing the novel. The outline of the rest was clear, and, whatever the difficulties, they would be overcome step by step. Even correspondence must take second place, and the stack of letters awaiting him he would turn over to Katia and Hilde Kahn—though this was a resolve only partially fulfilled. The secretary came for an extra hour on her days, and Katia was by now so practised an imitator of his style that he was able to sign hers as his own. His birthday passed, naturally, very quietly, and he withstood the stream of afternoon callers only with some difficulty, noting a tendency to breathlessness in company. Through June, he gradually recovered his strength, with a regular gain in weight and return to normal breathing, resumed daily outings, at first in the car but later on foot, with a camp-chair to rest on; and he worked steadily on revising the manuscript so far, more often on the sofa than at the desk, before turning at the end of the month to the next chapter. Smoking had not been forbidden: his attempts to resume with cigarettes and an occasional half a cigar were not encouraging, but though alarmed at the thought of provoking a relapse, he was loath to abandon the pleasure from misplaced hypochondria, and was not long regaining the normal moderate level, which, it seemed, did him no harm.

Little was in fact changed in his daily routine, as his condition improved. The former avid follower of political events, both in America and Europe, took now a more detached view, and began before long to feel it was only from a 'stupid sense of duty', pedantry almost, that he continued to read the papers. Although he noted with foreboding later in June the 'criminal' atomic bomb tests on Bikini Atoll, and would later lend his support to a movement for a federal world government, the apparent preparations for another war seemed 'no longer my business', and he was able to find consolation in continuing the narrative.

The severe trial had softened the harsher edges of his character. On his birthday evening, in the course of a champagne dinner with Bruno Walter and his wife, he brought himself to propose to this friend of nearly forty years' standing that they should henceforth be on first-name terms—a sign of how much he had mellowed. The news of Hauptmann's death, from a heart attack after his expulsion from the new Poland, moved him only to reflection on the comparison with his own loss of hearth and home in 1933, and the memory of their avoided encounter then in Zurich, when Hauptmann had said this must await better, 'more neutral' times: 'was he ashamed, or did he regard talking to an *émigré* as treachery towards "the new Germany"?' As Golo recalled, he said Hauptmann was his only peer in Germany (who else could have called him brother?); and although he had abhorred the other's subservient behaviour towards the new Reich, Golo doubted whether he would have continued to hold this against him had he survived.

Writing to Golo, after an appeal from a new 'German League for Peace' to accept its presidency, he was greatly preoccupied over the general problem of 'reconciliation'—a word much used now over there in the less acceptable sense of reconciling Germany herself, rather than as a sign of remorse. He did not wish, he said, to hold himself aloof, to separate himself from Germany for good, and was inclined to accept this responsibility, but had doubts over the status of such an apparently small group. Golo, from his closer knowledge of conditions there, evidently advised against, and in the end he declined. Contributing to this decision, probably, had been a satirical article by Erich Kästner (the writer of children's books who had returned to Dresden from Zurich before 1939 to stay, despite the banning of his work), and his own sustained aversion for the 'inner *émigrés*', which he expressed in forceful terms to those, like Blunck, who, as he put it, had remained blind to the horrors of the regime as they served it. As he wrote later to others remaining, like himself outside, Germany was not cured: 'her writers celebrate the dishonourable bankruptcy of criminal stupidity as a tragedy and a wonderfully distinguishing destiny which once again elevates that unfortunate country above all others. But what better can they do, since they all conformed?'[64] For himself, he would never return. The satisfaction later afforded him by the offer from Bonn University to restore his doctorate, which he immediately accepted, did not alter this resolve, and he was glad that the act of restitution could not remove from the record his response so widely publicized at the time. Later, he refused an invitation to translate John Hersey's 'Hiroshima' report: 'as a piece of American self-criticism, it is very good, but the Germans already have enough to feed their *schadenfreude*'.

Going over *Faustus* to date, and noting the unacceptable *longueurs* of this 'misshapen giant snake',[65] he had been inclined to see these as a matter for a later editor to correct (with Erika in mind)—to view the whole undertaking in fact as a kind of testament for posterity. But he was determined still to carry it forward, and through summer and autumn made steady progress towards 'an end still somewhat unclear to me'. Erika was at hand to correct his 'old man's verbosity' with substantial cuts of some forty pages in the manuscript, particularly in the early parts, so that by the end of August the first 275 pages could be sent to Helen Lowe-Porter in Oxford for translation (she had agreed to step in after Agnes Meyer had finally refused).

At the end of September a new visit from Michael and his family was timely, for the moment was near for the long-planned episode of the life and tragic death of Leverkühn's little nephew Nepomuk, the elf-like 'Echo'. To have his model there for a month—listening to his chatter in a German strongly influenced by the Swiss, making drawings for him as before, even if often finding him disturbing—was an inspiration: when he came to the writing, he was moved to a tenderness which he himself found surprising, and worked on these chapters with an eager zeal he thought he had never before experienced. From his doctor he had sought full details of the course of the meningitis which was to be the Devil's way of depriving his cold hero, for whom love was not permitted, of the solace of the 'divine child'; and the result was the most moving passage of the book—as he found when he read it to the family, and when on New Year's Day 1947 Erika, back in New York, telegraphed: 'Shall go into New Year with reddened eyes but happy heart. Wondering only how on earth you do it.'

By then, he was near the close, with Leverkühn's time run out and his lapse into madness after completing his cantata 'The Lamentation of Doctor Faustus', on its twelve-note theme 'For I die as a bad and a good Christian', and running through it, as Zeitblom notes, the reference to 'the promise and the blood pact'. The advice of Adorno, his 'Privy Councillor', was here of capital importance, less in the musical sense than in the theological or religious: he rightly criticized the over-emphasis on the comfort of grace, as

---

[64] 46/335, 46/337.　　　[65] 46/311.

too strong a light after all the darkness of the story, and Mann reworked the passage to its final more cautious and less optimistic form. By 29 January, he had set the last line to Zeitblom's epilogue: his friend's burial, after years of mental darkness, on 25 August 1940, while Germany was reeling on the hectic heights of triumph by virtue of the 'one pact she was minded to keep, signed with her blood', but now as he writes 'tumbles surrounded by demons . . . from despair to despair. When will she reach the bottom of the abyss? When . . . will the light of hope dawn? A lonely man folds his hands and speaks: God be merciful to thy poor soul, my friend, my Fatherland.'

After over three and a half years, it was done. Though he wondered whether Katia's words of congratulation were deserved, he could justifiably see a moral achievement in completing the most important work of his life. It was one in which he had 'never felt more passionately engaged',[66] which had come close to destroying him, but which he had been able to complete in the curious 'mixture of sensitivity and phlegm . . . that brought me through and allowed me with the right hand steadfastly to continue my labour and with the left to fight'.[67] They celebrated that evening with a bottle of Veuve Clicquot; but he still spent some time in the following days on retouching and changes before he could feel he had finished, even though the manuscript had already gone off to Helen Lowe-Porter and to Bermann, who had begun printing in Switzerland. As he wrote later to Reisiger, the four volumes of the *Joseph* had been 'pure operatic enjoyment' in comparison. 'That was epic, this is something else, more terrible', despite its lighter passages, for it held so much of himself: the sad and wicked story of Adrian Leverkühn was not only a symbol of the ruin of Germany, but also 'a displaced, transferred, distorted, demonic rendering and exposure of my own life'.[68] The whole thing had been like an open wound; and he was concerned over the way he had sacrificed so many of his friends— like Reisiger, Annette Kolb, even Caroline Newton and Ida Herz—and his own relatives, Carla and his mother, to the 'cold glance' of Leverkühn, with the accursed montage technique, dictated to him by the Devil, which had pasted so much reality on to the picture. And during the months to come he awaited the effect on readers, especially German, with no little trepidation (with the Anglo-Saxons, who would see it later, he was already resigned to hear it branded as a 'terrible mess, excessively German').[69]

Katia had done wonders to give him the quiet he needed. There had been constant problems with servants, house and kitchen often left entirely to her or whoever else happened to be on hand, and post-war shortages had given no little trouble. Things had not been made easier by the arrival in November of her twin, Klaus, from Tokyo, with his son, in the hope of

[66] *DüD*. iii, 92.    [67] *DüD*. ii, 621.    [68] *Tb*. vii, 608 f.
[69] To Joachim Maass, 2 Feb. 1948 (Stargardt auction cat. 612, 1977).

finding a post with his brother-in-law's help, and they stayed till past Christmas. That festival had of necessity been quiet, with no children apart from Golo and Monika able to come; and throughout the final months of 1946 the work could continue without interruption. Golo, the 'civilian lieutenant-colonel', had decided to quit the occupation forces; temporarily with the State Department, he finally accepted a history professorship at Claremont College, Pomona, in the New Year, to start in the autumn, and the prospect of having him so close was a welcome one for his father. Over the holiday period there had been only sparse contact with Heinrich, but Golo kept him company one evening after the New Year. During 1946 he had been several times urged to return to Germany, to the Soviet Zone, where his books were being reissued while almost totally ignored in the Western zones: though he decided now not to accept the invitation, later in the year he was awarded an honorary doctorate by the East Berlin Humboldt University.

His brother, now thoroughly restored and relieved of the burden of the novel, had returned to thoughts of the long-deferred lecture-tour in the spring of 1947, with the Nietzsche text he had planned: beginning with the Library of Congress, which his illness had kept him from, and going on to Europe—Sweden, London, Brussels, Amsterdam, and Switzerland, with a visit too to Germany. Between mid-February and mid-March, as he awaited confirmation of his dates, he completed 'Nietzsche's Philosophy in the Light of Contemporary Events', the further contribution he had long envisaged to the psychology of 'Germanness' and the Germans. His close study in the course of *Faustus* had given him a sense of the continuity and unity of Nietzsche's thought, with its later undoubted degeneration into anti-morality and a 'lamentable glorification of evil' under the effect of syphilis. The world's recent experience of evil in its more 'ordinary imbecility'[70] could lend his theme actuality both in America and Europe, though his versions must clearly differ in these presentations. As with earlier lectures, therefore, Erika's editorial blue pencil was successfully brought into play, not only to simplify the English text for Washington and London ears, but also to bring the German version down to lecture length, leaving his original for later publication as an essay.

By early April she had 'murdered' the text sufficiently, and they could prepare their departure for the tour, on which she would accompany them. The American assignments—Library of Congress and Hunter College, New York—remained firm, but for Europe, the original programme was now limited to England, Switzerland, and Holland, omitting, as he had decided after much heart-searching, the visit to Germany. The Americans, as he

---

[70] *DüD.* iii, 330 f.

told Viktor, feared disturbances if he appeared there: was he to go around with a military police bodyguard? and what could he say to the Germans in their present state? Instead he would try to arrange a meeting in Switzerland during his stay. They set off on 22 April on the familiar night-train for Chicago; a few days' break there with the Borgeses gave the opportunity of a check at the Billings Hospital, which left the doctors fully satisfied with his condition (any troubles now, as he noted, came from nerves and disposition, which was not their concern). Michael was there, on tour with the orchestra, and had news of Gret's visit to Zurich with the children, who were getting on famously with their Swiss grandfather. A trial run for the family of the English lecture-text left him exhausted but content with it, despite Borgese's reservations over his approach to Nietzsche.

The Washington occasion followed its now traditional course, with the Meyers' unfailing hospitality, long-lasting applause for the lecture from a packed Coolidge Auditorium on 29 April, and the customary reception afterwards at Crescent Place, attended by, among others, Walter Lippmann and the French and Swiss ambassadors. He found himself well able to withstand it all, though it gave him a restless night, and felt it had been a success. Calling next day at the British embassy for their visas, he was received by Ambassador Clark-Kerr (Lord Inverchapel)—'a Scottish noble-man, very literary'—and found atmosphere, accent, and sense of humour of this British cultural environment highly entertaining. Inverchapel was at the station on 1 May to see off the Duke of Windsor, who was taking their same train to New York and was treated with notable respect by the Americans.

In New York for ten days, they were welcomed by Erika, Klaus, Golo, and Monika. His performance at Hunter College, on 3 May, seemed even more successful than in Washington: he felt he had spoken well, the audience of 2,000 was closely attentive, he had to respond many times to the applause, and the whole evening was like that of a magnificent concert. 'Such an incomprehensible passion for lectures is only to be found in this country.'[71] In an interview for the *New York Times* next day ('Nobel Prize Winner Says "A New War is not Inevitable"'), he enlarged on the needs of what he called the 'post-bourgeois era', for which 'neither Russian communism nor American democracy with its somehow antiquated economic doctrines points in the right direction'. What was required was a compromise between the two, a synthesis of liberty and equality with social necessities and individual rights. If Soviet Russia abandoned her radicalism and the United States revised her democratic principles for the require-

---

[71] Letter of 4 May 1947 to Wolfgang Born (in private ownership).

ments of a new age, as both eventually must, 'then and only then we shall
strive towards a true world democracy'.[72] This view had at its root his
concern over the anti-communist witch-hunt recently started by the House
Unamerican Activities Committee, and his support for the Civil Rights
Congress's protest over the case of Gerhart Eisler, the communist *émigré*
whose attempts to leave for Germany had been thwarted by his arrest and
threatened prosecution. But he was loath to get further involved, and
refused now in New York to sign another protest, as too clearly communist
in inspiration.

The none-too-comfortable passage to England, on the crowded *Queen
Elizabeth*, which they boarded on 10 May, brought feelings of regret and a
certain loss of confidence: but he had set his hand to the plough, and was
himself again when they landed at Southampton on 16 May. During their
week's stay at the Savoy, he was plunged into a heavy round of engagements, both social and official, with Erika as always a tower of strength for
him. In the immediate Reuter interview in Southampton he took the same
world political line as in New York, adding his earlier advocacy of a loose
federal solution for Germany. (The remark, however, on his reluctance to
revisit Munich and Bonn 'under the Allied bayonets' was so misrendered in
the German news-agency translation as to appear as if Bonn had renewed
his doctorate only 'under Allied pressure'[73]—an important discrepancy
which would later cause him much trouble.)

At a big reception on the evening of his arrival in London, attended
among others by Vansittart, he met Harold Nicolson again: a curious
experience, as the latter wrote in a later article, to recall his last encounter
nearly twenty years earlier in Munich with 'this great humanist' who had
subsequently had 'the tragic experience of seeing his gloomiest prophecies
fulfilled'. Mann's aim was to discover whether socialism—for 'we are all
socialists today'—could be rendered 'humanistic', and he believed that
Britain and the Commonwealth, with their long experience, toleration, and
dislike of extremes, had a major role to play in this (as he told Nicolson on
a later occasion, he truly feared America was going fascist, and he was not
inclined to become for a second time a martyr to freedom). On 19 May he
visited the BBC, to record an abbreviated version of his 'Germany and the
Germans', and the following day came his Nietzsche lecture.

He spoke before the largest audience ever assembled in the university
Senate House, the pressure in fact so great that all doors to the building had
to be closed early and an overflow room arranged for microphone relay. In
brief introductory words, he expressed his emotion at beginning his return
to Europe in Britain, the land which 'in 1940 saved mankind by her

---

[72] *Tb.* vii, 567.      [73] *Fr./Antw.* 268 f.

steadfastness from the most horrible slavery' and was now perhaps 'furthest
on the road to that new humanism' which was the fundamental theme of
his lecture. His performance proved as successful here as in Washington,
the occasion as triumphal as at Hunter College. In this 'simple' form,
designed for 'ignorant Anglo-Saxons', the lecture would be heard more
critically in Zurich, was his comment in a letter to Heinrich: here, however,
as telephone calls, visits, and press coverage assured him, the reception was
unanimously favourable.

At a further interview, for the Hamburg paper *Die Welt*, where the first
question concerned a visit to Germany, he chose his words carefully:
though his mind was still open, on balance a visit was better left to a later
date, 'when minds there have quietened and become more clear', and that
was probably the German view too, since he had received no official
invitation. The Germans had not yet realized that their suffering resulted
from their own earlier actions, not from the occupation, and in their old
'national egoism' had no eyes for the misery of the rest of the world. And
he concluded with his same hope for the future, in that 'synthesis of
freedom and equality, socialism and individualism' once hoped for by
Roosevelt and now possible under the guidance of Britain.[74] In a short
'Message to the German People', recorded for the BBC on 21 May, and
published later in the *Frankfurter Zeitung*, his line was rather sterner:
responsibility could not be laid only upon the Nazi leaders, National
Socialism had certain roots in the German character and tradition, and
their eradication and any re-education could effectively come only from
within. He had in fact firmly decided not to visit Germany, and made this
clear in a final interview for United Press, before boarding an air-taxi for
Zurich on 24 May: 'I am not eager to go and see the wreckage—either stone
wreckage or human wreckage.' 'I wonder what rubble-strewn alley it is that
they have named after me in Dresden,' he had written to Erika the previous
October: 'it certainly won't be very grand.'[75]

The stay in Switzerland, which lasted over two months, marked his real
return to Europe. The familiar Zurich scenes, over mild Whitsun days,
recalled the relatively happy times of his first years of exile from Germany,
and the reunion with so many friends, as well as Gret, her children, and
Therese Giehse, were a lift to the heart. Through June, he was almost
overwhelmed by the stream of visitors and a 'calamitous' flood of mail, the
calls for interviews, and the growing disorder in his papers in his room in
the Baur au Lac. A written programme had to be prepared daily, in which
a number of lecture engagements figured prominently—foremost, of
course, the Nietzsche, which he gave during the week of the Zurich PEN

---

[74] Ibid. 270 ff.      [75] *Br.* ii, 511.

Congress, on 3 June, and repeated in Berne on 11 June, apparently well received each time, but also a reading from *Faustus* in the Zurich Schauspielhaus on 8 June, to great applause, and a talk to students in the university. These were weeks of considerable pressure, increased by renewed attempts to rouse him to visit Germany, notably from Munich for an 'International Youth' meeting: he maintained his refusal, even when a delegation from Munich arrived to try personal persuasion. 'Too much argues against it, both there and in my still greatly embittered heart,' he wrote later to Reisiger.[76] The unceasing attacks on him, some provoked by the mistranslation of his London interview, some misrepresenting his 1933 letter to the Interior Ministry, he found sickening, but resigned himself to regarding 'those over there [as] three parts crazy'. Watching the antics of Knappertsbusch as he conducted a *Götterdämmerung* performance was a thoroughly sinister experience.

On 20 June he and Katia escaped to spend a month in Flims, Erika leaving them to visit Prague and Poland, and after the tumult he found welcome refuge in some work—the proofs of *Faustus*, which also appeared to be circulating among certain privileged readers in Stockholm, for he began to hear enthusiastic comments even at this early stage. He was reminded again of how he had 'murdered' his friends in his 'ruthlessly autobiographical' approach (many placatory letters would later have to be written, after the book's appearance in the autumn), but felt he had paid for his sins with the lung operation. *Faustus*, he wrote later, whatever criticism it aroused, would at least certify him as a 'true son of his unhappy country, deeply concerned with its character', and not a deserter.[77] Meanwhile, he was worried over production delay in the preliminary small edition in America to preserve his copyright, and had written to seek Luther Evans's help in securing a relaxation of the rules.

After their return to Zurich on 20 July the remaining weeks were publicly less demanding, with only two readings from *Faustus*, and socially less of a whirl, with leisure for excursions to Lucerne, for a rewarding evening with Hesse, and Stresa. Viktor and his Nelly arrived on 24 July, with Heinz Pringsheim and his wife: but the reunion, not surprisingly, proved difficult, uneasy as Thomas was at the excited and over-affectionate manner of the young brother who had stayed throughout in Germany. The continuing adverse criticism there remained a thorn in the flesh, and he decided to publish in the *Neue Zürcher Zeitung* the full text of his 1933 letter to the Interior Ministry, in order to disarm those who claimed he had really endeavoured to make his peace with the Reich. His current thoughts on Germany were altogether gloomy: there would be a rebirth of nationalism,

[76] *Bl.* 8, 16.      [77] *DüD.* iii, 97.

Germany would be restored and rearmed, and in fifty years, if not sooner, would once more 'have non-Russian Europe in her pocket'. The ideal, as he noted later, was a unified Europe without German (or Russian) hegemony—but the priority was to ensure that Germany's power should not be restored.

He longed to be back under his Californian palms. First, however, there were engagements in Holland to be discharged. Flying to Amsterdam on 10 August, they were met by Klaus, who had been back there for some time with Fritz Landshoff (dreaming once more of starting a journal, but meantime helping with the selection for a Goethe anthology, to mark the coming bicentenary, which his father had undertaken to edit for the Dial Press). An elaborate press-conference in the hotel, with radio and film in attendance, was followed on 13 August by a reception in the PEN Club, at which he improvised a brief address, recalling his friend Menno ter Braak and the other victims of Nazism, explaining his reluctance for the moment to visit Germany, but affirming his faith in Europe's youth for a brighter future, saying he intended to write an introductory essay for Frans Masereel's 'novel in pictures' *La Jeunesse*. After the relative luxury of Switzerland, he found conditions, like those in England, spartan indeed —nothing to buy, in the hotel no coffee or eggs, reduced to their own supply of honey—and began enquiries for a stay by the sea in the probably more congenial Noordwijk, with its memories of 1939. His Nietzsche lecture was given in the Indian Institute on 14 August, before a quiet and no more than polite audience, and they were glad of the peace in the familiar beach-hotel in Noordwijk for the final weeks. Though there too food and service were anything but satisfactory, he was happy to be back at work. Interrupted only for the last public appearance, a *Faustus* reading in Amsterdam, which proved popular, he completed the Masereel essay, read in Huizinga's study on Erasmus, and began to think about the introduction for the Goethe anthology which would have to be produced soon after his return to California.

The slow crossing on the small Dutch steamer *Westerdam*, which they joined on 29 August in Rotterdam, gave ample time for reflection over the tour. It had made great demands on his endurance, and he could fleetingly envy Heinrich, who did not burden himself with this life of a stage virtuoso or let the world lead him thus by the nose.[78] (An article by Melvin Lasky in the *New Leader*, which he saw only later, had rightly stressed the invigorating effect of his visit on 'broad European cultural circles', his curious position and personality serving 'to touch (and scandalize) them at any number of literary, political, and national points'—a sign of Europe's

---

[78] 47/267.

recovering intellectual health. In the light, wrote Lasky, of his refusal to visit Germany, incensing both the Americans, with his reference to Allied bayonets, and the Germans, who had always seen him as a traitor to their traditions though grudgingly recognizing him as an immortal of world letters, his performance in London and Zurich had been a *tour de force*, and his choice of Nietzsche 'a master-stroke of Mann irony'.)[79]

For himself, as he settled on board to his backlog of correspondence, the months away from his desk had not been unfruitful: ideas for new work were not lacking (a medieval novella was already in mind, and *Felix Krull* still remained to be completed)—and the expensive stay in Switzerland had been well covered by the influx of 'Fränkli' from fees and royalties. Reading more on Erasmus, he was impressed, if a little put out, by the similarity with his own character—and with Goethe's, who would have been equally evasive over the Reformation, and as negative towards Luther's tumult as he himself had been towards Hitler's. There was something Erasmian too about his fame, which he felt he failed in the end, like the indecisive humanist, to vindicate. The visit to Europe had seemed like a return to where he belonged, though it was still too insecure to consider making a home there; he was impatient to see Pacific Palisades again, and the words of the immigration officer as they landed in New York—'you are *the* Thomas Mann, welcome home'—struck the note he wanted to hear. After an interview for the *New York Times*, in which he urged the Americans to realize the need for a planned economy in shattered Europe, not simply a return to nineteenth-century capitalism, the transcontinental journey was then literally a playback: seen into their air-conditioned train by Monika; in Chicago met by Elisabeth and burdened by the anti-Semitic vapourings of Borgese; tested again and pronounced fully fit at the hospital; the final leg to Los Angeles in welcome American comfort, and at last driven by Golo back to Pacific Palisades on 14 September.

No more novels, he had said after finishing *Faustus*; and as he resumed the Californian routine, his references to his work during the last months of 1947 were disparaging—merely passing the time, he often said, no more than a hobby and of little consequence. This he felt certainly applied to the essay and selection work for the Goethe anthology. During October and November the sometimes boring effort consisted mainly of recycling his earlier material—'old stuff newly arranged and smartened up'; but it presented problems, for one ill-versed in English, over the choice of good translations, even with Klaus's help, and he thought the fee of 2,000 dollars would be small recompense for his trouble. His income at the moment was in fact considerably reduced, while awaiting the publication of *Faustus*, and

[79] *Tb.* vii, 617 f.

calls on his purse from friends, from Erika (whose lecture plans were finding little interest), and particularly from Heinrich, were giving cause for some concern. A little ashamed over the disparity between his circumstances and Heinrich's, he found it difficult to talk to him, and was glad, if only for Katia's sake, that inviting him to stay was impossible as he was forbidden to climb stairs. Problems clearly lay ahead, with his brother's worsening health and advancing age. Nevertheless, despite his anxiety over the reception of *Faustus* when it appeared, his idea for the medieval novella-legend was taking shape, and he had not forgotten *Felix Krull*: he was 'thirsting', he told Agnes Meyer on 10 October, for 'comedy, laughter, humour' after the scantily lightened terrors of *Faustus*: 'One who could write the *Joseph* at the time of Hitler's victories will not be got down by what is to come—if he survives.' As Erika said on 17 October, the day of publication of *Faustus*, that book, far from making him ill, as he had thought, had in fact given him perfect health and readied him 'for new exploits on paper'.

What was to come he could discern in the current trend towards a hysterical anti-communism. The move early in October to deport the composer Hanns Eisler, after his 'trial' before the House Unamerican Activities Committee, as a 'driving force of international communism' and an illegal immigrant, was a depressing sign for Mann of America's dwindling sense of justice, the advent even of fascist rule. At the end of the month, appearing in Hollywood as a confessedly hostile witness before a subcommittee of the HUAC investigating alleged communist influence in the movie industry, he argued powerfully against 'spiritual intolerance, political inquisitions, and declining legal security' in the name of a spurious state of emergency, only too symptomatic of the way fascism had started in Germany. It was satisfying to speak his mind to these 'illiterates', and he recorded his statement for ABC, in their radio series 'Hollywood Fights Back' (later, in the hysteria of the so-called McCarthy era and the intensification of the cold war, it would be used against him, to show him as a dupe and willing tool of the communists). Interviewed in San Francisco in November, after a repeat of his Nietzsche lecture, he pleaded for *détente* with Soviet Russia, despite its false idea of democracy, and called communism 'an empty word', wrongly used to condemn all kinds of socialism or left-liberal ideas and its danger greatly exaggerated. But, whatever his sympathy in the particular case of Eisler, whom he considered by no means a communist, he was reluctant to get further involved, as unbecoming to one who felt himself, though a citizen, still a guest of the country. From now on, eager only for 'quiet and invisibility', he was more cautious over lending his name to liberal causes, though never backward in support for Jewish resettlement and the fight against anti-Semitism.

He had begun studies and the search for material for the novella-legend, but could not settle to it until his worries over the reception of *Faustus* had been relieved. By December, the first reviews from Switzerland had made clear how unwarranted these had been: 'since Werther's days there has perhaps never been so much talk of tears'.[80] Korrodi, over two October numbers of the *Neue Zürcher Zeitung*, had run a discussion on the book between a theologian, a biologist, and the musical scholar Willi Schuh—surely unique, Mann thought, as a journalistic review. In Germany, where an edition with Suhrkamp under licence was in preparation, it would probably be another matter, he felt, but his euphoria was unconcealed over the unexampled excitement shown by this, the other reviews (including one from Michael in a Swiss musical journal), and the many letters he continued to receive through January. Never had a book of his had such an echo—and never before had he awaited reactions so eagerly or collected them with such 'true piety'. Nor, perhaps, had he entered into so much correspondence over a single work.

His first sight of it between hard covers had been the copyright-preserving mimeographed edition Bermann brought out in October, and he had qualms of conscience again at the over-heavy theoretical and pedagogical passages. During November therefore he had worked with Erika on substantial cuts, not only to ease the translation problem for the foreign editions, but also, if possible, to give the German text a stronger narrative line. These were successfully made for Bermann's successor edition in Vienna, and Suhrkamp's in Frankfurt, during 1948, and undoubtedly made for easier reading. *Faustus* and its reception remained a constant preoccupation through 1948, and any unfavourable reaction did not fail to rouse him to extensive response and explanation, in February in particular to the Germanist Käte Hamburger, whom he upbraided for total lack of understanding for the role of the book in his life's work and its quality as a confession. The London *Times Literary Supplement* review was far from adverse—'bold grandeur', 'highly entertaining digressions [gathering] the memories and thoughts of a lifetime into the loosely-woven net of an ironically glittering prose'—though from his previous experiences with the *TLS* he may well have suspected this as damning with faint praise.

He had written soothing letters at length to all the friends who might feel themselves pilloried in his admittedly ruthless portraiture. There were more difficult problems, however, with Adorno, who, though silent, gave the impression of discontent over the lack of acknowledgement of his collaboration, and especially with Schönberg, to whom he sent a copy inscribed 'to the real one', but who was clearly infuriated by the flagrant misappropriation of his intellectual property in Adrian Leverkühn's 'invention' of the twelve-tone system. Adorno was pacified when Mann told him he intended to write a full autobiographical account of the genesis and development of the novel, in which he would receive full credit for his invaluable assistance. Schönberg, on the other hand, moved to the attack, sending Mann a fictitious encyclopaedia-article in which their roles were reversed: Mann the inventor of the system, revealing his achievement only in *Faustus*, with Schönberg the thieving composer and plagiarist appropriating it for himself. 'I know I can only count on posthumous fame, and I should not have to defend that too,' Schönberg wrote him.[81] It was not until the end of February that they could make an uneasy peace, Mann undertaking to add an afterword, for the English and other foreign editions, and all future German editions, establishing the other's legitimate claim. But Schönberg continued to make himself heard publicly, and even at the end of the year Mann was worried over the possibility of a lawsuit. More interesting were enquiries whether with Leverkühn's music he had had Benjamin Britten's in mind. That, he averred, was coincidence, the effect purely of contemporaneity, for he had never heard it; when he did, in March, he agreed his hero might well have been glad to set to music Tennyson's poem 'Nocturne' or Keats's 'Ode to Music'. For the moment, though, listening again to the song of the Rhine maidens, he was moved to tears: 'I'd sacrifice all Schönberg, Berg, Krenek, and Leverkühn for that passage.'

He had felt an aversion to starting something new: but in January 1949 the first tentative lines of what would become *The Holy Sinner* were on paper. 'I'm reading a lot of Middle High German (with dictionary),' he told Agnes Meyer in February—Hartmann von Aue's religious legend *Gregorius*—and planned a modern version of this 'variation on the Oedipus myth, the election by God himself of a fearfully incestuous sinner as the Roman Pope', its theme 'actually that of *grace*'.[82] Though he spoke of the amusement he was finding in this 'pious grotesquery' (and found much too in the simple humour of Jack Benny's weekly radio-programme), he was not yet in light enough mood, after the dark terrors of *Faustus*, to make more than hesitant progress. He was in a 'nervous and unsteady state of transition';[83] a fracture of the left shoulder from an unlucky fall at the end of February, though quickly mended, was not helpful; and it was not until April that he felt the too long 'period of melancholy and hangover after *Faustus*'[84] was past.

It was a year at least of rest from travel: there would be no more until 1949, when the Goethe bicentenary would require another lecture-tour,

[81] *Tb.* vii, 715.    [82] *AM Brw.* 694.    [83] *Amann Br.* 68.    [84] 48/317.

with perhaps, at last, a visit to Germany. To a large extent also, he held himself aloof from politics and from events which in earlier days would have exercised him more deeply: the murder of Mahatma Gandhi in January, the communist take-over in Prague in February, the Allied repression of the Left in Greece, Henry Wallace's presidential campaign against Truman for a third party and for a foreign policy of peace with the communists. He recognized the events in Prague as naked assumption of power by the communists, the 'suicide' of Jan Masaryk as obviously murder, and sent a telegram of sympathy to Beneš. Klaus was there, invited for lectures by the communist Ministry of Culture, but, as his father said, 'we're all counted as reds and menials of Wallace anyway, and haven't much to lose',[85] and where formerly he would have been active in protest, he had no public statement to make now. If anything, he considered the events in Greece far worse than those in Czechoslovakia, and his diary noted only shame at his earlier optimism over 'The Coming Victory of Democracy'.

There was no secret of his support for Wallace, but he resisted any public endorsement. He was, however, persuaded to appear at a conference of the Hollywood 'Peace group' in June, at which he stressed that peace for him was by no means just a communist slogan, but 'the categorical imperative' for humanity; and in October, in the final stages of the presidential campaign, he broadcast a statement in support of Wallace, 'the only candidate . . . for democratic progress', coming out clearly 'against the division of the earth into two hostile camps'. (Though he voted for Wallace, and did not regret his demonstration, he was not unhappy when Truman won—'a clear posthumous victory for Roosevelt'.)[86] Heinrich, in the current climate more determinedly pro-Soviet than ever, had toyed in the spring once again with the idea of moving to East Germany, but in a new apartment in the autumn grumblingly decided to stay, ungrateful, it seemed, for Katia's help over the move. All this had hardly been conducive to the new work, which was broken off in June in favour of the detailed account of the genesis of *Faustus*, and he completed it, to book length, by the end of October.

In America the novel surprised him with its success. Knopf's first printing of 25,000 in the summer had been largely sold out by September, and in August it was announced as November Book of the Month choice—admittedly a dual selection with Maugham's *Catalina*, which, as he reflected ironically, might sweeten the pill for all those 'average readers'. (Had he read *Catalina*, which it seems he did not, he might have acknowledged the sense of appending to *Faustus* this novel of old Spain with some

[85] Bl. 5, 9.        [86] KlM Br. Antw. 602.

affinities to *Krull* and *The Holy Sinner*; but he would probably not have been amused by Maugham's avowed shunning of the 'Mandarin' style with its 'trifling disadvantage of taking a long time to say what can be said in brief'.) *Faustus* reviews, contrary to his forebodings, were broadly favourable, many with the highest praise, though he was sensitive to the exceptions. For Orville Prescott, never an indulgent critic, in the *New York Times* in October, the philosophizing smothered the story-telling: as a literary *tour de force* 'brilliant in its massive, ponderous, pedantic way', but as a novel 'clumsy, stilted and wonderfully tedious'. He was impudent enough too to carp at Mann's 'lack of political understanding'—aware only 'late' of the Nazi danger, and now supporting Wallace, 'whose ideas and associates have so little in common' with Western democracy. To this shot in the cold war, and falsification of the record, Mann was quick to react with a letter to the editor: as opponent of the Nazis from ten years before they came to power, his bitter experience of the road to fascism, war, and ruin was precisely the source of his present political attitude.

He was unreasonably depressed, in fact, over the hostility of this and some other reviews, and of the American press in general, notwithstanding many letters of approval and support, and more justifiably over the 'world constellation' of sharpening division into two opposing camps. A future in America for anyone, especially a writer, who counted as left wing, and was therefore branded as a communist, was becoming impossible; and it was primarily this, he felt, which had accounted for Klaus's startling attempt at suicide by gas on 11 July. They were alerted by the police and the press, Katia at once went to the hospital and arranged for private nursing, and the Walters took him in, with Erika, until he had recovered. The immediate motive had been the apparent defection of his latest friend, a stupid but devoted young sailor; but, as his father realized, the fatal urge in his character was like that of his aunt Julia, and all the circumstances of his present life conspired to encourage it—'except that of a parental house on which he can always rely ... but on which he naturally does not wish to be dependent'.[87] There was a dark background to Klaus's outwardly bright disposition, and though ashamed of his weakness, and disgusted with the inevitable publicity, he still regretted he had not succeeded (a psychiatrist, as Golo recalled, had said 'in nine months, you'll try again').[88] Now, at any rate, he had promised to go on living; and by the end of August was back in Amsterdam working with Querido, duly reminded by his father of the sympathy and support he had found, and urged also to help in London with Alexander Korda's film-treatment of *The Magic Mountain*.

[87] *Br.* iii, 37.     [88] KlM *Br. Antw.* 657.

For Christmas the house at San Remo Drive was once again full, overfull in fact. Erika, and Monika, whose moods on an earlier stay had become intolerable for Katia, had to be boarded out to make room for Michael and his family, Golo, and Klaus back for a while from Amsterdam. For Thomas Mann, still concerned over the Schönberg affair, and with worrying commitments looming for the coming Goethe year, the crowd and disorder in the home became a real irritant, whatever his efforts to distance himself from the children's problems. He had accepted the award of East Germany's newly instituted Goethe Prize, but had grave doubts over the visit there that it might imply: his inclination was to keep out of Germany altogether, but if he did consider going, to enter the Eastern Zone in the increasing chill of American–Soviet relations would obviously cause a major political stir. Through a year of very mixed experiences, his main comfort had been the aid and support of Erika, who on her frequent stays had taken over much of his routine work, dealing herself with correspondence, as 'Homer Smith, secretary', and a sensible sifter of the mass of material flowing to him. She had vague plans for a biography, and as he had noted earlier in the year he wanted nothing better than that she should live with them as a 'daughter-adjutant'—secretary, biographer, keeper of his *Nachlaß*. The hope would be largely fulfilled in the years to come.

# VIII

# THE ISOLATED WORLD CITIZEN 1949–1951

'Almost too good to be true in his perfectly genuine role of
"world citizen", Thomas Mann remains apart, both in his art and
in the peculiar atmosphere which surrounds him . . . a great and
dignified and humorous product of our age'
(Philip Toynbee in the London *Observer*, 27 November 1951)

1

*'This meeting again, after sixteen years of estrangement, I can't but
look on as an eerie adventure, and a real trial'*
(TM, 19 March 1949)

By January 1949 Mann's plans for the lecture tour, to begin in April, were
firm: Chicago, Washington, New York, Oxford (where yet another
honorary doctorate awaited him) and London; Sweden and Denmark;
Switzerland—but not yet Germany, on which he still could not bring
himself to decide. On Goethe, he had said in mock-despair, 'j'ai vidé mon
sac', wondering how on earth he was to scratch together yet another
presentation to appeal to both America and Europe. 'Goethe and Democracy' soon suggested itself—that could well occupy an hour or so, turning
this way and that, now left, now right, like the pendulum on his mantel-
piece clock, and sow interesting confusion among the Anglo-Saxons.[1] Early
in February he sent the draft, for once not excessively long, to Erika for her
ideas on cuts: one passage in particular, where he speculated whether
Goethe might today, for the future liberty of art and science, have set his
sights on Russia rather than on America, she agreed, with him and Golo, it
would be politic to omit.

[1] *DüD.* iii, 454.

His personal 'German problem' was still unresolved. Attacks in the Munich press on Erika and Klaus as communist agents, 'Stalin's Fifth Column', had angered him; but though he had pressed *Aufbau* to publish Erika's response, he took no public action. His earlier reluctance even to visit Germany had abated somewhat, for despite continuing personal attacks on him, he had received many enthusiastic letters from young students and Germanists. As far back as the previous July he had been mild in his judgement of Ernst Bertram's support for Nazism, and though not recommending his reinstatement as professor, after the ruling of the Denazification Court, considered he at least deserved his pension rights. His aversion to personal contacts with the 'inner emigration' persisted, however; and he was still anxious to avoid the political implications that would inevitably arise from a visit.

From the American viewpoint, East Germany seemed ruled out: he had already made clear to the authorities there that his acceptance of their Goethe Prize must be *in absentia*, and to Hans Mayer in Leipzig that a student support foundation should use his name without announcement of his specific agreement, to avoid any appearance of a 'solidarity with Russian-East German cultural policy which could be publicly exploited'.[2] On the other hand, to go to West Germany would imply a political stance to which he was by no means inclined. There, to the proposal of his election as a member of the Bavarian Fine Arts Academy, he had suggested honorary membership only. This was eagerly accepted, as he learned now in March, with an invitation to attend the Munich Goethe festival in July. There was word of an invitation to speak in Frankfurt-on-Main and of the award of the Goethe Prize there as well. He was confused and uncertain, receiving much advice against a visit, particularly from Klaus, who had now decided to move to the south of France to work on a new novel, and even from Bermann Fischer; and it was not until May, when he had reached Washington after Chicago, that he finally decided to attend the prize award in Frankfurt at the end of July—though realizing it would mean preparing *en route* a different speech and extending his tour much longer than planned. Frankfurt must stand symbolically for Germany as a whole, he felt—any more extensive trip (to Lübeck for instance, where he was also invited) would be beyond his powers—and be the best opportunity to show his goodwill: he could then at last say 'I've been there,' as he wrote to Reisiger, hoping they could meet in Frankfurt.

But he wanted his attitude to Germany to be seen as evenly balanced between East and West—and that was obviously going to be difficult, not least because in America he was more and more regarded as pro-commu-

---

[2] *Br.* iii, 59.

nist. His 'hatred' now for the Unamerican Activities Committee was almost as great as that once for Hitler, he had confessed to Agnes Meyer; the award in February of the Bollingen Prize for poetry to Ezra Pound made him wonder whether the verdict of T. S. Eliot and the other jurors would have been equally 'objective' had Pound been a communist and not a renegade to Fascist Italy. At the end of March a 'Conference for World Peace' was convened by the National Council of Arts and Sciences in New York, of which he was a member. It was branded in advance in the *New Leader* as a 'soapbox for Red propaganda', and *Life* magazine's later report—'Red Visitors Cause Rumpus'—showed a rogues' gallery of the 'friends of the communists': himself (though he had not attended), Einstein, Chaplin, Norman Mailer, Arthur Miller, Lillian Hellman, Dorothy Parker. He was neither dupe nor fellow-traveller, nor an admirer of the current dangerous phase of the Russian revolution, he wrote in protest to Assistant Secretary of State Biddle, but every effort had to be made to avert the catastrophe of a war between America and Russia.[3] After the conclusion of the Atlantic Pact on 4 April, clearly setting the seal on the East–West divide, he was prominent among the 500 signatories of a letter to Congress demanding its refusal and advocating direct negotiations with the Soviet Union to resolve the differences.

All this was amid the complicated preparations for the tour and much correspondence over the forthcoming lecture-dates. As he was about to depart with Katia and Erika for Chicago, there came a cable from Nelly Mann with news of the death of Viktor, not yet 60, in Munich—a disturbing *memento mori* on which there was little time to brood. Though their meeting in Zurich had not been easy, he had exchanged many cordial letters with his younger brother over the past two years, sent parcels of food and clothing, and discussed with him the possible recovery of family possessions and his hope that some of the heirlooms might find their way to Frido. He had also taken trouble to assist him with the memoirs he was writing, a project which he found faintly amusing, but which Viktor had pursued with an energy and dispatch more like Heinrich's than his own: extracts had been published as early as January 1948, and the whole lengthy book, *We Were Five: A Portrait of the Mann Family*, dedicated to the memory of their mother, was out only six months after his death. (As both Thomas and Heinrich later recognized, this unexpected production by one who had led a wholly unliterary life had an admirable warmth and no little narrative skill, even if his memories were not always reliable.)

The transcontinental journey was broken as usual for a few days in Chicago at the end of April, for the first performance of the 'Goethe and

[3] 49/281.

Democracy' lecture and another full check at the hospital, again with satisfactory results. In Washington, once more hosted by the Meyers, he found Hallstein, former rector of Frankfurt University and now teaching in America, with the formal invitation to Frankfurt, which (although much concerned by Erika's disapproval) he had decided to accept. His lecture on 2 May in the Library of Congress was well received, and was followed by the usual exhausting reception afterwards at the Meyers'; from New York it was repeated twice, in Mount Holyoke College, Massachusetts, and Hunter College; and they set off on 10 May on a night flight for England (his first Atlantic air-crossing).

The stay of over a week, in material conditions greatly improved since his last visit, was marked by a reception whose warmth surprised him after what he had considered cool reviews of *Faustus*; and for the exceptionally busy round of engagements he was more than glad of the support of wife and 'daughter-adjutant'. Based at the Savoy in London, he was in Oxford on 13 May, where a special ceremony in the medieval lecture-hall of the Divinity School, with 'indescribably old-fashioned solemnity', had been arranged for the conferral of his honorary D. Litt., after which he gave his Goethe lecture in German at the Taylorian, to be published later by the Clarendon Press. It was repeated, in English, before the Goethe Society on 16 May in London University Senate House. For the BBC he recorded a short talk on 'Goethe, the German Miracle' (part of an essay on Goethe, Luther, and Bismarck as the three giants of German history), which he considered later as his best contribution to the centenary celebrations, and which was used for many other publications both in Germany and America. The following day, at a London PEN Club reception, he warned of the need for vigilance and protest against infringements of 'spiritual freedom and independent thinking' wherever they occurred; and at the Wiener Library, on 18 May, with its documentation of the horrors of the Reich, of the importance of remembering those twelve years. The Germans were only too ready now to forget and suppress them, but they must remember, and from the memory gain the will to make amends: 'German writers will have to work long and hard before they can create a library capable of holding the balance against what stands on those shelves.'[4] His days were filled with interviews and meetings, notably with the musicologist Ernest Newman, whom he found receptive to *Faustus*, and time had to be found for Ida Herz and Katia's cousins.

Flying on 19 May via Göteborg to Stockholm, they were received by Edgar von Üxküll, his friend and admirer since the twenties, arrested for complicity in the July 1944 plot against Hitler, and emigrating to Sweden

---

[4]  xiii 791.

soon after the war. In contrast to the friendly Swedish press, Mann found in the Frankfurt *Täglicher Rundschau* a collection of readers' letters to the editor fulminating against his Goethe Prize award, and felt if there were much more of this he would cancel his visit. As they returned on 21 May to the Grand Hotel, after a morning of touring with Üxküll, there was shattering news: Klaus had committed suicide in Cannes, with an overdose of sleeping-pills. A letter from Klaus to Katia and Erika, written the previous day, was in his usual jaunty style: trying to continue writing despite money difficulties and the uncertainties over his books, looking forward to meeting Erika later, apparently cheerful in the character of 'morbid hermit and neurotic mouse' he had assumed, and giving no sign of what must have been a sudden impulse to end it all.[5]

His father's immediate reaction was concern for Katia and Erika—'he should not have done this to them'—and they sat long together in sorrowful recall of the 'irresistible urge to death' that had so long beset Klaus. As his father saw it, such a deed showed irresponsibility and a grievous lack of consideration for others—but he supposed that, for one who had reached that point, such feelings were impossible: his 'obsession with death' was clearly stronger than any love or loyalty, any tie. His thoughts dwelt sadly on this life that had been cut short, he wrote to Hesse later: their relationship had been difficult, and on his part not without guilt for the shadow he had cast over Klaus's existence, though he had done his best to praise and encourage him. 'His was an outstanding talent. Not only his "Gide", his "Tchaikovsky" too is a very good book, and his "Volcano" . . . perhaps the best novel of the emigration. Putting his finest things together, it will be seen what we have lost.'

It was decided not to cancel the lecture engagements, and to continue the tour as planned, while cutting out as far as possible all social functions; but the Germany visit was once again in the balance. Both Katia and Erika were deeply affected; Erika, as her parents realized, most of all, for she had been closest to her brother. Only the previous week she had written to encourage his latest attempt in a Nice clinic to break his morphine habit, suggesting they should get together for 'a little healthy fun so you can recover', in Switzerland or Austria. 'We were part of each other,' she wrote in June: 'so much so, that I'm simply not conceivable without him.'[6] She could not bring herself to journey to Cannes, and at the funeral only Michael, in the area on an orchestra tour, was able to attend to play a largo for his brother.

'Goethe and Democracy' was successfully performed in the University of Uppsala on 23 May, the following evening before the Academy in

[5] KlM *Br. Antw.* 624.   [6] EM *Br. Antw.* i, 257, 261.

Stockholm, both to massive applause, and at Copenhagen University on 28 May. There they separated from Erika, who was to rejoin them in Switzerland, and travelled back to Lund on 30 May, for a repeat of the lecture and a rehearsal of the doctorate ceremony to be held next afternoon in the cathedral. Elaborate, very long, and not without some amusing moments, this nevertheless impressed him as the most beautiful he had ever experienced: the candidates in procession to cannon-fire from university to cathedral, his place in full evening dress next the bishop, children in white to hand up the laurel wreaths, more cannon-fire with each capping, his short speech (rapidly prepared that morning, and with a slight *faux pas* in referring to Lund's favourite son as Jeremias instead of Esaias Tegnér), the procession back to the university to the acclaim of the students. (The local paper felt it necessary to explain, in a photograph showing him alongside the verger of the cathedral, that the one on the right was the famous one.) But he was glad it was over, and looking forward eagerly to the escape to Switzerland—were it not for two letters from the mayor of Frankfurt, making it clear that cancellation there would be difficult, and with his realization that it had taken courage to invite him at all.

Arrival at the airport in Zurich on 1 June was just as he had dreamed, with everyone there—Erika, Michael and Gret and the children, Monika, the Oprechts, Therese Giehse—and they did not refuse an invitation that evening to the new production of *Faust* in the Schauspielhaus, which was the scene two days later for his first Goethe lecture. Given before the Federal President, the mayor of Zurich, and a large audience, it was received with lengthy applause, and made a warm welcome back to the land which he once again thought was where they should spend their last years. On 7 June, after a quiet birthday, he travelled to Berne for a repeat performance, to similar acclaim, and gave three readings from his work, including *The Holy Sinner* manuscript, in Zurich, Basle, and Küsnacht, before they left at the end of June for some weeks' rest in the Engadine, at Vulpera.

A rest, but not without work: for he had now decided, not only to go ahead with the Frankfurt visit, but also to accept for Weimar, where, according to press reports, he was to be offered honorary citizenship. A different address was required, and he set himself to this, later enlisting the help of Erika when she joined them for a while. Georges Motschan, the wealthy young Swiss friend and admirer of long standing, who had generously driven them to Vulpera in his elegant Buick, was keen to act as their chauffeur on what would now become an extensive German tour, including Munich and Nuremberg, from where he had also received an invitation; and they welcomed the convenience and independence this would offer, as well as the benefit of their own interpreter in the Eastern Zone, for

Motschan, though Swiss, had been born in Russia. Mann was still unsettled and nervous over his first personal appearance where so much hysteria had been generated, vitriolic articles alternating with cries of longing to see him, and with not a few actually threatening letters. 'The malice of the Germans is not to be appeased': how much easier, he felt, to speak before Anglo-Saxons, Swedes, and Swiss. He could only hope the peace of the mountains would prepare him for the ordeal, and that, while political exploitation was probably unavoidable, he would not become a target for investigation in America through the Weimar visit. His aim with that, as he said in an interview, was to underline the unity of Germany and disregard its current division. But he feared the Weimar announcement would lead to trouble with the occupation authorities over his Frankfurt engagements, and Erika, before leaving for Amsterdam, did her best to guard against this by telephoning her many American contacts there. He started the journey with the feeling he was setting off to war.

That there were official security worries over the tour, not only American and German, but even Swiss, became clear when they reached Basle with Motschan on 22 July. The plan was to take the sleeper that night to Frankfurt, where Motschan would join them with the car: their young friend learned that the police had had the Manns under discreet surveillance since Zurich, having been apprised of the threatening letters, and there was a strong police presence at the station. The French occupation forces across the frontier had mounted a guard of honour at the Badischer Bahnhof, the first stop across the frontier—but by then the Manns had retired, hearing with regret only later from the conductor that they had missed this singular sign of respect. In Frankfurt the following morning they were whisked off to the city guest-house in the Taunus foothills at Kronberg, where they were guarded against possible intruders by a force of police, but where Motschan's big Swiss-registered car gained him easy access to join his charges. Tutti Bermann Fischer, self-appointed press secretary, kept the large assembly of international journalists at bay.

At a crowded reception given by the social democrat mayor Kolb, as all and sundry—especially sundry—pressed themselves forward with any excuse to be near the guest of honour, Motschan was impressed by Thomas Mann's calm demeanour, and his presence of mind as he greeted many whose names for so long had had little significance for him, and which, in some cases, he would have preferred to forget. Motschan noted too his disappointment at the absence of Ernst Bertram, and was asked to ensure that the police guard admitted him should he turn up later. To the press on 24 July, Mann was cautious, stressing that he was awaiting the arrival next day of a delegation from Weimar before deciding whether to go there. 'I know, of course, that there are people who are not in favour of my presence here, but I think no one will misunderstand my good intentions.' It was not true that he was planning to return for good to Germany: 'I am an American citizen and will be going home to the States. But I hope this will not be my last visit here.'[7]

Driving with police escort to the Paulskirche on 25 July, he was applauded by a large crowd, and his reception by the high officials at the door was a media event. Within, every seat was filled by an invited audience, the East German delegation among those in the front row, but with his long experience of such occasions he gave no sign of the tension he must have felt on his first appearance in Germany since the Wagner lecture in February 1933. As a Goethe celebration, the programme naturally included readings from the poet, with musical prologue and epilogue, but for his audience it was undoubtedly Thomas Mann's hour. He had no need of excuse for opening his address on a personal note: due thanks, of course, for the honour of the prize, which recognized that his work in exile had been in the service of the country whose language was its medium, and which he intended now to use to alleviate need in his homeland; but mainly his experience of Germany from afar through those sixteen years—his hatred for, and revulsion from, the Nazi regime, the part he had played in the war with his broadcasts, the conflict in himself, as in all Germans, when the end brought not only Hitler's downfall but total catastrophe and the tearing-apart of their country.

*Faustus*, though the work of an *émigré*, showed how deeply he had felt, and how intimately he had shared, that fate. After long and only too understandable hesitation, he had come now to meet foes and friends alike—for, welcome or not, it would have been inexcusable had he honoured Goethe only elsewhere and avoided Germany. He was there, not as 'preacher of repentance or prophet of truth', but as one suffering like everyone else under the painful confusion of the times, who without the refuge of his art, the diversions of his fables, would simply not know how to survive, let alone how to advise others. Perhaps, however, such 'very serious jests', as Goethe had called his *Faust*, might be of better service than any attempt at counsel. Praise for Goethe simply as representative of a 'good' Germany would be misplaced, for in his greatness there was both good and bad, he was both Faust and Mephistopheles: the admired harmony and balance in his long life was the result not only of constant striving for perfection in his work, but of his readiness for life in all its aspects, establishing his claim to representation of all humanity.

The performance had been a clear presentation of his personal position, courageous and with little or no concession to hostile criticism, and he had

[7] Fr./Antw. 304 f.

combined with it the obligatory tribute to his great predecessor with only indirect implication of his own claim to the inheritance. (He could hope, as he wrote later, that his appearance would be of some slight help, if only morally, for the hard-pressed better elements in Germany, whose situation was by no means favoured by the current unhappy world situation.)[8] The audience probably comprised more friends than foes, and the ovation left no doubt of their welcome for what he had to offer. Microphones had relayed him to the thousands outside, and amid the applause from there he heard gratifying shouts of 'Come back soon!' But the event had left him exhausted, and after the official banquet given for a hundred guests in the Kronberg guest-house that evening ('I wonder how much blood there is on all the hands I've had to shake this evening?'),[9] Katia made sure they retired early—fortunately, as Motschan found, for the feast lasted far into the night as an orgy of gluttony, with Nazi nostalgia in riotous wartime song.

On 26 July, after a city-organized tour of Frankfurt and its ruins, a visit to the restored Goethe House, and a press conference, there came a welcome reunion: not with Bertram, as Mann had hoped, but with Reisiger, who had come over with an official invitation to visit Stuttgart on their way next day to Munich. With some difficulty, he was squeezed into the Buick—the Manns' luggage, though less than at the start in California, still comprised eleven pieces—but the planned early start was delayed by a visit Mann had promised to the chief editor of the *Frankfurter Rundschau*. This developed into a leisurely interview, in which, as at the press conference, he again rebutted the 'malicious fiction' that he had turned his back on Germany, expressed his reserved attitude towards 'totalitarian communism', which had inherited the autocracy of the Tsars, and emphasized that Germany's future must lie in incorporation into a federation of European states.

The result was considerable delay for the timetable. Though late for the official lunch in Stuttgart, they could not decline the programme and hospitality offered: speeches, another police-escorted tour of ruins, dinner with the mayor, and installation in the city guest-house for the night. The onward journey to Munich, a day late on 28 July, took them past the sign to Dachau—the concentration camp, as Mann drily remarked, where 'Heydrich wanted to humiliate and murder me'[10]—and into evidence of destruction of more poignant significance for them, as young Motschan noted from their silence (his suggestion of a visit to Poschinger Strasse was firmly ruled out). At the Hotel Vier Jahreszeiten they had known so well, now damaged but in reasonable working order, Mann was chiefly impressed by the contrast between the luxurious menu and the very spartan

---

[8] *Br.* iii, 95; *DüD.* iii, 467.     [9] Motsch, 96.     [10] Ibid. 107.

food to which they had lately been treated in London's Savoy: the losers, it seemed, were faring better than the victors. There was time at last to review the papers spread here for him, with the agreeable surprise that the reception of his Frankfurt address had been overwhelmingly favourable, before the reception that evening in the Bavarian Fine Arts Academy, of which he had accepted honorary membership. To speeches of welcome by Hans Carossa, Preetorius, and Ernst Penzoldt, his improvised reply asked for understanding for his feelings of mingled joy and sadness at returning to the city which had been his home of nearly forty years: 'the blows of fate have dealt severely with us all, and tonight at least we will let joy prevail'.[11]

Munich for him was 'the past in rags, for which I have little heart': such joy as the brief stay brought was in the reunion with a number of old friends, including Carl Ehrenberg, and at last a contact with Ernst Bertram, from whom he received a letter by hand of a young American, a former student of his friend's, next day. That letter alone, he told Motschan, would have justified the whole journey. It was moving to hear from this 'pariah' (graded 'III' by the Denazification Court and allowed to publish only subject to censorship), with memories of happier days, his sorrow at missing a personal meeting, and his appreciation of the peacemaking words of the Frankfurt address; but an adequate reply would have to wait till the return journey. At a big press conference, the questions concentrated on his coming visit to Weimar and the strong criticism of his already publicized refusal to include on his itinerary the Buchenwald concentration camp, now housing opponents of the new regime. He repeated that his presence in Weimar was to symbolize the basic unity of Germany (who better for that than an independent writer 'whose homeland is the German language unaffected by the separation into Zones?'), and it would do no good to make demands on the East German authorities which under the Soviet occupation would be impossible of fulfilment. His theme there would be humanism; and he stressed his, and the world's, optimism over Germany's future.[12]

For his official speech, instead of using the Frankfurt address, he read his 'Goethe and Democracy' text. The great applause, and the banquet offered afterwards, convinced him that he had stood the Munich test well; and he felt fresh enough to accept the invitation from the mayor and the newly founded Thomas Mann Society in Nuremberg to visit there on 30 July *en route* to East Germany. This was a more muted occasion. On the short city-tour, he politely declined a look at the war criminals' trial-hall and execution-site in favour of the scene of the gigantic 'Party Day' rallies, to stand where Hitler had once acknowledged the salute of the faithful—at his feet

---

[11] *Tb.* viii, 435.     [12] *Fr./Antw.* 308.

the remains of a great concrete swastika destroyed by the Americans, a symbol, as he remarked, of Germany's condition today. From there it was on to Bayreuth, for a night's rest at the Bayerischer Hof before entering the Eastern Zone, and to meet, as had been agreed in Frankfurt, the emissaries from there who would arrange the border crossing. As he signed the hotel's 'Golden Guest Book', he was taken aback to see the most recent entries were of the 'whole devil's brood', Hitler, Himmler, Goebbels, and the rest— but mollified by the sixteen empty pages between, 'one for each year of my exile'.

Elaborate plans for the border reception next day were thrown into some confusion by Motschan's sensible insistence on the shortest route to Weimar, using a different crossing-point, and the expectant East German delegation had to improvise a welcome on the autobahn at Hermsdorf. From there, in an impressive convoy, they proceeded on through Jena to Weimar, to be greeted by a great crowd and, in due course, by full media attention. In the Hotel Augusta—the old Hotel Elephant, familiar to Goethe enthusiasts (and readers of *The Beloved Returns*), being too badly damaged—a whole floor had been reserved, and every arrangement made for comfort and quiet for the guests, including plain-clothes police guards. At the international press conference, held at once, Mann had to face questions more political than literary, but adroitly avoided being drawn on to thin ice, notably in response to provocation from West German journalists. He intended, he said, to urge his brother Heinrich to accept the offered presidency of the Berlin Academy of the Arts.

On the evening tour of the city which followed, exchanging his trilby now for a more suitable cloth cap, he joined the Thuringia *Land* Governor in an open car, Katia in the Buick remarking to Motschan on the solemn faces of the people lining the route, not a smile to be seen: 'they take all this much too seriously, yet my husband waves to right and left as if he were on an official state visit'.[13] In effect, this was what it was for the East Germans, as a beflagged 'Free German Youth' parade at one point showed—children too young to have much idea whom they were cheering—and, more clearly still, the programme organized for the award of the prize and of his honorary Weimar citizenship the following day. The crystallization of the occupation zones into two separate German republics had taken legal form in May; and for the Eastern German Democratic Republic, not yet officially proclaimed or entirely a one-party state, and the Soviet authorities behind it, the Thomas Mann visit was a diplomatic asset they had concluded should be exploited to the full (after initial hesitation and communist arguments against receiving this 'lackey of Wall Street'.)

[13] Motsch. 126.

Before the official ceremonies in the National Theatre on 1 August there was time to admire the restoration of Goethe's house on the Frauenplan, and to erect a great wreath, thoughtfully provided for him, at the Goethe-Schiller tombs—pondering during his few moments' silence there, as he told Motschan afterwards, chiefly on the rumoured plan to open them and verify the remains. In the packed theatre, making his way through a large throng outside, he was greeted with a standing ovation, and long applauded when he mounted the stage to receive his honours. He prefaced his text (the same as his Frankfurt address), not only with thanks for the symbolic recognition of German unity in the award to him of both Goethe prizes, but also with his oft-repeated hope that from its troubled times the world could find the way to a new humanism, based on the preservation of 'freedom, justice, and the dignity of the individual . . . even if constrained by a heightened sense of social obligation'—a tactful bow to the politics of his hosts, but also in line with his own ideas at this time.

Cool and unsentimental by nature, even he was greatly touched by the enthusiastic reception for his address and the warm appreciation of the crowd, as he struggled through for the ride to the Hotel Augusta, where the senior Russian representative and his family were expecting them for lunch. General Tulpanov, East Berlin city commandant and information chief of the Soviet Military Administration's political department, was fluent in German—to the relief of Motschan, whose Russian was needed only for the wife and daughter—and the discussion with his guest was mainly on German and Russian literature, though he did not omit to mention his satisfaction with the 'independent' progress in East Germany towards a people's democracy (a progress, as Mann thought later, doubtless assisted by the strong policing so much in evidence, and the outward forms with a dire similarity to those of the Nazis.)[14]

At the farewell banquet that evening, his words were of thanks at having been received, not as an old fogy murmuring of times past, but as one who might be able to help a little towards the construction of a new world: if his work had made some contribution to that, no one could be happier than he. And he took the opportunity to announce that his prize of 20,000 marks would go to the restoration of the Herder Church in Weimar: support for needy writers, he said, to which he was dedicating the Frankfurt prize, was not required here, where writers 'enjoyed higher esteem and material encouragement than in the Western Zone'. Their journey next day to the border at Wartha on the way back to Frankfurt, in a long convoy through fervent crowds in the villages he had missed on the road in, garlands and banners everywhere, and sometimes bands, was a triumphal

[14] xi 509.

progress such as he had never before experienced. There was a mayoral address in Erfurt; a final lunch in Eisenach, at which he received the personal thanks of the bishop for his donation, and where his 'Auf Wiedersehen!' was greeted with overwhelming enthusiasm; at Wartha never-ending expressions of gratitude for his visit from the accompanying officials.

Looking back after his return to America, he felt he had kept his head amid all this, flattering though it had been. He had noted the iron discipline in the effort of this 'people's democracy' to realize a vision which, though he could not fully share it, was not without attraction for him, and which he had seen represented there by many men of goodwill. Indeed, as he watched what looked to him like a renazification of the new Western Federal Republic, after the currency reform, this discipline in the East seemed a boon in stifling the 'stupidity and insolence' so common in the West's public life (it had been striking that while over there he had not been the target of a single slanderous attack). He had made no secret of his reservations over the autocratic regime of Soviet Russia, not so different from that of the Tsars; but he would continue to resist the 'hysteria' of the anti-communist witch-hunt and incitement to war, and to speak in favour of peace 'in a world whose future has long been unimaginable without communist characteristics'. The respect shown him in the East, as he wrote later to Agnes Meyer, was for his work, not by any means for pro-communist statements: 'I am no "fellow-traveller". But it seems a few clever communists are fellow-travellers with me.'[15] All too evidently, the controversy over his position was only at its beginning. As they boarded the train for Amsterdam at Frankfurt station on 4 August, however, and said good-bye to the loyal Motschan, whose support had been indispensable, he could feel tolerably content with his first visit to Germany, which had passed off better than he had expected, and satisfied with the tour as a whole, clouded though it had been by the death of Klaus. (Motschan was later warmly invited to pay them a visit in California.)

Remarkable nevertheless, and indicative of the true character of Thomas Mann, is that, with the exception of a brief report for the *New York Times*, nowhere—neither in diary nor letters—did he record any *reaction* to the vast destruction of his country which he had seen everywhere he went. Through these sixteen years he had 'suffered from Germany', from the 'open wound' which had found so moving a reflection in his *Faustus*, where he asked for God's mercy towards his Fatherland. His only desire after that had been to avoid the sight of the wreckage, material and human, and his overriding interest the reaction of Germany, and the Germans, to *himself*

---

[15] *AM Brw.* 723.

personally. Seeing now the destruction on the spot roused him, it seems, to little or no emotion—except where his personal position was concerned, when he was prepared to defend himself with all the polemical skill at his command. Understandably, perhaps, he might feel that the Germans who had embraced the disastrous policy of Nazism, either in enthusiasm or helplessly like sheep, had deserved all they got, and that his Fatherland had abandoned him, as he would now abandon it until one day it might return to a proper appreciation of his worth. In this apparent indifference was reflected once again the self-centredness dominant in his character.

2

*'Once again, once again! How exactly the old story with its grief and its bright moments'*          (TM, 12 July 1950)

It was fortunate that their original plan to fly from Frankfurt had been changed, so that the press hounds waiting at the airport were evaded, and the onward journey to Rotterdam, where they took up comfortable cabins in the *Nieuw Amsterdam*, was out of the glare of publicity. The short crossing to New York, where they landed on 12 August, made a complete rest, and even his correspondence was neglected, except for the overdue letter to Ernst Bertram. 'Our warm good wishes are with you,' he wrote, with his great regret that they had been unable to meet. 'You know me, I think, as one for whom nothing in his life is lost, but lives on with him to the end—and foremost of all, old friendship!'[16] Their estrangement was at an end, and Mann, as he had promised, later did what he could to ease Bertram's difficult position.

They did not linger in New York, nor very long over the accustomed stopover in Chicago, but he began now the report on the Germany visit which had been requested by the *New York Times*, and continued it on the long train-journey back to Los Angeles. In this largely anecdotal account, he did at least confess his deep shock at the sight of the ruined cities; while criticizing the shortcomings of the denazification procedures in the West, he was careful not to play down the less attractive side of the East German regime, and to stress his personal non- rather than anti-communist position. As also in an interview for the *Herald Tribune* in New York, he underlined the importance of supporting the 'dangerously small' minority of democratically minded Germans resisting the trend to a rebirth of nationalism among the great majority, who refused to admit the true reasons for their condition and cried how much better things had been

[16] EB Br. 191.

under Hitler; and he urged again the vital need for an understanding between East and West.[17] His immense relief at returning home, safely hidden once more, as he hoped, from the strident controversies of the world, was tempered by the mass of press material awaiting him, in which he detected further evidence of creeping 'renazification' in West Germany. It seemed he had made his visit 'at the last moment', he wrote gloomily to Reisiger.[18] Good though it had been to see Carl Ehrenberg flourishing as a professor in Munich's Academy of Music, it was an indication of the favour now enjoyed by former Nazis. Herbert von Karajan, once an SS Obergruppenführer, could plan a tour of the States. 'The wind sets strongly to the advantage of the perpetrators of those deeds, and all the unpleasantness, according to everything I heard, falls to the others.'[19] Even in America democracy appeared no more than a shadow, to be dispersed by the first serious economic crisis; and the devaluation of the pound and other European currencies in September (bringing him incidentally a loss in his European income) he looked on as blatant economic imperialism, on the part of a country deranged 'by the discrepancy between power and immaturity'.

Whatever his hopes for a winter of peace from the demands of the world, and for a quiet return to work on *The Holy Sinner* or completion of *Krull*, they were dashed by his political unease, further calls for lectures, and the letters which flowed in unceasingly. He longed for a more private and less exposed life, he wrote to Frans Masereel in November: there were so many attacks, and at the same time a world-wide correspondence 'taking more time than is endurable at my age and for my still-experimental work'.[20] Erika, who had joined them in August, took an even blacker view of the strengthening of West Germany, seeing in it a yielding to blackmail against the perceived Russian threat, and the likely result a German domination of all Europe. This outlook, and her growing hostility towards Golo, whom she regarded as 'heartless' in his anti-Russian and pro-capitalist views, found favour with her father, and there were arguments during a weekend visit in September from her brother, whose attitude irked them both. At a press conference in Berkeley, on the occasion of his performance there in October of 'Goethe and Democracy', Mann reproached the Western powers for sympathizing with Nazis rather than with social democrats and for appearing to see the former as potential shock-troops against the Soviet Union: communism, he urged, should be combated by democracy, not by fascism. Nehru, with whom he spent an hour in San Francisco and who invited him to visit India, impressed him as a fine and kindly character, 'cleverer than those in charge of this country':[21] the best statesman of the

[17] *Fr./Antw.* 311.    [18] 49/436.    [19] *DüD.* iii, 237.
[20] Letter of 17 Nov. 1949 (Bassenge auction cat. 59, 1992).    [21] *HH Brw.* 217.

time, steadfastly refusing to take sides in the cold war (and so not likely to get financial support). Heinrich's disgust with America's politics was, if anything, even more extreme, and he was eager to accept the invitation to East Berlin, making plans in September for a flight via Paris; but, old and ill, he hesitated, and finally decided to defer his journey until the spring.

All in all, the final months of 1949 for Thomas Mann were in unsatisfactory contrast to the success of the European tour. He did manage to settle to continuing *The Holy Sinner*, still with the feeling that it was no more than a pastime, a private entertainment, for after *Faustus* it was hard to take anything seriously. But it was unlike him to feel so reluctant to deal with the mass of letters that swelled with every post, loath to write even to the correspondents he liked best; and the political pronouncements he could not resist brought bursts of regret that he had not kept silent, for they did nothing but provoke hostile reactions and draw him into further controversy. In December a 'maniacal' article in the anti-Soviet journal *Plain Talk*, entitled 'The Moral Eclipse of Thomas Mann', pilloried him as America's 'fellow-traveller No. 1' for his support of Wallace and of the World Peace Conference, and especially for his Weimar visit—it was not the last he was to hear from the author, the journalist Eugene Tillinger.

On the more personal front, he was not best pleased to find Schönberg still on the attack over *Faustus*, publicly reminding him that he had failed to return the loaned copy of his tract on harmony and treating the post-script acknowledging Schönberg's claims as an 'act of revenge'. Hastening to return the loan, with apologies, he recalled the other's earlier full satisfaction with the postscript: 'you are attacking a bogy of your own imagination, not me. . . . If you insist on being my enemy—you won't succeed in making yourself one to me.'[22] Disturbing though all this was, by the end of the year he had reached more of an equilibrium. The reluctance to take up his letter-pen had soon dissipated, and with the help of Hilde Kahn the backlog of correspondence was once more under control; there had been some steady progress with *The Holy Sinner*; and his normal routine seemed re-established.

Christmas promised to be a lively festival, with a large house-party assembling during December: Golo and a young American friend Ed Klotz, Erika, the Borgese family (though Michael and his were still in Switzerland, and Monika remained in New York), with Klaus Pringsheim and his son visiting, and an expansive champagne dinner-party planned for Christmas Eve. Erika's highly irritable frame of mind, however, was proving a grave disturbance to the harmony of the crowded house, for she was at odds with them all, especially Elisabeth. It was small wonder, for since Klaus's death, everything had combined to make her despondent and depressed. Her application for American naturalization was held up by the continuing FBI investigations, which were likely to bar her from foreign travel for lack of a re-entry permit; the personal attacks in the German press had continued, while protracted attempts at a lawsuit over her earlier denunciation as a fifth-columnist for Stalin were coming to nothing. Her sex-life had never been satisfactory, and her marked homo-erotic tendencies made her a difficult companion; recently a surprising passion for the widowed Bruno Walter, which, of an age with her father, he could not reciprocate, had greatly cast her down. She had never been reconciled to Thomas Mann's decision to visit Germany, and though they saw eye to eye on much of the political scene both there and in America, she had been bitter in condemnation of what she regarded as his devious conduct, while he for his part was seriously concerned at her excessive intolerance.

Her role as her father's 'adjutant' was now to some extent assumed by Golo, who was more compliant, during December for instance writing a review for him. He and his parents were in anxious conclave over her future—whether she might find conditions better in England, perhaps in a job with the BBC—though her father was more than reluctant to lose her, and felt such a decision had to mean a total uprooting for him in favour of a return to Europe, not a move he was ready, yet, to consider. It was all most unsettling; but he was relieved, as he went on quietly with his work, to find a happier mood and a spirit of reconciliation when Christmas Eve arrived. Katia had seen to presents for all, including the guests; Erika's 'newspaper' pasted up from incongruous headlines was as popular as ever; he himself was delighted with the modernization of his gramophone to take the new long-play records, and for recording too; the young American, for whom such a 'Continental' evening was something new, exclaimed 'Gee, Golo, the champagne, the conversation—it was out of this world!' A diversion for Erika had suggested itself when Joseph Angell, in a nervous breakdown over the introduction to his long-planned Thomas Mann Reader, appealed for help, and over the New Year she and Golo worked together to complete it for him. Before the Borgeses left on 2 January their father was glad to hear she and Elisabeth had made up their quarrel.

The start of another of his 'round years'—fifty since *The Buddenbrooks*, twenty-five since *The Magic Mountain*, and his seventy-fifth birthday in prospect—found a Thomas Mann in typical form: pursuing the usual daily routine of morning work, on the 'little novel' of *The Holy Sinner* or other tasks, afternoon correspondence, evening relaxation with the gramophone or very often in the cinema, and already considering the year's lecture-tour; but depressed over ailments, more or less minor, of ear and throat, and by the unaccountable disappearance of his dog Niko, faithful companion of all his years in America (soon replaced, fortunately, by another presented by the eager Caroline Newton). Depression was more deep-seated, however, in the 'more and more unbreathable' atmosphere of the cold war: the moral dilemma over the production of the hydrogen bomb, the sentencing of Alger Hiss, which he found dreadful, and nearer to home the initial refusal of the Beverly Wilshire Hotel to house a dinner of the local chapter of the Council of Arts, Sciences, and Professions if 'a communist like Dr Mann' was to speak. The February issue of *Esquire*, spreading the Karsh photographs of himself and Jascha Heifetz in respectful tribute to these 'welcome expatriates', weighed little against his political disquiet, as he noted daily signs of America's incipient fascist trend—was the demand for a 'loyalty oath' from academics any different from the Nazis' pressure for conformity?

A great public outcry meanwhile forced the Wilshire Hotel to capitulate, and, as he wrote to Adorno on 9 January, he intended to have his say there—his latest tax demand, for 16,000 dollars to be 'thrown into the maw of the cold war', surely gave him the right as a citizen to speak out. His draft gave him concern, over its possibly too pro-communist a line, but at the dinner, on 14 January, he left his audience in no doubt where he stood. 'If communism means power and illegality, concentration camps, totalitarian management of culture, with its level determined from below to the taste of little people, then I am decidedly no communist': but as he had written decades ago, a new socially organized world, unified and planned, had to be created, and as long as the bourgeois world had nothing to oppose to communism other than a market economy and the struggle of competition for profit, then there was little hope of success against it. The current dialectical process between old and new must one day—perhaps in fifty years—bring the resolution of the socio-economic conflict between East and West, and it would probably be found then that Eastern ideas had had a greater influence on the West than the other way round. But all hope for this must depend on peace: war could today no longer be the solution.[23]

In the months that followed he took many opportunities of public support for this necessity of reaching an understanding between East and West now both were capable of annihilating the world. But, as he ruefully admitted, to speak the truth was to tread on everyone's toes, and please neither side. He watched with revulsion the intensification of the cold war, with the arrest in London of the Soviet spy Klaus Fuchs (the German *émigré* with a major role in the Manhattan project for the atomic bomb), and in America the continuing hearings and investigations, for him a disgusting exhibition of 'primitive puritanism', hatred, 'fear, corruption

[23] *Tb*. viii, 685 f., 679 f.

and self-righteousness', while the FBI director Hoover pressed the Senate for large increases in his staff, alleging there were 54,000 communists in the States and ten times that number of fellow-travellers. Orwell's *Nineteen Eighty-Four* Mann found hard to bear, in its horrific vision of a future that had seemingly already arrived.

Plans for Heinrich's transfer to East Berlin were now advanced, and by early February his passage, with a Czech passport, had been arranged in the Polish ship *Batory* for Gdynia, the opening of the Berlin Academy of Arts under his presidency having been deferred till his arrival. Great honours and much money awaited him there, noted his brother—for whom this recognition in Heinrich's declining years brought a welcome lightening of the burden on himself; for both of them the adventure seemed scarcely believable. During the night of 10–11 March, however, Heinrich, already attended by a nurse in his Santa Monica apartment, suffered a stroke while asleep: the cerebral haemorrhage brought a coma, from which he could not be awakened, and under which he finally succumbed during the following night. In the hours of waiting, while Katia did all that could be done, Thomas fixed his attention on his work, carried on with letters to keep himself busy, listened to *Don Giovanni*, and noted laconically in his diary, shaken though he was, only his lack of protest against this blow 'which does not come too early and is the most merciful solution'.[24] The discovery among his brother's papers of a mass of obscene sketches—Heinrich's lifelong penchant for drawing had turned recently to fat nude women—roused him to musing on the sexual problems of the whole family, including himself and even Viktor, who, though of more straightforward character, had apparently not shrunk from recurrent adultery. There was no will; among the few documents left in the desk was a tribute to Klaus, which Erika published later in her memorial volume for her brother. At the funeral on 14 March in the Santa Monica mortuary, a simple and only sparsely attended ceremony, Lion Feuchtwanger gave the address.

Thomas's main emotion, it seems, was at being left now as the last of the five—but also (understandably in his present political mood) over the lack of any word of recognition for his brother's life and work from West German officialdom. He dispatched with due care his thanks for the lengthy and effusive telegrams of sympathy, respect, and praise from the GDR leaders (Grotewohl, Pieck, Johannes R. Becher), which Heinrich would not have taken too seriously, as he wrote a week later to a Heidelberg editor. But to hear 'from Bonn, Frankfurt, Munich . . . and from his birthplace Lübeck *not a single word*, is *miserable*'.[25] Though his differences with Heinrich had long been laid to rest, even for one usually so

---

[24] Ibid. 175.    [25] *Br.* iii, 138.

ready with a memorial article it was still far from easy to consider for publication a tribute which might have restored the balance against his country's neglect. His only effort in this respect was in the form of a letter to the editor of the New York *Germanic Review*—significantly, to appear in the special number in preparation for his own seventy-fifth birthday. 'He knew that his work—a mighty work!—was done. . . . The fact that [he] was one of the greatest writers in the German language will sooner or later dawn even on the reluctant consciousness of the Germans.'[26]

The problem of his brother—thirty-five years earlier 'the most difficult of my life', and still one that had never left him—had been finally resolved, and he could turn his attention back to the more pressing question of the projected next visit to Europe with the annual lecture-tour. This was to be built round the launch of the French edition of *Faustus* in Paris, preceded by a preliminary tour of America, including, of course, the Library of Congress, and Sweden, and ending once again in Switzerland. There he would celebrate his seventy-fifth birthday—in the back of his mind, as he privately admitted, the idea of a reconnaissance for a permanent move there. His first idea for a theme had been Schopenhauer, but he had abandoned this as too academic, and decided instead on the more personal approach of a talk on his times, a review of the epoch through which he had lived his seventy-five years, appropriate enough now at the mid-century, and offering ample scope for some verities *in politicis*. He regarded it in fact as 'a historical act', more important even than his 'German Address' given in Berlin in 1930. 'How insupportable people find the truth!' he wrote to Hesse, as he completed the lecture on 21 March. 'But I'm going to tell it soon, on my trip. And in Washington into the bargain.' (His 'truth', indeed, was mild and conciliatory enough, but it would not escape the criticism of the extreme Right.)

He had already suggested a date to Agnes Meyer for Washington, but learned now from her, as she enclosed a letter from the Librarian of Congress, that his hitherto untroubled relationship with the Library had been gravely affected, in the current cold-war hysteria, by the publicity over his visit to East Germany and his many statements so readily inter-preted as pro-communist. Luther Evans, confronted with a comprehensive FBI dossier of these, was reluctantly compelled to omit the lecture, so far unannounced, from the programme, the Library's hundred-and-fiftieth anniversary offering sufficient excuse for so doing. Mann made no protest, saying he fully understood and accepted the decision. 'My talk, it is true, apart from a word in favour of peace, concludes with a decisive and well-founded disowning of communism, but I can see that I have forfeited the

[26] x 521f.

chance of making this statement in the Library.' To Agnes, however, he stressed again the great dangers of the cold war: 'Russia it makes even more evil, if that's possible, and here with us it is ruining democracy. . . . It is hard to describe my depression, fuelled by all the losses of a single year— first my son, in Germany my youngest brother, and now the eldest . . .' He trusted that at least the lecture might be given as planned in Chicago and New York—it would be shaming to have to confess in Europe that he was banned from speaking in America.[27]

In the weeks before leaving for Chicago on 19 April his depression deepened, and thoughts recurred of a flight for good from this 'land of gangsters'. He was firmly against the annexation of the word 'peace' by the communists; but he was not about to make himself a martyr, he wrote, for a cause that was not his own, for a totalitarian state of which he could never approve. On the other hand, any man here risked martyrdom who protested against the destruction of democracy under the pretext of preserving it, as in the Mundt–Nixon bill before Congress, which demanded registration of all communists and communist-controlled organizations and provided for their internment in a national emergency. If that went through, 'I shall *flee* head over heels, taking my seven honorary doctorates with me.'[28] Troubling too was a legal dispute over the future of the Fischer Verlag, re-established since the war by Suhrkamp but its return demanded now by Bermann Fischer, in whose eyes he had been merely a temporary trustee. (It was not until the end of April that this could be resolved by their agreement to set up the separate houses of Suhrkamp and Fischer, Mann remaining with Bermann in the latter, not without concern over the future of his books and some sympathy for Suhrkamp, who he considered had behaved admirably.) The coming change of air might do him some good, he thought—except that the 'air' was probably the same everywhere now.

He felt sure, however, that he still enjoyed massive support in America, and at the first performance in the University of Chicago on 22 April found this amply confirmed. The pressure for tickets was so great that the venue was changed to the bigger chapel, and he spoke to more acclaim and with more satisfaction for himself than he had anticipated. Erika, who had accompanied them, had been of great help in last-minute revisions and cuts to this English version, and during their few days in Chicago, which included a family dinner for Elisabeth's birthday, did the same with the German text for New York. There too, on 26 April, the reception at the performance arranged by *Aufbau* was most encouraging. Excerpting his lecture in a press release, and in a recorded message for the Mid-Century

[27] AM Brw. 735f.    [28] Br. iii, 140.

Conference for Peace in Chicago, he returned to his theme of the cold war's threat to democracy: emphasizing how much America and Russia had in common, the similarity of the peoples in their 'innate openness and affability, an absence of reserve in human intercourse', he called for America to seize the initiative for a universal peace-conference and a plan for consolidation of the world's resources to eliminate poverty. 'This would be humanistic communism, outdistancing the inhuman brand; and not until Russia scorned such world planning would the proof be manifest that [it] does not want peace', a proof now too prematurely taken for granted.[29] For the launch of the 'Thomas Mann Reader' (more like a necrology, sniffed the *New Yorker*—he might be a major author but 'not that major'), Knopf arranged a press conference, and there too his burden was political. Germany's future was dark, amid the understandable American and British fear of communism which tempted them to take fascism as a brother-in-arms: everything would be better if America were sincerely anti-fascist and not bent on the suppression of socialism throughout the world.

In Stockholm, where they arrived on 2 May after a wearisome twenty-hour flight via Scotland, Hamburg, and Copenhagen, his talk in the Academy next evening was introduced by Prince Wilhelm, president of the PEN Club. It was equally well received, and if anything more successful than that of the year before. After repeating it in the University of Lund, he flew with Katia to Paris on 8 May, to spend a week of relative tumult there, constantly dogged by journalists: a crowded reception given by the publishers Albin Michel at the Ritz, three hours of signing copies of the French *Faustus* in Martin Flinker's bookshop, and the lecture before a large audience at the Sorbonne, all interspersed by excellent but over-lavish restaurant meals. For his talk, in German and curtailed for broadcasting purposes, he made a brief preamble in passable French—recovering quickly from his slip of the tongue in thanking his introducers, the Germanist Edmond Vermeil, and the writer Jules Romains, as 'M. Merveil' and 'M. Romain Rolland' (to some amusement, though not apparently for Romains)—and was well pleased with the ovation which followed.

The evident success of *Faustus* in its French version, he wrote towards the end of the year, was psychologically remarkable: that so thoroughly German a novel should appeal to the French was almost an abdication, and he would not like to see Europe's integration founded on the 'intellectual disarmament' of France. What was needed was a 'European Germany, not a German Europe'.[30] In the numerous interviews in Paris, he often concentrated on the problem of Germany and its current sterile artistic life in the cold war situation, correcting any impression from his previous statements,

---

[29] Manfred George papers, Deutsches Literaturarchiv, Marbach; xi. 322 ff.        [30] *Br*. iii, 176.

or from his visit to Weimar, that he favoured communism in its Stalinist form, though admitting he had found in the East a moral ideal of promise for the future.

But it was an overtiring stay. He confessed to his diary how he was beginning to detest the French-language ambience, and over the last day or two successfully resisted the pressure of further invitations and the insistence of journalists. As soon as Katia had arranged the rental of a little car— a Hillman Minx, in decided contrast to young Motschan's luxurious Buick of the previous year—they were glad to escape on 16 May, heading for Zurich. His first assignment there was the birthday celebration—his lecture to be given on 5 June, and a dinner next evening—so they would be able first to rest for a week in Lugano, joined by Erika for part of the time. During the few days in Zurich, however, he was persuaded to record his lecture for Bavarian Radio for a birthday broadcast—without cuts, he hoped. Delightful spring weather, and not least the chance of exchanging frequent visits with the Hesses in Montagnola, made the stay ideal. Katia had begun to suffer from varicose veins, but to him made light of this, making do with massage; her doctor, however, diagnosed a more serious internal condition (perhaps the sequelae of her trouble early in 1940 in New York) which would probably need operation. This she resolutely concealed from her husband, deciding to wait until the festivities were over.

Hesse, for whom on one of his visits he read two chapters from the *Holy Sinner* manuscript, found him surprisingly youthful, his lively and gently mocking manner unchanged: simply listening to him speak was pure pleasure in language. Such contact with people 'whose eyes have been opened', as Hesse wrote later to Erika, 'brothers with understanding also for our troubles . . . which no one otherwise sees', was one of the few joys of life left.[31] For Mann too there was comfort and encouragement in exchanging views with one whose political stance was so close to his own—even if this scene of his first months of emigration brought melancholy recall of all that had happened to him since, and Hesse, more resigned and averse to any form of intervention in the public debate, seemed to him—though they were much of an age—an old man. 'For me, many blessings, and much sorrow: world fame, trouble, pain,' he noted in his diary. 'Now my house stands in California. All very strange, this life. People are astonished at my youth and capacity for work. But often, how profound the fatigue!'

The return to the Baur au Lac in Zurich on 31 May brought a welcome reunion with Gret and the grandchildren, Frido little changed, eager to show him his 'Doctor Doolittle' book, and as affectionate as ever. The

[31] EM *Br. Antw.* i, 274.

lecture in the Schauspielhaus earned great applause: somewhat surprisingly, he thought, with a text so contrary to current opinion, but evidence perhaps that his words expressed what many privately felt. An extraordinary man, commented Korrodi in the *Neue Zürcher*—critical of liberalism and indulgent towards socialism, yet not whole-heartedly, for he finds the ideal political solution in Goethe, the self-confessed 'moderate liberal'.[32] Telegrams, letters, flowers had begun to stream in, and this time more than ever a printed card would be needed for the acknowledgements. For his birthday, at least some of the family were there: Erika, of course, Elisabeth, who had crossed from America, and Michael joining Gret and the boys from a tour in Austria. A delegation from Lübeck was in attendance, presenting him ceremoniously with a cartwheel-sized cake of traditional marzipan. At the dinner that evening, given by Swiss friends in one of Zurich's ancient guild houses, the historian J. R. von Salis spoke of his close associations with Switzerland, with Zurich in particular, the Lübecker's orderliness and punctuality so very like that of the Zürcher, but also of the significance of his work, thoroughly German yet transcending the purely national to European status, as had been shown in the Paris reception of *Faustus*. The quiet and harmonious festival touched him greatly, his only regret that in his few words of thanks he had omitted any word of memorial for Klaus.

Once this was safely over, Katia could tell him she was due now for hospital. On 9 June Erika took her to the Hirslanden Clinic, on the northeastern outskirts of the city, for a period of preliminary treatment designed to reduce the risk of embolism, before the actual operation on 20 June. The doctors' prognosis was reassuring; with Erika, then Golo, who arrived on 18 June, there were daily visits to Hirslanden; and with their support, and the services of a locally recruited secretary, he was able to pursue essential tasks; but in the loneliness he felt without Katia at hand he could concentrate only on the pile of correspondence. During the waiting-period he drove with Motschan to Basle on 11 June, to repeat his lecture, to applause in the Stadttheater there. There were anxious days after the operation, which had given some complications and caused Katia considerable pain, but her case was soon well in hand and she was never in serious danger. A lengthy convalescence would, however, be needed before they could think of the return to California, and they planned a stay in Sils-Maria during July. He and Erika settled meanwhile into the luxury Hotel Dolder, well-situated near the clinic and above the city's heat, but he was in too low spirits to turn back to the manuscript of *The Holy Sinner*, which had lain so long untouched.

---

[32] *Tb*. viii, 558.

It had become clear to him that his repeated plea for East–West understanding and for a 'humanistic communism' had not been universally welcomed either in Switzerland or in West Germany. Already in May a projected invitation to Berne by the Free Students organization there had been refused for this 'pilgrim to the East'; and among the West German articles on the occasion of his birthday which began now to flow in there was repeated denigration, not only of his political advocacy of the 'oppressive regime of the East' but also of his literary achievement ('Thomas Mann can write, but is incapable of thinking'). Bermann, proposing to publish a compilation of all his political statements, was persuaded to desist from this recall of so much that was 'outdated', which could 'only give rise to renewed spiteful discussions and comments I can honestly do without'. It was the first time in his life he had ever forgone such a reprint of earlier pronouncements, blithely confident always in his ability to withstand controversy over the changes in his politics, and maintaining an Olympian serenity in quoting Goethe's words

> Confuse me not with plaints of contradiction:
> To speak at all's at once an aberration.

The conservative-turned-democrat, and the outspoken anti-fascist since the thirties, had had no difficulty in turning aside criticism of his changes of view; it was a different matter now for the American citizen with unwelcome left-wing views.

In the weeks that followed, he worried continually over the wisdom of a return to America, weighing the attraction of his Californian existence, which offered the peace he needed to finish *The Holy Sinner*, against that of a permanent resettlement in Switzerland—but who, as he wrote to Adorno, would have thought yet another emigration possible? His exposure to attacks over there, 'long since denounced by *Life* and company as a fellow-traveller',[33] would hardly be favourable for quiet work, and the hot war in divided Korea, which had just broken out between Russia and the 'United Nations'—that is, the Americans, though later joined by Britain and others—could not but make the atmosphere there worse for him. There was much anxious discussion with Elisabeth (who, with many of his friends, was firmly in favour of Europe for him now), Golo, Katia when she was better, and Erika. Compounding his and Katia's concern was that over Erika herself, the daughter on whose support they had both come to lean so heavily. In near-desperation over the refusal of her provocative articles for publication in Germany, and her virtual excommunication in America, she was eating little, drinking rather too much, and had grown alarmingly

---

[33] 50/322.

thin. Her occasional resort to a morphine preparation, prescribed earlier for gall-bladder trouble, was, she assured him, well under control, but he was none the less greatly worried for her, and it was hard to find the mood for continuing with the manuscript.

Soon after his move with her into the Dolder Hotel, to await Katia's release on 11 July, there had come for him a disturbance of a very different kind—one of those experiences he had thought long since over for him —through an irresistible attraction to a young Bavarian waiter occasionally at their table. He could not take his eyes off the handsome nineteen-year-old, Franz Westermeier from familiar Tegernsee, Erika tugging at his sleeve in concern at the attention he was arousing, and only half accepting his denial that there was anything sexual about it. Physical desire indeed played only a small part: this was 'something for the heart', long missing in his life. He lost no opportunity of a sight of the boy, who he thought realized his interest; contrived to draw him into talk of his prospects, his hopes for a job in Geneva, and gave him surreptitious tips. All this once more, he confided to his diary: '*once again love*, emotion, deep longing for another—not felt for twenty-five years, yet to happen to me one more time'. The sexual drive was there, as he found—not without 'a certain pride in the vitality of my years'—during the night before Katia's return, but it was firmly repressed. 'Banal activity, aggressivity, testing how far he might be willing, is not for my life with its demands for secrecy. . . . Shrinking from a reality very dubious in its chances for happiness . . .'

In the few days remaining before they left for Sils-Maria, this half-melancholy mood gave way to a comfortable resignation, if still with thoughts of giving way to his desires.

World fame is worthless enough for me, but how little it weighs against one smile from him, his glance, the gentleness of his voice! . . . Three more days, and I won't ever see the boy again, shall forget his face. But not the adventure of my heart. He has been taken into the gallery which no 'literary history' will report, and which reaches back through Klaus H[euser] to those now dead, Paul, Willri, Armin. . . . Fell asleep in thoughts of the darling. . . . 'When we still suffered from love.' It happens still, at 75. Once again, once again! How exactly the old story with its grief and its bright moments. . . . Farewell for ever, you charming one, late and painfully exciting dream of love!

In Sils-Maria, from where discontent over cold, sunless, and uncomfortable rooms soon provoked a transfer to better quarters in St. Moritz, his thoughts were still full of this 'last love', which had awakened all the deepest memories of his life, and recalled the old passions which had found a 'certain immortality' in his work: Armin Martens in *Tonio Kröger*, Willri

Timpe in *The Magic Mountain*, Paul Ehrenberg in *Faustus*, Klaus Heuser, for whom he had written the introduction to the Kleist essay.

To 'Franzl' he wrote, in guarded propriety, enquiring about his Geneva project, and offering any recommendation which might be useful. Would he reply? 'Writing of course comes hard for him. Yet how I long to receive something from the hand which shook mine so cordially.' Chancing now to receive for review a translation into German of Michelangelo's poems, with the originals, he found it remarkable how the homo-erotic love they expressed was devoted so much to the countenance, the compelling 'forza d'un bel viso'—exactly his own experience with Franz: it must be delightful to sleep with him, but he could not picture himself in actual physical contact. 'My tenderness for him would be on account of his eyes, of something almost "spiritual" therefore . . .' The message for him from these verses was the 'empowering' of old age to love, which he himself shared with the melancholy sculptor as with those 'powerfully enduring natures' Goethe and Tolstoy: eroticism lasting well into old age, 'untameable infatuation with beautiful eyes'. The essay-review which he began at once and which was published in a Zurich journal later in the year, would be his immortalization of Franz Westermeier, anonymously but clearly indicated, like Klaus Heuser in the Kleist essay, and the general theme of love erupting late in life remained in his mind, to figure in work still to come.

For days, his diary entries were exceptionally lengthy. He recalled almost daily the immense pleasure at a simple word from the boy, with news of a position in Geneva after the Dolder season was over; mused over the Michelangelo parallel as he continued his essay, and the difficulty of resuming the novel; noted how he rose from his desk to watch with 'deep erotic interest' a young tennis-player at practice with his trainer on the St. Moritz courts, irresistibly attracted by the Hermes-like legs in white shorts. There had been a certain harmony in the outcome of the Dolder experience, and he could accept with equanimity the sarcastic comments of Erika, who, like Katia, was well aware of it: but the effect now, he recognized as he watched this new object of desire, had been a relapse into melancholy over his sex-life—'this all-pervading, illusory, yet passionately persistent enthusiasm for the *incomparable attraction, unsurpassed by anything in this world*, of male youth, which has ever been my happiness and misery, not to be spoken . . . no "promesse de bonheur", only renunciation . . .' The god of the tennis-court too had to be left behind and forgotten.

Constantly, however, there was his rehearsal of the pros and cons of a return to America, on which a decision could not be postponed much longer. Much had seemed against, not least his worsening American income, apparent from Knopf's most recent accounts; and the risk of the

Korean war broadening into a more general conflict, with attendant McCarthyite persecution of all types of nonconformists, coupled with his memories here of the days of 1933, had turned the debate with Erika and Katia to serious consideration of how a discreet re-emigration might be contrived. 'The question of citizenship and papers at all events very difficult. But probably certain that if we return we would never get out again, and the country would be a major trap for us.' Golo, said Erika, had now joined the many who advised staying in Europe; Michael with his family had decided in any case to do so. Yet their father felt his position over there must be still intact; there was the coming Thomas Mann exhibition at Yale, to commemorate the seventy-fifth birthday, and so many friends to welcome him back; despite the similarities with 1933, he could not imagine they would ever be regarded in America as the 'undesirables' they would have been in Nazi Germany.

As he later realized, their fears were grossly exaggerated. At the moment, however, they seemed very real, and when the time came on 9 August to leave St. Moritz, he was still vacillating. They drove first to Innsbruck, for a final leave-taking from Michael, Gret, and the boys—with Gret he left his gold wrist-watch for Frido, for it would be a long time before they met again, if ever—and returned then to Zurich. It had been depressing enough to learn from Michael that he had had a concert appearance in West Berlin refused (impossible, said the director of the Staatstheater, for a son of Thomas Mann), and to find in St. Anton that a bookseller's display of Mann books needed police protection; now in Zurich there was a letter from Elisabeth urging him not to return to America, which raised once again all the problems this would entail. To his diary, he confided that on this journey he had lost far too much of himself 'to the charms of youth, to beguiling faces. . . . Back now to the exhaustion, the pressing questions of life, 1933 brand, and in a way more difficult especially now we have become so old. Deeply reluctant to give up the support which Erika means for our age, at any rate for mine.' On her seemed to depend all his plans. For better or worse, they finally decided on return to California, flying to London on 17 August, and thence to New York, while she drove the Hillman Minx back to Paris and would join them in London.

He had accepted to lunch with Siegfried Trebitsch at the Hotel Dolder on 15 August, and was curious whether it would bring a last sight of young Franz. Erika, he suspected, actually arranged this, for he was found waiting as they left the dining-room. To Mann, who again could not take his eyes off him, he was servile, yet honest, in his gratitude for his letter and his interest. The news, however, that the Geneva post had been lost—he had been wanted at once, and the Dolder would not release him—brought for Mann a twinge of conscience at his own 'egoistic enjoyment' without the practical help he might have given. Now it was farewell for ever: 'the pressure of his powerful hand. His smile, his eyes. Unforgettable. . . . A love, a favour in the extreme, an affection from the depths of the heart. Or merely the delighted senses . . .' Singular: no longer now the reluctance for closer physical contact, yet the dubious, and now impossible, happiness from an actual embrace seemed unessential for a passion which must remain a distant tenderness. He would leave him his address, urging him to write with his news—a faint hope that contact might not be lost for ever.

There was more confusion then, before they said goodbye to the Zurich friends. According to her New York lawyer, Erika risked being held in Ellis Island if she returned with them direct, but she pressed her unwilling parents to carry on without her, and decided herself to fly via Canada. After three days in London—he fatalistic now and prepared for the worst, but looking to the positive advantage of a few months' quiet to finish *The Holy Sinner*—they took a Panamerican flight, and arrived in New York on 21 August. His hopes might or might not be vain, but his fears were certainly liars: their reception could not have been more friendly, the customs were particularly benevolent, and it seemed like a homecoming, his apprehensions of a threatening atmosphere quite unfounded. The Mann exhibition at Yale, which they visited briefly on 23 August, made a satisfying tribute, which, as Thornton Wilder said, no other author had received in his lifetime. Mann remarked with pleasure on the case where *The Magic Mountain* was aligned with the *Bildungsromane* of his great predecessors— Goethe's *Wilhelm Meister*, Stifter's *Nachsommer*, Keller's *Grüner Heinrich*— 'That's where I belong.' He regretted only being provoked at the press conference to reiterating his concern at German rearmament and his belief in Russia's fundamentally peaceable intentions.

The final stages of their journey they took as quickly as possible, with only two days in Chicago, where the relations between Elisabeth and her egocentric and bombastic husband, now planning a move to Italy, were clearly not of the best. For Mann, there and in the tedium of the train on to Los Angeles, it was a time to regain hope in the curative effect of the return to his normal existence, and in long diary-entries to strike a balance.

May [the future] grant me enough peace to bury and collect myself in the work which is still the strongest tie to life. May Erika soon come! May I see Frido again! May the boy from the Dolder write just once! . . . Too much suffering, too much gaping and staring for my own pleasure. I've let the world lead me too much by the nose. Better if it had all *not* happened? It *did*, and that handshake . . . remains a sadness to be treasured.—Why am I writing all this? To destroy it all in good time before I die? Or do I want the world to *know* me? I believe it knows anyway, at least some experts do, more of me than is admitted. . . . At home, in my own domain, I shall forget the torments of the journey, find myself again, in spite of Franz

Westermeier's eyes and those Hermes-like limbs on the tennis-court. I shall preserve within me those faces and those raptures, while I recover from them and from
that loss of myself which made me so old and dull. The fact remains that *all*
remembrance for me is essentially painful, and that the thing for me is to look
forward. . . . And yet [the past] holds much treasure. . . . Without a doubt, my
enthusiasm for the young male form has grown tempestuously recently, perhaps in
the feeling that closing time is near . . . axiomatic for me, how far worthier of
admiration is the 'divine youth' above all that is female, awakening a longing with
which *nothing* in the world can be compared.

Back at last on 29 August among his own things—uncertain yet whether to
be bored or pleased—his first thought was to get back to work as soon as
he could.

## 3

*'One's self-satisfaction is an untaxed kind of property which it is
very unpleasant to find depreciated'*

(*George Eliot,* Middlemarch)

Paradise regained? It could well seem so, as he relaxed in enjoyment of the
first real privacy for many months, a privacy he was resolved to maintain.
He took out the *Holy Sinner* manuscript, and made leisurely preparations
for continuing when the mass of correspondence, journals, and other
material awaiting his return had been dealt with. Politics, however, amid
the heightening war-mood in America, continued to intrude, reviving the
old worries over his personal position. Erika arrived shortly afterwards,
having had no trouble on the journey; but they put their heads together in
concern over the effect of the impending registration of 'communist' organizations, in view of his membership of the Arts and Sciences Council
long suspected as such. An important priority for him was to put Agnes
Meyer right, who had written bemoaning what she saw as an anti-patriotic
stance in his often-repeated lecture.

That, he told her, would be his last. If she would read again its closing
passage she would find it a 'very appropriate word of farewell from an old
man who means well with humanity and thus also with this country'. He
would never publish anything against America, and in Europe had been at
pains to stress his obligations and ties to his new country, speaking as a
patriot even when he urged the use of American power for the furtherance
of world peace. Nor was he trying to convert America to socialism (though
this might be an 'inescapable necessity for Europe'): what troubled him was
to see the land of freedom acting all over the world as the policeman of the
old, corrupt status quo. Even under the stress of internal politics and the

'criminal McCarthy campaign', however, the world catastrophe of a general war was unlikely, and he hoped he might be permitted to continue his life and his work for a while, in the house he loved on 'the piece of American soil that is my own', assured that here, as in Europe, he did not lack sympathy and respect. *Harpers* was to publish the shorter, lecture form of 'The Years of my Life' in October: 'daring people! Is publication not an un-American activity?'

His words might soothe her, but they did not allay his own disquiet over America's power-politics and the atmosphere of investigations and persecution. She was also not the only one to harbour misgivings over the lecture: Manfred George, the editor of *Aufbau* in New York, was pressing him in October to give an interview which would clarify his position. But for the moment he felt he had said enough. His financial position in America seemed more and more precarious, and over a proposal to improve that for Europe he had been at odds with Bermann. On the one hand the publisher was complaining of poor German sales, due to Mann's political attitude, yet on the other he was reluctant to permit Swiss editions under licence of *The Buddenbrooks*, and later of *The Holy Sinner*, under highly attractive conditions Mann had discussed while there. Their dispute was finally resolved, with reasonable proposals for book-club editions and better conditions in Germany. Before September was out his yearning to get away for good to Europe had returned, stronger than ever, in which he was seconded by Erika, who urged him to sell the house before the next European tour he was considering for the spring, and make that his final departure. A powerful argument in favour, he felt, as Erika's forty-fifth birthday approached, lay in her poor health, bringing her close to a nervous breakdown, and her need to get away from the atmosphere she found so stifling and repugnant in America—for he took it for granted that that she would remain with them and continue her valuable support. A somewhat alarming infection for Katia had meanwhile yielded quickly to treatment, and he was relieved when the 'dear one, so completely indispensable', was out of bed and active again.[34]

Whatever their decision, *The Holy Sinner*, which he had resumed at first half-heartedly, must at all costs be completed, if only for financial reasons, and his diary noted almost daily application with increasing vigour. From Zurich there arrived a case left behind for forwarding, with papers including a photograph of the frontispiece to the Michelangelo translations and Franz Westermeier's letter: both were inserted in his diary—a childish performance, he admitted, but 'nothing has changed in this relationship', and in the back of his mind there was the thought that he would anyway

[34] 50/351.

burn all the diaries at some suitable moment. Nothing had changed, indeed, and he surprised himself with his eager scanning of each day's post for a letter from Franz, though realizing this was probably a forlorn hope. 'Almost certainly he felt a slight exaggeration in my interest. It's asking too much that he should be glad of it.' The experience had been filed away, as it were; calmer and more relaxed now, he could only wonder at others' expressions or explanations of the homo-erotic—the psychoanalytical approach, perhaps by Havelock Ellis, in an English journal he had read soon after his return, attributing it to fear of incest with the mother ('academic ignorance personified'); the sex in Gore Vidal's *The City and the Pillar*, where he found the homosexual affairs incomprehensible (how was it possible actually to sleep with men?); or Dorothy Bussy's lesbian best-seller *Olivia*, 'situated remarkably between girlish kitsch and higher literature'. When Joseph Angell now proposed the purchase by Yale, not only of the loaned exhibits, but also of all his available manuscripts, including the diaries—these to be kept sealed, and opened to research only twenty or twenty-five years after his death—he quite welcomed the thought of the entertaining discoveries to be made when all was dead and gone and the world finally knew his secrets.

On 26 October the last lines of *The Holy Sinner* were written, and after an evening at the cinema, to see Gloria Swanson in *Sunset Boulevard*, Katia and Erika surprised him with flowers, caviare, and a bottle of Moët et Chandon in celebration. Two years and eight months, he calculated, less interruptions of about five months—a fair achievement in all the circumstances, and he was not displeased with the way he had contrived to maintain the ironic lightness of touch he had aimed for. To Reisiger he had said earlier that the good Hartmann von Aue would have been amazed at what was being made of the very serious poem *Gregorius* he had adapted from the twelfth-century French *Vie du pape Grégoire*. Though endeavouring to 'rein in his penchant for the comic in the interest of the religious gravity of the background', Mann had found the legend very humorous, as he told Helen Lowe-Porter: and 'comedy seems to me more and more the best thing in the world, a tonic, a relief, a true blessing'.[35]

As with the *Joseph*, he had followed the main lines of the story given, but here far less thorough background study had been needed to realize his aim of retelling the myth in realistic form, of creating the illusion of real events, if in fantastic form. Details of everyday medieval life he had found in Wolfram's *Parsifal*, and the verses of the *Nibelungenlied* made a model for a little of the narrative; but for the rest he gave his invention free rein to flesh out the story of fearful sin, great penance, and final grace, leading 'the

[35] *DüD.* iii, 366; 50/380.

child of shame, his mother's spouse, his grandfather's son-in-law, his father's father-in-law, monstrous brother of his own children, to St. Peter's seat', as the elect of God Himself. Not the least of his fun had been in the elaboration of a quite unhistorical, supranational time-scale and a linguistic mish-mash of Old French, Early English, and Middle High German: his fictional narrator an Irish monk, Clemens, sitting in Alemannic St. Gallen as the personification of the spirit of story-telling, 'free to the point of abstraction', the languages running together in his writing, and proud of his grammatical and dignified prose. For Mann, it had made an ideal pendant to *Faustus*, his interest first kindled as he gave the theme to Leverkühn to compose as a marionette play, and just what he needed for light relief afterwards, in preference to continuing *Felix Krull*, for which his outline plan was vastly longer. He had, as he said, worked for his own entertainment—of necessity, since contemporaries did not offer much in that line; it was 'light, serene, has a certain aloofness without being cold, and I think it *is* something that I could do it right after *Faustus*'.[36] But it could not be filmed: Cardinal Spellman, the Archbishop of New York, 'who himself wants to be Pope, though not born of incestuous parents and never marrying his mother, would not permit'.[37] And he was not surprised later at its banning in Eastern Europe, where a sense of humour was notoriously lacking, as 'formalist' and *volksfremd*.

The final chapter was not yet satisfactory to him, with a knotty problem still unresolved: should the pious abbess recognize in the wearer of the papal crown, to whom she has come to confess, the son, and husband, last seen twenty-two years before? In her confession, his identity must come out, for he would produce the ivory tablet with which she had set adrift the child of her incestuous union, and which later had proved to her the incest of her second marriage: it would now establish the trinity of child, husband, and Pope. She might be expected to realize that instinctively, but at what point of the audience? The whole story, improbable enough as it was, might well become totally absurd. Before he could tinker with his text to get the ending right, however, there came another, more urgent call on his time: a request from the BBC, following the death of Shaw, for a half-hour memorial talk to be broadcast in the Third Programme.

At first doubtful, he accepted: the Grand Old Man had never stood 'particularly close to my heart', but he thought it sensible to have a German speak about him in view of the contribution Germany, in Trebitsch's translations, had made to his fame. Applying himself diligently to this far-from-easy task, his respect and interest grew—not only reading *Heartbreak House*, *The Apple Cart*, the preface to *Androcles*, and *Saint Joan*, but also

[36] 51/147.     [37] *DüD*. iii, 374.

learning how similar to his own had been Shaw's approach to, and capacity for, work, even if he could not credit with true greatness a nature so 'lean, vegetarian, and frigid', so unerotic. (It was only a few years later, with the publication of Shaw's letters, that he realized how wide of the mark this latter judgement was.) 'He Was Mankind's Friend' was the title for the *Listener*'s publication of his talk after the broadcast in January 1951: 'the laughing prophet of a humanity emancipated from the gloom of tragedy', who had done his best with 'the gleaming weapon of word and wit' to raise it to a 'new level of social maturity'.

That done and recorded during November, he quickly completed *The Holy Sinner* to his satisfaction, with an adroitly humorous, yet still respectfully religious turn in the final dialogue of recognition, and the monk-narrator's valedictory to warn his readers not to draw the wrong moral from his tale. What was then to follow? Certainly there was no lack of occupation as such. After the Shaw, a short essay-review was soon completed of the edition in English of Wagner letters, many hitherto unknown, in the Burrell Collection in Philadelphia; in December, a New Year message to the Tokyo paper *Asahi Shinbun* with his belief in, or at any rate hope for, a religious humanism transcending all creeds. Politics too continued to exercise him. Though he kept to himself his concern over the Korean war, with China now involved, at most confessing to Agnes Meyer the sleepless nights it caused him, he made no bones in a letter in November to the liberal journal *Nation* over repeating his criticism of America's sacrifice of democracy in the cause of anti-communism. His own political position was still under fire, with an allegation that he had been a signatory to the communist Stockholm Peace Appeal, and a report in November that he had been elected to the presidium of the second World Peace Congress in Warsaw, this constraining him to issue a denial ('which of course has been far less visible than the false report'). 'If it was just a question of filling the day,' he had written to Hesse, 'one would need no work. But it leaves an insipid taste . . . and I must soon look around for some new entertainment to occupy me in the mornings, if only in order to say: "excuse me, I am so busy." '[38]

Logically, he thought, he should turn back to *Krull*, as he had in 1943, only then to take up *Faustus*: it would have to make an 'enduring task', however, not simply a pastime. He had nothing else; no ideas for novellas, no theme for a novel. Of his older plans, the Frederick the Great was unthinkable; 'Maya', 'The Loved Ones', and all the rest had already been largely exploited, even the Luther–Erasmus theme seemed difficult to take up now. To cast himself back over four decades and continue *Krull* was

[38] *HH Brw.* 226.

attractive, with the voluminous dossier of material accumulated and the personal experience of the world and of travel gained, not least in terms of homosexuality; yet he hesitated, in the fear that after all the intervening events this might have nothing to say to him, or not enough, 'and I would like to feel that my work has truly been done'. 'All I know is that I must do something, must somehow have a continuity of work and a life task. I cannot stay idle.' For want of better, it was *Krull* that began in December to engage him, as Katia and Erika set to work to sort and bring in order the 'thousands of scribblings' with which his cupboards were stuffed in preparation for their planned transfer to Yale: and on Christmas Eve he resumed where had broken off, on the same manuscript sheet, still in some doubt whether the subject would succeed in holding him.

His hesitations had been against a background of great depression. In the Korean adventure he saw the threat of a third world war, with atomic weapons as like as not, and the seeming impossibility of quick and effective action to sell the house and escape to Europe before a firm agreement could be reached with Yale over the purchase of his papers. Katia was less convinced than Erika over the need to leave the country without delay, and was against any over-hasty decision. There had been another family problem too: a crisis between Elisabeth and her husband in Chicago. Borgese, who had for some time been vaguely considering a move to Italy, telephoned excitedly on 20 November that she had confessed to a lover, an Argentine, Secretary-General of the 'World Government Movement', in which they had both been active: he was ready to forgive all, but was determined to start a new life in Italy with or without her and the children. It seemed vital, for the children's sake, to avoid the catastrophe of a divorce, and Katia left at once for Chicago; but while at first Elisabeth agreed to stay with her husband and go with him, impossible though the situation was, to Italy, leaving the children with her parents for three months or so, by the end of the year Borgese, unstable as ever, was talking of taking them with him alone. It would be a long time before a *modus vivendi* was reached, with Borgese havering between Italy and possible posts in America. The resultant uncertainty was less than helpful in moving them towards reaching their own decisions, although Elisabeth's future was more disturbing for Katia than for her husband, whose dependence on his 'adjutant' Erika had now become crucial for his plans.

However these might turn out, the coming year, as he noted on New Year's Eve, would not be without its upheavals, and it was hardly surprising that nervous apprehension and a certain weariness of life should make a leitmotif for his diary entries in the early months of 1951. The chosen task to fill his mornings was the completion of *Krull*, but he was going at it with only half a will: this parodying of eighteenth-century autobiographies, once an entertaining enterprise, seemed increasingly lack-lustre, amusing though it was to note how much of Goethe's *Dichtung und Wahrheit* read like ready-made parody. He had no lack of material, nor of ideas for continuing the story; but the occasional pleasure in a successful passage was not enough to overcome his feeling of dissatisfaction at mere working for work's sake, aimlessly spinning the tale further in day-to-day improvization. Time and again, he felt he was no more than temporizing until he could find his way to something more worthwhile, and the study on Erasmus, for instance, which he had long had in mind, often loomed now as a fallback position against the day when, as he feared, the vein of *Krull* would give out. With the experiment of *The Holy Sinner*, light relief though it was after *Faustus*, he had had a clear plan, a story of unusual interest and considerable power in itself, with, in addition, all the fun of the linguistic by-play. Here, however, he was back in a more traditional Thomas Mann style—'seeking distraction in these entertainments'—but fundamentally dubious of his power to sustain them in the absence of a truly firm purpose, despite the urgings of so many friends to complete the work.

It was inopportune, to say the least, to find now his own weapon of irony turned against him, in a January essay in the London *Times Literary Supplement* by the Germanist Erich Heller. Writing on 'The Artist and the Real World', Heller found the history of Mann's style itself 'highly ironical': 'the more radically he renounced his earlier German nationalism, the more untranslatably German became his books', commanding respect 'without affording much spontaneous pleasure', to the point where some critics questioned whether his later works held sufficient substance to be classed among the great achievements of world literature. Heller was unsurprised too to see a note of 'unconvincing naivety' in his political declarations, often like the appeals of a Hamlet who, having found the world out of joint, 'makes himself the spokesman of a committee for the prevention of royal assassinations. . . . Tonio Kröger's guilty conscience . . . compels Thomas Mann to play from time to time the part of a Lübeck senator, exhorting the citizens of a ruined city and world to fulfil their municipal duties.'[39] This was wit striking more nearly home than he cared to acknowledge or appreciate, and its effect was inhibiting, accompanied as it was in Pacific Palisades by the interminable discussions with Erika and Katia over their future.

Though he could not really see America's involvement in Korea as the prelude to a disastrous nuclear war, the fact remained that that danger was ever-present—the continuing bomb-tests in the Nevada desert made them-

---

[39] Quoted *Tb* ix, 367f.

selves felt as far as the coast, with the ground shaking, windows rattling, and unearthly lights appearing in the distant sky—and they all three no longer had any doubt that the time was approaching to exchange America for Europe: to spend his declining years on the ancient soil from which he had sprung, and to look on Switzerland as his final resting-place. In the America of which he had been proud to become a citizen, the political atmosphere continued to deteriorate through the McCarthyite investigations, extending now to the movie world of Hollywood and giving him reason to fear that he himself would soon be cited to appear, however he strove to remain aloof from controversy. Taxes were being heavily increased, and he felt America was 'reeling towards madness—yet the whole world is dependent on her'.

All the same, their settled existence in California was going to be hard to abandon. The house they had been to such trouble and expense to establish, despite constant problems over servants, continued to afford much pleasure; in their excursions in the surroundings, on shopping-trips to Westwood or regular visits to hairdresser or manicurist, he was a familiar figure, reserved in neighbourly relations but regarded with benevolence if as somewhat eccentric in insisting on walking where everyone preferred the automobile. No one here seemed to care about his political views, and the Californian world went its way regardless of Thomas Mann's forebodings of McCarthyite concentration camps and a rebirth of fascism in America. It would be a big step to give up such a congenial life, and, as Katia did not fail to point out, there were substantial administrative difficulties in the way of a complete 're-emigration'. There was no trouble in January over having their passports renewed, and enquiries in Switzerland showed no obstacles to their establishment there, even if residence depended on regular renewals. But if the house, now obviously too big for a family reduced to three, was to be sold, he foresaw the need for some considerable refurbishing, and with the tax increases and their diminishing American income, careful calculation was needed. They successfully sold off the adjoining plot; but much would depend on the disposal of the manuscripts to Yale, which Erika by early February had ordered and prepared for despatch and for which a figure of 40,000, or at least 30,000 dollars, was hoped for. (In the event, in spite of Angell's enthusiasm and Caroline Newton's readiness to contribute, this kind of sum could not be raised, one important sponsor withdrawing his support in view of the press reports on Mann's 'communism'; and the Yale collection was the loser, to the benefit of other repositories.)

The arguments were endlessly rehearsed during March, and finally yet another interim solution arrived at: in the summer, another visit with Katia to Switzerland, to reconnoitre for a small house near Zurich, while Erika remained to investigate rental or possible sale of Pacific Palisades, with a view to removal for good the following year—in Erika's bitterly pessimistic view, the very latest possible timing if they were not to be caught up in the anti-communist hysteria and perhaps prevented for ever from leaving. Meanwhile his name was as constantly in demand as ever for support in matters both private and public, whether for recommendations to appointments in Germany or America or on letterheads for liberal causes in which his sympathy, mostly rightly, was taken for granted. How dangerous this latter ground could prove was shown in the *New York Times* headline of 1 February 1951 reporting him as joining a 'new Peace Crusade' with the popular singer Paul Robeson, notorious for his pro-communist stance, made clear by an appearance in Moscow's Red Square.

A long letter to the *New York Times* explaining how he had been drawn into this, in ignorance of the communist wire-pulling behind it, was not published, thanks largely to Knopf's intervention with the editor: his publisher, probably rightly, considered the affair best ignored, and continuation in the correspondence columns counter-productive. All his troubles, wrote Knopf on 14 February, stemmed from his political naïvety: it behoved him not to print a denunciation of the story, but to live up to the last part of his draft and renounce any further sponsorship or political announcements of any kind. This Erika had in fact prepared for him in a declaration for the United Press on 12 February: 'I am convinced that any peace movement generally believed to be communist inspired or controlled is bound to hurt rather than help the cause of peace. . . . I wish to announce my determination not to sponsor any more "causes" . . . whether political or in a "cultural" guise. . . . Unless I were the sole signer, my signature appearing under any "protest", "appeal", "petition" etc. must henceforth be considered a forgery.' But Mann had been disgusted to find his friends unwilling to assist him to a more public defence in the case of the 'Peace Crusade', particularly Agnes Meyer, whose attitude he found hysterical, and to whom he wrote coolly, though with his usual tact.

The affair served as a powerful reinforcement of the plan to quit America sooner rather than later, for early in April his name appeared in a list, issued by the House Committee on Unamerican Activities, of those 'affiliated with various peace organizations or communist fronts'—along with Einstein, Feuchtwanger, Marlon Brando, Norman Mailer, Frank Lloyd Wright, and others. These months had told upon him heavily in nervous strain, aggravated by another article in *The Freeman* from the indefatigable Eugene Tillinger on 'Thomas Mann's Left Hand', accusing him of 'keeping company with Moscow-inspired operations' and denouncing his 'great propaganda value to the Kremlin'. To this, with Erika's assistance, he replied at some length, both in those columns and in the New York *Aufbau*.

But after further articles had appeared (including one read into the Congressional record by his local Congressman—'Mr Mann should remember that guests who complain about the fare at the table of their host are seldom invited to another meal') he finally renounced the struggle, to maintain what he hoped was a dignified silence. 'I keep my mouth shut—with a pretty good conscience,' he wrote at the end of March to Helen Lowe-Porter, 'for I frankly admit I have largely lost interest in this country.' It was galling, however, towards the end of June as they began preparations for the Europe trip, to see an article in *Time*, with its wide European circulation, rehearsing his 'sins', summarizing all the attacks, and implying that a summons for him to appear before the Committee on Unamerican Activities was imminent.

The strain of this 'poisoned atmosphere' was becoming intolerable. 'If only, as when Hitler was flourishing, one could know which side one belonged to . . . communism with its infantile amoralism is impossible, but so is any belief in the future of this corrupt, condemned, late-capitalistic world of profit.'[40] Further scandal was aroused in June by his letter of congratulation to Johannes Becher ('supreme Pontiff of Soviet–German culture') on his sixtieth birthday. Unnoticed at the time, however, was his lengthy plea to the GDR Deputy Prime Minister, Walter Ulbricht, for clemency towards a number of internees, condemned for collaboration with the Nazis, who had appealed for his aid. Writing as neither communist nor anti-communist, but as a fervent peace-lover, he argued against such inhuman judgements, all too similar to those of the fascist regime itself: a generous act of clemency in the cases of these 'average people' would be a significant gesture of peace and reduction of tension between the two power complexes. (Although Ulbricht did not reply, there seems reason to believe that his action may have contributed to the pardon and release in October 1952 of some 1,600 of those concerned.)

By the end of June he was in a condition of 'deep physical and mental fatigue', the coming visit to Europe a cause more for apprehension than pleasure with the hopeless uncertainty he felt in his work. Till then, he had tried to continue with the *Krull*—work for him, as he had written in April, had never been dependent on a good mood, 'my so-called humour is usually born of despair';[41] in May, he had at least one more chapter in mind, and if it petered out then, he would turn to a 'dignified historical novella on Erasmus, Luther, and Hutten'. Now it all seemed senseless. The 'pan-erotic amorality' of Felix Krull, in his progress from lift-boy to *commis* to fully-fledged waiter, with all the opportunities for theft and seduction this offered, was the wrong theme for the world of today; ideas for an Erasmus

---

[40] Letter to Reisiger, 30 Apr. 1951 (Stargardt auction cat. 591, 1969)     [41] *DüD*. i, 326.

work remained vague in the extreme; and all the time, in the background, the irreconcilables of the Korean conflict, with America likely to find herself at war with China, 'the wrong enemy'. 'Since our last European trip . . . I've had a hefty shove into old age'.[42] In this mood of depression, and with a painful arthritis in the right shoulder and arm, he began to see the main object on the new journey as an opportunity for a cure, in Bad Gastein, rather than the reconnaissance they had envisaged for a new home in the Zurich area.

Their itinerary followed the by now accustomed course—a brief stopover in Chicago, a day in New York, and passage in the French liner *De Grasse* to Le Havre, to be met there on 19 July by Erika, who had gone ahead by air and in Paris rented the familiar Hillman Minx for the ride to Zurich. Travel was usually a rapid restorative from ill humours; but this time, grumbling over conditions aboard the French ship and still feeling excessively tired, he did not begin to recover and relax until he could look forward to a week in the safe haven of the Hotel Baur au Lac, with suitcases unpacked and a proper order regained. They had allowed themselves barely two months before returning to New York at the end of September, and their programme was largely improvised: a brief visit to Munich, a week with Michael and his family at the Wolfgangsee, and a few days in Salzburg during the Festspiele until rooms could be secured for a three-week stay at the thermal baths of Gastein. No lectures had been arranged, his only public performances were readings in Salzburg and Zurich, for which he used passages from *Krull*, and he was a reluctant interviewee. As he told a friend, he had in personal terms nothing new to say, and the political brought only misquotation and unwelcome hubbub:[43] to the *Zürcher Woche* on 27 July, however, whose reporter rehearsed the doubts reflected here from America over his political position, he was firm in declaring 'I am a man of freedom, and no communist.' Public exposure was what he had left America to escape, and to a German journal at the end of the stay he reiterated his resolve to keep silent: 'the world needs [peace]— but I need it too'.

The tour in Europe this time was in effect little more than a recuperative change of scene, with conscientious attention to his arthritis in Gastein, a constant struggle against more minor ailments in the changes of altitude and temperature, and much discontent when conditions did not measure up to his standards of comfort. There were many friends to be seen, the mail that pursued him to be kept up with (with special attention to the reception of *The Holy Sinner*) and betweenwhiles a few pages added to the *Krull*, though he was still nagged by scepticism over its future. Theatre

---

[42] *Bl.* 12, 26.        [43] 50/341.

and musical performances that attracted him were fitted in where possible, and relaxation sought in the most varied reading, from Conrad's novels and Kafka's diaries to Duff Cooper's *Operation Heartbreak*. Quietly slipping into Munich at the end of July, and spending only one night there, they drove through Schwabing and the Herzogpark for a look at their ruined house, still full of displaced persons. The authorities had recently formally returned it to his ownership, with the associated tax-liability; but the sight confirmed him in refusal to have anything further to do with the lengthy and costly prospect of clearance and restoration. Even if he had ever envisaged a return to Germany, there could be no future for him in renewing this sad association (though he continued later to pursue compensation for their substantial financial losses under the Nazi regime). There was a touch of melancholy too in seeing Frido again, during the few days' stay which followed near Michael and Gret's lakeside house at Strobl on the Wolfgangsee. Grandfather could no longer be the comrade and playmate he had been to little 'Echo', whose hand could now span octaves on the piano and who was disappointed not to be joined in a swim or on a climb. Buying him a bicycle, however, made up for these shortcomings, and it was satisfying, if sad, to hear how the youngster longed to go back to California with them.

The few days in Salzburg during August on the way to Gastein brought mixed experiences. In dinner-jacket for the performance of Verdi's *Othello*, under Furtwängler, at which US High Commissioner McCloy under heavy military police escort stole the limelight, he found the poor seats to which they were ushered by the Festspielhaus management so demeaning that he marched Katia out in angry disgust at the end of the first scene; but a morning dress-rehearsal of Alban Berg's *Wozzek*—'my most powerful and interesting European impression'—more than compensated for this. He was well content too with the effect of his *Krull* reading, for the benefit of a local scholarship fund, in the *Aula Academica* on 13 August, with many friends in the large audience and praise next day from the press for the 'great humorist' and master of descriptive prose whose lively presentation belied his seventy-six years.

Gastein they found overcrowded when they arrived on 15 August, but the comfortable rooms Erika had arranged were soon free; and he settled to a quiet routine in which almost daily thermal baths, though very tiring, seemed to bring the relief he needed for his arthritis—and, as he noted, a surprising sexual stimulus. Nearly three weeks there, and a week afterwards in Lugano, were the opportunity even for work, of a kind: chiefly attention to correspondence, especially in response to many favourable comments on *The Holy Sinner*, but also some corrections to his Krull manuscript so far—though with the alternative project never far from his mind as he read in Luther and Hutten material. The mountains and rushing waters of Austria and Switzerland made a most refreshing contrast to California, and no praise was too high for the performance of the little car, in Erika's capable hands, which carried its heavy load magnificently over the passes to Lugano, exhausting though he found the journey. The Villa Castagnola there, familiar from their stay in 1933, brought 'life and diary' back to contact with old times and roused thoughts of all he had experienced in the eighteen years since. Best of all, it was near Hesse's home in Montagnola, and they spent many agreeable afternoons with him, in admiration of his settled existence and not without envy of the beautifully situated quarters he was fortunate to enjoy. Bruno Walter was also holidaying in Lugano, and on 12 September, as they prepared for the drive over the Gotthard back to Zurich, Mann left for him flowers and a letter—for it was his seventy-fifth birthday—in warm gratitude for the benevolent destiny that had brought them together over so many years, and the hope that it might let them celebrate together their eightieth.

It was in their final few weeks in the Hotel Dolder in Zurich, despite the abrupt change of altitude and temperature, that he could appreciate how much the tour had restored him. Now he was thoroughly back in his old form; and as he enjoyed the mostly favourable American reviews of *The Holy Sinner*, just out and already marked as Book of the Month choice, his friendly and respectful reception in the city, and the success of his *Krull* reading in the Schauspielhaus on 24 September, he felt renewed vigour to face the return to the 'controversial homeland' of America. But in the Zurich atmosphere, after the visits to Hesse in Montagnola and Walter's declared intention also to settle in Switzerland, there was revived for him and Katia, more firmly than ever, their own plan to do the same. It was embarrassing, after his return to California, to find himself elected to the New York American Academy of Arts and Letters, cited as 'a creative artist whose works are likely to achieve a permanent place in the nation's culture'. He had made, he admitted, too little effort to strike roots in the culture of the United States, had 'remained too much the man I was', and doubted whether his 'Germanic approach' meant much to 'our country', as so many *émigrés* insisted on calling it.[44] No matter: touching though the friendly, even courageous, gesture was, his mind was made up to return to his roots in Europe; and the final failure of the sale of his papers to Yale served only to reinforce the decision, towards which all his planning, as he thought, would now be directed.

----

[44] *Br.* iii, 236.

# IX

## RETURN TO 'EUROPE'S ANCIENT SOIL' 1952–1955

'Switzerland is a country where very few things start, but many things end'

(F. Scott Fitzgerald)

1

*'I'm looking forward to life near Zurich . . . with confidence, almost a youthful joy in novelty, and even some hope for productivity'*

(TM, 29 October 1952)

By the time he returned to California in October 1951, Mann was well into the third section of *Felix Krull*, still following his 1910 outline plan for the novel. The loot acquired during his erotic adventures has given his hero a certain cautious independence, adequate for him to resist the invitation to enter the personal service of hotel guest Lord Kilmarnock (an episode with echoes of Mann's own homosexual attraction to Franz Westermeier); and he is ready now for a more daring enterprise, which will require all his dubious talents—a transformation from waiter to bogus aristocrat. The young Marquis of Venosta proposes he should impersonate him on a year's world tour, arranged by the parents in the hope of weaning him from the disastrous attraction of a Paris mistress. Reaching this long-planned turn in the yarn, with the wider perspectives it offered, gave Mann for a while renewed impetus—scope indeed for his admitted tendency to make everything he touched, even something so light, 'degenerate into the Faustian mode' and become a 'pilgrimage into infinity'. During his few days in Chicago his fascinated impressions, noted at length, from the Museum of Natural History, with its tableaux of the origins and history of life, made excellent material for the wordy Professor Kuckuck, who would be Krull's chance companion on the train from Paris and his introduction to Lisbon *en route* to Buenos Aires; and during December this amusing chapter was rapidly completed.

Yet for Mann the many months of indecision over his future—even now when sure in his heart that 1952 would see his back turned on America for good—had had an inhibiting and often depressing effect on the work. The problems over the move (despite encouraging and flattering reactions from the Swiss authorities to his enquiries), worry over Erika's health, and a further hostile article by Tillinger on the 'Case against Thomas Mann' ('not a fellow-traveller, he already belongs in a more dangerous category') had combined to bring him almost to despair, in 'apprehension, fear and weariness of soul'. If he went to Switzerland, he began to think, it would be, not to live, but to die there—a death which, as the last of a large family, most of his relations and friends already gone, he felt he would welcome sooner rather than later after all the vexations and misunderstandings of a long life of fame. There was nothing for it but to continue with *Krull*, however doubtful of his ability ever to complete it. Through the first months of the New Year he began to groan under the burden of its demands on his inventive powers, and rail at his increasing boredom with the task—even if comforted in the knowledge that that had often been Tolstoy's complaint too. Hilde Kahn, bringing back her typescripts, noticed from his anxious questioning on her impressions how little there was of the *élan* that had characterized the earlier works.

There were diversions from the struggle, however, in the shape of two short pieces for American and British broadcasts, written rapidly in the first days of February and March respectively, and of more significance than their occasion would suggest for our picture of Thomas Mann as he prepared to quit the United States. The talk for the CBS series 'This I Believe', broadcast in October, was 'In Praise of the Transitory': a five-minute encapsulation of the philosophy he had drawn from the Chicago Museum's vivid tableaux. Earth, insignificant and peripheral to the wider scheme of the universe, had witnessed a three-fold creation—first, that of cosmic existence from the original chaos, then the awakening of life from the inorganic, and finally the development of human life from the animal. All must be transitory, with a beginning and an inevitable end, and human life could be an episode only brief on the time-scale of aeons so far known; yet man's very awareness of this transitoriness gave him the restless energy and the power to transform the transient into the imperishable. Science might reduce it all to relative insignificance: for himself, he firmly believed that life on earth held a deep meaning, and that man was the ultimate purpose of the three-fold creation—'a great experiment . . . any failure of which, through the fault of man, would represent the failure of creation itself, its negation. This may or may not be so—but it would be well for man to conduct himself as if it were so.'[1]

In contrast to these intimations of immortality, his words for the BBC's Third Programme during May concerned 'The Artist and Society': reflections, from a nature which he conceded was fundamentally sceptical, in justification of the standpoint which had attracted for him so much hostile criticism on both sides of the Atlantic. The work of the artist, and in particular the writer, could not fail to carry implications of moral and social criticism—whether from the Right, like Balzac, Hamsun, or Ezra Pound, or from the Left, the position to which he himself had been impelled by his aversion to fascism rather than by any liking for communism, and which had turned him into a roving advocate of democracy. Toynbee's article in the *Observer* had rightly expressed a certain distrust of Mann's optimistic faith in democracy—even of his 'world citizenship': for his books were 'maddeningly German', and whatever they expressed on social-political questions had had to be wrung from the pessimism of a spirit schooled in Schopenhauer. 'To be frank: I have not much belief, but also do not believe so much in belief as in the goodness which can exist without belief, and in fact be the product of doubt.'[2] Though probably little noticed in America, the statement made a suitable quiet valedictory before his departure; and he was sufficiently pleased with the formulation to make use of it for lectures later in the year in Switzerland, Germany, and Austria.

The *Krull* narrative began to languish, however, and he found it hard to recapture the style of the earlier text. By April, sending Agnes Meyer the completed Venosta chapter, he confessed to a crisis: 'I've burdened myself with something which is in no way . . . suitable to my age, and I often wonder whether I'd not do better to break off and leave it as an extended fragment.' These memoirs, he noted in his diary, were no *Faust* 'to engage the final powers of old age': a worthier subject was needed, with a foreseeable completion-date, and deciding to break off the attempt was perhaps more respectable than trying to complete it under pressure.

He had felt for some time an urge to turn to something new, a work which might be easier to bring to a conclusion, so as to get something at least done. One of his correspondents had suggested a prose continuation of Goethe's *Achilleis* fragment, an idea which held his attention for a while. However, when, early in April, Katia recalled a Munich anecdote she had heard long ago, he was spurred to a novella on its theme: a widow of 50' falling in love with her son's young English tutor and daring to declare her passion when deceived by the apparent renewal of her menstruation, only

---

[1] x 385.        [2] x 398.

to find that this is in fact due to a cancer of the womb. Typically, however, he wanted first to confirm whether such a cruel fraud on nature's part was a medical and physical possibility, and put many detailed questions to the doctor friend who had been the first to diagnose his own lung-condition four years earlier. Deciding on a Rhineland setting for the story also involved consultations with former Düsseldorfers, to make sure not only of his ground there but also of the local dialect. Thus, although he began the narrative during May, and had determined to keep it to short-story form, his hopes for rapid progress were as vain as those for *Krull*. It was clear that he could not get either work beyond the fragment stage before the departure for Europe, which was now being fixed for some time in June, and when the time came his document case included the notes and material for both: the manuscript for the novella already well advanced in setting the scene, the *Krull* in typescript as far as the 'Marquis's' arrival in Lisbon.

In anxious, almost over-anxious caution to avoid further public attention, he had kept to himself and a very few friends the fact that he would very likely not return. He took pains to discount speculation (which appeared even in the press) that he was being driven away by the witch-hunt atmosphere or an impending summons before the Unamerican Activities Committee, and to maintain, especially to American friends like Agnes Meyer and Caroline Newton, the impression of another, though longer, visit, on the now routine pattern of the previous years. It was not exactly duplicity, for in truth his plans were yet far from firm. In May he was even toying seriously with the idea of accepting invitations to India and Japan and turning the trip into a world tour back to California, but he eventually came sensibly to the conclusion that he was too old for such a stressful venture. Enquiries had shown good prospects for sale of the house, but he had a strange reluctance actually to put this in hand with agents, and did not do so till late in May. It was almost as though he was refusing to admit to himself the finality of this departure, as he continued in his normal routine, with much to occupy him and to distract him from the halting progress with his work, and he seemed loath to grapple with the big decisions on house and possessions. One of great personal importance, however, could not be neglected: the safe disposal of his diaries. On 5 June he had Hilde Kahn pack and seal them, ready for transfer to the bank, and marked: 'Daily notes from 33–51. Without literary value, but not to be opened by anybody before 20 years after my death.' (He had destroyed all the earlier diaries in May 1945, with the exception of those for 1918 to 1921, retained probably for reference for *Faustus*, and now also included in the parcel.) His injunction would be faithfully followed when the time came; and it was only after the twenty-year time-lapse that these personal revelations would finally allow the world to 'know' him. Meanwhile his daily record continued.

An additional project had had his attention since the turn of the year, more fitting, he thought, to his age than the still-doubtful literary fables: at Bermann's suggestion, the selection for another volume of his essays, speeches, and miscellaneous writings, to include much not so far reprinted. Delving back into the past, he surprised himself with the quantity of material available, and it began to develop into a fairly substantial collection of almost autobiographical character, particularly when he decided to include some of his correspondence. The posthumous effect seemed not inappropriate: he had reached the point of becoming 'historical' to himself, and felt it only right to lend later academic studies this kind of assistance.[3] It was a view in line with the trouble he had always taken in his responses to critics and with his forthcoming attitude to scholarly enquirers about his work, sources, and methods, which he showed now in his careful comments on doctoral dissertations reaching him in June (Yale on 'The Role of Love in the Works of Thomas Mann', Berlin on *The Holy Sinner*, and Toulouse on the music in *Faustus*). When finally published by Fischer in 1953, under the title *Old and New* (Minor Prose from Five Decades), the volume ranged from the 1906 polemic on *romans à clef*, 'Bilse and I', through the lectures and essays of the 1930s and 1940s to some of his most recent production: the CBS and BBC broadcasts, and even a speech in Frankfurt in November 1952 on the occasion of Hauptmann's ninetieth birthday. Included too was a brief reassessment of Stefan Zweig, written early in 1952 on the tenth anniversary of his suicide, acknowledging the over-harshness of his judgement at the time of that act, and stressing the positive values of the work and humanity of this latter-day Erasmus. (It was a noble admission; but, significantly, he did not see fit to publish it elsewhere, as was his practice on such anniversary occasions, even in the case of lesser figures. There was a touch of jealousy perhaps as he noted Zweig's world-wide literary fame, 'remarkable in view of the slender popularity enjoyed by German writing in comparison with French and English'.)[4]

While the *Old and New* collection, and the careful dispositions over his diaries, showed a proper care for his posthumous standing in literary history, he had for a long time been preoccupied with a more current problem: the lack of East German editions of his works. He had always been convinced that after the war his books in Germany would be 'sucked in like air into a vacuum'. With Fischer in the West this had been so (though Mann often found cause to complain at Bermann's slowness to reprint); but with the lack of any licensing for East German editions the lively appetite there for his work, of which his correspondence almost daily reminded him, had been frustrated. Bermann's efforts at his prompting to

---

[3] *DüD.* iii, 491.  [4] x 524.

remedy this had proved vain, largely because of the publisher's over-legalistic approach and insistence on hard-currency transfer of at least a proportion of the royalties—a measure to which the East German authorities in the end could not agree, so that Mann found himself in the unenviable position of appearing to seek only his own private gain. Bermann argued the importance of properly securing copyright, while Mann was prepared to accept almost any conditions, even royalties held in blocked East-mark accounts, if only the great demand could be satisfied. When in May unauthorized East German editions appeared of *The Buddenbrooks* and *The Beloved Returns*, his inclination was to legalize this after the fact, and he complained over Bermann's stiff-necked attitude. It was to be another two years before the situation could be clarified, when the East Berlin Aufbau Verlag began to plan a complete Thomas Mann edition on the occasion of his eightieth birthday.

To Erika was entrusted the editing of the *Old and New* volume, needed to obviate repetitions and overlapping, and she worked hard despite the poor health and persistent insomnia that plagued her. She herself was more determined than her father to break with America, where her bitterly outspoken critical attitude to the cold war and the Marshall Plan had attracted much more concrete suspicions of 'un-American activities', and virtually put an end to her hitherto successful career as lecturer there. The denial of re-entry to the States she feared if she travelled had so far not proved warranted, but the threat was always there; it was clear to her that her future must lie in Europe. She had turned back to the children's stories which she had always enjoyed writing: new editions of her first two had been arranged with a Munich house, and she had begun another as the start of a new series there. She was well aware, however, of her father's reliance on her as adjutant, and to a large extent manager, of the Thomas Mann enterprise, and was fully prepared to continue to live with the parents when they settled in Switzerland—as now seemed certain, even though, as the time for departure approached, her father still appeared to be keeping his options open and was sedulously avoiding any definitive farewells.

For their earlier moves her energetic aid had been invaluable, as she attended to many of the inevitable administrative chores, and she might have been expected this time to travel later in order to take charge of the sale of the house, for which prospective clients were now awaited at any time. She was impatient to get started, however, and although, as her father noted, still far from well, she took off alone on 1 June for New York, not yet decided whether her destination in Europe should be Zurich or Holland. Both Katia and he were deeply worried about her, 'she doesn't know whether she will ever see this house again, nor will we when we leave'. Discussing with her Klaus's autobiographical book *The Turning-Point*, he noted her tendency to morbid thoughts, and feared she might only too easily follow her brother: 'certainly she doesn't want to survive us'.[5] At all events, they could expect to meet later in Switzerland, and he seemed prepared to defer his own final decision until after a leisurely reconnaissance there.

He could at least feel free from any financial pressure to make that urgent. His income during this year was proving exceptionally good, both in Europe and America, and in May he had word of an unexpected bonus: the award to him, by the Rome Accademia dei Lincei, of the first International Literature Prize founded by the publisher Antonio Feltrinelli. The cash value of 5 million lire came to less in dollars than it might sound, but the 'miniature millions' would nevertheless yield 8,000 in the harder currency. What chiefly interested and heartened him, however, was the international prestige of the award itself, with its citation of the example he had given of a 'lively humanism transcending intellectually the divisions of our time and pointing the way for all spiritually creative people'. He regarded the accolade as a major boost to his defence against the continuing attacks on his position, and was greatly disappointed at the lack of publicity, particularly in America, when the award was officially announced in June. It would be a pity if this demonstration were not brought to the notice of his enemies, he told Agnes Meyer; on his urging she inserted a suitable announcement in the *Washington Post* on 29 June, and he took similar action with the New York *Aufbau*. In the event, his hoped-for visit to Rome, and a private audience with Pope Pius XII, who spoke German well, 'to discuss with him the world situation', had to be deferred until the following year.

He was more and more feeling his age, as the time drew near for departure. His usual complaints over minor ailments multiplied, and though quietly pursuing his normal routine—with work on the novella, a daily walk, dealing with his correspondence, relaxing in the evenings to recorded music, at a film show, or invited by friends—fatigue and lassitude often overcame him. Reading Tolstoy, he felt ashamed over his awards of literary prizes in the face of such true greatness. His birthday was celebrated with a dinner for a few friends only, whom he impressed with a reading from the Professor Kuckuck chapter in *Krull*, but it was all the same a surprising strain. Katia, though troubled by constant problems over domestic staff, was still reluctant to consider a permanent move and giving up the house, while he nursed his 'irrational desire for the ancient soil' of Europe and Switzerland as the site for his gravestone. The future still uncertain, it was decided to invite her nephew (her twin brother's son

[5] *Tb.* ix, 224.

Klaus Hubert) to act as caretaker at Pacific Palisades during their absence, and he was glad to agree, arriving from New York on 20 June as they began to clear the decks for departure four days later. If a suitable sale should offer, he would make a reliable representative.

This time the journey was to be made as easy as possible, by flying the whole way to Zurich via Chicago, New York, and Amsterdam. It was wise to avoid the long hours in the train, for by now Mann was in a genuinely weakened condition, his appetite was poor, and he was increasingly depressed by the American atmosphere of persecution and the hopelessness of persisting with the Korean war. In Chicago, where they stayed two nights, they were beset by a sweltering heat-wave, and were glad in New York to keep as far as possible to the air-conditioned rooms of the St Regis Hotel. Though not surprising, it was still something of a shock there to learn that Erika's request for a re-entry permit had been refused, with no reasons given; but he dissuaded the lawyer from raising more of a protest than letters to Senators (she herself, as they learned by cable, was now in a sanatorium in Berne). *En route* they had been able briefly to see Elisabeth and her husband, their plans for Italy still uncertain, and Monika, who was remaining in New York; but he was eager to reach his goal with a minimum of delay. The flight on 29 June to Amsterdam was by KLM, with gratifying personal attention, and, as on the final leg to Zurich, far better food than on the American lines, though he missed most of it in much-needed slumber.

Golo, on leave from California, and Emmy Oprecht met them at the airport, where the senior customs official saw them through promptly, and they were soon back once more in the Baur au Lac, surrounded by familiar faces in the dining-room (though he noted with pleasure a good-looking new young waiter). In his thoughts of where to settle in Switzerland he had considered not only the Zurich area but also the Ticino, which was Bruno Walter's goal and where Hesse's home was so attractive, and the problem was discussed at length with Golo, and with Erika, who came over from Berne next day, apparently making good progress with her treatment. It was agreed that a house in the Ticino and a *pied-à-terre* near Zurich might be the best solution; but his first priority was to restore his health, with an escape to some mountain-resort and later a renewed cure at Bad Gastein. Zurich, like New York, was suffering from an oppressive heat-wave, and he developed a throat infection which needed a doctor's attention. Katia's phone calls to likely resorts, including their favourite, Arosa, found them overcrowded, but she finally secured reservations in Kandersteg in the Bernese Oberland from 8 July; while waiting they moved to the cooler Waldhaus Dolder, from where he enjoyed gentle excursions with Golo and visits to the many old friends in the area.

In Kandersteg, which they reached by car, having picked up Erika from her sanatorium, the abrupt change of climate brought something of a relapse for him. He had continued to lose weight, his appetite was slow to return, and he was unable to do more than a little letter-writing; it was a week before he felt in a condition to resume work on the novella, albeit in some doubt over its continuation. This area of the mountains, however, with wonderful views on the glaciers, was new to them and a real discovery; plans for the coming few weeks began to crystallize—on the way to Gastein, a reading in Salzburg and a call on Michael and the family at the Wolfgangsee—and he, if not Katia, was at last confirmed now in the resolve not to return to America. Problems remained, he wrote to Feuchtwanger: 'that of my novella I'll soon deal with, but those of life are getting more difficult.'[6] They had good news of Pacific Palisades from young Pringsheim, though still with no word of a sale; but the thought of a return there thoroughly sickened him, especially after the Republican Convention had nominated Eisenhower, a likely winner, as presidential candidate (his forecast of an unpleasant Californian running-mate later proved correct, in the shape of Richard Nixon). Adlai Stevenson, the Democratic nomination, looked, however, like a good choice, with a chance of winning.

At the end of the month they drove with Erika to Lucerne, where she left them to continue by rail to Lugano for a view of some properties there. Only one, situated high at Barbengo and secluded, though with a disappointing view, seemed promising, at a price they could manage provided Pacific Palisades was sold before too long. Heating would have to be installed, however, among other adaptations to their needs; Katia was not much taken with the place; and a *pied-à-terre* near Zurich would still be essential, to compensate for the otherwise attractive isolation (he was not one to follow Hesse's example with a sign at the gate to bar visitors). They returned to Zurich with the promise of first refusal, grateful for the peace of the Waldhaus Dolder after an intolerably crowded train-journey ('inexpressible, how I hate having to push my way through people').

By now his condition had greatly improved, and he felt ready to meet demands, if not yet for public appearances, at least for radio recordings of the 'Artist and Society' piece, which he regarded as an important statement on his philosophical and political position. Erika had meanwhile been briefly in Munich, and may perhaps have arranged a session there for the South German radio; at all events, after he had recorded it for Zurich on 4 August (for a not unwelcome 400-franc fee), she returned to drive them to Munich, as the start of their journey through to Austria, and he repeated

---

[6] 52/218.

the performance there. The producer commented that controversy would probably be aroused by his political views; but he hoped to be able to ignore any press attacks which might follow. In an interview, he took trouble to stress that his stay in Europe, though perhaps for a year, was not to be permanent, he was by no means turning his back in ingratitude on America; but he remained a German writer, and it was increasingly difficult to maintain a due balance when subject to accusations of disloyalty to American ideas paralleling those in Germany after 1945. Between East and West, his position was like that of Erasmus between the Catholic Church and the Reformation; and his acceptance in 1949 of both the Frankfurt and Weimar Goethe prizes had been an attempt to bridge the gap. The Rome prize now, not for his literary achievements, but for his humanism, characterized his task in the world: 'I am no politician, and cannot talk propaganda. But perhaps through my example, through my existence, I can achieve something and influence the atmosphere around me.'[7]

In Salzburg, where they arrived on 9 August and listened to Michael in a Mozart concert in the Reitschule, he gave 'The Artist and Society' as a lecture in the Mozarteum next evening, a well-attended and, as he thought, successful performance (it brought Salzburg to life, in the words of one commentator). There followed ten restful days at St. Wolfgang, with some good progress on the novella, and even an occasional swim—restful, that is, as far as the grandsons, who often came over from Strobl, would leave him in peace, delighted though he was to see Frido again, and Erika's disturbingly persistent bitterness and intolerance towards others would allow. (Golo felt insulted to hear her brand Melvin Lasky, now editor of a monthly journal in Berlin and an acquaintance of his, whom he brought along to visit their father, as an 'American agent and spy'.)[8] She worked with a will, however, on Mann's English-language correspondence, so that with her and Katia's help he got well abreast of his letter commitments, and she was in better mood when the time came on 19 August for their farewells, both to Michael and family in Strobl, and to Golo, who was returning to his teaching-post in California. She drove them back first to Salzburg, for a performance of Strauss's *Danae*, before continuing to Gastein.

In their usual pension here it seemed like a return home, one of many homes. The 'cure' of thermal baths, which he dutifully began daily, proved as fatiguing as on the previous visits, and as before he had to space them out to find enough energy for work on the novella during their three weeks' stay. The first days were enlivened by a visit from Reisiger, the same 'old Reisi boy' as ever and a welcome companion on walks when the cold and

---

[7] *Fr./Antw.* 329.     [8] *Tb.* ix, 258.

constant rain allowed; but on the whole the cure was not a success, though he was eating better and his weight had stabilized, and their departure on 10 September could not come soon enough for him. They spent two days on the journey, spending the night in Munich and enjoying a Lucullan dinner as guests of the proprietor of the Vier Jahreszeiten Hotel, with a moving visit next day to the Herzogpark, past the remains of their house, now demolished down to the foundations.

Back in the Waldhaus Dolder, it took him a day or two to overcome a feeling of nervous depression, the reaction from the journey. He was out of temper to find that the separate rooms they had booked were not yet available, and the irritation in his longing for a room to himself vented itself in unaccustomed sharp words with Katia. Her task was by no means an easy one: falling in with his changeable moods, sustaining him in the multitude of obligations that he took on, standing ready with advice, secretarial notebook, and sympathy over his ailments, smoothing the path as far as possible in their still-uncertain installation in Switzerland, undoubtedly made greater demands than ever before during their long years together. The company of three of their children this summer had been a comfort for her, and, although worrying, like him, over Erika's unpredictable behaviour, she had been glad of her efficient support as driver and in seeing to the practical details her husband ignored. She would have preferred to stay in California: but now the die had been finally cast for Switzerland she could look forward to exchanging the hotel existence for something more settled, perhaps in the Zurich area, even if she still looked upon this as temporary. Action could not long be delayed, for further assignments were in the offing for November—an invitation to Frankfurt, for the commemoration of Hauptmann's ninetieth birthday, and lectures in Vienna—and commitments in Switzerland before then were accumulating; their thoughts turned now to renting rather than buying or building a house, though the latter appealed to Mann. But there was still hesitation. Why not winter in Italy, wrote Elisabeth from Fiesole, where she was now installed with Borgese and the children; for a while he was attracted by the idea, since he had promised a visit there after the Rome prize, but in the end abandoned it as too much for him.

For he was having to concede, with reluctance and some annoyance, that his powers were no longer what they had been. He complained of a work-load which was slight in comparison with those of earlier years, when he had had the major novels on the stocks but yet had found the energy and time to prepare wide-ranging lectures for performance on long and exhausting tours, to say nothing of his vast correspondence. Now, with the material for his public appearances already to hand (at two in Zurich during September he read from *Krull* and gave 'The Artist and Society'), he still felt overwhelmed by more minor tasks and the never-ending letter-writing. Even preparing the twenty-minute Hauptmann speech for Frankfurt, for which he would once have found a ready pen and energy for the research required, seemed a huge burden; and he appealed in despair to Reisiger, who had known him better, for 'a few tips, notes, suggestions, ideas, memories, and factual data'. To his friend's prompt and very full reply he responded with relief: aided by a 'ghost-writer whom Truman and Eisenhower might envy me' he would soon get done—if more and more convinced that the Peeperkorn portrait in his *Magic Mountain*, albeit grotesque and irreverent, gave a better idea of the Hauptmann phenomenon than any academic effort.

Completing the speech early in October helped to banish any feeling of inadequacy, but his days still seemed to be so taken up with a multitude of minor activities that he saw no hope of resuming work either on the novella or on *Krull*. That month brought, in the space of a few days, the deaths of three friends, numbered among the few who had come close to him, and all younger than he: the novelist Alfred Neumann, a neighbour in the twenties in Munich and later in California, and a valued adviser and critic; the translator Hans Feist, an early friend of Klaus and Erika in Berlin, later of the whole family, who nicknamed him 'Fog' because of his incoherent though always stimulating remarks; and Emil Oprecht, to whose goodwill and publishing enterprise since the early days of emigration Mann had owed much. It was melancholy to be left living on when the younger passed away like this: 'Nature seems to find it amusing that after so many other trials one can survive these too.'[9] For all three he wrote brief but sensitive obituary notices before flying to Munich to give a reading from *Krull*. His choice of the Professor Kuckuck chapter was enormously popular, and the applause lasted even after the lowering of the safety curtain, through which he emerged to calls of 'Come again!' 'Stay here!'—an appeal he was not likely to heed, although a semi-official offer later to provide him with a house found him half-inclined to accept. Immediately on return, he was in Berne, to give the 'Artist and Society' lecture in the university *Aula*, at the invitation of the Free Students organization (their earlier condemnation of the communist Thomas Mann now forgotten).

'When shall I get back to work again?' he sighed. 'I feel I'm using up my resources, capable of nothing more than the representational.' A settled residence was the first essential, but so far Katia's search had found nothing suitable. There was a friendly offer, however, from Pfisters, the leading Swiss furniture concern, to provide the full equipment for any rented house

---

[9] 52/302.

on free loan until their effects arrived from California. It was delightful to find so much goodwill and helpfulness here, even in the official world. On 27 October he received his Swiss residence permit, 'for the purpose', as it noted, 'of pursuing his literary activity and of spending the evening of his life'—a turn of phrase which caused them great amusement: in his whole life he had never pursued anything but literary activity, and even in depressed moments was not yet quite ready to admit the approach of its evening.

Two days later their search was over. In Erlenbach, just below Küsnacht on the lake, they were shown a newly built house on Glärnisch Strasse, through the good offices of Emmy Oprecht and the Pfisters, who lived hard by. More beautifully situated than their previous house at Küsnacht, it seemed to meet their needs very well, and at tea with Frau Pfister they reached an immediate deal with the architect-owner to rent the two available upper floors and garage from 15 December, after their return from Vienna, at a most reasonable price (annually the equivalent, as he wrote to Reisiger, of the cost of their servants in California). It was a red-letter day, he noted in his diary: nineteen years since they had left Munich, and after fourteen in America, they were back in Switzerland to 'spend the evening of their days'—old people certainly now, but 'looking forward to life near Zurich, in comfortable quarters and amid woods and meadowland I love, with confidence, almost a youthful joy in novelty, and even some hope for productivity'. The initial contract for four months was signed on 31 October. Much remained to be done, of course, with priority for the transport of furniture and books from Pacific Palisades: Michael and his wife were now over there, leaving the boys with the Zurich grandparents, and it was decided to recruit Gret to see to the packing of a lift-van, with suitable recompense for the loss of her job.

He was apprehensive over possible adverse criticism in America once it became known he was to settle in Switzerland, and in a long-overdue letter to Agnes Meyer on 7 November, just before leaving for Frankfurt, went to some trouble in explanation. They intended to sell Pacific Palisades, if they could get a good price: but although 'poor old Europe' seemed to welcome his return, he was definitely not turning his back on the land to which he owed so much. 'Please help, if there should be need, to counter that impression! I'm remaining, of course, an American citizen, and am on just as good terms with the American consul here as with the Swiss authorities.' He wrote in similar vein to Knopf. To Agnes, as a Republican, he expressed a cautious welcome for Eisenhower's victory in the presidential election, which he said would make McCarthy and his ilk less of a danger than if Stevenson had won. In fact, however, he considered the outcome only as the lesser of two evils, and was fearful, with Nixon as a possible successor

President, of what might follow, particularly as concerned his own position and the ever-present threat of withdrawal of his citizenship. Katia would meanwhile go ahead with the renewal of their passports; but the German press was already reporting his decision to settle in Erlenbach, and he would have to tread carefully on his coming 'representational' trips to maintain the balance between East and West and avoid upsetting either side.

In Frankfurt, fortunately, he was not pressed for interviews. At the high ceremonial of the Hauptmann commemoration he was accorded every honour, and for his speech was introduced as 'the greatest German novelist of our time on the greatest German dramatist of our epoch'.[10] With his concluding words on his inspiration for the Peeperkorn figure—'no mean caricature, no betrayal, but an act of homage' which could reveal for posterity more of his real existence than any critical monograph—it was received with long-lasting applause, and a kiss *coram publico* from the widow. Next day his reading from *Krull* (once again the Kuckuck chapter) to a large audience in the university was greeted with satisfying amusement and equal applause; it was followed by a crowded reception arranged by Bermann in the Fischer Verlag. It was all highly flattering; but he returned exhausted to Zurich, with a heavy cold and bad throat.

The thought of the Vienna tour, due to start in a few days' time, was daunting. East–West tension was on the increase: he noted with dismay the resignation, under Russian pressure, of United Nations Secretary-General Trygve Lie and the suicide of the American legal adviser to the UN Secretariat, Abraham Feller—a martyr, as he saw it, to persecution by the Senate Committee. Immediately after his arrival in Vienna, he knew, there was to be a press conference: it would be difficult to restrain his antipathy for American policy and maintain a suitably balanced position in this advanced outpost, in the light of his often-criticized 1949 visit to East Germany, and not least in view of the communist-organized 'World Peace Conference' being prepared for December in the Austrian capital, to be attended by prominent intellectuals like Picasso, Cocteau, and Sartre. Erika (who would not be accompanying him) therefore prepared a statement to open the conference, designed to disarm any attempts to exploit his visit for party-political ends, and explaining that his three public appearances, mainly under the auspices of the PEN Club—'The Artist and Society' (twice because of the demand) and, of course, a reading from *Krull*—were strictly non-political. While the lecture could not avoid politics in the broadest sense, neither in London, Switzerland, nor Germany had it provoked any misinterpretation for party purposes. As a citizen of the world,

---

[10]  *Tb.* ix, 725.

and no politician, he must be free to speak out clearly on matters of humanity 'without incurring the senseless reproach of addressing one part of mankind only'.[11]

Though he had thought of driving to Vienna, it seemed more sensible to fly, as he was not yet fully over his indisposition. Arriving with Katia on 17 November, he was met by Franz Theodor Csokor, president of the Austrian PEN Club, who would be introducing him at his appearances, and driven to the 'old-fashionedly European' Hotel Sacher. The press conference the following morning lasted two hours, but after his statement, which was also broadcast, he felt he had survived the many questions well and walked his tightrope successfully—'indulgent towards both sides'. The widely disseminated Associated Press report was a very fair summary of the proceedings, though the extracts elsewhere varied a great deal, notably in America, where one report, he was incensed later to hear, quoted him as declining to say what political system he preferred. Press criticism, however, was not lacking, as he had expected: the *Neue Wiener Tageszeitung* presented Thomas Mann as two-faced and his professed avoidance of the party-political as a charade, in view of his enthusiasm for East Germany in 1949 and his 'crypto-communist utterances': an attitude such as his was not impartial, but squarely 'in the camp of dictatorship and tyranny'.[12] It was a view apparently confirmed by the favourable reports in the communist press.

At his lecture that evening, to a packed house, his voice held out well, and the applause seemed never-ending; when he finally escaped the throng of autograph-hunters, for a quiet dinner at Sachers with the Fischer Verlag representative, he was well content, and telegraphed to Erika his satisfaction. But after a mass book-signing next day in a bookshop on the Graben his throat gave trouble again, a doctor diagnosed a severe bronchial catarrh, and he was able to stand up to the heavy programme of the next few days only by dint of inhalations and penicillin: a formal call on the mayor, a long reception and dinner by the PEN Club, his reading from *Krull* (the Kuckuck chapter once again), and finally the repeat of his lecture on 25 November in the Großes Konzerthaus. The success of the performances was undoubted; that of his political attempt to hold the balance between East and West seemed less sure: the Americans (still present in Vienna's four-power occupation) totally ignored his visit, whereas the communist press was over-friendly, and there was even an invitation from the Russians to a concert of Soviet artists—a harmless enough occasion but nevertheless declined on health grounds, for fear of giving yet another handle to accusations of crypto-communism.

[11] Ibid. 853.     [12] Ibid. 732.

He was in poor condition after the return flight on 26 September, the cough now bad enough to bring worries of emphysema (and envy, if that came, of Heinrich's more peaceful end). Among the pile of letters and books awaiting him there, which he felt unable yet to face, came good news from the Paris bookseller Flinker of the success of the intrigue he had himself instigated for the award of the Legion of Honour: official confirmation was imminent. This, and a telephone call confirming final approval for permanent residence in Switzerland, went a long way to compensate for the misreporting in America of the Vienna press conference, on which Erika drafted for him a long and detailed correction to the New York *Aufbau* and to Associated Press. It was more than a week, in fact, before he felt well enough to return to the novella, while Katia and Erika began preparations for the temporary furnishing of the Erlenbach house. As he had already said, the installation there would be a task for 'the women', and he was content to let it proceed without him, in the hope that they might be in before Christmas.

Concern over the family, however, was not conducive to a quiet return to work. Erika, though an ever-reliable aide, was despondent over the publication of her children's books in Germany, and in her irritability, her relationships with others remained problematic, particularly with Elisabeth, who arrived with her children on 29 November for a few days. Katia was anxious to bring Golo over, after he had written how unhappy he was in California: they began to look into possible openings for him in Switzerland, but his incompatibility with Erika seemed to rule out his living with them. On 4 December news came by telephone that Borgese in Fiesole had suffered a stroke, to die later that night in hospital, and Katia left with Elisabeth at once for the funeral in Italy. Mann was in no state to accompany them, for all his sympathy with the young widow, and—typically—was chiefly worried over being thus left alone (and exposed to the telephone, which Katia normally intercepted). It was not for long, for she returned on 9 December: there had been fulsome tributes to Borgese, Elisabeth's regard for him had been reawakened now he was no more, and she intended to stay in Italy with the children.

The preparations for the move now took up most of the women's time. He could confidently leave it all to them, but it was still a preoccupation for him as it emerged that the Erlenbach house living-rooms would scarcely be big enough, notably for the specially made tall bookcases to come from California. Cables went to and fro on possible sale of the house there, and it gradually became clear that the price they wanted would be hard to get: after much discussion, they finally accepted an apparently firm offer of 50,000 dollars, with cash down of 35,000 dollars and the balance to come as rental. This was less than its value (and even at that price the sale was subsequently to fall through); at the time, however, it seemed the burden was about to be disposed of, not without some pangs of regret for him. Through December, as he tried to keep abreast of the usual demands on his time—in particular a short piece on Zola for a French journal, a worthwhile labour in view of the Legion award—and to take up the novella again, he felt unconscionably depressed, eating badly and losing weight again, and suffering greatly from the cold. The signs in America of what he saw as an inexorable advance towards fascism did not help, and he began seriously to consider abandoning his citizenship, which in Switzerland was arousing some unfavourable comment. His condition, and the advance of age, it seemed to him, were an indication that love had disappeared from his life: for a long time now, he noted on 20 December, he had seen no human face over which he could mourn, only the sight of dumb creatures remained to give him pleasure (considering the devotion that surrounded him and the efforts to create for him the environment he needed, singularly ungracious remarks, but fortunately confined to the pages of his diary).

What he needed was something to bring joy back into his life. 'The final confirmation from Paris [of the Legion of Honour] would decidedly give me new life, I know. But it still doesn't come.' On 23 December, the day before Erlenbach was ready to receive him, it was at last in his mail: the official Foreign Ministry letter conferring the Officer's Cross of the Legion, as 'un hommage rendu par la France à l'exceptionelle valeur et à la signification mondiale de votre œuvre littéraire ainsi qu'à la lutte que vous n'avez jamais cessé de mener dans l'intérêt de la liberté et de la dignité humaine'. With it was a personal letter, with thanks for the dedicated copy of *The Holy Sinner* he had sent, from Prime Minister Robert Schuman, stout worker with Konrad Adenauer for a Franco-German *rapprochement*. This success for Flinker's long efforts to secure the distinction was certainly the morale-booster Mann needed now, an irresistible fillip to the vanity which had always been a major element in his character and which he took no trouble to conceal. When he wrote to Schuman and the Ministry in gratitude, he went so far as to ask for two ribbons immediately, which he would be proud to wear to the end of his days. To Agnes Meyer on Christmas Eve he confessed that no previous honour had ever given him so much pleasure, and he would be duly grateful if the news could be spread in America.

A reading, meanwhile, to Katia and Erika of the novella as so far written had been encouraging, and productive of ideas for its continuation, which he began during his final days in the hotel. The festive days then in Erlenbach, if quiet and necessarily somewhat improvised, made a happier occasion than he had expected: the Pfisters had sent a tree along with the furniture, and Michael's boys, Frido and Toni, who arrived on Christmas

Day to stay a while, could enjoy the right atmosphere. He was well content with his study and bedroom, even if, as forecast, the living-rooms were somewhat cramped, and it was uncommonly satisfying, after the long months of hotel life, to sit once more at his own desk, eat at his own table, and enjoy the unaccustomed privacy. He put off answering the mass of correspondence that had flowed in, and, now that the letters of thanks to Paris had been dispatched, could settle to the novella again, glad as the year drew to an end to be back at work—resolved too, when the lift-van with their effects from California arrived, to move back to the Dolder Hotel for two days to avoid the upheaval.

2

*'If I have a spacious, comfortable house in which I can truly feel at home, it's really a matter of indifference to me where it is'*
(TM, 1 November 1953)

Through the cold and heavy snowfalls of January 1953 Mann applied himself daily to the task of finishing *Die Betrogene*, as he was calling the novella (in English translation later, it would carry the title 'The Black Swan', less allusive to the cruel deception and 'betrayal' of the heroine). Elisabeth, always devoted and never able to stay away for long, came from Fiesole with the children on a short visit, and Frido and his brother were there from time to time—Frido now a plump young man, tall enough to be a support on walks through the snow. Welcome though the visits were, he did not allow himself to be diverted from his work, any more than by the workmen in the still relatively makeshift conditions in Erlenbach. On 14 January, with the lift-van due next day and as he prepared to escape with Katia to the hotel, he was overjoyed to receive from the French consulate the long-awaited Legion ribbons, mounting one at once into his buttonhole and proud to display it at dinner in the Waldhaus Dolder.

It was prudent to evade the disorder in the house, and the women were doubtless glad to have him out of the way. Katia, of course, went down each day, and while continuing quietly with the work, he followed in nervous anxiety her reports on progress amid the chaos. Despite the efforts of Michael and Gret, it had not been a good packing job, with damage to some books and lamps, though most of the effects had survived reasonably well. He was upset to hear that, as suspected, the bookcases were too tall to be fitted in and alternatives would have to be made, but he tried to look on this as a minor matter compared with finishing the book. For Katia and Erika, the work-load was exhausting; but he was able to continue his normal existence in the comfort of the hotel, until on 20 January the house was ready for his return to the enjoyable surroundings of long-familiar things. The order he longed for was still far from being restored, though: there was no room in his study for the sofa on which he liked to lie as he wrote, and his books were not yet properly to hand.

He still felt regret at having left the more spacious ambience of Pacific Palisades. A long time in fact was to pass before he overcame his homesickness for the house that had been so completely his own and that Erlenbach could not come up to; and acclimatization to Central Europe after the years in California was more difficult than he had expected. But he was firmly against going back to the 'air-conditioned nightmare' of investigations and persecution in America, which, as he learned from the papers, were in full spate—a 'slippery slope' on which it would be hard to stand,[13] and paralleled, he thought, by the anti-Semitic show trials in the Soviet Union following the so-called 'Doctors' Plot'. He was delighted, however, to see a powerful speech by Agnes Meyer, reported in the *New York Times* of 18 February, vigorously attacking McCarthy and advocating a campaign for the defence of academic freedom. The *Times* was pressing him for an interview or a statement on the current trend of American policy towards restriction of liberty—'everything, in short, that will be suggested to you by the names McCarthy and McCarran'; but on Erika's advice, a long response he drafted, recalling the *Times* headline coupling him with Robeson as a communist, and with dark references to Orwell forecasting a drift to fascism only too reminiscent of his experience with Nazism, was not sent. He finally replied on 3 February with a terse refusal of any contribution. Anything he could have said would be either too little or too much, and he had decided against any intervention in matters political: at 77, he was concerned only to complete his life's work, that from the start had stood in the service of Western civilization.[14] As he wrote to Erika, who had escaped for a well-earned break in Arosa, sending his thanks for her translation, if he had once started to spread himself on the matter, he might have ended with something like his 1918 *Reflections*.

For the typescript of *The Black Swan* he had meanwhile found an excellent copyist in the wife of the German cultural attaché in Berne, who was fascinated by the story and by February had completed the first forty pages. A further reading to Erika and Katia towards the end of January of the manuscript so far had evoked some valid criticism of his handling of the 'miracle' for his heroine, inadequate preparation they thought for the tragic deception she was to suffer. He took this seriously enough to make considerable amendments before going further, and was held up too during February awaiting the results of more enquiries on the Düsseldorf sur-

[13] 53/30.    [14] 53/42.

roundings, the minor details like tram connections he was always keen to get right. A week in bed with a virus infection did not help to make it a productive month. The personal visit of Robert Schuman on 9 February, however, for the official presentation of his decoration, and many further congratulations from France after the attendant publicity, did much to keep up his spirits. By March, with further touches to their installation in the house, some order in his bookshelves and the setting-up of his gramophone, he could feel ready for a renewed attack on the novella, if hesitantly when he compared its dullness in language and theme with the sprightly *Holy Sinner*. In his correspondence was an invitation to Cambridge for the award on 4 June of an honorary D.Litt.: an acceptance was one of the few letters he felt able to attend to, leaving other essential replies to Katia. An attempt from Yugoslavia to interest him in a visit there and a meeting with Tito on Brioni he did not look upon with favour, as likely to prompt far more unsuitable publicity.

Dissatisfied though he was with the quality of his prose, it was a question now of reaching the end at all costs, and through March his mornings marked such steady progress that he began in his reading to prepare for what might follow—his earlier idea of something on Luther. The death of Stalin, announced on 6 March, with the missionary tone of Eisenhower's message to the Russian people during his illness and the curt hostility of the official American condolences on his death, once more stirred unease over the world political situation. As Golo wrote, he should be thankful to be in Europe; but homesickness for California still persisted, and his discontent with the inadequacy of the Erlenbach house began to nag. Driving once past their former house in Küsnacht brought home to him how much more spacious that had been; an offer later in the month from the Erlenbach owner, to build for them a new house on a neighbouring plot at the same rental, was interesting, but he felt his real needs could not be met at that price. For the moment the form of existence he had reached was not unsatisfactory, and evenings with his records were a constant pleasure. With dictation he was able to reduce the mountain of correspondence; and there were excursions in the Fiat they had acquired as second car earlier in the year, making him and Katia more independent from Erika. At the cinema one evening he was greatly impressed with Chaplin's *Limelight*, thoroughly deserving, he thought, of its world success. He recorded 'In Praise of the Transitory' in the Zurich studios; and a reading in the PEN Club on 13 March from the early part of the novella was well enough received to make him think its narrative style was not so bad.

On 18 March, on the ninety-first manuscript page, he wrote his final lines, satisfied on the whole with the ten months' effort. Elisabeth and the children arrived that day, with vague ideas of returning to America, and she listened with approval to his reading of the last half of the text. It was something new in his work, after all, and though there were some passages of dry tedium, particularly in the latter part, he thought the conclusion had turned out well. For better or worse, it could go off to Berne for typing, and he began arrangements to make his planned visit to Rome during April, before turning to whatever new work might then be decided on (Luther was still uppermost in his mind, and he ordered more literature on the subject). The typescript was rapidly returned, and after some revision with Erika—softening passages which might give offence to women readers—it was dispatched to Bermann, who brought it out as a slim volume in October, and to the Stuttgart journal *Merkur* for pre-publication in serial form through May to July. The American copyright was preserved by the usual mimeographed edition, but it took some time to find a translator, Helen Lowe-Porter being too busy on her own work, and the English version did not appear until 1954.

For Klaus, as Erika recalled, all Thomas Mann's 'love stories'—contented husband though he was, with six children—belonged to the realm of the forbidden and of death: how much more, and more intensely, she thought, did this apply to the latest. For her father at the time, this seemed no more than a tribute to the strength of the story-line; but there is no doubt that with this somewhat distasteful theme, 'true' though it might be, he was back almost to the macabre atmosphere of early stories like *Friedemann* or *The Road to the Churchyard*. As he wrote later, he had always liked experimenting, with varying success: this problematic subject, trivial yet daring, ironically presented in the classical novella-form, was a late offering not deserving of great consideration.[15] That was a judgement with which Hesse agreed, regarding it as 'superfluous' to his major works; but the story found a surprisingly enthusiastic reader in Adorno, who greatly admired the subtlety of his interweaving of love and death in the almost musical variations of an 'incommensurable' production. Mann firmly denied any symbolic intent,[16] and an interpretation like that of the East Berlin *Aufbau* he thought best ignored—woman under capitalism as 'exploited, repressed and "deceived"', and an end to 'history's lie of bourgeois society as a natural, even rational order'.[17]

In delightful spring weather now, his days passed in a feeling of idleness without a major work on hand. Carrying on with *Krull* was the obvious task, yet he had no inclination for it; Luther and Erasmus were more attractive, but lacked a central theme; his ideas were still vague. There was no lack of occupation as such: his unceasing correspondence; the dispatch of dedicated copies of the *Old and New* essay-volume, which had now

---

[15] *DüD.* iii, 519; xi 529 f.     [16] 54/248.
[17] Cf. Lion Feuchtwanger, *Briefwechsel mit Freunden*, i (Berlin: Aufbau, 1991), 162, 469.

appeared; drafting a foreword to Klaus Jonas's comprehensive bibliography of secondary literature on his work; preparing for the coming journeys to Rome and later to Cambridge (which they now thought might take in Hamburg too); and spending much time with Frido and his little brother whose train-set and other playthings took up the living-room. His loss of weight, not likely to be made good in view of his minimal appetite, made alterations necessary to his suits, and for the ceremonies ahead new tails and dinner-jacket had to be ordered and fitted. He began to work on the speeches which would be required, and to think of what he might say to the Pope—always assuming *The Holy Sinner* would not have ruled out an audience. All the same, he needed the anchor of daily application to real work, and on 11 April finally decided, however reluctantly and still hankering after the Luther theme, to resume the *Krull*.

Flying with Katia to Rome on 20 April, in the Excelsior as the guests of his publisher Mondadori, he began a turbulent ten days of ceremonies, entertainments, and excursions. At the crowded reception given by the Accademia dei Lincei he could finally give official thanks for the prize award; there was a PEN Club dinner in his honour, and receptions were held by both Mondadori and the other publisher, Einaudi; the President of the Republic conferred on him the insignia of the Italian Service Order. Holding his own under the pressure, mainly in French, he was struck everywhere by the enthusiasm for his work, particularly for *Faustus* and *The Holy Sinner*. Visits to Tivoli and Ostia, to the Vatican Museum and San Clemente, to St Peter's and so many other sites, including Palestrina, awakened memories of his stay while still unknown, nearly sixty years earlier, and prompted reflection on his vicissitudes since—an exceptional life, no question, both favoured with grace and marked by misfortune.

Most moving, however, was the brief private audience with Pope Pius XII on 29 April, who received him with evident pleasure, in lively discussion of Mann's impressions of Rome and of his own time as Nuncio in Germany, his happiest years as it seemed. Mann recalled the then Cardinal Pacelli's words on the Wartburg, related to him in 1949 by the mayor of Eisenach ('this is a blessed castle!'): demonstrating for him the unity of the religious world, the fundamental agreement between all religious men, whatever their confession. *The Holy Sinner* did not apparently figure in the conversation, perhaps to his relief. He was flattered to receive as a parting gift a small silver medallion with the Pope's likeness. As he knelt before him—unbeliever though he was—and kissed the ring of the Fisherman, he felt he was faced, not with a human being, a politician, but with a white-robed idol of priestly gentleness, embodying two millennia of the Western world's history. Towards the Catholic Church his attitude was like that towards communism: he would have no word to say against either, whatever others' zealous criticism of theocracy and censorship. The deep impression of the interview stayed long with him—as he said it was perhaps 'a certain weakness of old age' to remain so touched by it.[18]

At all events, the journey had given him much, and returning to a glorious spring on 30 April he felt better than when he had left. Fortunately, perhaps: for he was able to begin vigorously on the mass of correspondence, books, and journals that awaited him, as well as on the proofs for *The Black Swan*. He had promised an article for the Paris journal *Comprendre* on Europe's significance for the world, and spent much of the first ten days of May on a very personal statement of his feelings over returning to the old continent: with all gratitude for America and admiration for its basically healthy democracy, he was uneasy at its 'cultural arrogance', and deeply worried by the current trend there to denial of freedom. Though Europe, steeped in its historical tradition, was 'at once of more sensitive nerves and less hysterical than the trans-Atlantic colossus', thoughtless abasement before American money and power, and over-readiness to follow her anti-Soviet line, could bring similar risks. Europe must hold firm to the idea of freedom, and despite its historic guilt be the mediator in the nuclear antagonism that had brought the world to the edge of the abyss. He was confident that Europe, ever the 'heart and brain of the world', could achieve unity 'in the spirit of knowledge, justice, and peace'[19]—a confidence that was reinforced soon afterwards as he read of a speech by Churchill, stressing England's duty to take the initiative and bring America to adapt to new world conditions.

His attempts to take up *Krull* again were desultory, lacking in conviction, and though he returned repeatedly to reading on Luther, he still gained no clear idea for a possible alternative task. Preparations had to begin for the next journey early in June, on which Cambridge was to be followed by two readings in Hamburg, needing introductory words. An invitation to Lübeck, however, he turned down, suspecting, in view of the meagre thanks earned by his contribution to the restoration of the Marienkirche, a certain lingering antipathy towards him in his native city. Appearances in Düsseldorf and Mannheim too he felt obliged to decline, at least for the moment: old now, he could not expect many years to be left to him, and he must conserve his strength for his work. A proposal from Caroline Newton on behalf of a group of American east-coast universities for an autumn lecture, with all expenses paid and a substantial fee, was attractive, but in the end he had to agree with Erika that it too should be refused. Apart from the stress, it would be too venturesome after the criticism of America in his *Comprendre* article, risking further provocation, as he wrote to Caroline, of

[18] Cf. Lion Feuchtwanger, *Briefwechsel mit Freunden*, i, (Berlin: Aufbau, 1991), 150.
[19] xii 974–7.

those powers for whom he had long been *persona non grata*. In the present state of the world, and his own anxiety to avoid political involvement, he felt a certain sympathy when Michael wrote from California of giving up his career and withdrawing to a small property in Italy which his father-in-law might purchase: such escape was the desire of every more decent person today, including Golo, said Michael. The Moser grandparents, though gladly playing their part in caring for Frido and Toni, had always looked askance on the prolonged separation from their parents, and no doubt proposed this as a proper restoration of family life; it was an idea Michael did not lose sight of, though it was to be some time before he and Gret returned to Europe.

Mann himself was more concerned over Erika, whose insomnia and excessive drinking made her a difficult companion when she was home. They had always made her lesbian and other friends welcome; but the apparent fixation on her of Strindberg's daughter Kerstin, recently released from psychiatric treatment in Germany and pressing to be brought to Zurich, threatened to be a little too much even for their hospitality. In his preparations for the brief England and Germany tour it was disturbing too to have Katia falling ill, but fortunately this proved only slight; and for the first time, in the splendid weather as summer approached, he could at least compare the view from the Erlenbach terrace favourably with that in Pacific Palisades.

Flying to London on 3 June—Elizabeth II's coronation now just over—they were taken on in a university car to Cambridge, guests there of Sir Charles Darwin, the grandson of the naturalist. In company with the Indian Prime Minister and the inventor of the jet engine, Frank Whittle, at the doctorate ceremonies next morning, he reflected on his rare distinction of holding the degree from both Oxford and Cambridge. Nehru—who was to attend the Commonwealth conference later in the day—once again seemed to him the best and wisest of contemporary statesmen, and his anxious bearing only too understandable. On 5 June, after visits to St John's and King's, they returned by train to London, where Ida Herz had succeeded in reserving rooms at the Savoy in spite of the Coronation crowds. The two days here he had determined to make as private as possible, and his birthday, for which telegrams and letters had begun to flow in, passed quietly over a lunch with his publisher Frederic Warburg, tea with Ida Herz, and dinner with Katia's cousins.

In Hamburg, which they reached by air on 7 June, it was otherwise. Accommodated in the city guest-house on the Elbchaussee, and as guests of the North German Radio and the Goethe Society, they faced a constant stream of visitors, and he had two public appearances for readings from *Krull*, the first on the next evening in the university. To the mainly student audience there his prefatory words, expressing an old man's joy in the Hanseatic atmosphere of his childhood, repeated much of his article for *Comprendre*, though with less of the criticism of America and with more stress on Europe's need for unity, and the dream of a reunified Germany one day creating 'not a German Europe, but a European Germany'.[20] At interviews he took a similar line, adding his hope for *détente* following Stalin's death and the final release of all German prisoners held by the Soviet Union, making this time quite clear his personal preference for the West over the East, and expatiating willingly on his own work.

After a dinner on 9 June given by the mayor—the excellent menu once again a contrast to England's still meagre fare—his second reading in the Konzerthaussaal was to a full house, the appreciative audience calling him forth again and again to load him with flowers and gifts. After receiving an official deputation from Lübeck, bearing gifts of marzipan and wine, he compromised with a meeting, on 10 June, in Travemünde, favourite haunt of his childhood summers, to be followed by only a brief car-tour round the city itself. The editor of the *Lübecker Nachrichten*, his host in Travemünde, who had correctly divined his disappointment over Lübeck's neglect in the post-war years, was amiably reassured that his feelings for his birthplace were unchanged, and he did not rule out a proper visit one day in the future. For the moment, however, he must make an end to travel and get back to the work awaiting him—unlike Hesse, who had decided to write no more, he had much in hand and, despite his age, had no intention of laying aside his pen. During the moments spent then in Lübeck, the first since 1931—the main streets, the damaged 'Buddenbrook House' in the Meng Strasse, the Marienkirche he had helped to restore, the Katharineum, with its memories of his schoolboy passion for Willri Timpe and recalling that earlier for Armin Martens—he was gratified to remain unrecognized and unexposed to the antipathy he was convinced still persisted, and stole quickly back to Hamburg. After a dinner given by the North German Radio that evening, the speeches witness to the warm sympathy his visit had evoked, they boarded the Scandinavian express sleeper for Basle on 12 June, not escaping a final television interview.

At 78, he felt he had borne the strain of the journey well; and in spite of a melancholy feeling that he had seen Travemünde for the last time, the acclaim he had met with, and the reverent and grateful tone of the pile of birthday letters awaiting him now, served to make his first few days back in Erlenbach a time of contentment. Seldom since Goethe's last days, he thought, had any writer received such tributes; and he read with approval shortly afterwards in a Swiss journal that his life was 'the most astonishing

[20] x 402.

of our century, comparable with that of Goethe'. On 16 June, after watching the London film of the Coronation (tedious and badly produced, he thought), they held a belated birthday-celebration, with the family presents, including, to his pleasure, a complete *Lohengrin* on record. But any assurance that he would quickly be back to work soon faded, as he toyed once more with the Luther theme and continued to hesitate over *Krull*: for Luther he lacked a starting-point, while *Krull*, despite Katia's urging, still seemed an inappropriate subject and its end impossibly far off. Refusing a request for a talk on the occasion of a Wagner exhibition, he felt his excuse of other work lame in the extreme. It was a fearful thought that he might have outlived his productive power, that *Faustus* would prove his truly final work, with *The Holy Sinner* and *The Black Swan*, whatever their merits, merely unnecessary appendages. *Krull* could scarcely be regarded as the crowning effort to be completed at all costs before his eightieth birthday, if this 'after-life' should last that long.

Nevertheless he took it up again, *faute de mieux*, between all the unavoidable incidental activity: the many letters and cards of thanks to be written, the mass of journals, reprints, and critical studies on his work to be read. His eyes, as always, were on developments in the cold war. Soon after his return he had addressed, signing as American Academy member and officer of the Legion of Honour, a lengthy cable of protest to Eisenhower against the impending execution of Julius and Ethel Rosenberg—not, as he said in an interview in July, because he approved of their espionage, but because the sentence offended against America's moral values. When it was none the less carried out, it seemed to him nothing less than an act of sabotage against peace. On the Russian side, a worker's revolt in East Berlin on 18 June, apparently not without Western provocation, and then in other East German cities, had been suppressed; but Erika, visiting East Berlin during July, heard Johannes Becher admit that socialism had been ill served. That month the power struggle between Stalin's successors, with Beria's dismissal in the customary show-trial and 'confessions', seemed deplorable; but he could not think the corruption and hypocrisy of America, or its actions in Korea, all that better.

As he stumbled on through July with *Krull* (experimenting as he called it), unwillingly laying aside reading on Luther and his times in favour of Balzac's *Illusions perdues*, his dissatisfaction with the Erlenbach house grew almost to hatred. The longing for the dry air and so much more congenial conditions of Pacific Palisades was such that he even spoke of going back there if Adlai Stevenson should succeed in three years' time to the presidency, conceding only with reluctance that then would probably be too late, and that the crisis in his work would be as bad there as here. At any rate no more lectures now, he averred, anything other than the purely academic would bring him on to dangerous ground; but he did at least expressly ask the July interviewer to give publicity to his protest in the Rosenberg affair. There were many distractions in his correspondence, particularly enquiries as to his attitude to communism, on which he spent more time than he should, stressing always that, while no communist, he deplored the current anti-communist campaign. He could not conceive of a world without communist elements, and he noted that in Italy no stigma attached to a scholar who declared himself for the party; but he felt he must refuse the offer of both the East German 'National Prize' and the Stalin Prize, in order to pursue his work in the cause of peace without the reproach of being in the pay of communism. A visit from Ida Herz was less than welcome, but he could give her 'something to nibble and gnaw on' in the shape of press clippings for her collection; a reading from his latest pages of the manuscript, to her and a visiting American woman academic, proved in fact a fresh fillip to his languishing narrative.

A larger distraction came with the preparations for Katia's seventieth birthday, due on 24 July, as the house began to fill with the family: Monika, Golo, Elisabeth with her children, and Klaus Pringsheim, as well as the 'Swiss boys' Frido and Toni, brought over by the Mosers to stay for part of their summer holidays. His nervous fatigue did not bear the crowd well. Erika's warning that a speech would be expected from him, at a celebratory dinner being prepared by Swiss friends for the morrow of the birthday, among them young Motschan, was hardly surprising. Settling to the draft, however, he found himself unusually moved, to tears even, recalling his long years together with Katia, the inestimable aid on which he had come to depend, the infinite patience with which she had followed the progress of his 'fearful novels . . . dragging out for years', and the comfort she had always offered in times of crisis. 'If posterity should find a good word for me, it will be for her no less, in reward for her . . . active loyalty and courage.'[21]

There were two days of delightful celebration. On her birthday itself, after the presents, a mass of flowers, telegrams, and letters, published articles from Bruno Walter and Erika, a morning serenade by members of the symphony orchestra, and a charming Festspiel by the grandchildren on the veranda; the following evening, the dinner in the Éden au Lac hotel, at which his speech made a fitting response to the tributes of the Swiss. In his letters, then and later, his tone was less sentimental and more realistic: like Philemon and Baucis now, they reminded him of Boecklin's well-known picture of an old couple, hand-in-hand on a bench but 'already leaning gently apart, each in the loneliness of his non-existence'.[22] In himself he felt

---

[21] xi 525f.     [22] *Bl.* 5, 13.

a deep longing for solitude, a sign, he supposed, of the downward path to the grave itself. He could not wait for the house to empty again, and prepared scarcely polite refusals of invitations and visitors who were proposing themselves. In the diversions, he had not neglected work, continuing his letters and steadily adding pages to *Krull*, but he was despondent when he compared the cultivated mediocrity of his own contribution to literature with the true greatness of Dostoevsky or Balzac. (Measured against the novelists of the nineteenth century, he said in an interview in August, today's were 'primitive miniatures'.) What matter, though: he would soon be gone and know no more. Meanwhile he worried, as always, over the fluctuations in his condition, and although Frido, successfully breaking a wishbone, made no secret of his one desire for Grandpa's continued health, the years which might remain did not promise to be trouble-free for him.

It was only slowly that the guests dispersed. At the end of July Elisabeth sent off her children alone to a holiday camp in England, returning herself to Fiesole for a few weeks; Monika, however, seemed to have nothing better to do than stay on, as usual an uncongenial guest; and Golo, after visiting the Wolfgangsee, returned later in August with Michael's dog, who had been left in Strobl, a welcome companion on walks. However delightful the company of Frido, especially at a circus which grandfather enjoyed as much as grandson, it was a relief, particularly for Katia, when he and Toni left at the end of August. Erika was off then too, for Göttingen, 'to save what could be saved' over a film of *Royal Highness*, which was already advanced in production without her collaboration when her father had made this a condition. (She succeeded in bringing the script up to a more acceptable standard, and was able afterwards to supervise the production, even taking over a minor character-role herself; but as a measure of protection for the book he insisted on 'freely adapted from the novel' being inserted in the credits.)

He was moderately pleased with the advances he was making in *Krull*, but as the weeks went by, and difficulties increased with the owner of the Erlenbach house, he decided an end must be made at all costs to these conditions restrictive beyond endurance: there must be no renewal of the lease after April, and a serious search started for a place to build or buy which would give him what he wanted and for which sufficient funds were now in sight. The Poschinger Strasse site in Munich, restored to his ownership in 1948, had been sold for 20,000 West marks; there was a really firm offer, at last, for Pacific Palisades—50,000 dollars, most of it cash down—and early in September came a transfer from East Berlin of 10,000 East marks. While not ruling out the area further along the lake from Zurich—Meilen, Stäfa—where they had inspected a number of possibilities, he and Katia, Erika driving, began their hunt on 12 September with a short stay in Vevey, to be followed by two weeks in Lugano.

The Lake Geneva coast, especially near Montreux, seemed attractive, with properties available of appropriate standing, more spacious, and more moderately priced than those round Zurich. His favourable impression was reinforced by a view of Charlie Chaplin's magnificent house and park above Vevey, where they were invited on two successive evenings more enjoyable than he had had for many a long month. Chaplin had been a victim of the McCarthy campaign, his alleged communism leading to refusal of re-entry to the States the previous year; and after Oona had succeeded in transferring capital, he had settled with her and the large brood of children in this enviable luxury. When the Manns left for Lugano, they had more than half decided, notwithstanding the French-speaking ambience, on a suitable house in Montreux, which, once the money arrived from California, would be financially possible. There was competition for it, but a further visit to what they came to call 'the hotel coast' was planned for later in the year, and in a long situation-report to Agnes Meyer from Lugano at the end of September, sending her the German version of *The Black Swan* just out, he said it was probably somewhere there that they would buy.

In Lugano they stayed once again in the Villa Castagnola, more in view of a rest and change than with the idea of further search. Exchanging visits with the Hesses and with Bruno Walter compensated for the indifferent weather. He continued every day with the *Krull* manuscript, given new impetus to stick it out by words of praise from Erika and some constructive criticism, of which he was glad to take account; Balzac, with further volumes sent on by Golo, made his almost exclusive reading. Erika had to leave them on 18 September to spend some weeks in Germany, mainly on the film work in Göttingen, from which some stills sent him looked not unpromising, but which was proving an enormously costly production; Elisabeth, always willing, agreed to come up from Italy to act as their chauffeur home on the first day of October. Later that month a cheque from California for just over 39,000 dollars arrived, so that—if they could only find the right house—the way was cleared for action. During the rest of the year the search continued, around Zurich and again near Geneva, which Katia revisited briefly early in November. His own mood fluctuated: now resigned to giving it up and accepting the drawbacks of Erlenbach, now thinking again of the Geneva area or even Lugano, now keen again on building in Stäfa (impossibly expensive, as it turned out) or a purchase near Zurich. In Erika's view, and in the end they agreed, the last would be the best choice, especially in view of the out-of-season desolation of the Lake Geneva coast.

Incidental to this uncertainty was concern over the family. Erika had returned at the end of October, bringing Kerstin Strindberg to Zurich, as he had feared—mercifully in more or less normal condition, but Erika herself exhausted and over-excited, so that towards the end of the year she was in the doctor's hands again. Relations between her and Golo, who had taken rooms nearby, were once more strained, her brother pointedly failing to look in on her birthday. Monika had at last removed herself, staying with a student boy-friend in the mountains not far from Winterthur; her future, like Golo's, remained uncertain, as she considered moving back to Italy. Michael, the business concluded in Pacific Palisades, had crossed with Gret to Tokyo, visiting Klaus Pringsheim and presumably looking for orchestral work there: what was to come after that, whether and when they would return to Europe, could not be foreseen, and it was worrying to think of the growing estrangement from their children. Only Elisabeth had achieved a certain stability, with plenty to occupy her in Fiesole but ready to be of service to her parents at any time.

A private showing of the *Royal Highness* film in Zurich on 19 December, which he attended with Katia, Erika, and Golo, made a pleasant relief. Though it was still in rather rough form, sound and movement not very well co-ordinated, he found it cleverly done and closer to the novel than he had expected, the hero just right but his Imma and her millionaire father less convincing. At a champagne supper afterwards in Erlenbach he expressed his appreciation to the film people, who presented him with a leather album of stills. Asked in a Berlin telephone-call for his comments, he was indulgent: book and film could not be compared, but as a film he found it cut a noble figure, with the colour and the interiors particularly successful. A Thomas Mann exhibition however, which opened in Basle during January, he left unvisited, having been plagued enough in sorting out material for the organizers.

Their thoughts were now turning to a winter holiday, in February perhaps, in warmer climes—Madeira, the Canaries, or Sicily. As time went on, with no end in sight for *Krull*, and perhaps never to come, Mann aired with Bermann the idea of satisfying the public's curiosity, following his successful readings, by issuing a first volume, *Part One of the Memoirs*. A line could be drawn at the end of Krull's stay in Lisbon, a point he now felt he could reach before their holiday, and sufficient to make a sizeable book. It had been, after all, a successful procedure with the *Joseph*, and would have the advantage of giving him then a breathing-space, to consider whether he could or should continue or abandon it in favour of something worthier. That decided, he seemed to be spurred on, and during the quiet Christmas days, though still preoccupied by the problem of a move and brooding over plans of various sites and houses, he managed to bring the work to this interim conclusion. However disparaging his private estimate of its worth, he gave diligent attention in the New Year to a full revision of the whole text, later enlisting Erika for a final review and attending carefully to the suggestions for corrections she sent from her convalescence in Arosa.

He was admittedly still unclear over what real work might follow. There had been an invitation for a lecture in the spring in Holland, but he was at a loss for a suitable subject; and he temporized with·a review for the Zurich *Weltwoche* of a newly published volume of letters of Fontane, for him a theme on which there was always plenty to say and which he had no trouble in finishing by 17 January. In the meantime Katia had seen a house likely to suit their—or more accurately his—needs: on the other side of the lake at Kilchberg, only 10 kilometres south of Zurich.

Like the others, including Elisabeth, who was visiting once more, he was enthused. The property, at 39 Alte Landstrasse above the main road south, with a magnificent view over the lake to the mountains beyond, came up to the standard of that in Munich, on three floors and throughout with the spaciousness he had longed for: a bedroom and bathroom to himself, and on the ground floor a fine study adjoining the library, with room at last for the sofa on which he written much of *Faustus*. At a 'four-power conference' (owner, agent, Katia, and himself) on 28 January the purchase was agreed, at 255,000 francs, with a mortgage of something over half that, and on 2 February the contract was signed—their fifth house, though not of their own building, and he could feel once again the pleasure of ownership, with a truly dignified *maison de maître* worthy of his standing. The first proper accommodation since leaving Pacific Palisades, it would be their final address, as he wrote later to Agnes Meyer; and even if Katia thought it did not compare with what they had left in San Remo Drive, he himself was well content. The agent needed firm handling over the prices for the fixtures being left, and doubts remained over the garage arrangements, but the financing presented no problem, their balance having been notably improved at the turn of the year when an emissary from the Soviet Embassy handed over 29,000 francs in cash by way of royalty for an edition of *The Buddenbrooks*. The move would be in March, he of course escaping the turmoil by staying again in the Dolder, once their winter holiday was out of the way.

The arrangements for this were now proving difficult. Tenerife, which Katia had preferred, was too far afield for him; Sicily he feared would probably be no warmer than Zurich; he had become more and more reluctant to leave at all, but they finally settled on Taormina. The long train-journey they began on 4 February, in acute discomfort, did not augur well, in spite of a short break in Rome, where both Elisabeth and Monika met them, and although the approach to Taormina from Messina was appealing, with cactus and orange-groves reminding him of California, there were few glimpses of the sun, neither then nor during the two weeks' stay. The guest-book of their Hotel Domenico showed it had been the haunt of crowned heads and well-known artists, as well as of Heinrich Himmler. Mann found himself in conversation, more often than he cared, with the writer Roger Peyrefitte, who had been curious to identify a German-speaking holder of the Legion of Honour and was delighted himself to be recognized as *homme de lettres*. He introduced them to former French President Vincent Auriol, also staying in the hotel, whose lively Provençal wit and robust anti-American views were appealing. Peyrefitte, openly homosexual, with the typical gestures which Mann had always found repellent, was full of scandalous gossip of his indiscretions in embassy circles during his four years in Greece.

Taormina indeed struck Mann as a place where 'queerness' flourished, many windows displaying pictures of boys which Mann failed to find attractive. Feeling far from well with bronchitis, with no relief from the hostile weather, and the hotel's mostly uneatable food tolerable only with plenty of wine, his mood grew steadily gloomier. He was touched by Erika's conscientious work on corrections for the *Krull* manuscript, many to expunge contradictions between the earlier and later parts, but, though applying himself to them, he often felt inclined to abandon the task and leave the evidence of his forgetfulness as it was. He thoroughly approved her proposal to reinsert the Lord Kilmarnock episode, earlier dropped: but where were the original pages? In California, he suspected, and if not destroyed, they would have to be found; but meanwhile he finished as much as possible for the Frankfurt printers during a few days in Rome, which they reached again on 22 February heartily glad to have done with the nonsense of a winter 'holiday' which had turned out a complete failure.

Their stay then in Fiesole with Elisabeth was a delightful contrast, her eagerness to do all she could for them more than making up for the relative discomfort of her house: good food at last, and many invitations from her friends. A visit to Bernard Berenson's splendid house was particularly impressive: the old man, dapper and thin, was proud to show them his renowned art-collection, comparable with the treasures in Florence if less well displayed, and to be left to Harvard, they learned. In the Palazzo del Bargello Mann marvelled once more at the tireless attention of the Renaissance to the young male form, the female represented only by a couple of Madonna reliefs. He was still in poor condition, however; and after an overnight stay in Milan on 3 March, where Mondadori had arranged seats at an excellent performance of Verdi's *Othello* in the Scala, was relieved to reach Erlenbach again, with the feeling of having survived a superfluous and exhausting journey.

His mail had followed him throughout, and had not been neglected, Katia acting as secretary when he did not write himself. Most friends, and the grandchildren, had been remembered, and with the news of the Pope's illness he had written, in fellow-feeling, a letter of good wishes. A request from America for a preface to an edition of Kleist's novellas, for the generous fee of 1,000 dollars, had been answered favourably, for it would make a welcome interim task until he could find something more substantial; he had also promised a foreword to an Italian edition of letters from European resistance fighters under sentence of death; and the Berlin *Aufbau* was asking for an article on Feuchtwanger's seventieth birthday. Extra income of this kind never failed to attract him, regardless of actual need. The finances, of course, were Katia's domain: he himself seemed to have little idea how comfortably off they were. Even in letters to friends he tended to stress the deep inroads into their purse the new purchase would make, while strangers' demands for help found a deaf ear. To an appeal in March from a Jewish victim of Nazism, who had been unwise enough to return first to the GDR and then to West Germany, he protested he was anything but wealthy, 'in old age I still have to work hard to maintain my household': a young man of 34 must surely be able to find work in a Federal Republic 'bursting with energy, diligence, and joy of life'.[23] In truth, however, it was the work, however minor, rather than the money which made the attraction for him: without that he would be lost.

On 25 March he withdrew as planned with Katia to the Dolder Waldhaus, while the preparations for the move to Kilchberg began. Both Golo and Erika were on hand to assist Katia—fortunately on good terms again, though Erika had been sharp-tempered and testy after their return from Italy, and a trial in her jealousy of the others, particularly Elisabeth. The foreword to the Italian book was quickly disposed of, but although pressed from America for the Kleist preface he had then to turn urgently to finalizing the *Krull* text: the original manuscript for the Lord Kilmarnock episode could not be found, and his rewrite was still not completed when the time came on 15 April to move into his new domain.

3

*'It is no less worthy to observe how little alteration, in good Spirits, the approach of Death make; for they appear to be the same Men till the last Instant'* (Francis Bacon)

Through all the changes and travels of the previous fifteen months, Mann had been able to follow his accustomed routine, the path smoothed for him

---

[23] 54/79.

by the devotion of Katia and the rest of the family. His general health gave no real cause for concern, though he worried over digestive troubles and lack of appetite, and a persistent throat-affection, with paroxysms of coughing, made sleeping-pills necessary almost every night. It was rare for a day to pass without application to the work on hand, such as it was, his walk, his afternoon rest, and some hours of reading whatever book seemed to suit the moment or could be selected from the flood sent him. Both at home and on the journeys abroad, his correspondence continued, with careful attention to the articles and critical comments on his work that arrived in ever-increasing numbers. When at home, his usual evening relaxation with recorded music—Wagner as always the favourite—was varied with visits to theatre, opera, or cinema: bored by a performance of Prokofiev's *Romeo and Juliet*, entertained by the miming of Marcel Marceau, enthused by the *Moulin Rouge* film with José Ferrer as Toulouse-Lautrec. Age, he recognized, was taking its toll, reducing greatly his staying-power. Writing to Reisiger, whose seventieth birthday was approaching, he said that the thought of his own eightieth, soon to come, was verging on the macabre. With the passing of the years, he felt a strong sense of decline, in his inability to find a substantial task that could bring his long life to a worthy conclusion.

During the first weeks in Kilchberg, however, his vigour seemed renewed, at least in the incidental work that remained to be finished. Within a week he had done with the final touches to *Krull*, Lord Kilmarnock satisfactorily reinserted and the whole manuscript of the final section sent off to Frankfurt (the discovery later of a real-life Kilmarnock family compelled a change in the English version to the less convincing 'Strathbogie'). Over three days after Easter the Feuchtwanger article was completed, and he could turn to the preparation of the Kleist preface. His work-room was all he could have wished for, and the remaining work on the house, including the building-in of the garage, was slowly going ahead towards a most gratifying elegance, so well that they could plan a house-warming party, American style, for 20 May. On walks he found the village more civilized and with more to offer than Erlenbach, and in the delightful spring weather—always his season—he felt a new euphoria. The only unsettling note was the insistence on an interview from the correspondent of *Unità*, the communist paper in Rome: reluctantly giving way, he dealt politely and at length with him, in English, hoping there would be no controversial consequences. The headline it received in the event—'The Great German Writer Speaks out against War and the H-bomb'—in fact scarcely represented the general drift of the journalist's benign essay on the European Thomas Mann, his works, and his moderate stance, neither anti-

American nor anti-communist[24] (the deep concern he actually felt over the hydrogen-bomb tests in the Pacific on Bikini atoll found expression only in his diary).

Alongside his labour on the Kleist preface, during which he reread most of the works, together with others' studies, and, he feared, made heavy weather of the task, there was plenty of business to occupy him. Journals were seeking to pre-print extracts from *Krull*, though he left this mainly to Erika to handle on visits to Germany. The financial position of the Fischer Verlag gave him some anxiety, with royalties due to him of 40,000 marks still outstanding in spite of excellent sales of *Royal Highness*, following the great success of the film, and an offer for a book-club edition. There were promising enquiries for the film from many other countries, and already vague plans for one in Germany of *The Buddenbrooks*: this too would be Erika's domain, but he intended to insist on a collaborative production which could be screened in both East and West Germany.

Most interesting of all, perhaps, was East Germany's continuing respect for his person and his work. On a visit in January to East Berlin, Erika had heard the promise of a gift for him of a fur coat, and there had been word of a plan for a twelve-volume edition of the collected works there to mark his eightieth birthday. He agreed now to accept a visit from Walter Janka of the Aufbau Verlag on 15 May, for discussion of the project. With the spur of this deadline, and of an interim payment from America of half the fee for the Kleist, he succeeded in completing it just before Janka arrived, accompanied by Professor Hans Mayer, the Leipzig Germanist who was to be the editor, and bringing for him the promised fur coat, magnificent in mink and quite the best he had ever owned. Not unnaturally, he was eager to back Janka's proposal, in the difficult negotiations with Bermann which followed, for direct transfer to himself of the royalties arising, which promised to be substantial. Mayer, long an *aficionado* of the works but meeting the author for the first time, was in some doubt how to address him: he settled for 'Professor', and it gave Janka some amusement to hear the two using the title to each other. It was embarrassing, however, over an impeccably served lunch reminiscent of *Lotte in Weimar*, when Mayer could not resist a quote from his host's works and entirely failed to remark the irony of the reply: 'Herr Professor Mayer, I must have read that myself somewhere.'[25]

When the emissaries departed, after detailed discussions on the edition, notably on the selections to be made by Mayer from the essay volumes and the 1918 *Reflections*, Mann was in high spirits at the wealth in prospect, and

[24] *Fr./Antw.* 377 ff.    [25] Janka 232.

was soon inspecting with Katia the possibilities for a new and larger car. With Janka had also come a renewed offer of the GDR National Prize, which would mean 100,000 East marks: on Erika's advice he maintained his refusal, to avoid controversy, but in his mind did not rule out acceptance for his eightieth birthday the following year. The eagerness of the East to show him honour seemed in marked contrast to the relative silence in West Germany. An enquiry soon afterwards, however, whether he would accept the award of the 'Pour le Mérite' order, and an invitation to Stuttgart in May 1955, to give the Schiller memorial lecture on the hundred-and-fiftieth anniversary of his death, restored the balance. Both these were more than welcome, he told Bermann, and he fully intended, if invited, to give the lecture in Weimar too, the seat of the Schiller Society whose honorary presidency he had just accepted. 'My role, as I see it, is that of intermediary and servant of unity':[26] as on his 1949 visit this action would be demonstrative of his even-handed regard for Germany as a whole, not in the two parts divided by the cold war.

During April, somewhat to his relief, Michael and Gret had finally returned, but they still nursed the notion of settling to a country existence in Italy, perhaps in Fiesole near Elisabeth. Mann, loath to lose Frido, who came so often to see him, was reconciled to this rather wild idea when they spoke of keeping with them only the younger boy, less bright than his brother, to attend the Swiss school there, while Frido would return to Zurich in the autumn to go on to secondary school; but it was a sad moment for him when the family left for Italy in July. Golo's future too was still unclear: he had been offered a post as professor in Berlin, but was doubtful whether to accept, and was meanwhile working as a journalist with the Zurich *Weltwoche*. Both sons were on hand for the house-warming party on 20 May, organized with admirable efficiency by Katia and Erika. Thirty-six guests from among the family's Swiss friends and acquaintances—including the president of the city council, the *feuilleton* editor of the *Neue Zürcher Zeitung*, Werner Weber, the writer Robert Faesi, and Georges Motschan, with their wives—were welcomed to sherry and music in the hall, Michael's viola accompanying violin and clarinet in Schumann and Mozart, and a lavish champagne-supper followed at tables spread in dining-room, library, and hall. For the Swiss, such an inaugural occasion was usually a simpler affair, and as they brought along their flowers and the traditional bread and salt in various forms, they were surprised and impressed by this more transatlantic form of entertainment, which went on till nearly midnight. The host himself, proud to show off his elegantly furnished residence, was well pleased with the success of the evening.

[26] *GBF Brw.* 623 f.

Erika departed a few days later for a clinic she knew well near Munich, in the hope of finding a solution to her persistent intestinal troubles. After a long and unpleasant gastroscopy, however, and three days of so-called healing sleep, drug-induced, the doctor could find no other advice to regain her health than to give up her sixty cigarettes a day and the use of soporifics. Her father, still sometimes plagued by coughing during the night, reflected that he too would be better off without smoking, and probably live longer: but was it worthwhile, if it meant giving up such comforts? With the *Krull* page-proofs nearly finished, and apprehensive of what he saw as the almost degrading effect of its appearance, he was now once again despondent at the lack of significant future work and his want of vigour, and feeling more and more out of temper with the demands of the world as congratulatory birthday letters began to arrive. What use congratulations, when he was so anxious and unsure of the life that remained to him? His thoughts turned only to the past, the days of *Faustus* or *The Holy Sinner* with a zeal for engagement which now seemed lost; ahead lay macabre and dubious festivities, and no prospect of the joy which only a similar enterprise could bring. Luther, or at any rate the sixteenth century, still lay nearest—perhaps a series of historical scenes with the widely different characters of the times—but he could not find an idea for its composition, still less the energy to start. 'I often think it would have been better to have departed this life after *Faustus*,' he wrote to Bermann on the eve of his birthday. 'That at least was a book of gravity and power, and would have rounded off a life's work whose loose epilogues often seem to me painfully superfluous.'[27]

The melancholy mood persisted through his birthday, despite Katia's words of encouragement, telephone calls to Erika and Elisabeth, and an excellent performance by Michael and Frido of a Mozart violin sonata, before a quiet dinner with Golo and Katia and Lotte Walter, Emmy Oprecht, and the von Salises as the only guests. The innumerable letters that continued to arrive, the telegrams by special delivery, seemed to him more a burden than a pleasure; even a lengthy telegraphic effusion from the GDR 'Minister of Culture', Becher, comparing him with Goethe, sounded an unmerited and inappropriate note. Retiring early, he pondered once more on this final stage of his life, the difficulty of summoning up the courage for artistic endeavour, for productive effort in the coming year. During the weeks that followed, in writing to friends, he could take a calmly resigned and satisfied view of a life not without achievement, at 25, 50, 60, 70, some 'small works completed to admired standards'. 'God knows I was not great. But a certain childlike intimacy in my relationship

27 Ibid. 619.

---

to greatness, a smile of allusion to it in my work, may bring pleasure now and later to initiated readers well-disposed and ready to be amused.'[28] In private, however, he thought only of Prospero's words 'my ending is despair': ashamed and grieved to contemplate a future empty of further work, as he read scholarly dissertations reminding him of his former immense capacity for absorption of material, and admired the heroism in achievement of Wagner, for all his faults.

At the end of June and into July even his diary was neglected for two weeks—a symptom of this accidie and disgust with an existence so devoid of promise—as he struggled to keep pace with the overwhelming routine demands: correspondence (though a printed card once again did duty in reply to the less intimate birthday wishes), the inescapable social and musical occasions, the flood of articles to be read. To a benevolent interviewer, however, his manner and smart appearance, the well-groomed hair and scarcely greying temples, seemed to show no sign of his age. Requests for appearances he tended to refuse, but a reading from *Krull* in Cologne was accepted for August, after a three-week break they were now planning in the mountains. Politeness towards the continual visitors was an effort when, as often, they outstayed their welcome, but a notable exception was the theologian and musician Albert Schweitzer: this noble figure inspired in him great admiration, as he listened in fascination to the account of his humanitarian work in Central Africa against sleeping sickness and leprosy, and to records of his organ music. From East Germany came representatives of the company planning the film of *The Buddenbrooks*, and a meeting was arranged on 12 July for detailed discussions with Erika in Lucerne, where she had moved by way of recuperation. He found, to some surprise, his demand of 150,000 Swiss francs for the rights accepted without demur, as well as his desire for a 'pan-German' production, with a firm promise for Erika's collaboration. It was disappointing, however, to learn later from Bermann of strong West German interest, with talk of 40,000 dollars for the rights, but excluding any co-operation with the East. Such a move he regarded as pure politics—after the defection on 23 July of the Bonn information chief Otto John, an East German *Buddenbrooks* production would be too much for Adenauer's regime, he thought sourly—and was inclined to refuse the rights altogether unless he could get his way.

His recent reading of Chekhov had suggested an essay, at the approach of the fiftieth anniversary of his death, as going some way at least towards restoring his productivity. He had finally summoned up the courage to start at the end of June, and it was completed before they left with Erika for St. Moritz at the end of July. A highly personal view of Chekhov's mastery of

[28] *AM Brw.* 786 f.

the short-story form, and bringing out in biographical detail his modesty and unpretentiousness in the relationship with great achievers like Tolstoy or Gorky, the essay's tenor closely reflected his own preoccupations: sceptical of his attainments, ironical in the face of renown, discontented with himself, yet still with the prospect of salvation through untiring work to the very end. No more than Chekhov could he find the 'saving truth' for the 'forlorn world of late capitalism':[29] but like him he must nevertheless 'work on, tell stories, shape the truth . . . in the dark hope, almost the confidence, that truth and serene form may liberate the soul and prepare the world for a better, more beautiful life, a life that does more justice to the spirit'.

St. Moritz, where they arrived on 27 July, in the new Plymouth car just acquired, was a disappointment: at exorbitant prices, only poor rooms, exposed to the winds over the Maloja pass and (as he noted in his diary) offering no opportunity for the observation of any interesting tennis-players who might appear. A thorough reconnaissance by Katia and Erika revealed better prospects in Sils-Maria, and they moved there immediately, well satisfied with the change. After his daily labour at the desk, absorbed now in preparatory study for the coming Schiller lecture, he had the good-humoured company of Hesse, staying in the same hotel, to act as relaxation and tonic. As always, he wrote to Reisiger, his place was at work, while everyone else sunned themselves outside: in fact, there was time most days to enjoy the sun to the full, and though callers were occasionally importunate, when the day came for return he could look back on the stay as a highly successful holiday.

There remained now barely a week before the journey to Cologne. From the organizer of his reading-evening there, at the university, he had been touched to hear of Ernst Bertram again: his old friend said he still thought often of him, indeed dreamed of him, and was longing for a meeting after the many years of separation. Nothing troubling remained from their differences through those years, he wrote in reply, 'all that is self-explanatory', and he would not omit a call at Bertram's home from his programme.[30] Cologne was to be followed by a further performance in Düsseldorf, and he prepared two extracts from *Krull* with suitable adaptations, returning then to his notes and extracts for the Schiller lecture. That assignment was still far enough ahead to allow time for the leisurely preparation he preferred, and his study was eventually as exhaustive as any he had undertaken before, enough, as Erika wrote later, for more than one book on the theme. From Michael, who arrived after music courses in Darmstadt and was on his way back to the family in Fiesole, he learned of

---

[29] *Br.* iii, 349.    [30] 54/270.

a possible change of plan for their future: an apparently firm offer of a post as professor in Ankara, which would mean yet another change of schools for the boys. Michael's idea of a business career for Frido he thought not inappropriate, for to his mind the boy seemed to have small intellectual or poetic bent.

He and Katia reached Cologne by sleeper early on 24 August, and were shown to a beautiful, if draughty, room in the Dom Hotel with picture windows affording a splendid view of the Rhine. Visiting the cathedral, they found its grandeur spoiled by works on the extensive war-damage shutting off a third of the interior, and were glad to keep to their room until evening, when he was due at the university. His reading, which was part of the programme for an international students' summer course, was not a success, he thought. Having to walk the length of the big lecture-room to the podium, to the traditional stamping of student feet, ruled out the theatrical presentation he always preferred, and though he read the Professor Kuckuck chapter well, to great applause, he was dissatisfied with the cuts he had made. The following day a car was at their disposal, and after a visit to an impressive exhibition of art treasures from São Paulo, a collection ranging from Titian and Holbein to Goya, the Impressionists, and Picasso, they made their way to Bertram's apartment in nearby Marienburg. He found his friend unchanged, if aged, with the same slightly old-fashioned eloquence; both probably realized it would be their last meeting, and it was not difficult to resume their old cordial relationship. A delegation of students awaited them at the hotel, for a lively discussion on the text he had read, before they started in the evening on the short drive to Düsseldorf.

Here his performance next day was less of an academic affair and much more to his taste. The inviting cultural organization—better funded, it seemed, for their hotel room was luxurious, and his fee would be 2,000 marks—had spread the net wide, and the Schumann Hall was packed with all the notables of the city to hear about Felix Krull in Paris. He had no doubt this time of his success, in a presentation that led his host to comment on his talent as an actor; and the applause and frequent curtain-calls, the flowers, the press of autograph-hunters and the festive dinner which followed, were as flattering as of old. From the parents of Klaus Heuser, who were present, he heard that the boy he had loved, conferring on him a certain immortality with the opening lines of his 'Amphitryon' essay, would soon be returning after eighteen years in China—now 40 and still unmarried. On 27 August, their last day, he called at the bookshop of Mann collector Hans-Otto Mayer, who had laid out a special exhibition of his works—many more editions, as he told him, 'than I myself now possess.

Mine were stolen from my house in Nidden under the Third Reich.'[31] A visit followed to Schloß Benrath—his first actual sight of part of his setting for *The Black Swan*—before they took the night train back to Zurich.

The excursion, not unexpectedly, had left him tired. More disturbing, however, was his inability, in the first September days, to take a firm grip on the Schiller work: he was assailed by an overpowering lassitude as he tried to continue his reading, and brooded over the strange infirmity of purpose that had overtaken him when circumstances should have been so favourable. Never before, it seemed, had he experienced such a block, a whole morning spent over simply preparing the paper to make a start. Was he really at the end, should he resign himself, like Hesse, to no more than the occasional *feuilleton* or a circular letter to his friends? He could not conceive how to pass the days without work, but was struggling for achievement without finding the energy it needed. 'To be celebrated for past work, as just now in Düsseldorf, is shaming rather than encouraging, and has an element of deception,' he wrote to Emil Preetorius: he was publishing the *Felix Krull* fragment and acting as though a further instalment were on the way, whereas in reality he had not written a word of it, in his heart he knew he would never complete 'the nonsense', and lacked the strength for the worthier task he longed for. First, however, the Schiller assignment had to be disposed of. In Sils-Maria he had formed a rough outline of the longer essay from which his lecture would be extracted: but, as he told Preetorius, he was in despair of finding the right 'naïve-personal' note, the lightness and warmth needed for the text to merit a place among the mountains of critical literature.[32] Remarkably enough, to have unburdened himself thus did some good. By mid-September he had made a tentative beginning on the waiting stack of paper, though his depressed mood took a long time to lighten, and a lengthy visit at the end of the month from Stuttgart representatives, to discuss plans for the May ceremonies, left him disturbed and exhausted.

The family were meanwhile in and out of the house on their various affairs. Golo had decided not to accept the Berlin post, in favour of continuing with the *Weltwoche*, but at the end of July had suddenly been given notice from the journal; his plans were as nebulous as ever. His visits were the occasion once more of differences with Erika, whose outspoken, sometimes wild political ideas were not to his taste. She, though still a prey to insomnia, was a frequent visitor to Munich, where her contacts led to a remunerative script-writing assignment and where she could also watch developments with the still-embryonic but promising project for the

---

[31] *Chr.* 246.    [32] *Br.* iii, 356f.

*Buddenbrooks* film. Michael, arriving from Italy in September for a chamber concert, had to abandon it because of a finger infection, and returned, taking the dog with him: a relief for his father with winter approaching, fond though he was of the animal.

When Katia's brother Peter Pringsheim came with his wife for a few days' stay at the end of the month, it was pleasing to hear, as with every visitor, their admiration for the Kilchberg house, and he was not displeased to see photographs of his domain in an article in the *Münchner Illustrierte*, with text by Erika, likely though this was to attract even more unwanted visitors. Publication date for *Krull* now approached, to the accompaniment of great publicity—to his mind unwarranted, for he was still doubtful of its success, despite Bermann's report of advance orders for half the first print of 20,000. The excellent press it received during October therefore came as a genuine and agreeable surprise, reviews delighting in its humour, and the *Neue Zürcher Zeitung* calling it a 'master work'. He was astonished to hear in November that the rapid sales had made reprints necessary and, later that month, that, with the number of copies sold approaching 40,000, it was named book of the month. Knopf, reading the English version in manuscript, had cabled 'absolutely magnificent': 'the old master still puts the young ones to shame'.

Thomas Mann in his eightieth year was becoming altogether the man of the hour. A bust now being completed by an East Berlin sculptor was to be erected in some public square in the GDR, to stand in stone for ever through sun, rain, and snow, he noted wryly: for him a strangely comforting affirmation of his existence, as he contemplated his time soon to run out, and compared his work to no more than the track of a snail, admired briefly for its 'beautiful silver filigree', until it disappeared.[33] At the Zurich première of the *Royal Highness* film on 7 October the family's entry became a ceremonial, greeted with flowers and applause and more ovations after the show in the lobby, followed by a press reception at the Baur au Lac. To be treated himself like a Royal Highness appealed to his vanity, and he felt he had behaved to suit the role. But all these celebrations at the start of what promised to be a festival year had an overtone of finale: 'curious, curious', he reflected, recalling his words in *The Buddenbrooks*, to be repeated, no doubt, at the end, soon to come, for the remarkable dream that had been his life.

Through all this time he had resisted involvement as far as he could in matters political. He was as critical as ever of American policy, of the McCarthy hearings, and particularly of the pressure for German rearmament, and in two minds over the embryonic European Economic

---

[33] *Br.* iii, 359.

Community, based on Franco-German *rapprochement*, but had maintained a resigned silence, which seemed the only possible course for those, like himself, placed 'between two stools'. In the sunset of one's life, one could only wish the best for those with theirs still ahead of them. His personal dilemma remained: caught between the extraordinary welcome for his work in East Germany, evidence—naturally—of the GDR's 'colossal respect for culture', and what sometimes seemed an almost criminal regime in Adenauer's Federal Republic, it was hard to know what to think.[34] To a request, however, from the Paris *Express* for his views on Germany's progress since 1945, he had prepared a reply in September, with some reluctance and with Erika's help. Published there on 23 October, it concluded from the social democratic majority in the recent Federal elections, slender though it was, a deep-seated will to peace in Germany, a renunciation of power-politics, and a resistance to the rearmament being pressed by America. The nuclear stand-off seemed to him an assurance of peace—if only time could be allowed to exert its powerful effect, to raise 'the contradictory elements of democracy, liberty, and equality to a new synthesis and to bring reconciliation to mankind under a humane socialism. Heaven grant us time!'[35]

He had taken pains to stress that, as an American citizen, he felt these views were in America's true interests, even though they ran contrary to the current pressure there for conformism; his apprehensions over the possible effect of the article were, however, quietened by the news of poll forecasts favourable to the Democrats in the coming American elections, and signs there of a less 'fascist' atmosphere. The 'Pour le Mérite' order promised by the Federal Republic should be assured, he had written to Ida Herz on 15 October, provided he did not commit 'further acts of high treason'.[36] That was an interpretation which part of the German press did not fail to place on his subsequent message to the Warsaw preparatory committee of the 'World Youth Festival for Peace and Friendship', reaffirming peace as the overriding concern for the 'salvation of mankind's honour and its preservation from . . . destruction in blood and shame';[37] and he had to stress in protest his purely non-party intentions.

In November, however, he was greatly taken with Erika's proposal, suggested to her by an English friend, for a serious manifesto to be signed by four or five prominent world personalities and issued as a solemn warning against the course being followed by the West, which could lead only to catastrophe. It would need a dignified and measured text, with signatories like Schweitzer and Einstein and some Englishmen and Americans of sufficient standing, to give it the weight and deep earnestness needed. But his own energies were fully absorbed by the Schiller essay, with which he was now pressing furiously ahead, sticking at it for four hours every morning, and neglecting for a while even his daily diary-entry. It was only when the whole mass was on paper, whatever the quality, that the actual lecture-text could be distilled from it—and that task seemed beyond his own powers. 'It worries me that it is turning out so long,' he wrote to Erika on 7 November, 'and so far I've not reached a firm concept for a concise formal speech. Never mind, I'm ruthlessly shaking the whole lot out, and then it will be up to you, I can't help you with it . . .' When she came back from Munich two weeks later, however, and heard him read the first twenty pages, he was greatly reassured: she found it all beautiful, and foresaw no difficulty with the editing needed. His work continued, in more relaxed mood, but it was not until after the turn of the year that the massive manuscript was ready for his transcriber, now in Bonn, and Erika's attentions as editor.

There had been plenty to fill the remainder of the day. He had rarely known such a spate of correspondence, books, and journals; letters and reviews of *Krull* continued to arrive in large quantity; and, although dictating much, he also found the energy for handwritten replies, as well as for several readings recorded in Zurich for German radio. Michael, on a brief visit at the end of November, was the first he had heard notice the self-portrait in the figure of Lord Kilmarnock (a likeness which he himself pointed out in a letter treating of today's much more liberal attitude towards homosexuality). He was often in the theatre: a German version of Molière's *L'École des femmes* and an impressive performance of Shakespeare's *Henry IV*, both parts; *The Caine Mutiny*; Kleist's *Penthesilea*; a piece by Anouilh; a play with Elisabeth Bergner.

During October and November there were visitors for discussion of the events of the coming year. Emmy Oprecht was planning a multiple celebration of his eightieth birthday, at her home, in the Schauspielhaus, and also in the Kilchberg church, to be attended by ranking officials from canton and Federation. Behind this role for the Kilchberg commune, it seemed, lay the possibility of the grant to him of honorary Swiss citizenship—a highly exceptional honour and a splendid prospect, certainly, but most improbable, as he thought (and as indeed it proved). A talk with Janka from East Berlin—on the Weimar Schiller ceremony, the collected edition of his works, and the renewed offer of the GDR National Prize—left him feeling indifferent to what looked like a most precarious and possibly damaging journey. He was ready in fact to cancel altogether the appearance in Weimar if it risked upsetting the present tenor of his life and spoiling the celebration of his birthday; but in December, after discreet enquiries had shown no apparent objection from President Heuss, he kept it on his programme. The Soviet offer, however, of the 'Stalin Peace Prize'—a gold star and 100,000 roubles—was really impossible for him to accept, galling though it was to throw away such wealth merely to please the 'free world', its vaunted freedom of speech in his view a fraud while it remained subservient to America.

His Schiller draft was now approaching a conclusion, though still in unsatisfactory form, as preparations began for the Christmas celebrations. It had been a great joy to hear that Golo planned to bring Frido up from Italy, and as he left his study on 23 December, the final lines written, the boy was there to greet him—over 14 now, growing up fast, and voice about to break, but for him still the child he had loved so deeply. A reader now of grandfather's works, he had understood and enjoyed *Royal Highness* alongside *The Three Musketeers* and *The Last Days of Pompeii*: his Christmas present, along with a chemistry set, was to be *The Buddenbrooks*. He and his brother, brought over from the Mosers, and Golo and Erika, were the only family members at this first Christmas Eve in Kilchberg, but with the decorated tree, the punch prepared by Erika, and the traditional songs, it was as pleasurably festive an occasion as ever.

Work, however, was the watchword for the household, now and into the New Year: Katia, delegated to deal at her discretion with much of the massive mail that had arrived, Erika completing an abridged English version of the Chekhov lecture for the BBC, and her father the Schiller. On New Year's Day he read the final pages, to enthusiastic praise from the family. More was still needed on *Wallenstein*, however, and it was only on 11 January that he could pronounce the great effort at an end—for better or worse. As always after a completed work, he was dubious, felt it a touch pedestrian and with little new, and could only await the effect—the same doubts, as Erika wrote later, that had overcome him with *Death in Venice*, when he thought it 'not good enough' for the *Rundschau*. Once again encouragement came from the family: Golo, himself much later to be a biographer of Wallenstein, thought he had never heard so good a treatment of Schiller's trilogy. The greatest relief, however, had been the effect of his New Year's Day reading of the solemn concluding words. Here he had found a truly high style, he noted in his diary with some satisfaction: the essay would be a definitive discharge, once and for all, of the obligations unceasingly laid upon him.

It was true—though he could not yet know it—that the 'Essay on Schiller: Dedicated to his Memory in Affection, on the Hundred and Fiftieth Anniversary of his Death' was to be his last major work, discharging the duty to German literature imposed upon him by his venerable standing as its undisputed laureate. In parallel with the, to him, astonishing success of the *Krull*, now in its third impression, it was published later in the year as a slim book by Fischer and in East Germany, and its essence extracted for his lecture at the Stuttgart ceremonies in May. By no means, however, could it be a once-for-all escape from the demands on his time to which he so often yielded and which to him were no less a duty even as he turned again to the idea of writing on Luther. In the coming months his complaisance in such minor matters, combined with the strain of preparation for the public appearances, would not be without effect on his health.

Now, for example, his promise to the BBC of the English version of the Chekhov essay had urgently to be fulfilled, and scarcely was the Schiller manuscript sent off for transcription than he was bidden to a Zurich studio for the recording. Much rehearsal had been needed, with the help of Elisabeth visiting briefly from Italy, and he was left overtired and restive at the disproportionate effort it had cost him. A recuperative break later in January, once more in Arosa, had been planned with Katia and Erika, where he hoped to receive the first typescript of the essay, to return to study for the Luther theme, and above all with their help to reduce the mass of unanswered letters. A week after their arrival, however—whether as a result of the recent exertions, of the long and difficult train-journey, or of the unaccustomed height—he virtually collapsed under a virus infection, in fever and with alarmingly low blood-pressure. Though these symptoms seemed to yield to antibiotics prescribed by the local doctors, Erika insisted on summoning a doctor from Chur as consultant, and on his recommendation the patient was taken down by ambulance to the hospital there. Thorough tests, including even a bone-marrow biopsy, showed his basic condition to be sound, and, with the gradual recovery of normal blood-pressure, he was sufficiently restored to allow a return to Kilchberg on 5 February, though still very weak.

Katia had remained throughout at his side, an admirable aid, as the doctor noted, in calming the fears of a patient ever inclined to hypochondria. Erika, however, had stayed on in Arosa, in order not to alarm him by a show of over-great concern, but also to concentrate on the work of distilling the Schiller text to one-sixth of its length for the lecture— experienced though she was in such editing, a more difficult task than she had at first imagined. Within a few days he was convalescent, largely thanks to home cooking, where Katia saw to favourite delicacies. Though still spending part of the day in bed, receiving daily vitamin injections, and forbidden actual work, he resumed his reading; pondered on a Schiller letter sent him by Reisiger, mentioning a hitherto unknown plan for an idyll on Olympus (important, he thought, to insert somewhere in the text); and was able to take an occasional short walk. When their golden-wedding day arrived, on 11 February, Elisabeth joined Erika and Golo in the celebratory present of a new dog—another Niko, to follow the one lost in California. Two years old, and already well trained by Golo in his new home on Lake Constance, he made a charming complement to the household, even if he could never give up barking when the postman approached. It was a welcome surprise when Michael too turned up, between orchestral appearances in Austria, so that all the children except for Monika were there for the quiet family dinner, with a champagne and white-wine punch. Significantly now, continuing his reading on Luther, he began to conceive a dramatic sketch on his marriage, though still without any firm idea.

In a long-overdue letter to Agnes Meyer, on which he spent several days, he had recalled that their anniversary was the exact day, twenty-two years ago, on which they had left Munich, without any idea that they would not return: life was indeed 'strange, I couldn't award it more praise than that, and would not willingly go through it again'. Before the effort ahead of the Schiller celebrations, both in Stuttgart and Weimar, and those planned by others for his birthday, he felt despondent, he said, unable to foresee his frame of mind at the time; the sixth of June, at any rate, he would face with the upright bearing of Andersen's tin soldier, 'basically the symbol of my life'.[38] A deputation from Lübeck arrived on 1 March, announcing the award of the honorary citizenship of the city and proposing a visit to receive it after his Schiller tour, with a stay also in Travemünde. Though this would extend his public exertions well into the summer, and, as he well realized, was a by no means unanimous demonstration of goodwill after so much ill-concealed hostility, the gesture of official reconciliation made an appropriate biographical rounding-off, he felt, in sentimental recall of his father; and to the mayor he wrote his acceptance, agreeing also to give a reading while there.

Erika's hard work had by the end of February reduced the lecture text from 120 to 34 pages—still too long for the hour he would be allowed, but near enough for the draft to be sent to President Heuss and Hoffmann, president of the Schiller Society, to avoid overlaps with their own speeches. Time was beginning now to press, and his days during March to be taken up by a thousand and one things requiring attention—film projects, more invitations to extend his tour, extracts from the Schiller essay to be prepared for a number of journals, proof-reading for its full publication, more correspondence than he could cope with. It was a programme such that he was amazed at his own endurance, fulfilling too a reading-engagement on 22 March in a Zurich hotel, with the shortened version of the Chekhov: the audience had to be extended over two rooms, with many turned away, and

---

[38] *AM Brw.* 796f.

their applause was for him unexpectedly tumultuous. He was even able to make a tentative start on the Luther sketch. The many invitations from other German cities were refused, but one from Holland to repeat his lecture in July gladly accepted, for that would afford a stay in his beloved Huis ter Duin in Noordwijk for the recuperation he expected by then to need.

On 27 March Golo, engaged now on a history of Germany, came for a quiet celebration of his forty-sixth birthday. As his father reminded himself, it was the same day as Heinrich's, whose work now, five years after his death, continued to be neglected by literary criticism, in the West at least, in favour of his own: he was still the Royal Highness looking up to his elder brother and representing him before the people. There were earnest discussions on developments with Michael and his family: Gret was again pregnant, and he proposed, instead of continuing a precarious career as soloist in Europe, to fly at his father's expense to America in search of an orchestral appointment. (He returned having secured a contract with the Pittsburgh Symphony; Gret shortly afterward suffered a miscarriage.) Erika, meanwhile, the lecture text abbreviated as far as she dared, was again travelling to and from Munich, on film affairs and for the publication of her book for children—her health still precarious, and her continued intake of tranquillizers sometimes alarming to her parents when she was home.

Mann's own final reduction of the lecture text to twenty-two pages—an operation so radical that it brought on a nightmare of nothing being left at all—was completed over Easter, on 10 April, stimulated perhaps by the news that in the Netherlands a distinguished decoration from the Queen was in store for him, and reasonably satisfied that the result was not too impoverished. Finishing the final editing, on 23 April, he had become heartily sick of the whole thing. In the short time left before his Stuttgart appearance, the usual travel-fever beginning to assail him and not feeling at his best, he was still beset by commitments—a brief review, a much lengthier recording for Hamburg Radio. He had been asked for a reading of the whole text of *Tonio Kröger*, and made the recording over five days towards the end of April—an effort which would have strained many a younger man, and not made easier by the news of the death of Einstein, for whom, with Erika's help, he at once prepared a short obituary: 'a light went out that over many years was a comfort to me in the gloomy disorder of our times'.[39]

Martin Gumpert too had just died in New York, old friend of the family and one-time unsuccessful suitor for Erika. Mann was deeply affected by

[39] x 549.

these tidings, and no less by the passing a few days later of Alfred Polgar, in his eighty-second year, the Viennese essayist whose work had always appealed to him. One after the other: when would it be his own turn? before his birthday, or soon after? 'I have the impression that the world wants to do all it can to prevent me getting very much older,' he wrote good-humouredly on 29 April: 'one should not be immodest, and at 80 one has long become superfluous'.[40] In fact, however, his nerves suffered, and he began to wonder how he could stand up to the coming stress, even at a season of the year that was usually his best. To a friend protesting against the Weimar visit, he explained his motives and how this had been cleared with Heuss: it could hardly be ruination for him if he spoke about Schiller 'to the poor Soviet Germans, for after all they too are Germans'. He listed the distinctions that awaited him, there and in Holland and Switzerland— but not from euphoria, 'for I'm very, very tired, and Fontane's words "What is the nonsense for?" have taken full possession of the short life-span that remains to me'.[41] Normally firm on his legs, to fall at the sideboard and break the cup he was holding was a symptom of this extreme fatigue. Erika was to drive him and Katia to Stuttgart; and in the days before their departure, behind his assurances to her that any shortcomings in the lecture were not her fault—'you have done what you could, and anyway in fifty-five minutes it's impossible to say *much* more'—she sensed a foreboding of the finality of the performances ahead.

Once on the road, he seemed to relax, and in the Park Hotel on arrival in Stuttgart on 7 May, after a friendly first meeting with President Heuss, also staying there, spent a quiet evening with Reisiger, Bermann, and others from the Fischer Verlag. At the ceremony in the Staatstheater the following morning, after a Bach overture and introductory words by the Württemberg Prime Minister and the president of the Schiller Society, he took the stage, Katia remaining in the auditorium but his attentive adjutant Erika standing in the wings. With the excellent acoustics, as she wrote later, not a word was missed by an audience held spellbound in tense and devout attention, and, like them, though knowing the text virtually by heart, she was caught by the Magician's own emotion as he brought out everything he had invested in this work. 'My father's swan-song! Should I not have been anxious at heart over such moving words? But I was happy.'[42] He too was happy, she thought, when he had finished, to a standing ovation, and she received him back-stage after the final curtain-call. Heuss followed him, bringing the ceremony to a most satisfactory close. The speeches were broadcast nation-wide, as well as to Austria and Switzerland, and many were the letters of appreciation received later, even

---

[40] 55/153.     [41] 55/154.
[42] Erika Mann, *Das letzte Jahr: Bericht über meinen Vater* (1956), 30.

from those initially inclined to disparage Thomas Mann's ability to do justice to Schiller.

There followed two hectic days of receptions and dinners, a performance of Schiller's *Maria Stuart*, and a press of people which he stood up to with astonishing vigour; and he was more favourably impressed than he had expected by the prominent figures of a regime he had hitherto regarded with considerable political suspicion. Two days of rest were then planned in Bad Kissingen: but, as Erika had noted on the American tours, he was not a good 'rester' between assignments, and here, as always, was impatient to get on. The East Berlin publisher Janka joined them as their pilot to the badly marked frontier-crossing at Wartha on 13 May. From there their slightly comic triumphal progress through Eisenach and the villages to Weimar, in slow convoy with Culture Minister Becher, was reminiscent of his previous visit in 1949: the same banners across the road, the parties of schoolchildren, the flowers, the zealous traffic-control, but this time rather fewer signs of state-organized regimentation.

His lecture too the next morning, in the National Theatre, seemed a replay of 1949, the auditorium overfilled and the same crowds outside listening to the loudspeaker relay. After Becher's introductory words, Mann was somewhat disturbed by an over-high lectern, too much coughing in the audience, and the continual flashes of the photographers; but the applause, both within and as he emerged in the square, restored him, and he felt he had done reasonably well. There was the same banquet-style lunch, this time in the Hotel Elephant, and in the evening a performance of Schiller's *Maid of Orleans*; but by then he was really tired, and was able to escape before the end. A caller at the hotel in the afternoon had remarked what a delicate figure he made, very much showing his age and less imposing than expected, more like a retired archaeology professor than a great artist. There was a final ceremony in the castle next morning, to receive yet another honorary doctorate, this time from the Schiller University of Jena, with rector and all the professors in attendance. In his improvised reply to an impressive *laudatio* he also included thanks to the Berlin Academy of Sciences for the foundation of a Thomas Mann Archive. Less pleasing, as they prepared to leave for Göttingen that afternoon, was the insistence of the defector Otto John on a talk with him: John published shortly afterwards a garbled and tendentious account of this pointless exchange, which Mann was obliged to counter with a *démenti* through United Press. Becher, who throughout had shown immense respect and care for the visitor, accompanied them again to the frontier, and seemed much moved at their farewells.

After a night in Göttingen, as the guests of the film company that had made *Royal Highness*, Erika left them taking the train for Lübeck while she drove back to Zurich (very nearly being carried off too when, after an alarming struggle to get them aboard, the train pulled out without warning and she barely had time to jump from the running-board). Welcomed by the mayor, they were taken to comfortable rooms in the Kurhof in Travemünde, with a car at their disposal for frequent visits to Lübeck, before the ceremonial presentation, in the Town Hall on 20 May, of the charter of honorary citizenship. His brief speech of thanks marked as much of a biographical rounding-off as was possible—short of actually returning to Lübeck to live: not without robust reference to the critical voices there of his work, but more in sentimental recall as a survivor, his family and school-friends now all gone. He wished only that his official commemoration of Schiller in both Germanies could have been heard by his former teacher, whose enthusiasm for the poet had so inspired him, or that the present occasion could have been witnessed by his father, the one-time Senator who had not lived to see the tribute paid by his son—if in sometimes strange fashion—to his origins.[43] At this, and at his reading the following evening in the Staatstheater, few if any critics seemed to remain, to judge by the great applause. He had chosen extracts from *Tonio Kröger*, *Young Joseph*, and *Krull*: the performance lasted an astonishing hour and a half, and was concluded by the prelude from *Lohengrin*, which he had first heard at 14 in the same theatre, the proceeds at his request going to an old people's home in Lübeck. Everywhere his reception was princely; and though exhausted by the throng curious to see or meet him, as he toured the city or arrived for the functions arranged, he could justifiably feel that he had stood up well to the strain. It was an infinite relief all the same to escape to blessed solitude on the train for Zurich in the afternoon of 24 May, and the next morning, met by Erika, to reach the haven of Kilchberg again.

Among the immense accumulation of mail, which there was time only to scan, he found encouraging news of the possible grant of Swiss citizenship, which now meant more to him than ever but which he did not really expect. After the honours shown him in East Germany, anything comparable from the Federal government seemed unlikely by the time his birthday arrived: the Dutch decoration, and the 'Hommage de la France' which reached him on 2 June, counted for more than a 'Pour le Mérite' from Bonn, already worn by men, in his eyes, of lesser worth. He began some preparation for his 'improvised' words of thanks at the various birthday celebrations, if only in note form, and made a brief recording on the occasion for Radio Free Berlin. First priority, however, were two short memoirs, recalling earlier days and once more reminding him of his lonely position

---

[43]  xi 535 f.

as a survivor: one on the tenth anniversary of Bruno Frank's death, another on the passing of Ernst Penzoldt, the whimsical and witty essayist, seventeen years his junior, who had not hesitated to visit him in exile and had been among those welcoming him back to Munich in 1949.

He had resumed as far as possible his normal quiet routine, with daily walks with the dog and evening relaxation with music, even a theatre performance of Steinbeck's *Of Mice and Men*. But from early June the birthday post and telegrams, the tributes in journals and papers, began to pour in, a steadily growing avalanche physically impossible to do more than sort, some for later replies but most to receive a printed card, with a general text he strove to make as personal as possible. The ceremonies began on 4 June, with a lunch in Zurich at which the mayor transmitted the good wishes of the city, and later in the day the celebration arranged by the Kilchberg commune in the Conrad Ferdinand Meyer House, with an address of congratulation by the Federal President Petitpierre—the only time in living memory that the holder of this office had appeared at such a local festival. Mann had been prepared for this honour, but not for a further distinction he now received, an honorary doctorate of science from the university, presented by the rector. It was a first in many senses: never before had this taken place outside the university (a special Senate decree had been required); and it stood out, among all those he had gained, as the only one from Switzerland and the only one in a discipline other than the humanities. Writing to the rector later with his thanks for the 'bold, free, original idea', he said this single Swiss degree had given him, and continued to give, more pleasure than all those together that he already possessed.[44] A banquet followed given by the town council in the local Gasthaus zum Löwen. As a sign of his gratitude, he later donated 5,000 francs to be used by the commune for cultural and welfare purposes: a gift as he said of 'symbolic character only', hardly necessary for so wealthy a community, 'and I am not a rich man', but a symbol of his pride and happiness in the privilege of spending his last days here.[45]

It was well he could rest next day, for a more elaborate evening had been arranged in the Schauspielhaus, and the auditorium was packed, with many standing, for what was clearly regarded as a historic occasion and was to be widely broadcast. He was particularly touched to find Bruno Walter had flown over unexpectedly from New York to conduct the musical prologue, Mozart's *Kleine Nachtmusik*, after which there were readings from the works by five actors and actresses, Therese Giehse among them. With the presence of these two reminders of former times, it was perhaps understandable that in his few words of introduction for his own reading,

---

[44] 55/195.     [45] 55/188.

a passage from *Krull*, he should refer to the 'receptivity of the Munich public' instead of that of Zurich—a *lapsus linguae* which caused great amusement. Afterwards Gottfried Bermann Fischer was the host at a reception in one of the guild-halls, the Manns surrounded by a hundred or so guests from among their Swiss friends and the prominent of Zurich, and glasses raised on the stroke of midnight as Thomas Mann entered upon his ninth decade.

Alfred Knopf had also come over specially from New York to be present at all the festivities, despite his lack of German, and was inviting the family with Reisiger to a lunch in the Hotel Eden au Lac on the birthday itself, after the morning spent at home to receive gifts and personal congratulations from far and wide. The house was crowded with flowers, the telephone never still, letters, parcels, and especially telegrams delivered every half an hour. The Kilchberg post office itself was stimulated by such unusually 'edifying telegraphic work' to add its own congratulations; and local firms were proud to send their offerings of stationery or a carpet, as though they enjoyed Royal Warrant status. Official callers arrived: from East Berlin, Janka bringing the newly issued collected works, and the sculptor the bust; a delegation of culture ministers from the Western *Länder*, with a document of a 'Thomas Mann award' of 50,000 marks for the support of needy writers, and his honorary membership of the Darmstadt Academy for Language and Letters (no word however of a 'Pour le Mérite'). Bermann presented the Fischer edition of the works in leather, the original drawings by Günther Böhmer for an edition of *A Man and his Dog*, as well as a beautiful head of Osiris, and there was a special commemorative issue of the *Rundschau*. The 'Hommage de la France', which he now had time to look through, included messages from the President of the Republic and other major political figures as well as leading intellectuals—among them Camus, Malraux, Martin Du Gard, François Mauriac, Picasso, Schweitzer, and Marguerite Yourcenar. Knopf's lunch, and in the evening a dinner given by Emmy Oprecht, Motschan, and other Swiss friends, closed an exhausting day.

For this of all birthdays, none of the family could be absent, not even Monika, who had now settled on Capri; and of the gifts accumulating in the library, that which perhaps gave him the greatest pleasure was their joint present, a splendid gold ring set with a tourmaline, which he had put on at once. As Erika wrote, he loved to gaze into clear stones, especially while at work, and had often expressed the wish for a ring with an immaculate jewel, preferably green. But the overwhelming influx of offerings—he counted well over 1,000 letters, telegrams, books, manuscripts, and other gifts—left him confused and tired; the duty in the days which followed of sending so many words of thanks, even in the printed form and with secretarial help, oppressed him; and he was beset by the anxious feeling that his life was in solemn process of dissolution.

In a letter a week later, he said the birthday turmoil had been 'decidedly overdone': in earlier times writers had had it easier and quieter, without all this 'hypertrophic publicity'. Many messages had spoken of the 'miracle' of his life, and to friends he could say he was himself full of wonder at it, thankful for 'a gracious guidance from above';[46] in fact, privately, he felt only worry and shame to be so completely at a loss over future work and his lack of any concept for the Luther. The childlike delight in presents and tributes gave way to irritation at the disorder all this had brought into the house, his days were passed in fruitless clearing-up, seemingly endless letter-writing, and unproductive reading, and he lacked energy to prepare for his departure with Katia for Amsterdam at the end of the month. She too had felt the stress, concerned into the bargain by Erika's fluctuating and often negative moods. Her hope as well as his was that in Holland, after the final public honours, rest and relaxation in the always congenial Noordwijk might banish his depression and show him the road back to settled work, bringing reality to the façade of Olympian serenity he had maintained through the celebrations.

Flying with Katia and Erika to Amsterdam on 30 June, he was welcomed next evening at the university by Professor Donkersloot and the Foreign Minister before appearing in the crowded great hall for his Schiller lecture. On a high stool before the lectern, he spoke his lines well, he thought, and was gratified by the applause on his entry and the ovation which followed from an understanding audience. Invested then by the Minister, on the Queen's behalf, with the cross of Commander of the Oranje-Nassau Order, he made a brief speech asking for his gratitude to be conveyed to Her Majesty, whom he hoped also to thank personally. It was a symbol of sympathy from a country he had always admired, not least for its steadfastness, in 'faithful unity with the Royal House', in the face of a 'fearfully disfigured Germany' which had brought so much sorrow not easily to be forgotten. 'To be honoured by a land which bore so much suffering without yielding is a high distinction indeed, which will be my pride and joy to the end of my days.'[47] The rest of the evening was mercifully quiet, in the hotel with the publisher Landshoff, with whom Klaus had worked, and Donkersloot, whom he knew from his visit in 1945. He wore the interim ribbon of the Oranje-Nassau order, instead of the Legion of Honour, for the remainder of his stay.

Very much in his mind still was his earlier idea for a peace manifesto to be issued by prominent Western intellectuals, which the deepening East–

---

[46] *Bl.* 12, 29.  [47] xi 541.

West polarization after the end of the Korean war, the accession of a sovereign Federal Germany to NATO, and the establishment of the Warsaw Pact made more urgent than ever. He had thought of some names for an initial approach—among them Pearl Buck, Faulkner, Hesse, the Chilean writer Gabriella Mistral—but as a first step Erika was delegated to visit England, with a view to sounding out Bertrand Russell, E. M. Forster, and Arnold Toynbee; she would fly over on 4 July immediately after a dinner with the German ambassador, which was their next commitment. Driven to The Hague by embassy Mercedes on 3 July and installed in the Hôtel des Indes—markedly better than the accommodation in Amsterdam—they had time for a restful afternoon before being fetched for the dinner. It proved a formal diplomatic affair, with the Swiss and American chargés in attendance, and introductions afterwards to the whole staff (though this did not prevent Erika from getting into an argument, no doubt political, with the German minister). It was over early enough for them to see the final acts of an excellent performance of Rossini's *Italians in Algiers* by a visiting company from the Milan Scala, a highlight of the first 'Holland Festival' to be held since the war, the programme of which included his final appearance the following evening, a repeat of the Schiller lecture.

After reconnoitring the church which was to be the venue, Erika took the afternoon plane for London. Her father was embarrassed, after his declared intention to seek an audience with Queen Juliana, when the private secretary of the Queen Mother telephoned an invitation to tea with her: it was too far from Noordwijk, he felt, and sent a polite refusal—surprising, perhaps, seeing that Queen Wilhelmine as a refugee in England had been the symbol of Netherlands resistance in wartime. But the embassy were at a loss for advice, and he could only hope for understanding between the royal competitors, as he prepared the lecture for his fourth and last performance. He felt fit as he took his place at a rostrum placed below the pulpit, facing a crowded assembly, and thought he read his text effectively despite amplification less than adequate for such a big auditorium. Duty well fulfilled, he passed his last night in The Hague in sound sleep, notwithstanding the Dutch habit of serving coffee at all hours, and they set off next day at noon for Noordwijk, in a car provided by the local film company who were to present a Dutch première of *Royal Highness* in Amsterdam.

Though the weather was hardly summery, with a stiff nor' wester, the familiar surroundings in the Huis ter Duin were a comfort, and he looked forward to working in his accustomed beach-hut when, as forecast, the wind dropped. Landshoff had thoughtfully provided a radiogram for their room, and Mann found evening relaxation with Bach and Prokofiev. He had brought his notes for the Luther, but in the accumulated mail awaiting him there were some minor demands on his time which had first to be met. For both a Bremen performance of *Fiorenza*, and a new publication of 'The World's Best Stories', of which the proofs now arrived, he was asked for introductory words; and as soon as he was installed in his beach hut, with coat and rug, he began to clear these away. As in Zurich, the film première on the evening of 8 July was an occasion of regal ceremony: they were escorted to a central box in the theatre, to listen to an introductory talk by a university professor, and after the show, which the audience clearly enjoyed and which he himself found more pleasing than before, were accorded an ovation both in the theatre and as they emerged. This too had to be commemorated, and in the following days he wrote a short article on 'Film and Novel' for an Amsterdam journal.

On the morning of 11 July came the call on the Queen at Soestdijk, a contrast of informality after their reception by a uniformed adjutant. They found no need for Katia to curtsey, or for a 'Your Majesty' address, as they were led into the garden to take coffee with Juliana; her conversation was dignified yet homely, and she was in no hurry to give the signal for their departure, so that they were with her much longer than expected. He was pleased to see that all the papers had carried the visit, and to hear later that the conferral of the Oranje-Nassau Order had been given great publicity in the German press. A week later, at last, came the offer from Bonn of the 'Pour le Mérite', to which he telegraphed his acceptance.

The days passed in a rare feeling of well-being, by his standards almost laziness: mornings spent in his beach hut as the weather improved, at continuous but desultory work on letters or the articles, undisturbed by the summer crowds and children at their games; afternoons with walks, shopping, or visitors; an occasional excursion with Landshoff; evenings at a concert or with his music. He was absorbed in Melville's *Billy Budd*— one of the 'Best Stories'—and Shaw's *Getting Married*, of which the preface bore on the Reformation; but that was as near as he came to work on the Luther drama. After Erika's report on her mission to London—support for the project promised by Russell and Forster, but at Chatham House only 'three-fifths of a possible Yes' from Toynbee—he wrote to all three with his ideas on the next steps, particularly the need to keep the number of signatories small, and in the hope of convincing Toynbee (if need be, however, he considered replacing him by Trevelyan). News of his personal wealth now was reassuring: a large compensation-payment from Germany, and the old-age pension from America, had arrived to comp-lement the already ample royalties from *Krull*, so that although they could expect correspondingly high taxes, he could admit to himself, for the first time, that they were rich—no longer just 'well-to-do', as his mother used to say.

On 18 July, however, he began to feel the onset of what he thought was rheumatism in the left leg, then in the right, and on 20 July, late for lunch, admitted the climb from beach to hotel over the dunes had become 'a bit difficult'. He made light of it, jubilant at having completed the 'Best Stories' preface—'I enjoyed doing it, especially the passage on *Billy Budd.*' Katia, however, did not share his confidence that the trouble, as so often before, would soon pass, and insisted that afternoon on calling in a doctor from a nearby rheumatological institute. He found the left leg badly swollen, hesitated to pronounce, and ordered complete bed-rest while he consulted a specialist professor in Leiden. By telephone later from there Katia was shocked to learn a thrombosis was diagnosed, but this she resolutely concealed from her husband, letting him believe it was phlebitis, less serious but bad enough to give the prospect of a long time in bed.

He was greatly cast down to have the holiday interrupted on which he had been feeling 'so well—as well as it's possible for me now to feel'—and to be immobilized like this, not even able to see the sea from his bed. Vein trouble was something new for one who through his long life had had, or suspected he had, such a variety of complaints, but he was convinced it must be a delayed reaction to the stress of the past two months. Next day the specialist confirmed to Katia his diagnosis, while wisely leaving Mann in this belief, but recommended urgent transfer as a stretcher-patient to a clinic for treatment, either his own in Leiden or, if they preferred, in Zurich. But he warned Katia that all would depend on the thrombosis not being merely a secondary symptom of something more deep-seated, which only thorough hospital surveillance and treatment could confirm. They naturally decided on Zurich; once adequate anti-coagulants had been administered, the flight was arranged from Amsterdam on 23 July, and that evening he was installed in the Cantonal Hospital. Erika, meanwhile following a cure of her own in Lucerne after her return from England, had been in daily touch, but in order not to show over-concern had not come to Noordwijk. Visiting next day in Zurich she found him looking tanned and well, with no pain, somewhat perplexed over his situation but despondent mainly over having had to abandon the holiday, and, though aware of the real diagnosis, she could return to Lucerne easier in mind, if not without a certain premonition.

He was in the best of care under Professor Löffler, whom he found sympathetic if something of a prima donna, but whose treatment he felt sure was 'of great scientific precision'. Alcohol and acetic acid compresses were applied to the leg, bringing down the swelling, penicillin and anti-coagulant injections continued, and by the end of July progress seemed marked, with an apparent resorption of the thrombosis, which made the doctors cautiously optimistic. Mouth and throat, however, were inflamed, he found eating difficult, with anyway little appetite, and his nights passed in some discomfort from an irritating eczema in the feet. Golo, and Michael and Gret with the boys before leaving for a holiday in Ischia, came to see him, though not, it seems, Elisabeth or Monika; Erika came daily after her return from Lucerne on 8 August. He could read, and write a few letters; and soon was allowed to sit a short while in a chair in the afternoon, when Katia, who was with him through the day, played some of his favourite records on a gramophone provided by Motschan. Music, however, he found tolerable only in small doses, preferring to reread Alfred Einstein's book on Mozart—a subject which he began to feel might attract him when, as he hoped, he could return to work.

In letters he was cheerful over this tedious 'magic-mountain time': 'a trial of patience of the first order, but as it happens patience is my strong suit', and his progress through the 'dreary intermezzo' gave him hope that it might be a matter of only four or five weeks.[48] But both Katia and Erika were struck by his lack of interest in what was happening in his beloved house, the small changes, the new building below it, the dog. On 11 August he was ready for a short walk down the corridor, but a slight relapse that afternoon was followed overnight by a near-total collapse, the blood pressure in the morning practically no longer measurable. Through the day of 12 August the doctors did all they could, with blood transfusions, an intravenous drip-feed, and when breathing became difficult, oxygen. He was conscious, though very weak, and towards evening, after morphine injections, fell asleep—asking Katia first for his spectacles, which gave her a faint hope that he might yet recover. She stayed by his bedside, sending Erika and Golo home: but they had scarcely reached there when the doctor telephoned, at ten minutes to eight, to say the end had come, peacefully in his sleep.

As the autopsy revealed, and as the Leiden professor had feared, the thrombosis had been a symptom of a more deep-seated illness: though the treatment for it had given signs of progress, these had been illusory against an extreme and very long-standing arteriosclerosis in the leg, which had finally led to a breach in the main artery and a painless end—as Professor Löffler said, probably 'the most merciful to be expected at such an advanced age'. 'Though I was sitting at his bedside,' wrote Katia afterwards to Knopf, 'I did not notice his passing away. . . . It was really a miracle that he could go on as he did, working until the outbreak of his last illness . . . his Schiller lecture in Germany [was] the most successful probably he ever gave . . .'

---

[48] *Br.* iii, 415 f., 419.

4

*'A throne has been left empty'*        *(German press obituary)*

For Katia, it was perhaps some comfort to learn that medically there was no doubt over the cause of death. In no way could it be attributed to the cumulative stress of his final years: on the contrary, the autopsy had shown the arteriosclerosis to be affecting all the blood-vessels save those of the brain, and, unsuspected, to have advanced to the point where his life had for a long time hung literally by a thread. It was all the more remarkable, and a testimony to his will-power, that he had been able to carry the strain of the final tour of lectures, celebrations, and birthday ceremonies success-fully, and, apart from fatigue, without apparent physical disability. Before the war he had disclaimed any wish to be buried in the family vault in Lübeck; for Mann the European the ancient soil to which he had returned from America was above all that of Switzerland, which he had for long now looked upon as his last resting-place. Though the city of Zurich offered one of its big churches, Katia felt that Kilchberg, the scene of his final years, would be in accord with his wishes, and the small fifteenth-century church there appropriate to the simple Protestant ceremonial he had wanted rather than one of pomp or ostentation.

After a brief lying-in-state in Zurich on 15 August, the funeral was fixed for the following afternoon, on a day miraculously free from the months-long rain. As befitted such surroundings, the service was indeed simple; the numbers arriving, however, and the vast array of wreaths sent from far and wide, inevitably lent the occasion the tone of an affair of state, and raised difficult problems of their placement in the limited space. Very notice-able—and a sad commentary on Thomas Mann's view of Germany as an entity, and his efforts to bridge the gap between East and West—was the difference between the representation of the Federal Republic and the GDR. From each had come messages of condolence from the highest level—President Heuss and Chancellor Adenauer, President Wilhelm Pieck and Prime Minister Grotewohl—and each now furnished elaborate wreaths; but at the service West Germany was represented only by the ambassador and the Zurich consul-general, with no one from the 'Pour le Mérite' order, while from the East came a whole delegation, headed by Culture Minister Becher and including the Rector of the Schiller University in Jena. Their conflicting demands for precedence were solved by placing them to right and left of the aisle, in the second row behind the dignitaries of Zurich canton. The two enormous GDR wreaths ('to the writer for peace and a truly democratic Germany', 'to the greatest German writer of the century, our unforgettable Thomas Mann',[49] arriving late and in any case too big to be admitted easily, were firmly left with their bold display of hammer and sickle at the church portals—as Mann would doubtless have commented, a symptom of Western Europe's subservience to American interests in the cold war, and it drew later an official protest from the GDR government.

There were far too many mourners to be accommodated within, and the police had difficulty in freeing a passage for the family when they arrived. All, including the grandchildren, attended, and as they left house for church it was a rare occasion of tears hardly to be controlled, wrote Golo much later: the only time he could recall his mother unable to master her emotion, and Michael unexpectedly deeply affected, while he himself had had to seek from Erika a morphine injection when other forms of tranquillizer failed in effect.[50] After the organ prelude, the Kilchberg pastor's brief homily seemed, to many of those present, over-stern in its dry and unsentimental approach. And yet his text, from the 90th Psalm—'the days of our years are threescore and ten, and if by reason of strength they be fourscore years, yet is their strength labour and sorrow, for it is soon cut off, and we fly away'—was not inappropriate at the obsequies of a man whose whole life had been one of unremitting toil, if generally little affected by sorrow.

An interlude of music from among Mann's favourites—the slow fifth movement from Beethoven's string quartet in B major, Op. 130, and one of Brahms's songs—preceded a dignified speech, not by any celebrated personality, but by the more modest Richard Schweizer, director of the Schauspielhaus and friend of the family since the early exile years in Zurich. Recalling the fulfilment of his long life in the celebrations of golden wedding, Schiller year, eightieth birthday, to find rest now from the 'cease-less effort' of its creativity, Schweizer quoted his words on the completion of *Faustus*: 'In truth, I did not have the feeling I had done, simply because the word "End" had been written.' 'Even if the word "End" has been written under the life of Thomas Mann, that does not mean all is over. His spirit remains, here and now—who among us would not feel it?'[51] To those waiting outside the one-and-a-half-hour service had seemed inter-minable, and the many wandering around the cemetery made for some disorder as the cortège emerged. But a respectful distance was observed, even by press and newsreel cameras, as, to final prayers, the coffin was lowered into the grave allocated in perpetuity by the Kilchberg Council, near the south-west corner of the cemetery, looking towards the distant Alps.

---

[49] Sprecher 292 f.      [50] GM *Erinn.* 62.      [51] *Chr.* 257.

'A life has been fulfilled that was dedicated to one single aim: the work of the German language and the survival of the European spirit,' wrote the dramatist Carl Zuckmayer—emigrant like Mann, and also choosing Switzerland on his return to Europe.

You carry, so it is said, the fatherland on the soles of your feet. Thomas Mann carried it like a burden under his heart, as if he had to give it new birth: and painful, often insupportable, was his struggle in exile over a Germany sorely tried, convulsed, and torn apart. His memory and the gift of his great work remain the enduring possession of that indivisible Germany to which we all belong, today and for ever, wherever we may live.[52]

Twenty years later, at the centenary of Thomas Mann's birth, it would still be a divided Germany laying wreaths on successive days at his Kilchberg grave.

[52] Ibid.

# EPILOGUE

'I shall be like that tree—I shall die at the top'
(Swift)

KATIA outlived her husband by a quarter of a century, dying in 1980 shortly before her ninety-seventh birthday. The Kilchberg house remained a permanent residence for her and Erika, and from 1959 it became home for Golo too, who never married; it was the family meeting-point on all the traditional occasions. There she continued, with Erika's assistance, to preside over the progress and prosperity of the Thomas Mann enterprise. At his death, almost exactly fifty years had passed since the young Katia Pringsheim had consented to marriage with a man for whom she was not at first overwhelmed by love, but who had pressed her to become his 'Princess', and whom, for all his growing renown as a writer, her father at least considered only a moderate catch. Her decision had meant the sacrifice of any hope she may have had during her university studies for an independent career: as she said in her *Unwritten Memoirs*, edited from talks and interviews and published in 1974 soon after her ninetieth birthday, 'I have never in my life been able to do what I might have wanted.'[1]

From the start, she had had to realize that the cause of emancipation and women's rights, dear to the heart of her grandmother Hedwig Dohm, could not be hers, any more than her mother's; but it had taken some time for her strong personality to acquiesce in apparent subservience, and the earlier years of constant child-bearing and frequent separation had not been without effect on her health. She was committed to becoming an 'accessory' to her husband, as she once put it, a role of which she made a notable success and in which she found fulfilment. As wife and housekeeper, chauffeuse, social secretary, cook, accountant, nurse, and manageress, she took off his shoulders the entire organization of their day-to-day existence,

[1] KM 182.

down to the smallest detail, sheltering him from disturbance to his work at home or wherever they might find themselves, and ensuring efficient handling of their financial affairs. She brought understanding for his hypochondria and sexual ambivalence, which, after all, had little effect on his procreative powers, and took a dignified place at his side through the last thirty years of his increasingly representational life. Her devotion suited well his self-centred nature: his every wish, seemingly, was law. From his diary, however, it is evident how greatly dependent he was on her support, and in moments of decision and times of stress, as their discussions turned this way and that, it was very often her clear appreciation and strength of will which prevailed.

Such indefatigable service to his cause, overriding all other considerations, undoubtedly spoiled and pampered him, bolstering his vanity and encouraging his self-importance. In an only natural compensation for his aloof attitude towards the children, even his favourites Erika and Elisabeth, she tended also to be over-indulgent in her attentions for them. He probably never knew how far she personally saw them through the financial straits brought on by their sometimes headstrong behaviour. In different ways, all were talented, but theirs was a problematic heredity: it was not surprising that their lives should show unusual features, and that in the end none, save Golo and in later life Elisabeth, could achieve a balanced realization of their potential. Unsurprising also the homo-erotic element in their make-up, strongest and unashamedly declared in Klaus, but evident in Erika too, and more discreetly in Golo.

ERIKA survived her father by only fourteen years, dying from a brain tumour in August 1969. Successive falls, in which a measure of drug dependence probably played a part, made her last years a story of increasing disability, until after an unsuccessful hip-operation in 1964 she was virtually wheelchair-bound. Still first and foremost her father's 'adjutant', she published in 1956 a tenderly sympathetic eyewitness account of his final year, and went on, between 1961 and 1965, to the difficult task of editing a selection from his vast correspondence, with the avowed intention of making it an 'autobiography in letters', to show 'a man in his contradictions'.[2] The three volumes included only about 1,200 of the 10,000 or so letters then available to her (many more have since come to light), with much abbreviation and omitting references to matters she considered still too intimate. They have been the subject of criticism, especially from academics: but whatever their shortcomings, they remain the only attempt so far at a representative picture of the literary output to which Thomas Mann devoted so much of his time and whose publication

[2] Lühe 263.

one day had never been far from his mind. She also gave a long broadcast on her father, and edited a volume of his autobiographical writings, as well as a selection of his works for young readers.

But with characteristic energy she also toiled to the memory of Klaus, securing new editions in West Germany of many of his books. An important exception was Klaus's novel *Mephisto*: though this thinly disguised and bitterly critical story of her one-time husband Gustaf Gründgens and his theatrical successes under the Third Reich appeared in the GDR in 1956, publication in the Federal Republic was finally stopped by court decision at the instance of Gründgens's heirs, after much excitement in the press, and incidentally for herself a successful libel-action against journals which had implied an incestuous relationship with her brother. Just before her death she had in hand an edition of his essays. Not unnaturally, she was less active than before in publishing her political views, describing herself as a 'militant liberal', 'conservative with a social conscience';[3] but she made no secret of her support for the student movement of 1968 and for opposition to the Vietnam war, earning for her the old stigma of fellow-traveller. Looking back in 1964 on the days of the 'Peppermill' and her lecture tours in America, she contrasted the clear-cut issues then with the complications now: 'the place of honour, to my mind, is that between all the stools, a very uncomfortable position to which I have long been condemned'.[4] She did not live to see a new generation's recognition of Klaus's literary legacy which she had done so much to foster. Its editor, Martin Gregor-Dellin, at her funeral in Kilchberg, remarked how out of place sadness must be now for one who had always been uneasy at the sight of distress: 'who could ever picture her otherwise than with the elasticity of youth and untroubled spirit, shrill with irony, bright and active, many-sided, indefatigable'.[5]

She and Elisabeth had been alone among the children in resisting intimidation by their father's personality. GOLO, as he admitted in memoirs of his youth up to 1933, was by nature submissive to authority, whether parental or governmental, and inclined to conciliation. Somewhat eclipsed by the more venturesome Klaus, he had been able quietly to make his own way to a successful academic career as a historian, begun in minor colleges in America and continued after his father's death with professorships in Münster and Stuttgart. His 1946 biography of Friedrich von Gentz ('attractive', thought his father, 'highly praised in the *New York Times*'),[6] and a series of essays, were followed in 1958 by a history of Germany in the nineteenth and twentieth centuries, and finally in 1971 with the outstanding Wallenstein biography, the fruit of long years of study and much

<hr>

[3] Lühe 278 f.      [4] EM *Br. Antw.* ii, 169.      [5] Lühe 283.      [6] *Tb.* vii, 4.

praised as his *chef d'œuvre*. He was awarded the Büchner and Gottfried Keller prizes, and after retirement followed his father in receiving the Goethe prize in 1985. Like him, he remained unwilling to return to live permanently in Germany, and after settling in Kilchberg was granted Swiss citizenship in the 1960s. He died on a visit to Germany, to the widow of a son adopted earlier, in April 1994, shortly after his eighty-fifth birthday.

Golo regarded himself as a writer rather than a historian, and history as narrative writing, not a vehicle for theories: his *Wallenstein* was 'the life narrated by Golo Mann'. Only a thorough study of the sources could furnish intuition, 'it doesn't fall from heaven'.[7] There was no comparison between him and Klaus in terms of their writings, he said in his memoirs: and he thanked God that their relationship had never experienced the pain of that between their father and Heinrich. It was possible, he wrote there, that his serious writing could begin only after Klaus had gone, even only after his father's death, but if so, he was unconscious of it at the time.[8] He had been very much aware of the shadow of Thomas Mann; but although ready to be enlisted in his aid, whether for minor tasks or more important assignments like the editorship of *Standards and Values*, he had kept a firm eye to an independent course. It was significant, perhaps, that he chose to be buried in Kilchberg, not alongside his parents and Erika, but in a separate grave a little distance away.

MONIKA, the other of the two middle children, had never found in either parent an affection equal to that for the others, least of all in her father, with his marked preference for her sisters. The tragic end to her apparently happy marriage with Jenö Lányi, when their ship was torpedoed in 1940 and he drowned before her eyes, had left her for a long time withdrawn and difficult, and though a capable writer, as can be seen in her memoirs *Past and Present*, published in 1956, she never succeeded in a career. She remained bitter over her outsider role in the family: in a television interview in 1984 she said she could not recall ever having had a talk with her father, and had deliberately avoided reading his diaries, the publication of which had begun in 1977—perhaps just as well, in view of his generally disparaging remarks about her. After settling on Capri in 1955, however, she had found happiness with a simple fisherman, Antonio Spadaro, living in great contentment with him in a delightful villa, built by himself, that had once housed Oscar Kokoschka, and where, after leaving the sea, he made souvenirs for tourists. After his death in 1985, she joined Golo in Kilchberg before finally moving to Germany, where she died just before her eighty-second birthday in 1992.

[7] Speech on receiving Goethe Prize, 1985, qu. *Neue Zürcher Zeitung*, 11/12 June 1994, 68.
[8] GM *Erinn*. 434.

ELISABETH, though only 34 when her husband died, did not remarry, but found a full life in writing on international affairs and in an absorbing interest in the ecology and conservation of the sea. She was the only woman member at the foundation in 1970 of the Club of Rome, and herself founded and led the International Ocean Institute in Malta, primarily for the training of maritime scientists from the developing world. She organized over the years a succession of world seminars and congresses, notably those for an international forum on the theme 'Pacem in Maribus', and played a major part in drafting the United Nations Convention on the Law of the Sea. Her book *The Drama of the Seas*, published in 1974, describes them as 'the mirror of our soul'; if they are not treated and administered as an inheritance held in common, she said in a 1987 interview, 'mankind will lose its last not yet exhausted asset of infinite mineral wealth and resources of energy and nutrition'.[9] Her daughters also followed scientific careers, Angelica as physicist and Dominica as biologist; married and with children, they live in Italy.

Since 1978 Elisabeth has been Professor for Political Science at Dalhousie University in Halifax, Nova Scotia, in vacations an indefatigable speaker, conference-organizer, and fund-raiser for the cause. Hers has been a life widely divergent in its intellectual interests from those of the rest of the family—as she confessed in the 1987 interview, she had always been the silent one when it came to discussion of her father's readings *en famille* from his work—and though admiring him, and aware of his great tenderness for her, she has remained firmly independent on her chosen path in fields away from 'literature'. Her home at Ketch Bay is always full of dogs, and communication with animals has been an abiding interest: her 1963 book *The White Snake* described experiments in teaching a dog to type, and she has a one-octave 'piano' with large keys on which her setter bitch can, more or less, pick out 'Silent Night' with its muzzle. This touch of eccentricity, and a merrier disposition than any of her siblings, have effectively protected her from the darker side of the Mann inheritance. 'We were a large family, and a lot is bound to happen.'[10] Characteristically, her favourites among Thomas Mann's works are *The Transposed Heads* and *The Holy Sinner*.

Her younger brother MICHAEL was not so fortunate, in spite of the promise of his musical talent. He had shown from his early days a volatile and rebellious temperament, to which marriage with Gret, the arrival of the children, and his mastery of the viola had not brought the stability or contentment that might have been expected. After his father's death, he took up his contract for two seasons with the Pittsburgh Symphony, Gret

---

[9] Quoted in interview by Barbara Ungeheuer, *Die Zeit*, Nr. 51, 11 Dec. 1987, 83.
[10] Ibid.

at his side while Frido and Toni were once again left behind at school in Zurich, in the care of his mother. In 1957, however, he turned seriously towards a total change of career, beginning studies at Harvard in German literature which led him in 1961 to a professorial appointment at Berkeley (a post which he earned, not because of his parentage, but through a hard-won doctorate). A certain preoccupation with his father's work had sooner or later inevitably to follow, and it was he who persuaded Katia, soon after her ninetieth birthday in 1973, to agree to publication of her *Unwritten Memoirs*. At the Thomas Mann centenary in 1975 it was natural that he should be in demand, not only for a series of lectures ranging through America, Canada, and Europe, but also for editing the diaries after they had been unsealed that year. On New Year's Eve 1976, however, not yet 58, he followed Klaus in suicide, with a combination of alcohol and barbiturates, in California.

To friends he had spoken of earlier 'playful' experiments with the drugs, 'just to find out how far I can take it' rather than with the end actually in view.[11] As early as 1935/6, however, Klaus had noticed in him, still a teenager, a certain likeness to, a copy almost of, his friend Ricki Hallgarten, that earlier suicide, and wondered how deep this went. He had the 'slightly painful feeling' that Michael was imitating his own and Erika's 'past—and present'.[12] For Klaus at that time the present meant daily shots of morphine; but the drug for Michael, though like the others too ready to reach for pills, was alcohol, to the point where he had now become something of an alcoholic. His friends were convinced that it was the pressures of preparation of the centenary lectures, and more particularly the study of the diaries, their editing completed by the end of 1976, that had brought him to his fatal decision. It had been mortifying to read how, before his birth, his mother's health early in pregnancy had on the doctors' advice nearly led to an abortion, until she and Thomas finally decided to let nature take its course. It also disturbed him to note his father's 'ruthlessness' in exploiting family and friends for the purposes of his art, 'acting out the myth of his own work'.[13] (His own dubious immortality as Snapper, in *Disorder and Early Sorrow*, Michael found less forgivable, he said, than the montage of Frido in *Faustus*;[14] all the same, he chose for a short story of his own, a 'professorial idyll', the same name as the protagonist in his father's *Disorder*.)

Certainly too, in these final months, Michael thought much upon the fate of his eldest brother, as was evident from 'suicide poems' he read to his friends towards the end of 1976: Klaus's escape from the 'tangled web' of life to 'reality' in death by his own hand. The inheritance of Thomas Mann

[11] Tubach 219.  [12] KlM *Tb*. 1935, 143, and 1936, 58.  [13] Tubach 117.
[14] Ibid. 151.

could well have seemed to him, as to Klaus, a burden for which he felt inadequate. At all events, the solace of a devoted wife, his sons, and in the last few years a daughter adopted from India, was not enough to deter him from the 'unutterable horror' of the final step.[15] His widow has remained in California; his ashes lie alongside his parents in Kilchberg.

Something of his uncertainty in life was reflected in FRIDO, whose career has also followed a changeable though successful course, from music to theology, then to psychology, with practice in Germany as a psychiatrist and studies latterly in medicine. In his 1985 autobiographical novel, *Professor Parsifal*, he too has acknowledged the burden of his grandfather's 'misuse for his own purposes' of that 'blind affection' for him as a child, Echo's condemnation to death lying on him like a lifelong curse.[16] Not so his brother TONI, who remained in Zurich and has found a contented existence as a gardener.

Harold Nicolson, in the 1930s, had called the Manns an 'amazing family'—thinking then of the literary (and political) careers of Thomas and of the more startling Erika and Klaus. That the rest should have followed their father into writing, one way or another, was perhaps not so amazing. For Katia, looking back in her eighties with Golo, that had been a disappointment: 'I always wanted one of them to choose a sensible bourgeois career, doctor or engineer, and none did. Writers!' At least a historian, and now Michael in his progress from musician to academic, were 'serious'. Maybe, thought Golo; it was regrettable that some of his generation had not followed 'normal, practical' careers, but the atmosphere of a family home frequented mostly by literati and professors had been more influential than inherited talent, and hardly conducive to the note of protest needed for a complete break from the tradition.[17]

Thomas Mann had indeed cast a long shadow, from which it was not easy to emerge. The predominance of literary activity in their home was one thing; more determinant was the character of its ruler, around whom everything revolved. Life outside, wrote Monika, faded into insignificance against 'the power and unity of my father's strong and reserved personality and the dynamic counterpoint of my mother'.[18] Thomas Mann dominated the family less by his actions than by his mere existence, she thought, as a conductor commands the orchestra by his presence alone;[19] and there is no doubt that this effect persisted in different ways through their later years. All the same, in Elisabeth's view, the 'shadow of the father' syndrome has

---

[15] Tubach 208 f.
[16] Frido Mann, *Professor Parsifal: Autobiographischer Roman* (Munich: ed. Spangenberg, 1985), 180, 156.
[17] KM 62 ff.          [18] MM *Erinn.* 13.          [19] Ibid. 73 f.

been greatly exaggerated: Klaus, as we know from his diary, was bitter over his father's 'icy coldness', but in fact it concealed great fondness, and a real interest in his progress. In Thomas Mann there was a deep inhibition from showing and expressing his feelings towards his children, a difficulty reinforced by his single-minded application to his work. Self-awareness, and the knowledge of his own importance, always took priority over any more natural feelings.

Though he often liked to emphasize the streak of the Latin in his make-up, he acknowledged the coolness others found to reproach, but seems to have regarded it as the defensive cloak essential to the ambitious artist. Like his irony, it was part of his 'halo of self-defence', as Giuseppe Borgese called it in 1945. To critics in his early days he appeared a 'cold artist', but, as he said then, he only wished he were more so, it would then be less distracting for his work.[20] He cultivated a detachment which lent him the outward dignity required for his constant representational activities, and was an important element in the 'latter-day Goethe' role, of which he was very conscious (Goethe in his later days, as contemporaries noted, was also a man of glacial stiffness with whom people were rarely at ease). How deeply he was affected by the suicides of his sisters, and later of Klaus, is impossible to discern from anything he wrote: the impression is only of disappointment at a weakness frustrating the expectations of the family of which he felt himself the effective head. Self-centred to a degree, he lacked true feeling for others, and in personal relationships, whether with family or friends, never found it easy to cast off his innate reserve. 'To love you, my friend,' said Agnes Meyer in 1941, 'is a high art not everyone can attain to—a complicated solo-dance.'[21]

Alongside this frigidity, however, was the continual urge to project himself and seek the acclaim he knew he deserved—'artist enough', as he said of Goethe, 'to need applause, to absorb praise greedily'.[22] Like Dickens, he was always ready with readings from work in progress, both at home and from the podium, compulsively eager to see the reaction; with published autobiographical statements, like 'In the Mirror', 1907, and the 'Sketch' of 1930; with highly egocentric lectures ('On Myself', 'Lübeck as a Way of Life', 'The Days of my Life'); and neglecting no opportunity, in letters and interviews, to comment and enlarge on his work and on himself. In their confessional style, their narcissism, the 1918 *Reflections of a Non-Political Man*, permeated by the conviction that he represented a paradigm of German 'culture', were the supreme example of this self-centredness. And he had the egotism of the actor, of the little boy who had once played the prince: his lectures were in every sense stage performances, well stud-

[20] *Br. OG-BE* 150.      [21] *AM Brw.* 264.      [22] ix 348.

ied and with an urge to please which was coquetry, Adorno thought, rather than mere vanity.

Vain, however, he undoubtedly was. With the extreme care for correctness and elegance in his personal appearance went a constant expectation of deference and respect for his position. On a transatlantic voyage it seemed almost a snub not to be treated as well as the Duke of Windsor. In the interminable searches for the right Thomas Mann residence, as important as its suitability for work was its representational character, and he was flattered in the final years to find Küsnacht and Kilchberg becoming places of pilgrimage faintly comparable with Weimar. His accumulation of honorary doctorates, awards, and distinctions gave immense pleasure, and the ceremonial of his public appearances was as satisfying as their success.

The vanity was not simply selfishness or conceit, however. More important was his deep interest in his own biography, as he accounted for himself, with an ironic superstition, its satisfying symmetry of events over the passage of the years and its curious alignment on that of Goethe. He could exploit it for his works, which, taken together, make a selective autobiography, discreetly and ironically veiled in *The Buddenbrooks*, *Tonio Kröger*, and *Death in Venice*, less direct but with powerful effect in *Faustus*. Arthur Eloesser, his biographer at 50, after *The Magic Mountain*, could ask in fact whether, outside his writings, anything was left: was there anything to be said about him which he had not already said himself? At the start of his career, he had noted with approval Nietzsche's dictum that poets and writers were shameless exploiters of their experiences.[23] As he said in 1906, in the controversy over *romans à clef*, novels 'à la Bilse', he portrayed and presented a world that was purely his own, revealing only himself, however much he drew on observation of others. But his experiences remained those of the observer, rarely more than vicarious—from a tower that was objectively always of ivory, through a life that was never troubled by material discomfort or anything even approaching financial straits, despite its vicissitudes and the trauma of exile. A later critic has rightly pointed out that from a minimum of personal experience he drew a maximum of literature—'in exaggeration, one might say that he experienced practically nothing but described almost everything'.[24] 'The little out of which he makes much emerges with aplomb,' as Adorno said of Richard Strauss;[25] his novels were almost always originally conceived as short stories or novellas.

[23] *Nb.* I, 34.
[24] Marcel Reich-Ranicki, *Thomas Mann und die Seinen* (Stuttgart: Deutsche Verlagsanstalt, 1988), 21.
[25] *Jb.* 3, 83.

To see him, however, as his own best interpreter, 'his own literary historian' (Robert Faesi), seems hardly justified: for his various statements, collected together (as they have been, in three large volumes) are often contradictory, while the directly autobiographical pieces, also not always consistent, give him as he wanted to be pictured rather than as he actually was. He was assiduous in cultivating his renown—like Wagner, as Klaus once wrote—and always much occupied, in a kind of 'personal archaeology' (Manfred Dierks), with seeing to his posthumous reputation. Yet with the conceit he could combine a disarming modesty—not a genius, as he said in 1951, at most 'a certain intimacy with greatness', and a self-esteem with enough sense never to go beyond Correggio's 'Anch'io sono pittore'.[26] And the decision to leave his later diaries, warts and all, for posthumous inspection showed at least a desire for the truth eventually to be known.

In a literary life spanning over sixty years, he spent part of every day with pen to paper, and most of his waking hours were spent planning his work or thinking (and talking) about it. With this prodigious application, however (work like a beaver, said Ferdinand Lion), went an inordinately slow production-rate. He was by nature *slow*, in every sense, as he wrote to Freud in 1930: 'everything has to be thoroughly mature before I can communicate it'.[27] His apparent facility with the pen was not the expression of fertility in creative effort. The collected works of Thomas Mann, famed after all primarily as a novelist, show only eight volumes of fiction, while five more are taken up with his essays, lectures, and ephemeral writings, those omitted probably making up another volume. To these must be added the diaries (1918 to 1921, and 1933 to his death), now published *in extenso* (not in Michael's edited version) in nine volumes, with the tenth shortly to follow. And the letters, which also took up much of every day, and of which over 13,000 are so far known. In these, he gave a great deal of himself, and although a large number are mere bread and butter, there are enough gems of brilliant phrasing, even to correspondents of no significance, and certainly enough of biographical interest, to warrant fuller publication than Erika's edition. Should this one day be attempted, Mann would be a step nearer the Goethe status which his true literary production never attained.

He lacked imagination, in the purely creative sense, as he confessed himself, but was blessed with a rich fantasy which, as Kurt Martens noted as early as 1906, ran to transforming rather than creating.[28] A scrivener might be the word for him, in its historical meaning of copyist—but with a marvellous talent for illuminating his manuscripts with minute and finely executed detail, personifying the omniscient 'spirit of narration', as he put

---

[26] *DüD*. ii, 532.      [27] *Br*. i, 296.      [28] *Jb*. 3, 230.

it in *The Holy Sinner*, and 'covering the parchment with my small and fine, learned and decorative script'. He mistrusted inspiration, in favour of the discipline of the hard slog. If thereby he gained the reputation of a 'universal writer', he was ready to admit that that was just a question of cribbing from the available sources: 'you can't know everything, but you can look it up!'[29] This was factually the case in many notable instances—medicine in *The Magic Mountain*, archaeology and Egyptology in *Joseph*, music in *Faustus*—and the technique of montage became almost an obsession, often leading him to a display of acquired knowledge many readers were to find tedious.

More: nothing he committed to paper, in letters or ephemeral pieces, was lost, but hived away, in copy or in his excellent memory, as 'material' to be exploited for his work (quite apart from the habit, common to us all, of repeating a telling passage or quotation to several correspondents at a time). In his enthusiasm after the Schrenck-Notzing seances early in 1923, the detailed record he made was not only worked into many letters and transformed to the lecture 'Occult Experiences' and a piece for the *Rundschau*, but also then adapted for incorporation into *The Magic Mountain*. The great themes to which he was always returning—Wagner 'without end', Goethe, Tolstoy, Nietzsche, even Fontane—were a process of fruitful recycling and development. It was his way, he said in 1949, to 'allow nothing to drop out of my life, but to take the earlier with me into the later, so that it can at any time become productive again'.[30] He was thus never at a loss for the contributions journals constantly demanded of him; extracts or pre-prints from work in progress were always available (over the lengthy gestation of the *Joseph*, many of the chapters seemed almost to be written with this in mind), while pages discarded from his manuscript for the 1923 'Goethe and Tolstoy' lecture were sent in unsolicited as a 'thoroughly complete little study' in themselves.[31]

In short, he was the literary businessman, as well as the magician his children called him because of both the arcane aura of his out-of-bounds sanctum and his histrionic powers as story-teller and reader. That was a sobriquet which others, in exaggerated adulation, have adopted for him, and is not exactly that suggested by a more dispassionate view. His is anything but a sorcerer's work: the spell cast by these involved fables lies in their narrative skill and intricate composition of fine detail, while his well-constructed essays, though models of their kind, can hardly be thought of as bewitching. His powers as a wordsmith always exercised great charm, most notably in *Royal Highness*, *Joseph*, and *The Holy Sinner*; but his works of art might more properly be described by the French term

---

[29] Motsch., 28 f.        [30] *Br.* iii, 118.        [31] Bl. 7, 9.

*ouvrage d'art*, used for those marvels of construction, bridges, viaducts, or tunnels, on the motorways. They are *tours de force* of architecture and engineering rather than of pure artistic creativity.

That they should be more to German than Anglo-Saxon taste is not to be wondered at. The *Gründlichkeit*, the enormous spread of the narrative and its brilliant detail in composition, the ironic, almost professorial tone in Mann's minute analysis of complicated characters, made that assured. Before he was 30, the success of *The Buddenbrooks* had earned him immediate acceptance into the German pantheon, a respect and an oracular status comparable with that of an eminent philosopher, for which English literature has no parallel. That reputation, if more muted, followed him to the United States; in England, however, it generally did not prevail. He felt that England did not know what to make of him, and as late as 1952 said he was determined, whether or not he produced another book, certainly never to bring another out there. A factor in English puzzlement was perhaps his humour, which he often protested was his essential quality: 'in truth my books . . . are full of fun and music, and I am essentially a humorist'.[32] He had himself a keen sense of the comic, retailed anecdotes with relish and effect, loved to hear Karl Valentin and, in America, Charlie Chaplin; but he went so far once as to admit that 'my so-called humour is actually the child of despair'.[33] With German readers, and especially with those listening to his readings or recordings, the subtle effect has been well appreciated: but to English ears it appears stilted, except perhaps in *The Holy Sinner*. And in spite of his sometimes daring modernity, the themes and style—and the prolixity—have for an English reader an air of the antique: for long novels of that sort, and the more marked and boisterous humour that goes with them, Anglo-Saxons look to Trollope and Dickens, and may prefer the chronicles of nineteenth-century London or Barchester to those of Lübeck or Davos.

In his dispassionate, slightly academic way, he acknowledged his position was something of an archaism. He saw himself as the last of a line, a 'late comer', his novels marking the end of the nineteenth-century tradition and representative of capitalist society in its final stages. 'Late-bourgeois', 'late-capitalist' became convenient tags with which to classify him, well suited to current literary-historical theory and conforming to the fashionable materialist—Marxist—notion of literature as a superstructure to social organization. Though far from being a communist himself, he had progressed politically to a broad affirmation of socialism, which favoured his reception in post-war communist Germany despite its stricter Marxist views. Thomas Mann in his early-won status as a 'classic' could continue

---

[32] *DüD*. iii, 218 f.    [33] *DüD*. i. 326.

safely to be revered both there and in the Federal Republic as the supreme German representative of a past, or at any rate passing, epoch.

In the innumerable studies and dissertations which began in his lifetime (and show no sign yet of diminishing), the 'late capitalism' classification and a quasi-religious reverence towards the master broadly set the tone, even in the non-German and non-communist world and however different the themes chosen. By the centenary of his birth in 1975, however, the reaction, the demythologizing tendency of a later generation, inevitable with a writer of such stature, had set in, and adulation was giving way to a more critical and antagonistic approach. He was a poseur, said some, his prose was hard work to read; for those dangerously lost in trying to escape what they saw as the bourgeoisie's 'process of disintegration', he had nothing to say; he could be admired, but never loved.[34] As the diaries then began to appear, with frank admission of homo-erotic inclinations till then only suspected, and an image more vacillatory than the mask of firmness hitherto accepted, a new and different interest developed. Though probably only academics bought and read the lengthy and expensive volumes, the general public was eager to devour the extracts in the media: an investigative reporter, rather than a professor, was first to track down in New York the 'last love', Franz Westermeier, and sensationalized reports began to rival those so common now with prominent politicians and royalty. Students flocked to lectures on Thomas Mann from this new, all-too-human angle; and, so far from being toppled from its pedestal, the monument stood firmer than ever. To prescribe publication of the diaries after twenty years in fact turned out to be a shrewd stroke in aid of his posthumous success: these more intimate writings were as attuned to the temper of the times as his earlier publications. His sales have continued to prosper, while on television an adaptation of *Felix Krull* and programmes about Thomas Mann, his family, and his life, and operatic productions, as well as films like *Buddenbrooks* and Visconti's *Death in Venice*, continue to attract large audiences.

Since 1990, capitalism, socialism, and communism have been transformed, and to label Thomas Mann as the representative of late capitalism—of the 'post-bourgeois era', as he called it himself in 1947[35]—no longer makes much sense. Communism in the form he knew it has disappeared, and the world as a whole has now taken to capitalist market economics as an imperfect but workable solution. If there is ever to be a late capitalism, and one day an end to it, that time seems a long way off still; and the decline depicted in *The Buddenbrooks*, or less directly in his other works, like that in Galsworthy's or Waugh's novels, has to be seen as a

---

[34] M. Reich-Ranicki (ed.), *Was halten Sie von TM? 18 Autoren antworten* (1986), 68, 73.
[35] *Tb.* vii, 567.

phenomenon more transient than previously appeared. Today's broad acceptance on left and right of a market economy makes a new look at Mann's personal political activities and development of particular interest. As has rightly been pointed out, he is sometimes undervalued as a political writer and thinker: though his ideas were often vague, and sought-after less for their content than for the authority of his standing as an artist, they were far from being those of a merely careerist conservative.[36] From immediately after the First World War he had seen social concern, the 'social state',[37] as the road for the future, and after the defeat of fascism in 1945 could call for a new synthesis 'half-way between the Russian and American systems', to secure human rights and liberties.[38] In 1950 he thought the 'wild squabble' of the cold war would in fifty years' time have dissolved in civilization, 'when the West will be seen to have learned more from the East than the other way round'[39] (an interesting prediction as we approach the millennial year). Two years before his death, he was firmly convinced that the attainment of mankind's distant goals—'world government, a common administration of the earth, and peace between the peoples'—was inconceivable without communist elements.[40] Admittedly, these ideas are only a selection from a mass less coherent and often contradictory: but they give a distinctly different picture of the representative of the so-called late-bourgeois era. Though a firm individualist, he could say with more truth than Harold Macmillan that 'we are all socialists nowadays'.

Seeing himself as the last of a traditional line, writing 'final books' but with elements of experimentation to suit a time of transition, he could sometimes feel, he said in 1951, that his work was 'nothing more than a rapid recapitulation of the myth of the Western world and its cultural heritage before . . . the final curtain falls, to rise again only for a very different production to which we, precisely as harbingers of the end, already have certain affinities'.[41] His readers in the twenty-first century may find it hard to acknowledge any such affinities, and could well feel his 'classic' works have even less to say to them than they had to many in the 1970s.

What is certain, however, is that the historical figure of Thomas Mann will remain of absorbing interest, above all for his personal perception of the 'German problem' and the painful road to its solution. He was through and through German, as he always insisted; but even amid the patriotic fervour of the First World War, as he began the *Reflections*, he recognized the meaninglessness of German nationalism: 'we are no nation, like the others . . . more like a Europe in extract. In our soul, indeed in that of the

---

[36] Cf. Reed 306 f., 310.   [37] Matter iii, 7.   [38] *Tb.* vii, 567.   [39] *Br.* iii, 125.
[40] E. Hilscher, *Thomas Mann: Leben und Werk* (Berlin: Volk und Wissen, 1966), 196.
[41] Ibid. 192.

individual German, are expressed the antitheses of [all] Europe. . . . There is never anything to be made of us . . .'[42] And later, in the years of the approach and arrival of the second war, he admitted it was no easy matter to be a German writer, with conflicting feelings towards one's country 'of rage, revulsion, the desire for its destruction, yet an attachment that is inalienable'.[43] Germany seemed condemned for ever to start again from the beginning, 'schoolchildren who never pass their leaving exam', and Nietzsche was right to say that if Germany would not renounce the principle of right through might, nor admit the might of right, her fate must be sealed.[44] To Mann in his anguish over Germany, Heine's judgement a century before seemed only too prophetic, and Vansittart's *Black Record* of Germany's three characteristics—'envy, self-pity, cruelty'—incontrovertible. Hitler was no accident, but a truly German phenomenon; and in *The Beloved Returns* Goethe could be made to castigate the Germans for their ready submission to 'any ecstatic rogue who arouses their basest qualities, reinforces their vices, and teaches them to see nationality as isolation and brutality' (an anachronism which he could not bring himself to omit).[45]

Pity was out of place after the 1945 collapse he said. The Germans were not born for power, and must at all costs never possess it again. Their fate was not just destiny, or tragedy, but the 'dishonourable bankruptcy of criminal stupidity'.[46] True, they would see anything that happened to *them* as unheard-of injustice: 'they have learned nothing, understand nothing, regret nothing'.[47] Europe had everything to fear from the recrudescence of German nationalism which in 1949 he saw being fostered during the cold war; and although, with his symbolic visits that year to both East and West, he looked forward to their eventual reunification, he despaired of any lesson being drawn there from his *Faustus*. Germany 'has never descended to hell, and doesn't give a damn for guilt and redemption through grace'.[48]

The lesson he himself drew was to reduce it to a federation of German states, created under the occupation by the Germans themselves with due regard for their individualism, and self-administered. That stage, after many vicissitudes, has in fact been reached, and reunification has finally brought the Eastern *Länder* into the federal fold. Mann went further, however: it was imperative not only to avoid a German Europe, but to achieve a *European* Germany. That, in the European Union of our century's final decade, is proving far from easy, to put it no higher. If the coming years can achieve it, it will constitute not the least important element of the legacy of Thomas Mann.

---

[42] *Amann Br.* 49.     [43] *Br.* ii, 221.     [44] *Fr./Antw.* 148; *Tb.* iii, 52 f.     [45] 41/333.
[46] *DüD.* iii, 73.     [47] *AM Brw.* 616; *Br.* ii, 397.     [48] *DüD.* iii, 248.

# Select Bibliography

Publisher S. Fischer, Frankfurt a. M. (or Berlin, before 1945) unless otherwise stated.

*Blätter* = *Blätter der Thomas-Mann-Gesellschaft*, Zurich.

## I. THOMAS MANN'S WORKS

*Gesammelte Werke in dreizehn Bänden* (Frankfurt a. M.: Fischer Taschenbuch Verlag, Sept. 1990).

*Tagebücher*

1. ed. P. de Mendelssohn
   i: *1918–1921* (1979); ii: *1933–1934* (1977); iii: *1935–1936* (1978); iv: *1937–1939* (1980); v: *1940–1943* (1982)
2. ed. Inge Jens
   vi: *1944–1.4.1946* (1986); vii: *28.5.1946–31.12.1948* (1989); viii: *1949–1950* (1991); ix: *1951–1952* (1993).

*Notizbücher*, ed. H. Wysling, *1–6* (1991), *7–14* (1992).

*Altes und Neues*: Kleine Prosa aus fünf Jahrzehnten (1976).

*Aufsätze—Reden—Essays*, ed. Harry Matter (Berlin/Weimar: Aufbau), i: *1893–1913* (1983); ii: *1914–1918* (1983); iii: *1919–1925* (1986).

*Pro and Contra Wagner*, transl. Allan Blunden, introd. Erich Heller (London: Faber, 1985).

'Reisebericht', in: *Neue Schweizer Rundschau*, 8 (Dec. 1949) (German orig. of his article for *New York Times* on the 1949 journey to Germany).

## II. LETTERS

**Thomas Mann**

*Die Briefe Thomas Manns: Regesten und Register*, ed. H. Bürgin and H.-O. Mayer, i–v (1976–87).

*Briefe*, ed. Erika Mann, i: *1889–1936* (1961); ii: *1937–1947* (1963); iii: *1948–1955*, and addenda (1965).

*Briefwechsel mit Autoren*, ed. H. Wysling (1988).

*Briefe an Paul Amann 1915–1952*, ed. Herbert Wegner (Lübeck: Schmidt-Römhild, 1959).

'Briefe an *Otto Basler*', *Blätter*, 5 (1965), 5–15.

*Briefwechsel mit seinen. Verleger Gottfried Bermann Fischer 1932–1955*, ed. P. de Mendelssohn (1973).

*Briefe an Ernst Bertram 1910–1955*, ed. Inge Jens (Pfullingen: Neske, 1960).

'Briefe an *The Dial*', ed. H. Wysling, in *Thomas Mann Studien*, iv (Berne: Francke, 1974).

*Briefwechsel mit Robert Faesi*, ed. R. Faesi (Zurich: Atlantis, 1962).

'Aus dem Briefwechsel mit *Kuno Fiedler*', ed. H. Wysling, *Blätter*, 11 (1971), and 12 (1972).

'Briefwechsel mit **Samuel** und *Hedwig Fischer* 1897–1946', in Samuel Fischer/ Hedwig Fischer, *Briefwechsel mit Autoren*, ed. D. Rodewald and C. Fiedler, introd. Bernhard Zeller (1989), 394–466.

*Briefe an Otto Grautoff 1894–1901 und Ida Boy-Ed 1903–1928*, ed. P. de Mendelssohn (1975).

*Briefwechsel mit Hermann Hesse*, ed. Anni Carlsson and Volker Michels (Frankfurt a. M.: Suhrkamp/S. Fischer, 1975).

'In Exile: The Friendship and Unpublished Correspondence between Thomas Mann and **Heinrich Eduard Jacob**', ed. J. B. Berlin, Deutsche Vierteljahrsschrift Schrift für Literaturwissenschaft und Geistesgeschichte, 64 (1990), 172–87.

**Erich von Kahler:** (a) 'Briefwechsel im Exil', sel. and ed. Hans Wysling, in *Blätter*, 10 (1970), 5–61; (b) *An Exceptional Friendship* (different selection), trans. and ed. R. and C. Winston (Cornell University Press, 1975).

*Thomas Mann–Karl Kerényi: Gespräch in Briefen*, ed. K. Kerényi (Zurich: Rhein-Verlag, 1960).

'On the Making of the *Magic Mountain*: The Unpublished Correspondence of Thomas Mann, *Alfred A. Knopf*, and *H. T. Lowe-Porter*', ed. J. B. Berlin, *Seminar*, 28/4 (Nov. 1992), 283–320.

'"Ein Lese- und Bilderbuch von Menschen": Unpublished Letters of Thomas Mann, **Alfred A. Knopf** and **H. T. Lowe-Porter** 1929–1934, With Special Reference to the *Joseph* Novels', ed. J. B. Berlin and J. M. Herz, *Seminar*, 30/3 (Sept. 1994), 221–80.

*Briefwechsel mit Karl Loewenstein*, ed. Eva Schiffer: 1933–8 in *Blätter*, 18 (1981); 1938–55 in *Blätter*, 19 (1982).

*Briefwechsel mit Heinrich Mann*, new enlarged edn., ed. H. Wysling (1984).

*Briefwechsel mit Kurt Martens*, ed. H. Wysling with T. Sprecher, I: 1899–1907, *Thomas Mann Jahrbuch*, 3 (1990), 175–247; II: 1908–35, *Thomas Mann Jahrbuch*, 4 (1991), 185–260.

*Briefwechsel mit Agnes E. Meyer 1937–1955*, ed. H. R. Vaget (1992).

*Briefwechsel mit Alfred Neumann*, ed. P. de Mendelssohn (Heidelberg: Lambert Schneider, 1977).

*The Letters of Thomas Mann to Caroline Newton*, foreword Robert F. Goheen (priv. printed at Princeton University Press, 1971).

'Dichter oder Schriftsteller? Der Briefwechsel zwischen Thomas Mann und *Joseph Ponten*', ed. H. Wysling with W. Pfister, in *Thomas Mann Studien*, viii (Berne: Francke, 1988).

'Aus dem Briefwechsel Thomas Mann–**Emil Preetorius**', ed. H. Wysling, in *Blätter*, 4 (Dec. 1963), 3–24.

'Thomas Mann–**Hans Reisiger**, Briefe aus der Vor- und Nachkriegszeit', ed. H. Wysling, in *Blätter*, 8 (1968), 8–38.

'Briefwechsel Thomas Mann–**Max Rychner**', ed. H. Wysling, in *Blätter*, 7 (1967), 5–38.

*Jahre des Unmuts: Thomas Manns Briefwechsel mit René Schickele 1930–1940*, ed. H. Wysling with C. Bernini (*Thomas Mann Studien*, x) (Frankfurt a. M.: Klostermann, 1992).

'Briefwechsel mit *Arthur Schnitzler*', ed. Hertha Krotkoff, in *Modern Austrian Literature*, 7/1–2 (1974), 1–33.

'Briefwechsel mit *Bruno Walter*', sel. and ed. H. Wysling, in *Blätter*, 9 (1969), 12–43.

Jonas, Klaus W., 'Thomas Mann, *Hermann J. Weigand* und die Yale University: Versuch einer Dokumentation', pt. i, *Philobiblon*, 38/2 (June 1994), 97–147; pt. ii, ibid., 38/3 (Sept. 1994), 217–32.

'Briefe an *Franz Werfel* und Alma Mahler-Werfel', ed. Glenys A. Waldman, in *Blätter*, 17 (1979), 5–8.

Jonas, Klaus W., '*Stefan Zweig* und Thomas Mann: Versuch einer Dokumentation', *Philobiblon*, 25/4 (Nov. 1981), 248–75.

*Others*

Feuchtwanger, Lion, *Briefwechsel mit Freunden 1933–1958*, i, ed. H. von Hofe and S. Washburn (Berlin: Aufbau, 1991).

Mann, Erika, *Briefe und Antworten*, ed. Anna Z. Prestel (Munich: ed. spangenberg), i: *1922–1950* (1984); ii: *1951–1969* (1985).

Mann, Heinrich, *Briefe an Karl Lemke 1917–1949* (Berlin: Aufbau, 1963).

Mann, Klaus, *Briefe und Antworten 1922–1949*, ed. M. Gregor-Dellin (Munich: ed. spangenberg (new rev. edn.), 1987).

Walter, Bruno, *Briefe 1894–1962* (1969).

III. SECONDARY LITERATURE

Abusch, Alexander, 'Unsere besonderen Freunde', *Sinn und Form*, 27/3 (1975), 475–82.

Bahr, Hermann, 'Thomas Mann' (review of *Königliche Hoheit*), in id., *Essays* (Leipzig: Insel, 1912), 85–92.

Bauer, Arnold, *Thomas Mann und die Krise der bürgerlichen Kultur* (Berlin: Deutsche Buchvertriebs- und Verlagsgesellschaft, 1946).

——*Thomas Mann* (Berlin: Colloquium, 1960).

Berendsohn, Walter E., *Thomas Mann: Künstler und Kämpfer in bewegter Zeit* (Lübeck: Schmidt-Römhild, 1965).

*Blätter der Thomas-Mann-Gesellschaft*, 2, 4, 5–20 (Zurich, 1963–84).

Bludau, Beatrix; Heftrich, Eckhard; Koopmann, Helmut (eds.), *Thomas Mann 1875–1975: Vorträge in München, Zürich, Lübeck* (1977).

Blume, Bernhard, 'Der Briefschreiber Thomas Mann', in *Lebendige Form: Festschrift für Heinrich Henel*, ed. Jeffrey Sammons (Munich: Fink, 1970).

Böhm, Karl Werner, *Zwischen Selbstzucht und Verlangen: Thomas Mann und das Stigma der Homosexualität* (Würzburg: Königshausen & Neumann, 1991).

Bürgin, Hans, and Mayer, Hans-Otto, *Thomas Mann: Eine Chronik seines Lebens*, (1965).

Carstensen, Richard, *Thomas Mann sehr menschlich* (Lübeck: Weiland/Oprecht, 1974).

Craig, Gordon, *Germany 1866–1945* (Oxford: Oxford University Press, 1978).

Dierks, Manfred, 'Der Wahn und die Träume in *Tod in Venedig*', *Psyche*, 44/3 (Mar. 1990), 240–68.

——'Schreibhemmung und Freud-Lektüre: Neuer Blick auf die Novelle *Tod in Venedig*', *Neue Zürcher Zeitung*, 23–24 June 1990.

*Dichter über ihre Dichtungen:* see Wysling and Fischer.

Dietzel, Ulrich, 'Julia Mann: Tante Elisabeth—zur Entstehungsgeschichte der *Buddenbrooks*', *Sinn und Form*, 15/2–3 (1963), 482–502.

*Du, Schweizerische Monatsschrift*, 15/6 (June 1955): 'Zum 80. Geburtstag Thomas Manns'.

Dvoretzky, Edward, 'Thomas Manns *Doktor Faustus*: Ein Rückblick auf die frühe deutsche Kritik', *Blätter*, 17 (1979), 9–24.

Ebermayer, Erich, *Denn heute gehört uns Deutschland . . .* (Hamburg: Zsolnay, 1949).

Eloesser, Arthur, *Thomas Mann: Sein Leben und sein Werk* (1925).

Fischer, Brigitte B., *Sie schrieben mir* (Zurich: Classen, 1978).

Fischer, Ernst, 'Dr Faustus und die deutsche Katastrophe', in *Dichtung und Deutung* (Wien: Globus, 1953), 305–70.

Franke, Peter R., *Der Tod des Hans Hansen: Unbekannte Dokumente aus der Jugend Thomas Manns* (Saarbrücken: Landesbank Saar) (catalogue of exhibition 2–20 Sept. 1991).

Frey, Erich A., 'Thomas Mann', in *Deutsche Exilliteratur seit 1933*, i: *Kalifornien*, pt. 1, ed. J. M. Spalek and J. Strelka (Berne: Francke, 1976), 473–526.

Hamilton, Nigel, *The Brothers Mann* (London: Secker & Warburg, 1978).

Hampton, Christopher, *Tales from Hollywood* (London: Samuel French, 1983).

Hansen, Volkmar, and Heine, Gert (eds.), *Frage und Antwort: Interviews mit Thomas Mann 1909–1955* (Hamburg: Knaus, 1983).

Häntzschel, Hiltrud, ' "Pazifistische Friedenshyänen"? Die Friedensbewegung von Münchner Frauen . . . und die Familie Mann', *Jahrbuch der deutschen Schiller-Gesellschaft*, 36 (1992), 307–32.

Hatfield, Henry, *Thomas Mann* (Norfolk, Conn.: New Directions, 1951).

Heftrich, E., and Wysling, H. (eds.), *Thomas Mann Jahrbücher*, 1–5 (Frankfurt a. M.: Klostermann, 1988–92).

Heilbut, Anthony, *Exiled in Paradise* (Boston: Beacon Press, 1984).

Heller, Erich, *Thomas Mann der ironische Deutsche* (Frankfurt a. M.: Suhrkamp, 1959).

Herz, Ida, 'Erinnerungen an Thomas Mann 1925–1955', in *German Life and Letters*, NS 9/4 (July 1956), 281–90.

——'Freundschaft und Korrespondenz mit Thomas Mann', *Publications of English Goethe-Society*, 55 (1985), 1–21.

Hilscher, Eberhard, *Thomas Mann: Leben und Werk* (Berlin: Volk und Wissen, 1966).

Hummel, Ursula (ed.), *Klaus und Erika Mann: Bilder und Dokumente* (Munich: ed. spangenberg, 1990) (catalogue of exhibition Munich 10 Oct.–30 Nov. 1989).

Janka, Walter, *Spuren eines Lebens* (Berlin: Rowohlt, 1991).

Jasper, Willi, *Der Bruder Heinrich Mann* (Munich: Hanser, 1992).

Jens, Inge, *'Es kenne mich die Welt, auf daß sie mir verzeihe'*—*Thomas Mann in seinen Tagebüchern* (1989).

——'" . . . eingeholt von der Vergangenheit": Der späte Thomas Mann und die Politik' (lecture 1991, MS).

Jonas, Ilsedore B., ' "Ich sah ein kleines Wunder": Porträts von Thomas Manns Lebensgefährtin', *Philobiblon*, 26/4 (Nov. 1982), 318–28.

Jonas, Klaus W., *Die Thomas-Mann- Literatur: Bibliographie der Kritik* (Berlin: Erich Schmidt), i: *1896–1955* (1972); ii: *1956–1975* (1979).

——'Thomas Mann und Hans Bürgin: Versuch einer Dokumentation', *Philobiblon*, 31/3 (Sept. 1987), 178–200.

——'Thomas Mann, Joseph W. Angell und die Yale University: Versuch einer Dokumentation', *Philobiblon*, 34/2 (1990), 97–137.

Kahn-Reach, Hilde, 'Thomas Mann, mein Boss', *Neue deutsche Hefte*, 20/2 (1973), 51–64.

Keiser-Hayne, Helga, *Beteiligt euch, es geht um eure Erde: Erika Mann und ihr politisches Kabarett die 'Pfeffermühle' 1933–1937* (Munich: ed. spangenberg, 1990).

Kellen, Konrad, 'Reminiscences of Thomas Mann', *Yale Review*, 76/2 (winter 1987), 238–46.

Koopmann, Helmut, ' "German Culture is where I am": Thomas Mann in Exile', *Studies in Twentieth Century Literature*, 7/1 (autumn 1982), 5–20.

——(ed.), *Thomas-Mann-Handbuch* (Stuttgart: Kröner, 1990).

Krüll, Marianne, *Im Netz des Zauberers: Eine andere Geschichte der Familie Mann* (Arche, 1990).

Lehnert, Herbert, 'Bert Brecht und Thomas Mann im Streit über Deutschland', in *Deutsche Exilliteratur seit 1933*, i: *Kalifornien*, pt. 1, ed. J. M. Spalek and J. Strelka (Berne: Francke, 1976), 62–88.

Lindken, Hans-Ulrich, 'Thomas Mann und E. T. A. Hoffmann in Warschau', in id. (ed.), *Das magische Dreieck: Polnisch-deutsche Aspekte zur österreichischen und deutschen Literatur des 19. und 20. Jahrhunderts* (Frankfurt a. M.: Lang, 1992), 152–79.

Lion, Ferdinand, *Thomas Mann: Leben und Werk* (Zürich: Oprecht), 1947.

Lühe, Irmela von der, *Erika Mann: Eine Biographie* (Frankfurt a. M.: Campus, 1993).

Mádl, Antal, and Györi, Judith (eds.) (bibliog. Ferenc Szász), *Thomas Mann und Ungarn* (Budapest: Akadémiai Kiadó, 1977).

Mann, Erika, and Mann Klaus, *Escape to Life* (Boston: Houghton-Mifflin, 1939).

Mann, Erika, *Das letzte Jahr: Bericht über meinen Vater* (1956).

Mann, Frido, *Professor Parsifal: Autobiographischer Roman* (Munich: ed. spangenberg, 1985).

Mann, Golo, *Erinnerungen und Gedanken einer Jugend in Deutschland* (1986).

Mann, Heinrich, *Ein Zeitalter wird besichtigt* (Berlin: Aufbau, 1947).

Mann, Julia, *Ich spreche so gern mit meinen Kindern* (Berlin: Aufbau, 1991).

Mann, Julia (sister), 'Tante Elisabeth', *Sinn und Form*, 15/2–3, (1963), 482–502.

Mann, Katia, *Meine ungeschriebenen Memoiren*, ed. Elisabeth Plessen and Michael Mann (Berlin: Buchverlag Der Morgen, 1975).

Mann, Klaus, *Der Wendepunkt: Ein Lebensbericht* (Berlin G. B. Fischer, 1960).

——*Kind dieser Zeit*, afterword William H. Shirer (Munich: Nymphenburger, 1965).

——*Prüfungen: Schriften zur Literatur* (Munich: Nymphenburger, 1968).

——*Woher wir kommen und wohin wir müssen* (Munich: ed. spangenberg, 1980).

——*Tagebücher 1931–1937*, ed. J. Heimannsberg, P. Laemmle, W. F. Schoeller (Munich: ed. spangenberg), i: *1931–1933* (1989); ii: *1934–1935* (1989); iii: *1936–1937* (1990).

Mann, Michael, *Das Thomas-Mann-Buch: Eine innere Biographie in Selbstzeugnissen* (1965 (Fischer-Bücherei 710) ).

——'Schuld und Segen im Werke Thomas Manns' (Lübeck: G. Weiland, 1975) (lecture on centenary 6 June 1975).

——'Thomas Mann und Österreich', in *Austriaca, Festschrift für H. Politzer* (Tübingen: Niemeyer, 1975), 376–9.

——*Fragmente eines Lebens*, ed. Frederic C. and Sally Tubach (Munich: ed. spangenberg, 1983).

Mann, Monika, *Vergangenes und Gegenwärtiges: Erinnerungen* (Munich: Kindler, 1956).

Mann, Viktor, *Wir waren fünf* (Konstanz: Südverlag, 1949).

Mayer, Hans, *Thomas Mann: Werk und Entwicklung* (Berlin: Volk und Welt, 1950).

Mendelssohn, Peter de, *Der Zauberer: Das Leben des deutschen Schriftstellers Thomas Manns*, i: *1875–1918* (1975); ii: *(nachgel. Kapitel 'Jahre der Schwebe 1919 und 1933'*, ed. A. von Schirnding) (1992).

Mertz, Wolfgang (ed.), *Thomas Mann: Wirkung und Gegenwart* (produced by S. Fischer Verlag for centenary 6 June 1975).

Michels, Volker (ed.), *Hermann Hesse in Augenzeugenberichten* (Frankfurt a. M.: Suhrkamp, 1987).

Middell, Eike, *Thomas Mann: Versuch einer Einführung in Leben und Werk* (Leipzig: Reclam, 1966).

Motschan, Georges, *Thomas Mann—von nahem erlebt* (Nettetal: Matussek, 1988).

Pascal, Roy, 'Thomas Mann 1875–1955: The German Problem', in id., *The German Novel* (Manchester University Press, 1957), ch. ix, 258–96.

Piana, Theo: *Thomas Mann* (Leipzig: VEB Bibliographisches Institut, 1968).

Pringsheim, Klaus, 'Thomas Mann in Amerika', in *Neue deutsche Hefte*, 13/1 (1966), 20–46.

Reed, T. J., *Thomas Mann: The Uses of Tradition* (Oxford: Clarendon Press, 1974).

Reich-Ranicki, Marcel, *Thomas Mann und die Seinen* (Stuttgart: Deutsche Verlagsanstalt), 1968.

——(ed.), *Was halten Sie von Thomas Mann? 18 Autoren antworten* (1988).

Schoeller, Wilfried F. (ed.), *Heinrich Mann: Bilder und Dokumente* (Munich: ed. spangenberg, 1991) (catalogue for Heinrich Mann exhibition Frankfurt a. M./ Munich 12 Dec. 1990–3 Mar. 1991).

Schröter, Klaus, *Thomas Mann im Urteil seiner Zeit: Dokumente 1891–1955* (Hamburg: Wegner, 1969).

Schulte, Hans H., and Chapple, Gerald (eds.), *Thomas Mann: A Colloquium* (Bonn: Bouvier, 1978).

Sprecher, Thomas, *Thomas Mann in Zürich* (Munich: Fink, 1992).

Stahlberger, Peter, *Der Zürcher Verleger Emil Oprecht und die deutsche politische Emigration 1933–1945* (Zurich: Europa, 1970).

Stepanauskas, Leonas, 'Drei Sommer in Nida', *Sinn und Form*, 28/2 (1976).

Stern, J. P., 'Mann in his Time', *TLS* 6 June 1975, 621–3 (lecture on centenary, London).

Storck, Joachim W., 'Deutsche Sprache im Exil: René Schickele und Thomas Mann' (lecture Ludwigsburg 4 Feb. 1991, Gesellschaft für deutsche Sprache).

Thimann, Susanne, *Brasilien als Rezipient deutschsprachiger Prosa des 20. Jahrhunderts* (Frankfurt a. M.: Lang, 1989).

Thirlwall, John C., *In another Language: A record of the 30-year Relationship between Thomas Mann and Helen Lowe-Porter* (New York: Knopf, 1966).

Tubach, Frederich C., and Tubach, Sally (see Mann, Michael, *Fragmente eines Lebens*).

Unseld, Siegfried, *Peter Suhrkamp—zur Biographie eines Verlegers* (Frankfurt a. M.: Suhrkamp, 1991 (new enl. edn. on centenary)).

Vaget, Hans Rudolf, 'Vorzeitiger Antifaschismus und andere unamerikanische Umtriebe: Aus den geheimen Akten des FBI über Thomas Mann', in *Horizonte, Festschrift für Herbert Lehnert* (Tübingen: Niemeyer, 1990), 173–204.

Walter, Bruno, *Thema und Variationen: Erinnerungen und Gedanken* (Stockholm: Bermann Fischer, 1947).

Weber, Evelyn, *Dichter privat* (Oberwil: Kugler, 1981).

Wiedemann, Hans-Rudolf (ed.), *Thomas Manns Schwiegermutter erzählt*, foreword Golo Mann (Lübeck: Graphische Werkstätten, 1985).

Winston, Richard, *Thomas Mann: The Making of an Artist 1875–1911*, afterword Clara Winston (London: Constable, 1982).

Wysling, Hans (ed. with Yvonne Schmidlin), *Bild und Text bei Thomas Mann: Eine Dokumentation* (Berne: Francke, 1975).

——*Dokumente und Untersuchungen: Beiträge zur Thomas-Mann-Forschung* (*Thomas Mann Studien*, iii) (Berne: Francke, 1974).

—— et al., *Thomas Mann Studien*, iii, iv, viii, x (Berne: Francke/Frankfurt a. M.: Klostermann, 1974–92).

—— and Fischer, M. (eds.), *Dichter über ihre Dichtungen*, xiv: *Thomas Mann* (Munich: Heimeran/Frankfurt a. M.: S. Fischer), pt. i *1889–1917* (1975); pt ii *1918–1943* (1979); pt. iii *1944–1955* (1981).

Zweig, Stefan, 'An den Genius der Verantwortlichkeit', in *Neue Rundschau*, 36/6 (June 1925), 624–6.

# Index of Thomas Mann's Works

# General Index